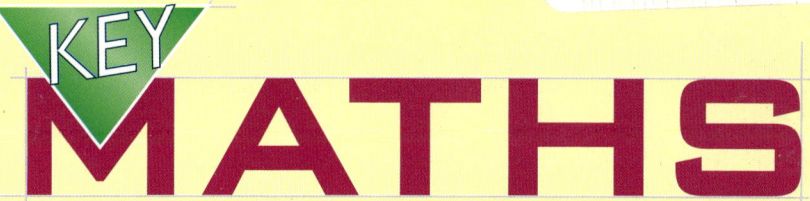

KEY MATHS

AQA (Modular) Specification B

GCSE

▶ **David Baker**
The Anthony Gell School, Wirksworth

▶ **Jim Griffith**
The Bishop of Hereford's Bluecoat School, Hereford

▶ **Paul Hogan**
St. Wilfrid's Church of England High School, Blackburn

▶ **Chris Humble**
Gillotts School, Henley-on-Thames

▶ **Barbara Job**
Christleton County High School, Chester

▶ **Peter Sherran**
Weston Road High School, Stafford

Series Editor: **Paul Hogan**

First published in 1998 by:
Stanley Thornes (Publishers) Ltd

This edition published in 2002 by:
Nelson Thornes Ltd
Delta Place
27 Bath Road
CHELTENHAM
GL53 7TH
United Kingdom

02   03   04   05   06   /   10   9   8   7   6   5   4   3   2   1

A catalogue record for this book is available from the British Library.

ISBN 0-7487-6738-X

Illustrations by Maltings Partnership, Peters and Zabransky, Oxford Illustrators, Clinton Banbury
Page make-up by Tech Set Ltd

Printed and bound in China by Midas Printing International Ltd.

Acknowledgements
The publishers thank the following for permission to reproduce copyright material:
Alton Towers: 465, 473, 521, 522; Ann Ronan Picture Library: 331, 341; Axon Images: 443 (Nichola-Jane Iddon); Colorsport: 37; Empics: 357 (Tony Marshall), 381 (Tony Marshall); Eye Ubiquitous: 395 (T Futter), 396 (T Futter); Genesis Space Photolibrary: 155 (NASA); Getty Images: 140 (Tony Stone Images/S Lowry/Univ. of Ulster), 221 (Tony Stone Images/Willard Deni McIntyre), 235 (left – Will and Deni McIntyre); Image Bank: 293 (Pete Turner); John Birdsall Photolibrary: 25; John Walmsley Photography: 411 (top), 412; Martyn Chillmaid: 30, 31, 43, 150, 379; Science Photolibrary: 235 (right – John Sanford), 420 (bottom – Dr Gopal Murti), 420 (Dr Gopal Murti); Stockmarket: 53, 54; Sygma: 58 (Philippe Eranian); Topham Picturepoint: 85 (Press Association), 86 (Press Association)
All other photographs Nelson Thornes Archive.

The publishers have made every effort to contact copyright holders but apologise if any have been overlooked.

Contents

1 Dealing with data

CORE

QUESTIONS

EXTENSION

TEST YOURSELF

1 Types of data

Ria and John are helping to collect data for a school census.

Ria is collecting data on hair and eye colour.

John is collecting data on height and age.

Statistics is all about data.
There are two types of data.

Quantitative data   Data that is numerical is called **quantitative data**.
Height and age are both examples of quantitative data.
Number of people in your family is also an example of quantitative data.

Qualitative data   The second type of data does not use numbers.
It is non-numerical data. It is called **qualitative data**.
Hair and eye colour are examples of qualitative data.
Favourite TV programme is also an example of quantitative data.

Exercise 1:1

1   As part of the census Ria has to collect data on each person.
These are some of the questions that she asks.

   a How many people are there in your family?
   b Are you left or right-handed?
   c What type of house do you live in?
   d How long have you lived in your present house?
   e How many rooms does your house have?
   f What colour is your bedroom?

For each question write down if the data is quantitative or qualitative.

2   You are testing people's knowledge of the British Parliamentary system.

   a Write four questions to collect quantitative data.
   b Write four questions to collect qualitative data.

Ria and John have completed their survey.
They have collected the information themselves. This is an example of **primary data**.

Primary data	**Primary data** is data that is collected by the person who is going to use the information. The data can be obtained by asking questions, taking measurements, or counting. It can be very time consuming to collect primary data and you need to avoid any possible bias. However it is possible to collect exactly what information is required.
Secondary data	**Secondary data** is data that is not collected by the person who is going to use the information. It is obtained from published statistics or databases. Tables in science books and temperature charts on the internet are both examples of secondary data. It can be very cheap to obtain large quantities of secondary data but the data may not be exactly what is required. Also the data may be out of date.

3 Write down whether each of these is an example of primary data or secondary data.

  a Ken looks at the local police records to find out how many crashes each week involved cyclists.

  b Paul mesures the time each pupil takes to complete a maths test.

  c Barry gets his data from the magazine 'Annual Abstract of Statistics'.

  d Carl wants to invest some money. He gets information on interest rates from the internet.

  e Louise measures the times that people wait in the express checkout of her local supermarket.

  f Tom writes down the colour of each car that passes his school between 10:30 a.m. and 11:30 a.m.

4 A sports company decides to market a new range of sports clothes. Explain how they could use both primary and secondary data to help them decide on the new range.

2   Presenting data

Ian Hatem is the Headteacher of Adeney School. He is preparing a report for parents on the Key Stage 3 results in Maths, English and Science.

He has to report separately on boys' and girls' results. He has to decide which diagrams are best to make the results clear to the parents.

One of the diagrams Mr Hatem is considering is a pie-chart.
All the data he is using is in percentages.

Pie-chart

A **pie-chart** shows how something is divided up.
The angle of the sector represents the number of items.
It is not useful for reading off accurate figures.

Example

This table shows the percentage of boys gaining each level in the Key Stage 3 Maths exams.

Level	2	3	4	5	6	7	8
% of boys	1	6	15	24	24	18	12

Show these results in a pie-chart.

(1)   Divide up the 360°.
The total is 100%   1% = 360° ÷ 100 = 3.6°

(2) Work out the angle for each level.
You will need to round the angles to the nearest degree.

Level	Percentage	Working	Angle	Angle (rounded)
2	1	$1 \times 3.6°$	3.6°	4°
3	6	$6 \times 3.6°$	21.6°	22°
4	15	$15 \times 3.6°$	54°	54°
5	24	$24 \times 3.6°$	86.4°	86°
6	24	$24 \times 3.6°$	86.4°	86°
7	18	$18 \times 3.6°$	64.8°	65°
8	12	$12 \times 3.6°$	43.2°	43°

(3) Check that the angles add up to 360°.
When the angles have been rounded, they might not add up to 360°. If this is the case, add or take 1° from the biggest angle. It will never be noticed!

(4) Draw and colour the pie-chart. Always add a key.

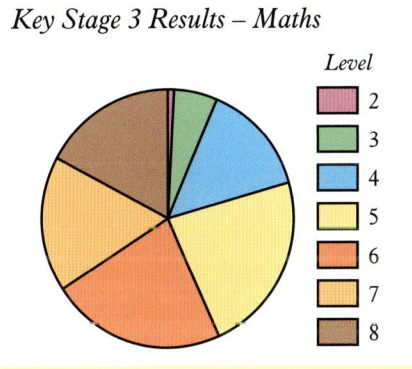

Key Stage 3 Results – Maths

Level
2
3
4
5
6
7
8

Exercise 1:2

W You need Worksheet 1:1 for this exercise.

1 **a** Look at the data for Adeney School boys' Maths results.
   b Draw a table like the one in the example.
   c Draw a pie-chart of this data.

2 **a** Look at the girls' Maths results at Adeney School.
      Draw a pie-chart for these data.
   b Write a couple of sentences about any differences between the two pie-charts that you have drawn.

3 **a** Draw pie-charts for the boys' and girls' Maths results at Bishop's School.
   b Write about all four pie-charts. Comment on the differences and the similarities.

The Head also wants to compare the Maths, Science and English results. He wants to see if the students are doing equally well in all three subjects. He decides to plot the students' results in Maths and Science on a scatter graph.

He uses the actual test scores rather than the levels.

Scatter graph

A **scatter graph** is a diagram that is used to see if there is a connection between two sets of data.

One value goes on the x axis and the other on the y axis. It doesn't matter which way round they go.

This is a scatter graph showing exam results in Maths and Science. If a student scores 35 in Maths and 40 in Science, a point is plotted at (35, 40).

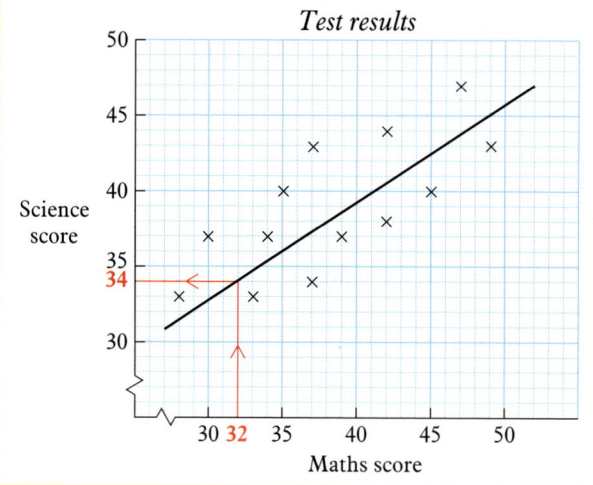

Line of best fit

The points on this graph lie roughly in a straight line. This line is called **a line of best fit**. It goes through the middle of the points.

The line of best fit is used to estimate other data values. To do this, draw from one axis to the line and then to the other axis.

Example

Ben scored 32 in Maths but missed the Science test. Work out an estimate for his Science score.
(1) Find **32** on the Maths axis.
(2) Draw a line up to the line of best fit.
(2) Draw across to the Science axis.
(4) Read off the Science score.
The estimate is shown by the red line on the graph.
The estimate for Science is **34**.

Exercise 1:3

1 Here are some of the results for class 9P in Maths and Science.

Maths	27	34	26	28	34	27	40	21	35	27	29
Science	29	38	22	29	27	32	43	20	32	25	31

    a Plot a scatter graph for this data.
       Scale both your axes from 20 to 45.
    b Draw a line of best fit on your graph.
    c Dave scored 33 in Maths. Use your line to estimate his score in Science.

2 These are the English results for the same students in 9P.

English   35   40   20   22   28   21   35   29   30   26   40

    a Draw a scatter graph of Maths against English.
    b Draw a line of best fit on your graph.
    c Liam scored 37 in English. Use your line to estimate his score in Maths.

3 **a** Draw a scatter graph of the Science and English scores.
    b Draw a line of best fit on your graph.
    c Louise scored 37 in English. Use your line to estimate her score in Science.

Correlation **Correlation** is a measurement of how strongly connected the two sets of data are.
There are different types of correlation.

Positive correlation This scatter graph shows the weights and heights of people. As the weight increases so does the height.
This is **positive correlation**.

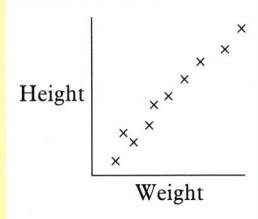

Height

Weight

Negative correlation	This graph shows the value of a car and its age. As age increases, value decreases. This is **negative correlation**.	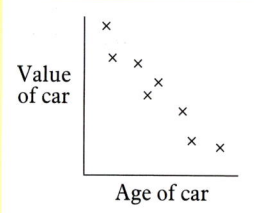

Zero correlation	This graph shows the height of some students against their Maths scores. There is no connection between these two things. There is **zero correlation**.	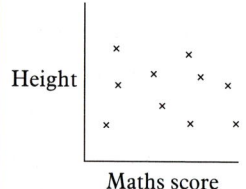

Correlation can be strong or weak.

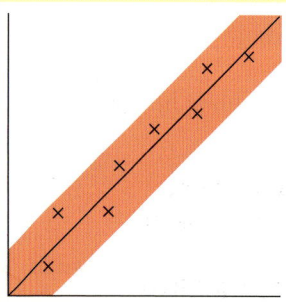 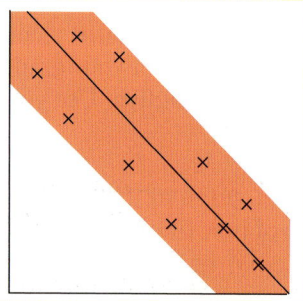

Strong correlation
The points all lie close to the line of best fit.

Weak correlation
The points are well spread out from the line of best fit but still follow the trend.

Exercise 1:4

1 The age of 10 Ford Escorts and their values are shown in this table.

Age	3	6	5	4	2	6	5	3	6	5
Value in £	6000	2500	2900	3500	6500	2300	3100	5800	2100	3300

a Plot a scatter graph to show this data.
b Draw a line of best fit.
c Describe the type of correlation that this data shows.
d Estimate the age of a car that is worth £5500.
e Estimate the value of a $3\frac{1}{2}$ year old car.

2 Two judges awarded marks in an art competition.
Judge A scored out of 20. Judge B scored out of 15.
Here are the results of the judging for 10 paintings.

Judge A	15	12	8	19	7	6	17	8	15	16
Judge B	12	9	7	13	8	3	12	5	12	14

a Plot a scatter graph to show this data.

b Draw a line of best fit.

c Describe the type of correlation that this data shows.

d Judge A gives a piece of work 14 marks.
Estimate the score Judge B would give.

3 LoPrice supermarkets are doing a survey of their customers.
They asked how many visits people made to the supermarket during a
3 month period.
They also asked how far away from the store the people lived.
Here are the results for 14 customers.

Number of visits	9	7	12	11	14	12	6
Length of journey (miles)	7	5	5	8	3	4	8

Number of visits	8	15	13	5	12	2	9
Length of journey (miles)	5	3	6	10	1	7	6

a Plot a scatter graph to show this data.

b Draw a line of best fit.

c Describe the type of correlation that this data shows.

d Estimate the number of visits made by a shopper living 9 miles away.

e Say how reliable you think this estimate is.
What other factors could affect your answer?

| Frequency polygon | **Frequency polygons** are often used to compare two sets of data. You join the mid points of the groups with straight lines. |

This table shows the scores of Year 7 pupils in a French test.

Score	0 up to 10	10 up to 20	20 up to 30	30 up to 40	40 up to 50
Number of pupils	4	8	16	20	12

To draw a frequency polygon

(1) First work out the mid point of each group in the table. This is easy to do by adding a row to the table.

Score	0 up to 10	10 up to 20	20 up to 30	30 up to 40	40 up to 50
Number of pupils	4	8	16	20	12
Mid point	5	15	25	35	45

(2) The scale along the bottom of a frequency polygon must be like a graph scale. It must not have labels like a bar-chart.

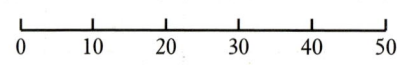

(3) The vertical axis shows the frequency or number of pupils.

(4) Plot the mid-points and join them with straight lines.

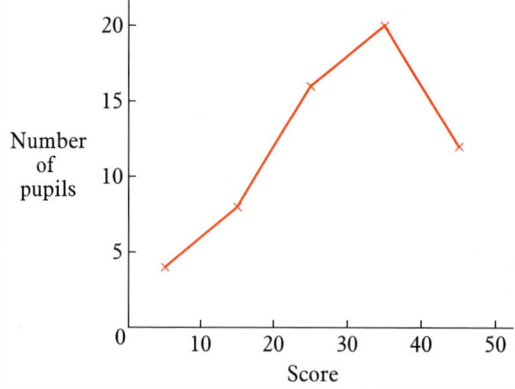

(5) You can label the vertical axis 'Frequency' if you want to.

Exercise 1:5

1 Here are the scores for the English tests at Adeney School.

Score	0 up to 10	10 up to 20	20 up to 30	30 up to 40	40 up to 50
Number of pupils	2	8	12	18	20
Mid-points	5	15	25		

Score	50 up to 60	60 up to 70	70 up to 80	80 up to 90	90 up to 100
Number of pupils	22	15	1	0	2
Mid-points					

a Copy the table.
b Fill in the mid-points.
The first few have been done for you.
c Draw a frequency polygon of the results.

2 Here are the results of the Science tests at Adeney School and Bishop's School.

Score	0 up to 10	10 up to 20	20 up to 30	30 up to 40	40 up to 50
Pupils at Adeney	3	10	9	16	18
Pupils at Bishop's	2	7	6	10	19

Score	50 up to 60	60 up to 70	70 up to 80	80 up to 90	90 up to 100
Pupils at Adeney	16	14	9	3	2
Pupils at Bishop's	22	15	7	8	4

a Draw a frequency polygon for both schools on the same graph.
b Write a brief report describing the trend of each graph and the differences between the graphs.
Look carefully at the two frequency polygons.
Here are some hints to help you write your report.
  ● Which school has the most pupils scoring in the 0–45 range?

- How do the graphs show you this?
- Which school is doing better in this range?
- Which school has the least pupils scoring in the 45–95 range?
- How does the graph show you this?
- Which school is doing better in this range?
- What do you notice about the general trend of both graphs?
- Which school do you think produced the 'better/worse' set of results?

3   Miss Carver is a new Mathematics teacher at Bishop's School.
She is helping her Year 10 class with their coursework.
They have collected information on weekly pocket money from the pupils in the school.
This table shows their results.

Pocket money (£)	0 up to 2	2 up to 4	4 up to 6	6 up to 8	8 up to 10	10 up to 12
Girls	38	68	88	32	22	18
Boys	34	58	106	56	30	12

a   Draw a frequency polygon for boys and girls on the same graph.
b   Write a brief report for Miss Carver comparing boys' and girls' pocket money.

4   Bishop's Belters and Adeney Acers
are two cycle clubs.
This table shows the number of
cyclists from each club that
achieved various speeds in a time
trial.

Speed in mph	5 up to 10	10 up to 15	15 up to 20	20 up to 25	25 up to 30	30 up to 35
Bishop's Belters	13	23	36	20	6	2
Adeney Acers	20	25	32	19	9	0

a   Draw a frequency polygon for both clubs on the same axes.
b   Write a report about the differences between the two clubs for the local newspaper.

3 Equal and unequal histograms

In this section you will see how exam results can be represented as histograms.

Discrete data

When data can only take certain individual values it is called **discrete**.

Shoe size is an example of discrete data.
The values can only be 5, $5\frac{1}{2}$, 6, $6\frac{1}{2}$, 7, etc.
There are no shoe sizes in between these.

Continuous data

Data is **continuous** when it can take any value in a certain range. The *lengths* of earthworms, the *heights* of trees and the *weights* of guinea pigs are all examples of continuous data.

Exercise 1:6

1   Describe the following as examples of discrete or continuous data.
   a   A shirt collar size.
   b   The number of children in a family.
   c   The weight of a defrosting chicken.
   d   The number of words a 4-year-old child can read.
   e   The length of toothpaste squeezed from a tube.

Bar-charts

Bar-charts are used to show discrete data.

There are gaps between the bars when data is not numerical.

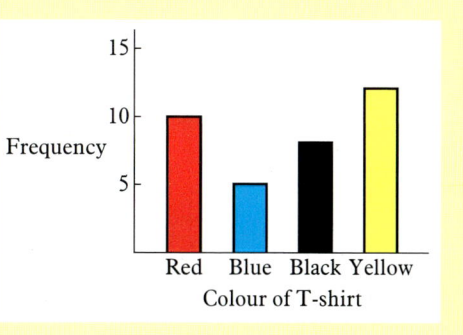

There are no gaps between the bars when the data is grouped.

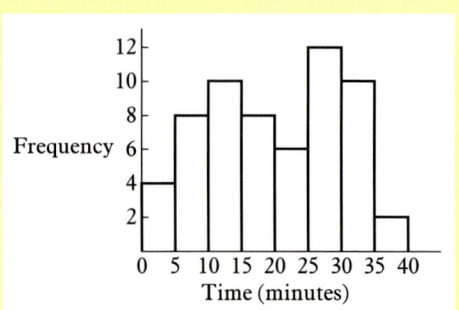

Histogram

A **histogram** looks like a bar-chart but there are several important differences.

(1) It can **only** be used to show continuous data.
  This means that you cannot draw a histogram of favourite colours. You would have to draw a bar-chart.
  A histogram can only show numerical data.

(2) Data for a histogram is always grouped.
  You can use equal width groups or unequal width groups. We will start with equal width groups.

(3) The scale along the bottom of a histogram must be an evenly spaced graph scale like this:

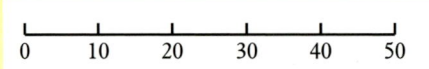

You **never** label it in categories like this:

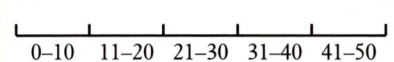

Exercise 1:7

1 Look at these diagrams.
Write down which diagram is a bar-chart and which is a histogram.
Give **two** reasons for each answer.

a

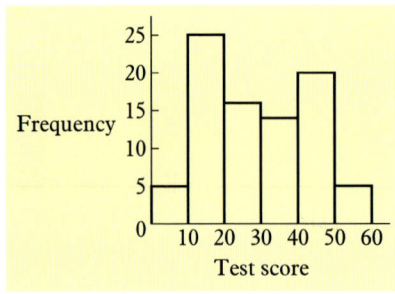

b

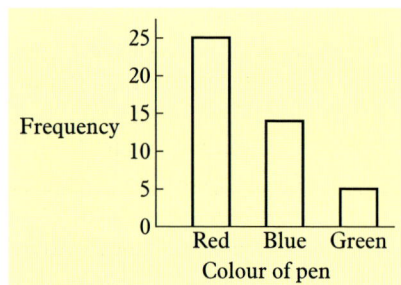

2 Look at this histogram.
   a How many pupils scored between 0 and 10?
   b How many pupils scored between 30 and 60?
   c How many pupils scored 70 or more?

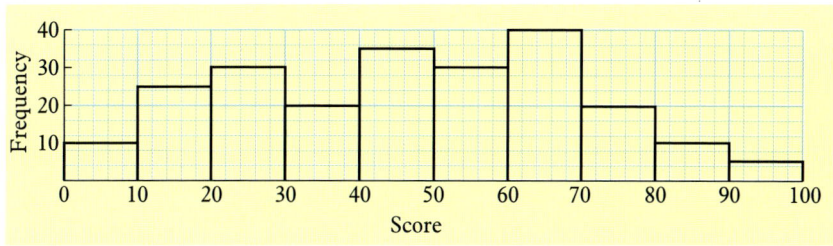

3 Here are the scores for the Key Stage 3 Science exam at Bishop's School.

Score	$0 \leqslant s < 10$	$10 \leqslant s < 20$	$20 \leqslant s < 30$	$30 \leqslant s < 40$	$40 \leqslant s < 50$
Number of pupils	2	7	6	14	19

Score	$50 \leqslant s < 60$	$60 \leqslant s < 70$	$70 \leqslant s < 80$	$80 \leqslant s < 90$	$90 \leqslant s < 100$
Number of pupils	20	13	8	7	4

Draw a histogram of these results.

4 The Headteacher at Adeney School is looking at the attendance figures. Each pupil can attend a maximum of 380 half days per year. Here are the attendance figures for Year 7 and Year 9 last year:

Number of sessions attended	Number of pupils Year 7	Number of pupils Year 9
$100 \leqslant s < 140$	3	1
$140 \leqslant s < 180$	5	2
$180 \leqslant s < 220$	5	4
$220 \leqslant s < 260$	11	9
$260 \leqslant s < 300$	18	15
$300 \leqslant s < 340$	30	37
$340 \leqslant s < 380$	28	32

   a Draw this scale on graph paper. Continue the vertical scale up to 40 and the horizontal scale across to 380.
   b Draw a histogram to show the attendance data for Year 7.
   c Draw a histogram to show the attendance data for Year 9.
   d Compare the histograms. Write down what the histograms tell you about the attendance of Year 7 and Year 9.

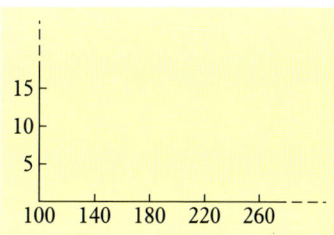

Histograms with unequal groups

So far all the histograms that you have seen have groups that are the same width.

You can put data into groups with unequal widths.

Exam results are done this way.

The width of each group depends on how many marks are needed for each grade.

All the pupils with the same grade need to be in the same group.

The marks that are used for each group are different each year.

The groups may be something like this:

Grade	U	C	B	A	A★
Mark (m)	$0 \leqslant m < 50$	$50 \leqslant m < 60$	$60 \leqslant m < 70$	$70 \leqslant m < 90$	$90 \leqslant m \leqslant 100$

You need a percentage between 90 and 100 to get an A★ and between 70 and 90 to get an A.

90 to 100 is a width of **10**   **70 to 90** is a width of **20**

When you draw a histogram of different width groups you have to change some of the heights of your bars.

This is because it is the **area** of each bar that represents the frequency and not the height.

There are two ways of drawing a histogram.

For the first, you have to choose a 'standard width'.

Then, if your one is twice as wide as the standard width you need to halve the frequency to get the height of the bar. If the group is three times as wide then you divide the frequency by three and so on.

This table shows you the results of Year 11 at Adeney school in the GCSE higher mock exam. Their teacher has grouped the results.

Mark (m)	$0 \leqslant m < 50$	$50 \leqslant m < 60$	$60 \leqslant m < 70$	$70 \leqslant m < 90$	$90 \leqslant m \leqslant 100$
Number of pupils (frequency)	10	10	14	22	8

He wants to draw a histogram of these results.

He adds a third row to the table.

This shows the width of each group.

He chooses 10 as his standard width.

The standard width can be any value but it is best to use the most common width.

He adds two more rows to the table.

The fourth row shows how many standard widths each group is.

The fifth row is the frequency divided by the number of standard widths. This is the **frequency per standard width.** Here, it is the **frequency per 10 marks.**

Mark (m)	$0 \leqslant m < 50$	$50 \leqslant m < 60$	$60 \leqslant m < 70$	$70 \leqslant m < 90$	$90 \leqslant m \leqslant 100$
Number of pupils (frequency)	10	10	14	22	8
Width	50	10	10	20	10
Number of widths of 10 marks	5	1	1	2	1
Frequency per 10 marks	$10 \div 5 = 2$	$10 \div 1 = 10$	$14 \div 1 = 14$	$22 \div 2 = 11$	$8 \div 1 = 8$

Now the teacher can draw a histogram. He draws an evenly spaced graph scale on the mark axis. He labels the vertical axis 'Frequency per 10 marks'.

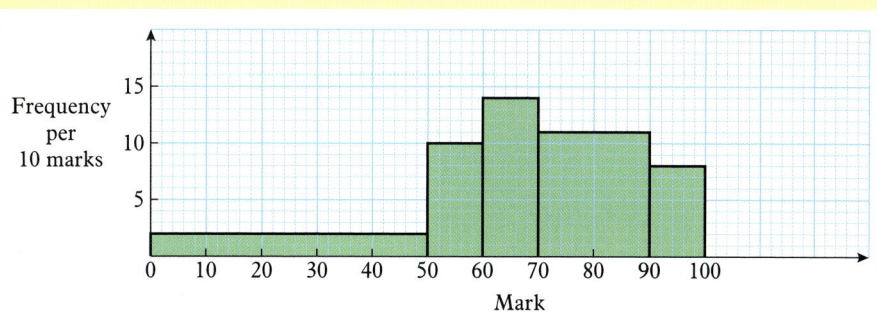

When you draw a histogram:

(1) work out the width of each group

(2) choose your standard width

(3) divide the frequency by the number of standard widths. This gives the heights of the bars

(4) draw the histogram and label it properly.

Exercise 1:8

1 Mr Baljit gave his French class of 32 pupils a vocabulary test.
The results are shown in a table.

Mark (m)	$0 \leqslant m < 20$	$20 \leqslant m < 40$	$40 \leqslant m < 50$	$50 \leqslant m < 70$	$70 \leqslant m \leqslant 100$
Number of pupils (frequency)	2	4	5	12	9
Width	20	20	10		
Number of widths of 10 marks	2	2	1		
Frequency per 10 marks	$2 \div 2 = 1$	$4 \div 2 = 2$	$5 \div 1 = 5$		

   a Copy the table.
   b Fill it in. The first few have been done for you.
   c Draw the histogram for this data. Don't forget the key, labels and title.

2 Rebecca and Phillip time their assemblies at school for a term.
These are their times.

Time taken (min)	$0 \leqslant m < 6$	$6 \leqslant m < 10$	$10 \leqslant m < 14$	$14 \leqslant m < 16$	$16 \leqslant m < 18$	$18 \leqslant m < 25$
Frequency	3	12	16	14	4	7
Width	6	4				
Number of widths of 2 minutes	3	2				
Frequency per 2 minutes	$3 \div 3 = 1$	$12 \div 2 = 6$				

   a Copy the table.
   b Fill it in. The table has been started for you.
   c Draw a histogram of these results.

The second way to draw a histogram is to work out frequency density.

The **frequency density** is the frequency divided by the class width.

This method has the advantage that it doesn't matter if there isn't an obvious standard width to use.
You work out the frequency divided by the class width for all of the groups.
Here is the data from the last example.

Mark (m)	$0 \leqslant m < 50$	$50 \leqslant m < 60$	$60 \leqslant m < 70$	$70 \leqslant m < 90$	$90 \leqslant m < 100$
Number of pupils (frequency)	10	10	14	22	8

This time you only need to add two extra rows to the table.
The third row is still the width of each group.
The fourth row is the frequency divided by the width.
This is the frequency density.

Mark (m)	$0 \leqslant m < 50$	$50 \leqslant m < 60$	$60 \leqslant m < 70$	$70 \leqslant m < 90$	$90 \leqslant m < 100$
Number of pupils (frequency)	10	10	14	22	8
Width	50	10	10	20	10
Frequency density	$10 \div 50 = 0.2$	$10 \div 10 = 1$	$14 \div 10 = 1.4$	$22 \div 20 = 1.1$	$8 \div 10 = 0.8$

Now you draw the histogram.
You label the vertical axis frequency density.

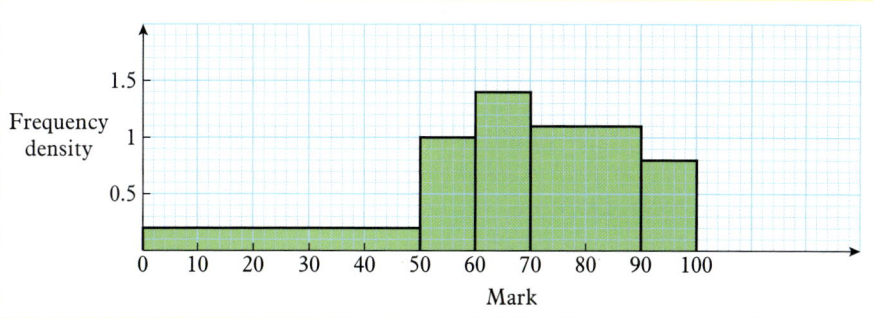

Notice that the final histogram is exactly the same shape as the one you drew when you used a standard width.
The frequency density is actually the frequency per unit width. Here it is the frequency per 1 mark. You can work out the number of people in each group by multiplying the height of the bar by the width.

3 Surjinda looks after 41 children during her work experience.
She organises an obstacle race for them.
These are the times that the children take to finish the course.

Time in seconds (t)	$0 \leqslant t < 30$	$30 \leqslant t < 40$	$40 \leqslant t < 60$	$60 \leqslant t < 90$
Number of children (frequency)	6	8	12	15

   a Copy the table.
   b Add a third row to your table. Label it 'Width'. Fill it in.
   c Add a fourth row to your table. Label it 'Frequency density'. Fill it in.
   d Draw a histogram of these results.

4 This histogram shows the
distribution of marks in a
trial mathematics exam.

   a How many pupils are
shown in each bar?
   b Draw a frequency table
to show this data.
   c What percentage of the
pupils scored more than
60%?

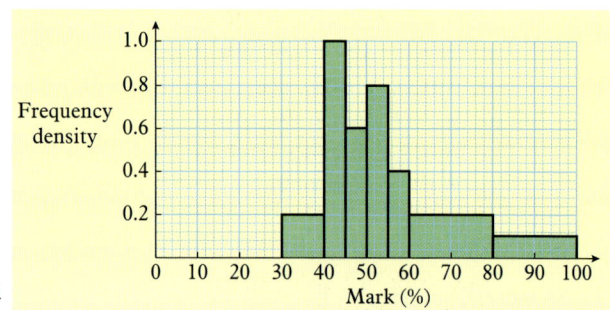

5 Whitecross School Parent Teacher Association have arranged for helpers to
organise their annual show. The table shows the ages of the helpers.

Age (years)	0 up to 5	5 up to 10	10 up to 15	15 up to 20	20 up to 25	25 up to 30	30 up to 35	35 up to 40	40 up to 45	45 up to 50
Frequency	1	0	2	1	6	11	14	8	1	3

The first four age groups from 0 to 20 have low frequencies. John decides to put
these frequencies into one group from 0 up to 20.
   a Which other groups would it be sensible for John to put together?
   b John decided to use 5 years as the standard width. Explain why John did this.
   c Copy the table. Fill it in.

Age (years)					
Frequency					
Width					
Number of widths of 5 years					
Frequency per 5 years					

Mary decides to use a different table to record the data.

d Copy this table. Fill it in.

Age	0 up to 25	25 up to 30	30 up to 35	35 up to 50
Frequency				
Width				
Number of widths of 5 years				
Frequency per 5 years				

e Draw John's histogram. Use this scale on graph paper. Continue the vertical axis up to 15.

f Draw Mary's histogram on another piece of graph paper. Use the same scale.

g Look at the two histograms. Whose histogram is better for showing this information? Give a reason for your answer.

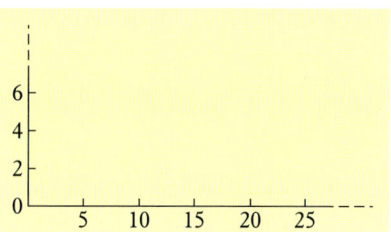

Histograms of continuous data

Frank is a forestry ranger.
One of his jobs is to measure the girth of the trees to measure their rate of growth.
The girth is the circumference around the base of the tree.

He measures the girth in centimetres correct to the nearest centimetre.
This is a table of his results.

Girth in centimetres (to the nearest cm)	40 to 44	45 to 49	50 to 54	55 to 59	60 to 64
Frequency	10	15	21	27	12

The girth is an example of **continuous data** because the lengths have been rounded to the nearest centimetre. Length can be any value.
For example, you could have a length of 46.8 cm.
This would round to 47 cm and would go in to the 45 to 49 group.

Frank wants to draw a diagram to show his results.
He has to draw a histogram because he is showing continuous data.
He knows that he must label the edges of the bars in a histogram.
He draws a new table to show the groups more accurately.

Girth (cm) (to the nearest cm)	40 to 44	45 to 49	50 to 54	55 to 59	60 to 64
Girth (cm)	$39.5 \leqslant g < 44.5$	$44.5 \leqslant g < 49.5$	$49.5 \leqslant g < 54.5$	$54.5 \leqslant g < 59.5$	$59.5 \leqslant g \leqslant 64.5$
Frequency	10	15	21	27	12

Now Frank can draw a histogram to show the results. All of the groups have a width of 5 cm so he does not have to change any of the heights.

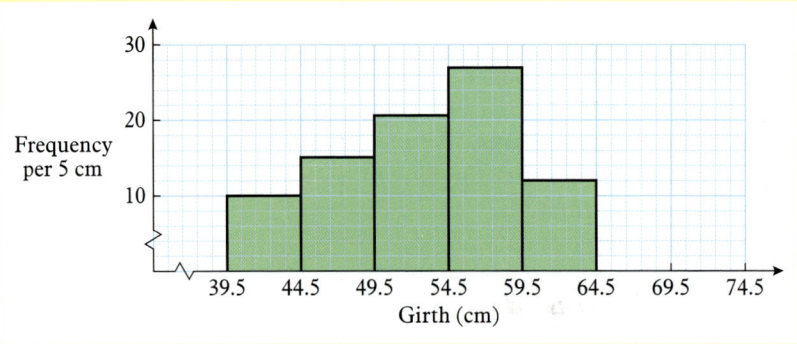

Exercise 1:9

1 An engineering student is completing her study on the expansion of certain metals. She has measured a sample of brass pins correct to the nearest millimetre. Her results are shown below.

> 1.9, 4.1, 4.9, 2.5, 3.3, 5.8, 1.8, 5.9, 2.9, 3.3, 2.4, 5.1, 1.2, 5.1, 3.2,
> 2.8, 4.0, 2.4, 4.7, 2.8, 3.5, 1.2, 5.4, 2.7, 1.7, 2.8, 2.2, 3.8, 2.7, 3.1,
> 2.4, 2.1, 3.4, 1.6, 4.2, 2.5, 5.6, 1.8, 3.5, 5.6, 2.5, 3.2, 1.9, 3.9, 2.7,
> 1.3, 2.6, 3.7, 2.1, 4.4, 1.6, 3.4, 2.0, 3.1, 2.3, 2.6, 1.7, 5.5, 2.6, 2.9

a Group the data into intervals of 5 millimetres.
b Draw a histogram. Remember to put some of the groups together if it is appropriate. Don't forget labels, title and a key.

2 Suzanne and her friends are doing a survey for their mathematics coursework. They asked a number of pupils how long they took to work through a list of multiplication questions given to them the previous night. They used this table to record the pupils' times in minutes to complete the questions.

Time (min)	$0 \leqslant m < 5$	$5 \leqslant m < 15$	$15 \leqslant m < 25$	$25 \leqslant m < 40$	$40 \leqslant m \leqslant 70$
Frequency		16			42

a Copy and complete the histogram to show the results of the survey.

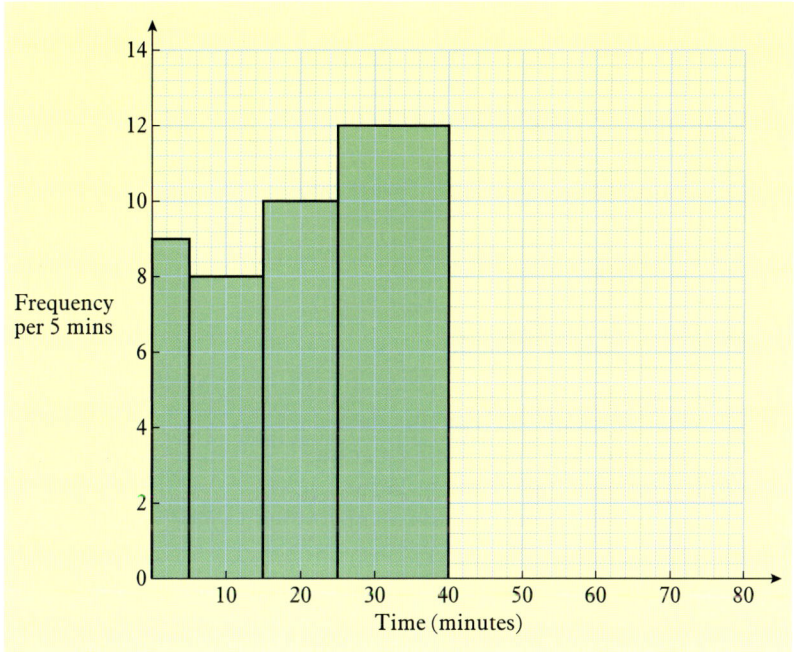

b Calculate the total number of pupils who did the multiplication questions for Suzanne and her friends.

3 The ages of 34 town councillors in Ross-on-Wye are shown in the histogram. Put the information into a table.

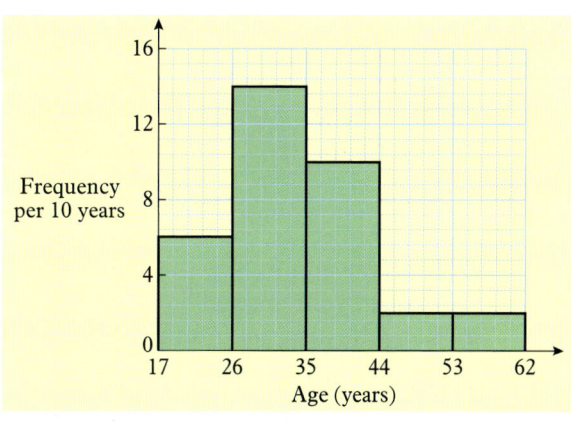

1 This table shows you the marks scored by pupils in a Geography test and a History test.

History	16	24	37	29	18	24	26	34	17	20
Geography	20	26	34	24	20	22	30	28	21	17

a Draw a scatter graph of these marks.
b Draw a line of best fit on your diagram.
c Alan scored 27 for the Geography test, but missed the History test. Use your line of best fit to estimate his History mark.

2 The world record time for running the mile has gradually reduced. The table shows some of the records.

Year	Athlete	Time (secs)
1934	Glenn Cunningham	247
1954	Roger Bannister	239
1965	Michael Jazy	234
1975	John Walker	230
1993	Noureddine Morcelli	224

a Plot a scatter graph to show this data.
b Draw a line of best fit on your diagram.
c Steve Cram held the record in 1985.
Use your graph to estimate his record time in 1985.

3 This scatter graph shows the scores of some pupils in a mental arithmetic test.

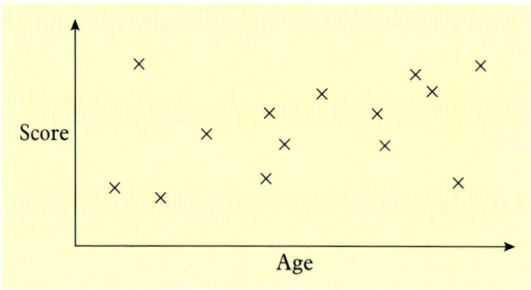

a Does the graph show the sort of result you would expect? Explain your answer.
b Copy the diagram. Add a line of best fit.
c Taking age into account, circle the point that you think shows the best pupil.

4 Sixty-nine Year 10 pupils sat an end-of-term examination.
Their results are shown in the table.

Mark	0 up to 10	10 up to 15	15 up to 20	20 up to 25	25 up to 30	30 up to 35	35 up to 50
Frequency	7	8	14	20	11	6	3

a Copy the table and add three more rows.
b What is a sensible standard width to choose?
Explain your answer.
c Fill in the table.
d Draw a histogram to show the data.

5 The following table shows the ages of the residents of a small village.

Age (years)	0 up to 10	10 up to 20	20 up to 30	30 up to 40	40 up to 50	50 up to 60	60 up to 70	70 up to 80	80 and above
Frequency	6	12	5	7	15	14	12	7	0
Mid-point									

a Copy the table and fill it in.
b Draw a frequency polygon to show the data.

6 The number of bottles of wine sold on fifty-eight consecutive days at Saxty's restaurant is shown in the table.

Number of bottles of champagne	15 up to 20	20 up to 25	25 up to 30	30 up to 35	35 up to 45	45 up to 55
Frequency	10	12	15	9	7	5

Draw a histogram to show the data.

7 Harold celebrated his 100th birthday by having a party with his relations.
The table shows the number of people in each age group at the party.

Age group (years)	10 up to 20	20 up to 30	30 up to 45	45 up to 50	50 up to 70	70 up to 100
Frequency	2	0	6	4	22	12

Draw a histogram to represent the data.

8 The average hourly distances travelled by the 'reps' of an insurance company are shown in the table.

Average daily distance (miles)	0 up to 20	20 up to 30	30 up to 40	40 up to 50	50 up to 80
Frequency	6	8	10	12	6

a Look at the four histograms.
Which **one** of them is the correct diagram?
b Give a reason why each of the others is incorrect.

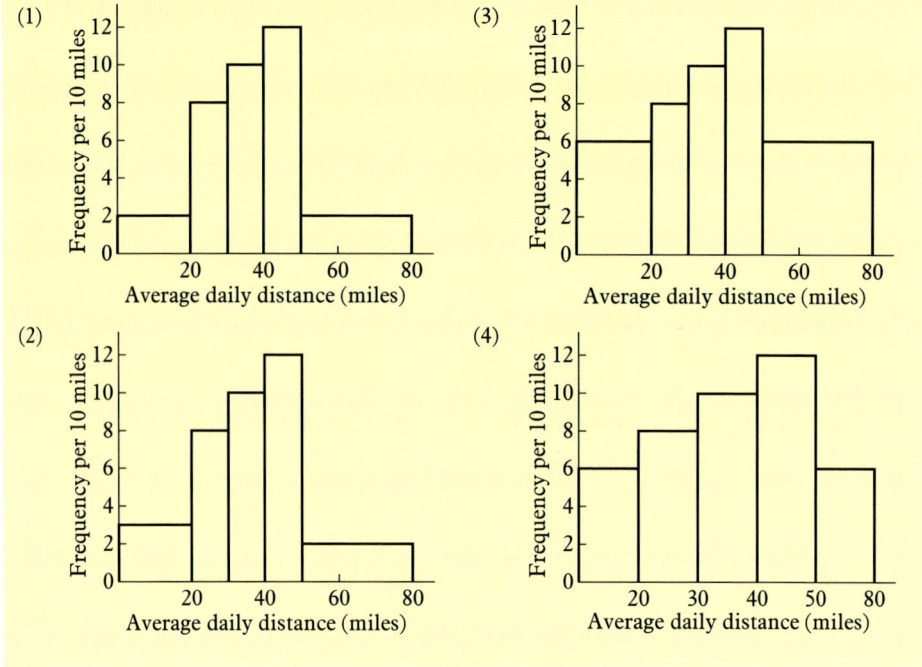

9 Sian is recording the distances that Year 11 boys throw the javelin. She displays the results in a histogram.

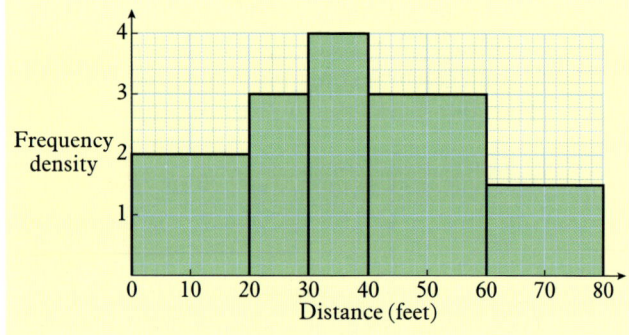

a How many boys threw the javelin less than 40 feet?
b How many boys took part?

1 This histogram shows the results of an experiment to find the lifetime of a batch of video tapes. Work out the total number of tapes that were tested.

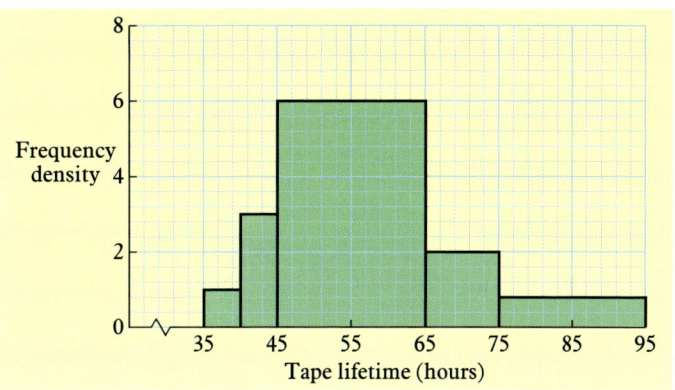

2 The two frequency polygons show the casualties in the population of barn owls studied during 75 days of winter in 1995 and 1997.

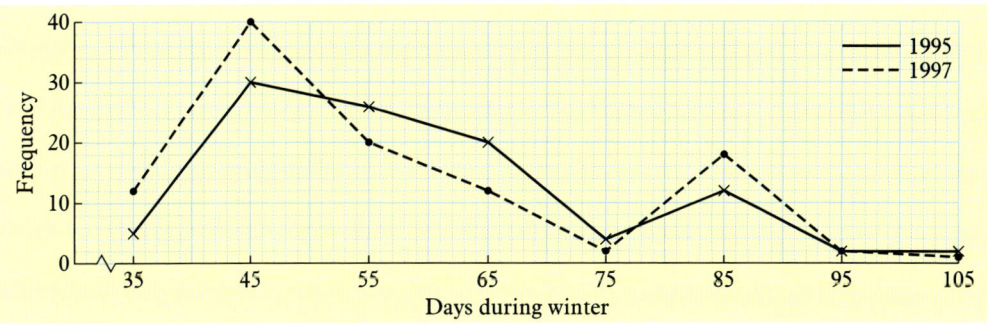

    a What were the possible group intervals in the original table?
    b What conclusions can you draw from the frequency polygons?

3 The histogram shows the distribution of the ages of badger sets.
Show the data in a frequency distribution table.
What is the total number of badger sets?

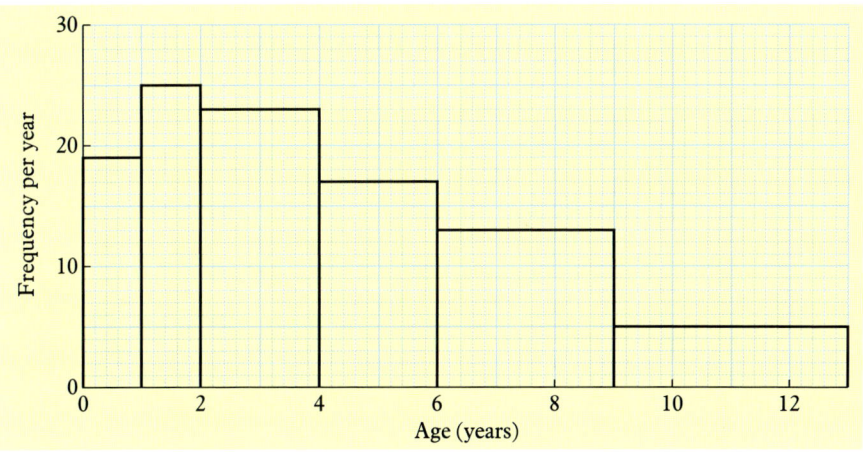

1 Doctor Young and Doctor Old work at St George's Surgery.
The practice manager wants to compare the times that they spend with patients.
This is the data that she has collected.

Time spent in minutes (t)	Number of patients Dr Young	Dr Old
$0 \leqslant t < 5$	16	10
$5 \leqslant t < 10$	14	11
$10 \leqslant t < 15$	10	15
$15 \leqslant t < 20$	6	9
$20 \leqslant t < 25$	4	5

a Draw a frequency polygon for each doctor on the same axes.
b Write down two conclusions that you can draw from this data.

2 Holly buys a bumper box of Christmas cards.
She measures the area of each card. This is her data.

Area in cm² (A)	Number of cards
$20 \leqslant A < 40$	8
$40 \leqslant A < 60$	18
$60 \leqslant A < 80$	17
$80 \leqslant A < 100$	15
$100 \leqslant A < 140$	12
$140 \leqslant A < 180$	11
$180 \leqslant A < 240$	6
$240 \leqslant A < 300$	3

Draw a histogram to show this data.
Use 20 cm² as the standard width.

3 The data shows the rainfall in mm for 30 days for Town A and Town B.

Rainfall in mm (r)	Town A	Town B
$0 \leqslant r < 2$	12	4
$2 \leqslant r < 5$	9	3
$5 \leqslant r < 10$	4	8
$10 \leqslant r < 15$	2	12
$15 \leqslant r < 30$	3	3

a Draw two histograms to show the data for the two towns.
b Comment on the differences between the rainfall in the two towns.

2 Probability diagrams

1 Sample space diagrams
Drawing sample space diagrams
When two events are independent
Using notation in probability
Events that cannot happen at the same time

CORE

2 Tree diagrams
How to draw tree diagrams
Using tree diagrams to find probabilities
How to find probabilities when the words
'at least one' are used

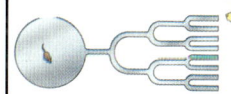

QUESTIONS

EXTENSION

TEST YOURSELF

1 Sample space diagrams

Nicola and her father are buying paint. They are trying to find the best colour to use for redecorating her bedroom. They have to decide which paint colours to mix. They are using a paint chart to help them.
You can use diagrams to help in probability.

Sample space	A **sample space** is a list of all the possible outcomes.
Sample space diagram	A table which shows all of the possible outcomes is called a **sample space diagram**.

Example Toby rolls a dice and spins a £1 coin.
  a Draw a sample space diagram to show all the possible outcomes.
  b Write down the probability that Toby gets a Head and a 5.

a

		Dice					
		1	2	3	4	5	6
Coin	H	H, 1	H, 2	H, 3	H, 4	H, 5	H, 6
	T	T, 1	T, 2	T, 3	T, 4	T, 5	T, 6

b There are 12 equally likely possible outcomes.
(H, 5) appears once.
The probability of getting a Head and a 5 is $\frac{1}{12}$.

Exercise 2:1

1 Ben rolls an 8-sided dice and an ordinary dice.
  a Draw a sample space diagram to show all the possible outcomes of rolling the two dice.

  Write down the probability of getting:
  b a 7 on the 8-sided dice and a 4 on the ordinary dice
  c double 6
  d a number less than 3 on both dice

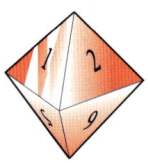

2 David is playing in a football match and Roz is playing in a netball match after school. Both David and Roz are equally likely to win, lose or draw.

    a Draw a sample space diagram to show all the possible outcomes.

Write down the probability that:
b they will both win
c only one of them will win

3 A red dice and a black dice are thrown together.

    a Draw a sample space diagram to show all the possible outcomes.

Write down the probability:
b of getting two odd numbers
c of getting an even number and a prime number
d of getting a prime number and a triangle number
e that the sum of the two numbers is $\leqslant 12$
f that the difference between the two numbers is 3
g that the product of the two numbers is > 12
h that $r < b$, where r is the number on the red dice and b is the number on the black dice

4 Mrs Jones has decided to change the flowers in one of her garden tubs. She has two bags of tulips. Each bag contains one bulb of each of these colours: red, yellow, black, pink, orange, violet and white.
She takes one bulb at random from each bag.

    a Draw a sample space diagram to show all the possible outcomes.

Write down the probability that the tulips will be:
b the same colour
c different colours

5 Jenny has made these two spinners to use in a game to raise money at the school's summer fair.

To play the game you spin both spinners. You only win if both spinners land on the same colour.

    a Draw a sample space diagram showing all the possible outcomes.
    b Write down the probability that a player will win.

Independent events	Two events are **independent** if the outcome of one has no effect on the outcome of the other.

If you roll a fair dice and toss a coin you can get 1, 2, 3, 4, 5 or 6 on the dice and either a head or a tail with the coin.

Whatever you get on the dice has no effect on what you get with the coin.

Exercise 2:2

Look at the events in questions **1–5**.
Write down whether each pair of events is independent.
Give a reason for each answer.

1 Peter throws a dart and scores double 20.
He removes his dart from the board.
Rebecca throws a dart and scores 18.

2 Alison chooses a red smartie at random from a tube and eats it.
Richard then chooses a red smartie at random from the same tube.

3 Jenny draws a red playing card from a pack of 52 cards. She puts the card back and shuffles the pack. Jenny then draws a black card.

4 Tim wins in his next tennis match and Louise passes her music exam.

5 Anna spins this spinner and it lands on 6.
She spins it again and it lands on 2.

Probability of an event A happening	The **probability of an event A happening** can be written as $P(A)$. If A is the event 'getting an ace from a pack of 52 playing cards' then $P(A) = \frac{4}{52} = \frac{1}{13}$
Probability of an event not happening	The **probability of an event not happening** is 1 minus the probability that it *does* happen. For the event A, the event 'not A' is written A'. and $P(A') = 1 - P(A)$ The probability of not getting an ace: $P(A') = 1 - \frac{1}{13}$ $= \frac{12}{13}$

Exercise 2:3

1 The probability that it will snow on the 10th January is $\frac{2}{15}$
Write down the probability that it will not snow on that day.

2 Barbara has three times as much chance of passing the driving test as Jim. Let B be the event that Barbara passes her test and J be the event that Jim passes his test.
If $P(B) = 0.9$
Write down:
a $P(B')$
b $P(J)$
c $P(J')$

3 Look at the word STATISTICS. One of the letters is chosen at random.
V is the event 'getting a vowel' and C is the event 'getting a consonant'.
a Find: (1) $P(V)$ (2) $P(V')$ (3) $P(C)$ (4) $P(C')$
b Explain why $P(V) = P(C')$.

4 Peter's Geography project contains 30 pages (numbered 1–30).
N is the event 'a page chosen at random contains the digit 5'.
a Find $P(N)$
b Find $P(N')$

5 The four teams in a league are Ashley, Livingstone, Cheshire and Shaftesbury. The probability that Ashley will win the sports cup is $\frac{1}{5}$, that Livingstone will win is $\frac{1}{4}$ and that Cheshire will win is $\frac{3}{10}$.
Let S be the event 'Shaftesbury will win the cup'.
  a Write down $P(S)$.
  b Write down $P(S')$.
  c Which team would start as the favourite?

6 *Humble Pi* is a mathematics magazine. Chris is analysing part of the magazine to find the number of letters in each word. He puts the information into a table.

Number of letters	1	2	3	4	5	6	7
Number of words	8	7	12	10	5	4	2

What is the probability that the number of letters in a word chosen at random is:

  a 6   **d** more than 4   **g** a prime number
  b 3   **e** 3 or less
  c 5   **f** between 2 and 7 inclusive

Probability of independent events

If two **events** A and B are **independent** then the **probability** of them both happening is called $P(A \text{ and } B)$

and $P(A \text{ and } B) = P(A) \times P(B)$

Example

Mary throws a dice and tosses a coin.
Find the probability that she gets a head and a 4.

Let H be the event 'getting a head' and F be the event 'getting a 4',

then $P(H) = \frac{1}{2}$ and $P(F) = \frac{1}{6}$

So $P(H \text{ and } F) = \frac{1}{2} \times \frac{1}{6} = \frac{1}{12}$

Exercise 2:4

1 R and S are independent events.
$P(R) = 0.23$ and $P(S) = 0.65$
Find $P(R \text{ and } S)$.

2 Anna and Richard are auditioning for different parts in a play.
The probability that Anna will get her part is $\frac{3}{5}$ and the probability that
Richard will get his part is $\frac{5}{8}$.
Write down the probability that:
a both Anna and Richard will get a part
b neither will get a part
c only Richard gets a part

3 Carmen is responsible for checking the components of the braking
system for new cars. A component has a 2% chance of being faulty.
Two components are selected at random.
Write down the probability that:
a both components are faulty
b neither component is faulty

4 A and B are independent events.
$P(B) = \frac{3}{5}$ and $P(A \text{ and } B) = \frac{12}{45}$
Find the value of $P(A)$.

Mutually exclusive	Events are **mutually exclusive** if they cannot happen at the same time.

When a coin is tossed it can land showing either a head or a tail.
It cannot show *both* a head and a tail at the same time.
One outcome automatically excludes the other.
The events 'showing a head' and 'showing a tail' are mutually exclusive.

Probability of mutually exclusive events

For two **mutually exclusive events** A and B, the **probability**
that *either* event A *or* event B will occur can be found by *adding*
their probabilities together.

$$P(A \text{ or } B) = P(A) + P(B)$$

When a dice is thrown, E is the event 'getting an even number'
and T is the event 'getting a three'.
The events E and T are mutually exclusive.

$$P(E) = \tfrac{1}{2} \quad \text{and} \quad P(T) = \tfrac{1}{6}$$

So $P(E \text{ or } T) = \tfrac{1}{2} + \tfrac{1}{6} = \tfrac{2}{3}$

Exercise 2:5

1 State whether each pair of events is mutually exclusive.
- **a** When tossing a dice:
  'getting a 2' and 'getting an even number'.
- **b** When picking a card at random from a pack of cards:
  'getting a red card' and 'getting an ace'.
- **c** When choosing a person at random from a group of people:
  'getting a man with brown hair' and 'getting a woman with grey hair'.

2 In a school raffle Michelle buys 5 tickets and Jonathan buys 10 tickets. 300 tickets are sold altogether.
What is the probability that:
- **a** Michelle wins first prize
- **b** Michelle or Jonathan wins first prize?

3 A tin of biscuits contains 3 shortbreads, 9 custard creams and 6 bourbons. Jemima chooses a biscuit at random.
Find the probability that Jemima chooses:
- **a** a shortbread
- **b** a bourbon
- **c** a shortbread or a bourbon
- **d** a custard cream or a bourbon

4 The events G and H are mutually exclusive:
$$P(G) = \tfrac{1}{3} \qquad P(H) = \tfrac{3}{5}$$
Find $P(G \text{ or } H)$.

5 The events M and S are mutually exclusive:
$$P(M) = \tfrac{2}{5} \qquad P(M \text{ or } S) = \tfrac{3}{4}$$
Find $P(S)$.

Exercise 2:6

In this exercise you need to decide whether the events are independent or mutually exclusive before you work out each probability.

1 The probabilities that Damon and Michael will pass their driving test are $\tfrac{2}{3}$ and $\tfrac{1}{5}$ respectively. Find the probability that:
- **a** Damon *and* Michael pass
- **b** they both fail
- **c** only Damon passes.

2 In an accident during a game of
rugby, the probabilities that a player
will break an arm, a leg or a rib are
$\frac{1}{8}, \frac{1}{12}$ and $\frac{1}{6}$ respectively.
Write down the probability of breaking:
a an arm and a rib
b an arm and a leg and a rib
c none of these

3 Harry is taking his end of year exams. These are
the probabilities of Harry passing each exam:

P(passing Maths) $= 0.65$

P(passing English) $= 0.8$

P(passing French) $= 0.45$

Assuming that the events are independent find the probability that
Harry will:
a pass all three exams   **c** pass English but fail Maths
b fail all three exams   **d** pass Maths but fail French

4 Katy checks the oil and screenwash containers in her car every two
weeks to see if they need topping up.
The probability that she needs to top up the oil is 0.25 and the
probability that she needs to top up the screenwash is 0.3
Find the probability that the next time Katy checks her car:
a both need topping up
b only the oil needs topping up
c neither needs topping up

5 Sian prints pictures onto sweatshirts. She has four designs and three
colours.
The four designs are: animal, bird, insect, fish
The three colours are: red, blue, black
Sian chooses the design and colour at random.
Find the probability that she chooses:
a an animal design
b a bird design in red
c a fish or insect design
d an animal or bird design in black
e a design in blue
f a bird or fish design in blue or red

2 Tree diagrams

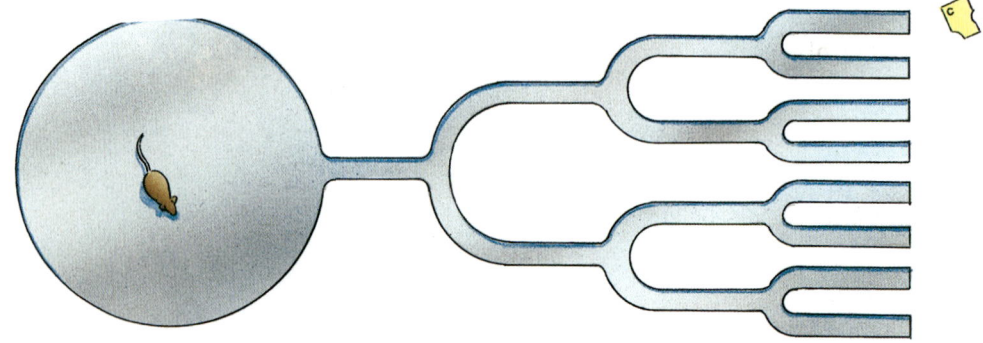

There are many paths that the mouse can take through the maze of tunnels. Only one of these paths leads to the food.

Tree diagrams   You can use **tree diagrams** to show the outcomes of two or more events.
Each branch represents a possible outcome of one event.
The probability of each outcome is written on the branch.
The final result depends on the path taken through the tree.

Example   The probability that a new company will fail in the first 5 years is 0.6
Two new companies are chosen at random.

   a Show all the possible outcomes on a tree diagram.
   b Use the diagram to find the probability that both will fail.
   c Find the probability that only one company fails.

  a The first set of branches of the tree shows what can happen to the first company.

    The second set of branches shows what can happen to the second company.

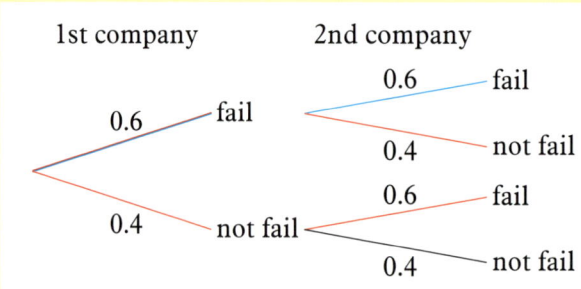

Each path through the tree gives a different outcome.
The tree has four paths so there are four outcomes.

b The blue path gives the outcome 'both companies will fail'.
You *multiply* the probabilities on the branches of this path.
This gives you the probability of this final outcome.

The probability that both companies will fail is $0.6 \times 0.6 = 0.36$

c Each red path gives an outcome of one of the two companies failing.

The top red path gives the probability
of the first company failing $\quad = 0.6 \times 0.4$
$\quad = 0.24$

The lower red path gives the probability
of the second company failing $\quad = 0.4 \times 0.6$
$\quad = 0.24$

Now you *add* the probabilities of each path to find
the probability that only one company fails $\quad = 0.24 + 0.24$
$\quad = 0.48$

Remember: You **multiply** the probabilities along the branches.
You **add** the probabilities when more than one path is used.

Exercise 2:7

1 Jenny posts two letters at her local post office. The probability that a
letter posted will be delivered the next morning is 0.96
  a Copy this tree diagram to show all the possible outcomes.
  Fill in the probabilities.

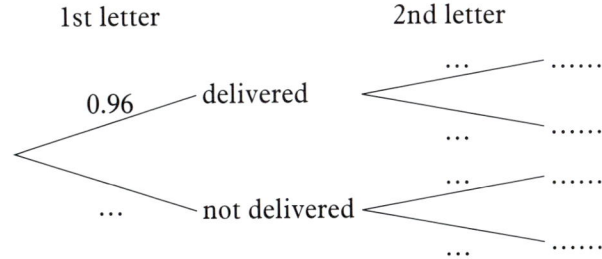

Find the probability that:
  b neither letter will be delivered the next morning
  c only one letter will be delivered the next morning

2 Gary uses two buses to get to work.
The probability that the first bus is late is 0.2
The probability that the second bus is late is 0.3
Use a tree diagram to find the probability that:

a both buses are late

b both buses are not late

c the first bus is late but the second bus is not late

d only one bus is late

3 The probability that a new car will develop a fault in the first 6 months
is $\frac{1}{10}$. Three new cars are chosen at random.
Copy this tree diagram. Finish it off.
Fill in the probabilities.

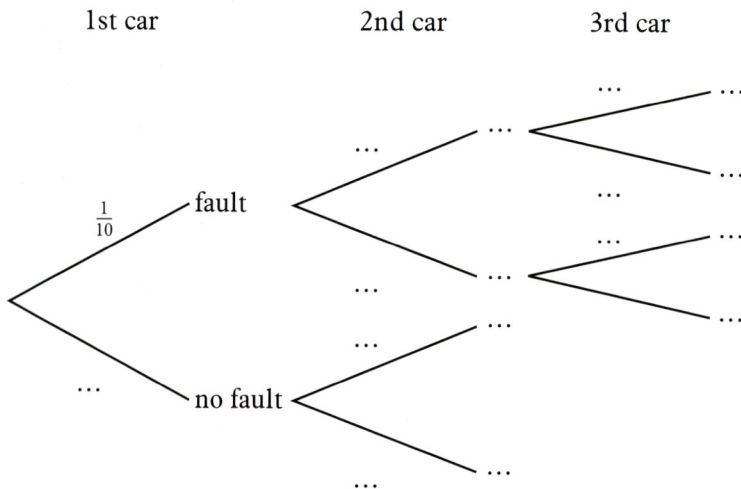

Use your tree to find the probability that:

a all three cars will develop a fault

b none of the cars will develop a fault

c exactly two cars will develop faults

4 Jenny tosses a coin three times.

a Draw a tree diagram showing all the possible outcomes.

Use your tree diagram to find the probability that Jenny gets:

b three heads

c exactly two heads

d exactly one head

e more heads than tails

Tree diagrams can take a long time to draw if all outcomes are included. You can simplify them by only drawing paths that are needed.

Example

Penny rolls a dice three times.
Find the probability that she gets exactly two 6s.

Although the possible outcomes are 1, 2, 3, 4, 5 and 6 the question only involves 6s.
You only need to draw paths to show 'a 6' or 'not a 6'

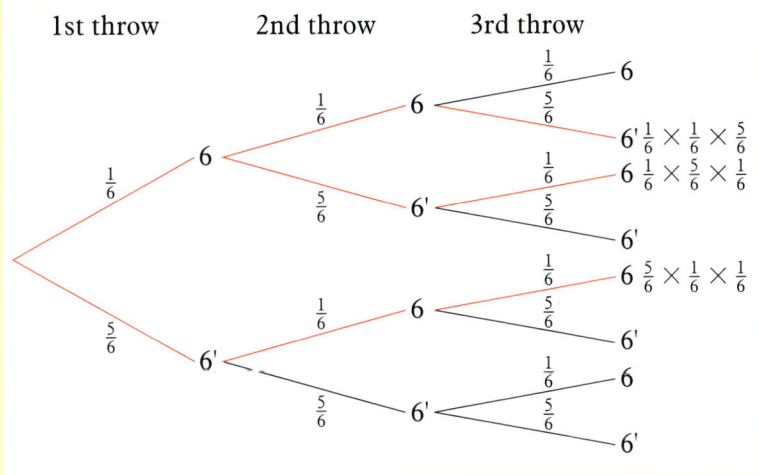

The three red paths give exactly two 6s.

$P(\text{exactly two 6s}) = (\frac{1}{6} \times \frac{1}{6} \times \frac{5}{6}) + (\frac{1}{6} \times \frac{5}{6} \times \frac{1}{6}) + (\frac{5}{6} \times \frac{1}{6} \times \frac{1}{6})$

$= \frac{15}{216} = \frac{5}{72}$

Exercise 2:8

1 Graham has a box containing 20 counters. Four are red, six are green and the rest are blue.
Graham picks out one counter at random and then replaces it.
He then picks out a second counter at random.
Use a tree diagram to find the probability that:
a both counters are red **b** only one counter is red

2 Keith uses this spinner three times.
Use a tree diagram to find the
probability that Keith gets:
a only two blues
b only one blue

3 Ellen chooses one card at random from a pack of cards and then replaces
it. She does this two more times.
Use a tree diagram to find the probability that Ellen gets:
a three hearts
b only one heart
c no hearts

You have been drawing tree diagrams for independent combined events.
Sometimes the events are not independent.

Example

Sally has two tennis matches to play.
The probability of her winning the first match is $\frac{3}{5}$
If she wins the first match the probability of her winning the
second is $\frac{7}{10}$
If she loses the first match the probability of her winning the
second match is $\frac{2}{5}$
Use a tree diagram to find the probability that Sally:

a wins both matches   **b** wins only one of her matches

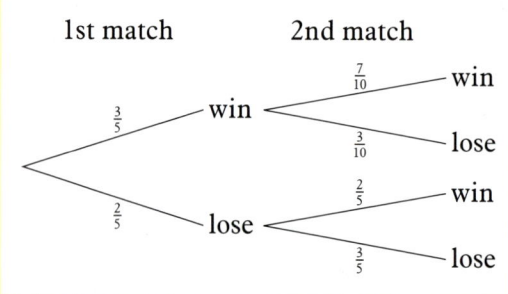

1st match   2nd match

a $P(\text{Sally wins both matches}) = \frac{3}{5} \times \frac{7}{10} = \frac{21}{50}$

b $P(\text{Sally wins only one of her matches}) = (\frac{3}{5} \times \frac{3}{10}) + (\frac{2}{5} \times \frac{2}{5})$
$$= \frac{17}{50}$$

Exercise 2:9

1 Sam has a box of chocolates containing 12 milk and 8 plain chocolates.
Sam takes out two chocolates and eats them.
Use a tree diagram to find the probability that:
- **a** both chocolates are plain
- **b** only one chocolate is plain
- **c** neither of the chocolates are plain

2 A swimming team consists of four
girls and six boys.
Three of them are chosen at
random to represent the team.
Use a tree diagram to find the
probability that:
- **a** all three will be girls
- **b** only one girl will be chosen
- **c** only one boy will be chosen

3 A box contains 20 balls. Five are red, seven are blue and the rest are green.
Two balls are removed at random from the box.
By drawing a tree diagram find the probability that:
- **a** both balls will be green
- **b** only one ball is blue
- **c** neither of the balls is red

4 Dale has a probability of 0.2 of being late for lectures.
When he is late he has a probability of 0.8 of finding the car park full.
Otherwise he has a probability of 0.4 of finding the car park full.
- **a** Draw a tree diagram to show the possible outcomes.

Use your tree diagram to find the probability that:
- **b** Dale is late and finds the car park full
- **c** Dale finds the car park full

5 One lunchtime three times as many men as women ordered meals at a
restaurant. 70% of the men and 30% of the women ordered chips.
Find the probability that a diner chosen at random is:
- **a** a woman
- **b** a man who ordered chips
- **c** a person who ordered chips
- **d** a woman who didn't order chips

Sometimes one of the paths of a tree diagram stops before the others.

Example   Julia is taking a music exam. The probability of her passing the first time is 0.6
If she fails and resits, the probability of her passing the second time is 0.7
a Draw a tree diagram to show the possible outcomes.
b Find the probability of her failing both times.

a

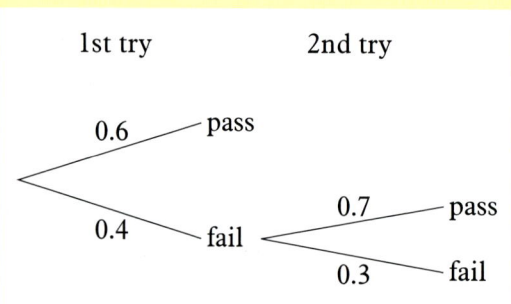

1st try   2nd try

0.6 ——— pass

0.7 ——— pass

0.4 ——— fail

0.3 ——— fail

The first pathway stops because she has passed the exam. There is no need for her to resit.

b *P*(her failing both times) $= 0.4 \times 0.3$
$= 0.12$

Exercise 2:10

1 The probability of pupils using Parry's driving school passing their driving test for the first time is 0.6. If they fail the first time the probability of their passing the test the next time is 0.7
   a Draw a tree diagram to show all the possible outcomes.
   Find the probability that a pupil chosen at random will:
   b pass on the second try
   c fail on both tries

2 Harry has three chances to lift a set of weights.
The probability of him succeeding on the first try is 0.8
On each try after that he has a probability of 0.4 of succeeding.
   a Draw a tree diagram to show all the possible outcomes.

Find the probability of Harry:
   b failing on the first try
   c failing on the first two tries
   d succeeding on the third try
   e failing on all three tries

You can use mutually exclusive events to find a quick method for finding probabilities which involve the words *at least one*.

Example

A bag contains 4 yellow and 6 red balls.
Two balls are picked out at random.
Find the probability that *at least one* ball is red.

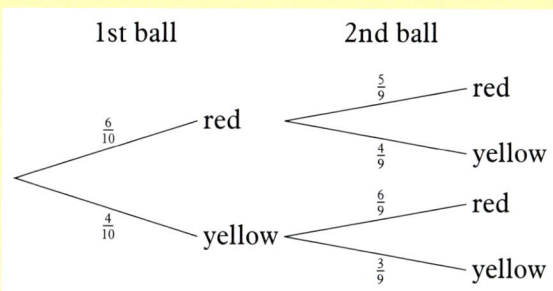

The events P '*at least one* ball is red' and P' '*no* balls are red' are mutually exclusive and nothing else is possible.

Either *no* balls are red or *at least one* of them is red.

P(at least one ball is red) $= 1 - P$(no balls are red)
$$= 1 - (\tfrac{4}{10} \times \tfrac{3}{9})$$
$$= 1 - \tfrac{12}{90}$$
$$= \tfrac{13}{15}$$

Exercise 2:11

1 Carl throws two dice. Find the probability of Carl getting at least one six.

2 Mia picks two cards at random from a pack of cards.
Find the probability that at least one of them is a spade.

3 Geoff spins three coins.
Find the probability of him getting at least one tail.

4 Kiran buys 6 raffle tickets. Two hundred tickets are sold altogether.
There are three prizes. Find the probability that Kiran wins at least one prize.

Exercise 2:12

Answer these questions with or without a tree diagram.

1 Emma is making jewellery with semi-precious stones. The probability of a stone having a flaw is 0.3
Emma has made a pendant using 3 stones.
Find the probability that, of the stones she used:
  a none is flawed
  b only one is flawed
  c at least one is flawed

2 Cara sorts plates in a china factory. Of the plates made 70% are perfect, 25% are seconds and the rest are chipped.
The chipped ones are destroyed.
Cara picks out two plates at random.
Find the probability that:
  a they are both perfect
  b they both have to be destroyed
  c at least one is a second

3 Dariel drives through two sets of traffic lights on his way to work. The probability that he has to stop at the first set is $\frac{3}{5}$ and that he has to stop at the second is $\frac{1}{2}$
Find the probability that he has to stop at:
  a both sets of lights
  b just one set of lights
  c at least one set of lights

4 Tom is practising his archery. He says his probability of hitting the bull's-eye with an arrow is 0.4. If there is an arrow already in the bull's-eye then his probability of hitting the bull's-eye falls to 0.3
Tom shoots three arrows. Find the probability that:
  a all three arrows miss the bull's-eye
  b at least one arrow misses the bull's-eye
  c two arrows hit the bull's-eye

5 Veena is taking exams in Maths, English and History. The probability that she passes Maths is 0.6
The corresponding probabilities for English and History are 0.8 and 0.3
Find the probability that Veena:
  a passes all three exams
  b fails just one exam
  c passes at least one exam

1 Ian spins a 5-sided spinner numbered 1 to 5 at the same time as rolling a fair dice numbered 1 to 6. He writes down the two numbers he gets. Draw a sample space diagram to show all the possible outcomes and use it to find the following probabilities.

   a The total score is 7.

   b The score is the same on the dice and the spinner.

   c The total is less than 5.

   d The score on the dice and the spinner is the same and the total score is less than 5.

2 Which of the following pairs of events are independent and which are mutually exclusive? Give reasons for your answers.

   a Peter chooses at random the ace of clubs from a pack of cards and then replaces it. Surjinda then chooses at random the queen of hearts.

   b Mr McCavity wins the 2:30 race at Newbury this Saturday. Mr McCavity wins the 2:30 race at Haydock this Saturday.

3 A bag contains 5 white discs, 3 black discs and 2 green discs. Robert takes a disc from the bag at random. Let the events 'getting a white, black or green disc' be W, B or G. Write down:

   a $P(W)$ **b** $P(B')$ **c** $P(G')$ **d** $P(W \text{ or } B)$

4 Birth statistics show that the probability of a baby being male is 0.51 The Fletcher and Edmundson families are each expecting a baby. What is the probability that both babies are girls?

5 Write four questions based upon birthdays where the answers are the following probabilities.

   a $\frac{1}{365}$ **b** $\frac{31}{366}$ **c** $\frac{335}{365}$ **d** $\frac{1}{7}$

6 An archery target has a bull's-eye worth 25 points, a middle ring worth 15 points and an outer ring worth 5 points. When Amanda fires an arrow at the target, the probability that she scores 5 points is $\frac{2}{5}$, the probability that she scores 15 points is $\frac{1}{3}$ and the probability that she scores a bull's-eye is $\frac{1}{5}$.

   a What is the probability that Amanda misses the target?

Amanda fires two arrows at the target. Find the probability that she:

   b misses the target with both arrows

   c scores a total of 20 points

   d scores a total of 0 points or 30 points

7 The probability of Sara having carrots for Sunday dinner is $\frac{3}{4}$
The probability of her having apple pie for pudding is $\frac{1}{10}$

Find the probability that Sara has:
a carrots but not apple pie
b apple pie but not carrots
c neither carrots nor apple pie

8 Ruth chooses three numbers at random from the numbers 1, 2, 3 and 4. She can choose the same number more than once.

a List the twenty different possible selections of the three numbers.

Write down the probability that these numbers could be the lengths of the sides of:
b an equilateral triangle
c a triangle that is isosceles but not equilateral
d any triangle

9 Two drawing pins are dropped. The probability that a drawing pin lands point up is $\frac{1}{4}$

a Draw a tree diagram to show all the possible outcomes.

Find the probability that:
b both drawing pins will land point up
c only one drawing pin will land point up

10 The probability that a family has three or more children is $\frac{1}{9}$
Two families are chosen at random.

a Draw a tree diagram to show all the possible outcomes.

Find the probability that:
b neither family has three or more children
c only one family has three or more children

11 The probability that a light bulb will fail in the first year is 0.3
Three bulbs are chosen at random.

a Draw a tree diagram to show all the possible outcomes.

Find the probability that:
b all three will fail in the first year
c only two will fail in the first year
d none will fail in the first year

12 Tarvin Tennis Club have two matches to play.
One is at home and the other is away.
The probability that they will win the home match is $\frac{4}{5}$
The probability that they will win the away match is $\frac{3}{5}$
Use a tree diagram to find the probability that:
a they win both matches
b they lose both matches
c they lose only one of the matches

13 The probability that the Stone cricket team will win their next match is 0.6
The probability that they will draw is 0.15
a Copy and complete the tree diagram showing the outcomes of their next two matches.

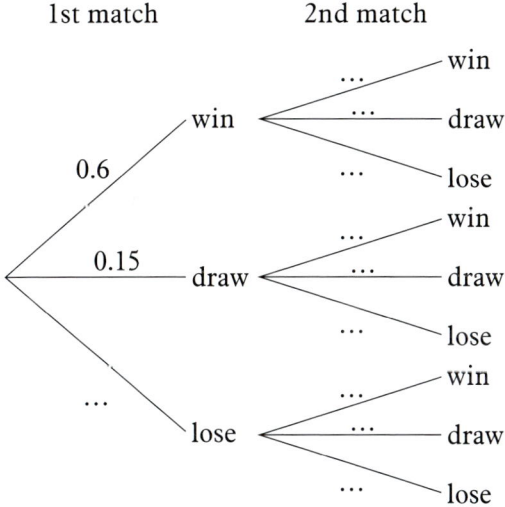

1st match   2nd match

Use your tree diagram to find the probability that:
b they draw the next two matches
c they draw the first match and win the second
d they win only one match

14 A box of fruit contains 6 apples and 4 oranges.
Two pieces of fruit are removed at random.
By drawing a tree diagram, or otherwise, calculate the probability that:
a both will be apples
b only one will be an apple
c at least one will be an apple

1 In a school survey of 36 girls, the numbers playing the piano, flute and clarinet are shown in the diagram. If a girl is picked at random from this group, write down the probability that she plays:

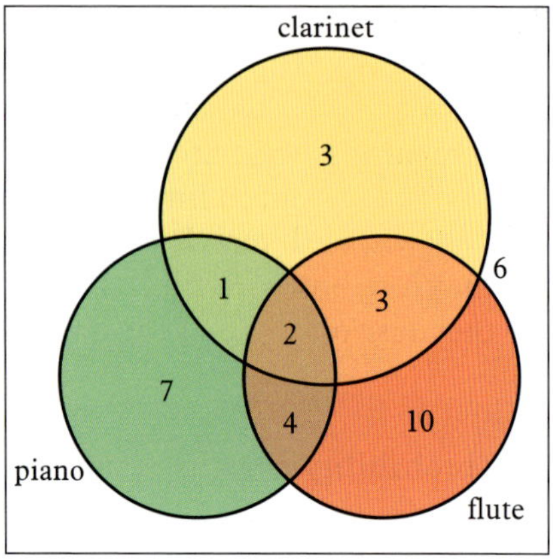

  a the piano
  b only the flute
  c the clarinet
  d the piano and the flute but not the clarinet
  e all three instruments
  f none of the instruments
  g only the clarinet and the piano
  h If a girl who plays the piano is chosen at random, what is the probability that she plays the flute?

2 A box contains x yellow discs, $2x$ green discs, and $3x$ red discs.
A disc is chosen at random. Let Y be the event when a yellow disc is chosen.
Similarly G and R are the events when a green or red disc is chosen.
Write down the following probabilities:

  a $P(Y)$ **c** $P(R)$ **e** $P(G')$
  b $P(G)$ **d** $P(Y')$ **f** $P(R')$

3 Pat uses the underground each day. The table shows how long she waited for a train each day for the last 50 days.

Time t (min)	$0 \leqslant t < 2$	$2 \leqslant t \leqslant 5$	$5 < t < 10$
Frequency	12	30	8

  a Write down the probability that she has to wait more than 5 minutes.

  Use a tree diagram to find the probability that, for the next two days, she will have to wait:
  b less than 2 minutes on both days
  c between 2 and 5 minutes on only one day

4 Paul applies for membership of a very popular club. He has a 50% chance of being accepted the first time. If he is not accepted he reapplies. Each time he reapplies the chance of him being accepted increases by 10%.
Find the probability that Paul is accepted on his:
  a second try   **b** third try   **c** sixth try

1 Paul and his sister, Eileen, both have to play a match this weekend.
Paul plays squash and Eileen plays tennis.
The probability that Paul wins his squash match is 0.85
The probability that Eileen wins her tennis match is 0.6

Find the probability that

a Paul does not win his squash match

b they both win

c they both lose

d Paul wins his match but Eileen loses her match

e one wins and the other loses

2 a Two events Q and R are independent.
$P(Q) = \frac{1}{4}$, $P(R) = \frac{1}{3}$. Find $P(Q$ and $R)$.

b Two events S and T are mutually exclusive.
$P(S) = \frac{2}{5}$, $P(T) = \frac{1}{2}$. Find $P(S$ or $T)$.

c $P(A) = 0.4$, $P(B) - 0.2$, $P(A$ and $B) = 0.075$
Explain how you can tell from these values that the events A and B
are not independent.

d $P(C) = 0.85$ and $P(D) = 0.3$
Are C and D mutually exclusive?
Explain how you can tell.

3 Mia spins both of these fair spinners.

a Draw a sample space diagram
to show all the possible outcomes.

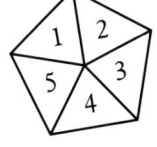 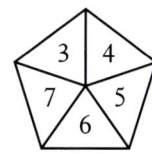

Write down the probability that

b both spinners show an even number

c both spinners show the same number

d the total score is 8

e the total score is a number less than 6

f the total score is more than 4 but less than 10

4   The weather forecast gives a 35% chance of rain.
    Write down the probability that it will not rain.

5   Danny picks a counter at random from a box of counters.
    The table shows the probability that Danny gets a red, blue or green
    counter.

Colour	red	blue	green
Probability	0.38	0.29	0.19

   a Are there any other colours in the box?
      Explain how you can tell.

   b Write down the probability that Danny picks out a red or blue
      counter.

6   Selena serves three balls in a game of tennis.
    The probability that she serves an ace on any one serve is 0.15

   a Copy and complete the tree diagram to show all the possible
      outcomes of the three serves.

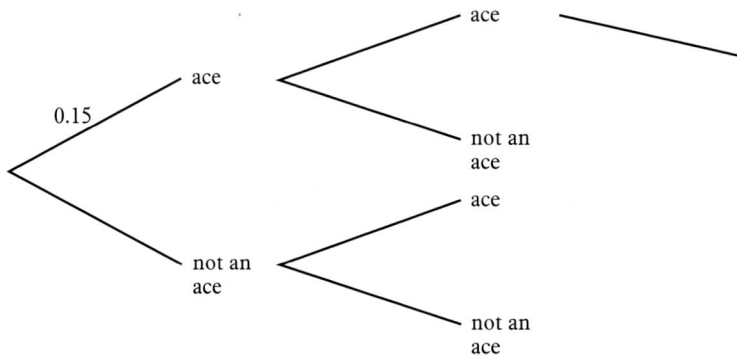

   1st serve   2nd serve   3rd serve

   Find the probability that Selena will serve:
   b   three aces   d   just two aces
   c   at least one ace   e   less than three aces

3 Statistics: about average

CORE

QUESTIONS

EXTENSION

TEST YOURSELF

1 Averages and range

During most races, cars will make at least one pit-stop to change the tyres. Mechanics have been known to change all four tyres in less than 5 seconds.

W You need Worksheet 3:1.
The worksheet helps you to understand the need for more than one kind of average.

Mode

The **mode** is the **most common** or most popular data value. It is sometimes called the **modal value**.

The mode is most useful when one value appears much more often than any other. If the data values are too varied then the mode should not be used.

Median

To find the median of a set of data, put the values in order of size.
The **median** is the **middle** value.

When the number of values is even there are *two* middle values. In this case, choose the value half way between the middle pair. If you have n data values, $\frac{1}{2}(n + 1)$ gives the position of the median.

The median can be used even if the data values are all different. It is possible to make big changes to some of the data without affecting the median. This lack of sensitivity is sometimes an advantage but it can make it unsuitable for some applications.

Mean

To find the **mean** of a set of data:
(1) find the total of all the data values
(2) divide the total by the number of data values.

Every value in the data affects the mean. This sensitivity to change can be useful, but extreme values can have too much influence.

You can find averages from frequency tables.

This table shows the number of pit-stops taken by Formula 1 drivers in one race.

Number of stops x	Frequency f
1	2
2	11
3	10
4	1

The **modal number** of stops is the number with the highest frequency.
The mode is 2
Unfortunately, in this case, there are almost as many 3s in the data, but this is ignored if the mode is used.

The **median** is the middle value.
You find the total number of drivers by adding together all of the frequencies.
The total frequency is written as $\sum f = 2 + 11 + 10 + 1 = 24$
So the position of the median is $\frac{1}{2}(24 + 1) = 12.5$

You need to look at the 12th and 13th values and choose the value in the middle.
Write the data in order of size. The 12th and 13th values are both equal to 2
So the median is 2
In this case, the median gives the same result as the mode. Both methods fail to take the high number of 3s into account.

The **mean** is $\dfrac{\text{Total number of stops}}{\text{Total frequency}}$

You find the total number of stops by adding together the values of $x \times f$.
Do this by adding another column to the table.

Number of stops x	Frequency f	$x \times f = fx$
1	2	$1 \times 2 = 2$
2	11	$2 \times 11 = 22$
3	10	$3 \times 10 = 30$
4	1	$4 \times 1 = 4$
	$\sum f = 24$	$\sum fx = 58$

Mean number of stops is $\bar{x} = \frac{58}{24} = 2.41\ldots = 2.4$ to 1 dp.

In this case, even though it is impossible to have 2.4 stops, the mean gives a representative value that takes account of all the data values.

Exercise 3:1

1 The average number of children per family in the UK is often quoted as 2.4 even though it is impossible to have 2.4 children.
  a Which average has been used to give this figure?

A recent newspaper article claims that the figure for Scotland has fallen to 1.5 children per family. The article goes on to say that the Scottish race will disappear within 20 generations unless the trend is reversed.

  b What does the average number of children per family need to be to keep the population stable?
  c Round 2.4 and 1.5 to the nearest whole number.
  d Explain why the mean number of children per family should be given to at least one decimal place.
  e What advantage does the mean have over the mode and median to represent the number of children per family?

2 The times that some Formula 1 teams took to change a set of tyres have been rounded to the nearest second. One of the teams struggled with a faulty wheel-nut.

The table shows the number of teams for each time.

Time (seconds) x	Frequency f	$x \times f = fx$
5	2	
6	3	
7	7	
8	1	
87	1	

  a Write down the modal time.
  b Work out $\sum f$
  c Find the median time.
  d Copy the table. Fill in the last column.
  e Find the mean time to the nearest second.
  f Explain why the mean does not give a good representative value in this case.

Sometimes the data in a table is grouped.

When data is grouped you cannot tell which data value is the most common.
You can only say which group has the most values in it.
This group is called the modal group.

The table shows the number of seasons that drivers have completed with their present teams.

Number of seasons	Frequency f
0–2	18
3–4	9
5–10	5
11–20	2

In the table the modal group is 0–2 seasons because it has the highest frequency.

You cannot find the exact value of the mean when the data has been grouped.
You can **estimate** the mean by using the mid-value of each group.

To find a mid-value you add the values at the ends of the group and divide by two.
In this case, the data is **discrete** and so the end values are as shown in the table.

The mid-value for the top row is $\frac{1}{2}(0 + 2) = 1$

The mid-value for the second row is $\frac{1}{2}(3 + 4) = 3.5$

Write these values in a third column and use them as the x values.

Number of seasons	Frequency f	Mid-value x	fx
1–2	18	1	18
3–4	9	3.5	31.5
5–10	5	7.5	37.5
11–20	2	15.5	31
	$\sum f = 34$		$\sum fx = 118$

The estimate of the mean can then be found in the usual way.

Estimate of the mean $= \dfrac{\sum fx}{\sum f} = \dfrac{118}{34} = 3.5$ seasons to 1 dp.

Exercise 3:2

1 The table shows the number of all time driver wins in Formula 1 racing.

Number of wins	Frequency f	Mid-value x	fx
1–5	44		
6–10	13		
11–15	8		
16–25	6		
26–55	5		

a Write down the modal group.
b Copy the table. Fill in the missing values.
c Estimate the mean number of wins.

2 The data that you used to estimate the mean in question **1** was grouped from the following original information.

Number of wins	1	2	3	4	5	6	7	8	10	11	12
Frequency	20	11	6	2	5	6	1	2	4	1	3

Number of wins	13	14	16	21	23	24	25	27	31	41	51
Frequency	1	3	1	1	1	1	2	2	1	1	1

a What is the modal number of wins?
b Explain why the mode does not give a good representative value in this case.
c Work out the true value of the mean.
d Comment on the accuracy of your estimate.
e Use the original information to replace the 1–5 group with two new groups 1–2 and 3–5. Find a new estimate of the mean.
f Explain how the new grouping has affected the estimate of the mean.

3 Use the original data given in question **2**.
a What is the median number of wins?
b Which average do you think best represents the data. Give a reason for your answer.

When the grouped data is **continuous**, care is needed with the end-values. These are some of the ways that the size of groups can be written.

21–30

31–40 $\longleftarrow$ This means 30.5 up to, but not including, 40.5

41–50   You use 30.5 and 40.5 to work out the middle value.

100–

200– $\longleftarrow$ This means 200 up to, but not including, 300

300–   You use 200 and 300 to work out the middle value.

Special care is needed with age, for example, which is counted in **completed** years.

21–30

31–40 $\longleftarrow$ This means 31 up to, but not including, 41

41–50   You use 31 and 41 to work out the middle value.

Sometimes algebra is used in a table to show the size of the groups.

$10 < x \leqslant 20$ 10 is not included in the group but 20 is included. You use 10 and 20 to work out the middle value.

$10 \leqslant x < 20$ 10 is included in the group but 20 is not included. You still use 10 and 20 to work out the middle value.

4 The table shows the times spent by people travelling to a race meeting.

Time in minutes (x)	$0 \leqslant x < 60$	$60 \leqslant x < 120$	$120 \leqslant x < 240$	$240 \leqslant x < 360$
Number of people	29	145	204	31

a Write down the modal group.
b Estimate the mean time spent travelling.

5 The table shows the ages of 100 spectators at a race meeting.

Age in years	10–15	16–25	26–35	36–45	46–55
Frequency	6	24	37	22	11

a Write down the modal group.
b Estimate the mean age of these spectators.

Moving averages

Averages can be used to show trends in data.
Look at this graph.
It shows Rob's weekly scores in cricket.
The lines drawn on the graph are trend lines.
The blue line shows that Rob is improving.
The red line shows that Rob is getting worse.
But which line is correct?

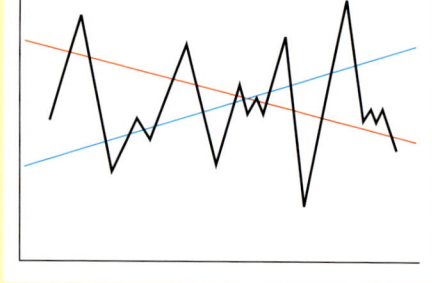

To answer this question we can use a moving average.

Here are Rob's scores for the first 10 weeks of the season:

    15   25   10   15   13   20   12   18   15   17

The average of the first 4 week's scores is $(15 + 25 + 10 + 15) \div 4 = 16.25$

Now remove the first week and add in the fifth week.
The average of these scores is $(25 + 10 + 15 + 13) \div 4 = 15.75$

Now remove the second week and add in the sixth week.
The average of these scores is: $(10 + 15 + 13 + 20) \div 4 = 14.5$

This is called a 4-point moving average.
It is called a moving average because the data values you are using move along one each time.
It is called a 4-point because it always includes 4 data values.

These are the values you get if you calculate all the moving averages.

    16.25   15.75   14.5   15   15.75   16.25   15.5

These moving averages show that the trend is actually that Rob's scores are staying steady.

The moving average can be plotted on the graph to show the trend.
You do not have to use a 4-point moving average.
You can use 3-point, 5-point or any other number.

Moving averages are used by businesses to show trends in their sales.
They are useful when sales are affected by seasonal trends. Ice-cream or wellys are examples of goods that are affected by the season!

Exercise 3:3

1 These are the number of people travelling on a train each day for 10 days.
45 31 50 36 48 38 46 39 49 56
  a Work out the average of the first 4 values.
  b Remove the first value and add in the fifth value.
    Work out the average of these values.
  c Remove the second value and add in the sixth value.
    Work out the average of these values.
  d Continue to work out the 4-point moving average for the rest of
    the data.
    Show your working and write down each value.

2 Alan records his golf scores over a period of 8 weeks.
These are his scores:
84 87 81 92 86 95 79 83
Work out a 3-point moving average for Alan's scores.
Show your working and write down each value.

You can plot the moving average on a graph to produce a trend line.

This graph shows a
company's profits in
each quarter of the year
over a period of three years.
A 4-point moving average
has been calculated for
this data.
The first average is from
quarters 1 2 3 and 4.
On the graph the average
is plotted in the middle
of these values.
The first value is plotted
between quarters 2 and 3.

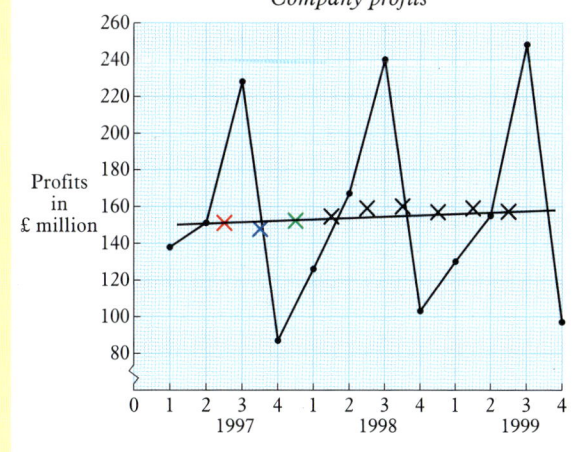

The second average value
covers quarters 2 3 4 and 1.
It is plotted between quarters 3 and 4.

Once all the points are plotted, a line of best fit is drawn through them.
This is the trend line.

3 This table shows the number of computers a shop sold in each quarter of the year over a period of 3 years.

	1998	1999	2000
1st quarter	315	340	351
2nd quarter	571	590	592
3rd quarter	446	470	491
4th quarter	963	989	

  a Copy the axes below onto graph paper and draw a graph to show this data.
  b Calculate a 4-point moving average from the data in the table.
  c Plot the moving average as a set of points onto your graph. Use a different colour if you can.
  d Draw a line of best fit through your points to produce a trend line.
  e Why is it difficult to use your trend line to predict the sales for the last quarter of 2000?

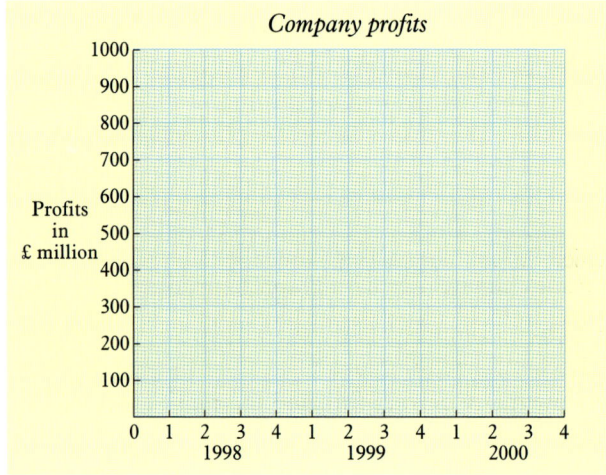

4 A school wants to publish data on its GCSE exam results. The Headteacher uses the data on the percentage of pupils gaining 5 or more A★–C grades.

Year	1993	1994	1995	1996	1997	1998	1999	2000
% 5 A★–C	46	49	50	45	40	48	45	50

  a Plot this data on a graph
  b Work out a 3-point moving average for this data.
  c Plot the averages on your graph. The first point should be plotted at 1994.
  d Draw a line of best fit to show the trend of the data.

Cumulative frequency

Cumulative frequency	Cumulative frequency is a running total of the frequencies.

Exercise 3:4

1 The table shows the number of laps completed by drivers in a 50-lap race.

No. of laps	Frequency	Cumulative frequency
$0 < x \leqslant 10$	3	3
$10 < x \leqslant 20$	1	4 (3 + 1)
$20 < x \leqslant 30$	7	11 (3 + 1 + 7)
$30 < x \leqslant 40$	4	
$40 < x \leqslant 50$	10	

  a Copy the table. Fill in the missing values.
  b How many drivers completed 30 or less laps?
  c How many drivers completed more than 20 laps?
  d How many drivers started the race?
  ● **e** Can you tell how many drivers finished the race? Explain your answer.

2 The table shows the ages of a number of drivers.

Age (years)	Frequency f
16–20	2
21–25	7
26–30	14
31–35	8
36–40	2

  a Draw a cumulative frequency table for this data.
  b How many of the drivers are aged 25 or less?
  c How many of the drivers are more than 30 years of age?
  d How many drivers are included in the data?

Cumulative frequency diagram	A **cumulative frequency** diagram shows how the cumulative frequency changes as the data values increase. The data is shown on a continuous scale on the horizontal axis. The cumulative frequency is shown on the vertical axis.

You plot the upper end of each group against the cumulative frequency. You then join the points with a straight line or a curve.

Example

The table shows the age distribution of people in a survey.
a Draw a cumulative frequency diagram for the data.
b Estimate the number of people in the survey who are:
  (1) less than 28 years old   (2) at least 36 years old

a The values given in the Age column are all at the upper ends of their groups. You plot these against the values in the cumulative frequency column. The points to plot are (20, 3), (25, 11) and so on. You could also plot the point (0, 0) since no one is less than 0 years old but, in this case, it is too far from the other points to be helpful.

Age (years)	Cumulative frequency
<20	3
<25	11
<30	28
<35	40
<40	46
<45	50

b (1) Find 28 on the Age axis, move up to the graph and across. Read the value off the scale.

Approximately 20 people.

(2) Repeat the process for 36, but subtract the answer from 50.

Approximately 8 people.

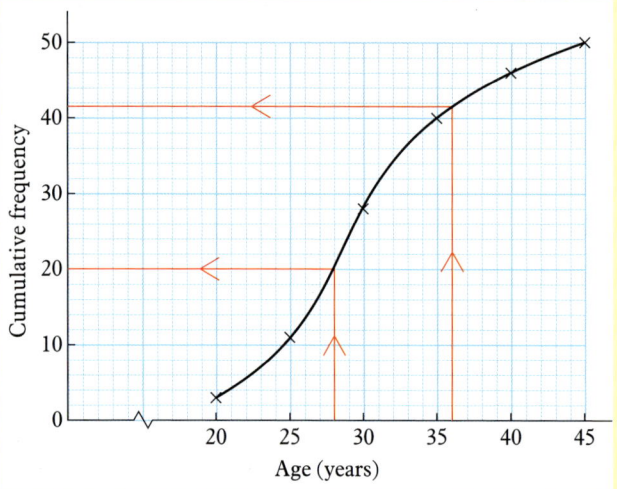

3 **a** Draw a cumulative frequency curve for the data in question **1**.
b Estimate how many drivers completed:
  (1) less than 15 laps   (2) more than 35 laps   (3) the last five laps

It is possible to obtain other information from a cumulative frequency diagram.

The **median** is the middle value. To get an estimate of the median:
(1) divide the total cumulative frequency by 2
(2) find this point on the cumulative frequency axis
(3) draw a line across to the curve and down to the horizontal axis
(4) read off the estimate of the median

The **lower quartile** is the value one quarter of the way through the data values. To find the lower quartile:
(1) divide the total cumulative frequency by 4
(2) find this point on the cumulative frequency axis
(3) draw lines as you did for the median
(4) read off the lower quartile

The **upper quartile** is the value three quarters of the way through the data.

Range

To find the **range** of a set of data you subtract the smallest value from the highest value. This tells you how spread out the data is but it is badly affected by extreme high or low values.

Interquartile range

The **interquartile range** is the difference between the upper and lower quartiles. This tells you how spread out the central half of the data is. Only the middle half of the data is used so the interquartile range is not affected by extreme values.

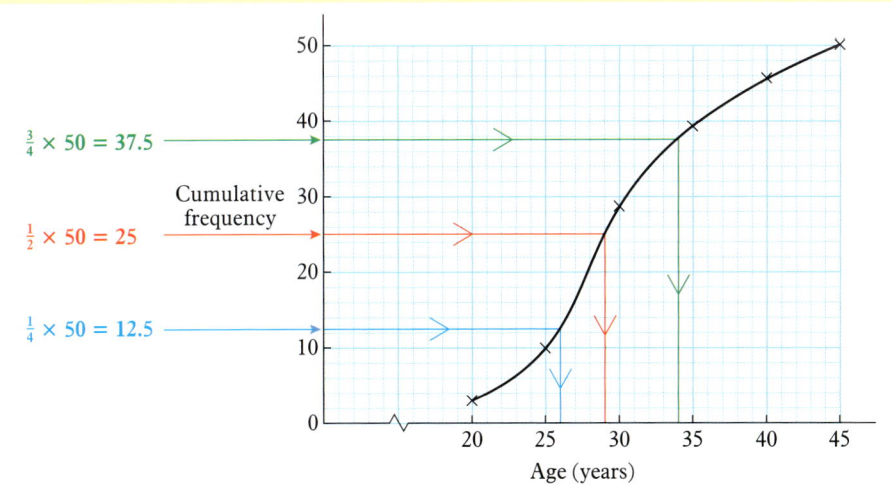

Median = 29 years   Lower quartile = 26 years   Upper quartile = 34 years
Interquartile range = 34 − 26 = 8 years.

Exercise 3:5

1 The table shows the length of time, in minutes, that cars stayed in a short stay car park.

Time t	$0 < t \leqslant 20$	$20 < t \leqslant 40$	$40 < t \leqslant 60$	$60 < t \leqslant 90$	$90 < t \leqslant 120$
Frequency	6	21	39	11	3

a Complete a cumulative frequency table for the data.
b Draw a cumulative frequency curve.
c Use your graph to:
    (1) estimate the median
    (2) find the interquartile range

Comparing two sets of data

To compare two sets of data you need:
(1) a measure of average for each set of data
    (this can be the mean or the median)
(2) a measure of spread
    (this can be the range or the interquartile range)

The table gives the median and interquartile range of the heights, in centimetres, of sunflowers grown from two types of seed.

	Median	Interquartile range
Type A	110	72
Type B	110	35

Both types of seed give the same median height. The interquartile range shows that the heights for seed A are much more spread out than the heights for seed B.

You would use seed A when you wanted to try to grow a really tall sunflower. You would use seed B when you wanted to produce flowers all with much the same height. The smaller the interquartile range, the more uniform the heights of the flowers.

2 Natalie is the manager of a factory. She needs to buy some new machines to fill bags of nuts. The bags must weigh at least 500 grams.
She has two machines to choose from.
She tests the machines by filling 100 packets of nuts with each one and then weighing the packets.
The table shows her results.

	Median	Interquartile range
Machine A	501	6
Machine B	503	2

Which machine should she choose?
Explain your answer.

3 The times of treatment for 100 patients at a clinic are shown in the table.

Time (mins)	0–	10–	20–	30–	40–	50–
Frequency	16	30	27	18	9	0
Cumulative frequency	16	46				
Time (mins)	<10	<20				

a Copy the table. Complete the last two rows.
b Draw the cumulative frequency curve.
c Use your graph to:
　(1) estimate the median　　(2) find the interquartile range

This table shows the times of treatment for 100 patients at a surgery.

Time (mins)	0–	10–	20–	30–	40–	50–
Frequency	7	42	38	11	2	0
Cumulative frequency						
Time (mins)						

d Copy the table. Complete the last two rows.
e Draw a cumulative frequency curve for this data.
f Use your graph to:
　(1) estimate the median　　(2) find the interquartile range
g Use your results to compare the waiting times at the clinic and surgery.

67

2 Statistical diagrams

A cat uses its whiskers to tell how wide an opening is.

In statistics we use a box and whisker diagram to show how wide the data is spread.

Box and whisker diagrams are another way to compare several sets of data.

A box and whisker diagram is sometimes called a box plot or a box and whisker plot.
The box is used to show the middle 50% of the data.
The whiskers are used to show the extreme points of the data.
Here is a box and whisker plot showing train journey times in minutes.

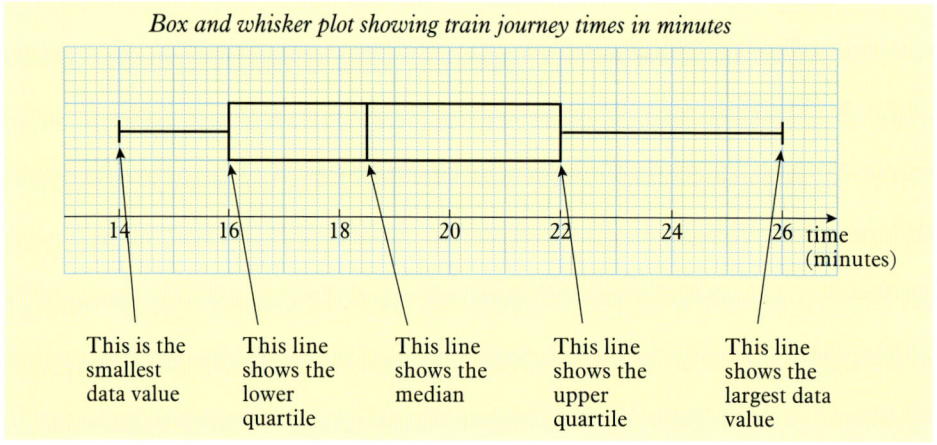

Box and whisker plot showing train journey times in minutes

This is the smallest data value | This line shows the lower quartile | This line shows the median | This line shows the upper quartile | This line shows the largest data value

From a box and whisker plot you can read off:

the smallest data value
the lower quartile
the median
the upper quartile
the largest data value
the range of the data.

But you can't tell how many data values there are.

Exercise 3:6

For each of these box and whisker diagrams:

     a Write down the smallest data value.
     b Write down the lower quartile.
     c Write down the median.
     d Write down the upper quartile.
     e Write down the largest data value.
     f Calculate the range of the data.

1

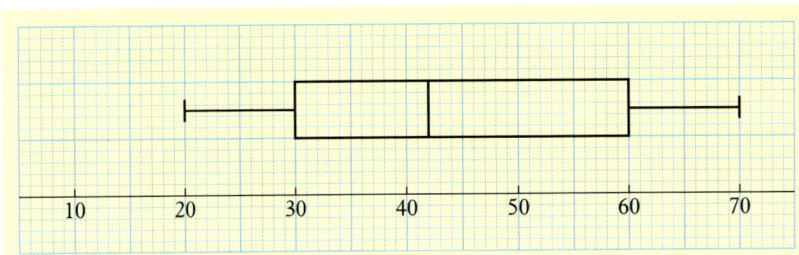

2

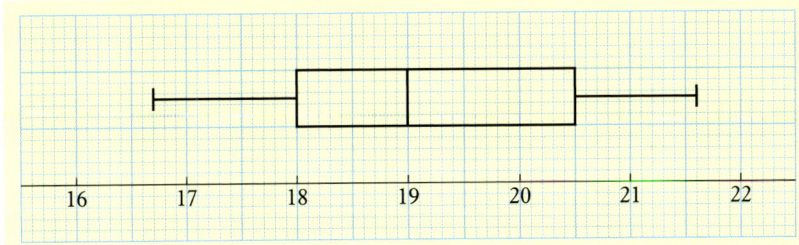

3

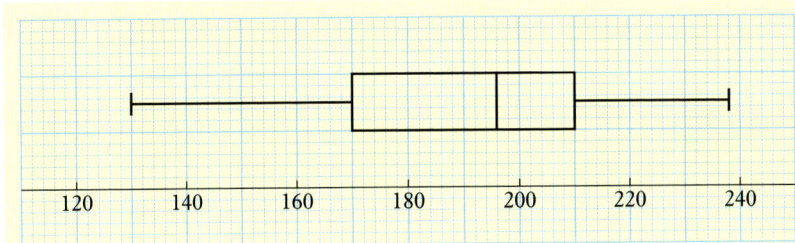

4

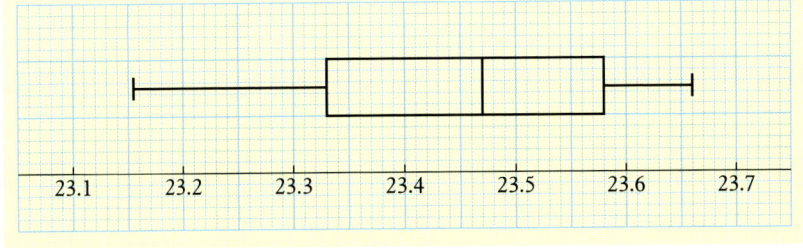

To draw a box and whisker plot you need to work out:

the smallest data value   the median   the largest data value
the lower quartile   the upper quartile

Example   These are the numbers of pages in 21 editions of a newspaper.

76   82   66   80   92   74   84   70   78   86   84
82   74   68   90   78   64   68   86   70   82

Draw a box and whisker plot to show this data.

First put the data in order of size. Start with the smallest.

64   66   68   68   70   70   74
74   76   78   78   80   82   82
82   84   84   86   86   90   92

Smallest value = 64   Median = 78   Largest value = 92

LQ = median of 64 66 68 68 **70** **70** 74 74 76 78
Lower quartile = 70

UQ = median of 80 82 82 82 **84** **84** 86 86 90 92
Upper quartile = 84

Now you can draw the box and whisker diagram.

First draw the scale and mark on the lower quartile, median and upper quartile.

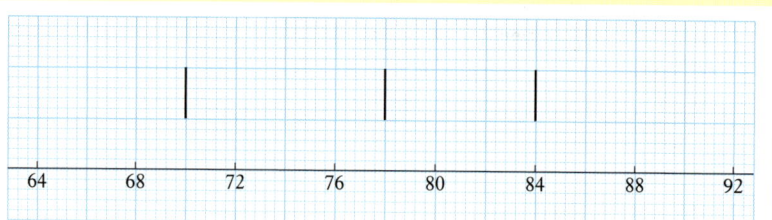

Join these lines to form the box.

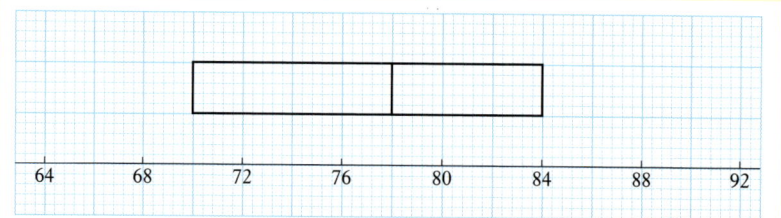

Mark the smallest and highest values and draw in the whiskers.

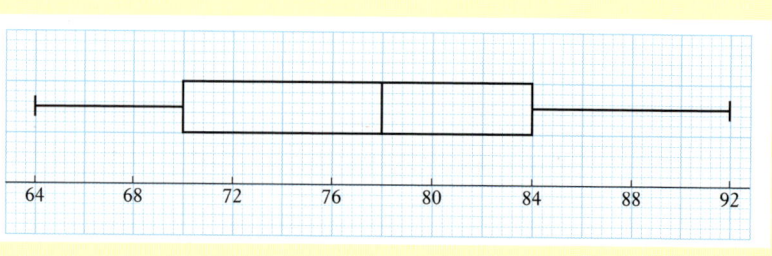

Exercise 3:7

1 Katy measured the length of some caterpillars for a biology experiment.
She measured the lengths in centimetres.
She used her data to work out the following:

smallest data value = 3.4   upper quartile = 4.8
lower quartile = 3.8   largest data value = 5.1
the median = 4.2

Draw a box and whisker diagram to show this data.

2 Andrew did a survey on how much the people in his form earned from
part time jobs in a week.
Here are his results.

£10   £20   £17   £19   £23   £0   £29   £18   £17   £24
£16   £15   £26   £10   £0   £0   £19   £27   £17   £14
£28   £13   £0

   a Rewrite the data in order of size. Start with the smallest.
   b Find the median earnings.
   c Find the lower quartile of the data.
   d Find the upper quartile of the data.
   e Draw a box and whisker plot to show Andrew's data.

3 Ned is a keen swimmer.
He records the times taken by members of his club to swim 100 m.
These are the times to the nearest tenth of a second.

29.3   26.4   32.4   28.9   27.3   20.7   27.6
25.3   23.5   21.7   24.7   28.9   23.6

   a Rewrite the data in order of size. Start with the smallest.
   b Find the median time.
   c Find the lower quartile of the data.
   d Find the upper quartile of the data.
   e Draw a box and whisker diagram to show Ned's data.

4 The maximum temperatures in Derby over a period of 14 days in July
were as follows. The temperatures are in degrees Celsius.

16   19   23   25   24   17   18   18   23   24   19   20   25   27

Draw a box and whisker diagram to show this data.

3

Exercise 3:8

1 These box and whisker plots show the test scores of two different classes.

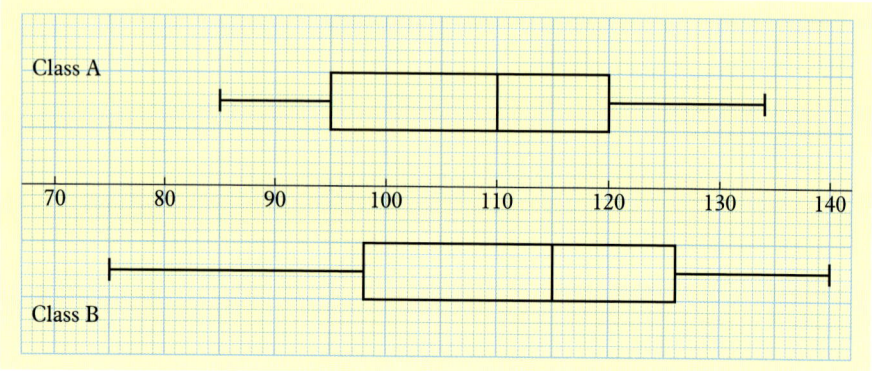

a For each class, write down (1) the range
(2) the interquartile range
(3) the median

b Write a few sentences about the differences between the two sets of marks.

2 This data shows the response times of two ambulance services to 999 calls. The times to get to the emergency are in minutes.

Service A

| 9 | 10 | 13 | 8 | 19 | 12 | 5 | 14 | 13 | 12 |
| 10 | 9 | 12 | 15 | 18 | 7 | 14 | 12 | 13 | 5 |

Service B

| 12 | 13 | 15 | 12 | 14 | 13 | 11 | 14 | 17 | 19 |
| 13 | 14 | 12 | 16 | 15 | 17 | 14 | 11 | 12 | 14 |

a For each ambulance service calculate
(1) the median
(2) the range
(3) the lower and upper quartiles.
b Draw box and whisker plots for both services.
Put them both on the same diagram.
c Write about the differences in the response times of the two services.
d Which service do you think is better? Explain your answer.

72

Time series graphs are used to show trends in statistics.
This graph shows the trends in work over the last 50 years.

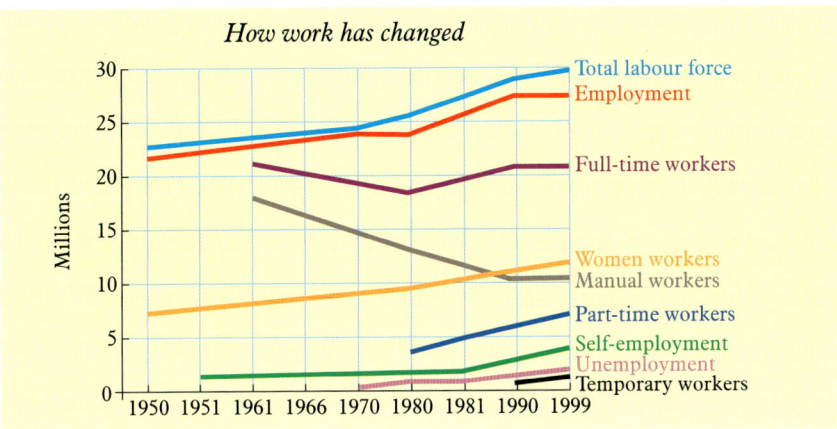

How work has changed

Exercise 3:9

Answer questions 1 and 2 by reading the information from the graph above.

1 **a** How many people were working full time in 1961?
   b How many people were working full time in 1999?
   c How many manual workers were there in 1961?
   d How many manual workers were there in 1999?

2 Copy these and fill in the gaps.
   a Between 1961 and 1999 the number of full time workers has ………
   b Between 1961 and 1999 the number of manual workers has ………
   c The trend is for ……… people to work part time.
   d The trend is for ……… people to be self-employed.
   e The trend is for ……… people to have manual jobs.

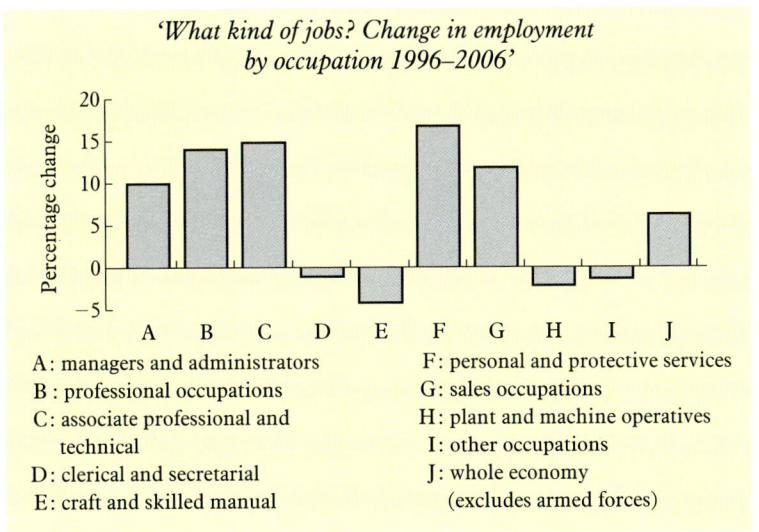

'What kind of jobs? Change in employment by occupation 1996–2006'

A: managers and administrators
B: professional occupations
C: associate professional and
   technical
D: clerical and secretarial
E: craft and skilled manual

F: personal and protective services
G: sales occupations
H: plant and machine operatives
I: other occupations
J: whole economy
   (excludes armed forces)

3 Look at the graph on the previous page which shows changes in the types of job that people may have. The graph is a prediction.
  a Which type of job is predicted to increase the most?
  b Which type of job is predicted to decrease the most?
  c Which type of job is predicted to increase by 10%?
  ● **d** Which type of job is predicted to increase the least?

4 Look at this graph. It shows car ownership since 1950.

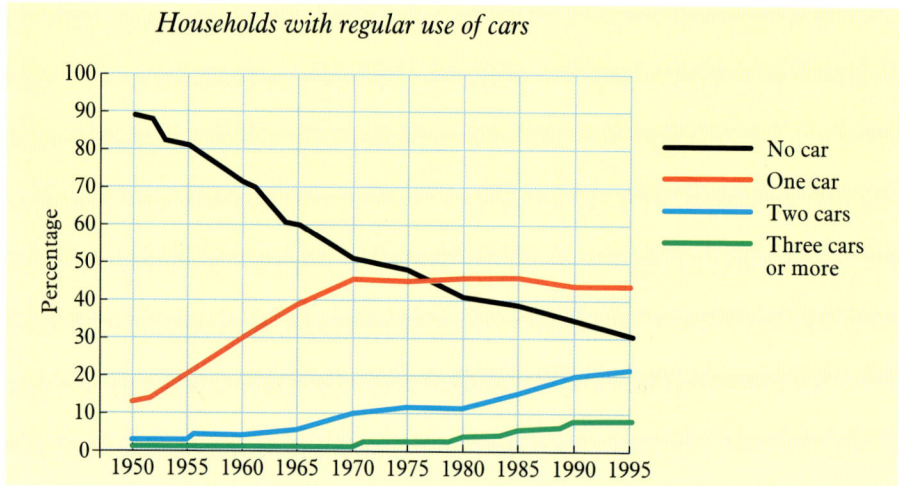

Households with regular use of cars

  a What percentage of families did not have a car in 1950?
  b What percentage of families did not have a car in 1995?
  c Describe the trend in families without a car.
  ● **d** Why has the number of families with one car levelled out whilst the total number of cars has gone up?

5 This table shows the number of people who attend different types of churches.
The numbers are in thousands.

	1980	1985	1990	1995	2000	2005
Anglican	968	921	918	839	794	748
Baptist	201	196	198	213	224	230
Methodist	438	421	395	347	313	279

a Copy these axes onto graph paper.
b Plot a graph to show the number of people who attend an Anglican church in each year.
c Plot the graphs for the Baptist and the Methodist churches **on the same graph.**
d Write a sentence to describe the trend for each type of church.

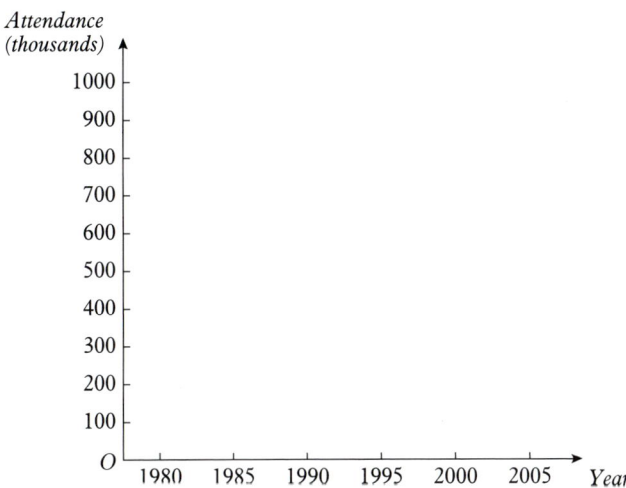

6 This table shows how spending on certain items has changed since 1971. The numbers in the table come from setting the amounts in 1971 at 100 and then comparing the amounts in each of the other years to this. These are called index numbers.

	1971	1981	1986	1991	1996
Food	100	104	109	115	125
Alcohol	100	127	134	132	131
Tobacco	100	89	74	71	59
Recreation	100	142	156	182	206

a Copy the axes on the next page onto graph paper.
b Plot the graph for Food.
c Plot the graphs for Alcohol, Tobacco and Recreation on the same graph.
Use a different colour for each if you can.

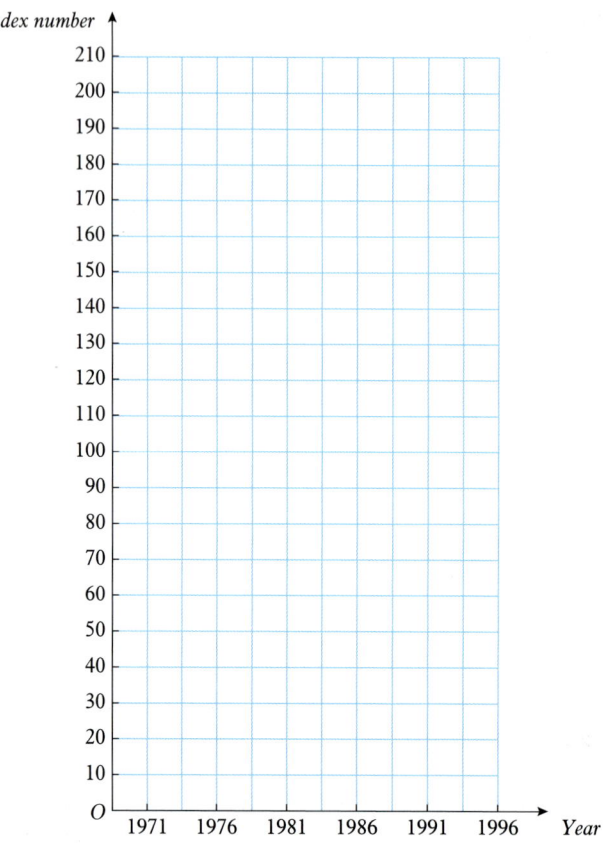

Index number

210
200
190
180
170
160
150
140
130
120
110
100
90
80
70
60
50
40
30
20
10

O   1971   1976   1981   1986   1991   1996   *Year*

d Which type of spending has increased the most?
e Which type of spending has decreased the most?
Say why you think this is.

7 This graph shows how the UK poulation is expected to change up to the year 2051. Write about the trends in this graph.

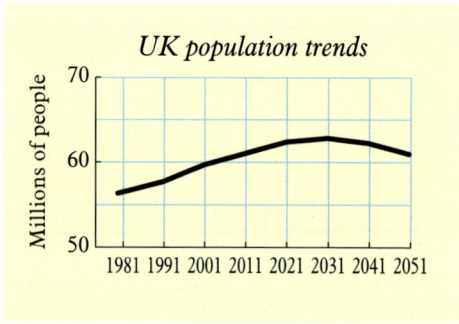

UK population trends

Millions of people

70

60

50

1981 1991 2001 2011 2021 2031 2041 2051

3 Sampling

Samples of goods on a production line are selected and checked for quality.

The process is known as quality control. It is a cost-effective way of making sure that the goods are of the right standard.

Population	The complete set of people or objects that information is collected about is called the **population**.
Bias	Anything that distorts data so that it doesn't fairly represent the population is called **bias**. You need to take care to avoid bias in the way that you collect data so that any results you produce are reliable.
Sample	Information is normally taken from a small part of the population called a **sample**. The key idea is that if you choose the sample without bias then the results will apply to the whole population.

The size of your sample is important. It needs to be large enough to represent the population but small enough to be manageable. |

Exercise 3:10

1 Say what is wrong with the way that each of these samples is selected.
   a The headteacher of a school wants to choose a new school uniform that pupils will be happy to wear. She asks 5 pupils in Year 7 for their ideas. The new uniform is to be based on their replies.
   b Clothes pegs are produced at a factory. One peg in every three produced is selected for rigorous testing.
   c A bakery works 24 hours a day making bread. A sample from the first batch of loaves produced each morning is taken for testing.
   d As a check on safety standards, every thousandth car made on a production line is given a complete safety check.

Random sample

In a **random sample** every member of the population has an equal chance of being selected. This is one of the ways of avoiding bias.

Scientific calculators have a random number key. Pressing the key displays a number between 0 and 1. The number usually has 3 decimal places but the calculator will not show zeros at the end.

You can use these random numbers to choose a random sample. Let's say that you want to choose some pupils at random from a group of 30. You start by giving everyone in the group a number from 1 to 30. This can be done alphabetically.

Now use the calculator to produce a random number. Multiply this number by 30 and round the answer to the nearest whole number. This value is used to pick a person at random. You keep repeating the process until you have enough people in your sample.

Stratified sample

A population might contain separate groups or strata. To represent each group fairly in a sample you choose a number from each one in proportion to its size. The selection is made at random from each group. A sample produced in this way is called a **stratified sample**.

Example

A survey about careers is to be carried out among pupils in Years 11, 12 and 13. The number of pupils in each year group is:

Year 11	207
Year 12	81
Year 13	58
Total	346

How many Year 11 pupils should be included in a stratified sample of 30 pupils?

$\dfrac{207}{346}$ of the population belong to Year 11

You need to find this fraction of 30

$$\dfrac{207}{346} \times 30 = 17.947\ldots$$

18 Year 11 pupils should be included in the sample.

2 Look again at question **1**. Describe a better way of selecting sample data in each case.

3 Use your calculator to produce 10 numbers at random from 0 to 100

4 A hair salon has 2872 female customers and 1653 male customers. A survey on customer care is to be made involving 150 customers. How many male customers should be included in a stratified sample?

5 A chocolate factory produced 429 boxes of milk chocolates and 164 boxes of plain chocolates in one hour. How many boxes of each type should be selected in a stratified sample of 20 boxes?

6 Give an example of a situation where a stratified sample is likely to be better than a random sample. Explain your answer.

What do you think?

The trend in recent years is for girls to do better than boys in most subjects at GCSE. One explanation given for this is that girls show better concentration in lessons than boys.

A guest speaker at a school made the following statement.

'Research shows that the average concentration span for girls is 10.5 minutes, but for boys the figure is only 3.5 minutes.'

a Make a list of questions that you would like to ask about the way that the research was done in order to be:
(1) clear about what the statement means
(2) convinced that it is unbiased

b Do some research of your own.
Take into account all of the questions that you thought of in part **a**.
Present your findings in a report.
Describe all of the steps taken to avoid bias.
Compare your results with the figures given by the guest speaker.
State your conclusions and justify them from the data collected.

1   These are Penny's marks for tests in five subjects

Maths (%)	65	53	57	71	60	72
English (%)	82	64	51	74	64	49
History (%)	64	50	58	63	59	66
Art (%)	58	64	78	56	71	66
French (%)	57	46	62	49	56	63

  a   Find the mean mark for each subject.
  b   Find the range for each subject.
  c   Use your answers to parts **a** and **b** to decide which is Penny's best
     subject.
  d   What assumption is made about the marks in making this comparison?

2   George has scored an average of 12 runs in the last four cricket matches.
  a   What is his total number of runs in all four matches?
  b   His mean score must be 15 or more for him to be picked for the school
     team. How many runs must he make in the next match if he is to be
     picked for the school team?

3   The noon-day temperature was measured at Silverstone on
   30 consecutive days. The results are shown in the frequency table.

Temperature (°C)	12	13	14	15	16	17	18
Number of days	1	7	4	3	5	3	7

  a   Find the mean temperature to 1 dp.
  b   Write down the modal temperatures.
  c   Find the median temperature.

4   The height distribution of Year 11 pupils in a class is shown in the table.
   The heights were measured to the nearest centimetre.

Height (cm)	160–164	165–169	170–174	175–179	180–184	185–189
Frequency	2	3	6	10	7	2
Cum. freq.						
Height (cm)	<164.5					

  a   Copy the table. Fill in the missing values.
  b   Draw a cumulative frequency curve for the data.
  c   Use your graph to estimate the median height of the pupils.

5 This data shows the response times of two taxi firms.
The times to get to each passenger are in minutes.

Terry's Taxis

7	19	23	18	19	30	15	19	23	17
20	16	17	19	18	21	14	20	22	16

Katy's Karrs

17	13	15	17	19	18	21	16	19	21
13	16	22	19	17	17	13	14	19	17

  a For each taxi firm calculate
     (1) the median (2) the range (3) the lower and upper quartiles
  b Draw box and whisker plots for both firms.
     Put them both on the same diagram.
  c Write about the differences in the response times of the two firms.
  d Which firm do you think is best? Explain your answer.

6 A school wants to publish data on its A level exam results.
The Headteacher uses the average A level points score.
This is the data for the last 8 years.

Year	1993	1994	1995	1996	1997	1998	1999	2000
points	15.7	16.3	16.8	15.1	17.8	16.3	18.0	17.5

  a Plot this data on a graph
  b Work out a 3-point moving average for this data.
  c Plot the averages on your graph.
     The first point should be plotted at 1994.
  d Draw a line of best fit to show the trend of the data.

7 Six years ago the mean age of the players in the village football team was
29.6 years. The same team is still playing. Write down the present value
of the mean age of the team.

8 A large building in the centre of town has become vacant. One proposal
is that it should be turned into a multi-storey car park. Local opinion is
tested by asking drivers as they queue for a space in a nearby car park on
a Saturday morning.
  a Predict the outcome of the survey.
  b Explain what is wrong with the method used.
  c Describe, in detail, how you would measure local opinion.
     Explain the steps that you would take to make sure that the results
     are reliable.

1 Anna is testing a new route to work. These are her times, in minutes, for the first five journeys.

$$23 \quad 17 \quad 22 \quad 19 \quad 21$$

a Find the mean of these times.
b After her sixth journey her new mean time is 20 minutes. How long did she take for this journey?
c Anna drives to work another four times. She works out the overall mean to be 22.5 minutes. Find the mean for these last four journeys.

2 **a** Copy the table.
b Fill in the missing values.
c Estimate the mean.

x	Mid-value	Frequency
$30 < x \leqslant 36$		5
$36 < x \leqslant 44$		11
$44 < x \leqslant 60$		9
$60 < x \leqslant 70$		3

3 A 3-point moving average starts at the value 106.
The second average is 107.
The first three data values are 102, 109 and 107.
What is the 4th data value?

4 The first three values in a set of data are x, $x + 10$ and $x + 20$
a Work out the first value of a 3-point moving average.
b What is the 4th data value if the second moving average is $x + 7$?

5 Howard did a survey into the length of TV adverts.
Here are his results in seconds

$$30 \quad 45 \quad 60 \quad 30 \quad 30 \quad 30 \quad 45 \quad 60 \quad 90 \quad 15$$
$$15 \quad 30 \quad 15 \quad 20 \quad 20 \quad 5 \quad 30 \quad 45 \quad 10 \quad 20$$

a Find the median and quartiles of these times.
b Draw a box plot to show this data.
c Calculate the values (1) median – LQ and (2) UQ – median.
What do these values tell you about the distribution of the data?

6 A sales representative uses a 3-point moving average to monitor her weekly sales figures. The first three weeks figures are £1300, £1250 and £1020. What is the smallest value of sales she can have in the 4th week to ensure that her average will not drop?

1 These are the attendances at a safari park for 5 days.

   256   328   156   208   297

   a Find the mean attendance.

   b After the 6th day, the mean attendance was 259. How many attended on the 6th day?

2 The table shows the amount of money, in £s, that families spent on transport in one week.

Amount, A (£)	Number of families
$0 < A \leqslant 10$	6
$10 < A \leqslant 20$	14
$20 < A \leqslant 30$	22
$30 < A \leqslant 40$	17
$40 < A \leqslant 50$	8

   a Work out an estimate for the mean amount spent on transport.

   b Explain why the mean you calculated in part **a** is only an estimate for the actual mean.

3 The table shows the number of pupils in a village primary school for a period of 8 years.

Year	1993	1994	1995	1996	1997	1998	1999	2000
Pupils	40	32	41	39	37	40	45	44

   a Copy the axes. Plot the data on your axes.

   b Work out a 4-point moving average for the data.

   c Plot the moving average as a set of points on your graph.

   d Draw a line of best fit through your points to produce a trend line.

   e Why is it difficult to use your trend line to predict the number of pupils for Year 2001?

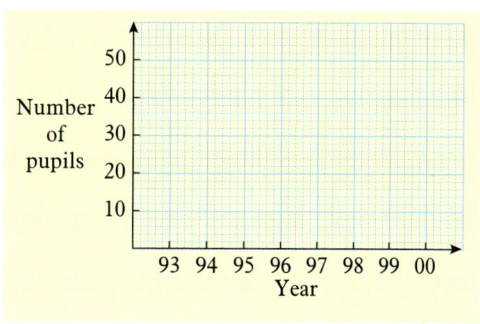

4 Aman has done a survey on the ages of people attending a cinema and a bowling alley.
She has put the results into a table.

Age in years	1–10	11–20	21–30	31–40	41–50	51–60
Frequency – cinema	1	15	24	17	32	11
Frequency – bowling	8	29	28	13	8	2

a For both the cinema and the bowling alley:
  (1) draw a cumulative frequency curve
  (2) estimate the median and the interquartile range

b Compare the ages of the people attending the two places.
Write a sentence explaining what you've found.

5 Cara records the time it takes to drive to work each day.
She does this for 20 working days.
This is her data. The times are in minutes.

    21   17   34   20   39   19   27   31   24   33
    19   41   36   38   26   17   20   27   23   37

a Find the median time.

b Find the lower and upper quartiles of the data.

c Draw a box plot to show the data.

Rudi drives the same distance to work.
He records the time for 20 days like Cara does.
This box plot shows his data.

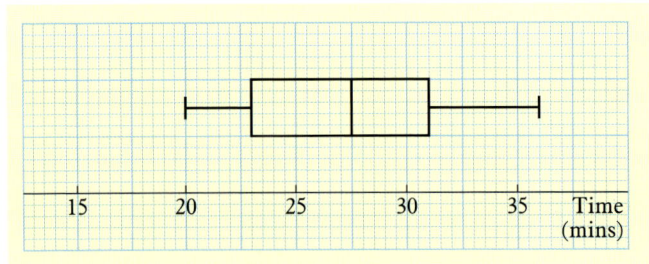

d Find Rudi's values for:
  (1) the median
  (2) the interquartile range
  (3) the smallest data value
  (4) the largest data value

e Compare the two sets of times.
Write a sentence or two to explain what you've found.

4 Probability: in theory

1 Finding probabilities
Finding the probability of something
happening more than once
Finding the expected number
Estimating probability in experiments
Deciding what method to use to find
probabilities

CORE

2 Conditional probability
Finding probabilities when outcomes depend
on each other
Using probability trees to help solve problems

QUESTIONS

EXTENSION

TEST YOURSELF

1   **Finding probabilities**

All the balls in the machine have an equal chance of being the first ball out.
The probability of one ticket matching the six numbers is 0.000 000 071 5

| **Independent events** | Two **events** are **independent** if the outcome of one has no effect on the outcome of the other. The probability of events A and B *both* happening is called $P(\text{A and B})$. |

$$P(\text{A and B}) = P(\text{A}) \times P(\text{B})$$

You can use this rule to find the probability of an event happening more than once.

Example

A dice is rolled three times. Find the probability of getting three 6s.

Probability of a 6 on one roll is $\frac{1}{6}$
Each roll is independent.

$$P(\text{three 6s}) = P(\text{6 on 1st roll}) \times P(\text{6 on 2nd roll}) \times P(\text{6 on 3rd roll})$$
$$= \frac{1}{6} \times \frac{1}{6} \times \frac{1}{6}$$
$$= \frac{1}{216}$$

Exercise 4:1

1   This spinner is used twice.
  Find the probability of getting two reds.

2   A dice is rolled twice.
  Find the probability of getting two 4s.

3 The spinner in **1** is used five times.
Find the probability of getting five blues.

4 The probability of Bill being late for work is 0.15
Find the probability that he is late on three consecutive mornings.

5 A coin is tossed ten times.
Find the probability that you get:
  a a head with the first toss
  b all heads with the first three tosses
  c all heads on all ten tosses
  ● **d** all heads on the first n tosses

Example   The probability of getting a red with this spinner is $\frac{1}{3}$
The spinner is used three times.
Find the probability of getting:
a a red on all three spins
b a red on just the first spin
c only one red on the three spins

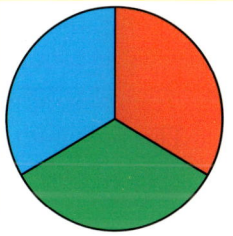

a $P(\text{red on all three spins}) = \frac{1}{3} \times \frac{1}{3} \times \frac{1}{3} = \frac{1}{27}$
b A red on just the 1st spin means that the 2nd and 3rd spins are *not* red.
$P(\text{not red on a spin}) = 1 - \frac{1}{3} = \frac{2}{3}$ so you have

$P(\text{red on 1st only}) = P(\text{red on 1st}) \times P(\text{not red on 2nd}) \times P(\text{not red on 3rd})$
$$= \quad \frac{1}{3} \quad \times \quad \frac{2}{3} \quad \times \quad \frac{2}{3}$$
$$= \frac{4}{27}$$

The events are independent so you multiply the probabilities.

c $P(\text{red on just}$
$\text{one spin}) = P(\text{red on 1st only}) + P(\text{red on 2nd only}) + P(\text{red on 3rd only})$
$$= \quad (\frac{1}{3} \times \frac{2}{3} \times \frac{2}{3}) \quad + \quad (\frac{2}{3} \times \frac{1}{3} \times \frac{2}{3}) \quad + \quad (\frac{2}{3} \times \frac{2}{3} \times \frac{1}{3})$$
$$= \quad \frac{4}{27} \quad + \quad \frac{4}{27} \quad + \quad \frac{4}{27}$$
$$= \frac{12}{27}$$

The three events are mutually exclusive so you add the probabilities.

6 Peter has to pass through three sets of
traffic lights on his way to work.
The lights are all independent of each other.
The probability that any one set of lights
will show red is 0.3
Find the probability that:
a all three lights will show red
b only the first will show red
c only one will show red

7 A dice is thrown three times. Find the probability of getting:
a three 6s
b a 6 on the last throw only
c only one 6 on the three throws

8 The probability that a patient seen in casualty received their injuries in
a road accident is $\frac{3}{8}$
Find the probability that, for the next four patients:
a all four will have received their injuries in a road accident
b only the last one received their injuries in a road accident
c only one received their injuries in a road accident

This probability tree shows all the possible outcomes when a dice is tossed
three times.

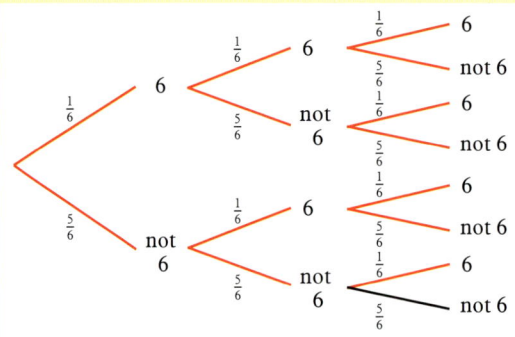

All the red paths satisfy the outcome 'at least one six'.
Only the bottom path is left.

$$P(\text{at least one } 6) = 1 - P(\text{no 6s})$$
$$= 1 - \tfrac{5}{6} \times \tfrac{5}{6} \times \tfrac{5}{6}$$
$$= 1 - \tfrac{125}{216}$$
$$= \tfrac{91}{216}$$

9   The probability of getting a black with a spinner is $\frac{1}{5}$
It is spun four times.
Find the probability of getting at least one black.

10   The probability that a customer buys a camcorder with cash is 0.15
Find the probability that at least one of the next three customers uses
cash to buy a camcorder.

You can work out how many times an event is likely to happen in a series of
trials.
You do this by first working out the probability of the event happening once.

A bag contains two red balls and three green balls.
A ball is chosen at random from the bag and then replaced.
This is done 40 times.

The probability of getting a red ball is $\frac{2}{5}$
This means that you expect two red balls in every five trials.

To find the expected number of red balls in 40 trials you divide by 5 to find
how many groups of 5 there are in 40.
You then multiply by 2 since you expect to get 2 red balls in every 5.

So the expected number of red balls $= \dfrac{40}{5} \times 2$

$$= 16$$

This is the same as $40 \times \frac{2}{5}$ where $\frac{2}{5}$ is the probability of getting a red ball.

The **expected number** = **number of trials** $\times$ **probability**

Exercise 4:2

1   The probability that a shopper in a supermarket buys cat food is 0.45
How many shoppers out of 800 would you expect to buy cat food?

2 a The probability that Martin is late for
school is 0.05
There are 75 days in the Autumn Term.
On how many days would you expect
Martin to be late?

b The Spring Term is 11 weeks long.
Martin is late on 3 days.
Is he more or less punctual?
Explain your answer.

3 A factory produces boxes of chocolates.
Each box of chocolates is tested twice.
The first test is a check on the contents, the second test is a check on the
packaging. The probability of a box passing the first test is 0.94 and the
probability of passing the second is 0.90. The two tests are independent.
Find the probability that a box of chocolates:

a fails the first test
b passes both tests
c passes the first test but fails the second
d fails the first test but passes the second
e fails at least one test

If a box of chocolates fails only one test it is sold as substandard.
If both tests are failed the box of chocolates is destroyed.
Out of 1000 boxes of chocolates produced, how many would you expect
to be:

f sold as substandard   **g** destroyed?

4 The probability that a letter sent by First Class post will arrive the next
day is $\frac{9}{10}$.
Five letters are sent by First Class post on the same day.
Find the probability that, on the next day:

a all five letters will arrive
b no letters will arrive
c only one letter will arrive

A firm sends out 250 letters by First Class post.

d How many would you expect to arrive the next day?

Laura has made a tetrahedral dice.
She throws the dice 100 times and
records her number each time.

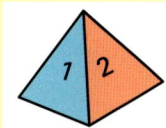

This table shows her results.

Number	Tally	Frequency
1	ⅢⅢ ⅢⅢ ⅢⅢ ⅢⅢ ‖	22
2	ⅢⅢ ⅢⅢ ⅢⅢ ⅢⅢ ⅢⅢ	25
3	ⅢⅢ ⅢⅢ ⅢⅢ ⅢⅢ ⅢⅢ ⅢⅢ	30
4	ⅢⅢ ⅢⅢ ⅢⅢ ⅢⅢ ‖‖	23

Frequency   The **frequency** of an event is the number of times that it
happens.

**Relative
frequency**   **Relative frequency** of an event $= \dfrac{\text{frequency of the event}}{\text{total frequency}}$

The relative frequency gives an *estimate* of the probability.

If the dice is fair the probability of getting each number is $\frac{1}{4}$
Laura checks her data to see if the dice is fair.
She uses the relative frequency from her experiment.

Relative frequency of 1 is $\frac{22}{100}$
Laura wants to see if $\frac{1}{4}$ and $\frac{22}{100}$ are about the same value.
She converts them both to decimals:
$\frac{1}{4} = 0.25$ $\frac{22}{100} = 0.22$
The two values are close so the dice is probably fair.

Laura can get a better estimate for the probability by repeating the experiment more
times.

Exercise 4:3

1   Darren tosses a coin 50 times.
This is his data.

Outcome	Tally	Frequency
head	ⅢⅢ ⅢⅢ ⅢⅢ ⅢⅢ	20
tail	ⅢⅢ ⅢⅢ ⅢⅢ ⅢⅢ ⅢⅢ ⅢⅢ	30

Find the relative frequency of: **a** a head   **b** a tail
c Is the coin fair? Explain your answer.

2 Kate wants to find out how many pupils are left handed in her school.
She asks twenty pupils in each year.
These are her results.

Year	7	8	9	10	11
left handed	4	3	8	7	5
right handed	16	17	12	13	15

a Find the relative frequency of left handed pupils in each year.
b There are 220 pupils in Year 8.
How many would you expect to be left handed?
c There are 1450 pupils in Years 7 to 11 altogether.
How many would you expect to be left handed?
Show your method clearly.
d How could Kate make her answer to part **c** more accurate?

3 Gemma is testing a biased spinner.
She has spun it 100 times.
The table shows her results.

Colour	Frequency
blue	20
green	45
yellow	35

Estimate the probability that on the next spin the colour will be:
a blue   **b** green   **c** not yellow

Gemma spins the spinner 500 times.
d How many greens would she expect?

4 A factory makes skirts. The waist sizes of 200 skirts were tested.
35 were smaller than the stated size and 62 were larger than the stated size.
Estimate the probability that a skirt made by this factory will have a waist
size that is:
a larger than stated
b smaller than stated
c equal to the stated size

The factory makes 1200 skirts.
d How many of these would you expect to have a waist size smaller than
stated?

You can use data from tables to find probabilities.

Example The table shows the type of person that took part in a survey.

	male	female
child	12	15
adult	5	8

a How many people took part in the survey?
b How many children took part in the survey?

A person is chosen at random from those surveyed.
Find the probability that the person is:
c a male adult   **d** a child

a You add up all the numbers to find the number of people.
Number of people = 12 + 15 + 5 + 8 = 40
b To find the number of children you look at the row for children.
Number of children = 12 + 15 = 27
c 5 male adults took part in the survey.
The total number of people was 40.

$$P(\text{the person is a male adult}) = \tfrac{5}{40}$$

d 27 children were asked.

$$P(\text{the person is a child}) = \tfrac{27}{40}$$

Exercise 4:4

1 The table gives the membership of a sports club.

	male	female
child	14	19
adult	46	55

a How many members does the sports club have?
b How many children are members?
c How many members are female?

A member is chosen at random.
Find the probability that this member is:
d a child   **f** a male adult   **h** a female adult
e female   **g** a girl   **i** male

2 The table shows the shoe sizes of a class of 30 pupils.

Shoe size	3	4	5	6
Number of boys	1	3	7	5
Number of girls	2	5	6	1

A pupil is chosen at random from the class.
Find the probability that the pupil will be:
a a boy
b a girl
c a boy with shoe size 5
d a girl with shoe size 4

3 A store sells duvet covers of different sizes and colours.
The table shows how many of each size and colour they have in stock.

	Single	Double	King size
white	5	11	3
blue	2	6	1
green	8	5	1

a How many duvet covers does the store have in stock?
A duvet cover is chosen at random.
Find the probability that it is:
b white
c double size
d blue and king size
e green and single size

4 A machine fills bags of sugar.
They should contain 2 kg sugar.
Rosemary tests the machine by
weighing 100 bags of sugar
chosen at random.
The table shows her results.

Weight of sugar	less than 2 kg	exactly 2 kg	more than 2 kg
Number of bags	5	64	31

Estimate the probability that a bag chosen at random will:
a contain exactly 2 kg
b not contain exactly 2 kg
c be underweight
d be overweight

Methods of finding probabilities

There are three methods of finding probabilities.

Method 1   Use equally likely outcomes
e.g. to find the probability of getting a 6 with a fair dice.

Method 2   Use a survey or do an experiment
e.g. to find the probability that a drawing pin will land point up when dropped.

Method 3   Look back at data
e.g. to find the probability that it will snow in Monaco this winter, look at the records of snow for previous years.

Exercise 4:5

Look at each of the probabilities in questions **1–9**.
Write down which method you would use to find each probability.
State whether your answer is the actual probability or an estimate.
If you say method 2 write down what experiment or survey you would do.

1   The probability that the next car to pass the school will be white.

2   The probability that a blue cube will be chosen at random from a box of 20 cubes, 7 of which are blue.

3   The probability that there will be a flu epidemic this winter.

4   The probability that a coin will show a tail when tossed.

5   The probability that a person chosen at random will vote Labour in the next General Election.

6 The probability of a biased dice giving a 5 when tossed.

7 The probability of a battery taken from the production line being faulty.

8 The probability of a cat living beyond 18 years.

9 The probability of Swansea winning their next football match.

Game: Win or lose?

This is a game for two players. You need to roll two dice.
Multiply the two numbers together.
The first player gets a point if the score is even.
The second player gets a point if the score is odd.
The first player to reach a score of 10 wins.

Investigating the game

Work with a partner.
You have to carry out an
experiment to see if the
game is fair.

Roll the dice.
Multiply the numbers and record whether the answer is odd or even.
Do this 50 times.

Work out the relative frequency of 'getting an odd number' and 'getting an even number'.
Is the game fair? Explain your answer.
What happens if you roll the dice 100 times?

Change the rules of the game and see if your game is fair.

2 Conditional probability

Peter's team have lost the match. They have another match next week and they think that they will lose that one too. They have lost confidence in themselves.

Hamish and his seven friends have just 1 ticket for the Cup Final. They put 8 counters into a hat. One of the counters is marked with a *. The person who picks out this counter gets the ticket. Hamish picks a counter at random.

The probability of him getting the * counter is $\frac{1}{8}$

Hamish doesn't get the ticket. He does not put the counter back.

Philip now picks a counter at random.

There are 6 plain counters and 1 with a * left.

The probability of Philip getting the ticket on his turn is $\frac{1}{7}$

What Hamish did affected the chances of Philip getting the ticket.

Conditional probability

When the outcome of a first event affects the outcome of a second event, the probability of the second event depends on what has happened. This is called **conditional probability**.

Example

Find the probability that the third person to pick out a counter gets the ticket.

The third person getting the ticket means that the first two people picked out plain counters.

$$P(\text{3rd person getting ticket}) = P(\text{1st plain}) \times P(\text{2nd plain}) \times P(\text{3rd } *)$$
$$= \frac{7}{8} \times \frac{6}{7} \times \frac{1}{6}$$
$$= \frac{1}{8}$$

The numbers in the denominators go down in 1s because each time a counter is taken it is not replaced.

4

Exercise 4:6

1 Tom has a bag of mixed toffees. There are 5 plain, 7 mint and 4 nut toffees.
He picks out a toffee at random and eats it. This toffee was a mint one.
He now picks out another toffee at random.
Write down the probability that the second toffee is:

   a mint   **b** plain   **c** not plain

2 Louise has bought 5 raffle tickets. One hundred tickets were sold.
   a A ticket is picked at random for the first prize.
      Write down the probability that Louise wins first prize.
   b Louise wins the first prize. Another ticket is chosen at random for the
      second prize. Write down the probability that Louise wins the second
      prize.
   c Find the probability that Louise does not win the first and second
      prizes but does win the third.

3 A player in the school football team has a probability of 0.2 of suffering an
injury during the football season. If a player suffers an injury one season
then the probability that they will get an injury next season increases to 0.4
Find the probability that a player gets:
   a an injury in each of his first two seasons
   b an injury in each of his first three seasons
   c his first injury in the second season
   d no injuries in his first three seasons

4 The probability of the school team winning their next football match is 0.4
If they win then the probability of them winning the following match is 0.5
If they do not win the match the probability of them winning the following
match is 0.3
Find the probability that:
   a they win the next two matches
   b they do not win either match
   c they win at least one match

5 Rhian has a 60% chance of passing her driving
test first time. If she fails her test the probability
of her passing it next time increases by 10%.
Find the probability that Rhian passes her test:
a on her second attempt
b on her third attempt
c on her fifth attempt
d on either the third or the fourth attempt

You can use probability trees to help with conditional probability.

A bag contains 4 red and 6 green balls.
A ball is chosen at random and not replaced.
This is done twice.

You can draw a probability tree to show the possible outcomes.

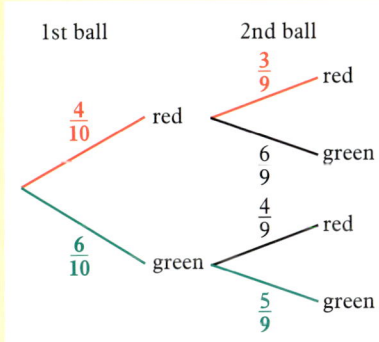

The probabilities in the branches for the second ball are out of 9
because there are only 9 balls in the bag if the first ball is
removed and not replaced.

If the red path is followed then the probability of the second ball
being red is $\frac{3}{9}$ not $\frac{4}{9}$. This is because one red ball has already been
removed.

Example

Find the probability that:
a both balls are red   **b** both balls are the same colour

a $P(\text{both balls are red}) = \frac{4}{10} \times \frac{3}{9} = \frac{12}{90} = \frac{2}{15}$

b $P(\text{both balls are the same colour}) = P(\text{both red}) + P(\text{both green})$
$$= \frac{2}{15} + \left(\frac{6}{10} \times \frac{5}{9}\right)$$
$$= \frac{7}{15}$$

Exercise 4:7

1 Karen is choosing two kittens from a rescue centre.
She chooses them at random.
The centre has 20 kittens. These are the colours.
    6 black   10 tabby   4 golden
  a Draw a tree diagram to show all the possible outcomes.

Find the probability that:
  b both kittens are tabby
  c one kitten is black and one is golden
  d at least one kitten is black

2 A bag contains 12 counters. 5 are yellow and the rest green.
Two counters are picked out at random.
This is the same as picking out one counter and not replacing it, then
picking out a second counter.
  a Draw a probability tree to show all the possible outcomes.

Find the probability that:
  b both counters are the same colour
  c the counters are different colours

3 Richard chooses a two-course meal from a menu. He chooses either fish
or meat for each course.
The probability that he will choose fish for his first course is 0.6,
otherwise he chooses meat.
The probability that he chooses fish for his second course is either 0.3 if
he has fish for the first course or 0.8 if he has meat for his first course.
  a Copy and complete this probability tree.

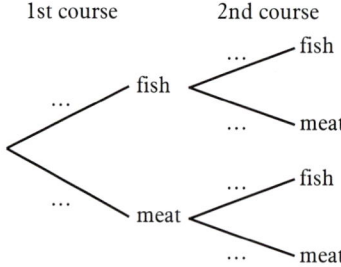

Find the probability that he chooses:
  b fish for both courses
  c fish for at least one course
  d fish for only one course

1 William has a biased coin. The probability of a head when it is tossed is 0.6
He tosses the coin three times.
Find the probability that he gets:
a 3 tails
b 3 heads
c at least 1 tail

2 20% of the calls to a fire station are false alarms.
Find the probability that for the next three calls:
a all three are false alarms
b at least one is false
c only one is false

3 A bag contains 60 beads. There are four different colours.
A bead is chosen at random from the bag.
The probability that it is red is $\frac{1}{4}$, blue is $\frac{1}{5}$ and white is $\frac{1}{3}$
The fourth colour is black.
a Find the probability that a bead chosen at random is black.
b How many beads are there of each colour?

4 Deidre has carried out a survey on the main sport played by people during
the last month. These are her results.

	Tennis	Golf	Swimming	Squash
Men	17	34	19	29
Women	21	27	26	27

a How many people took part in the survey?

Deidre chooses a person at random from her survey.
What is the probability that this person:
b is male and swims
c is female and plays golf
d is female
e plays tennis
f plays golf or squash
g is a male squash player

5 A journalist asked 12 spectators at a tennis match what their favourite sport was. Nine out of the 12 said tennis.
In his article on sport the journalist said that 75% of the population prefer tennis.

a Explain why his statement is misleading.

b Would the statement still be wrong if he got the same answer after asking 2000 spectators? Explain your answer.

c How would you get a better estimate of people's favourite sport?

6 Clay pots have to go through three stages of manufacture: throwing, firing and painting.
The pots either remain perfect or become flawed as a result of each stage.
The probability of the pot remaining perfect is $\frac{3}{5}$ for each stage.
Find the probability that, after passing through the three stages, a pot chosen at random has:

a no flaws

b at least a flaw from one stage

c flaws from all three stages

On one day, 1000 pots are made.

d How many would you expect to have no flaws?

7 The probability of Alan going to France for his summer holiday is 0.6
If he went to France for his last holiday then the probability drops to 0.3
Alan went to France for his last holiday.
Find the probability that Alan:

a goes to France this year

b goes to France for the next two years

c goes to France at least once in the next three years

8 A bag contains six counters. Four are black and two are white.
Three counters are taken out at random.
Find the probability that:

a all three are black

b all three are white

c at least one is black

d only one is white

9   The school canteen has estimated the probability that a pupil chooses coke, milk or fruit drink to drink at lunchtime. The estimated probabilities are 0.57, 0.29 and 0.14, respectively.
About 350 pupils eat in the canteen each day.
How many of each type of drink should the canteen order for the next five school days?

10   Mary always does the crossword on her way to work on the train.
The probability that she finishes the crossword is 0.7 if the train is late and 0.55 if the train is not late.
The train is late 20% of the time.
  a   Copy and complete this tree diagram.

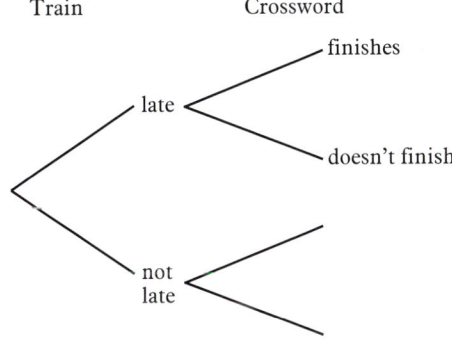

  b   Find the probability that:
      (1) the train is late and Mary finishes the crossword
      (2) Mary finishes the crossword.

  c   Which is more likely:
      'Mary finishes the crossword on a late train' or
      'Mary finishes the crossword on a train that is not late'
      Explain your answer.

1 This spinner is used n times.
Find the probability that you get:
a n blues
b no blues
c at least one blue
d only one blue

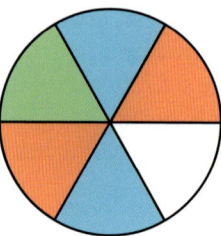

2 Tom drives to work and is sometimes late because of traffic jams.
The ratio of late : not late is 1 : 4
The car park is full 90% of the time when he is late.
It is full one quarter of the time when he is not late.
a Copy and complete this tree diagram.

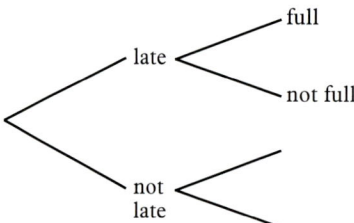

Use the diagram to find the probability that:
b he is late and the car park is full
c he is not late and the car park is full
d the car park is full when he gets to work
e the car park is not full when he gets to work

Tom drives to work 300 times in one year.
f How many times would you expect the car park to be full?

3 This dice is biased.
The probability of getting each number is shown in the table.

	1	2	3	4	5	6
Probability	x	$2x$	$3x$	$2x$	x	x

a Find the value of x.
b The dice is tossed n times. Find the probability of getting:
(1) n prime numbers
(2) at least one prime number

1 **a** Pam uses this spinner once.
Write down the probability that she gets a black.

b John uses the spinner 3 times.
Find the probability that he gets 3 blacks.

c Sue uses the spinner twice.
Find the probability that she gets a red followed by a black.

d Pete uses the spinner n times.
Write down the probability that he gets n blacks.

e Sean uses the spinner 3 times.
Find the probability that he gets the same colour on all 3 spins.

f Jan uses the spinner 3 times.
Find the probability that she gets at least one black.

g The spinner is used 200 times.
How many blacks would you expect to get?

2 A machine in a factory fills bottles of cola.
For any one bottle the probability that it:
(1) has a faulty label is 0.06
(2) has a faulty screw cap is 0.05
(3) is not filled properly is 0.02

Find the probability that a bottle chosen at random has:

a both a faulty label and a faulty cap

b a faulty label and a faulty cap, and is not filled properly

c none of these three faults

d at least one fault

The machine produces 12 000 bottles in a day.

e How many of these bottles would you expect to have at least one fault?

3 Police stopped 50 cars at random to check their tyres, lights and seatbelts. 7 cars had faulty tyres, 3 had faulty lights and 1 had faulty seatbelts. The police stop another 200 cars.

a Estimate the probability that the first car will have faulty lights.

b How many of the 200 cars would you expect to have faulty tyres?

4 Judy has 10 yoghurts in her fridge.
Four are strawberry and six are chocolate.
She chooses a yoghurt at random each day for breakfast.
She does this for three days.

    a Copy and complete this probability tree diagram.

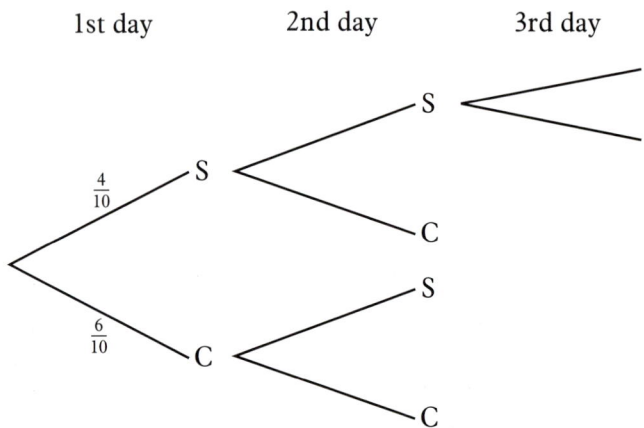

    Find the probability that Judy will choose:

    b 3 strawberry yoghurts

    c just 2 strawberry yoghurts

    d at least one strawberry yoghurt

5 Harry's factory makes duvet covers in three colours and sizes.
The table shows the number of duvets made in one day.

	red	white	black
Single	14	21	17
Double	22	19	12
King size	8	5	2

    A duvet is chosen at random. Find the probability that it is:

    a a red single duvet   **c** a king size duvet

    b a black duvet   **d** either a white or a red duvet

6 Kate is going to cross the Irish Sea in her yacht.
She wants to know the probability that the wind will be greater than
force 3.
How could she work out this probability?

5 Types of number

1 Rational numbers
Defining real numbers
Factors and multiples
Looking in detail at decimals
  – terminating decimals
  – recurring decimals
Writing fractions as decimals
Writing decimals as fractions

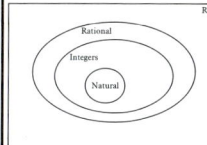

CORE

2 Irrational numbers
Defining rational numbers and irrational numbers
Defining and using surds

QUESTIONS

EXTENSION

TEST YOURSELF

1 Rational numbers

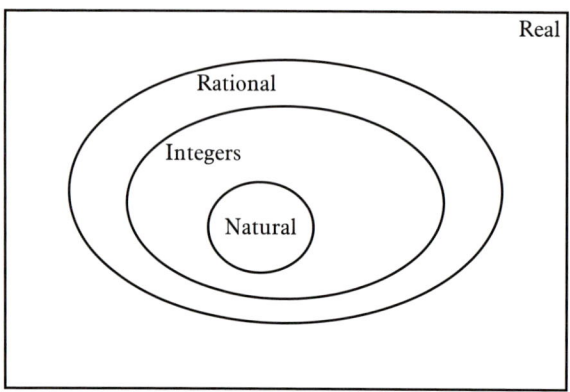

This diagram shows you the different types of real numbers.

Real numbers include rational numbers, integers and natural numbers.

The rational numbers include integers and natural numbers.

The integers include natural numbers. The natural numbers are the numbers you started with when you were a child!

Natural numbers	**Natural numbers** are the counting numbers: 1, 2, 3, 4, 5, … The set of natural numbers is sometimes called $\mathbb{N}$.
Integers	**Integers** include all whole numbers and zero. … $-4, -3, -2, -1, 0, 1, 2, 3, 4, …$ The set of integers is sometimes called $\mathbb{Z}$.
Rational numbers	**Rational numbers** include all the integers together with fractions. The set of rational numbers is sometimes called $\mathbb{Q}$.
Real numbers	**Real numbers** include all the rational numbers together with numbers that cannot be written as fractions. These numbers are called irrational numbers and you will see them in Section 2. The set of real numbers is sometimes called $\mathbb{R}$.

Natural numbers

Within the natural numbers there are other special types of numbers that you have already seen.

Factor

If **a** and **b** are both natural numbers,
a is a **factor** of **b** if **b** ÷ **a** is also a natural number.
So 2 is a factor of 10 because 10 ÷ 2 = 5.

Prime number

A **prime number** has only two factors, itself and 1.
1 is not a prime number because it does not have two factors.
2, 3, 5, 7, 11, 13, ... are prime numbers.

Prime factor

A factor of a number that is also a prime number is called a **prime factor**. You can write any number as a product of prime factors in exactly one way.

Example

Write 24 as a product of prime factors.

Look for the smallest prime factor of 24:

$$24 \div 2 = 12$$

write the 12 under the 24 and repeat the process.

Carry on until you reach 1:
$$24 = 2 \times 2 \times 2 \times 3$$
$$= 2^3 \times 3$$

You cannot write 24 as a product of any other prime numbers. Try it!

2	24
2	12
2	6
3	3
	1

Exercise 5:1

1 Write down all the prime numbers between 1 and 100.

2 Write each of these numbers as a product of primes.

a	12	**d**	34	**g**	78	**j**	256
b	18	**e**	44	**h**	82	**k**	405
c	22	**f**	48	**i**	126	**l**	750

3 **a** Write 900 as a product of primes.
  b Look at your list of factors. Write down what you notice.

Common factor	If a number is a factor of two numbers then it is a **common factor**.
Example	Find the common factors of 15 and 40.
	The factors of 15 are 1 3 5 15
	The factors of 40 are 1 2 4 5 8 10 20 40
	The common factors of 15 and 40 are 1 and 5
Highest common factor	The **highest common factor** of two numbers is the biggest number that is a common factor to both numbers.
	In the example above, the highest common factor of 15 and 40 is 5.
HCF	Highest common factor is written as **HCF**.

4 Find the HCF of each of these pairs of numbers.
Write out all the factors of each number to help you.

    a 10 and 25   **b** 16 and 24   **c** 48 and 60

5 Find the HCF of the numbers 100, 48 and 56.

It is possible to calculate the HCF of two numbers using prime factors.

Example	Find the HCF of 24 and 30.
	First, write each number as the product of prime factors:
	$24 = 2 \times 2 \times 2 \times 3$
	$30 = 2 \times 3 \times 5$
	Then mark the common prime factors: $24 = 2 \times 2 \times 2 \times 3$
	$30 = 2 \times 3 \times 5$
	The numbers have a 2 and a 3 in common.
	This means that the HCF of 24 and 30 is $2 \times 3 = 6$

6 Use the method of prime factors to find the HCF of these numbers.

    a 27 and 32   **d** 49 and 56   **g** 45, 60 and 99

    b 35 and 48   **e** 72 and 100   **h** 36, 60 and 91

    c 30 and 52   **f** 24, 35 and 56   **i** 150, 300 and 450

| Multiple | A multiple of 5 is the result of multiplying 5 by an integer. 5, 15, 50 and 125 are all multiples of 5. |

| Lowest common multiple | The **lowest common multiple** of two integers is the smallest number that is a multiple of both integers. You can also find the lowest common multiple of three or more numbers. |

| LCM | Lowest common multiple is often written as **LCM**. |

To find the LCM of some numbers:
1 Write each number as the product of prime factors.
2 List all the factors of the largest number.
3 Add to the list any factors from the smaller numbers that are not already in the list.
4 Multiply all the numbers in the list together.
   The result is the LCM of the numbers.

Example   Find the LCM of each of these sets of numbers.
a 8 and 12   **b** 9, 11 and 15

a $8 = 2 \times 2 \times 2$ $12 = 2 \times 2 \times 3$
Write down the factors of the bigger number: $2 \times 2 \times 3$
Now look at the factors of the smaller number.
It is made up of three 2s. We already have two 2s in the list so we need just one more.
The LCM of 8 and 12 is $2 \times 2 \times 3 \times 2 = 24$.

b $9 = 3 \times 3$ $11 = 1 \times 11$ $15 = 3 \times 5$
The factors of the largest number are 3×5.
9 has two 3s as its prime factors, so we need to add a second 3.
11 is prime and so we need to add an 11 to the list.
The LCM of 9, 11 and 15 is $3 \times 5 \times 3 \times 11 = 495$.

7 Find the LCM of each of these sets of numbers.

a 2 and 10	**d** 9 and 45	**g** 6, 8 and 10
b 5 and 8	**e** 15 and 24	**h** 5, 9 and 16
c 8 and 14	**f** 16 and 24	**i** 12, 15 and 28

Square numbers

The **square numbers** are   1,   4,   9,   16, ...
They can be shown as square patterns of dots.

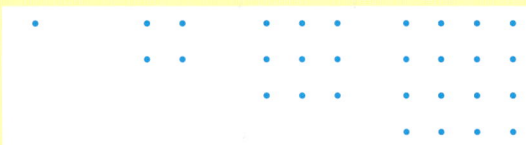

You work them out by doing 1×1 2×2 3×3 4×4
or 1^2 2^2 3^2 4^2

Cube numbers

The **cube numbers** are   1,   8,   27,   64, ...
They can be shown as cubic patterns of dots.

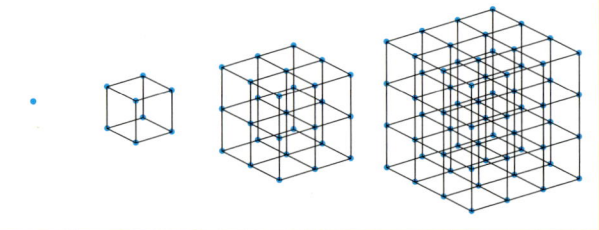

You work them out by doing $1 \times 1 \times 1$ $2 \times 2 \times 2$ $3 \times 3 \times 3$ $4 \times 4 \times 4$
or 1^3 2^3 3^3 4^3

Triangle numbers

The **triangle numbers** are   1,   3,   6,   10, ...
They can be shown as triangular patterns of dots.

You work them out by doing   1 $1 + 2$ $1 + 2 + 3$ $1 + 2 + 3 + 4$

or $\dfrac{1 \times 2}{2}$ $\dfrac{2 \times 3}{2}$ $\dfrac{3 \times 4}{2}$ $\dfrac{4 \times 5}{2}$

Exercise 5:2

1   Write down the first 10:
    a   square numbers
    b   cube numbers
    c   triangle numbers

2 The nth square number is $n \times n$ or n^2
Write down an expression for:
  a the nth cube number
  b the nth triangle number

3 **a** Write each of these numbers as a product of primes.
    (1) 36   (2) 225   (3) 144   (4) 324
  b These are all square numbers. How can you tell this from the prime factors?

4 **a** Find two square numbers which add together to give a square number.
  b Can you find two cube numbers which add together to give a cube number?

5 What do you get if you add together any two consecutive triangle numbers?

If you have a fraction in the form $\dfrac{a}{b}$

you can divide a by b to turn the fraction into a decimal.

$a \div b$ will give you either a terminating decimal
              or   a recurring decimal

Terminating decimal

A **terminating decimal** is one which stops.
0.5, 0.867, 0.373 645 651 2 are all terminating decimals.

Recurring decimal

A **recurring decimal** is one which does not stop but which repeats.

$1 \div 9 = 0.111\ 111\ 111...$
The 1s carry on forever.
You cannot carry on writing forever so you put a dot over the 1 to show that it repeats.

$0.111\ 111\ 111...$ is written $0.\dot{1}$

$1 \div 7 = 0.142\ 857\ 142\ 857\ 142\ 857...$
The 142 857 carries on forever.
You put a dot over the beginning and the end of the part that repeats.

$0.142\ 857\ 142\ 857\ 142\ 857...$ is written $0.\dot{1}42\ 85\dot{7}$

Exercise 5:3

1 Work out $1 \div 2$, $1 \div 3$, $1 \div 4$, $1 \div 5$, up to $1 \div 20$.
Write each answer as a terminating or recurring decimal.

2 **a** Work out $1 \div 9$ as a decimal.
b Work out the decimals for each of the fractions.

$$\frac{2}{9} \quad \frac{3}{9} \quad \frac{4}{9} \quad \frac{5}{9} \quad \frac{6}{9} \quad \frac{7}{9} \quad \frac{8}{9}$$

Write down what you notice.

3 Work out the decimals for each of these fractions.
Write down what you notice about the answers.

a $\frac{1}{7} \quad \frac{2}{7} \quad \frac{3}{7} \quad \frac{4}{7} \quad \frac{5}{7} \quad \frac{6}{7}$

b $\frac{1}{13} \quad \frac{2}{13} \quad \frac{3}{13} \quad \frac{4}{13} \quad \frac{5}{13} \quad \frac{6}{13} \quad \frac{7}{13} \quad \frac{8}{13} \quad \frac{9}{13} \quad \frac{10}{13} \quad \frac{11}{13} \quad \frac{12}{13}$

Every terminating decimal can be written as a fraction.
0.5 is 5 tenths because the 5 is in the tenths column.
Then you can simplify the fraction.

So $0.5 = \frac{5}{10} = \frac{1}{2}$

0.32 is 32 hundredths because the 2 is in the hundredths column.
Then you can simplify the fraction.

so $0.32 = \frac{32}{100} = \frac{8}{25}$

0.129 is 129 thousandths so $0.129 = \frac{129}{1000}$

Every recurring decimal can also be written as a fraction.
To do this you need to look at the recurring part.

If the recurring part is a single digit $\qquad 0.\dot{2}$

the fraction is that digit over 9 $\qquad = \frac{2}{9}$

If the recurring part has two digits $\qquad 0.\dot{3}\dot{1}$

the fraction is the two digits over 99 $\qquad = \frac{31}{99}$

If the recurring part has three digits $\qquad 0.\dot{4}8\dot{7}$

the fraction is the three digits over 999 $\qquad = \frac{487}{999}$

and so on.

Exercise 5:4

1 Write these decimals as fractions. Write each fraction in its simplest form.

   a 0.3   **c** 0.375   **e** 0.4728   ● **g** 2.52

   b 0.56   **d** 0.275   **f** 0.1825   ● **h** 3.145

2 Write these recurring decimals as fractions.

   a $0.\dot{2}$ **c** $0.\dot{3}\dot{7}$ **e** $0.3\dot{3}\dot{2}$ **g** $0.576\,\dot{3}\dot{2}$

   b $0.\dot{6}$ **d** $0.\dot{6}\dot{9}$ **f** $0.2\dot{8}\dot{2}$ **h** $0.142\,41\dot{3}\dot{5}$

Example
   Write $0.821\,212\,121\ldots = 0.8\dot{2}\dot{1}$ as a fraction.

In this example you have to split the decimal into two parts. The first part does not recur and the second part does.

$$0.8\dot{2}\dot{1} = 0.8 + 0.0\dot{2}\dot{1}$$

$$= 0.8 + 0.\dot{2}\dot{1} \div 10 \qquad \text{dividing by 10 moves the digits one place to the right}$$

$$= \frac{8}{10} + \frac{21}{99} \div 10$$

$$= \frac{8}{10} + \frac{21}{990} \qquad\qquad \frac{21}{99} \div 10 = \frac{21}{990}$$

$$= \frac{8 \times 99 + 21}{990} \qquad \text{adding the fractions using 990 as the common denominator}$$

$$= \frac{813}{990}$$

---

3 Write these recurring decimals as fractions.

   a $0.8\dot{2}$ **c** $0.4\dot{1}\dot{7}$ **e** $0.7\dot{1}\dot{1}\dot{2}$ **g** $2.6\dot{7}$

   b $0.6\dot{4}$ **d** $0.7\dot{4}\dot{2}$ **f** $0.6\dot{2}\dot{5}\dot{2}$ **h** $3.1\dot{4}\dot{2}$

4 **a** What is the fractional equivalent of the recurring decimal $0.\dot{9}$?

   b What does this tell you about the number 0.999 999 999 9 …?

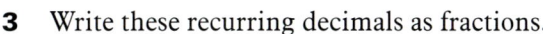

You can also use prime factors to spot recurring and terminating decimals. To use this method, the fraction must be cancelled down to its lowest terms. Some fractions always produce recurring decimals. These are fractions that include $\frac{1}{3}$s $\frac{1}{6}$s, $\frac{1}{7}$s and $\frac{1}{11}$s.

Fractions like $\frac{1}{2}$ and $\frac{1}{5}$ always produce terminating decimals. These are decimals that do not go on forever. For example $\frac{1}{2} = 0.5$ and $\frac{1}{5} = 0.2$

To tell if a fraction produces a recurring or a terminating decimal, write its denominator as a product of prime factors. If these prime factors are only 2s and 5s then the fraction will produce a terminating decimal. If you find any other prime numbers then the fraction will produce a recurring decimal.

Example

Decide if the following fractions are recurring or terminating.
a $\frac{2}{15}$ b $\frac{1}{50}$ c $\frac{7}{16}$

a Write 15 as the product of prime factors.
$15 = 3 \times 5$
Because of the 3, $\frac{2}{15}$ will produce a recurring decimal.

b Write 50 as the product of prime factors.
$50 = 2 \times 5 \times 5$
Because there are only 2s and 5s, $\frac{1}{50}$ will produce a terminating decimal.

c $16 = 2 \times 2 \times 2 \times 2$
Because there are only 2s, $\frac{7}{16}$ produces a terminating decimal. The 7 on the top does not affect this.

5 Decide whether the fraction $\frac{5}{18}$ produces a recurring or a terminating decimal.

6 Decide whether the fraction $\frac{7}{20}$ produces a recurring or a terminating decimal.

7 Decide whether the fraction $\frac{11}{45}$ produces a recurring or a terminating decimal.

8 Decide whether the fraction $\frac{13}{28}$ produces a recurring or a terminating decimal.

2 Irrational numbers

Georg Cantor was a famous mathematician who did a lot of research into numbers. He struggled for many years to understand the full implications of irrational numbers. His work gave us a new insight into this area.

Real number A **real number** is a number which can be written as a decimal.

Rational number A **rational number** is a number which can be written as a fraction $\frac{a}{b}$ where a and b are integers and $b \neq 0$.

Irrational number An **irrational number** is a number which is not rational. It cannot be written as a fraction.

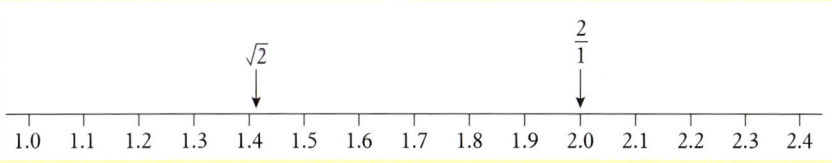

The number line goes on forever.
Every point on the number line is a real number.
There are no gaps on the number line.

Some of the points on the number line are rational numbers.
Rational numbers include integers like $\frac{2}{1}$
and recurring decimals like $0.\dot{3} = \frac{1}{3}$

You already know one irrational number. This is π.
π is a non-recurring decimal that goes on forever.
A lot of square roots are also irrational.
These include $\sqrt{2}, \sqrt{3}, \sqrt{5}, \sqrt{6}, \sqrt{7}, \sqrt{8} \dots$
$\sqrt{4}$ is not irrational because $\sqrt{4} = 2$

Example

Are these expressions rational or irrational?

a 4.1   **b** $\sqrt{3}$

a 4.1 is rational. It can be written as $4\frac{1}{10}$ which is $\frac{41}{10}$

b $\sqrt{3}$ is irrational. On a calculator $\sqrt{3} = 1.732\,050\,808$ (9 dp)
There is no sign of the digits recurring.
The calculator **rounds** the answer.
$\sqrt{3}$ to 15 decimal places is $1.732\,050\,807\,568\,877\ldots$
The digits are still not recurring.

Assume that if your calculator display does not repeat, the number is irrational.

Exercise 5:5

1 Are these numbers rational or irrational?
Explain your answers.

a 11	**d** π	**g** $\sqrt{25}$	**j** $\sqrt{66}$
b $\sqrt{2}$	**e** $0.\dot{3}$	**h** 2.3	**k** 66.6666
c $\frac{2}{5}$	**f** $\sqrt{12}$	**i** $\frac{5}{11}$	**l** 0.142 857

2 Ed is going over to see his Uncle Ric in New York. Ric hasn't seen Ed since he was a baby. Ed says he will wear a T-shirt with numbers on to make himself easy to find at the airport. When Ric arrives at the airport he finds students arriving for a Maths Conference! Some of these have mathematical T-shirts. All Ric knows is that Ed's mum said 'Well like most teenagers he's completely irrational and doesn't like pie!' Which student below will Ric approach?

Example

Are these expressions rational or irrational?

a $4.1 + 5.2$ **b** $\sqrt{2} + 5.2$

a $4.1 + 5.2 = 9.3$

$9.3 = 9\frac{3}{10}$

$9\frac{3}{10} = \frac{93}{10}$

Any fraction is rational.
So $4.1 + 5.2$ is rational.

b $\sqrt{2} = 1.414\,213\,562...$

$\sqrt{2} + 5.2 = 1.414\,213\,562... + 5.2$

$= 6.614\,213\,562...$

When you add 5.2 to the value of $\sqrt{2}$ it does not change the number beyond the first decimal place.
The digits still don't recur so the number is irrational.

3 Are these numbers rational or irrational?
Explain your answers.

a $4.79 \mid 2.328$ **c** $\pi + 7$ **i** $\sqrt{2} + \sqrt{3}$

b $\sqrt{2} + 17$ **f** $0.\dot{6} + 0.\dot{6}$ **j** $\sqrt{2} + \sqrt{5}$

c $\sqrt{3} + \sqrt{5}$ **g** $\frac{5}{9} + 0.\dot{3}$ **k** $\frac{2}{3} + \sqrt{7}$

d $2.37 - \frac{2}{3}$ **h** $19 - \sqrt{8}$ **l** $5\frac{4}{7} - \sqrt{7}$

4 Copy the tables below.
Fill them in using your results so far.
Write 'rational', 'irrational' or 'either'.

+	Rational	Irrational
Rational		
Irrational		

−	Rational	Irrational
Rational		
Irrational		

Example

Are these expressions rational or irrational?

a 2.1×3.3 **b** $\sqrt{2} \times \sqrt{3}$ **c** $\sqrt{32} \div \sqrt{8}$

a $2.1 \times 3.3 = 6.93$ and $6.93 = \frac{693}{100}$

Any fraction is rational, so 2.1×3.3 is rational.

b $\sqrt{2} \times \sqrt{3} = 1.414\,213\,562... \times 1.732\,050\,807...$
$$= 2.449\,489\,742...$$

There is no sign of the digits recurring.
So $\sqrt{2} \times \sqrt{3}$ is irrational.

c $\sqrt{32} \div \sqrt{8}$
$$= 5.656\,854\,249... \div 2.828\,427\,125...$$
$$= 2$$
$$2 = \frac{2}{1}$$

Any fraction is rational, so $\sqrt{32} \div \sqrt{8}$ is rational.

5 Are these numbers rational or irrational?
Explain your answers.

a 2.4×5.9 **e** $\sqrt{8} \times \sqrt{2}$ **i** $(\sqrt{6})^2$

b $5 \times \sqrt{2}$ **f** $(0.\dot{3})^2$ **j** $6 \times \sqrt{6}$

c $\sqrt{3} \times \sqrt{5}$ **g** $\frac{2}{3} \times \sqrt{8}$ **k** $(\sqrt{8})^3 \times (\sqrt{2})^3$

d $7 \times \pi$ **h** $\frac{4}{9} \times \pi$ **l** π^2

6 Are these numbers rational or irrational?
Explain your answers.

a $4.2 \div 1.8$ **e** $\sqrt{8} \div \sqrt{2}$ **i** $\sqrt{128} \div \sqrt{32}$

b $\sqrt{2} \div 4$ **f** $\frac{2}{3} \div 0.9$ **j** $6 \div \sqrt{6}$

c $\sqrt{3} \div \sqrt{5}$ **g** $\frac{7}{9} \div \sqrt{8}$ **k** $(\sqrt{32})^3 \div (\sqrt{2})^5$

d $\pi \div 6$ **h** $\frac{4}{\sqrt{2}} \div \pi$ **l** $\frac{1}{\pi^2}$

7 Copy the tables below.
Fill them in using your results so far.
Write 'rational', 'irrational' or 'either'.

$\times$	Rational	Irrational
Rational		
Irrational		

$\div$	Rational	Irrational
Rational		
Irrational		

Finding rational numbers within a given range

There is a rational number between every pair of numbers on the number line.
To find a rational number between any two numbers write the numbers as decimals.

Example   Find a rational number between   **a** $1\frac{5}{9}$ and $1\frac{5}{8}$ **b** $\sqrt{17}$ and $\sqrt{19}$

a On a calculator $1\frac{5}{9} = 1.555$ (3 dp) and $1\frac{5}{8} = 1.625$
So 1.6 is one possible correct answer. There are lots of others!

b On a calculator $\sqrt{17} = 4.123\,105...$ and $\sqrt{19} = 4.358\,898...$
So 4.2 is one possible correct answer. There are lots of others!

Finding irrational numbers within a given range

There is an irrational number between every pair of numbers on the number line.
Remember that   **irrational + rational = irrational**
and that   **irrational − rational = irrational**

π is a useful irrational number to start from.
It is approximately 3.14...
You then add or subtract a rational number to get into the range you need.

Example   Find an irrational number between **a** 1.2 and 1.3   **b** $\sqrt{22}$ and $\sqrt{23}$

a Subtract terminating decimals from π. Use trial and improvement.
$\pi - 2 = 1.141\,59...$ (too small) $\pi - 1.9 = 1.241\,59...$ ✓

b On a calculator $\sqrt{22} = 4.690\,415...$ and $\sqrt{23} = 4.795\,831...$
Add terminating decimals to π. Use trial and improvement.
$\pi + 1 = 4.141\,59...$ (too small) $\pi + 1.6 = 4.741\,59...$ ✓

Exercise 5:6

1 Find a rational number between:
a 1 and 2   **b** 4.9 and 5   **c** $2\frac{3}{5}$ and $2\frac{2}{3}$ **d** $\sqrt{2}$ and $\sqrt{3}$

2 Find an irrational number between:
a 1 and 2   **c** 4.9 and 5   **e** $2\frac{3}{5}$ and $2\frac{2}{3}$ **g** $\sqrt{95}$ and $4\sqrt{6}$
b 1.4 and 1.5   **d** 7.01 and 7.02   **f** $\sqrt{2}$ and $\sqrt{3}$ • **h** $3\frac{1}{9}$ and $3\frac{1}{7}$

| Surd | A **surd** is an irrational number that contains an irrational square root. |

$$2\sqrt{3}, \quad 4 + 3\sqrt{5}, \quad 10 - 4\sqrt{6}, \quad \frac{\sqrt{2}}{5}, \quad \frac{9}{\sqrt{7}} \quad \text{are all surds.}$$

Simplifying surds

You can write some surds in an easier way.
You have already seen that $\sqrt{2} \times \sqrt{3} = 2.449\,489\,742\ldots$
$\sqrt{6}$ is also $2.449\,489\,742\ldots$
So $\sqrt{2} \times \sqrt{3} = \sqrt{6}$

You can generalise this.
For any natural numbers m and n

$$\sqrt{m} \times \sqrt{n} = \sqrt{mn} \quad \text{or the other way round} \quad \sqrt{mn} = \sqrt{m} \times \sqrt{n}$$

This rule is useful to simplify some surds.
It works if one of the surds has a square number as a factor.
So to simplify surds look for a square number that is a factor.

Example   Simplify these expressions.   **a** $\sqrt{24}$ **b** $\sqrt{72}$

a   First use the rule $\sqrt{mn} = \sqrt{m} \times \sqrt{n}$
Look for a factor of 24 that is a square.
4 is a square number. $\sqrt{24} = \sqrt{4} \times \sqrt{6}$
Take the square root of 4. $= 2 \times \sqrt{6}$
This is the simplest form of this surd $= 2\sqrt{6}$
because 6 does not have a square number as a factor.

b   First use the rule $\sqrt{mn} = \sqrt{m} \times \sqrt{n}$
Look for the biggest square number you can. $\sqrt{72} = \sqrt{36} \times \sqrt{2}$
Take the square root. $= 6 \times \sqrt{2}$
This is the simplest form of this surd. $= 6\sqrt{2}$

You can start with $\sqrt{72} = \sqrt{9} \times \sqrt{8}$ and you will still get $6\sqrt{2}$ eventually.
Try it!

Sometimes it is helpful to use the rule the other way round.

Example   Simplify $\sqrt{8} \times \sqrt{2}$

First use the rule $\sqrt{m} \times \sqrt{n} = \sqrt{mn}$ $\sqrt{8} \times \sqrt{2} = \sqrt{16}$
Take the square root of 16. $\sqrt{16} = 4$

Exercise 5:7

1 Simplify these expressions.

a $\sqrt{3} \times \sqrt{2}$ **d** $\sqrt{3} \times \sqrt{12}$ **g** $\sqrt{10} \times \sqrt{6}$ **j** $(\sqrt{6})^2$

b $\sqrt{2} \times \sqrt{5}$ **e** $\sqrt{8} \times \sqrt{7}$ **h** $\sqrt{15} \times \sqrt{6}$ **k** $\sqrt{3} \times \sqrt{2} \times \sqrt{6}$

c $\sqrt{3} \times \sqrt{3}$ **f** $\sqrt{8} \times \sqrt{3}$ **i** $\sqrt{27} \times \sqrt{3}$ **l** $\sqrt{10} \times \sqrt{8} \times \sqrt{6}$

2 Simplify these expressions.

a $5\sqrt{2} \times \sqrt{2}$ **c** $2\sqrt{15} \times 3\sqrt{6}$ • **e** $(5\sqrt{15})^2$ • **g** $(\sqrt{5})^4$

b $2\sqrt{3} \times \sqrt{3}$ • **d** $(2\sqrt{8})^2$ • **f** $\sqrt{8} \times (\sqrt{3})^3$ • **h** $(\pi\sqrt{2})^2$

3 Simplify these expressions.

a $\sqrt{12}$ **c** $\sqrt{28}$ **e** $\sqrt{56}$ **g** $\sqrt{63}$

b $\sqrt{20}$ **d** $\sqrt{27}$ **f** $\sqrt{54}$ **h** $\sqrt{200}$

To simplify bigger surds, you might find it easier to use prime factors.

Example   Simplify $\sqrt{540}$

At each stage divide by the smallest prime number that you can.

Pair the factors up to make square numbers.

So $\sqrt{540} = \sqrt{(2 \times 2 \times 3 \times 3 \times 3 \times 5)}$

$= \sqrt{(2 \times 2)} \times \sqrt{(3 \times 3)} \times \sqrt{(3 \times 5)}$

$= 2 \times 3 \times \sqrt{(3 \times 5)}$

$= 6\sqrt{15}$

2	540
2	270
3	135
3	45
3	15
5	5
	1

4 Simplify these expressions.

a $\sqrt{120}$ **c** $\sqrt{288}$ **e** $\sqrt{596}$ **g** $\sqrt{5280}$

b $\sqrt{176}$ **d** $\sqrt{600}$ **f** $\sqrt{968}$ **h** $\sqrt{99\,225}$

Game: Absurd Snakes and Ladders

This is a game for 2 players. You need two counters.
Each player needs a different colour.
You will need a dice marked with the following numbers:

$1 \quad \sqrt{2} \quad \sqrt{3} \quad 2 \quad \sqrt{5} \quad \sqrt{7}$

Take it in turns to throw the dice.
On your first throw put your counter on your score.
On your next throw multiply your score by the value of the square you're on.
Play the game just like snakes and ladders.
If you land at the foot of a ladder, go to the top of the ladder.
If you land on the head of a snake, go to the bottom of the snake.
The winner is the first player to get a score higher than $2\sqrt{78}$.

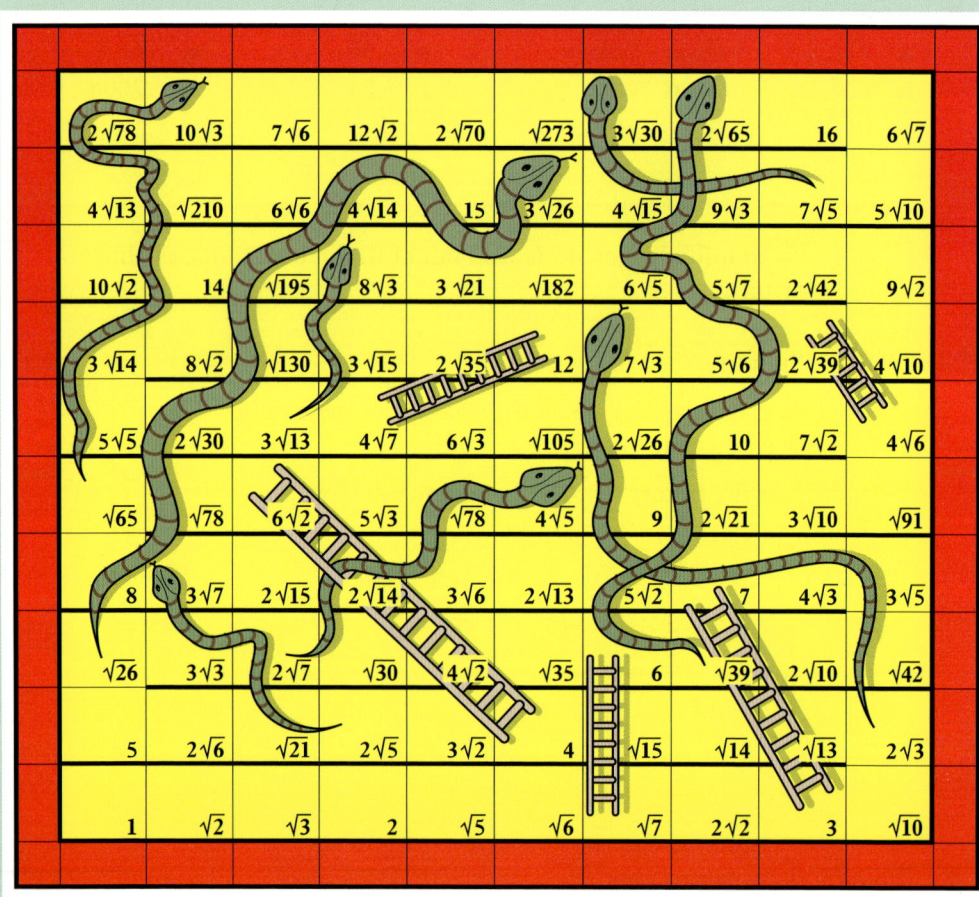

You have already seen that $\quad \sqrt{32} \div \sqrt{8} = 2$

This is because $\quad \dfrac{\sqrt{32}}{\sqrt{8}} = \sqrt{\dfrac{32}{8}} = \sqrt{4} = 2$

You can generalise this.

$\dfrac{\sqrt{m}}{\sqrt{n}} = \sqrt{\dfrac{m}{n}} \quad$ or the other way round $\quad \sqrt{\dfrac{m}{n}} = \dfrac{\sqrt{m}}{\sqrt{n}} \qquad$ This works as long as m and n are positive.

Example Simplify: **a** $\sqrt{8} \div \sqrt{2}$ **b** $\sqrt{180} \div \sqrt{24}$ **c** $\sqrt{1\tfrac{7}{9}}$

a First use the rule $\dfrac{\sqrt{m}}{\sqrt{n}} = \sqrt{\dfrac{m}{n}} \qquad \dfrac{\sqrt{8}}{\sqrt{2}} = \sqrt{\dfrac{8}{2}} = \sqrt{4}$

Take the square root of 4 $\qquad \sqrt{4} = 2$

b First use the rule $\dfrac{\sqrt{m}}{\sqrt{n}} = \sqrt{\dfrac{m}{n}} \qquad\qquad \dfrac{\sqrt{180}}{\sqrt{24}} = \sqrt{\dfrac{180}{24}}$

Find the prime factors of 180 and 24

$$= \sqrt{\dfrac{(\cancel{2} \times \cancel{2} \times \cancel{3} \times 3 \times 5)}{(\cancel{2} \times \cancel{2} \times 2 \times \cancel{3})}}$$

Cancel to give the simplest form of this surd $\qquad = \sqrt{\dfrac{15}{2}}$

c Convert this to an improper fraction $\quad \sqrt{1\tfrac{7}{9}} = \sqrt{\tfrac{16}{9}}$

(An improper fraction has a bigger numerator than denominator.)

Use the rule $\sqrt{\dfrac{m}{n}} = \dfrac{\sqrt{m}}{\sqrt{n}} \qquad\qquad \sqrt{\dfrac{16}{9}} = \dfrac{\sqrt{16}}{\sqrt{9}}$

Take the square root $\qquad\qquad\qquad \dfrac{\sqrt{16}}{\sqrt{9}} = \dfrac{4}{3}$

You can convert this to a mixed number $\qquad \tfrac{4}{3} = 1\tfrac{1}{3}$

(A mixed number is an integer and a proper fraction.)

Exercise 5:8

1 Simplify these expressions.

a $\sqrt{12} \div \sqrt{3}$ **d** $\sqrt{12} \div \sqrt{6}$ **g** $\sqrt{84} \div \sqrt{7}$ • **j** $\sqrt{420} \div 2\sqrt{3}$

b $\sqrt{27} \div \sqrt{3}$ **e** $\sqrt{42} \div \sqrt{2}$ **h** $\sqrt{180} \div \sqrt{8}$ • **k** $(\sqrt{15})^3 \div 3\sqrt{5}$

c $\sqrt{32} \div \sqrt{2}$ **f** $\sqrt{56} \div \sqrt{7}$ **i** $\sqrt{72} \div \sqrt{24}$ • **l** $3\sqrt{8} \div 2\sqrt{32}$

2 Simplify these expressions.

a $\sqrt{1\frac{9}{16}}$ **d** $\sqrt{\frac{1}{4}}$ **g** $\sqrt{\frac{4}{25}}$ • **j** $2\sqrt{1\frac{4}{5}}$

b $\sqrt{2\frac{1}{4}}$ **e** $\sqrt{\frac{1}{9}}$ **h** $\sqrt{1\frac{4}{25}}$ • **k** $\sqrt[3]{3\frac{3}{8}}$

c $\sqrt{\frac{4}{9}}$ **f** $\sqrt{\frac{4}{9}}$ **i** $\sqrt{2\frac{1}{16}}$ • **l** $\sqrt[4]{5\frac{1}{16}}$

Rationalising the denominator

You can simplify a fraction by removing a square root from the denominator.

You can do this by multiplying the top and bottom by the **same square root**.

This is allowed because you are effectively multiplying by 1.

This makes the denominator rational. It doesn't have a square root in it. This process is called rationalising the denominator.

Example   Simplify these: **a** $\dfrac{2}{\sqrt{3}}$ **b** $\dfrac{5}{7\sqrt{2}}$

a Multiply by $\dfrac{\sqrt{3}}{\sqrt{3}}$ $\dfrac{2}{\sqrt{3}} \times \dfrac{\sqrt{3}}{\sqrt{3}} = \dfrac{2\sqrt{3}}{(\sqrt{3})^2} = \dfrac{2\sqrt{3}}{3}$

b Multiply by $\dfrac{\sqrt{2}}{\sqrt{2}}$ $\dfrac{5}{7\sqrt{2}} \times \dfrac{\sqrt{2}}{\sqrt{2}} = \dfrac{5\sqrt{2}}{7 \times 2} = \dfrac{5\sqrt{2}}{14}$

Exercise 5:9

1 Simplify these expressions.

a $\dfrac{3}{\sqrt{2}}$ **c** $\dfrac{7}{\sqrt{3}}$ **e** $\dfrac{8}{\sqrt{6}}$ **g** $\dfrac{5}{3\sqrt{2}}$

b $\dfrac{5}{\sqrt{2}}$ **d** $\dfrac{5}{\sqrt{7}}$ **f** $\dfrac{6}{\sqrt{2}}$ • **h** $\dfrac{2\sqrt{8}}{6\sqrt{18}}$

Multiplying out brackets containing surds

You may have already seen the face method for multiplying out brackets in algebra. You can do this with surds.
You can multiply out $(2 + \sqrt{3})(5 - \sqrt{3})$ like this:

$2 \times 5 \quad \sqrt{3} \times -\sqrt{3}$

$(2 + \sqrt{3})(5 - \sqrt{3})$
$= 10 - (\sqrt{3})(\sqrt{3}) - 2\sqrt{3} + 5\sqrt{3}$
$= 10 - 3 - 2\sqrt{3} + 5\sqrt{3}$
$= 7 + 3\sqrt{3}$

$5 \times \sqrt{3}$
$2 \times -\sqrt{3}$

You can also use the box method to multiply out brackets.
Multiplying out brackets is sometimes called expanding brackets.

Example Expand $(2 + \sqrt{3})(5 - \sqrt{3})$

You use the grid like a multiplication table.

$\times$	5	$-\sqrt{3}$
2	10	$-2\sqrt{3}$
$\sqrt{3}$	$5\sqrt{3}$	-3

$(2 + \sqrt{3})(5 - \sqrt{3}) = 7 + 3\sqrt{3}$

Exercise 5:10

Expand these sets of brackets.
Give each answer in its simplest form.

1 $(1 + \sqrt{2})(1 + \sqrt{2})$

2 $(2 + \sqrt{3})(1 + \sqrt{3})$

3 $(3 + \sqrt{5})(1 + \sqrt{5})$

4 $(2 + \sqrt{3})(2 + \sqrt{3})$

5 $(3 + \sqrt{3})(5 + \sqrt{3})$

6 $(7 + \sqrt{3})(5 + \sqrt{2})$

7 $(6 + \sqrt{2})(5 + \sqrt{5})$

8 $(7 - \sqrt{5})(2 + \sqrt{3})$

9 $(2 - \sqrt{3})(5 - \sqrt{3})$

10 $(1 - \sqrt{2})(1 - \sqrt{3})$

11 $(\sqrt{3} - 2)(5 - \sqrt{5})$

12 $(\sqrt{7} + 2)(5 - \sqrt{6})$

13 $(\sqrt{3} + 9)(\sqrt{5} - \sqrt{6})$

14 $(\sqrt{3} + 2)^2$

15 $(5 - \sqrt{2})^2$

16 $(2 + \sqrt{3})(2 - \sqrt{3})$

● 17 $(2\sqrt{7} - 5\sqrt{2})(5\sqrt{7} - 3\sqrt{2})$

● 18 $(3\sqrt{5} - 5\sqrt{3})(3\sqrt{5} + 5\sqrt{3})$

Further simplification with surds

When you add or subtract surds, it may be possible to collect like terms.

Example   Simplify the expression $\sqrt{50} + 2\sqrt{72} + 3\sqrt{98}$
Look for the common factors in each surd.
To do this simplify each surd.
$\sqrt{50} \quad = \sqrt{25} \times \sqrt{2} \quad = 5\sqrt{2}$
$2\sqrt{72} = 2 \times \sqrt{36} \times \sqrt{2} = 2 \times 6 \times \sqrt{2} = 12\sqrt{2}$
$3\sqrt{98} = 3 \times \sqrt{49} \times \sqrt{2} = 3 \times 7 \times \sqrt{2} = 21\sqrt{2}$

All of these terms now contain $\sqrt{2}$
So $\sqrt{50} + 2\sqrt{72} + 3\sqrt{98} = 5\sqrt{2} + 12\sqrt{2} + 21\sqrt{2}$
$= 38\sqrt{2}$

Exercise 5:11

Simplify these expressions as far as possible.

1 $\sqrt{2} + \sqrt{8}$

2 $\sqrt{12} + \sqrt{8}$

3 $\sqrt{20} + \sqrt{12}$

4 $\sqrt{3} + \sqrt{18}$

5 $\sqrt{18} + \sqrt{27}$

6 $\sqrt{18} + \sqrt{45} + \sqrt{54}$

7 $\sqrt{50} + \sqrt{125} + \sqrt{175}$

8 $4\sqrt{50} + \sqrt{200} + \sqrt{50}$

9 $4\sqrt{24} + 2\sqrt{48} + 3\sqrt{72}$

10 $\sqrt{32} + \sqrt{72} + \sqrt{128}$

11 $\sqrt{104} + \sqrt{234} + \sqrt{650}$

12 $\dfrac{2}{\sqrt{2}} + \dfrac{5}{\sqrt{2}}$

● 13 $\dfrac{5}{\sqrt{12}} + \dfrac{6}{\sqrt{3}}$

● 14 $(\sqrt{12} - \sqrt{2})(\sqrt{20} - 3\sqrt{2})$

1 Look at this list of numbers.

$$2 \quad -4 \quad 3.4 \quad \tfrac{2}{3} \quad 0 \quad 17 \quad \tfrac{3}{7} \quad 5 \quad 0.\dot{1} \quad 25 \quad 10$$

Write down the numbers in this list which are:
a integers
b natural
c rational
d prime
e square
f triangle

2 Write down the first 10 prime numbers.

3 Write these numbers as a product of prime factors.
a 16   **b** 32   **c** 357   **d** 600

4 **a** Work out the decimals for each of these fractions.

$$\frac{1}{11} \quad \frac{2}{11} \quad \frac{3}{11} \quad \frac{4}{11} \quad \frac{5}{11} \quad \frac{6}{11} \quad \frac{7}{11} \quad \frac{8}{11} \quad \frac{9}{11} \quad \frac{10}{11}$$

b Look at the recurring part of each decimal.
Write down what you notice.

5 Write these decimals as fractions.
a 0.6   **c** 0.236   **e** 0.3472   **g** 2.7
b 0.18   **d** 0.834   **f** 0.1812   **h** 8.15

6 Write these recurring decimals as fractions.
a $0.\dot{3}$ **c** $0.\dot{3}\dot{9}$ **e** $0.3\dot{5}\dot{5}$ **g** $0.5\dot{7}2\dot{2}$
b $0.\dot{7}$ **d** $0.\dot{4}\dot{7}$ **f** $0.4\dot{5}\dot{6}$ **h** $0.442\,\dot{7}\dot{5}$

7 Write these recurring decimals as fractions.
a $0.7\dot{3}$ **b** $0.5\dot{2}\dot{8}$ **c** $0.6\dot{2}5\dot{3}$ **d** $4.7\dot{8}$

8 Write down in your own words the meaning of:
a a rational number
b an irrational number

9 Find the HCF of these sets of numbers.

    a 24 and 45   **b** 36 and 72   **c** 28, 35 and 60

10 Find the LCM of these sets of numbers.

    a 4 and 10   **b** 6 and 14   **c** 12, 16 and 18

11 Use prime factors to decide if the following fractions produce terminating or recurring decimals.

    a $\frac{2}{17}$ **b** $\frac{3}{50}$ **c** $\frac{7}{90}$ **d** $\frac{9}{45}$

12 Simplify these expressions.

    a $\sqrt{2} \times \sqrt{7}$ **c** $\sqrt{3} \times 2\sqrt{6}$ **e** $\sqrt{65}$ **g** $\sqrt{268}$

    b $\sqrt{2} \times \sqrt{12}$ **d** $\sqrt{12} \times \sqrt{3} \times \sqrt{6}$ **f** $\sqrt{252}$ **h** $\sqrt{650}$

13 Simplify these expressions.

    a $\sqrt{24} \div \sqrt{2}$ **b** $\sqrt{30} \div \sqrt{2}$ **c** $\sqrt{75} \div \sqrt{5}$ **d** $\sqrt{2\frac{4}{25}}$

14 Rationalise the denominator in each of these.

    a $\dfrac{2}{\sqrt{6}}$ **b** $\dfrac{7}{\sqrt{5}}$ **c** $\dfrac{8}{\sqrt{6}}$ **d** $\dfrac{7}{2\sqrt{3}}$

15 Expand these brackets.

    a $(1 + \sqrt{3})(2 + \sqrt{3})$ **c** $(3 + \sqrt{2})(5 - \sqrt{5})$

    b $(2 + \sqrt{5})(5 + \sqrt{2})$ **d** $(7 - \sqrt{3})(2 - \sqrt{3})$

16 Simplify these expressions as far as possible.

    a $\sqrt{18} + \sqrt{8}$ **b** $\sqrt{27} + \sqrt{48}$ **c** $2\sqrt{24} + \sqrt{54}$ **d** $\sqrt{125} - \sqrt{45}$

17 Which of these numbers can be written as recurring decimals?

    a $\sqrt{3}$ **b** $\sqrt{\frac{9}{49}}$ **c** 2π **d** $\sqrt[3]{15}$ **e** $\frac{2}{11}$

1 The nth triangular number is $\dfrac{n(n+1)}{2}$

   a Write down the $(n+1)$th triangle number.
   b Multiply out the brackets in the nth and the $(n+1)$th triangle number.
   c Add these two expressions together. Simplify your answer.
   d The $(n+1)$th square number is $(n+1)^2$. Multiply this out.
   e What do you notice about the answers to parts **c** and **d**?

2 Prove that the difference between any two consecutive square numbers is an odd number.
You will need to use algebra to prove this. Write down the expressions for the nth square number and the $(n+1)$th square number to start with!

3 You have written recurring decimals as fractions by using ninths, ninety-ninths etc. So you know that

$$0.\dot{2} = \frac{2}{9} \qquad 0.\dot{3}\dot{1} = \frac{31}{99} \qquad 0.\dot{4}8\dot{7} = \frac{487}{999}$$

Here is a more mathematical way of showing that this is true!

To show that $0.\dot{4} = \frac{4}{9}$
Start by using algebra and saying $\qquad\qquad\qquad\qquad x = 0.4444\ldots$ (1)
Then multiply by 10 to get $\qquad\qquad\qquad\quad 10x = 4.4444\ldots$ (2)
Subtract these two equations $(2) - (1)$ $\qquad\quad 10x - x = 4$
    and all the recurring decimal disappears. $\qquad\quad 9x = 4$
This gives the value of x $\qquad\qquad\qquad\qquad\qquad x = \dfrac{4}{9}$
    which is the value of $0.\dot{4}$

Use this method to write these decimals as fractions.
   a $0.\dot{2}$ **b** $0.\dot{6}$ **c** $0.\dot{2}\dot{3}$ **d** $0.\dot{1}2\dot{3}$ **e** $0.8\dot{3}$

4 Simplify these expressions.
   a $\dfrac{(\sqrt{2})^3(2-\sqrt{5})}{\sqrt{7}}$ **c** $\dfrac{\sqrt{5000} \times \sqrt{2000}}{(\sqrt{3000})^3}$ **e** $(2 - \sqrt{3} - 5\sqrt{7})(4 - \sqrt{3})$

   b $(1-\sqrt{3})^2$ **d** $\sqrt{32} - \dfrac{1}{\sqrt{2}}$ **f** $(3 + 2\sqrt{3})^3$

5 Write down a number between 9 and 10 which has a rational square root.

1   Write these decimals as fractions.

    a   0.4   **b** $0.\dot{7}$ **c**   0.45   **d** $0.\dot{4}\dot{5}$ **e** $0.6\dot{7}\dot{2}$

2   Find the HCF of:

    a   20 and 26   **b**   30, 45 and 60

3   Find the LCM of:

    a   6 and 14   **b**   12 and 18

4   Write 124 as the product of prime factors.

5   Use prime factorisation to decide if the fraction $\frac{4}{60}$ produces a recurring or terminating decimal.

6   Simplify these expressions.

    a $\sqrt{18}$ **c** $\sqrt{99}$ **e** $(\sqrt{7})^2$

    b $\sqrt{80}$ **d** $\sqrt{450}$ **f** $(3\sqrt{11})^2$

7   Simplify these expressions.

    a $\sqrt{3} \times \sqrt{5}$ **c** $\dfrac{3}{\sqrt{5}}$

    b $\sqrt{7} \times \sqrt{12}$ **d** $\sqrt{24} \div \sqrt{2}$

8   Expand these brackets.

    a $(1 + \sqrt{3})(1 + \sqrt{5})$ **b** $(3 + \sqrt{2})(3 - \sqrt{2})$

9   Simplify these expressions as far as possible.

    a $\sqrt{6} + \sqrt{24}$ **c** $\sqrt{12} + \sqrt{24}$

    b $\sqrt{8} - \sqrt{2}$ **d** $\sqrt{180} + \sqrt{45}$

10   Write $\frac{5}{7}$ as a decimal.

11   Write down:

    a   the first 6 square numbers

    b   the first 6 cube numbers

    c   the first 6 triangle numbers

6 Ratio and proportion

QUESTIONS

EXTENSION

TEST YOURSELF

1   Ratio

Blackpool Tower was opened in 1893 and was the second tallest building in the world. It is a copy of the Eiffel Tower in Paris which was then the tallest structure in the world.
The Blackpool Tower is not an exact copy.
It is only 0.53 of the height of the Eiffel Tower.

Ratios can be used to compare two measurements.

Example   Write down the ratio of the number of pages in a writing pad with 100 pages compared with one of 300 pages.
The ratio is 100 : 300. The second pad has 3 times the number of pages.

Ratios can be simplified like fractions.

Example   Simplify these ratios if possible.
   a 9 : 6   **b** 20 : 15   **c** 9 : 2

   a 3 divides into 9 and 6 exactly.
      9 ÷ 3 = 3 and 6 ÷ 3 = 2 so 9 : 6 = 3 : 2
   b 5 divides into 20 and 15 exactly.
      So 20 : 15 = 4 : 3
   c No whole number divides exactly into 9 and 2.
      9 : 2 cannot be simplified.

Exercise 6:1

1   A mouse weighs about 30 g. An elephant weighs about 6 000 000 g.
Write down the ratio of their weights. Simplify your ratio.

2   Simplify these ratios if possible.

a 21 : 14	**d** 7 : 28	**g** 35 : 24	**j** $\frac{3}{8} : \frac{5}{8}$
b 18 : 6	**e** 75 : 125	**h** 21 : 10	**k** $\frac{1}{2} : \frac{1}{4}$
c 17 : 2	**f** 10 : 36	**i** 18 : 72	**l** $\frac{1}{6} : \frac{7}{24}$

You can use a calculator to simplify ratios. You use the fraction key.

Example   Simplify the ratio 72 : 24

You must enter the smaller number first because of the way the calculator works.

Key in: **2** **4** **$a^b/_c$** **7** **2** **=**

You should see ⌐⌐ or ⌐⌐

Remember to write the ratio back around the right way.
So 72 : 24 = **3 : 1**

---

3   Use a calculator to simplify these ratios.
    a 52 : 39   **d** 45 : 54
    b 28 : 21   **e** 42 : 75
    c 34 : 85   **f** 28 : 39

4   Simplify these ratios. Make sure they are in the same units first.
    a 5 kg : 100 g   **d** 500 kg : 3 tonnes
    b 2.5 m : 50 cm   **e** 50 ml : 6 *l*
    c 4 hrs : 30 mins   **f** 750 ml : 7 *l*

Example   Write the ratio 272 : 57 in the form $n : 1$

To get the right-hand side of the ratio to be 1 you need to divide by 57.
This means that both parts of the ratio need to be divided by 57.
    272 ÷ 57 = 4.77 (2 dp)

The ratio 272 : 57 is the same as 4.77 : 1

In questions **5–7**, round your answers to 2 dp when you need to.

5   An average carrot weighs about 40 g. The world's biggest ever carrot
weighed 7000 g. Write the ratio 7000 : 40 in the form $n : 1$

6   Write the following ratios in the form $1 : n$
Notice that the 1 is on the left-hand side this time.
    a 34 : 98   **c** 23 : 60
    b 21 : 54   **d** 0.5 : 17

7 The following table has some more world records in it.
Copy the table and fill it in.

	Vegetable	Record weight (kg)	Average weight (kg)	Ratio	Ratio in the form $n : 1$
a	cabbage	56.24	2.3	56.24 : 2.3	
b	courgette	29.25	0.7		
c	leek	5.5	1.2		
d	pumpkin	449	8		
e	potato	3.5	0.3		
f	radish	17.2	0.1		

Ratios can also be used to show how a quantity is divided up.

Example   Divide £160 in the ratio 3 : 5

Find the total number of parts in the ratio   3 + 5 = 8
Find the value of one part   £160 ÷ 8 = £20
Work out the value of each share   3 × £20 = £60
                                                                              5 × £20 = £100

It is possible to divide a quantity into more than 2 parts.

Example   Divide 3 kg in the ratio 1 : 4 : 7

Change 3 kg to g   3 kg = 3000 g
Find the total number of parts in the ratio   1 + 4 + 7 = 12
Find the value of one part   3000 ÷ 12 = 250 g
Work out the value of each share   1 × 250 = 250 g,
                                                                              4 × 250 = 1000 g,
                                                                              7 × 250 = 1750 g

Exercise 6:2

2 Midnight Orange paint uses red and yellow in the ratio 4 : 3
How much red and yellow paint is needed to make these amounts of
Midnight Orange?
a 700 ml   b 7 litres   c 350 ml

2 Linden and Alex are partners in a T-shirt company.
To set up the company, Linden invested £7000 and Alex invested £3000.
  a Write their investments as a ratio. Simplify your ratio.
  b The company makes £13 000 profit in its first year.
    Linden and Alex split the profit in the same ratio as their
    investments. How much does each person get?

3 The £10 000 profits of a company are shared out amongst the three owners.
They are shared in the ratio 3 : 2 : 5
Calculate how much each person gets.

4 The three angles in a triangle are in the ratio 1 : 2 : 3
Calculate the size of each angle.

5 A tin of paint is made by mixing red, yellow and white paints.
The three colours are mixed in the ratio 2 : 3 : 5 and 300 ml of red paint
is used.
Calculate how much of the other two paints is used.

6 Three sisters share out a Premium Bond win.
They share the money in the ratio of their ages, 12 : 14 : 16
The middle sister gets £56.
Calculate how much each of the other two sisters get.

Ratios are really just another way of thinking about fractions.

Example   A concrete mix is made from sand and cement in the ratio 5 : 2
              What fraction of the concrete is sand and what fraction is cement?

              5 parts sand + 2 parts cement = 7 parts altogether.
              The fractions will be **sevenths**.

              The sand makes up $\frac{5}{7}$ of the mix and the cement makes up $\frac{2}{7}$ of the mix.

---

7 A metal alloy contains iron and tungsten in the ratio 6 : 1
What fraction of the alloy is iron?

8 Profits from a business are shared between three people in the ratio 7 : 2 : 3
  a What fraction of the profits does each person get?
  b If the profits are £29 400, find out how much each person gets.

2 Using multipliers

Ivan has a large sheet of paper.

He tears the sheet in half and puts the two pieces on top of each other.
Then he tears the two pieces in half and puts all four pieces on top of each other.

He plans to do this 50 times.

Estimate how high his stack of paper would be.

1000 pieces of paper make a stack that is about 4 inches high.

In the sequence 1, 2, 4, 8, 16, ... each new term is **2 ×** the previous term. The number **2** is the **multiplier** for the sequence.

Example

Write down the first five terms of the sequence with first term 5 and multiplier 3.

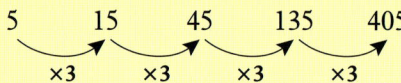

5   15   45   135   405
   ×3   ×3   ×3   ×3

The first five terms are 5, 15, 45, 135 and 405.

Exercise 6:3

1 For each of these sequences:
  (1) Work out the multiplier.
  (2) Write down the next two terms.

  a 7, 14, 28, 56, ...

  b 1, 3, 9, 27, ...

  c 2, 10, 50, 250, ...

  d −3, 3, −3, 3, ...

  e 11, −22, 44, −88, ...

  f 128, 64, 32, 16, ...

  g 81, 27, 9, 3, ...

  h 0.96, −0.48, 0.24, −0.12, ...

  i 1, 0.1, 0.01, 0.001, ...

 • **j** $1, \dfrac{1}{\sqrt{2}}, \dfrac{1}{2}, \dfrac{1}{2\sqrt{2}}, \ldots$

2 Find the two missing terms in each of these sequences.

    a 1, ..., 25, ..., 625   **e** 16, 24, ..., 54, ...

    b 8, ..., ..., 64, 128   **f** 50, 55, ..., 66.55, ...

    c 48, ..., 12, ..., 3   • **g** 80, ..., ..., 58.32, 52.488

    d 23, ..., 23, −23, ...   • **h** 1, ..., 2.56, ..., 6.5536

3 Use the given information to write down the first 5 terms of each sequence.

    a first term: 6, multiplier: 5   **e** second term: 21, multiplier: 3

    b first term: 0.5, multiplier: 4   **f** second term: 54, multiplier: $\frac{1}{3}$

    c first term: 9, multiplier: −2   **g** third term: 16, multiplier −4

    d first term: −0.1, multiplier: −5   **h** fifth term: −8, multiplier: −2

You can use your calculator to produce a number sequence.
This allows you to see what happens when the number of terms is large.

Example   Use your calculator to produce the sequence 1, 2, 4, 8, 16, ...

            You need to enter the first term and the multiplier.

Key in: **1** **=** **2** **Ans** **=** **=** **=**

If you have a graphic calculator then you will need to press **EXE**
or **ENTER** in place of **=**

You may need to experiment to find the right key sequence.
If the one above doesn't work, then try these:

           2 **×** **1** **=** **=** **=**

or   **2** **×** **×** **1** **=** **=** **=**

or   **2** **×** **→** **1** **=** **=** **=**

or   **2** **×** **K** **1** **=** **=** **=**

Exercise 6:4

1 The first term of a sequence is 4.

Find the twentieth term when the multiplier is:

    a 2   **b** 1.2   **c** 0.8   **d** 0.6

Give your answer correct to 3 sf.

2 The first term of a sequence is 100. Look at the sequence produced on your calculator when the multiplier is:

a 0.5   **b** 1   **c** 1.5   **d** -1 **e** -0.5

Write down what is happening to the terms in each sequence.

3 Under ideal conditions a sample of bacteria will double its population every 30 minutes. Use your calculator to produce a sequence to show how the population changes. Start from a single cell.

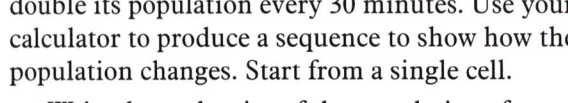

a Write down the size of the population after:
   (1) 4 hours   (3) 10 hours
   (2) 6 hours   (4) 15 hours

After 1 hour, the population can be written as 2^2.
After 2 hours, the population can be written as 2^4.

b Write the population as a power of 2 after:
   (1) 3 hours   (2) 10 hours   ● (3) n hours

4 The half-life of a drug is the time taken for half of the drug to be eliminated from the body. The half-life of a particular drug is 3 hours.

a A dose of 20 mg of the drug is given. Write down how much is left after:
   (1) 6 hours   (2) 9 hours   (3) 15 hours

b What fraction of the drug remains in the body after 12 hours?

 ● **c** What fraction of the drug remains in the body after n hours?

5 The half-life of a radioactive substance is the time taken for half of the substance to decay.
Carbon-14 has a half-life of 5730 years.
How long will it take for 8 g of carbon-14 to decay down to 1 g?

6 Look again at the puzzle given at the start of this section (page 132). One way to find the number of sheets of paper is to continue the sequence 2, 4, 8, 16, … to find the 50th term. Even with a calculator this can take a long time but there is a quick way.

a Write each of the first 4 terms as a power of 2.

b Write the 50th term in the same way.
Use the $\boxed{x^y}$ or $\boxed{y^x}$ key on your calculator to get the value of the 50th term.
The answer is too big for the calculator to display in the usual way.
Don't bother writing down the display that you get.
Carry on and do the rest of the calculation.

c Find the height of the stack to the nearest million miles!

Multipliers can help you do calculations that involve percentage change.

Example **a** Find the multiplier for increasing an amount by 17.5%.
b VAT at 17.5% is added to a bill of £67. Calculate the total amount to be paid.

a

$$100\% \quad + \quad 17.5\% \quad = \quad 117.5\%$$

The final amount is 117.5% of the original amount.

$$117.5\% = \frac{117.5}{100} = 1.175 \text{ so the multiplier is } 1.175$$

b Total paid = £67 × 1.175 = £78.725
= £78.73 to the nearest penny.

Exercise 6:5

1 Write down the multiplier for each of these percentage increases.
a 3%   **d** 87%   **g** 12.5%
b 21%   **e** 100%   **h** 37.5%
c 0.9%   **f** 120%   **i** 246%

2 Add VAT at 17.5% to each of these amounts.
a £14   **b** £98   **c** £2140   **d** £60 000

3 Last year 2460 tickets were sold for a firework display. This year ticket sales increased by 7%. How many tickets have been sold this year?

4 Jenny earns £1400 each month. How much will she earn per month after a pay rise of 2.6%?

5 To qualify for a Formula 1 Grand Prix race, a driver must complete the circuit within 107% of the pole position time. In the 1997 Australian Grand Prix, Jacques Villeneuve took pole position with a lap time of 1 minute 29.369 seconds. Find the qualifying time to the nearest $\frac{1}{1000}$th second.

To reduce an amount by a percentage you need a multiplier that is between 0 and 1.

Example

A chocolate bar weighs 250 g. Ben eats 15% of the bar.
  a Find the multiplier for reducing an amount by 15%.
  b Use the multiplier to work out how much chocolate is left.

a Percentage remaining = 100% − 15% = 85%

$$85\% = \frac{85}{100} = 0.85 \text{ so the multiplier is } 0.85$$

b Amount remaining = 0.85 × 250 g = 212.5 g

6 Write down the multiplier for each of these percentage reductions.
  a 25%   **c** 12.5%   **e** 93.2%
  b 30%   **d** 1.6%   **f** 0.7%

7 In a sale, all items are reduced by 12.5%. Find the sale price for each of these original prices.
  a £18   **b** £63   **c** £41.50   **d** £149.99

8 A farmer owns 120 acres of land. He sells 35% to a property developer. How much land does the farmer have left?

You can describe a change as a percentage by working out the multiplier.

Example

Calculate the percentage change in each of these.
  a In one year, Sally grew from a height of 5 ft 3 in to 5 ft 7 in.
  b A local Neighbourhood Watch scheme has shown some success. Annual crime figures have fallen from 1476 to 1231.

a 5 ft 3 ins = 63 ins, 5 ft 7 ins = 67 ins.

$$\text{Multiplier} = \frac{67}{63} = 1.0634\ldots = 106.344\ldots\% = 106.3\% \text{ to 1 dp.}$$

The final amount is **106.3%** of the original, so the change is an increase of **6.3%** to 1 dp.

b $$\text{Multiplier} = \frac{1231}{1476} = 0.83401\ldots = 83.401\ldots\% = 83.4\% \text{ to 1 dp.}$$

The final amount is **83.4%** of the original, so the change is a reduction of 100 − **83.4** = 16.6% to 1 dp.

9 Write down the percentage change for each of these multipliers.

    a 1.03   **c** 1.362   **e** 0.275   **g** 5.62

    b 1.47   **d** 0.84   **f** 2.3   **h** 0.068

10 Describe the change from the first amount to the second as a percentage.
Round your answers to 1 dp.

    a 36, 42   **c** £6.20, £15.30   **e** 0.56 g, 3.84 g

    b 5.79, 3.82   **d** 53 kg, 16 kg   **f** £750, £290

Multipliers are the best way of dealing with repeated percentage change.

Example

Bill opens an investment account with £3000.
The money gains 8% per year compound interest for 5 years.
This means that the interest earns interest too.
No money is withdrawn during this time.

    a How much is in the account at the end of 5 years?

    b Find the overall percentage increase on the amount invested.

You can use a multiplier of 1.08 to find how much is in the account at the end of each year.

a
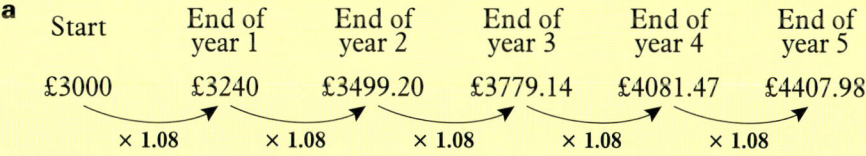

Start	End of year 1	End of year 2	End of year 3	End of year 4	End of year 5
£3000	£3240	£3499.20	£3779.14	£4081.47	£4407.98

  × 1.08   × 1.08   × 1.08   × 1.08   × 1.08

The value of the account at the end of 5 years will be £4407.98

b £3000 × 1.08 × 1.08 × 1.08 × 1.08 × 1.08 = £3000 × $(1.08)^5$
$$= £3000 × 1.469\,328\,077$$

The single multiplier for the change over the 5 years is 1.**469** 328 077

This gives the overall percentage increase as **46.9**% correct to 1 dp.

Exercise 6:6

1 Annabel invests £5000 at 7% compound interest for 6 years.

    a What is the value of the account at the end of this time?

    b How much interest is gained?

    c What is the percentage increase on the sum invested?

2 The Meadens have just bought a house for £142 000.
   a Assume its value increases by 6% each year. Predict its value in:
      (1) 5 years   (2) 10 years   (3) 20 years
   b What is the predicted percentage increase over 20 years?
      Give your answer correct to 1 dp.

3 The length of a rectangle is increased by 10%. The width of the rectangle is reduced by 10%. What is the overall percentage change in the area?

You can use the multiplier method to undo a percentage change.

Example   The cost of a computer is £1163.25 including VAT at 17.5%. What was the price before VAT was added?

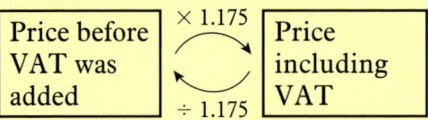

You need to divide to undo a percentage change.

The price before VAT was added = £1163.25 ÷ 1.175 = £990

Exercise 6:7

1 Each of these prices includes VAT at 17.5%.
   Find the price before VAT was added.
   a £58.75   **b** £112.80   **c** £28 200   **d** £399.50

2 Over a period of 33 years the world record for the long jump had improved by less than 23 cm. Then one day in 1968, Bob Beamon improved the record by 6.587% to 8.90 m. How much further did Beamon jump?

3 When Steve Cram broke the world record for the mile in 1985 he achieved a time of 3 minutes 46.32 seconds. Cram had reduced the time set by Roger Bannister in 1954 by 5.464%.
   a What was Bannister's time to the nearest tenth of a second?
   b Why was Bannister's time so significant?

3 Proportion

Bill is digging holes in the road.
It takes him 3 hours to dig each hole.
The holes are all the same size.
If he digs for 6 hours he digs 2 holes.
If he digs for 9 hours he digs 3 holes.
This is an example of direct proportion.

Directly proportional	Two quantities are **directly proportional** if when you multiply one quantity by a number, the other quantity is also multiplied by that number. They must also both be zero at the same time.

Example Which of these pairs of quantities could be directly proportional?

a	cost of packets of crisps	number of packets bought
b	time taken to do homework	number of homeworks set
c	time taken to run a mile	speed that you run

a and **b** could be directly proportional.

In **a** the more bags of crisps you buy the more it will cost.
If you buy no crisps it will cost nothing.
2 bags cost twice as much as 1 bag.

In **b** the more homework you get the more time it will probably take.
If you get no homework it takes no time.
2 pieces of homework will probably take twice as long as 1 piece.

In **c** the faster you run the less time it will take.
So this cannot be direct proportion.

Exercise 6:8

1 Which of these pairs of quantities could be directly proportional?
Explain your answers.

a	cost of packets of cornflakes	number of packets bought
b	number of lemonade bottles filled by a machine	time that the machine is working
c	area of a square	length of one side
d	volume of a cube	length of one side
e	volume of a prism with a fixed cross section	length of the prism

The cost of petrol is an example of direct proportion.
2 litres will cost you twice as much as 1 litre.
3 litres will cost three times as much as 1 litre.

Example Find the missing entries in this table.

Amount of petrol (litres)	1	2	b
Cost (£)	0.70	a	25.55

You can use the ideas that you saw in Section 1.
Use multipliers. You can look horizontally and vertically.

a Look at the horizontal multiplier.
2 litres costs 2 × as much as 1 litre.

So multiply £0.70 by 2 to get £1.40

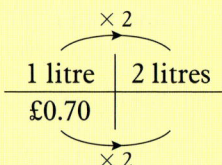

b Look at the vertical multiplier. 1 litre costs £0.70
You multiply by 0.70 downwards.

So to go upwards you divide by 0.70
Divide 25.55 by 0.70 to get 36.5 litres.

2 This table shows the price of apples.

Amount	1 kg	2 kg	5 kg	c	d
Price	38 p	a	b	£3.04	£5.32

Find the missing entries.

3 This table shows the area of wall covered by amounts of paint.

Area	5 m²	15 m²	b	55 m²	d
Paint needed	1 litre	a	7 litres	c	9.5 litres

Find the missing entries.

4 A recipe for 4 people needs 600 g of sugar.
  a How much sugar is needed for 16 people?
  b How much sugar is needed for 6 people?
  c How many people could the recipe be made for with a 1.2 kg bag of sugar?

5 When a photograph is enlarged the shape of the photo has to stay the same, otherwise the picture will be distorted.
This means that the length and width stay in the same ratio.
The table shows the length and width of some enlargements.

Length (cm)	10	15	20	**c**	50
Width (cm)	8	**a**	**b**	24	**d**

Find the missing entries.

6 1 litre of Coke costs 70 p.
The cost is proportional to the volume of Coke that you buy.
a Copy this table. Fill it in.

Volume, V (litres)	0	1	2	3
Cost, C (pence)		70		

b Copy these axes. Draw a graph of cost against the volume of Coke.

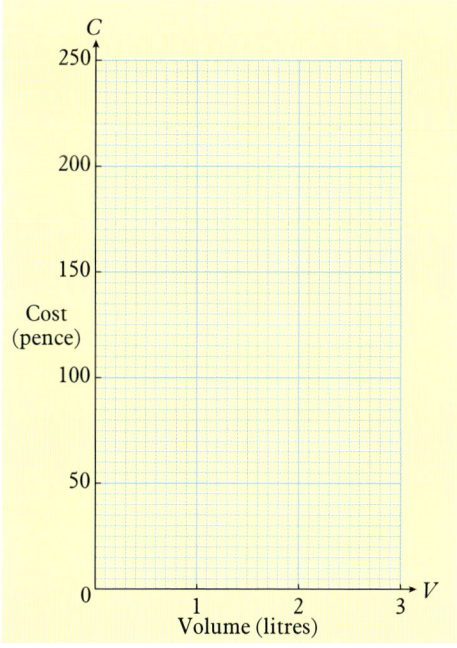

You should have drawn a straight line.
c What is the gradient of the line?
d What is the intercept on the C axis?
e What is the equation of the line?

7 A kilogram of bananas costs 90 p.
The cost is proportional to the weight of bananas that you buy.

a Copy this table. Fill it in.

Weight, W (kg)	0	1	2	3
Cost, C (pence)		90		

b Copy these axes.
Draw a graph of cost against the weight of bananas.

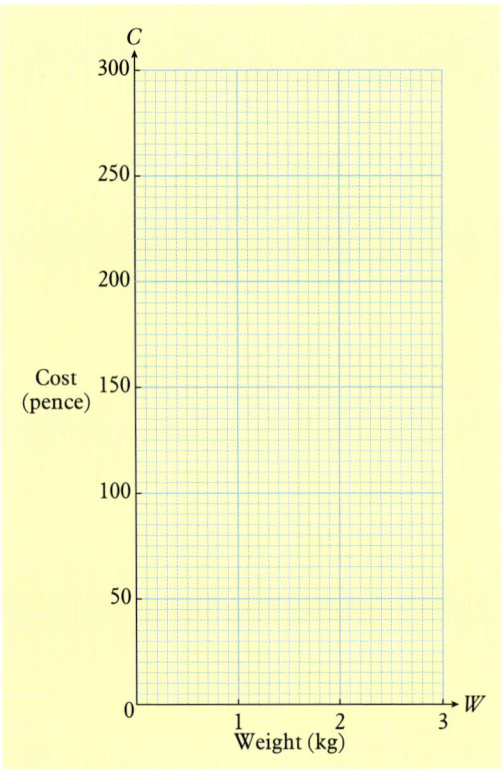

c What is the gradient of the line?

d What is the intercept on the C axis?

e What is the equation of the line?

Direct proportion using algebra

Bill is still digging holes.
The *t*ime that he needs is
proportional to the *n*umber
of holes that he has to dig.
You can write this as

$t \propto n$

The symbol $\propto$ means
'is proportional to'.

Bill takes 3 hours to dig each hole.

This is a graph of t against n. It shows the
time that it takes him to dig holes.

The equation of the line is $t = 3n$.

So $t \propto n$ is the same as $t = 3n$ in this example.

In general $a \propto b$ tells you that $a = kb$ where
k is a constant.

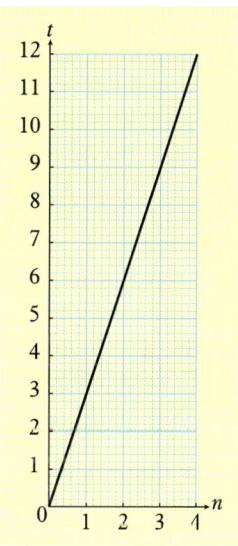

Proportionality statement	$a \propto b$ is an example of a **proportionality statement**. It tells you that a is proportional to b.
Proportionality equation	The proportionality statement $a \propto b$ can be replaced by the **proportionality equation** $a = kb$ where k is a
Constant of proportionality	constant called the **constant of proportionality**.

Example a is proportional to b. $a = 12$ when $b = 6$.

a Find the proportionality equation that connects a and b.
b Use your equation to find the value of a when $b = 14$.

a $a \propto b$ so $a = kb$ where k is a constant.
        $a = 12$ when $b = 6$ so $12 = 6k$ $k = 2$
        So the proportionality equation is $a = 2b$.
b When $b = 14$ $a = 2 \times 14 = 28$

Exercise 6:9

1 A is proportional to b. $A = 15$ when $b = 5$.
   a Find the proportionality equation that connects A and b.
   b Use your equation to find the value of A when $b = 4$.
   c Draw a graph of A against b.
   d Write down what you notice about your graph.

2 P is proportional to x. $P = 10$ when $x = 5$.
   a Find the proportionality equation that connects P and x.
   b Find the value of P when $x = 4$.
   c Find the value of x when $P = 12$.

3 y is proportional to m. $y = 14$ when $m = 4$.
   a Find the proportionality equation that connects y and m.
   b Find the value of y when $m = 6$.
   c Find the value of m when $y = 2.5$

4 The extension of a spring is directly proportional to the **weight** attached to the spring.
   When the weight is 30 g, the extension is 6 mm.
   Find the extension when a weight of 25 g is attached to the spring.

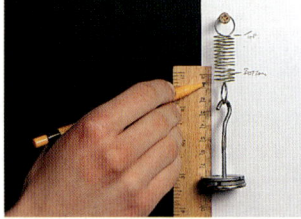

5 The volume of a prism is directly proportional to the length.
   The volume of a prism of length 14 cm is 217 cm³.
   Find the length of a prism with the same cross section that has a volume 376.65 cm³.

Squared and cubed terms

You can have direct proportion that involves squared terms and cubed terms.

The area of a circle is directly proportional to the square of the radius.
Because $A = \pi r^2$ and π is a constant, this is the same as $A = kr^2$. So $A \propto r^2$.

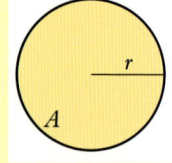

But A is *not* proportional to r.
$A = kr \times r$ and kr is *not* a constant.

So the area of a circle is not proportional to the radius. It is proportional to the **square** of the radius.

The volume of a sphere is proportional to the cube of the radius.

Because $V = \frac{4}{3}\pi r^3$ and $\frac{4}{3}\pi$ is a constant, this is the same as $V = kr^3$. So $V \propto r^3$.

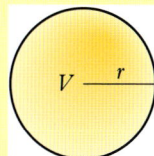

But V is *not* proportional to r.
$V = kr^2 \times r$ and kr^2 is *not* a constant.

So the volume of a sphere is not proportional to the radius. It is proportional to the **cube** of the radius.

You can still find rules of proportionality in the same way.

Example

P is proportional to x^2.
$P = 12$ when $x = 2$.

a Find the proportionality equation that connects P and x.
b Use your equation to find the value of P when $x = 14$.

a $P \propto x^2$ so $P = kx^2$ where k is a constant.
$P = 12$ when $x = 2$
so $12 = k2^2$
$12 = 4k$
$k = 3$
So the proportionality equation is $P = 3x^2$.

b When $x = 14$
$P = 3 \times 14^2$
$= 3 \times 196$
$= 588$

Exercise 6:10

1 A is proportional to b^2.
$A = 50$ when $b = 5$.
a Find the proportionality equation that connects A and b.
b Use your equation to find the value of A when $b = 4$.
c Copy this table. Fill it in.

b	4	5	6	7
b^2	16	25	36	49
A		50		

d Copy these axes.
Use them to draw a graph of A
against b^2.

e Write down what you notice
about the graph.

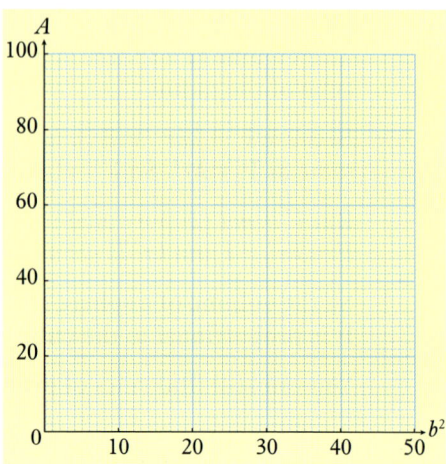

2 K is proportional to m^2.
$K = 10$ when $m = 5$.
a Find the proportionality
equation that connects K and m.
b Find the value of K when $m = 4$.
c Find the value of m when $K = 14.4$

3 y is proportional to m^3 and $y = 16$ when $m = 2$.
a Find the proportionality equation that connects y and m.
b Find the value of y when $m = 3$.
c Find the value of m when $y = 31.25$

4 The **v**olume of a bottle is directly proportional
to the **c**ube of the height.
When the height is 10 cm, the volume is 60 cm^3.
Find the volume of a similar bottle with height 20 cm.

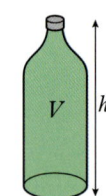

5 The *p*ressure under water is directly
proportional to the square of the *d*epth.
Sharon is at a depth of 20 metres.
The pressure is P N/m^2.
She dives to a depth of 40 metres.
What is the change in pressure?

Inverse proportion using algebra

Bill's supervisor is telling Bill that if he could
dig twice as fast, each hole would only take
him half as long.

This is an example of inverse proportion.

If you multiply the speed of digging by 2 you
divide the time taken by 2.

Inversely proportional	Two quantities are **inversely proportional** if, when you multiply one of them by a number, the other is divided by the same number.

You can solve inverse proportion questions as easily as direct proportion. The method is almost the same.

This table shows the time that it takes to travel 200 m at different speeds.

time (secs)	200	100	50	40
speed (m/s)	1	2	4	5

As the speed increases, the time decreases. This is an example of inverse proportion. Time is inversely proportional to speed for a fixed distance.

Here is a table of time and $\dfrac{1}{speed}$

$\dfrac{1}{speed}$	1	$\frac{1}{2}$ = 0.5	$\frac{1}{4}$ = 0.25	$\frac{1}{5}$ = 0.2
time	200	100	50	40

Look at the graph of *time* against $\dfrac{1}{speed}$

The graph is a straight line through the origin.
This tells you that *time* is directly proportional to $\dfrac{1}{speed}$

So $t \propto \dfrac{1}{s}$ and $t = \dfrac{k}{s}$

In general, if a is inversely proportional to b

a is directly proportional to $\dfrac{1}{b}$

so $a \propto \dfrac{1}{b}$ which gives $a = \dfrac{k}{b}$ as the proportionality equation.

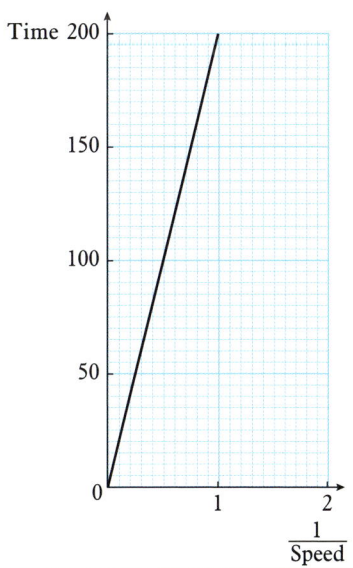

You can now do questions as before.

Example

P is inversely proportional to x.
$P = 12$ when $x = 2$.
  a Find the proportionality equation that connects P and x.
  b Use your equation to find the value of P when $x = 8$.

a $P \propto \dfrac{1}{x}$ so $P = \dfrac{k}{x}$ where k is a constant.

$P = 12$ when $x = 2$

so $12 = \dfrac{k}{2}$

$12 \times 2 = k$

$k = 24$

So the proportionality equation is $P = \dfrac{24}{x}$

b When $x = 8$

$P = \dfrac{24}{8} = 3$

Exercise 6:11

1 A is inversely proportional to b.
$A = 10$ when $b = 5$.
  a Find the proportionality equation that connects A and b.
  b Use your equation to find the value of A when $b = 4$.

2 K is inversely proportional to m.
$K = 70$ when $m = 2$.
  a Find the proportionality equation that connects K and m.
  b Find the value of K when $m = 4$.
  c Find the value of m when $K = 140$.

3 y is inversely proportional to m^2.
  a Write down what y is directly proportional to.
  b Copy this. Fill it in.

$y \propto \dfrac{1}{m^2}$ so $y = \dfrac{\cdots}{m^2}$

  c $y = 16$ when $m = 2$.
     Find the proportionality equation that connects y and m.
  d Find the value of y when $m = 1$.
  • **e** Find the values of m when $y = 0.25$

4 For a fixed distance, speed is inversely proportional to time.
When an object is travelling at 300 km/h it takes 2 hours to cover a
fixed distance.
How long would it take to travel the same distance at 200 km/h?

5 The force of attraction between two
bodies in space is inversely
proportional to the square of the
distance between them. The force
between two objects that are 200 km
apart is 1200 Newtons.
  a Find the proportionality equation
  that connects the force and the
  distance for these two objects.
  b Find the force between the two
  objects when they are 100 km
  apart.

6 It takes 3 hours for 4 men to dig a
hole. How long would it take 6 men
to dig the same hole?

4 Fractions

What do you think will happen to the sum of the fractions if the pattern is continued?

Writing fractions

You can write the same fraction in many different ways. This means that you can choose the best way to suit a particular problem.

Look at the fractions $\frac{5}{8}$ and $\frac{7}{12}$. It is difficult to say which is the bigger.

You can write both fractions using 24 as the denominator.

$$\overset{\times 3}{\frac{5}{8}} = \underset{\times 3}{\frac{15}{24}} \quad \text{and} \quad \overset{\times 2}{\frac{7}{12}} = \underset{\times 2}{\frac{14}{24}}$$

Now look at the numerators.

$$15 > 14 \quad \text{so} \quad \frac{15}{24} > \frac{14}{24} \quad \text{so} \quad \frac{5}{8} > \frac{7}{12}$$

This works for algebraic fractions too. Look at $\frac{9}{2x}$ and $\frac{5}{x}$.

First write the fraction $\frac{5}{x}$ using $2x$ as the denominator.

$$\overset{\times 2}{\frac{5}{x}} = \underset{\times 2}{\frac{10}{2x}}$$

Now compare the numerators as before.

$$\frac{9}{2x} < \frac{10}{2x} \quad \text{so} \quad \frac{9}{2x} < \frac{5}{x}$$

Exercise 6:12

1 Copy these. Fill in the gaps.

a $\dfrac{5}{11} = \dfrac{\cdots}{33}$ **d** $\dfrac{5}{x} = \dfrac{\cdots}{4x}$ **g** $8 = \dfrac{\cdots}{1} = \dfrac{\cdots}{x}$

b $\dfrac{4}{9} = \dfrac{32}{\cdots}$ **e** $\dfrac{3}{x} = \dfrac{21}{\cdots}$ **h** $5 = \dfrac{\cdots}{y}$

c $7 = \dfrac{\cdots}{1}$ **f** $\dfrac{9}{x} = \dfrac{9x}{\cdots}$ **i** $\dfrac{3x}{2} = \dfrac{\cdots}{2y}$

2 Copy these. Write $<$ or $>$ in the gaps. $x > 0$ in parts **c** and **d**.

a $\dfrac{5}{6} \cdots \dfrac{13}{18}$ **b** $\dfrac{7}{12} \cdots \dfrac{11}{18}$ **c** $\dfrac{5}{3x} \cdots \dfrac{2}{x}$ **d** $\dfrac{7}{4x} \cdots \dfrac{11}{6x}$

Adding and subtracting fractions

You can only add and subtract fractions that have the same denominator.

So $\dfrac{2}{9} + \dfrac{3}{9} = \dfrac{5}{9}$.

In the same way $\dfrac{2}{x+1} + \dfrac{3}{x+1} = \dfrac{5}{x+1}$ and $\dfrac{2}{(a+b)^2} + \dfrac{3}{(a+b)^2} = \dfrac{5}{(a+b)^2}$

You can use the same idea for subtraction.

$\dfrac{9}{11} - \dfrac{3}{11} = \dfrac{6}{11}$ so $\dfrac{9}{7yz} - \dfrac{3}{7yz} = \dfrac{6}{7yz}$

You can think of this as adding and subtracting like terms in algebra.

$\dfrac{2}{9} + \dfrac{3}{9} = \dfrac{5}{9}$ is the same as $2(\tfrac{1}{9}) + 3(\tfrac{1}{9}) = 5(\tfrac{1}{9})$ which is like $2x + 3x = 5x$.

Exercise 6:13

1 Simplify these expressions.

a $\dfrac{2}{7} + \dfrac{3}{7}$ **c** $\dfrac{11}{z} - \dfrac{4}{z}$ **e** $\dfrac{4}{pqr} + \dfrac{3}{pqr} - \dfrac{1}{pqr}$

b $\dfrac{8}{x} + \dfrac{4}{x}$ **d** $\dfrac{9}{5yz} - \dfrac{2}{5yz}$ **f** $\dfrac{5}{(2x-3y)} - \dfrac{1}{(2x-3y)}$

2 Copy these. Fill in the spaces.

a $\dfrac{2a}{x} + \dfrac{\cdots}{x} = \dfrac{5a}{x}$ **b** $\dfrac{3a+b}{xy} - \dfrac{\cdots}{xy} = \dfrac{a+b}{xy}$ **c** $\dfrac{a+3b}{x-y} + \dfrac{4a}{x-y} = \dfrac{\cdots}{x-y}$

You can add and subtract fractions that have different denominators.

Example Simplify **a** $\dfrac{7}{x} - \dfrac{3}{2x}$ **b** $\dfrac{3}{x} + \dfrac{4}{x+1}$

You need to choose a denominator that can be used for both fractions. It has to be a common multiple of both denominators.

a $2x$ is a common multiple of x and $2x$.

$$\dfrac{7}{x} - \dfrac{3}{2x}$$

$$\overset{\times 2}{\dfrac{7}{x}} = \dfrac{14}{2x}$$
$$\underset{\times 2}{}$$

$$= \dfrac{14}{2x} - \dfrac{3}{2x}$$

Now subtract the numerators as before.

$$= \dfrac{11}{2x}$$

b $x(x+1)$ is a common multiple of x and $(x+1)$

$$\dfrac{3}{x} + \dfrac{4}{x+1}$$

$$\overset{\times (x+1)}{\dfrac{3}{x}} = \dfrac{3(x+1)}{x(x+1)} \quad \text{and} \quad \overset{\times x}{\dfrac{4}{x+1}} = \dfrac{4x}{x(x+1)}$$

$$= \dfrac{3(x+1)}{x(x+1)} + \dfrac{4x}{x(x+1)}$$

Remove the brackets from the numerator.

$$= \dfrac{3x+3}{x(x+1)} + \dfrac{4x}{x(x+1)}$$

$$= \dfrac{7x+3}{x(x+1)}$$

3 Simplify these expressions.

a $\dfrac{5}{x} + \dfrac{3}{2x}$ **c** $\dfrac{a}{x} + \dfrac{a}{3x}$ **e** $\dfrac{a}{x} - \dfrac{a}{3x}$ **g** $\dfrac{1}{x+1} + \dfrac{1}{x+2}$

b $\dfrac{8}{3x} - \dfrac{1}{x}$ **d** $\dfrac{a}{x} - \dfrac{a}{2x}$ **f** $\dfrac{1}{x} + \dfrac{2}{x+1}$ **h** $\dfrac{3}{x+1} - \dfrac{2}{x+2}$

4 Copy these. Fill in the gaps.

a $5 + \dfrac{3}{x} = \dfrac{5x}{x} + \dfrac{3}{x} = \dfrac{\dots}{x}$ **c** $3x - \dfrac{1}{x} = \dfrac{\dots}{x} - \dfrac{1}{x} = \dfrac{\dots}{x}$

b $8 - \dfrac{1}{x} = \dfrac{\dots}{x} - \dfrac{1}{x} = \dfrac{\dots}{x}$ **d** $x + \dfrac{3}{x+1} = \dfrac{\dots}{x+1} + \dfrac{3}{x+1} = \dfrac{\dots}{x+1}$

Multiplying and dividing fractions

Fractions will cancel when the top line and the bottom line have factors in common. It is easier to cancel before you multiply.

$$\frac{{}^1\cancel{8}}{\cancel{9}_3} \times \frac{\cancel{15}^5}{\cancel{16}_2}$$

You multiply fractions by multiplying the top and bottom numbers separately.

$$= \frac{1 \times 5}{3 \times 2} = \frac{5}{6}$$

You do the same with fractions in algebra. Both of these lines have a factor of x.

$$\frac{2\cancel{x}}{3} \times \frac{x + 3}{\cancel{x}y}$$

3 and x are not factors of the top line so they cannot be cancelled.

$$= \frac{2(x + 3)}{3y}$$

You can always change division into a multiplication.

$$\frac{(x - 1)}{4} \div \frac{(x - 1)}{x}$$

To divide by a fraction you multiply by its reciprocal.

$$= \frac{{}^1\cancel{(x - 1)}}{4} \times \frac{x}{{}_1\cancel{(x - 1)}} = \frac{x}{4}$$

Exercise 6:14

1 Cancel these fractions as far as possible.

a $\dfrac{8x}{12}$ **b** $\dfrac{3x}{5x}$ **c** $\dfrac{x(x + 7)}{7x}$ **d** $\dfrac{3x(x - 2)}{6(x - 2)}$ **e** $\dfrac{4x + 2}{6x + 3}$

2 Simplify these expressions.

a $\dfrac{8}{x} \times \dfrac{x^2}{12}$ **c** $\dfrac{16xy}{15z} \times \dfrac{10z}{12x}$ **e** $\dfrac{2x + 6}{3} \times \dfrac{x}{x + 3}$

b $\dfrac{5x}{9} \times \dfrac{6}{x^3}$ **d** $\dfrac{x + 5}{x} \times \dfrac{x}{(x + 5)^2}$ **f** $\dfrac{(x + 5)}{5x} \times 10x^2$

3 Write these as multiplications. Simplify as far as possible.

a $\dfrac{15x}{7} \div \dfrac{3x}{14}$ **c** $\dfrac{x(x - y)}{y} \div \dfrac{(x - y)}{x}$

b $\dfrac{9}{2x + 1} \div \dfrac{3}{(2x + 1)^2}$ **d** $24x(x - 2) \div \dfrac{6x - 12}{x}$

1 The four angles in a quadrilateral are in the ratio $2:3:5:8$
Calculate the size of each angle.

2 **a** Write down the next two terms and the multiplier for each of these.
(1) 2, 6, 18, 54, ... (2) 256, 64, 16, ...
b Use the information to write down the first 5 terms of each sequence.
(1) first term: 8, multiplier: 3 (2) second term: 12, multiplier: 3

3 The first term of a sequence is 4.
Find the twentieth term when the multiplier is:
a 3 **b** 1.5 **c** 0.5 **d** 0.6

4 Write down the multiplier for each of these percentage increases.
a 2% **b** 82% **c** 32.5% **d** 8.25%

5 Add VAT at 17.5% to each of these amounts.
Give your answer to the nearest penny when you need to round.
a £12 **b** £67 **c** £2250 **d** £10 000

6 Write down the multiplier for each of these percentage reductions.
a 25% **b** 45% **c** 15.5% **d** 63.1%

7 Annabel invests £5000 at 7% compound interest for 6 years.
a What is the value of the account at the end of this time?
b How much interest is gained?
c What is the percentage increase on the sum invested?

8 A house increases in value by 9% each year for 5 years.
In 1980 the house cost £36 000.
a What was its value in 1985?
b What was the overall percentage increase in its value?

9 Each of these prices includes VAT at 17.5%.
Find the price before VAT was added.
a £32.25 **b** £89.30 **c** £2937.50 **d** £17 860

10 The $Circumference$ of a circle is proportional to the $diameter$.
a Write down a proportionality statement that connects C and d.
When $C = 785.4$, $d = 250$.
b Find the proportionality equation that connects C and d.
c What is the accurate value of the constant of proportionality?

11 P is proportional to x and $P = 15$ when $x = 5$.
  a Find the proportionality equation that connects P and x.
  b Find the value of P when $x = 3$.
  c Find the value of x when $P = 21$.

12 y is proportional to h^3 and $y = 32$ when $h = 2$.
  a Find the proportionality equation that connects y and h.
  b Find the value of y when $h = 4$.

13 K is proportional to m^2 and $K = 20$ when $m = 2$.
  a Find the proportionality equation that connects K and m.
  b Find the value of K when $m = 4$.
  c Find the value of m when $K = 180$.

14 A is inversely proportional to b and $A = 20$ when $b = 4$.
  a Find the proportionality equation that connects A and b.
  b Use your equation to find the value of A when $b = 10$.

15 J is inversely proportional to k^2 and $J = 70$ when $k = 2$.
  a Find the proportionality equation that connects J and k.
  b Find the value of J when $k = 4$.
  c Find the values of k when $J = 11.2$

16 What should be written between the fractions $\dfrac{4}{97}$ and $\dfrac{12}{301}$?
Choose from $<$ and $>$.

17 Simplify these expressions.

  a $\dfrac{2}{9} + \dfrac{3}{9}$
  b $\dfrac{10}{y} - \dfrac{4}{y}$
  c $\dfrac{5}{qr} + \dfrac{3}{qr} - \dfrac{1}{qr}$

18 Write each of these as a single fraction.

  a $\dfrac{3}{x} + \dfrac{2}{x^2}$
  b $6 - \dfrac{1}{x}$
  c $5 - \dfrac{2}{x+1}$

19 Simplify these expressions.

  a $\dfrac{9}{y} \times \dfrac{x^2}{12}$
  c $\dfrac{3p+6}{2} \div \dfrac{p+2}{p}$

  b $\dfrac{16pq}{15x} \times \dfrac{10xz}{12p}$
  d $2y(y-2) \div \dfrac{3y-6}{y}$

1   There is a very old story about the man who invented the game of chess.
    A King promised any prize in his kingdom to the person who could
    invent the greatest game ever.
    A wise man invented the game of chess. When the King saw the game
    he realised that this man had won the prize. The King promised him
    any prize he wanted. The wise man asked the King to imagine 1 grain of
    corn on the first square on the chessboard, 2 grains on the second
    square, 4 grains on the third square and so on. He would have the
    amount of corn on the last square of the board.
    The King was amazed. 'Is that all?' he exclaimed!

    a   Write each of the amounts of corn for the second square to the tenth
        square on the board as powers of 2.

    b   Write the amount for the 64th square in the same way.

    c   Use the $\boxed{x^y}$ or $\boxed{y^x}$ key on your calculator to get the value of the 64th
        square.

    d   Assume that 2 grains of corn weigh 1 g. Work out how many tonnes
        of grain the wise man would win.

    e   Explain why the King was unable to keep his promise and decided
        instead to have the wise man executed.

2   During a slump in the property market the value of a house fell by 15%.
    What percentage increase will restore the property to its previous value?

3   One year public spending fell by 15%, in the next year it fell by 7%, in
    the next year it rose by 3%, and in the next year it rose again by 8%.

    a   What is the overall percentage change?

    b   What percentage change is now needed to return to the original
        value?

4   L is proportional to $\sqrt{x}$ and $L = 24$ when $x = 16$.

    a   Find the proportionality equation that connects L and x.

    b   Find the value of L when $x = 4$.

    c   Find the value of x when $L = 18$.

5   z^2 is inversely proportional to $\sqrt{x}$ and $z = 3$ when $x = 4$.

    a   Find the proportionality equation that connects z and x.

    b   Find the values of z when $x = 81$.

    c   Find the value of x when $z = 6$.

6   Simplify these expressions.

    a $\dfrac{3}{(x + 2)} - \dfrac{6}{(x + 2)(x + 4)}$

    b $\dfrac{x + 3}{x} \times \dfrac{x}{2x + 6} \times \dfrac{y}{y + 4} \div \dfrac{y}{2x}$

1 Write down the multiplier for each of these percentage increases.

   a 7%   **c** 0.8%

   b 12%   **d** 150%

2 Add VAT at 17.5% to a garage bill of £96.

3 Write down the multiplier for each of these percentage reductions.

   a 28%   **c** 0.6%

   b 16.5%   **d** 99.3%

4 Last year, Tom paid £6520 in tax. This year he will pay 4.2% less. How much tax will Tom pay this year?

5 Write down the percentage change for each of these multipliers.

   a 1.08   **b** 2.36   **c** 0.789

6 Anna's pay increases from £386 per week to £405.30 per week.

   a Find the multiplier for Anna's increase in pay.

   b Write the increase as a percentage.

7 A prize of £6500 is to be shared between 4 people in the ratio of their ages. Alan, Pat, Luke and Katy share the prize in the ratio 40 : 38 : 10 : 6

   a Write the ratio of their ages in its simplest form.

   b Work out the amount each person gets.

8 The cost of a computer including VAT at 17.5% is £904.75 What was the cost before VAT was added?

9 A recipe for 1 litre of 'orange surprise' is:

       300 ml orange juice
       450 ml lemonade
       250 ml grapefruit juice

   a How much grapefruit juice would you need to make 5 litres of 'orange surprise'?

   b How much orange juice is needed if 1350 ml of lemonade is used?

   c How much lemonade is needed if 150 ml of orange juice is used?

10 Jo invests £8400 at 6% compound interest for 3 years.

   a What is the value of the account at the end of this time?

   b How much interest has been gained?

   c What is the percentage increase on the sum invested?

11 The cost of labels is proportional to the number ordered.

   a Copy this table.

Number of labels ordered	50	90	180	340
Cost	...	£2.25	...	...

   b Fill in the missing costs.

12 S is proportional to p.
$S = 12$ when $p = 8$.

   a Find the proportionality equation that connects S and p.

   b Use your equation to find p when $S = 126$.

13 P is proportional to r^2.
$P = 28.8$ when $r = 4$.

   a Find the proportionality equation that connects P and r.

   b Use your equation to find P when $r = 5$.

14 H is inversely proportional to t.
$H = 16$ when $t = 3$.

   a Find the proportionality equation that connects H and t.

   b Use your equation to find H when $t = 4$.

15 A bag of dried cat food contains enough food to feed 5 cats for 4 days.
Dave has 2 cats. For how long will the bag feed Dave's cats?

16 Simplify these expressions.

   a $\dfrac{3}{x} + \dfrac{5}{2x}$ **c** $\dfrac{10}{x^2} \times \dfrac{x^3}{15}$

   b $\dfrac{11}{3x} - \dfrac{1}{x}$ **d** $\dfrac{21x}{8} \div \dfrac{35x}{12}$

7 Formulas and graphs

CORE

1 Quadratic graphs
Drawing quadratic graphs
Substituting into quadratic expressions
Function notation

2 Solving equations using graphs
Seeing where graphs cross the x axis
Seeing where graphs cross horizontal lines
Looking for the intersection of two graphs
Re-arranging equations to use graphs
Using graphs to solve simultaneous equations

QUESTIONS

EXTENSION

TEST YOURSELF

1   Quadratic graphs

Each of the searchlights has a special mirror inside it. It is in the shape of a parabola. It focuses the light into a beam.

A parabola is the shape of graph produced by a quadratic equation.

Quadratic	A **quadratic** equation or formula is one which has an x^2 in it.
	It must not have any other powers of x such as x^3 or $\dfrac{1}{x}$.

Exercise 7:1

1 a Copy this table. Fill it in.

x	-5	-4	-3	-2	-1	0	1	2	3	4	5
$y = x^2$	25	16					1	4			

b Draw an x axis from -5 to $+5$ and a y axis from 0 to 25.
c Plot the points from your table.
d Join the points with a **smooth** curve.
Label your curve $y = x^2$.
This is a parabola.

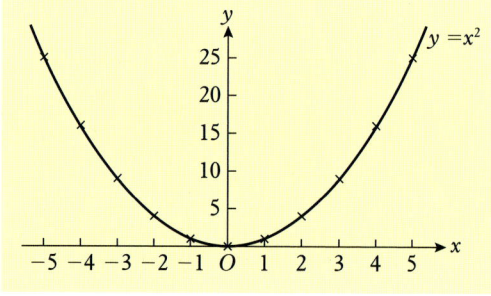

Often, the formula is a little more complicated.
It is then sensible to work out each part of the formula separately in your table.

Example

Draw the curve of $y = x^2 + 3x + 1$.
Use x values from -5 to $+3$.

(1) Complete a table showing each part of the formula
$y = x^2 + 3x + 1$ separately.

x	-5	-4	-3	-2	-1	0	1	2	3
x^2	25	16	9	4	1	0	1	4	9
$+3x$	-15	-12	-9	-6	-3	0	3	6	9
$+1$	1	1	1	1	1	1	1	1	1
y	11	5	1	-1	-1	1	5	11	19

(2) Draw an x axis from -5 to $+3$ and a y axis from -2 to 20.
(3) Plot the points from your table.
(4) Join the points with a **smooth** curve.
Your finished curve should look like this:

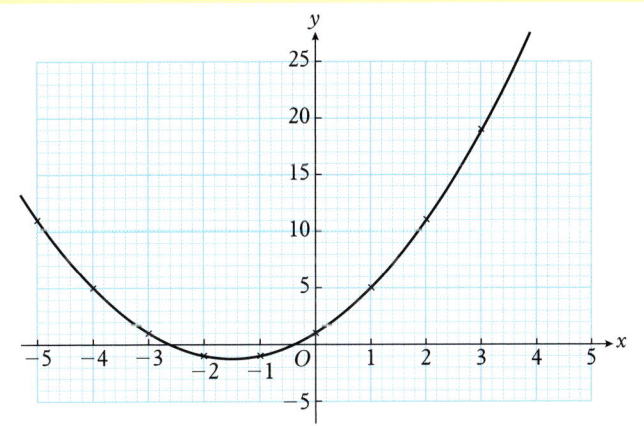

2 a Complete a table showing each part of the formula
$y = x^2 + 2x + 3$ separately.

x	-5	-4	-3	-2	-1	0	1	2	3
x^2	25	16				0			
$+2x$	-10	-8				0	2		
$+3$	3	3	3			3			
y	18	11				3			

b Draw an x axis from -5 to $+3$ and a y axis from 0 to 20.
c Plot the points from your table.
d Join the points with a **smooth** curve.

3 a Complete a table showing each part of the formula
$y = x^2 - x - 3$ separately.
Notice how the minus signs in the formula are included in the table.
Remember that if $x = -5$ then $-x = 5$.

x	-5	-4	-3	-2	-1	0	1	2	3
x^2	25	16							
$-x$	5	4					-1	-2	
-3	-3	-3							
y	27	17							

b Draw an x axis from -5 to $+3$ and a y axis from -5 to 30.
c Plot the points from your table.
d Join the points with a **smooth** curve.

4 For each part of this question:
(1) Draw a table using the x values given.
(2) Draw axes to fit the values in the table.
(3) Draw a graph from your table.

a $y = x^2 + 2x - 5$ x from -4 to $+4$
b $y = x^2 - x - 3$ x from -4 to $+4$
c $y = x^2 + 6$ x from -4 to $+4$
d $y = x^2 - 3x$ x from -4 to $+4$

Example   Work out $3x^2$ when: **a** $x = 4$ **b** $x = -3$

a $x = 4$ **b** $x = -3$

$$3x^2 = 3 \times 4^2 \qquad\qquad 3x^2 = 3 \times (-3)^2$$
$$= 3 \times 16 \qquad\qquad\qquad = 3 \times 9$$
$$= 48 \qquad\qquad\qquad\qquad = 27$$

---

5 Draw a graph of $y = 2x^2 + x - 3$.
Use x values from -4 to $+4$.

6 Draw a graph of $y = (x - 3)^2$.
Use x values from 0 to 5.

Function notation	It is sometimes easier to write the equations of graphs in **function notation**. You replace y with $f(x)$ so you write $y = x^2$ as $f(x) = x^2$. You read $f(x)$ as 'f of x'. It is short for 'function of x'. You can think of this as a formula written in terms of x. To show that you want the value of $f(x)$ when $x = 3$, you write $f(3)$.

Example	$f(x) = x^2 + 3x - 2$
	Work out: **a** $f(3)$ **b** $f(5)$ **c** $f(-2)$
	
	a $f(3)$ means replace x by 3 in $f(x)$
	       $f(x) = x^2 + 3x - 2$
	       $f(3) = 3^2 + 3 \times 3 - 2$ $= 16$
	b $f(5) = 5^2 + 3 \times 5 - 2$ $= 38$
	c $f(-2) = (-2)^2 + 3 \times (-2) - 2 = -4$

Exercise 7:2

1 $f(x) = x^2 + 3x - 2$
Work out: **a** $f(4)$ **b** $f(6)$ **c** $f(3)$

2 $f(x) = 2x^2 - 4$
Work out: **a** $f(5)$ **b** $f(0)$ **c** $f(-7)$

3 $f(x) = x^3$
Work out: **a** $f(1)$ **b** $f(-6)$ **c** $f(-9)$

4 $f(x) = \dfrac{1}{x} + 5$
Work out: **a** $f(1)$ **b** $f(-1)$ **c** $f(3)$

5 $f(x) = x^2 + 3$
Work out: **a** $f(4)$ **b** $f(-4)$ **c** $f(3)$ **d** $f(-3)$
Comment on your answers.

6 $f(x) = (x - 4)^2$
Work out: **a** $f(6)$ **b** $f(2)$ **c** $f(3)$ **d** $f(5)$
Comment on your answers.

2 Solving equations using graphs

This rocket needs to dock with the space station.

The trajectory of the rocket must meet the orbit of the space station at exactly the right point.

Timing is all important!

In maths, problems can be solved by looking at the points where two graphs intersect.

Exercise 7:3

In this exercise, write all the co-ordinates to 1 dp.

1 a Copy and complete this table of $y = x^2 - 3$

x	-5	-4	-3	-2	-1	0	1	2	3	4	5
y											

b Draw the graph of $y = x^2 - 3$ from your table.

Look at the points where the graph crosses the x axis.
c Write down the x co-ordinates of the crossing points.
d Solve the equation $x^2 - 3 = 0$ using algebra.
e Comment on the accuracy of your answers in part **c**.

2 a On your graph for question **1** draw the line $y = 5$
b Write down the points of intersection of the curve and this line.
The x co-ordinates of these points are the solutions to $x^2 - 3 = 5$

3 a On your graph for question **1** draw the line $y = 10$
b Write down the points of intersection of the curve and this line.
The x co-ordinates of these points are the solutions to $x^2 - 3 = 10$

4 a On your graph for question **1** draw the line $y = 17$
b Write down the points of intersection of the curve and this line.
c These x values are the solutions to an equation.
Write down the equation.

Sometimes you have to re-arrange an equation to fit the graph you have drawn.

Example Use the graph of $y = x^2 - 3$ to solve $x^2 - 22 = 0$

To solve this problem follow these stages.

(1) Write down the equation you want to solve: $x^2 - 22 = 0$

(2) Write down the equation of the graph: $x^2 - 3$

(3) Add an extra term to make this match the first equation: $(-3 - 19 = -22)$ $x^2 - 3 - 19 = 0$

(4) Take the extra term to the RHS of the equation: $x^2 - 3 = 19$

(5) Draw the line $y = 19$ on your graph of $y = x^2 - 3$.

(6) Write down the points of intersection of the curve and the line. The solutions to the equation are $x = -4.7$ and $x = 4.7$ (1 dp).

Exercise 7:4

1 **a** Draw axes with x from -5 to 5 and y from 0 to 30

b Copy and complete this table of $y = x^2 + 4$

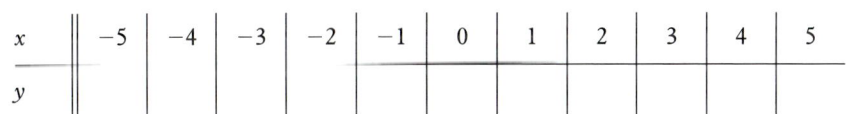

x	-5	-4	-3	-2	-1	0	1	2	3	4	5
y											

c Draw the graph of $y = x^2 + 4$ from your table.

2 Use your graph from question **1** to solve the equation $x^2 + 4 = 10$
Write your answers to 1 dp.

3 Use your graph from question **1** to solve the equation $x^2 - 1 = 0$
Write your answers to 1 dp.
Hint: $x^2 - 1 = x^2 + 4 - 5$

4 Use your graph from question **1** to solve the equation $x^2 - 6 = 0$
Write your answers to 1 dp.

5 a Draw axes with x from -5 to 5 and y from 0 to 30

b Copy and complete this table of $y = x^2 - x + 2$

x	-5	-4	-3	-2	-1	0	1	2	3	4	5
y											

c Draw the graph of $y = x^2 - x + 2$ from your table.

6 Use your graph from question **5** to solve the equation $x^2 - x + 2 = 10$
Write your answers to 1 dp.

7 Use your graph from question **5** to solve the equation $x^2 - x - 8 = 0$
Write your answers to 1 dp.

8 Use your graph from question **5** to solve the equation $x^2 - x - 13 = 0$
Write your answers to 1 dp.

You can solve more complicated equations by plotting graphs.
To solve an equation using graphs:
(1) draw graphs of both sides of the equation.
(2) write down the x co-ordinates of the points of intersection.

Example   Solve the equation $x^2 - 3x + 4 = 3x + 2$ graphically.

(1) Draw the graph of $y = x^2 - 3x + 4$
Draw the graph of $y = 3x + 2$

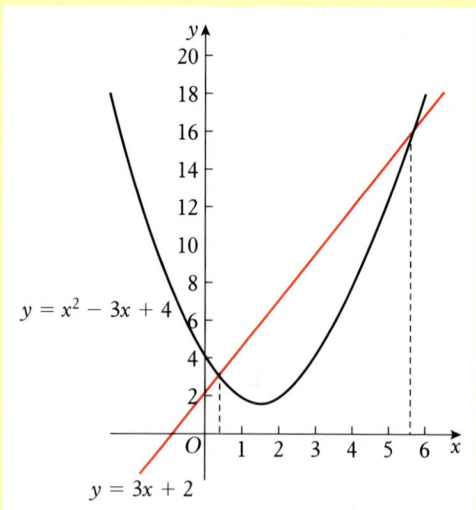

(2) The graphs intersect at
$x = 0.4$ and $x = 5.6$
These are the solutions of
the equation.

Exercise 7:5

1 **a** Draw axes with x from -5 to 5 and y from -5 to 30
b Copy and complete this table of $y = x^2 - 2x - 2$

x	-5	-4	-3	-2	-1	0	1	2	3	4	5
y											

  c Draw the graph of $y = x^2 - 2x - 2$ from your table.

2 **a** Copy and complete this table of $y = 2x + 2$

x	-5	-4	-3	-2	-1	0	1	2	3	4	5
y											

  b Draw the graph of $y = 2x + 2$ over the top of your graph from
     question **1**.
  c Write down the x co-ordinates of the points of intersection of the
     curve and the line to 1 dp.

  These are the solutions to the equation $x^2 - 2x - 2 = 2x + 2$
  More exact values are $x = -0.83$ and $x = 4.83$

3 Draw a graph to solve the equation $x^2 - 4x + 3 = 0$
  Draw your x axis from -2 to $+7$ and your y axis from -5 to 20

4 Use your graph from question **3** to solve $x^2 - 4x + 3 = 7$

5 **a** Draw the line $y = x + 2$ on to your graph from question **3**.
  b Use your graphs to solve the equation $x^2 - 4x + 3 = x + 2$

6 **a** Draw a graph of $y = x^3$
     Draw your x axis from -4 to $+4$ and your y axis from -70 to 70
  b Add a line to your graph to solve $x^3 = 10x + 10$

7 **a** Copy and complete this table of $y = \dfrac{1}{x}$

x	-5	-4	-3	-2	-1	0	1	2	3	4	5
y	-0.2	-0.25									

  b Draw the graph of $y = \dfrac{1}{x}$. Draw both axes from -5 to $+5$
  c Add a line to your graph to solve $\dfrac{1}{x} = 0.5x$

You can solve other equations by re-arranging them.

Example Use the graph of $y = x^2 - 2x + 2$ to solve $x^2 - 4x + 1 = 0$

To solve this problem follow these stages.

(1) Write down the equation you want to solve: $x^2 - 4x + 1 = 0$

(2) Write down the equation of the graph: $x^2 - 2x + 2$

(3) Add extra terms to make this match the first equation: $x^2 - 2x + 2 - 2x - 1 = 0$

(4) Take the extra terms to the RHS of the equation: $x^2 - 2x + 2 = 2x + 1$

(5) Draw the line $y = 2x + 1$ on your graph of $y = x^2 - 2x + 2$

(6) Write down the points of intersection of the curve and the line. The solutions to the equation are $x = 0.27$ and $x = 3.73$

Exercise 7:6

1 **a** Draw the graph of $y = x^2 + 2x - 1$ using x values from -4 to $+4$
  b Use your graph to write down the solutions to $x^2 + 2x - 1 = 4$
  c Use your graph to write down the solutions to $x^2 + 2x - 7 = 0$

2 **a** On your graph for **1** draw the line $y = x + 3$
  b Use your graphs to solve the equation $x^2 + x - 4 = 0$

3 **a** Draw the graph of $y = x^2 + 3x - 2$ using x values from -4 to $+4$
  b On your graph draw the line $y = 2x - 1$
  c Use your graph to write down the solutions to $x^2 + x - 1 = 0$

4 **a** Draw the graph of $y = x^2 - x + 3$ using x values from -4 to $+4$
  b Draw a straight line on your graph to solve the equation $x^2 - 6x + 5 = 0$

5 **a** Draw the graph of $y = 2x^2 - 3x + 2$ using x values from -4 to $+4$
  b Draw a straight line on your graph to solve the equation $2x^2 - 4x + 1 = 0$

Sometimes the equations of the line and the curve are written separately.

Simultaneous equations   When you solve two equations at the same time you are solving **simultaneous equations**.

To solve a pair of simultaneous equations:

(1) Draw the graph of each function.

(2) Write down the co-ordinates of any points of intersection. You need to write down both the x and the y co-ordinates.

Example   Draw graphs to solve the simultaneous equations $y = x^2 - 1$
$y = x + 1$

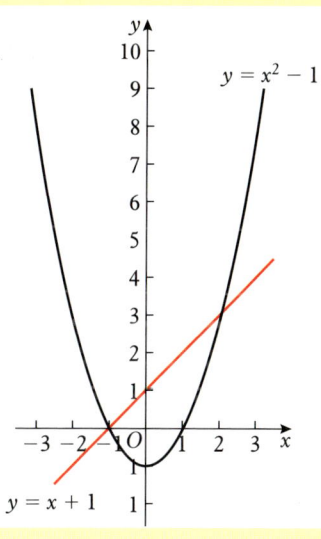

(1) Draw the graph of $y = x^2 - 1$
Draw the graph of $y = x + 1$

(2) The graphs intersect at the points
$(-1, 0)$ and $(2, 3)$

The solution to the simultaneous equations is

$x = -1, y = 0$ and $x = 2, y = 3$

Exercise 7:7

Solve each pair of simultaneous equations by drawing graphs.

1 $y = 2x - 3$
$y = 2 - 3x$

2 $y = 4$
$y = x^2 - x + 3$

3 $y = 8 - x^2$
$y = 5 - x$

4 $y = x^2 - 2x - 3$
$y = 2x - 3$

1 A pebble is thrown upwards from the top of a cliff.
The height of the pebble above sea level, h metres, after t seconds is given by the formula

$$h = 24 + 8t - 2t^2$$

a Copy this table. Fill it in.

t	0	1	2	3	4	5
h						

b Draw a graph to show the path of the pebble.
c Write down the height of the cliff.
d At what time does the pebble land in the sea?

2 A tunnel is constructed through a mountain.
The shape of the tunnel entrance is a parabola.

The equation of this parabola is $y = -\dfrac{1}{2}x^2 + 3x$

with x taking values from 0 to 6.
Draw the shape of the tunnel entrance.

3 $f(x) = \dfrac{1}{x^2} + 5$

Work out: **a** $f(1)$ **b** $f(-1)$ **c** $f(3)$ **d** $f(-3)$

4 $f(x) = x^3 + x - 1$

Work out: **a** $f(4)$ **c** $f(3)$ **e** $f(0)$
            b $f(-4)$ **d** $f(-3)$

5 **a** Draw the graph of $y = x^2 + 3x - 2$ using x values from -4 to $+4$
   b Use your graph to write down the solutions to $x^2 + 3x - 2 = 4$
   c Use your graph to write down the solutions to $x^2 + 3x - 5 = 0$
   d On your graph draw the line $y = x + 3$
   e Use your graphs to solve the equation $x^2 + 2x - 5 = 0$

6 **a** Draw a graph of $y = x^3$.
      Draw your x axis from -4 to $+4$ and your y axis from -70 to 70
   b Add a line to your graph to solve $x^3 = 5x + 6$

7 Draw graphs to solve the simultaneous equations $y = 3 - x^2$
                                                          $y = 1 - x$

1 **a** Copy and complete this table for $y = 4x - x^2$.

x	-1	0	1	2	3	4	5
y			3				

b Draw the graph of $y = 4x - x^2$.
Use an x axis from -1 to 4 and a y axis from -8 to $+8$
c Write down the values of x for which for $4x - x^2 > 1$
d Use your graph to solve the equation $2 + 3x - x^2 = 0$

2 $f(x) = x^4$
Work out: **a** $f(-3)$ **b** $f\left(\dfrac{1}{2}\right)$ **c** $f\left(\dfrac{2}{3}\right)$

3 $f(x) = x^3$
a Work out: (1) $f\left(\dfrac{1}{3}\right)$ (2) $f\left(\dfrac{7}{8}\right)$ (3) $f\left(-\dfrac{1}{4}\right)$

b Work out the value of a if
(1) $f(a) = 8$ (2) $f(a) = -27$ (3) $f(a) = -\dfrac{64}{125}$

4 Draw the curve of $y = \dfrac{1}{x}$.
The curve has two parts.

a Copy and complete this table of values to draw the first part of the curve.

x	$\dfrac{1}{4}$	$\dfrac{1}{3}$	$\dfrac{1}{2}$	$\dfrac{2}{3}$	$\dfrac{3}{4}$	1	2	3	4
y	4							$\dfrac{1}{3}$	

b Copy and complete this table of values to draw the second part of the curve.

x	$-\dfrac{1}{4}$	$-\dfrac{1}{3}$	$-\dfrac{1}{2}$	$-\dfrac{2}{3}$	$-\dfrac{3}{4}$	-1	-2	-3	-4
y	-4								

c Draw a set of axes and draw both parts of the curve $y = \dfrac{1}{x}$.
d Draw the line $y = 2x - 3$ on the same set of axes.
e Use your graphs to solve the simultaneous equations $y = \dfrac{1}{x}$
$y = 2x - 3$

5 Draw graphs to solve the simultaneous equations $y = 9 - x^2$
$y = x^2 - 3x - 4$

1   **a**   Copy and complete this table showing each part of the formula
$y = x^2 + 3x + 3$.

x	-5	-4	-3	-2	-1	0	1	2	3
x^2	25	16				0			
$+3x$	-15	-12				0	3		
$+3$	3	3	3			3			
y	13	7				3			

   b   Draw an x axis from -5 to $+3$ and a y axis from 0 to 25.
   c   Plot the points from your table.
   d   Join the points with a **smooth** curve.

2 $f(x) = 3x^2 - 7x + 14$

Find the values of

   a $f(5)$ **b** $f(0)$ **c** $f(-2)$

3 $f(x) = \dfrac{1}{x}$

Find the values of

   a $f(2)$ **b** $f\left(\dfrac{2}{3}\right)$ **c** $f(-5)$

4   **a**   Draw the graph of $y = x^2 - x - 3$ using x values between -3 and 4
   b   Write down the solutions to the equation $x^2 - x - 3 = 0$
   c   Write down the solutions to the equation $x^2 - x - 3 = 5$
   d   Draw the line $y = x - 3$ on the same set of axes.
   e   Write down the co-ordinates of the points of intersection of the line and the
curve.
   f   What is the equation of the line you would need to draw on the curve to solve
the equation $x^2 + x - 8 = 5$?

5   Solve each pair of simultaneous equations by drawing graphs.

   a $y = 2x - 4$ **b** $y = 6 + x - x^2$
       $y = 1 - 3x$ **b** $y = 2 - x$

8 Indices and standard form

1 Indices
Defining base and index
Working out an index of zero
Working out reciprocals
Learning the rules of indices
Looking at negative numbers
Solving exponential equations

CORE

2 Standard form
Defining standard form
Looking at large numbers
Looking at small numbers
Using the calculator
Working without a calculator

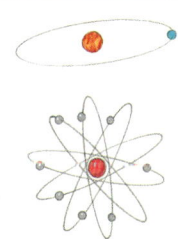

QUESTIONS

EXTENSION

TEST YOURSELF

1   Indices

You are given a pair of baby rabbits for Christmas. They start having baby rabbits themselves in two months. They have a pair of babies every month. Each pair of babies also starts having pairs of babies when they are two months old and so on. How many pairs of rabbits will you have by next Christmas?

This puzzle comes from a book written by Fibonacci in 1202.
The answers to various stages of the puzzle give the Fibonacci numbers.

You have already used powers.
2^4 means there are 4 twos multiplied together.
$2^4 = 2 \times 2 \times 2 \times 2 = 16$

Base   In x^n the number x is called the **base**.
In 2^4 the base is 2.

Index   In x^n the number n is called the **index** or power.
In 2^4 the index is 4.
The plural of index is **indices**.

Exercise 8:1

1   Copy this table.
   a Fill in the missing numbers.

2^4	2^3	2^2	2^1
...	8	...	...

   b Write down the pattern for the numbers in the second row.

   c Add an extra column to your table like this.

2^4	2^3	2^2	2^1	2^0
...	...	...	...	...

   d Use the pattern of numbers in the second row to fill in the value for 2^0.

2 Copy these.
Fill in the spaces.

a

3^4	3^3	3^2	3^1	3^0
...	...	...	...	...

b

4^4	4^3	4^2	4^1	4^0
...	...	...	...	...

Index of 0   Any number with an **index of 0** is equal to 1.
x^0 always equals 1 no matter what the value of x is.

You can extend your table further. In question **1** the numbers in the bottom line were divided by 2 each time.

2^4	2^3	2^2	2^1	2^0	2^{-1}	2^{-2}	2^{-3}	2^{-4}
16	8	4	2	1	$\frac{1}{2}$	$\frac{1}{4}$	$\frac{1}{8}$	$\frac{1}{16}$

So $2^{-1} = \dfrac{1}{2}$ and $2^{-2} = \dfrac{1}{4} = \dfrac{1}{2^2}$ and $2^{-3} = \dfrac{1}{8} = \dfrac{1}{2^3}$ and so on.

You can write this rule using letters: $x^{-n} = \dfrac{1}{x^n}$

Example   Find the values of **a** 12^0 **b** 7^{-1} **c** 9^{-2} **d** 10^{-3}

a $12^0 = 1$ Any number to the power 0 is equal to 1

b $7^{-1} = \dfrac{1}{7}$

c $9^{-2} = \dfrac{1}{9^2} = \dfrac{1}{81}$

d $10^{-3} = \dfrac{1}{10^3} = \dfrac{1}{1000}$

---

3 Find the values of:
a 8^0 **c** 11^{-2} **e** 27^{-1} **g** 20^{-3}
b 14^{-1} **d** 4^{-3} **f** 15^{-2} **h** 10^0

4 $10^{-3} = \dfrac{1}{10^3} = \dfrac{1}{1000} = 0.001$

Write each of these as a decimal.
a 10^{-1} **b** 10^{-2} **c** 10^{-4} **d** 10^{-5}

$$x^{-1} = \frac{1}{x}$$

Reciprocal $\frac{1}{x}$ is called the **reciprocal** of x.

Example Write down the reciprocal of: **a** 6 **b** $\frac{3}{5}$ **c** $2\frac{1}{2}$

a $\frac{1}{6}$ **b** $\frac{5}{3}$ **c** $2\frac{1}{2} = \frac{5}{2}$ so the reciprocal is $\frac{2}{5}$

5 Write down the reciprocal of:
a 8   **b** $\frac{1}{2}$ **c** $\frac{3}{4}$ **d** $1\frac{1}{4}$ **e** $5\frac{3}{4}$

6 Write down the value of:
a 6^{-1} **b** 24^{-1} **c** $\left(\frac{1}{5}\right)^{-1}$ **d** $\left(\frac{4}{9}\right)^{-1}$ **e** $\left(2\frac{7}{8}\right)^{-1}$

Multiplying numbers with powers

You have already simplified expressions like $3^2 \times 3^4$:
$$3^2 \times 3^4 = 3 \times 3 \quad \times \quad 3 \times 3 \times 3 \times 3 \quad = 3^6$$
The indices are added together like this: $3^{2+4} = 3^6$
This can only be done when the base numbers are the same.
You cannot simplify $3^2 \times 5^4$

You can write the rule using letters: $x^m \times x^n = x^{m+n}$

Example Simplify these:
a $x^4 \times x^7$ **b** $2a^3 \times a^5$ **c** $3d^2 \times 5d^4$ **d** $4x^3 \times 5y^2$

a x^{11} You *add* the indices 4 and 7 to give 11.
b $2a^8$ You *add* the indices 3 and 5 to give 8.
c $15d^6$ You *multiply* the numbers $3 \times 5 = 15$.
               You *add* the indices 2 and 4 to give 6.
d $20x^3y^2$ $4 \times 5 = 20$ You cannot simplify the x^3 and y^2 because they have different bases.

Exercise 8:2

1 Simplify:
a $a^5 \times a^6$ **c** $3d^4 \times 8d^9$ **e** $c^4 \times 5c$ **g** $2b^{-3} \times 4b^{-5}$
b $7b^6 \times b^2$ **d** $2g^3 \times 7h^5$ **f** $6x^{-2} \times x^7$ **h** $5h^{-4} \times 9h$

A power of a power

$(a^2)^3$ means $a^2 \times a^2 \times a^2$

so $(a^2)^3 = a^6$ The indices are multiplied.

You can write the rule using letters: $(x^m)^n = x^{mn}$

Example   Simplify: **a** $(f^{-2})^5$ **b** $(x^2y^3)^4$ **c** $(5ab^3)^2$

a f^{-10} $-2 \times 5 = -10$
b x^8y^{12} $2 \times 4 = 8$ and $3 \times 4 = 12$
c $25a^2b^6$ $5 \times 5 = 25$, $1 \times 2 = 2$, $3 \times 2 = 6$

2 Simplify:
  a $(b^3)^2$ **c** $(b^{-4})^{-1}$ **e** $(3f^5)^3$ **g** $(a^2b^3)^{-5}$
  b $(a^3)^{-4}$ **d** $(b^{-5})^0$ **f** $(6k^{-3})^2$ **h** $(2y^{-8})^5$

3 Simplify:
  a $(b)^{-1}$ **c** $(5b)^{-1}$ **e** $(3f^0)^{-1}$ **g** $(a^2b^3)^{-1}$
  b $(5)^{-1}$ **d** $(3y^2)^{-1}$ **f** $(a^{-1})^{-1}$ **h** $(7k^{-3})^{-2}$

Dividing numbers with powers

You can simplify $2^5 \div 2^3$ by cancelling pairs of 2s.

$$\frac{2^5}{2^3} = \frac{2 \times 2 \times \cancel{2} \times \cancel{2} \times \cancel{2}}{\cancel{2} \times \cancel{2} \times \cancel{2}} = 2^2$$

The indices are subtracted like this: $2^5 \div 2^3 = 2^{5-3} = 2^2$

You can write the rule using letters: $x^m \div x^n = x^{m-n}$

Example   Simplify: **a** $7^6 \div 7^2$ **b** $h^{-2} \div h^5$ **c** $y^8 \div y^8$

a $7^{6-2} = 7^4$ **b** $h^{-2-5} = h^{-7}$ **c** $y^{8-8} = y^0 = 1$

If numbers or more than one letter are involved you deal with each in turn.

Example   Simplify: **a** $d^6e^2 \div de^3$ **b** $8a^2b^{-3}c \div 16ab^{-2}c$

a $d^{6-1}e^{2-3} = d^5e^{-1}$

b $\dfrac{8a^{2-1}b^{-3+2}c^{1-1}}{16} = \dfrac{ab^{-1}}{2}$

4 Simplify:

a $y^7 \div y^4$ **c** $p^{-5} \div p^{-3}$ **e** $x^5y^4 \div x^2y$ **g** $4p^6q^{-2}r^4 \div 12p^5qr^{-3}$

b $w^3 \div w^{-4}$ **d** $m^{-5} \div m^{-5}$ **f** $10a^4bc^{-2} \div 5ab^7c^{-2}$ **h** $6r^4s^{-1}t^{-4} \div 12r^3s^{-2}t^{-7}$

Indices which are fractions

> You have already met surds.
> $$\sqrt{2} \times \sqrt{2} = 2$$
>
> If you write $\sqrt{2}$ as $2^?$ this means $2^? \times 2^? = 2^1$
> You need $? + ? = 1$ so $?$ must equal $\frac{1}{2}$.
> So $\sqrt{2}$ is the same as $2^{\frac{1}{2}}$.
>
> You can write the rule using letters:
> $\sqrt{x}$ means the same as $x^{\frac{1}{2}}$

5 $\sqrt[3]{2}$ means the cube root of 2.
So $\sqrt[3]{2} \times \sqrt[3]{2} \times \sqrt[3]{2} = 2$.
Copy this. Fill it in.
If you write $\sqrt[3]{2}$ as $2^?$ this means $2^? \times 2^? \times 2^? = 2^1$.
You need $? + ? + ? = 1$ so $?$ must equal ...
So $\sqrt[3]{2}$ is the same as $2^{\cdots}$.

You can write the rule using letters:
$\sqrt[3]{x}$ means the same as $x^{\cdots}$

6 Write down the value of:

a $\sqrt{25}$ **c** $\sqrt[3]{8}$ **e** $49^{\frac{1}{2}}$ **g** $\sqrt{64}$

b $36^{\frac{1}{2}}$ **d** $27^{\frac{1}{3}}$ **f** $\sqrt[3]{1000}$ **h** $1^{\frac{1}{3}}$

> Fractions are used to show other roots.
> You use $\frac{1}{4}$ to show the fourth root.
> $625^{\frac{1}{4}} = 5$ because $5 \times 5 \times 5 \times 5 = 625$.
>
> Similarly $\frac{1}{5}$ is used for the fifth root and so on.
>
> *Example*   Find   **a** $243^{\frac{1}{5}}$ **b** $1\,000\,000^{\frac{1}{6}}$
>
> **a** $243^{\frac{1}{5}} = 3$ because $3 \times 3 \times 3 \times 3 \times 3 = 243$
>
> **b** $1\,000\,000^{\frac{1}{6}} = 10$ because $10 \times 10 \times 10 \times 10 \times 10 \times 10 = 1\,000\,000$

7 Write down the value of:

a $16^{\frac{1}{2}}$ **c** $64^{\frac{1}{6}}$ **e** $729^{\frac{1}{6}}$ **g** $0.0016^{\frac{1}{4}}$

b $16^{\frac{1}{4}}$ **d** $1^{\frac{1}{4}}$ **f** $100\,000^{\frac{1}{5}}$ **h** $256^{\frac{1}{8}}$

You can combine the ideas of fractional indices with the rules for a power of a power.

Example   Simplify $8^{\frac{2}{3}}$

To work out $8^{\frac{2}{3}}$ write it as $(8^{\frac{1}{3}})^2$

$(8^{\frac{1}{3}}) = 2$ so $(8^{\frac{1}{3}})^2 = 4$

This means that $8^{\frac{2}{3}} = 4$

---

8 Write down the value of:

a $27^{\frac{2}{3}}$ **d** $16^{\frac{1}{4}}$ **g** $27^{-\frac{2}{3}}$

b $125^{\frac{2}{3}}$ **e** $16^{\frac{3}{4}}$ **h** $216^{-\frac{2}{3}}$

c $64^{\frac{2}{3}}$ **f** $81^{\frac{1}{4}}$ **i** $16^{-\frac{3}{4}}$

You already know that squaring and square rooting are the opposite of each other. This is also called the inverse.
You can find the inverse of any power.
The inverse of raising a number to a power n is to raise the result to the power $\frac{1}{n}$.

So $3^4 = 81$ and $81^{\frac{1}{4}} = 3$

You can also see this from the power to a power rule: $(3^4)^{\frac{1}{4}} = 3^1 = 3$

---

9 For each part: (1) write down the value of the letter
                 (2) work out the value of the expression to check your answer

a $(3^x)^{\frac{1}{4}} = 3$ **b** $(7^5)^x = 7$ **c** $(6^{\frac{1}{4}})^x = 6$ **d** $(9^{-2})^x = 9$

Exponential equations

Exponent	**Exponent** is another word for power or index.
Exponential equations	Equations where the variable is in the power are called **exponential equations**.

Example

Solve these exponential equations.

a $7^x = 49$ **b** $2^{x+1} = 32$

a You know that $7 \times 7 = 49$
so $7^x = 7^2$
x must be 2

b $2 \times 2 \times 2 \times 2 \times 2 = 32$
so $2^{x+1} = 2^5$
$x + 1$ must be 5 so $x = 4$

Exercise 8:3

1 Solve these exponential equations:

a $2^x = 8$ **d** $4^x = 16$ **g** $2^{x+1} = 128$

b $5^x = 125$ **e** $2^x = 16$ **h** $8^{x-3} = 64$

c $10^x = 1\,000\,000$ **f** $3^{2x} = 9$ **i** $7^{x-4} = 1$

You can draw graphs to solve exponential equations.

2 A type of cell divides into two every hour. Starting with a single cell, this formula gives N, the number of cells present at time t hours.

$N = 2^t$

a Copy this table for $N = 2^t$. Fill it in.

t	0	1	2	3	4	5
$N = 2^t$	...	2	4	...	...	...

b Draw a set of axes.
Use values of t from 0 to 5 for the horizontal axis.
Use values from 0 to 35 for the vertical axis.

c Use your graph to solve the equation $2^t = 14$.
This means find the value of t when $2^t = 14$ from your graph.
Draw dotted lines to show your method.

d Use your graph to find the number of cells present when $t = 4.5$
Show your method.

3 Sandra opens an investment account with £50.
The money gains 5% per year compound interest.
The amount of money, M, in the account is given by the formula
$$M = £50 \times (1.05)^n \text{ where } n \text{ is the number of years.}$$
a Copy this table.
Fill it in.

n	0	1	2	3	4	5	6
M	...	...	...	...	...	...	...

b Draw a set of axes.
Use values of n from 0 to 6 for the horizontal axis.
Use values of M from 0 to 70 for the vertical axis.
c Plot the points from the table.
d Use your graph to estimate when the money in the account will be £60.
Show your method clearly.

4 Brian buys a car for £12 000.
It loses 20% of its value each year.
a What do you have to multiply by to find the value after one year?
b Copy and complete the formula.
$$V - 12\,000 \times (\ldots)^t$$
V is the value of the car at the end of each year and t is the number of years.
c Draw and fill in a table showing V for values of t from 0 to 5.
d Draw a graph from your table.
e Can you use your graph to estimate when the value of the car will be zero? Explain your answer.

5 A drug has a half-life of two hours in the body. This means that half the drug is eliminated from the body every two hours.
A patient is given 60 mg of the drug.
Write down how much will be left in the body after:
a two hours   **b** six hours
The patient is not allowed alcohol until there is less than 1 mg of drug left in the body.
c How long will this take?

6 The half-life of a radioactive substance is 5 days.
How long does it take a sample of this substance to reduce from 100 mg to:
a 50 mg   **b** 25 mg   **c** 6.25 mg

d What fraction of the sample is left after 60 days?
Give your answer in index form.

2 Standard form

The distance between Pluto and the Sun is 5.907×10^9 km

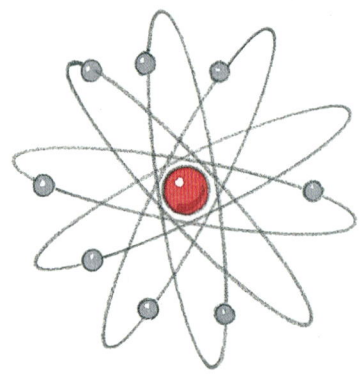

The diameter of an oxygen molecule is about 3.5×10^{-8} cm

Very large numbers are used in astronomy. Very small numbers are seen in atomic physics. You need to be able to write these numbers. A type of shorthand is used called Standard Form or Scientific Form. Standard form uses positive powers of 10 for very large numbers and negative powers of 10 for very small numbers.

Standard form   Any number can be written as **a number between 1 and 10 multiplied by a power of 10**. This is called **standard form**.

To write a number in standard form you split it into two parts multiplied together. The first part **must** be a number between 1 and 10.

For the number 34 000 you start with 3.4 to get a number between 1 and 10 but this then needs the decimal point moving to the right until it is in the correct place. Here it needs to move **4** places.

The number 4 is the power of 10

So 34 000 = 3.4 × 10⁴

$$34\,000 = 3.4 \times 10^4$$

$$3.4\,0\,0\,0.$$
$$1\ 2\ 3\ 4$$

Example   Write these numbers in standard form:
  a 2 000 000   **b** 120 000 000   **c** 460 000

  a 2 000 000 = 2 × 10⁶
  b 120 000 000 = 1.2 × 10⁸
  c 460 000 = 4.6 × 10⁵

Exercise 8:4

1 Which of these numbers are not written in standard form?

2.5×10^4 1×10^3 0.6×10^8 11×10^3 5×10^7

2 Write these numbers in standard form:

   a 30 000   **c** 104 000 000   **e** 23 470 000

   b 4 000 000   **d** 7 810 000   **f** 10 000 000 000

3 These numbers are written in standard form.
Write them as ordinary numbers.

   a 3.0×10^3 **c** 9.264×10^4 **e** 2×10^6

   b 8.3×10^7 **d** 6.07×10^5 **f** 1×10^{10}

4 Avogadro's number is a constant used in Physics.
It is $6.022\,57 \times 10^{23}$.
Write this as an ordinary number.

You use negative powers of 10 for very small numbers.

For the number 0.000 076 you start with 7.6 to get a number between 1 and 10.

This then needs the decimal point moving to the left until it is in the correct place. Here it needs to move 5 places.

$$0.000\,076 = 7.6 \times 10^{-5}$$

$$0.0\,0\,0\,0\,7.\,6$$
$$5\ 4\ 3\ 2\ 1$$

The minus sign in the power tells you that the movement is to the left.

Example   Write these numbers in standard form:

   a 0.000 000 8   **b** 0.000 000 056

   a $0.000\,000\,8 = 8 \times 10^{-7}$

   b $0.000\,000\,056 = 5.6 \times 10^{-8}$

5 Write these numbers in standard form:

   a 0.000 09   **c** 0.000 045   **e** 0.000 000 000 9

   b 0.000 000 007 8   **d** 0.003   **f** 0.6

6 These numbers are written in standard form.
Write them as ordinary numbers.

   a 4.0×10^{-5} **c** 8.034×10^{-4} **e** 3.905×10^{-2}

   b 1.7×10^{-6} **d** 5×10^{-9} **f** 1×10^{-12}

7 The diameter of an atom is about 0.000 000 000 1 cm.
Write this in standard form.

You can use a calculator to help you with numbers in standard form.

Use your calculator to do this calculation: 600 000 × 5000

Your calculator display will probably look like this: $3.^{09}$

This is the way the calculator shows a number in standard form.

$3.^{09}$ means 3×10^9.

Never write the calculator display as your answer for a number in standard form.

---

8 Write each calculator display as a number in standard form.

a $4.^{05}$ **c** 6.2^{13} **e** 1.4^{-15}

b $8.^{02}$ **d** $5.^{-12}$ **f** $9.^{23}$

9 Use the formula $s = 7t + 4.9t^2$ to find the value of s when $t = 37\,000$

10 Use the formula $N = A \div B$ to find the value of N when:
a $A = 4708$ $B = 0.000\,056\,1$
b $A = 4.5$ $B = 750\,000\,000$
c $A = 0.0004$ $B = 250\,000$

Most calculators have an **EXP** or **EE** key.

You use this key to enter numbers in standard form into your calculator.

To enter 5×10^6 press these keys. **5** **EXP** **6**

Your calculator display will look like this: $5.^{06}$

You use the **+/−** key to enter negative powers.

To enter 7×10^{-4} press these keys:

Your calculator display will look like this: $7.^{-04}$

Exercise 8:5

1 Enter these numbers into your calculator using the **EXP** key.
Write down the calculator display for each one.

  a 6×10^4 **c** 4.056×10^{12} **e** 2.7×10^{-23}

  b 7.2×10^9 **d** 7×10^{-7} **f** 6.003×10^{-13}

You can now use the calculator to do questions with numbers in standard form.

Example   Find the value of

    a $2.7 \times 10^4 \times 6.1 \times 10^{-9}$ **b** $7.75 \times 10^8 \div 2.5 \times 10^{-11}$

  a Key in:

               `Exp` `+/-` `9` `=`

        Key in: `2` `.` `7` `EXP` `4` `×` `6` `.` `1`

               `EXP` `(-)` `9` `=`

   Answer: 1.647×10^{-4}

  b Key in:

               `Exp` `+/-` `1` `1` `=`

        Key in:

               `EXP` `(-)` `1` `1` `=`

   Answer: 3.1×10^{19}

---

2 Work these out. Use your calculator.

  a $9.2 \times 10^5 \times 2.7 \times 10^7$ **c** $4.5 \times 10^{-4} \times 8 \times 10^{-6}$

  b $3.6 \times 10^3 \div 2.1 \times 10^{-7}$ **d** $1.5 \times 10^5 \div 8.3 \times 10^{-6}$

3 The thickness of the paper a firm produces is 6.0×10^{-2} cm.
They make a new paper which is twice as thick as this.
Calculate the thickness of the new paper.
Give your answer in standard form.

4 The population of the United Kingdom is about 5×10^7.
If the population increases by 20% what will be the new population?

5

	population 1990	area (km²)
England	4.8×10^7	5.0×10^4
Wales	2.9×10^6	2.1×10^4

Use the table to find:
a the total population of England and Wales
b how many times bigger England is than Wales
c the mean population per square km for Wales
d the mean population per square km for England

6 The capacity of a computer is 500 megabytes.
One megabyte is 10^3 kilobytes.
One kilobyte is 1.024×10^3 bytes.
Find the capacity of the computer in bytes.
Give your answer in standard form.

7 The diagram shows the rectangular end of a crystal.
a Find the area of the rectangle.
b Find the perimeter of the rectangle.

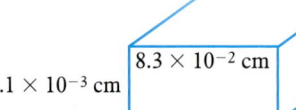

4.1×10^{-3} cm

8.3×10^{-2} cm

8 The table gives the masses of four planets.

Earth	5.98×10^{24} kg
Jupiter	1.25×10^{27} kg
Saturn	5.69×10^{26} kg
Venus	4.87×10^{24} kg

a Which planet has the largest mass?
b Write down the ratio of the mass of the Earth to the mass of Jupiter.
Give your ratio in the form $1 : n$ where n is correct to 2 sf.
c How many times heavier than the Earth is Saturn?
d How many times heavier than Venus is Jupiter?

9 You have 4.7×10^{12} blood cells in each litre of your blood.
Your body contains about 4.9 litres of blood.
About how many blood cells do you have?

You also need to be able to do standard form calculations without a calculator. To do this, you need to remember the power rules.

When you **multiply** powers of a number you **add** the powers: $10^3 \times 10^4 = 10^7$
When you **divide** powers of a number you **subtract** the powers $10^3 \div 10^7 = 10^{-4}$

Example   Work these out.
Do not use your calculator.
    a $(3 \times 10^4) \times (6 \times 10^8)$
    b $(6 \times 10^4) \div (4 \times 10^{-3})$

    a $(3 \times 10^4) \times (6 \times 10^8)$
The easiest way to do this is to multiply the **3** by the **6** and then the 10^4 by the 10^8.
$3 \times 6 = 18$ and $10^4 \times 10^8 = 10^{12}$
So $(3 \times 10^4) \times (6 \times 10^8) = 18 \times 10^{12}$

This is not in standard form because 18 is bigger than 10.
To change it into standard form think about 18 as 1.8×10
So $18 \times 10^{12} = 1.8 \times 10 \times 10^{12} = 1.8 \times 10^{13}$

    b $(6 \times 10^4) \div (4 \times 10^{-3})$
This time work out **6 ÷ 4** and $10^4 \div 10^{-3}$
$6 \div 4 = 1.5$ and $10^4 \div 10^{-3} = 10^{4 - -3} = 10^7$
So $(6 \times 10^4) \div (4 \times 10^{-3}) = 1.5 \times 10^7$
This is in standard form so you don't need to do any more work.

Exercise 8:6

1 Work these out. Give your answers in standard form.
Do not use your calculator.

    a $(4 \times 10^4) \times (2 \times 10^3)$ **i** $(4 \times 10^9) \div (2 \times 10^3)$

    b $(3 \times 10^3) \times (2 \times 10^7)$ **j** $(6 \times 10^{21}) \div (2 \times 10^8)$

    c $(6 \times 10^5) \times (7 \times 10^3)$ **k** $(8 \times 10^8) \div (5 \times 10^{-2})$

    d $(4 \times 10^4) \times (2 \times 10^{-2})$ **l** $(4 \times 10^7) \div (3 \times 10^3)$

    e $(2.1 \times 10^{21}) \times (3 \times 10^7)$ **m** $(8.4 \times 10^4) \div (2 \times 10^{-3})$

    f $(2.5 \times 10^4) \times (4 \times 10^9)$ **n** $(2 \times 10^{12}) \div (8 \times 10^3)$

    g $(7 \times 10^{-6}) \times (3 \times 10^9)$ **o** $(3.4 \times 10^4) \div (2 \times 10^{-9})$

    h $(5 \times 10^{-7}) \times (2 \times 10^{-8})$ ● **p** $(3 \times 10^{-5}) \div (8 \times 10^{-9})$

1 Find the value of:

  a 12^2 **b** 10^{-2} **c** 15^{-1} **d** 18^0

2 Write these as powers of 10.

  a 100 000   **c** 1000   **e** 0.0001   **g** 0.000 01

  b 0.001   **d** 0.000 001   **f** 100   **h** 0.000 000 01

3 This shows how three consecutive square numbers are added together.

$$2^2 + 3^2 + 4^2 = 4 + 9 + 16 = 29$$
$$3^2 + 4^2 + 5^2 = 9 + 16 + 25 = 50$$
$$4^2 + 5^2 + 6^2 = 16 + 25 + 36 = 77$$

Find three consecutive square numbers that add up to 1877.

4 Write down the reciprocal of:

  a 7   **b** $\frac{5}{6}$ **c** $2\frac{1}{3}$ **d** $\frac{1}{9}$

5 Simplify these.

  a $y^5 \times y^3$ **d** $4x^{-3} \times 7x^6$ **g** $(2x^5y^{-2})^4$ **j** $x^3y \div xy$

  b $a^2 \times 5a^4$ **e** $(b^5)^3$ **h** $(8r^2st^3)^0$ **k** $20ab^{-3}c^2 \div 5ab^{-5}c^{-1}$

  c $3m^5 \times 5m^2$ **f** $(4a^{-2})^2$ **i** $r^7 \div r^2$ **l** $40q^2r^{-4}t \div 8q^{-1}rt$

6 Solve these equations.

  a $4^y = 16$ **c** $2^x = \frac{1}{2}$ **e** $4^{x+1} = 64$ **g** $5^{\frac{x}{2}} = 125$

  b $2^x = 32$ **d** $5^y = \frac{1}{25}$ **f** $8^{3y} = 1$ **h** $(2^x)^{\frac{1}{4}} = 2$

7 Write these numbers in standard form.

  a 20 000 000   **c** 2 500 000   **e** 0.1   **g** 0.000 001

  b 0.0006   **d** 0.002   **f** 5 million   **h** 10

8 These numbers are written in standard form.
Write them as ordinary numbers.

  a 6.3×10^4 **b** 2.5×10^{-5} **c** 7×10^6 **d** 1.782×10^{-2}

9 These numbers are written in standard form.

  4.5×10^7 4.5×10^{-7} 4.5×10^{-8} 4.5×10^6

  a Write down the largest of these numbers.

  b Write down the smallest of these numbers.

10 The number 10^{100} is called a googol.
Write these numbers in standard form.
a 259 googols   **b** one thousand googols

A nanometre is 10^{-9} metres.
Write these numbers in standard form.
c 40 nanometres   **d** half a nanometre

11 A virus has a diameter of 15 nanometres.
1 nanometre = 0.000 000 001 metres.
a Write the diameter in standard form.
b A bacterium is 120 times as big as a virus.
  Write the diameter of the bacterium in standard form.

12 A pollen grain has a mass of 3.5×10^{-4} g.
Find the number of grains in 1 kg of pollen.
Write your answer in standard form.

13 The speed of sound is about 340 ms^{-1}.
a Write this number in standard form.

Work out how far sound travels in:
b 1 hour   **c** 1 week   **d** 1 year
Give your answers in standard form.

14 Work these out.
Don't use your calculator.
a $6 \times 10^{5} \times 3 \times 10^{8}$ **c** $6 \times 10^{15} \div 2 \times 10^{8}$
b $7 \times 10^{-3} \times 9 \times 10^{7}$ **d** $8 \times 10^{12} \div 4 \times 10^{-10}$

15 The diameter of an atom is about 0.000 000 000 1 cm.
How many atoms side by side would measure 1 cm?

16 The mass of an electron is 9.1×10^{-28} g.
a Find the mass of 5.6×10^{12} electrons.
b The mass of a proton is 1.7×10^{-24} g.
  Find the value of k in the formula:

   mass of a proton $= k \times$ mass of an electron

  Give your answer to the nearest whole number.

1　The first four terms of a sequence are:

(5×3)　　　　　(6×3^2)　　　　　(7×3^3)　　　　　(8×3^4)

　　a　Write down the fourth term as a number.
　　b　Write down the fifth term as a power of 3.
　　c　Write down an expression for the nth term of the sequence.

2　The formula for the nth term of a sequence is $5^{n-1} + 10$.
　　Find the first four terms of the sequence.

3　Look at this sequence of numbers:

　　　13　　61　　253　　1021　　...

　　The formula for the nth term is of the form $A^{n+1} - B$.
　　Find the values of A and B.

4　The value of an investment increases by 10% each year.
　　The sum invested at the beginning was £2500.
　　a　Write down a formula for the value V of the investment after n years.
　　b　How long will it take for the investment to double in value?

5　This is a formula used in a running event to work out the points, P:

$$P = 0.112(246 - t)^{1.87}$$

　　where t is the time taken in seconds.
　　P is always rounded to one sf.
　　a　Find the value of P when $t = 150$ seconds.
　　b　What time gives zero points?
　　c　Find a time that gives a score of 1000 points.

6　The volume of a cylinder is given by:

$$V = \frac{\pi d^2 h}{4}$$

　　Find the value of V when:
　　a　$d = 3.4 \times 10^5$ and $h = 7.2 \times 10^9$
　　b　$d = 9.2 \times 10^{-4}$ and $h = 1.2 \times 10^{-6}$

1 Write these as powers.

   a $7 \times 7 \times 7 \times 7 \times 7$ **b** $4 \times 4 \times 4$

2 Use your calculator to find the value of:

   a 12^3 **c** 23^2 **e** 10^5

   b $\sqrt{361}$ **d** $\sqrt[3]{1331}$ **f** $\sqrt[3]{1\,000\,000}$

3 Write down the reciprocal of:

   a 8 **b** $\frac{1}{5}$ **c** $\frac{2}{3}$

4 Write down the value of:

   a 11^0 **b** 4^{-1} **c** $\left(\frac{3}{4}\right)^{-1}$

5 Write each of these as a fraction.

   a 5^{-4} **b** 7^{-1} **c** a^{-1}

6 Simplify:

   a $y^4 \times y^3$ **e** $8x^7 \div 4x$ **i** $3x^3y^{-4} \times x^{-1}y$

   b $c^2 \times 6c$ **f** $a^5b \div a^2b^4$ **j** $(a^3)^5$

   c $5t^2 \times 7t^3$ **g** $h^4 \times h^{-2}$ **k** $\left(\frac{1}{a}\right)^{-2}$

   d $s^4 \div s^3$ **h** $w^8 \div w^{-1}$ **l** $(x^3)^0$

7 Write down the value of:

   a $16^{\frac{1}{2}}$ **b** $125^{\frac{1}{3}}$ **c** $27^{\frac{2}{3}}$

8 Work these out using a calculator.

   a $\dfrac{53.6 - 11.8}{13.2 - 9.4}$ **c** $\dfrac{40^2}{16 \times 25}$

   b $(3.9 + 2.8)^2$ **d** $\dfrac{328 \times 62 - 736}{3.2^2 - 7.74}$

9 Write these in standard form.
  a 450 000
  b 368 300 000
  c 0.0082
  d 0.3751
  e 3 million
  f 0.000 000 06

10 These numbers are written in standard form.
  Write them as ordinary numbers.
  a 6.9×10^4
  b 2.4×10^{-3}
  c 4×10^{-8}
  d 3.618×10^8

11 The table shows the populations of six cultures of bacteria.

Culture	Population	Culture	Population
A	6.5×10^{11}	D	9.25×10^{10}
B	7.8×10^{10}	E	7.5×10^{11}
C	8.1×10^{11}	F	8.9×10^{12}

  a Write the cultures in order of size. Start with the smallest number.
  b Find the difference in population between cultures A and F.

12 Water flows through a pipe at a rate of 25 m³ per minute.
  How long will it take to fill a pond of volume 6.34×10^9 m³?
  Give your answer in hours to 3 sf.

13 Work these out. Give your answers in standard from.
  Do not use a calculator.
  a $(7 \times 10^5) \times (5 \times 10^8)$
  b $(1.5 \times 10^4) \div (6 \times 10^{-5})$
  c $(4 \times 10^4) + (6 \times 10^3)$
  d $(3 \times 10^5) - (2 \times 10^4)$

14 Use a calculator to work these out.
  Give your answers in standard form to 3 sf.
  a $(3.82 \times 10^7) \times (2.84 \times 10^9)$
  b $(6.03 \times 10^{-3}) \div (6.221 \times 10^{-15})$
  c $(2.37 \times 10^{-6})^4$

9 Estimating and checking

1 Rounding and estimating
Rounding to 1 sf
Rounding to any number of sf
Solving problems and checking by estimating
Using inverses to check answers
Estimating square roots
Working out percentage errors
Rounding to a sensible degree of accuracy

CORE

2 Error bounds
Defining upper and lower bounds
Working with sums and products
Working with differences and quotients

QUESTIONS

EXTENSION

TEST YOURSELF

CORE

1 Rounding and estimating

How tall do you think this building is? When you answer that question you will probably give your answer to the nearest metre.

Even if you measure it you would probably only give your answer to the nearest centimetre. It would be silly to say that the height of the building is 3.494 632 m!

This would be far too accurate.
This length is given to the nearest ten thousandth of a centimetre!

You already know how to round numbers to a given number of decimal places. 3.494 632 m = 3.49 m to 2 dp. This is a sensible number of decimal places because it gives the answer to the nearest centimetre.

You can also round numbers to a given number of significant figures.
Most of the time you will be told what accuracy to use.

Significant figure	In any number the first **significant figure** is the first digit which isn't a 0. For most numbers this is the first digit. The first significant figure is the digit in red. 21.4 312 45.78 0.81
Rounding to any number of significant figures	To **round to any number of significant figures**: (1) look at the first unwanted digit (2) if it is 5, 6, 7, 8 or 9 add one on to the digit before. If it is 0, 1, 2, 3 or 4 ignore it (3) be careful to keep the number about the right size 341.4 to 2 sf is 340. It is *not* 34! The 1 is the first unwanted digit. This does not change the 4 when you round. 6845.78 to 1 sf is 7000. It is *not* 7! The 8 is the first unwanted digit. This changes the 6 to a 7 when you round. 0.002 034 5 to 3 sf is 0.002 03 Here the 0 after the 2 is significant because it comes after the first significant figure. A 0 is only significant when it appears on the right of the first significant figure.

Exercise 9:1

1 Round these numbers to 1 significant figure.

   a 15   **c** 3029   **e** 4.55×10^8

   b 549   **d** 9999   **f** 8.13×10^{-4}

2 Round these calculator displays.

   a 3.782497 to 3 sf   **c** 0.000273 to 1 sf   **e** 0.039898 to 2 sf

   b 58.34497 to 3 sf   **d** 255643 to 2 sf   **f** $5.25511^{\,07}$ to 3 sf

3 Write down the number of significant figures in each of these numbers.

   a 3.8457   **b** 0.243   **c** 0.000 30   **d** 2.103×10^{17}

4 Estimate the value of each of these by rounding each number to 1 sf.
Give your answers to parts **c** and **d** in standard form.

   a 18.7×426 **c** $(3.94 \times 10^7) \times (2.14 \times 10^{-3})$

   b $4217 \div 48.9$ **d** $(8.14 \times 10^{12}) \div (3.89 \times 10^4)$

You know that you can get an estimate by rounding each number to 1 sf.
Sometimes you will see a way of getting a better estimate.

Example   Work out: **a** 15×25 **b** $\dfrac{152.4 \times 6.42}{24.89 \times 1.59}$

a Calculation: `1` `5` `×` `2` `5` `=` Answer 375

   Estimate: 15 is 20 to 1 sf
             so 15 is rounded up a long way.
             You can compensate by rounding 25 *down* here.
             This is because 25 would only just round *up* to 30 to 1 sf.
             It gives a *better* estimate here to write:
             15×25 is about $20 \times 20 = 400$
             400 is near to 375
             so the answer is probably right.

b Calculation: `( 1 5 2 . 4 × 6 . 4 2 )`
`÷ ( 2 4 . 8 9 × 1 . 5 9 ) =`

Answer 24.4 (3 sf)

Estimate: You need to spot that:
152.4 is about 150
24.89 is about 25
and that $150 \div 25 = 6$
6.42 is about 6.4
1.59 is about 1.6
and that $6.4 \div 1.6 = 4$

so $\dfrac{152.4 \times 6.42}{24.89 \times 1.59}$ is about $\dfrac{\overset{6}{\cancel{150}} \times \overset{4}{\cancel{6.4}}}{\underset{1}{\cancel{25}} \times \underset{1}{\cancel{1.6}}}$ which is about $6 \times 4 = 24$

24 is near to 24.4 so the answer is probably right.

You must take care if you use methods like these.
You *cannot* use them if the question asks you to estimate by rounding each number to 1 sf.

Exercise 9:2

1 Work these out. Write down the answer and an estimate for each one.

a 1.5×2.5 **c** 251×1503 **e** $\dfrac{449 - 151}{44.89}$ **g** $\dfrac{1472 + 2494}{746.28}$

b 4.49×34.8 **d** $2498 \div 2.51$ **f** $\dfrac{1507 \times 1.409}{24.8 \times 4.21}$ **h** $\dfrac{25.2 - 14.8}{0.0675 + 0.0332}$

You know that you can estimate an answer to check that it is about the right size.

You can also check your answers by reversing the problem.
This is a different way of checking.

Example   Work out 234×45

`2 3 4 × 4 5 =`   Answer: 10 530

The reverse of multiplying is dividing.
So you can check your answer by doing a division question.

$234 \longrightarrow \boxed{\times 45} \longrightarrow 10\,530$

You can work out $10\,530 \div 45$
You should get 234

$234 \longleftarrow \boxed{\div 45} \longleftarrow 10\,530$

2 For each part:
   (1) work out the answer on your calculator
   (2) write down a question that you can use to check your answer

   a 24×367

   b 4.5×1967

   c $4335 \div 289$

   d $0.008\,972 \div 0.0056$

   e $6839 + 2897$

   f $19\,875 - 2876$

   g $(1.98)^2$

   h $\sqrt{347.8225}$

Where a calculation has more than one operation, you reverse the order of BODMAS to do a check.
If you are trying to do $285 + 52 \times 34$ you do 52×34 first then add 285
This gives an answer of 2053
To check this, *subtract* 285 first then *divide* by 52. This gives the answer 34.

• **3** $750 + 43 \times 27$ • **4** $7642 - 980 \div 35$ • **5** $(24.8)^2 \times 59$

Estimating square roots

You need to round the numbers to the nearest square number.

So $\sqrt{23} \approx \sqrt{25} = 5$

If you round $\sqrt{23}$ to 1 significant figure you get $\sqrt{20}$
This is just as difficult to work out as the question!

Sometimes you have to estimate in stages.

To estimate the answer to $\qquad \sqrt{\dfrac{23 \times 489}{35}}$

Start by rounding the numbers to 1 significant figure. $\qquad \approx \sqrt{\dfrac{20 \times 500}{40}}$

Work this out: $\qquad = \sqrt{\dfrac{10\,000}{40}}$

$$= \sqrt{250}$$

Now look for the nearest square number.
Square root to get the answer. $\qquad \approx \sqrt{256}$
$\qquad = 16$

Exercise 9:3

For questions **1–10**:
a estimate the answer
b work out the answer using your calculator
Give your calculator answer to 3 sf.

1 $\sqrt{\dfrac{197 \times 24}{38}}$

4 $\sqrt{\dfrac{86 \times 47}{153}}$

7 $\sqrt{\dfrac{189 \times 97}{22 \times 564}}$

2 $\sqrt{\dfrac{234 \times 46}{52}}$

5 $\sqrt{\dfrac{178 \times 68}{47}}$

8 $\sqrt{\dfrac{16^2 \times 13}{167}}$

3 $\sqrt{\dfrac{212 \times 64}{310}}$

6 $\sqrt{\dfrac{184 \times 43}{82 \times 31}}$

9 $\dfrac{-28 + \sqrt{18^2 - 4(12)(-35)}}{2(12)}$

Error   The difference between an exact answer and an estimate is called the **error**.

Always make the error positive. It is the size of the error that is important.

---

10 a Estimate the answer to this calculation by rounding each value to 1 sf.

$$\frac{84 \times 56}{96}$$

b Work out the answer using your calculator. You will get an exact answer.
c Work out the error using your estimate and your exact answer.

11 a Estimate the answer to this calculation by rounding each value to 1 sf.

$$\frac{2.025 \times 0.6}{0.243}$$

b Work out the answer using your calculator. You will get an exact answer.
c Work out the error using your estimate and your exact answer.

12 a Which estimate gives the biggest error, question **11** or question **12**?
   ● b Can you think of a better way of measuring the amount of error if you make an estimate?

You always work out a percentage error as a percentage of the exact value.

$$\text{Percentage error} = \frac{\text{error}}{\text{exact value}} \times 100\%$$

Example   The exact value of a length is 3.473 m.
John measures the length and gets 3.45 m.
Work out his percentage error.

$$\text{Percentage error} = \frac{3.473 - 3.45}{3.473} \times 100\%$$

$$= 0.66\% \text{ to 2 sf.}$$

Exercise 9:4

1 The table gives the exact answer and the estimated answers of some calculations. Copy the table. Fill it in.

	Estimate	Exact answer	Error	Percentage error
a	20	25		
b	42	39.8946		
c	60 000	66 048		
d	0.025	0.024		

2 Chris enters a competition at a fête to guess the number of potatoes in a bag. He estimates that there are 384 potatoes. There are in fact 392 potatoes, but he still wins the competition with the best estimate. What was the percentage error in his answer?

3 For each shape:
   (1) estimate the area by rounding each length to 1 sf
   (2) calculate the exact answer
   (3) work out the percentage error of the estimate

a

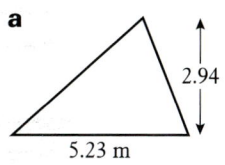

2.94

5.23 m

b

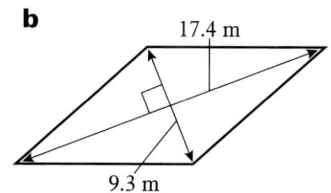

17.4 m

9.3 m

c

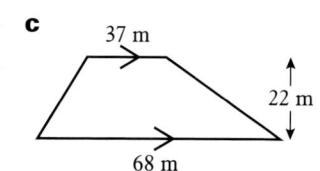

37 m

22 m

68 m

4 The height restriction sign on this bridge has disappeared.
Andy is standing under the arch. He is 1.82 m tall.

a Estimate the height of the arch.
The arch is a semicircle with an arc length of 12.23 m.

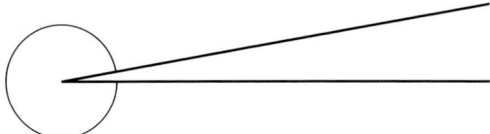

b Calculate the height of the arch.

c Using your calculator answer to part **b**, work out your percentage error.

5 **a** Estimate the size of this angle.
b Measure the size of this angle.
c Work out your percentage error.

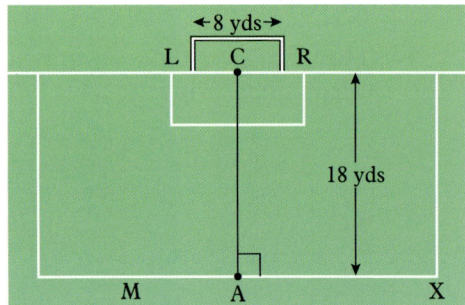

6 Mike is a football player. He is trying to score a goal from the edge of the box. He aims at the centre of the goal C from the point A, shooting along the ground.

a Work out the percentage error he can make in the angle XAC if his shot is off target, but still goes in the goal.

Later in the game Mike shoots from point M, 10 yards to the left of A. Again he aims at the centre of the goal C shooting along the ground.

b Work out the percentage error in the angle AMC if he scores:
(1) from a shot off the post L
(2) the goal of the season, in off the post at R!

You sometimes need to choose a sensible number of significant figures. Use your common sense to help you!

For an exact length given in centimetres you would give no more than 1 dp in your answer.
This would then be correct to the nearest millimetre.
For an exact length in metres you would give no more than 2 dp in your answer.
This would then be correct to the nearest centimetre.

The numbers that you are given in questions will also be a clue.
If numbers are only given to 3 sf then you should not give more than 3 sf in your answers.
So if a question has numbers like 127, 3.45 etc., which are only given to 3 sf, you should not give more than 3 sf in your answers.

Exercise 9:5

In each of these questions give your answer to a sensible degree of accuracy.

1 For each part:
  (1) write down the number of significant figures each number has
  (2) work out the answer
  a 270×49
  b $900 \div 70$
  c 0.0987×4.92
  d $0.009\,82 \div 36.8$
  e $0.001 \div 0.000\,09$
  f $2.3 \times 10^8 \times 3.9 \times 10^4$

2 The diagrams show two parks in a town.
Work out the lengths of the paths shown by red dotted lines.

a
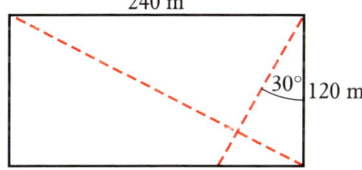

b
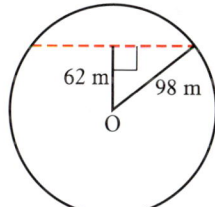

O is the centre of the circle.

3 Work out the distances marked with letters.

a
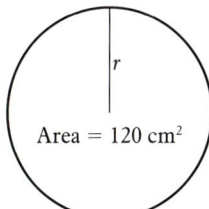

b
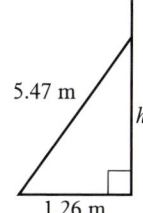

c
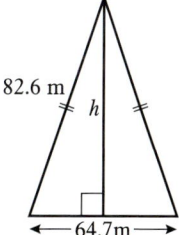

4 Jenny invests £122 for 3 years at a compound interest rate of 7.3% per year.
She leaves all the money and interest in the account for the 3 years.
Find the amount of money that she has at the end of this time.

2   Error bounds

When you put a plug in a plug hole you are happy to assume that it will fit.
When plugs are made they have to be made accurately so that you will not be disappointed!
The plug does not have to be *exactly* the right size.
There is a small error that is allowed.
This is called a tolerance.
A plug would probably fit if it is 0.5 mm too small.
But it won't fit if it is 2 cm too small!

The width of a plug is given as 30 mm to the nearest millimetre.
This does not mean that it is exactly 30 mm.
The width could be anywhere from 29.5 mm right up to, but not including, 30.5 mm.
You can show this on a number line.
    $29.5 \leqslant$ width < 30.5

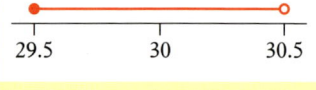

Lower bound   29.5 is called the **lower bound**.
It is the smallest number that will round up to 30 mm.

Upper bound   30.5 is called the **upper bound**.
The largest number that will round down to 30 mm is 30.499 999 99…
It is not convenient to use this value.
So 30.5 is used as the upper bound even though 30.5 would round up to 31 to the nearest whole number.

Exercise 9:6

1   Each of these numbers is correct to the nearest whole number.
Work out the upper and lower bounds for each number.
Show your answers on a number line.

a 4	**c** 15	**e** 86	**g** 1004
b 7	**d** 24	**f** 249	**h** 276 827

2 Each of these numbers is correct to 1 decimal place.
Work out the upper and lower bounds for each distance.
Give your answers in the form: lower bound $\leqslant$ distance $<$ upper bound.
  a 0.2 m   **c** 6.8 km   **e** 29.6 mm   **g** 197.0 miles
  b 5.2 cm   **d** 3.5 mm   **f** 2783.4 cm   **h** 400.2 light years

3 Each of these masses is correct to the number of significant figures shown in
brackets. Work out the upper and lower bounds for each mass.
Give your answers in the form: lower bound $\leqslant$ mass $<$ upper bound.
  a 20 g (1 sf)   **e** 0.05 kg (1 sf)
  b 780 kg (2 sf)   **f** 0.0007 mg (1 sf)
  c 45 mg (2 sf)   **g** 25 000 tonnes (2 sf)
  d 200 tonnes (1 sf)   **h** 2.4×10^7 tonnes (2 sf)

4 Simon buys a piece of wood at a DIY store. It is marked as 2.4 m long.
Assume this length is correct to 1 dp. Write down:
  a the lower bound   **b** the upper bound
Now take the marked value as the exact value of the length.
Calculate the percentage error in using:
  c the lower bound   **d** the upper bound

5 The radius of the Earth is 6380 km to 3 sf. Write down:
  a the lower bound, l **b** the upper bound, u
of the radius.
Now take the stated value as the exact value
of the radius.
Calculate the percentage error in using:
  c l **d** u
for the radius.
The radius of the earth is now given as 6378 km.
Calculate the percentage error in using:
  e l **f** u
for the radius.
  g Write down what you notice about your answers.

6 Roger is a weatherman.
He measures the temperature on the weather station thermometer.
He records it in his notebook as $-5.2\,°C$ to 1 dp.
  a Show the upper and lower bounds of this temperature on a number line.
Now take $-5.2\,°C$ as the exact value.
Calculate the percentage error in using:
  b the lower bound   **c** the upper bound
  d Write down what you notice about your answers.

There is a quick way of remembering how to work out the upper and lower bounds.

If you have a number correct to the nearest 10 then
      the upper bound is 5 more than this number
and the lower bound is 5 less than this number.   5 is half of 10

If you have a number correct to the nearest unit then
      the upper bound is 0.5 more than this number
and the lower bound is 0.5 less than this number.   0.5 is half of 1

If you have a number correct to the nearest 0.1
(which is the same as being correct to 1 dp) then
      the upper bound is 0.05 more than this number
and the lower bound is 0.05 less than this number.   0.05 is half of 0.1

The amount you add to get the upper bound and take away to get the lower bound is half of the place value of the accuracy.

7 Write down the amount to add to these values to get the upper bound. Each value is correct to the number of significant figures in brackets.
  a diameter 0.42 cm (2 sf)
  b mass 0.0246 kg (3 sf)
  c diameter 144 000 km (3 sf)
  d population 10 million (1 sf)

8 Write down the amount to subtract from these values to get the lower bound.
  a diameter 1.2×10^{-6} m (2 sf)
  b radius 1.81×10^{-10} m (3 sf)

9 Simon is back at the DIY store. He buys 2 pieces of wood.
One is marked 3.2 m long, and the other is marked 1.8 m long.
Both lengths are correct to the nearest 0.1 m.
  a Write down the upper and lower bounds of each of these lengths.
  b What is the maximum value of the lengths added together?
  c What is the minimum value of the lengths added together?
  d Write down what you notice about your answers.

10 Repeat question **9** if Simon now buys 10 pieces of wood, each 3.2 m long.

Working with errors

When you start doing calculations with lengths that are only correct to a given accuracy you must be careful!
As soon as you add or multiply lengths together you make the errors much worse.
You need to be able to work out the combined error.

Example Terry is the caretaker at a primary school.
He is making a playground for the pupils.
He needs to cover the ground with tarmac.
He also wants to put a fence around the ground.
He has measured the ground as a rectangle that is 45 m by 33 m.
His measurements are correct to the nearest metre.

a What are the upper and lower bounds for the length of the fencing?
b What are the upper and lower bounds for the area that needs to be covered in tarmac?

a The length of the rectangle is 45 m.
   $44.5 \leqslant$ length < 45.5
The width of the rectangle is 33 m.
   $32.5 \leqslant$ width < 33.5

The perimeter is 2 lengths and 2 widths added together.
The lower bound is obtained by finding the smallest possible length.
Lower bound $= 2 \times 44.5 + 2 \times 32.5 = 154$ m.
The upper bound is obtained by finding the largest possible length.
Upper bound $= 2 \times 45.5 + 2 \times 33.5 = 157$ m.

b The area of the ground is the length multiplied by the width.
The lower bound is obtained by finding the smallest possible area.
Lower bound $= 44.5 \times 32.5 = 1446.25$ m^2.
The upper bound is obtained by finding the largest possible area.
Upper bound $= 45.5 \times 33.5 = 1524.25$ m^2.

Exercise 9:7

1 For each shape, work out:
   (1) the upper and lower bounds of each length
   (2) the maximum and minimum area

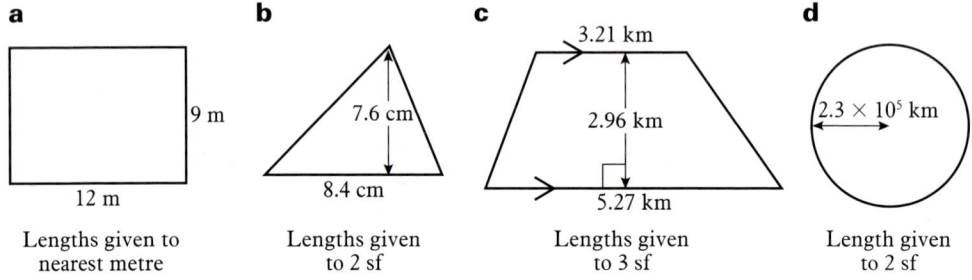

a

9 m

12 m

Lengths given to
nearest metre

b

7.6 cm

8.4 cm

Lengths given
to 2 sf

c

3.21 km

2.96 km

5.27 km

Lengths given
to 3 sf

d

2.3×10^5 km

Length given
to 2 sf

2 A football pitch has a length of 102 m and a
width of 72 m.
Each length is correct to the nearest metre.
David has to mark the perimeter with white lines.
He also has to re-seed the grass for the next season.
What are the upper and lower bounds for:
   a the length of the pitch
   b the width of the pitch
   c the perimeter of the pitch
   d the area that needs to be re-seeded?

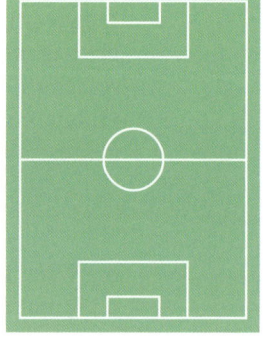

If the original measurements are exact, what is the percentage error in using:
   e the lower bound of the area   **f** the upper bound of the area?

3 A cylindrical paddling pool has a radius of 12.3 m to the nearest 0.1 m.
It is to be filled to a depth of 0.75 m, to the nearest centimetre.
What are the upper and lower bounds for:
   a the radius of the pool
   b the depth of the pool
   c the volume of water needed to fill the pool?

4 Eddie is loading a trailer with sacks of potatoes. His scales only weigh to
the nearest 2 kg. He is sure that each sack is 50 kg to the nearest 2 kg.
   a What are the upper and lower bounds for the mass of each bag?
The trailer will carry a mass of *exactly* 7 tonnes. It has a gauge that
measures the mass on the trailer *very accurately*.
   b What is the least number of sacks Eddie can put on the trailer?
   c What is the greatest number of sacks Eddie can put on the trailer?

You have to be even more careful if you subtract or divide!

Example   The length of a 100 m race track is correct to the nearest 10 cm.
Frank runs the length of the track in 10.4 seconds to the nearest 0.1 s.

   a What are Frank's greatest and least possible times?

   b What are the greatest and least possible distances that Frank has run?

   c What are Frank's greatest and least possible average speeds for his run?

   a The least time is **10.35** s.
The greatest time is the upper bound which is **10.45** s.

   b The length is 100 m to the
nearest 10 cm.
So the length is 10 000 cm to the
nearest 10 cm.
The least distance is
9995 cm = **99.95** m.
The greatest distance is the upper bound
which is 10 005 cm = **100.05** m

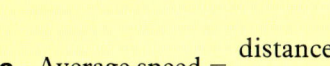

9995   10 000   10 005

   c Average speed $= \dfrac{\text{distance}}{\text{time}}$

To find the *least speed* you need to make the fraction as *small* as possible. To do this you want the numerator to be small and the denominator to be big.
So you want   the lower bound of the distance
and   the upper bound of the time.

Least speed $= \dfrac{99.95}{10.45} = 9.56$ m/s to 2 dp.

To find the *greatest speed* you need to make the fraction as *big* as possible. To do this you want the numerator to be big and the denominator to be small.
So you want   the upper bound of the distance
and   the lower bound of the time.

Greatest speed $= \dfrac{100.05}{10.35} = 9.67$ m/s to 2 dp.

Exercise 9:8

1 James has recorded his distances and times for four sections of a racing circuit.

Section 1   1.5 km   55.4 s   Section 3   1.1 km   48.3 s
Section 2   1.8 km   67.2 s   Section 4   2.1 km   61.9 s

Each time is correct to the nearest 0.1 s.
Each distance is correct to the
nearest 0.1 km.
For each section work out:

  a the greatest and least possible distances
  b the greatest and least possible times
  c James' greatest and least possible
     average speeds

2 Tracy is working out the density of a piece of steel.
The steel is in the shape of a cuboid.
Tracy has measured the lengths of the cuboid to the nearest millimetre.
Here are her results.

length 23 mm	width 31 mm	height 46 mm

Tracy measures the mass as 253 grams to the nearest gram. Work out:
  a the greatest possible density   **b** the least possible density
  c the maximum possible percentage error if Tracy assumes her data is exact.

3 Donna is a really fast sprinter.
The school sprint track is 100 m long to the nearest 20 cm.
She was timed at 12.49 s, to the nearest 0.01 s, for this distance.
Donna's mum, Ella, says she was faster than her daughter.
Ella's time for 100 yards was 11.5 s to the nearest 0.1 s, when she was Donna's age.
Assume the length of the track is correct to the nearest foot and take 1 yard to be exactly 0.9144 m.
  a Work out the maximum and minimum possible speeds of:
     (1) Donna   (2) Ella
  b Use your answers to part **a** to comment on Ella's statement.

4 Robert has a piece of copper piping 3.32 m long to the nearest centimetre.
He cuts off a piece of pipe 1.24 m long to the nearest millimetre.
  a Give the upper and lower bounds of the length of the pipe that he cuts off.
Use your answers to part **a** to work out:
  b the maximum length   **c** the minimum length
of the remaining pipe.

To find the upper bound for the difference $x - y$
use the upper bound of x
and the lower bound of y

To find the lower bound for the difference $x - y$
use the lower bound of x
and the upper bound of y

5 A train enters a tunnel. The train is
432 m long to the nearest metre.
The tunnel is 850 m long to the nearest metre.
The train stops at a signal so that the back of
the train is *exactly* level with the entrance to
the tunnel.
For the length of the train write down:
a the lower bound   **b** the upper bound
For the length of the tunnel write down:
c the lower bound   **d** the upper bound
Work out:
e the maximum distance   **f** the minimum distance
that the train must still travel to reach the other end of the tunnel.

6 Gavin wants to fit more shelves on the back wall of his garage.
He knows that his car is 4.3 m long to the nearest 0.1 m.
The house plans show the internal length of the garage is 5250 mm long
to the nearest 50 mm.
a Work out the minimum depth of the shelf that Gavin could fit.
b Work out the maximum depth of the shelf that Gavin could fit.
The table shows the widths of shelves
available from a local DIY store
c Which shelving would you advise Gavin
to buy? Explain your answer.

56 cm	80 cm	104 cm
68 cm	92 cm	116 cm

7 Private Quaypout is looking at his space map.
He tells General Vader that the galaxy they
are to survey is an annulus.
On the map it has an inner radius of 5.4 cm
and an outer radius of 7.9 cm to the nearest
millimetre. On the map 5 cm stands for 1 light year.
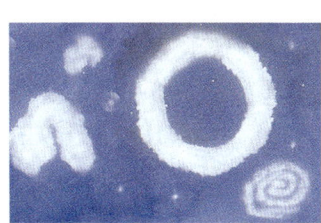
a Use the scale to convert these distances to
light years.
b Convert these distances to miles. You can assume that light travels at exactly
186 281 miles/s.
c Work out the maximum and minimum areas in square miles that they need
to survey.

1 Round these calculator displays.

a 4.9185723 to 3 sf   **c** 0.0209999 to 1 sf   **e** 2.1924^{-18} to 2 sf

b 68.939993 to 3 sf   **d** 34545454 to 2 sf   **f** 0.030999098 to 3 sf

2 Work these out. Write down the answer and an estimate by rounding each number to 1 sf for each one.

a 4.9×8.2 **b** 392×687 **c** $19\,692 \div 48.76$ **d** $0.9645 \div 0.00217$

3 Work these out. Write down the answer and an estimate by rounding each number to 1 sf for each one.

a $\dfrac{7.194 \times 807}{28.85 \times 39.3}$ **b** $\dfrac{983 + 615}{97 - 58.6}$ **c** $\dfrac{30\,159 \times 48.71}{392.15 \div 81.39}$ **d** $\dfrac{88\,867 - 7958.3}{0.005\,96 \div 0.029}$

4 Work these out. Write down the answer and an estimate for each one. You don't have to round to 1 sf.

a 14.8×243.7 **b** 352.1×2507 **c** $\dfrac{3489 - 1512.9}{55.12}$ **d** $\dfrac{3599 + 32\,494}{17492.67}$

5 For each part:
(1) work out the answer on your calculator
(2) write down a question that you can use to check your answer

a 428×71 **c** $\sqrt{2998.76}$

b $0.015\,48 \div 0.000\,369$ **d** $(197.36)^2$

6 For each part:
(1) estimate the answer
(2) work out the answer using your calculator
Give your calculator answer to 3 significant figures.

a $\sqrt{46}$ **c** $\sqrt{79}$ **e** $\sqrt{0.62}$ **g** $\sqrt{\dfrac{4889 \div 24.92}{0.0435 + 0.4517}}$

b $\sqrt{10}$ **d** $\sqrt{166}$ **f** $\sqrt{\dfrac{216 \times 32}{61}}$ **h** $\dfrac{14 + \sqrt{196 + 252}}{2 \times 9}$

7 For each shape:
(1) estimate the area by rounding each length to 1 sf
(2) calculate the exact answer
(3) work out the percentage error of the estimate

a
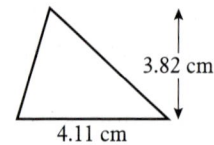
3.82 cm
4.11 cm

b
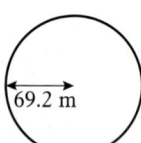
69.2 m

c
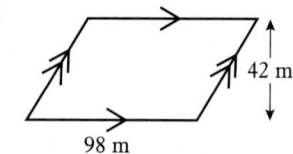
42 m
98 m

8 Here is a plan of the grounds of La Maising Towers. This is a hotel which grows all its own vegetables in a collection of ornate beds designed centuries ago. The crops are grown in the areas shown by the letters on the plan. This year the gravel needs renewing on the paths and fertiliser is needed on each bed of vegetables. The dimensions of each bed are shown in the table. Curiously, on an old plan, the accuracy of the measurements varies.

a For each crop area shown on the plan, work out the upper and lower bounds for:
(1) each length   (2) each area

b Work out the upper and lower bounds for the perimeter of beds A and E.

Bed	Shape	Dimensions from plan	to the nearest
A	square	length 118.7 m	0.1 m
B	parallelogram	base 180 m, height 120 m	10 m
C	triangle	base 18.43 m, height 14.56 m	0.01 m
D	kite	1st diagonal 185 m, 2nd diagonal 114 m	1 m
E	circle	radius 60 m	10 m
F	trapezium	parallel sides 262 m and 177 m, height 121 m	1 m

9 The population of Australia is 17.8 million, to the nearest 0.1 million. The area of Australia is 2 968 000 miles^2 to the nearest 1000 miles^2. Population density is defined as the number of people per unit of area.

Write down the upper and lower bounds for:
a the population of Australia
b the area of Australia
Using your answers to parts **a** and **b** work out:
c the maximum possible population density
d the minimum possible population density

If you are asked, you could give *one* answer for the population density of Australia to the number of significant figures you can justify. To do this, you need to take your answers to parts **c** and **d** above and round each of them until they agree exactly. This is the number of significant figures that you can justify.

e Give an estimate of the population density of Australia to as many significant figures as you can justify.

1 The half-life of a radioactive substance is given by

$$T = \frac{\ln 2}{d}$$

where T is the half life and d is the decay constant for the substance. The half-life of a radioactive substance is how long it takes for half of it to decay into another substance. Radioactive substances are used to find the age of historical items.

$\ln 2$ is the natural logarithm of 2. To get this as a number, key in:

Assume your calculator value for $\ln 2$ is the *exact* value.
Radium is a radioactive substance.
It has a decay constant of 1.354×10^{-11} per second to 4 sf.
Work out these values for the half life of radium:

a the upper bound in seconds **c** the upper bound in years
b the lower bound in seconds **d** the lower bound in years

Ian finds an old metal object with $\dfrac{1}{2^8}$ of the original radium in it.

e Use your answers to parts **c** and **d** to give the age range of the object.
f What is the most accurate age you could justify giving for the object?

2 Robin and Karl are two railway engineers. Karl wants to know how far away Robin is on a section of track. His father taught him a quick way to estimate this. Because the speed of sound is different through air and metal, his father told him he could do it by hitting the track with a mallet.

He knows that the speed of sound in air is 330 m/s, and the speed of sound through the track is 5940 m/s.
These speeds are both correct to the nearest 10 m/s.
Robin hits the track with a mallet.
Karl times the sounds on his watch.
He hears the 2nd sound 2.4 seconds after the first, to the nearest 0.2 seconds.

Use t seconds as the time until Karl hears the first sound.
a Form two equations in t for the distance, d, that Robin is from Karl.
b Work out the minimum and maximum possible values of t.
c Work out the minimum and maximum possible values of d.

1 Round these numbers.

    a 0.050 682 3 to 3 sf   **c** 600 070 to 4 sf   **e** 2.76×10^6 to 1 sf

    b 346 000 to 2 sf   **d** 0.090 057 42 to 3 sf   **f** 4.672×10^{-14} to 1 sf

2 Estimate the value of each of these by rounding each number to 1 sf.
Give your answer in standard form.

    a $(3.7 \times 10^{12}) \times (1.34 \times 10^{16})$ **c** $\dfrac{7.62 \times 10^{23}}{1.69 \times 10^{-5}}$

    b $(8.51 \times 10^{-15}) \times (4.7 \times 10^8)$ **d** $\dfrac{2.71 \times 10^{-17}}{6.29 \times 10^8}$

3 Work these out. Write down the answer and and estimate for each one.
Show clearly how you get each estimate.

    a $\dfrac{5.085 \times 3.471^2}{32.078 - 19.46}$ **c** $\sqrt{\dfrac{68.4 \times 53.2}{197 \times 10.39}}$

    b $\dfrac{62.83 \times 48.4}{6.71 \times 11.98}$ **d** $\dfrac{-15 + \sqrt{15^2 - 4 \times 4.87 \times (-29)}}{2 \times 4.87}$

4   **a** Calculate the value of $\dfrac{5}{\dfrac{1}{6.24} - \dfrac{1}{3.08}}$

    b Check your answer to part **a** by making an estimate.
Show your method clearly.

5 Laura says the error in her measurement is -0.5 cm.
What is wrong with this statement?

6 For this triangle:
    a estimate the area by rounding
each length to 1 sf
    b calculate the exact area
    c work out the percentage
error of the estimate.

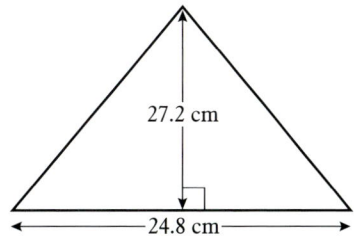

27.2 cm

24.8 cm

7 Australia has an area of 7.615×10^6 km² to 4 sf.
  a Write down the lower and upper bounds of this area.
  Give your answers in standard form.
  b In 1995 the population was 18 300 000 to the nearest 100 000 people.
  Write down the limits between which this population must lie.
  c The population density of a continent is the mean number of people
  per square kilometre.
  Find the minimum and maximum values of the population density
  of Australia.

8 Jamie is using the formula $v = u - 4t$ in a physics experiment.
  He measures u as 23 to 2 sf and t as 4.9 to 1 dp.
  Work out the lower and upper bounds for v.

9 $P = 34$ to 2 sf $Q = 5.71$ to 2 dp $R = 0.5$ to 1 sf
  Work out the lower and upper bounds for
  a $5P$ **b** $P - Q$ **c** $Q \div R$ **d** $3P - 4Q$

10 The sides of this container are given to 2 sf.
  a Write down the lower and
  upper bounds of the length.
  b Find the lower and upper
  bounds of the area of the base.
  c Find the lower and upper
  bounds of the length of the
  diagonal of the base.
  d Find the lower and upper
  bounds of the volume of
  the container.

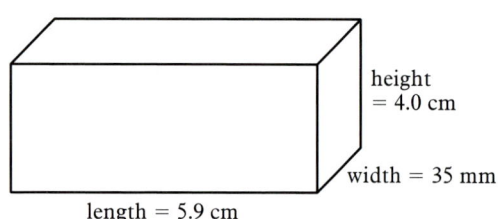

height = 4.0 cm

width = 35 mm

length = 5.9 cm

10 Transformations

1 Single transformations

Using translations
Using column vector notation
Using 'arrow' representation
Using inverses
Drawing enlargements and inverses
Using negative and fractional scale factors
Drawing rotations and inverses
Drawing reflections and inverses

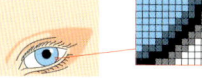

CORE

2 Combined transformations

Drawing successive transformations
Finding pairs of transformations to achieve an effect
Using equivalence of combined transformations to a single transformation

QUESTIONS

EXTENSION

TEST YOURSELF

1 Single transformations

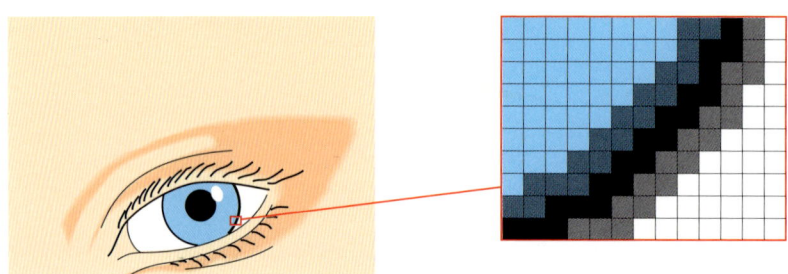

Pictures on a computer screen are made up of tiny squares called pixels. Storage of pictures based on single pixels can use too much memory. Patterns of pixels are often repeated in a picture and details of how they relate to each other can be stored as transformations. This saves memory.

A transformation can change the size or position of an object.

Translation   A **translation** is a movement in a straight line.

The movement shown is a translation of 5 places to the right and 3 places down.

The blue line and arrow represent the translation.

The translation can be written as $\begin{pmatrix} 5 \\ -3 \end{pmatrix}$

This is called a **column vector**.

Under a translation, the object and the image are congruent.

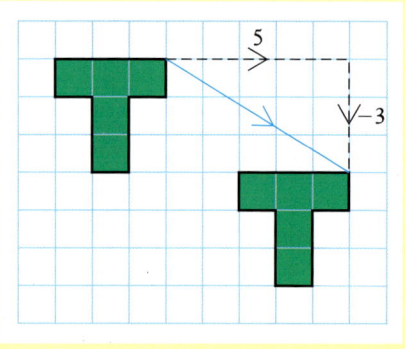

The sign of each number in a column vector gives the direction of movement.
This matches the way that axes are labelled.

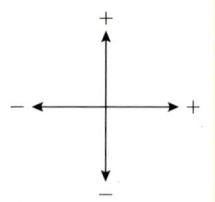

Exercise 10:1

1 Use column vectors to describe these translations.

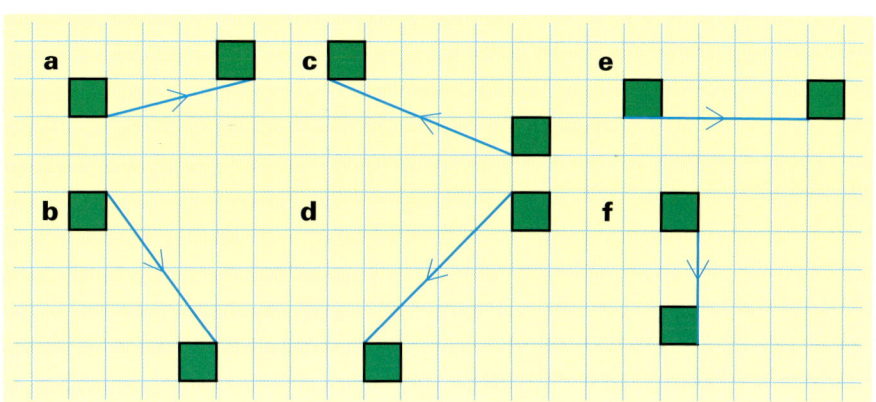

2 The lines below marked with arrows represent translations.
Write each translation as a column vector.

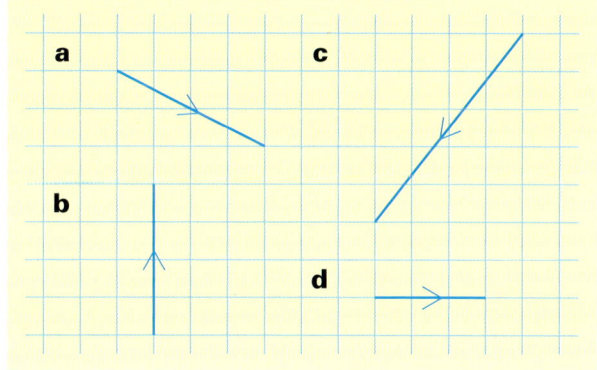

3 Show each of these on squared paper using lines marked with arrows.

a $\begin{pmatrix} 2 \\ 5 \end{pmatrix}$ **c** $\begin{pmatrix} 0 \\ -3 \end{pmatrix}$ **e** $\begin{pmatrix} 2 \\ -6 \end{pmatrix}$

b $\begin{pmatrix} 3 \\ -1 \end{pmatrix}$ **d** $\begin{pmatrix} -5 \\ 0 \end{pmatrix}$ **f** $\begin{pmatrix} -2 \\ 6 \end{pmatrix}$

Translations of single points are described in the same way.

4 P, Q and R have co-ordinates $(2, 3), (-2, 1)$ and $(0, -5)$ respectively.
Find the column vector for the translation from:

a Q to P   **d** P to Q
b Q to R   **e** R to Q
c R to P   **f** P to R

Inverse   A transformation that undoes the effect of another is called its **inverse**.

Example   This translation 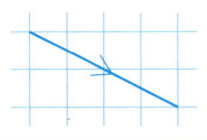 is written as $\begin{pmatrix} 4 \\ -2 \end{pmatrix}$

Write down the column vector of the inverse.

The movement is in the opposite direction so the arrow is reversed.

The inverse translation 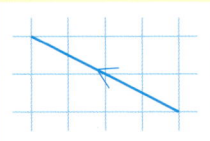 is written as $\begin{pmatrix} -4 \\ 2 \end{pmatrix}$

Exercise 10:2

1 Write down the inverse of the following transformations.
a move 3 places right   **c** move 11 km SW and 4 km NE
b move 7 km NW   **d** move 9 km NNE

2 These column vectors represent translations.
Write down the column vector of the inverse of each one.

a $\begin{pmatrix} 2 \\ 5 \end{pmatrix}$ **c** $\begin{pmatrix} 5 \\ -1 \end{pmatrix}$ **e** $\begin{pmatrix} -4 \\ -1 \end{pmatrix}$

b $\begin{pmatrix} 3 \\ 0 \end{pmatrix}$ **d** $\begin{pmatrix} -2 \\ 3 \end{pmatrix}$ **f** $\begin{pmatrix} 0 \\ 6 \end{pmatrix}$

3 A translation from A to B is given by the column vector $\begin{pmatrix} a \\ b \end{pmatrix}$

Write down the column vector for the translation from B to A.

4 In Logo, instructions are given to control the movement of the *turtle*.

Instruction	*Meaning*
fd 50	move forward 50 units
bk 30	move back 30 units
rt 90	turn to the right through 90°
lt 60	turn to the left through 60°

Write down the inverse of each of these Logo instructions.
a fd 60   **d** rt 60 bk 45
b rt 20   **e** fd 60 rt 75 fd 80
c fd 30 lt 90   **f** lt 120 fd 34 rt 70 bk 30

Enlargement

An **enlargement** changes the size of a shape.

Under an enlargement the object and the image are similar but not congruent.

All the lengths are multiplied by the same **scale factor**. Distances from the **centre of enlargement** are also multiplied by this scale factor.

When you describe an enlargement you must give these two things:
(1) the scale factor
(2) the centre

Example

Enlarge triangle ABC with scale factor 2 and centre O.

Draw lines from O through A, B and C. Mark the point A' so that OA' = 2 × OA. Repeat for B' and C'. Draw triangle A'B'C'.

A' is the **image** of A after the enlargement.
In the same way B' is the **image** of B and C' is the **image** of C.

Triangle A'B'C' is the **image** of triangle ABC.

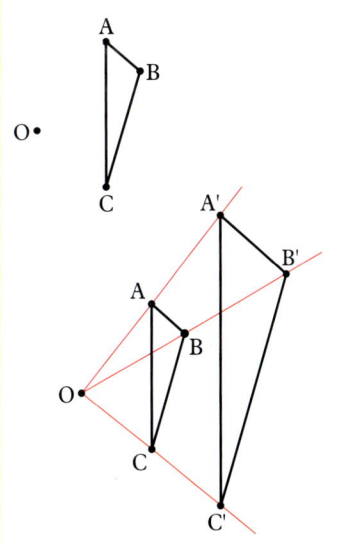

Exercise 10:3

1 **a** Copy the diagram. Enlarge triangle XYZ with scale factor 3 and centre O.

 b Label the image X′Y′Z′. Check that X′Y′ = 3 × XY.

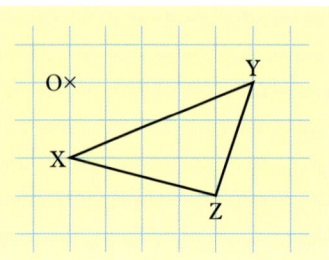

2 **a** Measure the lengths of PQ and P′Q′.

 b Use your answers to find the scale factor of the enlargement.

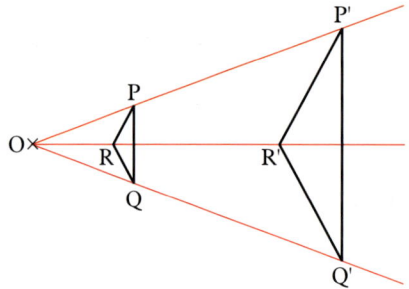

3 Jim has started to enlarge the rectangle with centre at O. Find the scale factor of the enlargement.

×D'

O×

For enlargements with centre at the origin:

co-ordinates of object × scale factor = co-ordinates of image

Example

Find the image of (4, 6) under an enlargement with centre at the origin and scale factor:

a 3   **b** $\frac{1}{2}$

a The image of (4, 6) is (12, 18).
You can write this as (4, 6) **maps to** (12, 18) or (4, 6) → (12, 18).

b (4, 6) maps to (2, 3).

A scale factor between 0 and 1 will make a shape smaller.

4 Find the image of these points under an enlargement with scale factor 4, centre the origin.

a (3, 2)   **d** (−3, −5)
b (1, 7)   **e** (2.5, 3)
c (2, −3)   **f** (−3.5, 1.25)

5 Find the image of these points under an enlargement with scale factor $\frac{2}{3}$ and centre the origin.

a (12, 3)   **c** (−12, −15)
b (9, −6)   **d** (7.5, −13.5)

6 **a** Copy the diagram. Enlarge triangle ABC with scale factor $\frac{1}{2}$ and centre O.
Label the image A'B'C'.
b Triangle A'B'C' can be mapped onto triangle ABC by an enlargement. Write down the scale factor.

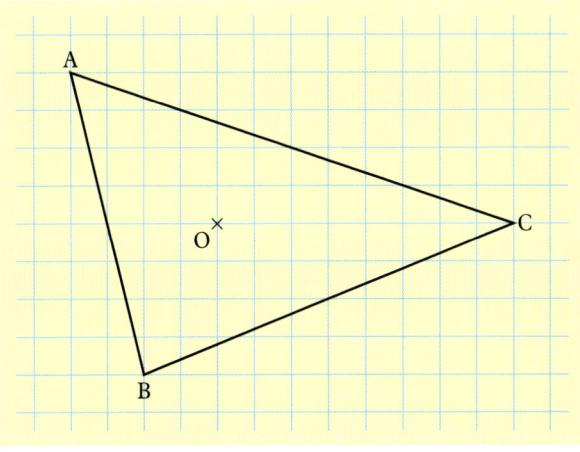

Inverse of an enlargement	The **inverse of an enlargement** with scale factor k is an enlargement with scale factor $\dfrac{1}{k}$.

The centre of enlargement must be the same for both.

$\dfrac{1}{k}$ is called the **reciprocal** of k.

Example

An enlargement has scale factor **a** 5 **b** $\frac{2}{3}$ **c** $4\frac{1}{2}$
Find the scale factor of the inverse in each case.

a $\frac{1}{5}$ **b** $\frac{3}{2}$ **c** $\frac{2}{9}$

$4\frac{1}{2} = \frac{9}{2}$ so the reciprocal is $\frac{2}{9}$

Exercise 10:4

1 These numbers are the scale factors of enlargements.
Write down the scale factor of the inverse of each one.

a 6 **d** $\frac{2}{5}$ **g** $\frac{a}{b}$

b 0.5 **e** $\frac{4}{3}$ **h** $1\frac{1}{2}$

c $\frac{1}{4}$ **f** $\frac{1}{n}$ **i** $2\frac{1}{3}$

2 **a** Find the scale factor of the enlargement that maps P onto Q.
  b Write down the scale factor of the inverse.

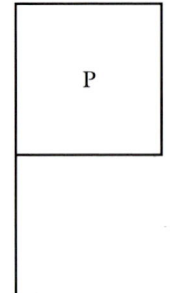

The scale factor of an enlargement may be **negative**. In this case, the object and image appear on opposite sides of the centre of enlargement.

Example

Show the image of P under an enlargement with scale factor -2 and centre the origin.

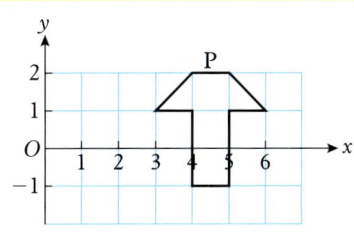

Co-ordinates of the image $= -2 \times$ the co-ordinates of the object.
$(3, 1) \rightarrow (-6, -2)$
$(4, 2) \rightarrow (-8, -4)$, and so on.

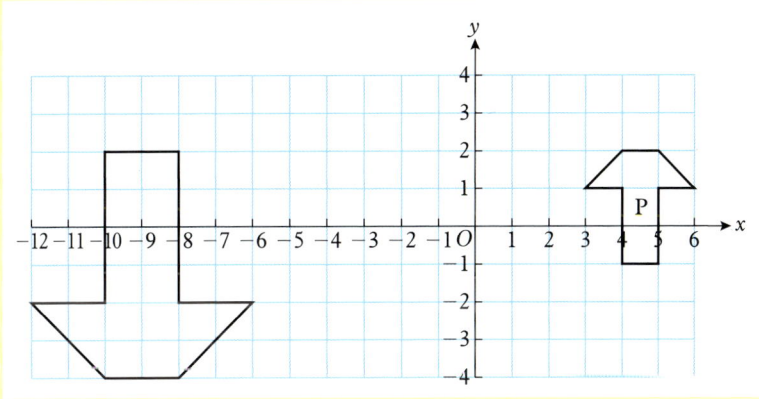

The scale factor of the inverse transformation is $-\frac{1}{2}$.

3 Find the image of each of these points under an enlargement with scale factor -3 and centre the origin.

a $(2, 3)$	**d** $(\frac{2}{3}, 0)$
b $(0, -4)$	**e** $(-\frac{4}{3}, 2)$
c $(-1, 2)$	**f** $(\frac{5}{6}, -\frac{1}{6})$

4 a An enlargement has scale factor -3
Write down the scale factor of its inverse.
b An enlargement has scale factor -0.4
Find the scale factor of its inverse.

5 **a** Copy the diagram. Enlarge triangle PQR with scale factor -1 and centre the origin. Label the image P'Q'R'.

    b Write down the scale factor of the inverse transformation.

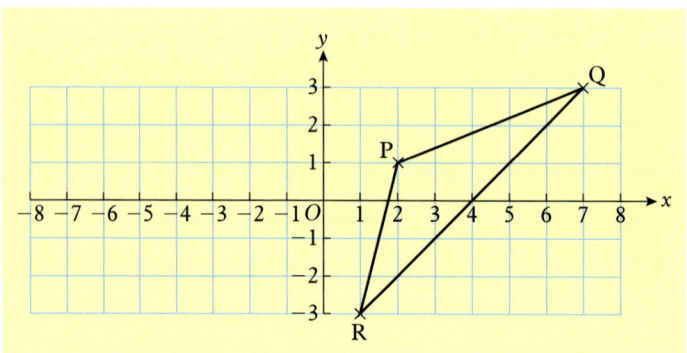

6 **a** Find the scale factor of the enlargement that maps P to Q.

    b Write down its reciprocal. What does this represent?

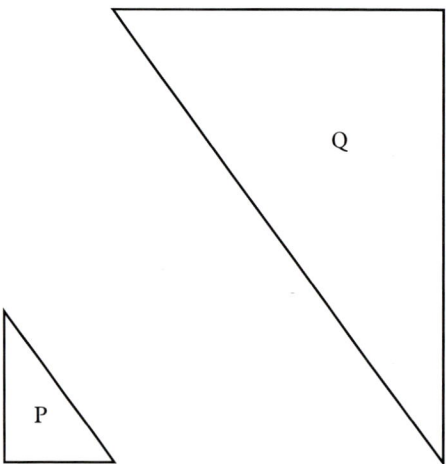

7 A(4, -2) is mapped to B(-2, 1) by an enlargement with centre at the origin.

    a Write down the scale factor of the enlargement.

    b Write down the scale factor of the inverse.

    c Give the co-ordinates of the point C that is mapped to A by the enlargement.

Rotation   A **rotation** turns a shape about a fixed point. This point is called the centre of rotation.

When you describe a rotation you must give these three things:
(1) the angle turned through
(2) the direction (clockwise or anti-clockwise)
(3) the centre

In the diagram, A is mapped onto B by a rotation of 90° clockwise, centre C(3, 2).

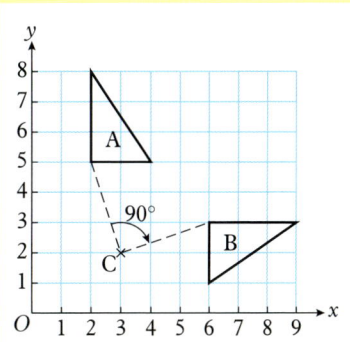

In a rotation, every line is turned through the same angle.

The object and the image are congruent.

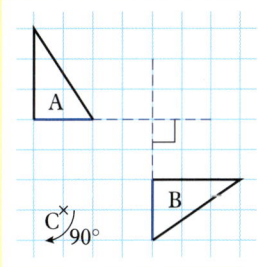

Exercise 10:5

1   **a**   Copy the diagram. Draw the image of F under a rotation of 90° anticlockwise about (2, 2). Label the image G.
    b   Rotate G through 180° about (2, 2). Label the image H.
    c   Describe the rotation that would map F on to H.

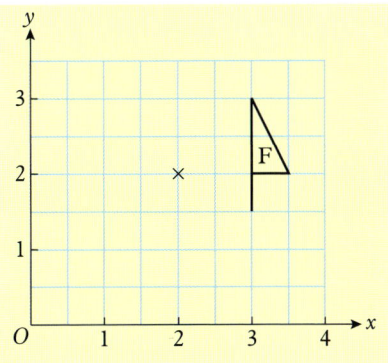

2 Describe fully a rotation that would map:
   a P onto Q
   b Q onto R
   c P onto R
   d Q onto S
   e S onto Q
   f R onto P

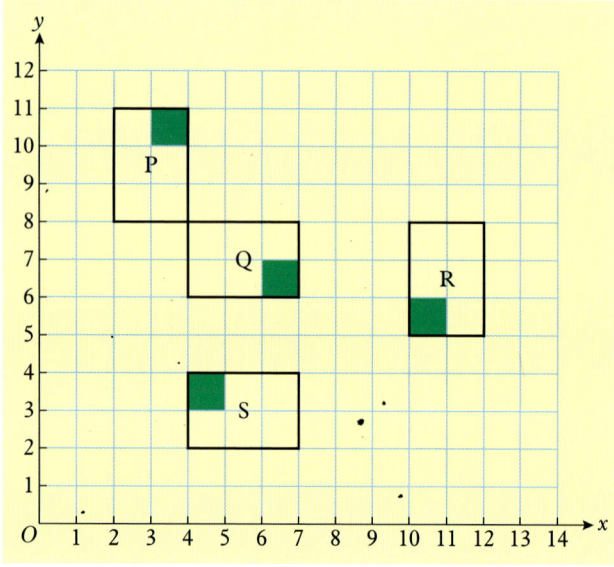

3 Describe each rotation fully.

   a

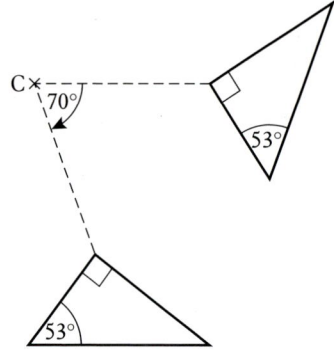

   b

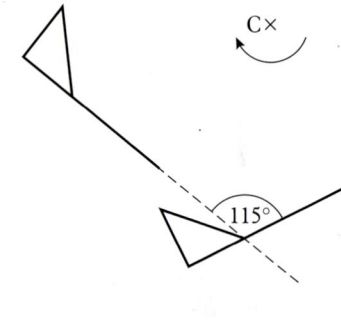

4 The diagram shows a regular hexagon ABCDEF with centre O.
   a Find the smallest angle of rotation about O so that A → B.
   b Describe a rotation so that every point on the hexagon is mapped to another point on the hexagon and A → C

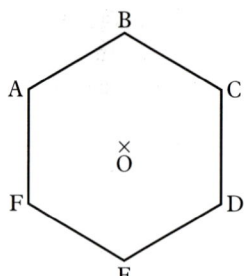

Inverse of a rotation	The **inverse of a rotation** is also a rotation. The angle and the centre are the same but the turn is in the opposite direction.
	The inverse of a rotation of 60° clockwise about (5, 7) is a rotation of 60° anticlockwise about (5, 7).

5 Write down the inverse of each of these rotations:
   a 90° clockwise about (8, 1)
   b 27° anticlockwise about $(-3, 5)$
   c 48° anticlockwise about $(-7, -10)$
   d 123° clockwise about $(11, -6)$

Reflection	In a **reflection** every point on the object moves to a point that is the same distance on the opposite side of a fixed line. The point and its image are directly opposite each other. The fixed line is called the mirror line. You can think of this as flipping the shape over the mirror line.

When you describe a reflection you must give the mirror line.

In the diagram P is mapped on to Q by reflection in the line AB.

The object and the image are congruent.

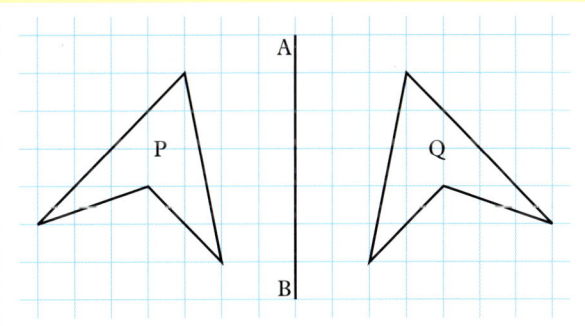

Exercise 10:6

1 Copy the diagram.
Reflect S in the line AB.
Label the image T.

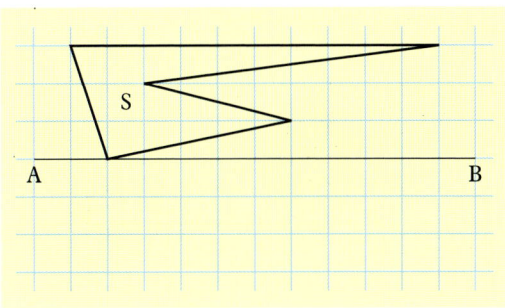

2 a Copy the diagram.

ABCD is mapped on to A′B′C′D′
after reflection in $y = x$.

b Write down the co-ordinates of
A′, B′, C′ and D′.
c Draw and label the image.

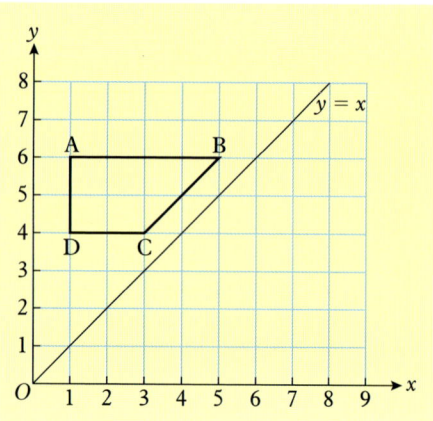

3 a Write down the image of (a, b) after reflection in $y = x$.
b Give the co-ordinates of a point that stays in the same position after
reflection in $y = x$.

4 a Plot the points A(2, 3), B(−1, 2), C(−2, −4), D(3, −1).
b Reflect the points in the line $y = -x$. Label the images A′, B′, C′, D′.
c Write down the image of (a, b) after reflection in $y = -x$.

Inverse of a reflection   A second reflection, in the same line, always undoes the effect of
the first. The **inverse of a reflection** is the same reflection.

5 Dave is exploring the effect of repeating reflections in the same mirror
line.

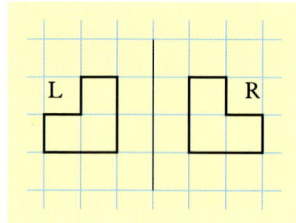

He finds that the image of L after one reflection is R
and the image of L after two reflections is L.

Write down the image of L when the number of reflections is:
a 5   **d** even
b 18   **e** odd
c 47   **f** a prime number that is bigger than 2

2 Combined transformations

The three Great Pyramids do not lie in a straight line. It has been discovered that if you take the position of the three stars in Orion's belt, then enlarge and rotate the diagram, it will fit exactly over the positions of the Great Pyramids.

Combination of transformations

You can often describe a movement by a **combination of transformations**.

P is mapped to the position Q by a combination of two transformations.

The first transformation is a translation $\begin{pmatrix} 5 \\ 3 \end{pmatrix}$

The second transformation is a rotation of 90° clockwise, about the point C.

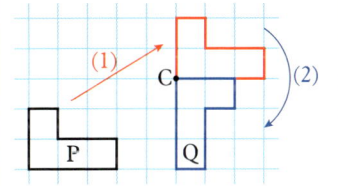

Exercise 10:7

1 T is mapped onto each of the other triangles by a translation of the point P followed by a rotation. Write down the combination of transformations that maps T to:
  a A
  b B
  c C

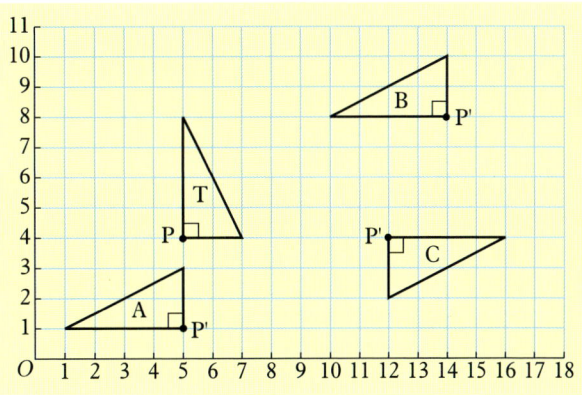

2 Part of a picture has been enlarged to give the pattern of pixels below.

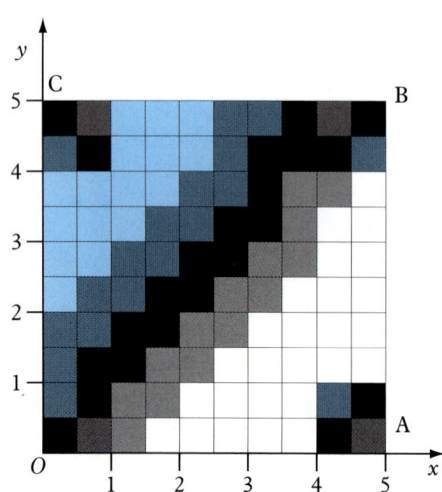

A block of 4 pixels appears in the corner at the origin.
You can transform this block to make the patterns at A, B and C.

a Give the translation that maps the block onto A.

b Give the rotation that maps the block onto B.

c Give the reflection that maps the block onto C.

● **d** Give the translation to do after a rotation of 180°, centre (1, 1) that maps the block onto B.

e Give the translation to do after a reflection in $y = 2$ that maps the block onto C.

f Give the rotation that maps A to C.

g B is translated through $\begin{pmatrix} 0 \\ -4 \end{pmatrix}$

Give the rotation so that the image maps to A.

Sometimes a combination of transformations can be replaced by a single transformation.

Shape A is reflected in the y axis to give the image B.

Shape B is rotated 180° anticlockwise about the origin to give the image C.

You can find a single transformation that maps shape A to shape C.

The transformation is a reflection in the x axis.

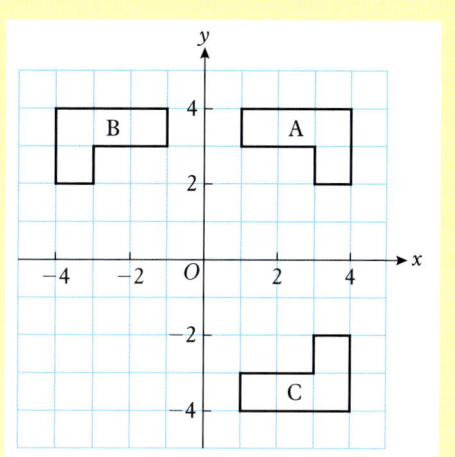

Exercise 10:8

1 **a** Copy the axes and the shape A on to squared paper.
  b Reflect A in the x axis. Label the image B.
  c Reflect B in the y axis. Label the image C.
  d Write down the single transformation that maps A to shape C.

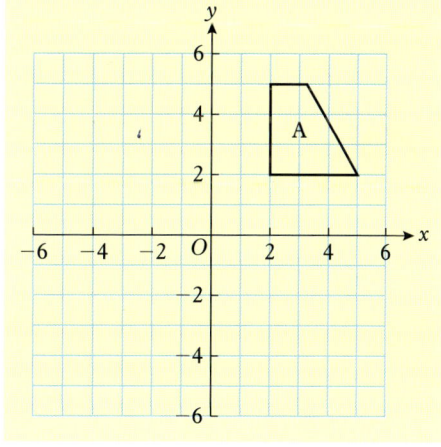

2 **a** Draw another set of axes like those in question **1**.
  b Draw the triangle with the vertices (−4, 2), (−2, 2) and (−4, 6). Label the triangle P.
  c Rotate triangle P 180° clockwise about the origin. Label the image Q.
  d Reflect triangle Q in the y axis. Label the image R.
  e Write down the single transformation that maps triangle P to triangle R.

3 **a** Copy the axes and triangle P on to squared paper.

   b Reflect triangle P in the *y* axis. Label the image Q.

   c Reflect triangle Q in the line $y = x$. Label the image R.

   d Write down the single transformation that maps triangle P to triangle R.

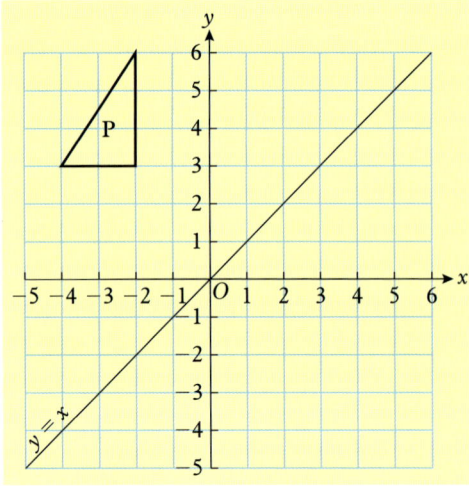

4 **a** Draw a set of axes with *x* and *y* from -6 to $+6$.
Draw the triangle with vertices $(2, 1)$, $(3, 1)$ and $(2, 4)$.
Label this triangle A.

   b Use triangle A to check if the following statement is true:

   'A reflection in the *x* axis followed by a rotation of 90° anticlockwise about the origin is the same as a rotation of 90° anticlockwise about the origin followed by a reflection in the *x* axis.'

5 **a** Draw the set of axes and the triangle A as in question **4**.

   b Use triangle A to check if the following statement is true:

   'A reflection in the *x* axis followed by a reflection in the *y* axis is the same as a reflection in the *y* axis followed by a reflection in the *x* axis.'

6 Here are some Logo instructions.
For each set of instructions, write down the instruction that would return you to the starting point.

   a fd 80

   b rt 45

   c fd 30 rt 60

   d fd 50 lt 30 fd 80

   e fd 50 rt 90 fd 50 rt 90 fd 50 rt 90

Transform – a game for two players

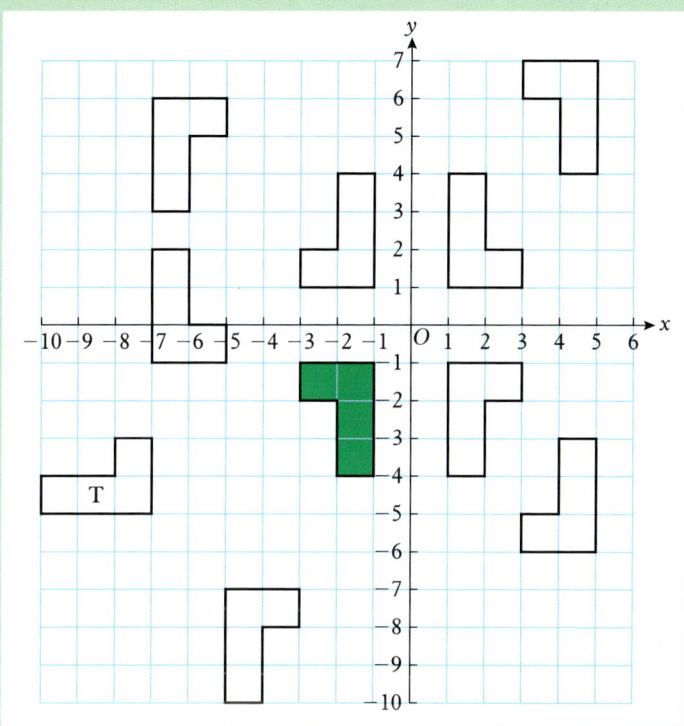

- Start with the shaded shape.

- Each player has three lives. Decide who is to go first.

- You throw a dice to decide which transformation to use:

1 – translation	4 – translation
2 – reflection	5 – reflection
3 – rotation	6 – rotation

- You now complete the details of the single transformation needed to move to one of the other shapes. Your opponent checks your transformation.

- If you are right then your opponent continues from the new position.

- If you are wrong then you lose a life and your opponent continues from the old position.

- You win either by landing on the target shape T or when all of your opponent's lives are lost.

1   Use column vectors to describe these translations.

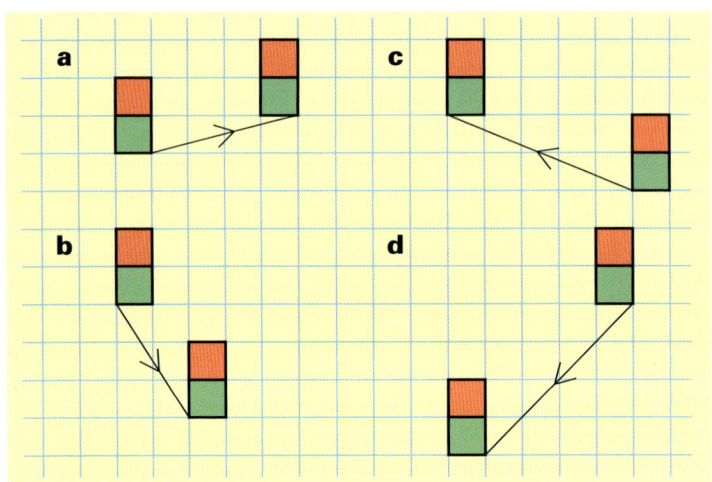

2   Give the translations from P to each of the other points in turn.

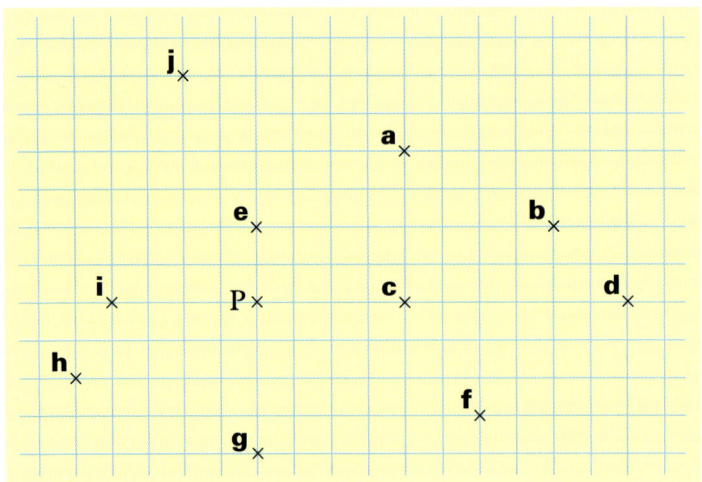

3   Copy each diagram. Reflect these shapes in the line AB.

a

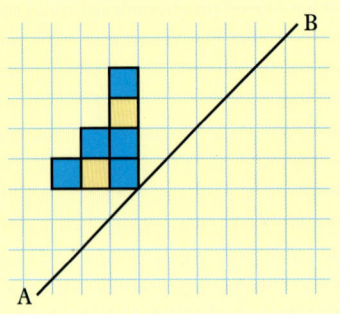

b

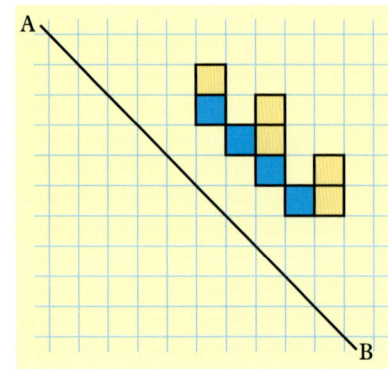

4 Triangle A has been enlarged to give triangle B.

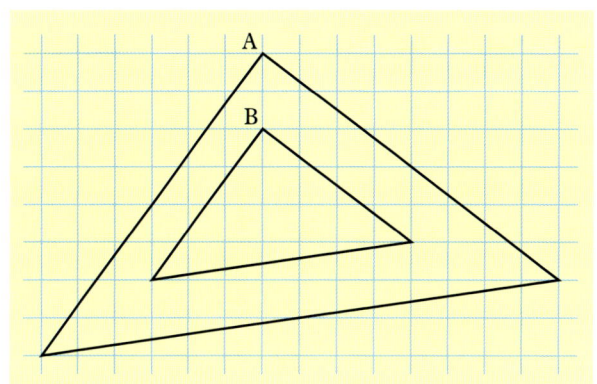

a Copy the diagram.
b Label the centre of enlargement C.
c Write down the scale factor of the enlargement.

5 A translation has vector $\begin{pmatrix} 3 \\ -2 \end{pmatrix}$. Find the image of the following points.

a $(1, 4)$ **e** $(4, -2.5)$
b $(-2, 3)$ **f** $(-3, 0)$
c $(0, -6)$ **g** $(-2.7, -10)$
d $(-3.5, 4)$ **h** (p, q)

6 Which shape cannot be mapped onto P by a rotation?

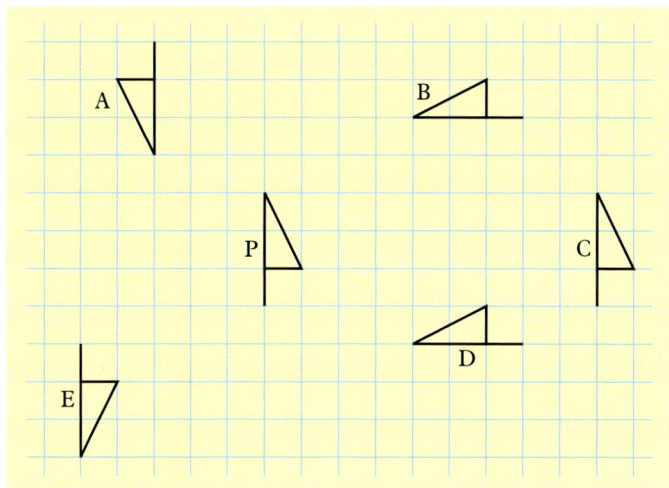

7 Each shape may be mapped onto L by a transformation. Describe each transformation fully.

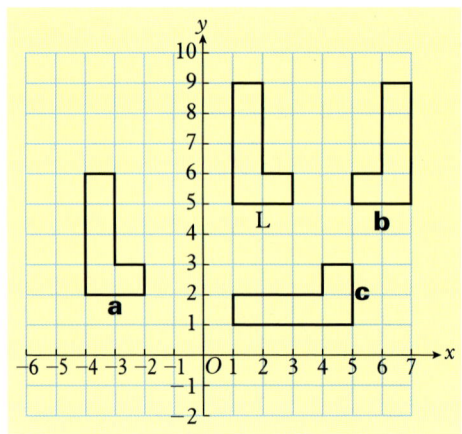

8 a The rectangle PQRS is reflected in the line $y = x$ to give rectangle P′Q′R′S′. What are the co-ordinates of S′?

  b The rectangle PQRS is enlarged with scale factor 2, centre of enlargement the origin, to give P″Q″R″S″. What are the co-ordinates of Q″?

  c The rectangle PQRS is rotated 90° clockwise about (0, 0) to give rectangle P‴Q‴R‴S‴. What are the co-ordinates of R‴?

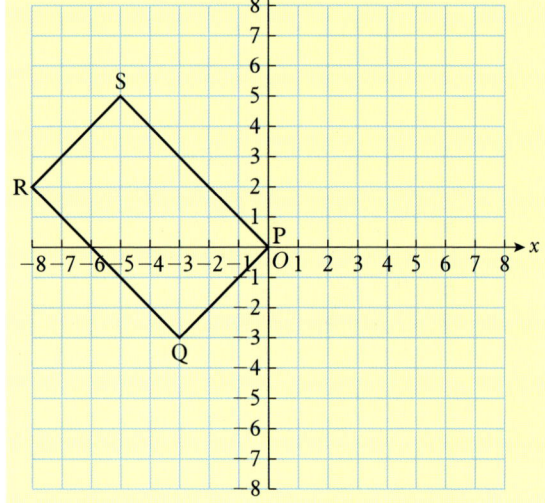

9 a Copy the diagram.

  b Reflect shape A in the line $y = 4$
Label the shape B.

  c Rotate the shape A 180° clockwise about the origin. Label the shape C.

  d Reflect shape A in the x axis. Label the shape D.

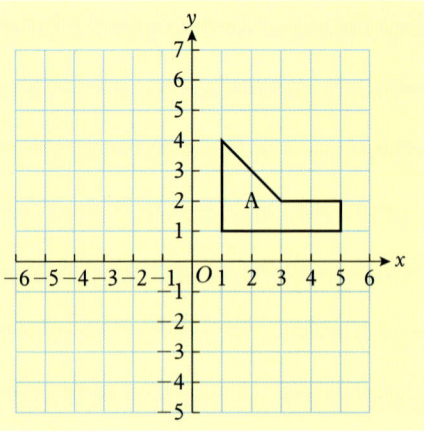

1 **a** Copy the diagram.
   b Translate shape A 5 units
      to the left and 2 units up.
      Label the image B.
   c Reflect shape A in the
      line $y = -x$.
      Label the image C.
   d Rotate shape A through
      $450°$ clockwise about $(-1, -1)$.
      Label the image D.

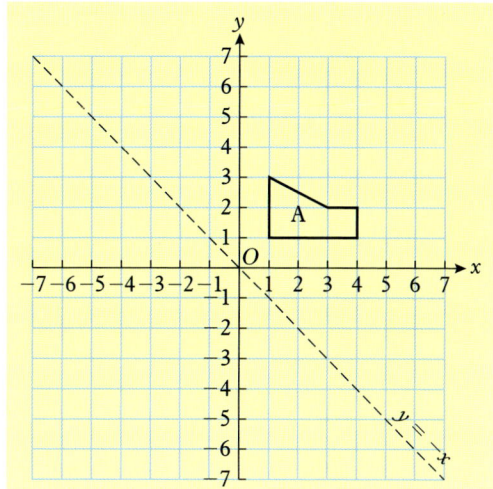

2 Describe the translation that maps $(3, 5)$ to the point:
   a $(6, 9)$ **b** $(3, 5)$ **c** $(0, -2)$ **d** $(-3, 6)$

3 **a** Draw a set of axes on to squared paper.
      Label the x and y axes from -6 to 6.
   b Plot the points $(1, 0)$ $(0, 3)$ $(3, 4)$.
      Join them up. Label the triangle A.
   c Reflect triangle A in the x axis. Label the image B.
   d Reflect triangle B in the line $y = x$. Label the image C.
   e Write down the single transformation that maps triangle A to
      triangle C.

4 **a** Draw a set of axes on to squared paper.
      Label the x and y axes from -8 to 8.
   b Draw the line $y = x$.
   c Reflect these points in $y = x$.
      A $(4, 5)$ C $(-3, 2)$ E $(-1, 0)$
      B $(2, 6)$ D $(0, -4)$ F $(-2, -1)$
      Label the image points A′, B′, etc.
   d Use your answers to part **c** to describe what happens to the
      co-ordinates of a point when it is reflected in the line $y = x$.
   e Investigate what happens to co-ordinates of points when they are
      reflected in:
      (1) $y = -x$ (3) $y = 1$
      (2) $y = 3$ (4) $x = 2$

5 **a** Draw a set of axes on squared paper.
Use values of x and y from -8 to 8.

    b Plot the points $(1, -1)$, $(3, -1)$ and $(3, -4)$.
Join them up.
Label the triangle P.

    c Reflect the triangle in the line $y = x$.
Label this triangle Q.

    d Reflect triangle Q in the x axis.
Label this triangle R.

    e Which single transformation maps triangle P onto triangle R?

6 **a** Copy the diagram.

    b Enlarge P with scale factor -3 and centre O.
Label the image Q.

    c Enlarge Q with scale factor $-\frac{1}{3}$ and centre $(3, 3)$.
Label the image R.

    d Describe the single transformation that maps P to R.

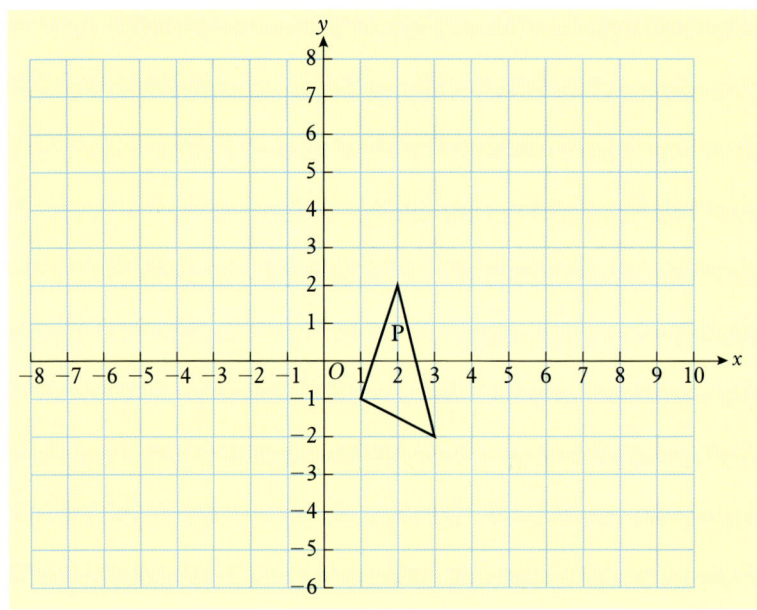

1 **a** Use a column vector to describe this translation.

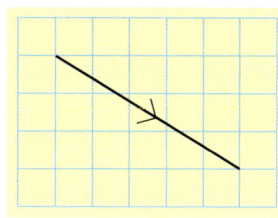

   b Draw a vector to show the translation:

     (1) $\begin{pmatrix} -2 \\ 3 \end{pmatrix}$ (2) $\begin{pmatrix} -3 \\ -4 \end{pmatrix}$

2 **a** Copy the diagram.
   b Reflect the shape in the y axis.
   c Rotate the shape 90° anti-clockwise about $(0, 0)$.

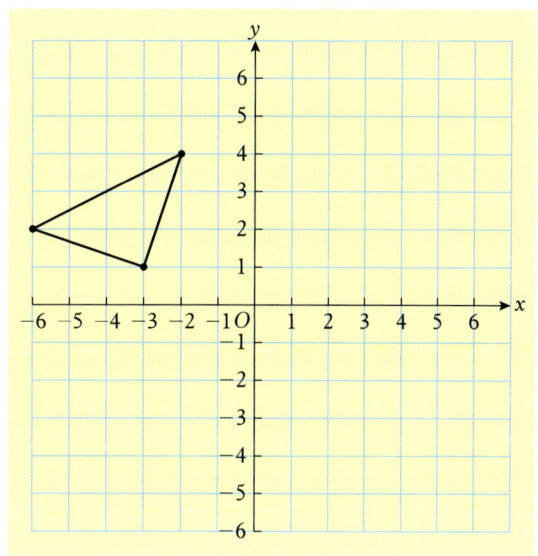

3 Write down the inverse of each of these:

   a a translation of 3 squares up and 2 squares to the left

   b a translation of $\begin{pmatrix} 5 \\ -4 \end{pmatrix}$

   c a rotation of 270° clockwise about the point $(2, -3)$

   d a reflection in the line $y = 2x$

4 **a** An enlargement has scale factor 4.
   Write down the scale factor of its inverse.

   b An enlargement has scale factor -0.5
   Write down the scale factor of its inverse.

5 **a** Copy the diagram.

   b Enlarge the triangle with scale factor −2, centre (0, 1)

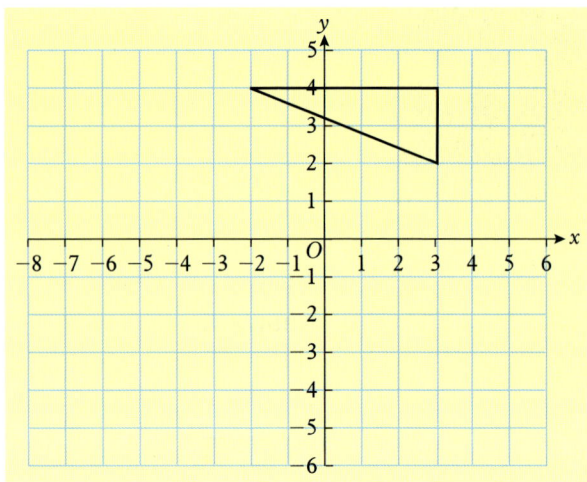

6 **a** Copy the diagram.

   b Reflect shape T in the *y* axis. Label the image B.

   c Rotate shape T 90° clockwise with centre the origin. Label the image C.

   d Write down the single transformation that maps B onto C.

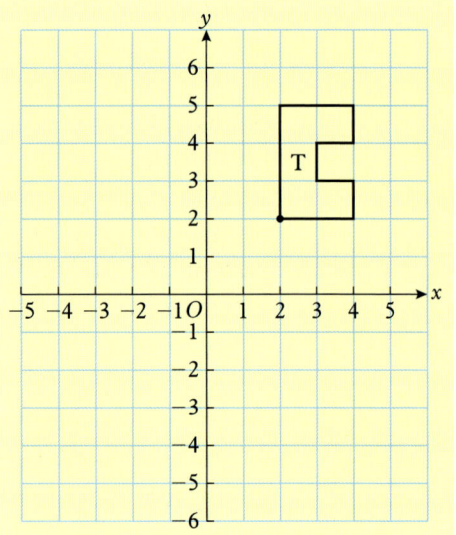

11 Algebra: lining up

1 Changing the subject
Rearranging simple formulas
Rearranging formulas with the subject
appearing twice

2 Sequences
Finding terms of linear sequences
Finding terms of quadratic sequences

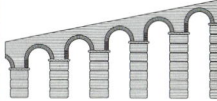

3 Straight lines
Looking at real life contexts for gradient
Looking at linear equations in context
Finding the gradient of a straight line given
two points on the line
Interpreting straight line graphs

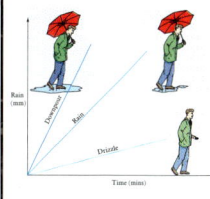

4 Solving equations
Solving one step equations
Solving two step equations

5 Simultaneous equations
Solving them using graphs
Solving them using algebra

CORE

QUESTIONS

EXTENSION

TEST YOURSELF

11 Changing the subject

Liz's mum is asking Liz what she's doing today.
Liz doesn't want to talk about it.
She is trying to change the subject.

You need to be able to change the subject in Maths too.
This doesn't mean getting your teacher to talk about something else!

The subject of a formula is the letter that appears on its own on the left-hand side. v is the subject in the formula $v = u + at$.
Changing the subject of a formula uses the same skills as solving an equation. But, instead of getting a number as an answer, you are now trying to get a different letter on its own.

Examples

1 Make u the subject of the formula $v = u + at$.

You need to remove the *at* term from the right-hand side.
This will leave the u by itself.
The *at* is *added* to the RHS at the moment.
So *subtract at* from each side.

$$v - at = u + at - at$$
$$v - at = u$$

Write the new formula the other way round with the subject on the LHS.

$$u = v - at$$

2 Make g the subject of the formula $v = 6g$.

Write the formula the other way round. This gets the $6g$ on the LHS.

$$6g = v$$

The g is *multiplied* by 6 at the moment.
So *divide* by 6 on each side.

$$\frac{6g}{6} = \frac{v}{6}$$
$$g = \frac{v}{6}$$

g is now the subject of the formula.

3 Make y the subject of the formula $x = 4y - 2z$.

First, you need to remove the $2z$ term from the RHS.
This will leave the $4y$ by itself.
The $2z$ is *subtracted* at the moment.
So *add* $2z$ to each side.

$$x + 2z = 4y - 2z + 2z$$
$$x + 2z = 4y$$

Now write the formula the other way round.

$$4y = x + 2z$$

The y is *multiplied* by 4 at the moment.
So *divide* by 4 on each side to leave the y on its own.

$$y = \frac{x + 2z}{4}$$

y is now the subject of the formula.

Exercise 11:1

Make the **red** letter the subject in each of these formulas.

1 $y = b + n$ **6** $v = 3t + u$

2 $u = f - 7$ **7** $k = 5r - 3z$

3 $e = s - 4u$ **8** $r = wx + yt$

4 $p = 6a$ **9** $5v = u + at$

5 $h = 5g$ ● **10** $k = 5t - 3z$

Example   Make u the subject of the formula $v = \dfrac{u}{5}$.

Write the formula the other way round. This gets the u term on the LHS.

$$\frac{u}{5} = v$$

The u is *divided* by 5 at the moment.
So *multiply* by 5 on each side.

$$5 \times \frac{u}{5} = 5 \times v$$

$$u = 5v$$

u is now the subject of the formula.

Exercise 11:2

Make the **red** letter the subject in each of these formulas.

1 $y = \dfrac{e}{5}$

2 $u = \dfrac{p}{15}$

3 $e = \dfrac{m}{5}$

4 $p = \dfrac{w}{5}$

5 $h = \dfrac{x}{5}$

6 $v = \dfrac{a}{5} - 5$

7 $k = \dfrac{y}{5} + 4$

8 $3r = \dfrac{5w}{8}$

9 $v = \dfrac{5v}{7} - 1$

10 $4k = 5t - \dfrac{k}{6}$

Some equations have lots of terms.
You need to remember BODMAS to help you to change the subject of these equations.

Example Make t the subject of the formula $c = \dfrac{zt + yb}{2}$.

Look at the letter t on the RHS of the formula.

Using BODMAS the t has

been	**multiplied** by z
then had	yb **added** to it
and then been	**divided** by 2

Undo these operations in the reverse order by using their inverses.

First	**multiply** by 2	$2c = zt + yb$
then	**subtract** yb	$2c - yb = zt$
and then	**divide** by z	$\dfrac{2c - yb}{z} = t$

So $\qquad\qquad\qquad\qquad\qquad\qquad\qquad\qquad t = \dfrac{2c - yb}{z}$

t is now the subject of the formula.

Exercise 11:3

Make the red letter the subject of each of these formulas.

1 $t = \dfrac{z + g}{7}$

2 $r = \dfrac{4h + 6j}{6}$

3 $3t = \dfrac{4f + 7r}{2}$

4 $at = \dfrac{pz + 5t}{y}$

5 $yk = \dfrac{ur + gj}{8}$

6 $\dfrac{r}{4} = \dfrac{h + 8e}{3}$

7 $3d = \dfrac{4h + 6j}{5}$

● **8** $5u = \dfrac{4h - 3d}{t}$

Some formulas have squares and square roots in them.
These two operations are the inverse of each other.
To remove a square, square root each side.
To remove a square root, square each side.

Examples

1 Make t the subject of the formula $s = \sqrt{t + r}$

To remove the square root, square each side.

$$s^2 = t + r$$

Now subtract the r.

$$s^2 - r = t$$

So $t = s^2 - r$

2 Make g the subject of the formula $r = 3g^2$.

First divide by the 3.

$$\frac{r}{3} = g^2$$

To remove the square, square root both sides.

$$g = \sqrt{\frac{r}{3}}$$

Exercise 11:4

Make the red letter the subject of each of these formulas.

1 $w = \sqrt{2t - s}$

2 $d = \sqrt{5t + 6p}$

3 $y = \sqrt{\dfrac{6x}{5}}$

4 $A = \pi r^2$

5 $e^2 = t^2 - 6f$

6 $k - 5 = gh - 2p^2$

You will need the skills of factorising and multiplying out brackets to solve some changing the subject problems.

In these formulas, the new subject appears twice.
You need to collect the terms with the new subject in together and then factorise.

Examples

1 Make *t* the subject of the formula $8tx = 3ty + s$.

First get any terms involving the new subject onto one side.
Get any terms not involving the new subject onto the other side.
$$8tx = 3ty + s$$
$$8tx - 3ty = s$$

Now factorise out the new subject.
$$t(8x - 3y) = s$$

Finally, divide by the bracket to leave *t* as the subject.
$$t = \frac{s}{(8x - 3y)}$$

2 Make *r* the subject of the formula $s = \frac{r + 4}{r}$

First multiply both sides by *r* to remove the fraction.
$$rs = r + 4$$
Then move all the *r* terms to the LHS.
$$rs - r = 4$$
Now factorise out the *r*.
$$r(s - 1) = 4$$
Finally divide by the bracket.
$$r = \frac{4}{s - 1}$$

Exercise 11:5

Make the **red** letter the subject of each of these formulas.

1 $3tx = 5ty - 4z$

2 $5nv = 6t - 3nm$

3 $7tx - 6y = 7z - 5tw$

4 $r = \dfrac{t + 3}{t}$

5 $z = \dfrac{3y + 3}{2y}$

6 $a = \dfrac{5b - 6c}{3b}$

7 $A = \pi r^2 h + 2\pi r h$

8 $t = \sqrt{\dfrac{3r - 2t}{2r}}$

● **9** $y = \dfrac{x - 4}{x - 3}$

2 Sequences

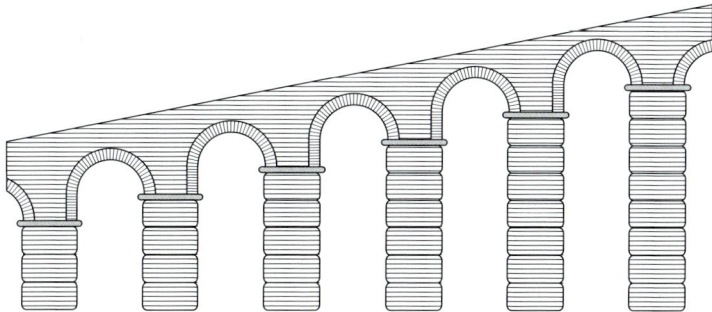

The number of blocks in the pillars give the sequence 3, 4, 5, 6, 7, 8, ...
You often find sequences of numbers in coursework.
It is useful to be able to find the formula for the sequence.

Formulas that contain n

Example   Find a formula for the *n*th term of this number sequence:

5, 8, 11, 14, 17, ...

You look at the differences between terms.
The differences are all the same.

5   8   11   14   17

+3   +3   +3   +3

If the **difference is a constant,** the formula for the *n*th term contains *n*.
The constant difference is the number that goes in front of *n*.
n is the term number.

For this sequence the first part of the formula is **3*n*.**
You need to make a table to help you find the rest of the formula.
Fill in the value of 3*n* for each term.

Term number	1	2	3	4	5
Sequence	5	8	11	14	17
	+2	+2	+2	+2	+2
Value of 3*n*	3	6	9	12	15

You now look for a number to add or subtract to get to the sequence.
In this sequence you need to **add 2.**

The formula for the sequence is **3*n* + 2.**

Exercise 11:6

Find a formula for the nth term of each of these number sequences.

1 5, 9, 13, 17, ...

4 5, 8, 11, 14, 17, ...

2 1, 3, 5, 7, 9, ...

5 11, 21, 31, 41, 51, ...

3 3, 5, 7, 9, 11, ...

6 4, 9, 14, 19, 24, ...

You can use the formula to find any term in the sequence.

Example   Find the 300th term in the sequence with the formula $3n - 8$.

You want the value of $3n - 8$ when $n = 300$
$$3n - 8 = 3 \times 300 - 8$$
$$= 892$$

The 300th term is 892.

---

7 Find the 25th term for each of these.

    a $4n + 5$ **b** $2n - 8$ **c** $10n + 40$

8 Find the 40th term for each of these.

    a $2n + 14$ **b** $8n - 10$ **c** $\dfrac{n}{2} - 30$

9 The formula for a sequence is $5n - 3$.
    Which term has the value:

    a 47   **b** 32   **c** 442

10 Which of these numbers belong to the sequence with the formula $5n + 12$?
     Remember that the term number can only be a whole number.

     a 38   **b** 53   **c** 72

Formulas that contain n^2

Example   Find a formula for the *n*th term of this number sequence.

5, 19, 41, 71, 109, …

Look at the differences between terms:

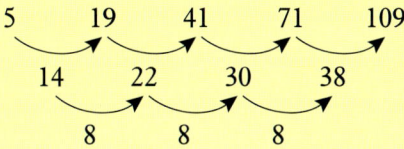

First differences are not the same.

Second differences are the same.

If the **second difference is a constant**, the formula for the ***n*th term contains n^2**.

The number in front of n^2 is **half** the constant difference.

In the example, the constant difference is 8.
The number in front of n^2 is half of 8, which is 4.
The first part of the formula is $4n^2$.

Make a table to help you find the rest of the formula.
Fill in the value of $4n^2$ for each term.

Term number	1	2	3	4	5
Sequence	5	19	41	71	109
	+1	+3	+5	+7	+9
Value of $4n^2$	4	16	36	64	100

Now look for what you need to add   +1   +3   +5   +7   +9
or subtract to get to the sequence.

Find the formula for the second part of the sequence as before.

Term number	1	2	3	4	5
	1	3	5	7	9

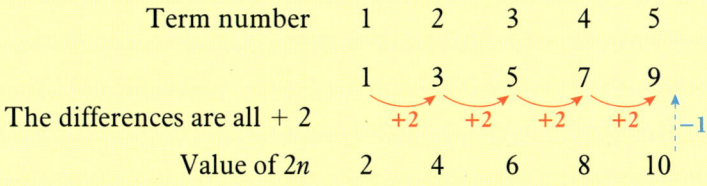

The differences are all $+ 2$ +2   +2   +2   +2   −1

Value of $2n$	2	4	6	8	10

The formula for the second part of the sequence is $2n - 1$.
The formula for the sequence is $4n^2 + 2n - 1$.
Check the formula by finding term number 5.

$n = 5$, $4n^2 + 2n - 1 = 100 + 10 - 1 = 109$ ✓

Exercise 11:7

For the number sequences in questions **1** to **8**:
a find the formula for the nth term
b find the 5th term using your formula.
Check to see if it is correct

1 15, 22, 31, 42, 55, …

5 3, 14, 31, 54, 83, …

2 4, 13, 26, 43, 64, …

6 6, 23, 48, 81, 122, …

3 3, 7, 13, 21, 31, …

7 8, 19, 34, 53, 76, …

4 5, 12, 21, 32, 45, …

8 2, 10, 24, 44, 70, …

9 The formula for a sequence is $3n^2 + n - 4$.
   a Find the first four terms.
   b Find the 20th term.

10 The formula for a sequence is $5n^2 - 2n - 7$.
   a Find the first four terms.
   b Find the 10th term.

11 The formula for a sequence is $4n^2 - 3n + 7$.
   a Find the 5th term.
   b Use trial and improvement to find which term has the value 1249.

12 The formula for a sequence is $3n^2 - 5n - 10$.
   a Find the first five terms.
   b Find the 12th term.
   c Use trial and improvement to find which term has the value 1462.

13 Which of these numbers belong to the sequence with the formula $4n^2 + 5n - 12$?
   a 624   **b** 1698   **c** 1229

3 Straight lines

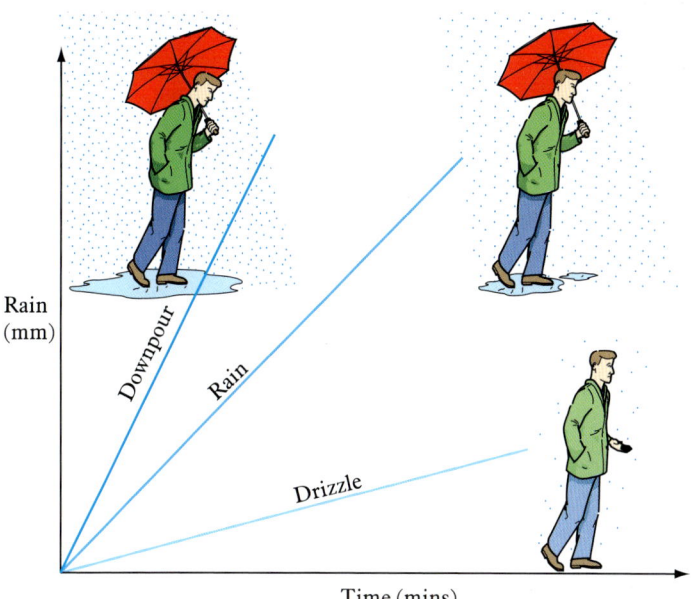

Rain (mm)

Downpour

Rain

Drizzle

Time (mins)

This graph shows different types of rainfall.
The heavier the rain, the steeper the line.

This graph shows the number of pages in a magazine and its cost. The magazines are *Computer World*, *Your Car* and *Pop Scene*.

The steeper the line the more pages you get per £1.

The best value magazine is *Computer World*.
You get about 320 pages for £1.
This magazine gives the most pages per £1.

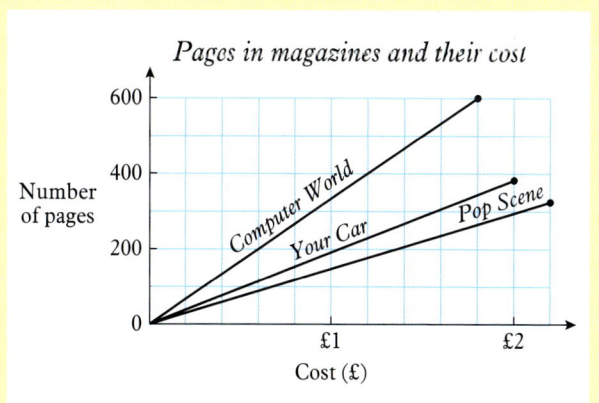

Pages in magazines and their cost

Number of pages

600

400

200

0

£1   £2

Cost (£)

Computer World

Your Car

Pop Scene

Exercise 11:8

1 Use the graph above to estimate the number of pages you get for £1 with:
    a *Pop Scene*   **b** *Your Car*

2 This graph shows the rates of climb on take-off for some planes.

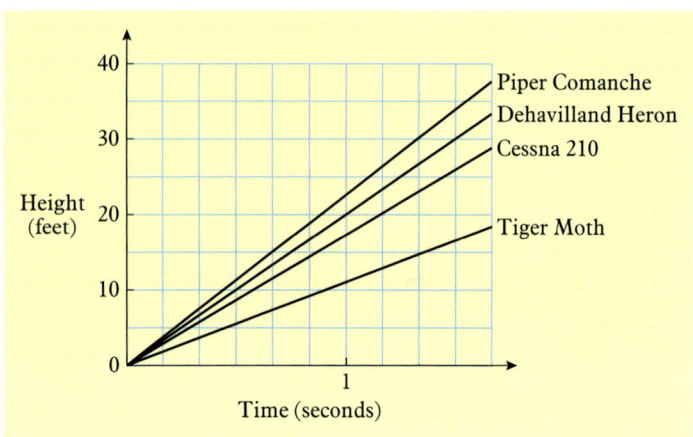

a Which plane takes off at a rate of 11 feet per second?
b Estimate the rate of climb for the other three planes.
c Which plane climbs the fastest?

Gradient   The **gradient** of a line tells you how steep the line is.

The graph shows the number
of complaints a shop expects
on average each week.
The number of complaints is
5 per week.

This can be written as a formula

$c = 5w$

This is the equation of the
straight line.
The number 5 is called the gradient.

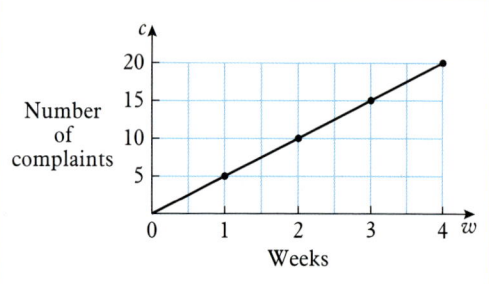

---

3 This formula gives the number of **telephone** calls received
by a computer helpline each **hour** $t = 50h$
a How many calls does the firm get each hour?
b You can draw the straight line with equation $t = 50h$
What is the gradient of this line?
c How many calls does the firm get in 4 hours?

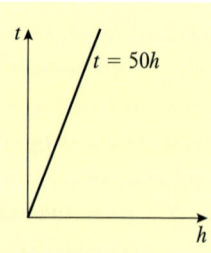

4 This graph shows the average number of computers sold by a shop each hour.

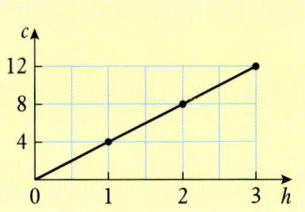

  a On average how many computers are sold in one hour?
  b What is the gradient of the line?
  c Write down the equation of the line. Use c for the number of computers and h for the number of hours.

5 Write down the gradient of each of these lines.

  a $p = 7h$ **b** $y = 4x$ **c** $y = \dfrac{2x}{3}$

This is the formula for the cost, in pounds, of hiring a mini-tractor for a number of days.

$$c = 20d + 10$$

The graph shows the straight line with equation

$$c = 20d + 10$$

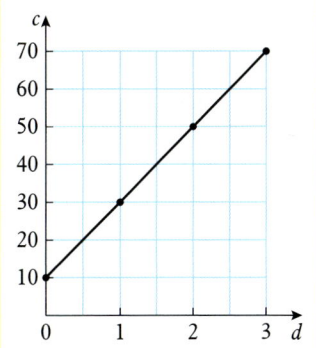

The gradient, 20, is the cost per day.
The line cuts the vertical axis at 10.
This is the deposit for the tractor.
So the deposit is £10 and it costs £20 per day to hire the tractor.

Exercise 11:9

1 Write down for each of these: (1) the cost per day   (2) the deposit
  a $c = 4d + 15$ **b** $c = 7d + 5$ **c** $c = 8d + 4$

2 Where will these lines cut the y axis?
  a $y = 3x + 4$ **b** $y = 7x + 2$ **c** $y = 4x - 7$

3 Write down the formula for each of these lines.

  a
  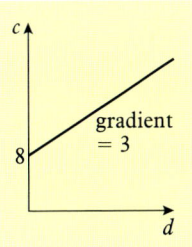

  b
  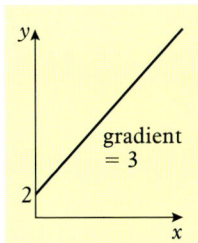

  c
  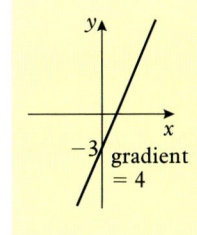

Finding the gradient of a line

To find the gradient of a line, choose two points on the line as far apart as possible.

You need to be able to read the co-ordinates of the points.

$$\text{Gradient} = \frac{\text{vertical change}}{\text{horizontal change}}$$

$$= \frac{7-1}{4-1}$$

$$= \frac{6}{3}$$

$$= 2$$

The gradient of the line is 2.

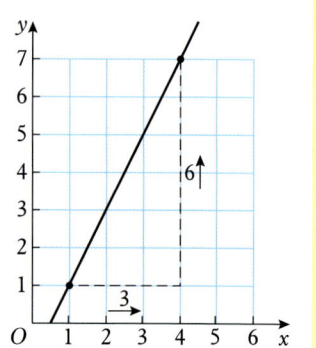

Exercise 11:10

1 Find the gradient of each of these lines.

a

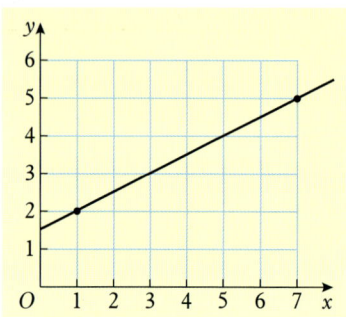

c

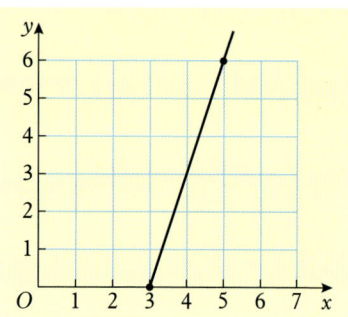

b

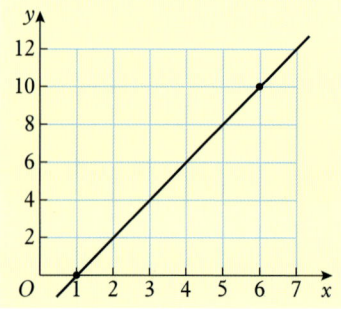

d

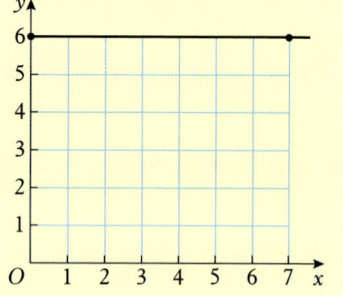

2   Work out the gradient of each of these lines.

a

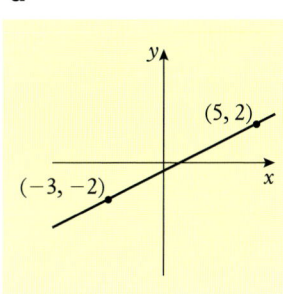

b

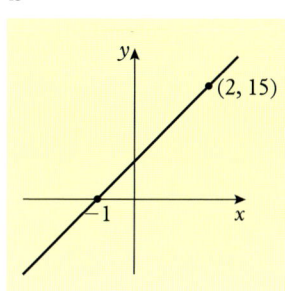

c

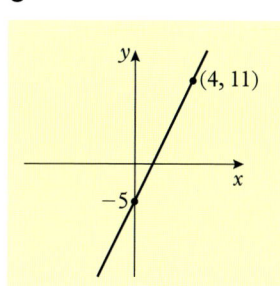

Negative gradients

This line has a negative gradient.
The vertical change is negative.

$$\text{Gradient} = \frac{\text{vertical change}}{\text{horizontal change}}$$

$$= \frac{-8}{2}$$

$$= -4$$

The gradient is -4

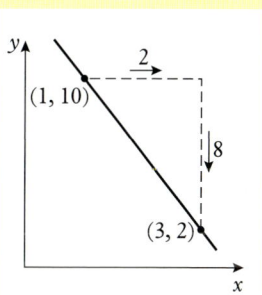

Exercise 11:11

1   Find the gradient of each of these lines.

a

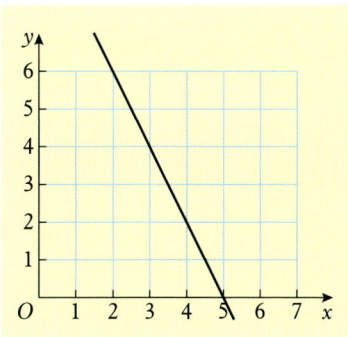

b

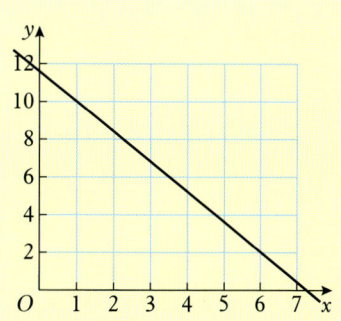

2 Work out the gradient of each line.

a

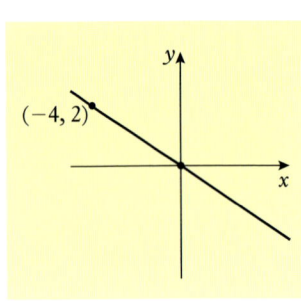

b

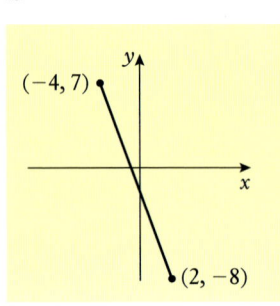

c

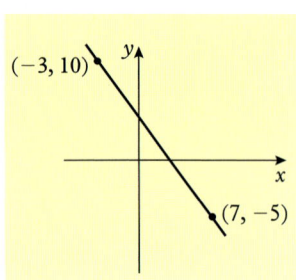

3 Find the gradient of the line passing through the following points.
Draw a sketch to see if the line has a positive or negative gradient to
help you.

   a (1, 1) and (6, 16)   **d** (−3, 0) and (0, 12)

   b (2, 9) and (4, 5)   **e** (−5, 4) and (−3, 10)

   c (−2, −12) and (4, 6)   **f** (−5, −14) and (−1, 4)

4 These lines have negative gradients.
Write down the equation of each line.

a

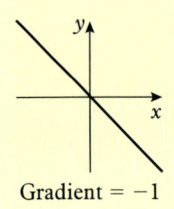

Gradient = −1

b

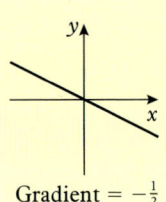

Gradient = −½

c

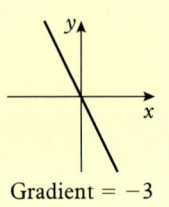

Gradient = −3

5 Write down the gradient of each of these lines.

   a $y = -6x$ **b** $y = -4x$ **c** $y = -\dfrac{1}{2}x$

6 **a** Find the gradient of the line
      shown.

    b Write the equation of the
      line in the form $y = mx + c$.

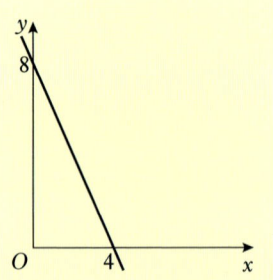

7 **a** Find the gradient of the line shown.

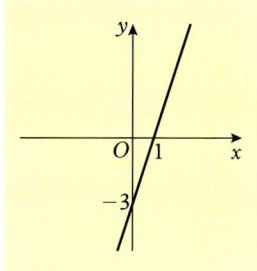

    b Write the equation of the line in the form $y = mx + c$

    c Use your equation to find the value of y when $x = 10$.

    d What value of x gives a y value of 12?

Parallel and perpendicular lines

Parallel lines always have the same gradient.

The lines $y = 2x$, $y = 2x + 5$ and $y = 2x - 3$ are all parallel.

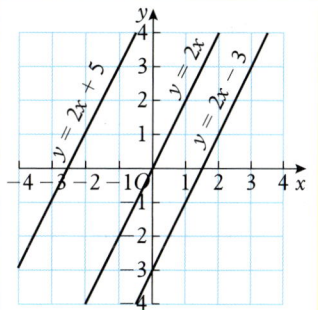

The lines $y = 2x + 5$ and $y = -\frac{1}{2}x - 2$ are perpendicular to each other. This means that they are at right angles to each other.

When you multiply their gradients together you get -1. This is always true of perpendicular lines.

This means that if a line has a gradient m, then the line that is perpendicular to it has a gradient of $-\dfrac{1}{m}$.

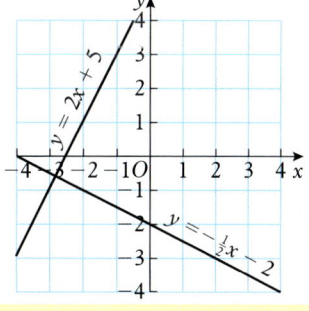

8 Write down the gradient of a line which is perpendicular to each of these lines.

    a $y = 2x + 3$ **d** $y = 4 - 2x$ **g** $y = -\frac{1}{2}x - \frac{1}{2}$

    b $y = 4x - 2$ **e** $y = \frac{1}{2}x + 3$ **h** $y = 6 - 3x$

    c $y = -5x + 2$ **f** $y = \frac{1}{4}x - 5$ **i** $y = 5 + \frac{1}{4}x$

9 For each of these pairs of points:
  (1) draw the line that passes through these points
  (2) work out the gradient of the line
  (3) write down the equation of the line
  (4) write down the equation of a perpendicular line.

  a $(0, -1)$ and $(4, 11)$

  b $(0, 2)$ and $(6, 5)$

  c $(-1, 3)$ and $(4, -2)$

The graph shows the cost of hiring a car. The cost is made up of a fixed charge and a daily rate.

The cost, C, is given by the formula
$$C = a + bn$$
where n is the number of days.

You can use the graph to find the values of a and b.

The fixed charge is the point where the line cuts the vertical axis.
This is a.
The daily rate is the gradient of the line.
This is b.

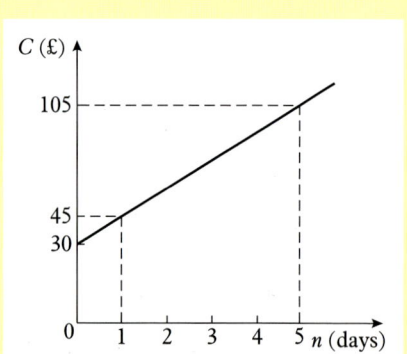

Exercise 11:12

1 Find the values of a and b in the example above.

2 This graph shows the cost, C, of a holiday. The formula is $C = a + bd$ where d is the number of days.

  a Find the value of a and b.

  b Write down the fixed charge and the daily rate for the holiday.

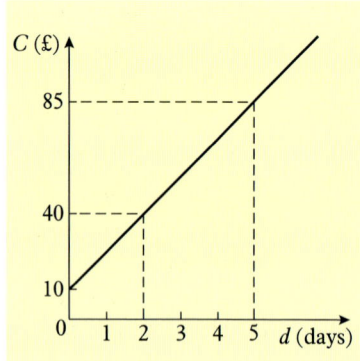

3 A car is travelling at a constant speed.
It then starts accelerating.
The graph shows how the speed of the
car changes.

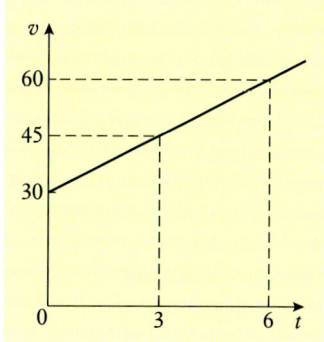

The formula for the new speed is
$$v = u + at$$
where v is the new speed and t is the time.
a Find the value of the acceleration a.
b Write down the value of u.
Explain what u is.

4 Alice has done an experiment in Physics.
She added masses to the end of a spring
and measured the new length L.

The formula is $L = a + bw$
where w is the mass in grams.
These are her results.

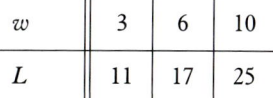

w	3	6	10
L	11	17	25

a Draw a graph using Alice's results.
b Write down the original length of
the spring.
c Find the extension per gram of
the spring.

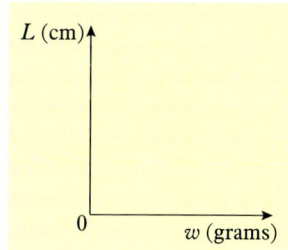

5 Chris is given a fixed amount of money to
spend on holiday. He spends the same
amount each day.
The amount of money that Chris has left is
shown on the graph.

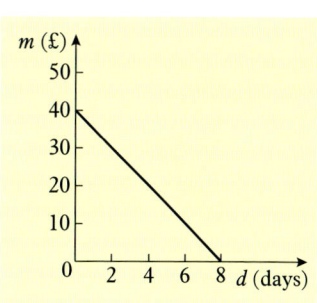

a Write down the equation of the line.
b Find the amount of money that he is
given.
c How much does he spend each day?
d How many days did the holiday last?

4   Solving equations

Alan, Andrew and Katy are brothers and sister.

Alan is the youngest. Andrew is three years older than Alan. Katie is three years older than Andrew.

Their ages add up to 39. How old are Alan, Andrew and Katie?

Problems like this can be solved using linear equations.

Linear equations

Equations with simple letters and numbers in them are called linear equations. Linear equations must not have any terms like x^2, x^3 or $\dfrac{1}{x}$ in them.

When you solve an equation, you are trying to work out the value of a letter.

You solve it by getting the unknown letter onto one side of the equation.

Example

Solve these equations:

a $x + 5 = 12$ **b** $2x = 7$ **c** $\dfrac{x}{6} + 3 = 5$

a To solve $x + 5 = 12$, notice that x has 5 *added* to it.
     To leave x by itself, *take* 5 from each side of the equation.
$$x + 5 - 5 = 12 - 5$$
$$x = 7$$

b In the equation $2x = 7$, the x has been *multiplied* by 2.
     To solve this equation, *divide* both sides by 2.

$$\frac{2x}{2} = \frac{7}{2}$$

$$x = 3.5$$

c You need to do two things to solve $\dfrac{x}{6} + 3 = 5$

The x has been **divided** by 6 and then 3 has been **added**.
To solve this, **subtract** the 3, then **multiply** by the 6.
This means doing the opposite operation in the opposite order.

$$\dfrac{x}{6} + 3 - 3 = 5 - 3$$

$$\dfrac{x}{6} \times 6 = 2 \times 6$$

$$x = 12$$

Exercise 11:13

1 Solve these equations.

a	$x + 4 = 16$	**j**	$3x + 1 = 16$
b	$3x = 18$	**k**	$4x - 3 = 13$
c	$x + 6 = 19$	**l**	$5x + 6 = 11$
d	$x - 12 = 14$	**m**	$7x - 6 = -13$
e	$x - 4 = 14$	**n**	$5x - 6 = 12$
f	$2x = -3$	**o**	$0.5x + 2 = 6$
g	$\dfrac{x}{5} = 6$	**p**	$\dfrac{x}{3} + 2 = 10$
h	$\dfrac{x}{7} = 4$	**q**	$\dfrac{x}{4} - 1 = 12$
i	$\dfrac{x}{3} = 9$	**r**	$\dfrac{3x}{2} + 5 = 26$

Some equations have letters on both sides.
To solve them, you need to change them so that they only have the letter on one side.

Example Solve $5x = 3x + 14$

Look to see which side has the *least* number of xs.
In this example, the right-hand side (RHS) has only $3x$.

Subtract $3x$ from each side	$5x - 3x = 3x - 3x + 14$
You now have x on just the LHS	$2x = 14$
Divide both sides by 2	$x = 7$

Exercise 11:14

1 Solve these equations.

    a $5x = 3x + 8$

    b $7x = 3x + 24$

    c $12x = 7x + 35$

    d $3x = x + 19$

    e $9x - 8 = 7x$

    f $11x = 6 + 8x$

    g $3.5x = 2.5x + 8$

    h $5x = 2x - 12$

    i $4.5x = 2x + 10$

    j $15x = 8x + 147$

2 Solve these equations.

    a $6x + 4 = 7x$

    b $4x + 7 = 11x$

    c $2x + 13 = 4x$

    d $3x + 9 = 6x$

    e $4x - 6 = 6x$

    f $4x - 21 = 11x$

    g $3x = 7x - 4$

    h $1.5x + 9 = 3.5x$

    i $3x - 6 = 5x$

    j $2x + 4.5 = 4x$

    k $5x - 3 = 7x$

    l $23x = 29x + 6$

Some equations have letters and numbers on both sides.

Example

Solve $11x - 20 = 6x + 15$

The RHS has the least number of x.

Take **6x** from each side $11x - \mathbf{6x} - 20 = 6x - \mathbf{6x} + 15$

$$5x - 20 = 15$$

Now remove the numbers from the side with the x.

Add **20** to each side $5x - 20 + \mathbf{20} = 15 + \mathbf{20}$

$$5x = 35$$

Divide both sides by 5 $x = 7$

Exercise 11:15

1 Solve these equations.

    a $4x + 4 = 2x + 10$

    b $2x - 7 = x + 3$

    c $6x - 13 = 4x + 5$

    d $8x + 9 = 4x + 13$

    e $4x + 6 = 6x + 2$

    f $7x - 21 = 3x - 5$

    g $3x - 15 = x - 4$

    h $6x + 2 = 17 + x$

    i $9x - 1 = 5x + 7$

    j $12x + 7 = 12 + 2x$

    k $3.5x - 15 = x + 5$

    l $5x + 25 = 3x + 25$

The method does not change if you have a minus sign in front of one of the letters.

Example   Solve $4x + 5 = 20 - x$

First, remove the x from the RHS $4x + 5 + x = 20 - x + x$
                                                           $5x + 5 = 20$

Subtract 5 from each side $5x + 5 - 5 = 20 - 5$
                                                        $5x = 15$

Divide both sides by 5 $x = 3$

2 Solve these equations.
   a $6x + 6 = 20 - x$ **e** $8x - 3 = 27 - 2x$
   b $5x + 7 = 21 - 2x$ **f** $-6x - 9 = 3 - 8x$
   c $x + 2 = 11 - x$ **g** $2.8x - 20 = 22 - 1.4x$
   d $10x - 7 = 12 - 2x$ **h** $7 - 3x = 4 + 2x$

Some equations have brackets in them.
To solve them, first multiply out the brackets.

Example   Solve $3(2x + 1) = 27$

Multiply out the bracket $3 \times 2x + 3 \times 1 = 27$
                                                    $6x + 3 = 27$
Now solve the equation as usual $6x = 24$
                                                     $x = 4$

Exercise 11:16

1 Solve these equations.
   a $3(2x + 1) = 21$ **g** $3(x - 1) = 2x - 2$
   b $4(7x - 4) = 40$ **h** $2(2x - 1) = x + 7$
   c $6(2x - 7) = 42$ **i** $2(x + 1) + 5 = 3(2x + 1)$
   d $5(8x - 1) = 35$ **j** $3(x - 2) - 2(x + 1) = 5$
   e $10(2x - 10) = 40$ **k** $6(7x - 2) = 6(5x + 3)$
   f $9(3x - 5) = -18$ **l** $10(3x - 4) = 5(6 - x)$

5 Simultaneous equations

Points of intersection are sometimes of interest.

You can find points of intersection of straight lines by drawing graphs.

Point of intersection	The point where two lines cross is called the **point of intersection** of the two lines.

Example In a sale, all compact discs are one price.
All tapes are also one price.
Jenny buys two *c*ompact discs and one *t*ape for £10.
Peter buys one *c*ompact disc and two *t*apes for £8.
Find the cost of a *c*d and the cost of a *t*ape.

You need to write down the equations that represent the information in the question. Then you find the points where these lines cross the axes.

Jenny's equation is $2c + t = 10$
When $c = 0$ $t = 10$
When $t = 0$ $2c = 10$
              $c = 5$

Two points on this line are $(0, 10)$ and $(5, 0)$

Peter's equation is $c + 2t = 8$
When $c = 0$ $2t = 8$
              $t = 4$
When $t = 0$ $c = 8$

Two points on this line are $(0, 4)$ and $(8, 0)$

Now you can draw the lines and find where they intersect.

These lines intersect at $(4, 2)$
This means that $c = 4$
and $t = 2$
So a compact disc costs £4
and a tape costs £2.

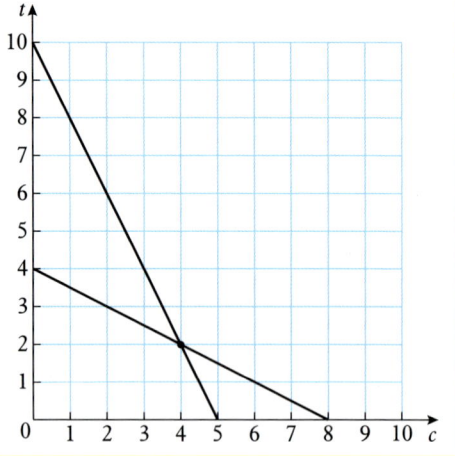

Exercise 11:17

Draw graphs to solve these problems.

1 Paul and Petra took part in a school quiz. They had to choose a *standard* or a *hard* question on each turn.
Paul answered 3 *standard* and 2 *hard* questions correctly and scored 7 points. Petra answered 1 *standard* and 4 *hard* questions correctly and scored 9 points.
Find the points awarded for a *standard* question and for a *hard* question.

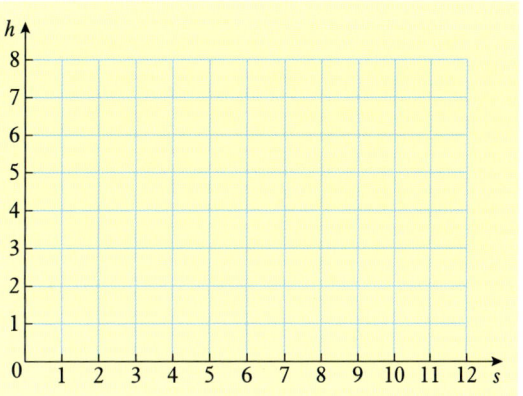

2 A school sells two types of calculator. One is a *basic* model and the other is a *scientific*.
The cost of 1 *basic* and 1 *scientific* is £10.
The cost of 3 *basic* and 2 *scientific* is £24.
Find the cost of a *basic* model and the cost of a *scientific* model.

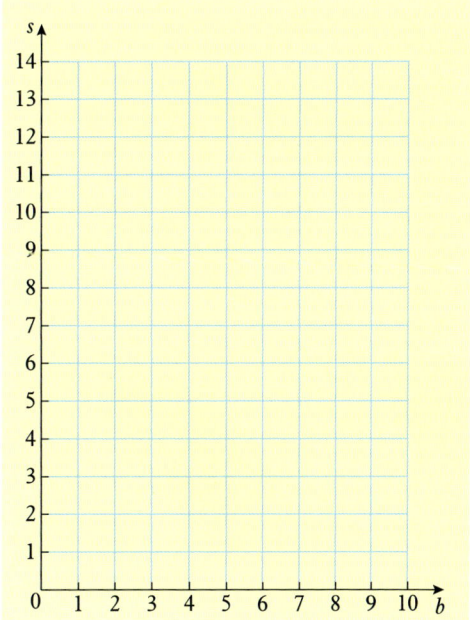

3 Find the point of intersection of these lines.

a $2x + y = 8$
$2x + 3y = 12$

b $x + 4y = 22$
$2x + y = 9$

You can also find points of intersection by using algebra.
You do this by solving the two equations at the same time.

| **Simultaneous equations** | When you solve two equations at the same time you are solving **simultaneous equations**. |

Examples

1 Solve this pair of simultaneous equations. $\qquad 5x + y = 20$
$\qquad\qquad\qquad\qquad\qquad\qquad\qquad\qquad\qquad\qquad\quad 2x + y = 11$

Number the equations. $\qquad\qquad\qquad\qquad$ (1) $5x + y = 20$
$\qquad\qquad\qquad\qquad\qquad\qquad\qquad\qquad$ (2) $\underline{2x + y = 11}$

Subtract to get rid of y. $\qquad\qquad\qquad\qquad\quad 3x \qquad = 9$
This finds x. $\qquad\qquad\qquad\qquad\qquad\qquad\qquad\qquad\quad x = 3$

Use equation (1) to find y. $\qquad$ Put $x = 3$ in equation (1)
$\qquad\qquad\qquad\qquad\qquad\qquad\qquad 5 \times 3 + y = 20$
$\qquad\qquad\qquad\qquad\qquad\qquad\qquad\quad 15 + y = 20$
$\qquad\qquad\qquad\qquad\qquad\qquad\qquad\qquad\qquad y = 5$
$\qquad\qquad\qquad\qquad$ The answer is $x = 3, y = 5$

Use equation (2) to check your answer.
$\qquad 2x + y = 2 \times 3 + 5 = 6 + 5 = 11$ ✓

2 Solve this pair of simultaneous equations. $\qquad 3x + 2y = 19$
$\qquad\qquad\qquad\qquad\qquad\qquad\qquad\qquad\qquad\qquad\qquad x - 2y = 1$

Number the equations. $\qquad\qquad\qquad\qquad$ (1) $3x + 3y = 19$
$\qquad\qquad\qquad\qquad\qquad\qquad\qquad\qquad$ (2) $\underline{\ x - 3y = 1}$

Add to get rid of y. $\qquad\qquad\qquad\qquad\qquad 4x \qquad = 20$
This finds x. $\qquad\qquad\qquad\qquad\qquad\qquad\qquad\qquad\quad x = 5$

Use equation (1) to find y. $\qquad$ Put $x = 5$ in equation (1)
$\qquad\qquad\qquad\qquad\qquad\qquad\qquad 3 \times 5 + 3y = 19$
$\qquad\qquad\qquad\qquad\qquad\qquad\qquad\quad 15 + 3y = 19$
$\qquad\qquad\qquad\qquad\qquad\qquad\qquad\qquad\quad 3y = 4$
$\qquad\qquad\qquad\qquad\qquad\qquad\qquad\qquad\qquad y = \tfrac{4}{3}$
$\qquad\qquad\qquad\qquad$ The answer is $x = 5, y = \tfrac{4}{3}$

Use equation (2) to check your answer.
$\qquad x - 3y = 5 - 3 \times \tfrac{4}{3} = 5 - 4 = 1$ ✓

Exercise 11:18

Solve these pairs of simultaneous equations.
You need to decide whether to add or subtract the equations.

1 $2x + y = 13$
   $3x - y = 12$

4 $3x + 2y = 12$
   $x + 2y = 2$

2 $4x + 2y = 6$
   $x - 2y = 9$

5 $4x + 2y = 13$
   $3x - 2y = 4\frac{1}{2}$

3 $6x + 3y = 21$
   $2x + 3y = 11$

6 $5x + 3y = 9$
   $4x - 3y = -3\frac{3}{5}$

You sometimes have to multiply one or both of the equations before adding or subtracting.

Examples **1** Solve this pair of simultaneous equations. $2x + 3y = 13$
                                 $4x - y = 5$

Number the equations.   (1) $2x + 3y = 13$
                (2) $4x - y = 5$

You need to multiply (2) by **3**
so that you have $3y$ in   (1) $2x + 3y = 13$
each equation.   (2) × **3** $\underline{12x - 3y = 15}$

Add to get rid of y. $14x\qquad = 28$
This finds x. $x = 2$

Use equation (1) to find y.   Put $x = 2$ in equation (1)
                    $2 \times 2 + 3y = 13$
                    $4 + 3y = 13$
                    $3y = 9$
                    $y = 3$
          The answer is $x = 2$, $y = 3$

Use equation (2) to check your answer.
   $4x - y = 4 \times 2 - 3 = 8 - 3 = 5$ ✓

2 Solve this pair of simultaneous equations. $3x + 5y = 30$
$2x + 3y = 19$

Number the equations. (1) $3x + 5y = 30$
(2) $2x + 3y = 19$

Multiply (1) by 2. (1) $\times 2$ $6x + 10y = 60$
Multiply (2) by 3. (2) $\times 3$ $6x + 9y = 57$

Now subtract to get rid of x. $y = 3$

Use equation (1) to find x. Put $y = 3$ in equation (1)
$3x + 15 = 30$
$3x = 15$
$x = 5$
The answer is $x = 5$, $y = 3$

Use equation (2) to check your answer.
$2x + 3y = 2 \times 5 + 3 \times 3 = 10 + 9 = 19$ ✓

Exercise 11:19

Solve these pairs of simultaneous equations.
You will need to multiply one or both of the equations.

1 $3x + 2y = 18$
$x + y = 7$

4 $4x - 2y = 7$
$3x + y = 11\frac{1}{2}$

2 $7x - 3y = 48$
$2x + y = 10$

5 $5x + 3y = 17$
$2x + 5y = 12\frac{1}{2}$

3 $3x + 4y = 41$
$4x - 5y = 3$

6 $x + 4y = -9$
$5x - 2y = -1$

7 Sam throws a ball into the air.
The height of the ball above the ground, s, after a time of t seconds is given by the formula $s = at + bt^2$.
When $t = 2$, $s = 20$ and when $t = 3$, $s = 15$.
Find a and b using simultaneous equations.

You sometimes have to rearrange the equations before you can start to solve them. You can also get some that give really horrible answers!

Example   Solve this pair of simultaneous equations. $2x = 3 - 4y$
$4x - y + 5 = 0$

Rearrange them so that they look like they usually do.
You want the xs and the ys on the same side.   (1) $2x + 4y = 3$
Now you can number these equations.   (2) $4x - y = -5$

Now multiply (1) by 2.   (1) × 2 $4x + 8y = 6$
(2) $4x - y = -5$

Subtract to get rid of x. $9y = 11$
$y = \frac{11}{9}$

Use equation (1) to find y.   Put $y = \frac{11}{9}$ in equation (1)
$2x + 4 \times \frac{11}{9} = 3$
$2x + \frac{44}{9} = 3$
$2x = 3 - \frac{44}{9}$
$2x = -\frac{17}{9}$
$x = -\frac{17}{18}$
The answer is $x = -\frac{17}{18}, y = \frac{11}{9}$

Use equation (2) to check your answer.
$4x - y = (4 \times -\frac{17}{18}) - \frac{11}{9} = -\frac{68}{18} - \frac{11}{9} = -\frac{68}{18} - \frac{22}{18} = -\frac{90}{18} = -5$ ✓

Exercise 11:20

Solve these pairs of simultaneous equations.

1 $y = 8 - 2x$
$x + y + 7 = 0$

2 $7x + 3y - 17 = 0$
$2x = y + 16$

3 $3x - 2y = 9$
$0 = 1 + y - 4x$

4 $4x + 2y - 6 = 0$
$3x - y + 17 = 0$

5 $3y = 18 - 5x$
$2x - y + 10 = 0$

6 $3x = 2y + 14$
$0 = 5x + 2y - 24$

1 Make the **red** letter the subject in each of these formulas.

a $p - 5 = q$

b $3m + 4 = n$

c $pq - r = s$

d $u(v + w) = x$

e $u(v + w) = x$

f $g = k - fh$

2 Make the **red** letter the subject in each of these formulas.

a $r = \dfrac{p}{q}$

b $h = \dfrac{j + m}{n}$

c $t = \dfrac{u}{r} + v$

d $w = \dfrac{x}{y}$

e $y = \sqrt{x - 3w}$

f $g = \sqrt{ax + b}$

3 Make the **red** letter the subject of these formulas.

a $k = \dfrac{3 + k}{7}$

b $y = \dfrac{4f + 7r}{f}$

c $t = \dfrac{5z - 3t}{y}$

d $g = \dfrac{4k + 6j}{6k}$

e $\dfrac{r}{4} = \dfrac{f + e}{3e}$

f $2d = \dfrac{5h - 2j}{5h}$

4 Find a formula for the nth term of each of these number sequences.
a 7, 10, 13, 16, 19, ...
b 1, 7, 13, 19, 25, ...
c $-1, 7, 15, 23, 31, ...$
d $-7, -3, 1, 5, 9, ...$

5 The formula for the nth term of a sequence is $3n + 15$.
Which term has the value:
a 45
b 39
c 93

6 Find a formula for the nth term of each of these sequences.
a 2, 9, 18, 29, 42, ...
b 6, 17, 32, 51, 74, ...
c 2, 3, 6, 11, 18, ...
d 3, 5, 11, 21, 35, ...

7 The formula for the nth term of a sequence is $3n^2 + n - 5$.
a Find the first four terms.
b Find the 15th term.
c Use trial and improvement to find which term has the value 2049.

8 Write down the gradient of each of these lines.

   a $c = 4d$ **b** $y = 3x$ **c** $d = -2t$

9 Write down the formula for each of these lines.

   a 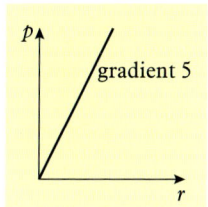   **b** 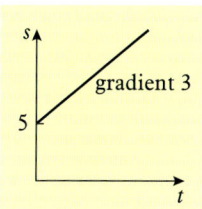   **c**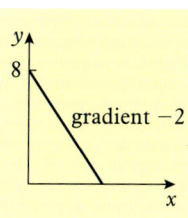

10 Where will these lines cross the **y** axis?

   a $y = 5x + 7$ **b** $y = 2x - 4$ **c** $y = 6x$

11 Which two of these lines are parallel?

   $y = 4x + 1$ $y = 3x - 4$ $y = 3x + 4$ $y = x - 4$

12 Find the gradient of each of these lines.

   a   **b**   **c**

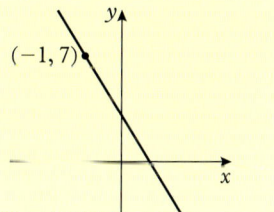 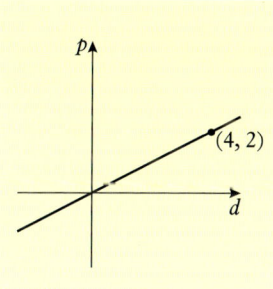 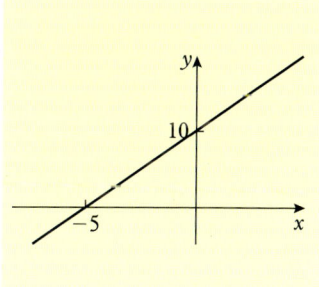

13 Find the gradient of the line passing through the points:

   a $(2, 1)$ and $(4, 7)$ **b** $(-2, 4)$ and $(3, -6)$

14 **a** Find the gradient of the line shown.

       b Write the equation of the line in the
           form $y = mx + c$.

       c Use your equation to find the value of
           y when $x = 25$.

       d What value of x gives a y value of 15?

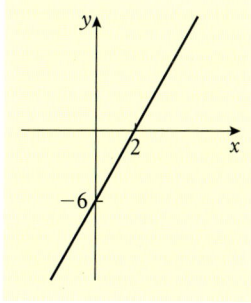

15 The table shows the co-ordinates of some points on a line.
The line has equation $y = mx + c$.
  a Plot the points and join them up with a straight line.
  b Use your graph to find the values of m and c.
  c Use the equation of the line to find the value of y when $x = -20$.

x	1	3	5
y	-5	-9	-13

16 John is trying to find the value of m in the equation $F = ma$.
He knows these values of F and a.
Find the value of m.

a	2	4	6
F	26	52	78

17 The graph shows the time, T, taken to cook a turkey.
The formula is $T = mw + c$ where w is the weight in pounds.
  a Find the value of m.
     What does this value tell you?
  b Write down the value of c.
     Explain what c is.

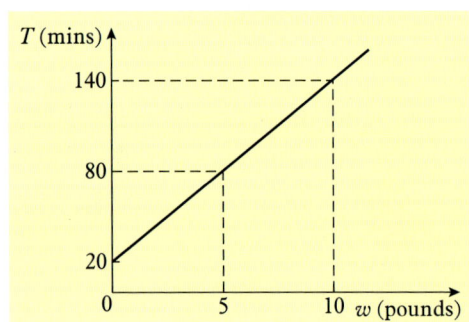

18 Solve these pairs of simultaneous equations.
  a $3x + 4y = 16$
     $3x + 6y = 21$
  b $3x - 3y = 8\frac{1}{4}$
     $4x + y = 22\frac{1}{4}$
  c $3x - 4y = 14$
     $5x + 3y = -54$
  d $x - 4y - 26 = 0$
     $2y = 8 - 3x$

19 Solve these equations.
  a $\dfrac{x}{3} = 6$
  b $\dfrac{x}{4} = -7$
  c $\dfrac{x}{2} + 3 = 14$
  d $\dfrac{x}{4} + 3 = 10$
  e $\dfrac{y}{5} - 4 = 8$
  f $\dfrac{y}{6} - 6 = 12$

20 Solve these equations.

  a $4x + 4 = 13 + x$

  b $6 - x = 14 - 3x$

  c $2x + 1 = 7 - 4x$

  d $1 + 4x = 25 - 2x$

  e $17 - 3x = 11 - x$

  f $5 + 2x = 8 - 4x$

21 Solve these equations.

  a $\dfrac{3x}{4} + 2 = 14$

  b $\dfrac{2x}{3} + 4 = 16$

  c $\dfrac{x}{2} + 3 = \dfrac{x}{4} + 12$

  d $\dfrac{x}{4} + 1 = \dfrac{x}{3} - 3$

22 Solve these equations.

  a $2(2x + 3) = 18$

  b $3(3x - 4) = 15$

  c $4(3x - 7) = 32$

  d $3(3x - 4x) = -15$

23 Write down the equation of the **red** line.

a

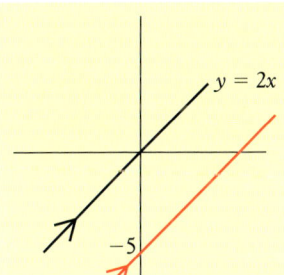

$y = 2x$

-5

b

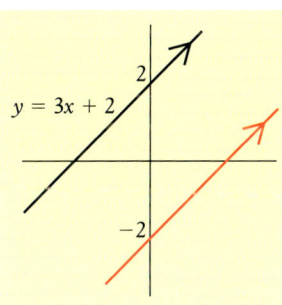

$y = 3x + 2$

2

-2

c

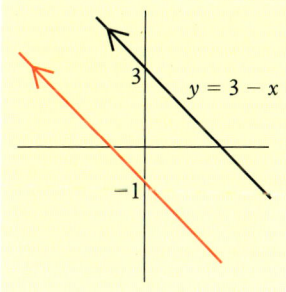

3

$y = 3 - x$

-1

24 Write down the gradient of a line that is perpendicular to each of these lines:

  a $y = 3x + 4$

  b $y = 5x - 7$

  c $y = 4 - 7x$

  d $y = \frac{1}{2}x - 7$

  e $y = -\frac{1}{2}x - \frac{1}{4}$

  f $y = 6 - 5x$

25 For each of these pairs of points:

  (1) Draw the line that passes through these points.

  (2) Work out the gradient of the line.

  (3) Write down the equation of the line.

  (4) Write down the equation of a perpendicular line.

  a $(0, 2)$ and $(2, 12)$ **b** $(0, 4)$ and $(6, 7)$ **c** $(-1, 5)$ and $(4, -5)$

1 The formula for a sequence is $-n^2 + n + 10$.
  a Find the first six terms.
  b Find the 20th term.
  c Use trial and improvement to find which term has the value -920.

2 **a** Write down the nth term of the sequence 3, 5, 7, 9, ...
  b Write down the mth term of the sequence 3, 5, 7, 9, ...
  c Use your answers to parts **a** and **b** to show algebraically that the product of any two terms of this sequence is also a term of the sequence.

3 Two variables x and y follow a relationship of the form $y^2 = ax^3 + b$.
  Here are two pairs of values of x and y.

x	2	4
y	5.9	16.1

  a Copy this table. Fill it in.

x	2	4
x^3		
y	5.9	16.1
y^2		

  b Copy these axes. They show y^2 plotted against x^3.
  c Plot the values for y^2 and x^3 that you have found in your table.
  d Join the points together with a straight line.
  e Find the values of a and b in the equation $y^2 = ax^3 + b$.

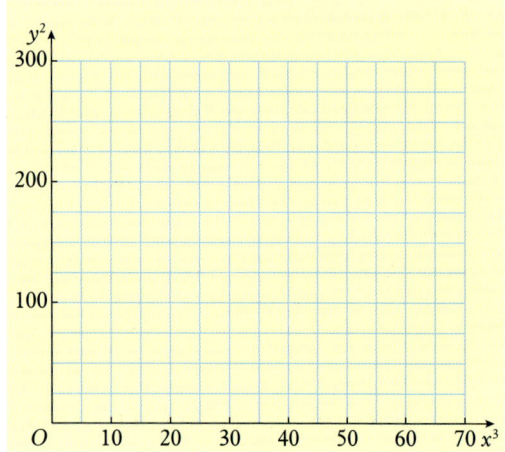

4 A snack bar sells burgers and sandwiches.
  John buys 3 burgers and 2 sandwiches and pays £4.05
  Muriel buys 2 burgers and 3 sandwiches and pays £4.20
  Find the cost of a burger and the cost of a sandwich.
  You must use simultaneous equations.

1 Make the **red** letter the subject of each of these formulas.

   a $t = \dfrac{3r + 4}{x}$ **d** $r = \dfrac{3t + 1}{t}$

   b $y = tx^2 + c$ **e** $3x + y = \dfrac{x}{t}$

   c $A = \pi r^2 h$ **f** $A = 2\pi rh + 2\pi r^2$

2 Find the formula for the nth term of this sequence.

   7, 12, 17, 22, …

3 These are the formulas for the nth term of two sequences.
Find the 20th term of each sequence.

   a $6n + 3$ **b** $\frac{1}{2}n - 7$

4 Find the formulas for the nth term of this sequence.

   4, 10, 18, 28, …

5 The formula for the nth term of a sequence is $2n^2 + 3n + 5$.
   a Find the first three terms of the sequence.
   b Find the number of the term that has value 95.

6 Write down the gradient of each of these lines

   a $y = 3x + 5$ **b** $y = \frac{1}{2}x - 4$ **c** $y = 2 - x$

7 Work out the gradient of each of these lines.

   a

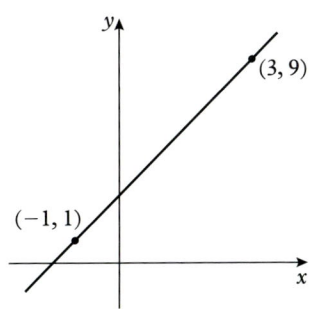

   b

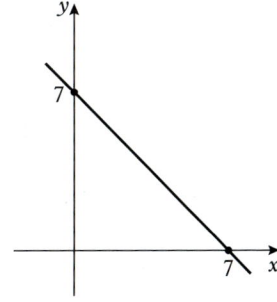

8 The table shows the co-ordinates of some points on a line.
The line has equation $y = mx + c$.

x	1	2	3
y	2	5	8

   a Plot the points and join them to form a straight line.
   b Use your graph to find the values of m and c.
   c Write down the gradient of a line that is perpendicular to this line.
   d Write down the equation of a line that is parallel to this line.

9 Solve these equations.
Give your answers as fractions where necessary.
   a $2x - 7 = 15$ **c** $4(6 - x) = 10$
   b $3x + 5 = 7x - 7$ **d** $10(3x - 2) = 5(2 - x)$

10 Solve each pair of simultaneous equations.
   a $4x + 2y = 6$ **b** $3x + 2y = 12$ **c** $y = 6 - 3x$
       $x - 2y = 4$ $x - y = -1$ $x + 2y = -13$

11 This graph shows the time taken to cook a chicken.
The formula is $T = mW + c$ where T is the time taken in minutes and W is the weight in pounds.

   a Find the values of m and c.
   b What does the value m tell you?
   c What does the value c tell you?

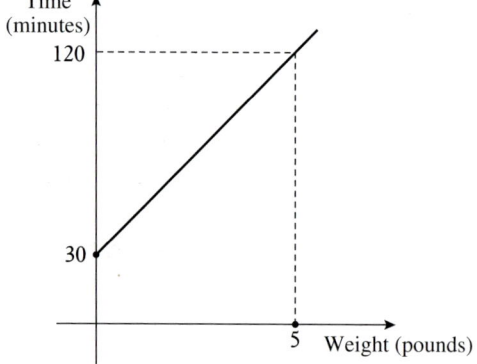

12 The equation of a line is $y = mx + c$.
The line is perpendicular to the line $y = 2x + 3$.
The line goes through the point $(0, 1)$.
Find the equation of the line.

12 Right-angled triangles

1 Pythagoras' theorem
Finding the hypotenuse
Finding Pythagorean Triples
Finding one of the shorter sides
Distance between two points

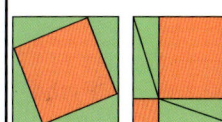

2 Finding an angle
Defining sine, cosine and tangent
Finding angles in basic triangles
Finding angles in worded problems
Finding sine, cosine and tangent for special angles

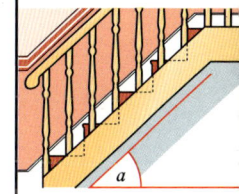

CORE

3 Finding a side
Finding sides in basic triangles
Doing problems involving components
Playing a game: 'Cop a load of this!'
Finding the hypotenuse

QUESTIONS

EXTENSION

TEST YOURSELF

1 Pythagoras' theorem

 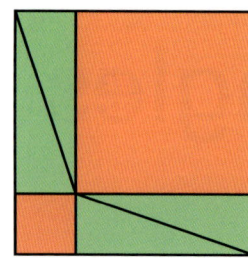

This picture shows you one of the many proofs of Pythagoras' theorem.

Can you see how it works?

| Pythagoras' theorem | **Pythagoras' theorem** says that in any right-angled triangle, the area of the square on the hypotenuse is equal to the sum of the areas of the squares on the other two sides. |

In this right-angled triangle, Pythagoras' theorem tells you that:

$$c^2 = a^2 + b^2$$

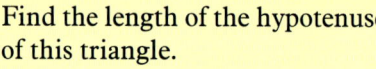

Although Pythagoras' theorem talks about areas, it is usually used to find the length of a side.

Example

Find the length of the hypotenuse of this triangle.

Using Pythagoras' theorem:

$$h^2 = 8^2 + 13^2$$
$$= 64 + 169$$
$$= 233$$

Now square root:

$$h = \sqrt{233}$$
$$h = 15.3 \text{ cm to 1 dp.}$$

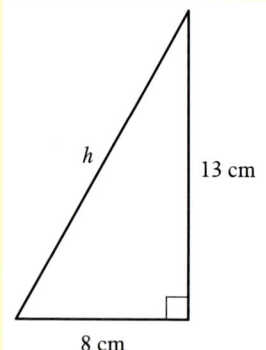

Always check that the hypotenuse is the longest side in the triangle.

If the answer that you get for the hypotenuse is smaller than one of the other sides you must have done something wrong!

Exercise 12:1

1 Find the length of the hypotenuse in each of these triangles.
Give your answers to 1 dp.

a

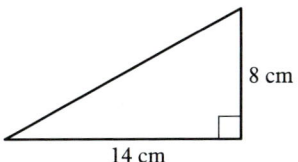

8 cm

14 cm

d

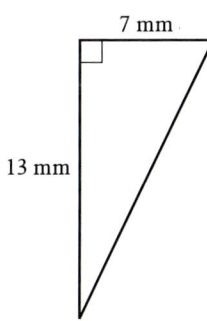

7 mm

13 mm

b

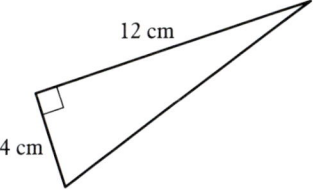

12 cm

4 cm

e

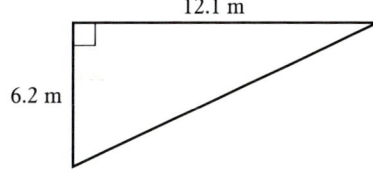

12.1 m

6.2 m

c

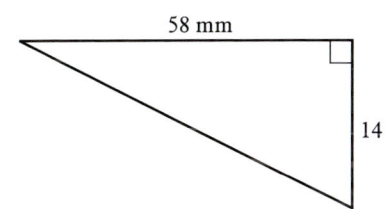

58 mm

14 mm

f

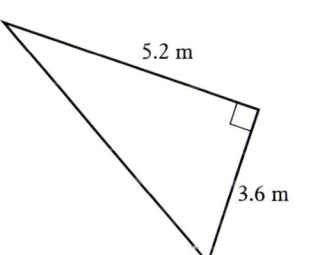

5.2 m

3.6 m

2 a Find the hypotenuse in each of these triangles.

(1)

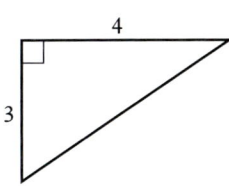

4

3

(3)

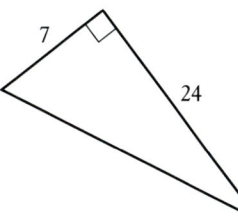

7

24

(2)

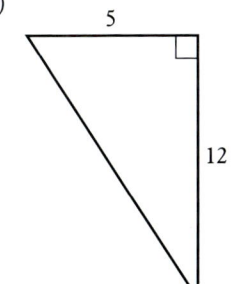

5

12

(4)

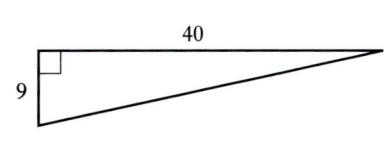

40

9

b Copy this table. Fill in the last column using your results from part **a**.

Triangle	Lengths of sides		Hypotenuse
1	3	4	
2	5	12	
3	7	24	
5	9	40	

The sides in the triangles in question **2** are all whole numbers.

Pythagorean Triple

When three whole numbers work in Pythagoras' theorem, the set of three numbers is called a **Pythagorean Triple**.

3 4 5 is a Pythagorean Triple because $3^2 + 4^2 = 5^2$

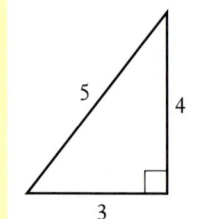

3 a Find the hypotenuse in each of these triangles.

(1)
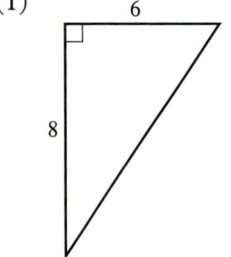

(3)
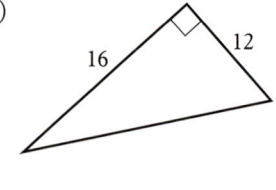

(2)
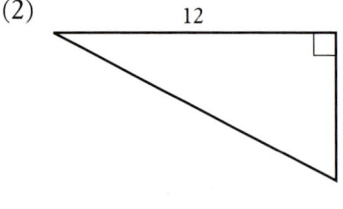

(4)
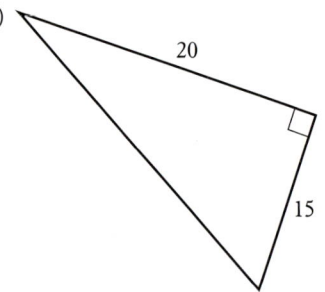

b All of the Pythagorean Triples in part **a** are based on one Pythagorean Triple. Explain how.

c Start with the Pythagorean Triple 5 12 13.
Write down four more Pythagorean Triples that are based on this one.

d Can you find a new Pythagorean Triple that is not based on any you have seen so far? Try 8 for the smallest side.

4 Jill takes a short cut across this field to get home.
She walks along the diagonal of the field.
  a How far does she walk?
  • **b** Jill walks at 4 km per hour.
    How much time does she save by taking this short cut?
    Give your answer in seconds.

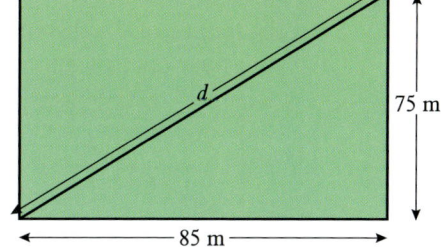

5 Farmer George is very proud of his square fields.
Every day he walks from his house along the diagonal of each field to get to his barn.
How far does he walk to get to his barn?

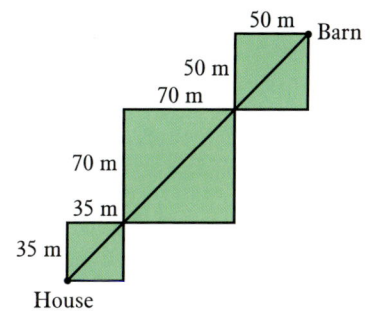

Finding one of the shorter sides

When you want to find one of the short sides, start by writing Pythagoras' theorem in the usual order.
$$\text{hypotenuse}^2 = {\dots}^2 + {\dots}^2$$

Then rearrange the equation to find the missing side.

Example

Find the length of side a in this triangle.

Using Pythagoras' theorem:
$$23^2 = 18^2 + a^2$$
$$23^2 - 18^2 = a^2$$
$$529 - 324 = a^2$$

So
$$a^2 = 205$$

Now square root:
$$a = \sqrt{205}$$
$$a = 14.3 \text{ cm to 1 dp}$$

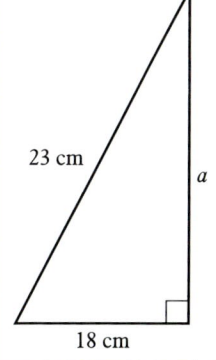

Check that the hypotenuse is the longest side. If the answer that you get for one of the shorter sides is bigger than the hypotenuse you must have done something wrong!

Exercise 12:2

1 Find the length of the missing side in each of these triangles.
Give your answers to 1 dp.

a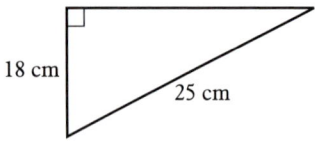

d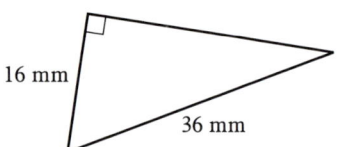

b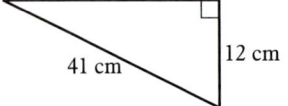

e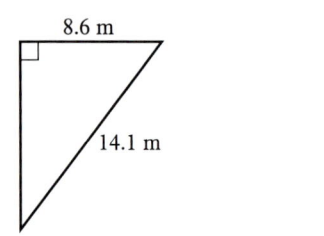

c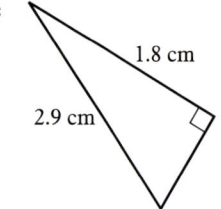

f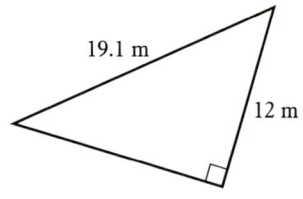

2 A mast is held in position by two wires.
Both wires are 20 m long.
The first is attached to the ground 14 m
from the base of the mast.
The second is attached to the ground 16 m
from the base of the mast.
How far is it between the two points where
the wires join the mast?

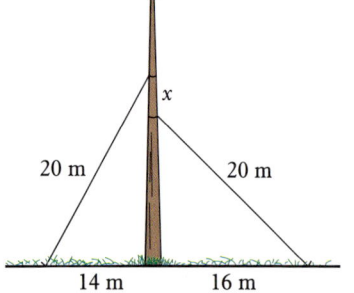

3 This is a cross section through the Great
Pyramid.
Each sloping side is about 180 m long.
The base of the pyramid is about 230 m.
How high is the pyramid?

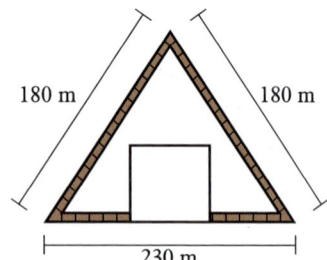

4   This is Katie's kite.
The wooden supports have cracked.
What length of wood does she
need to get to fix it?

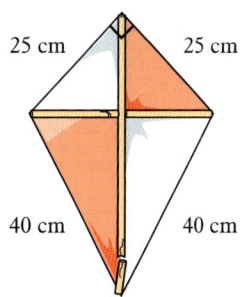

25 cm   25 cm

40 cm   40 cm

You can use Pythagoras' theorem to find the distance between two points.

Points A(**1**, **2**) and B(**6**, **5**) are marked on this diagram.
B is **6** – **1** = **5**cm to the right of A
B is **5** – **2** = **3**cm above A

You can use Pythagoras' theorem to find the
distance AB.

$$(AB)^2 = 5^2 + 3^2$$
$$= 25 + 9$$
$$= 34$$
$$AB = \sqrt{34} = 5.83 \text{ cm (2 dp)}$$

So the distance between A and B is 5.83 cm.

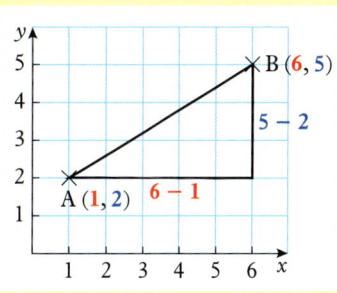

Exercise 12:3

1   Find the distance between each of the following
pairs of points. Give your answers to 2dp.
   a   A and B
   b   C and D
   c   E and F
   d   A and F

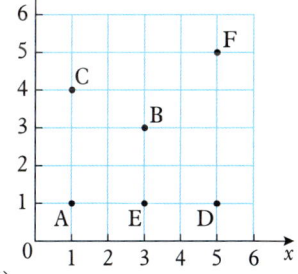

2   Find the distance between the points A(2, 3) and B(6, 6).

3   Three points are A(0, 1), B(3, 5) and C(6, 8)
Find the distances:
   a   AB   **b**   BC   **c**   AC

4   A triangle has vertices at points A(1, 2), B(4, 7) and C(5, 3)
Find the perimeter of the triangle.

● **5**   A triangle has vertices at points A(2, 3), B(6, 3) and C(x, y)
   a   Write down an expression for the length of the side AC.
   b   Write down an expression for the length of the side BC.
   c   If the lengths of AC and BC are equal, find the value of x.

How far is point C above point A?

One or more of the lengths might be given as a square root of a number.
This is because it is more exact than a rounded decimal.

In fact this makes it very easy to square.
Remember that when you square the square root of a number you get back to the original number!
This is because squaring and square rooting are inverses of each other.
So $\sqrt{8} \times \sqrt{8} = 8$

Example

Find the length of the hypotenuse of this triangle.

$$x^2 = (\sqrt{8})^2 + (\sqrt{6})^2$$
$$= 8 + 6$$
$$= 14$$

So $x = \sqrt{14}$ cm

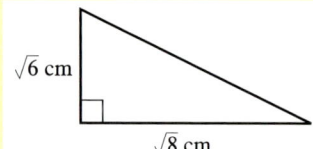

Exercise 12:4

1 Find the lengths of the sides marked with letters.
Give exact answers.

a 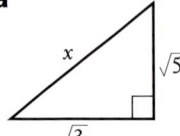   **b** 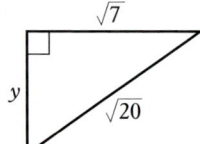   **c**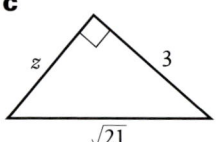

● **2 a** Find the area of the coloured equilateral triangles.
Leave your answers in surd form.
b Show that Pythagoras' theorem is still true for equilateral triangles.

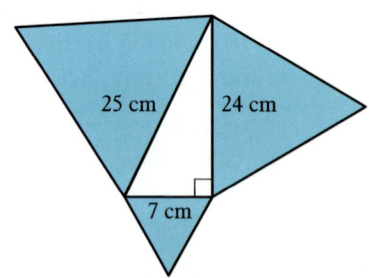

2 Finding an angle

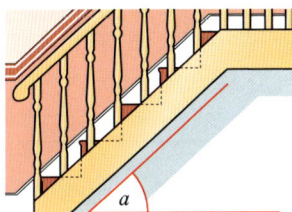

There is a legal limit on the value of angle *a* in houses. The maximum value is **42°**.

Stairs cannot be steeper than this.

You can use SOHCAHTOA to remember trigonometric formulas.

$$\text{Sin } a = \frac{\textbf{Opposite}}{\textbf{Hypotenuse}} \qquad \text{Cos } a = \frac{\textbf{Adjacent}}{\textbf{Hypotenuse}} \qquad \text{Tan } a = \frac{\textbf{Opposite}}{\textbf{Adjacent}}$$

To find the angle marked *a* in this triangle:

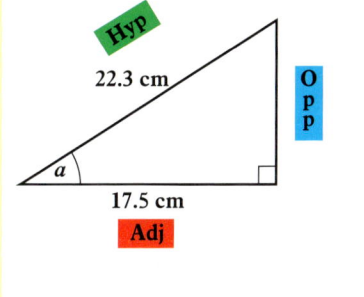

write out: **S O H C A H T O A**

Cross out the sides that you know.

S O H̸ **C A̸ H̸** **T O A̸**

The formula you need is where two sides are crossed out together.

$$\text{Cos } a = \frac{\text{Adjacent}}{\text{Hypotenuse}}$$

Substitute into the formula:

$$\text{Cos } a = \frac{17.5}{22.3}$$

Make sure that your calculator is working in degrees.

Key in:

 2nd F **cos** **(** **1** **7** **.** **5** **÷** **2** **2** **.** **3** **)** **=**

 SHIFT **cos** **(** **1** **7** **.** **5** **÷** **2** **2** **.** **3** **)** **=**

to get *a* = 38.3 ° (1 dp)

You can use the other two formulas in the same way.

Exercise 12:5

Find the angles marked with letters in each of these triangles.
Make sure that you always label the sides Hyp, Opp, Adj.
Round your answers to 1 dp.
Check that your answers seem reasonable.

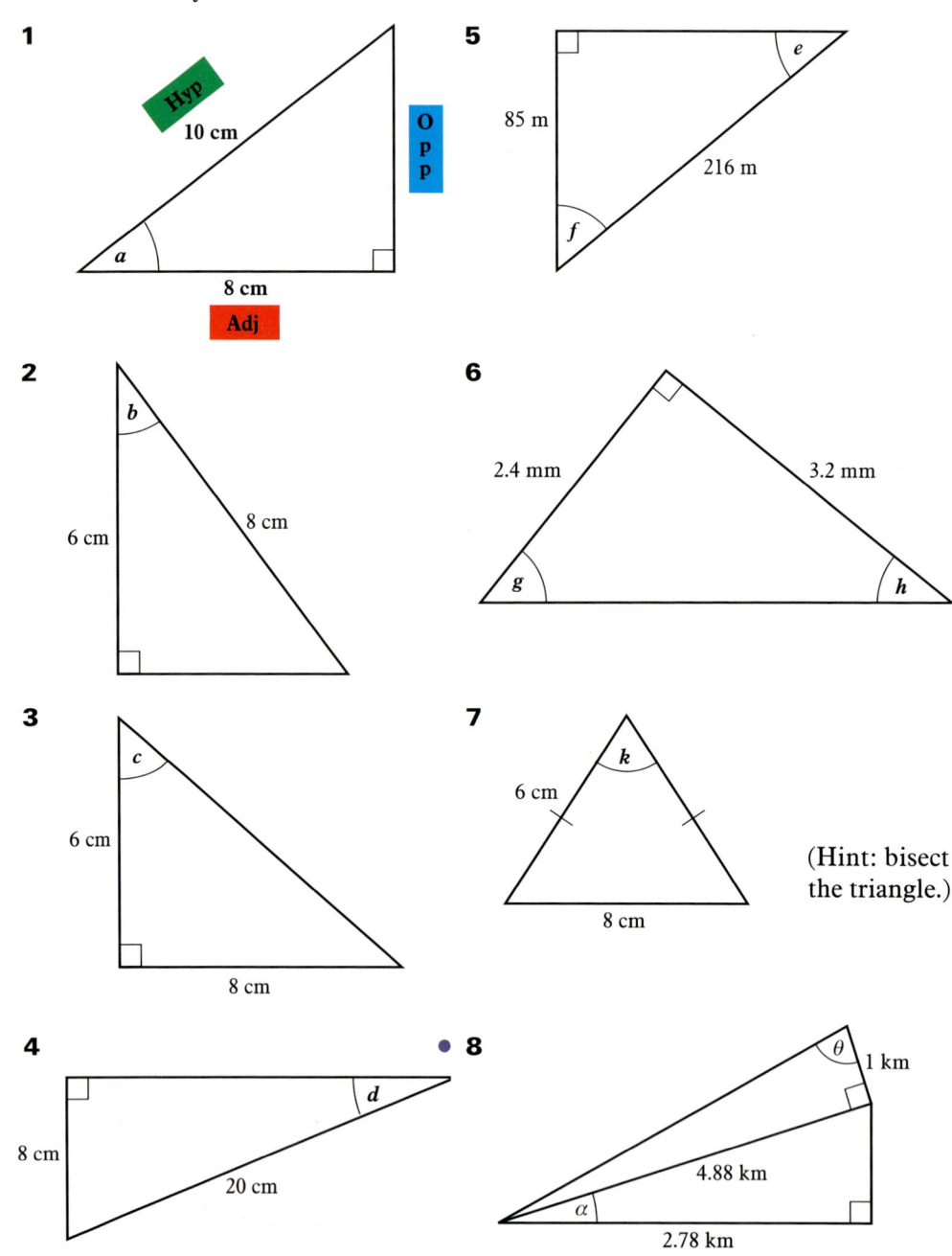

1

Hyp
10 cm

Opp

a

8 cm

Adj

2

b

6 cm

8 cm

3

c

6 cm

8 cm

4

8 cm

d

20 cm

5

85 m

e

216 m

f

6

2.4 mm

3.2 mm

g

h

7

k

6 cm

8 cm

(Hint: bisect
the triangle.)

8

θ

1 km

4.88 km

α

2.78 km

Exercise 12:6

In this exercise, round all your answers to 1 dp.

1 A flight of stairs rises 2.6 m. The horizontal distance under the stairs is 2.85 m.
  a What is the angle that the stairs make with the ground?
  b Is this angle legal ($\leqslant 42°$)?
  c How could it appear to be legal in a report?

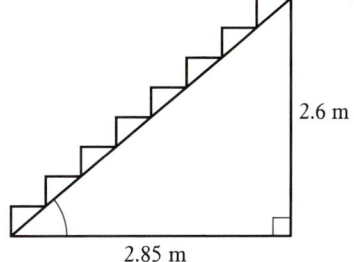

2.6 m

2.85 m

2 Mr Buss is a world famous motorcycle stuntman.
He jumps 19 coaches using this ramp.
What is his angle of take-off?

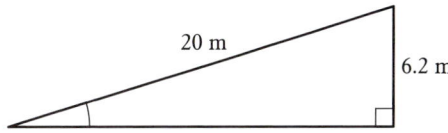

20 m

6.2 m

3 Claire Batin 'the human fly' is about to climb this overhang in the Pyrenees.
What angle does she need to climb out from the vertical?

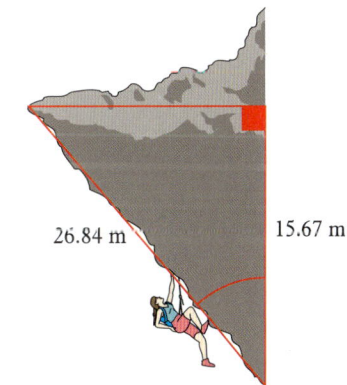

26.84 m

15.67 m

4 This is the descent slope of one of the world's tallest roller coasters.
What is the angle made with the ground?

50 m

28.4 m

5 The roundheads are coming!
They must be prevented
from entering the castle
by horse.
To ensure this, the drawbridge
must be raised 5 feet.
The drawbridge is 8 yards
long. What angle must it be
turned through?

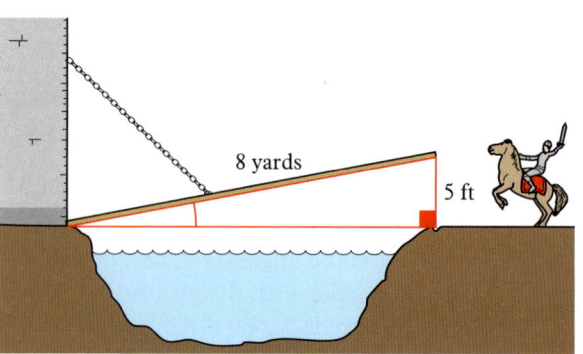

6 St Benedict's church spire is leaning
over.
The Reverend Ivor Leene needs to find
the angle of inclination to the vertical.
If it is more than 2°, he needs to take
urgent action. He calls you in to
measure the angle.
What do you advise him to do?

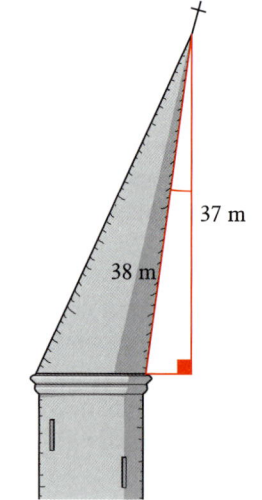

7 Madison Bridge has a roof.
The roof is not symmetrical.
Some special ironwork is needed
over the ridge.
a Find angles *p* and *q*.
b Use these to work out angle *r*.

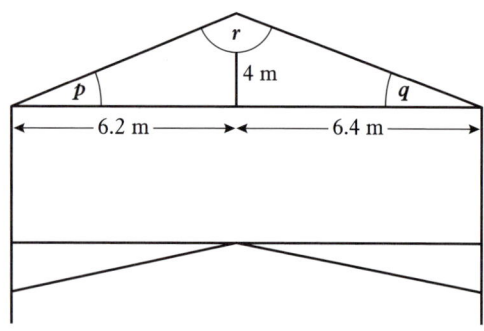

8 The picture shows the jib of a crane.
Using the information given, work out
the angle between the arms of the jib.

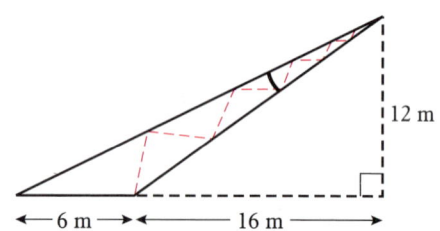

Using special angles

This is an equilateral triangle.
All the sides are 2 units long.
It is bisected to give a special triangle.
The lengths of this special triangle can be used to find sin 60°, cos 60° and tan 60° without using a calculator.

The opposite side is found using Pythagoras' theorem.

$$2^2 = 1^2 + (\text{opp})^2$$
$$2^2 - 1^2 = (\text{opp})^2$$
$$3 = (\text{opp})^2$$

So $\qquad \text{opp} = \sqrt{3}$

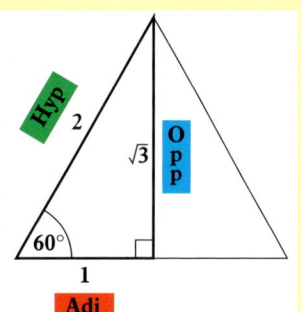

Using these sides gives:

$$\sin 60° = \frac{\sqrt{3}}{2} \qquad \cos 60° = \frac{1}{2} \qquad \tan 60° = \frac{\sqrt{3}}{1} = \sqrt{3}$$

Exercise 12:7

1 Use the special triangle above to find:
   a cos 30°
   b sin 30°
   c tan 60°

2 Draw this isosceles triangle.
   a Work out the hypotenuse using Pythagoras' theorem.
   Use this special triangle to find:
   b cos 45°
   c sin 45°
   d tan 45°

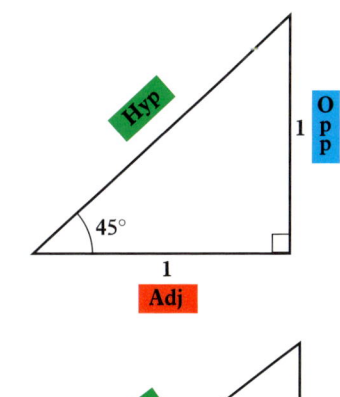

3 Draw this triangle.
   a Work out the hypotenuse using Pythagoras' theorem.
   Use this triangle to find, in their simplest form:
   b cos *a*
   c sin *a*
   d tan *a*

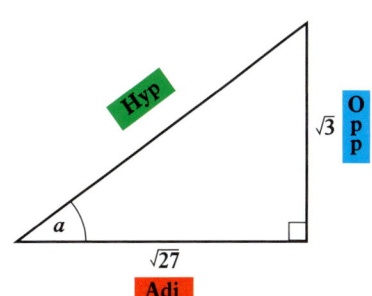

3 Finding a side

How could you find the width of the Grand Canyon without crossing it?

To find the side marked **a** in this triangle, write out:

SOHCAHTOA

Cross out the side that you know. Cross out the side that you need to find.

The formula you need is where two sides are crossed out together.

$$\text{Sin } 40° = \frac{\text{Opposite}}{\text{Hypotenuse}}$$

Substitute into the formula:

$$\text{Sin } 40° = \frac{a}{2} \qquad \text{So } 2 \times \sin 40° = a$$

Make sure that your calculator is working in degrees.

Key in:

 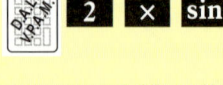

to get **a** = 1.29 m (3 sf).

You can use the other two formulas in the same way.

Exercise 12:8

Find the sides marked with letters in each of these triangles.
Make sure that you always label the sides Hyp, Opp, Adj.
Round your answers to 3 sf.
Check that your answers seem reasonable.

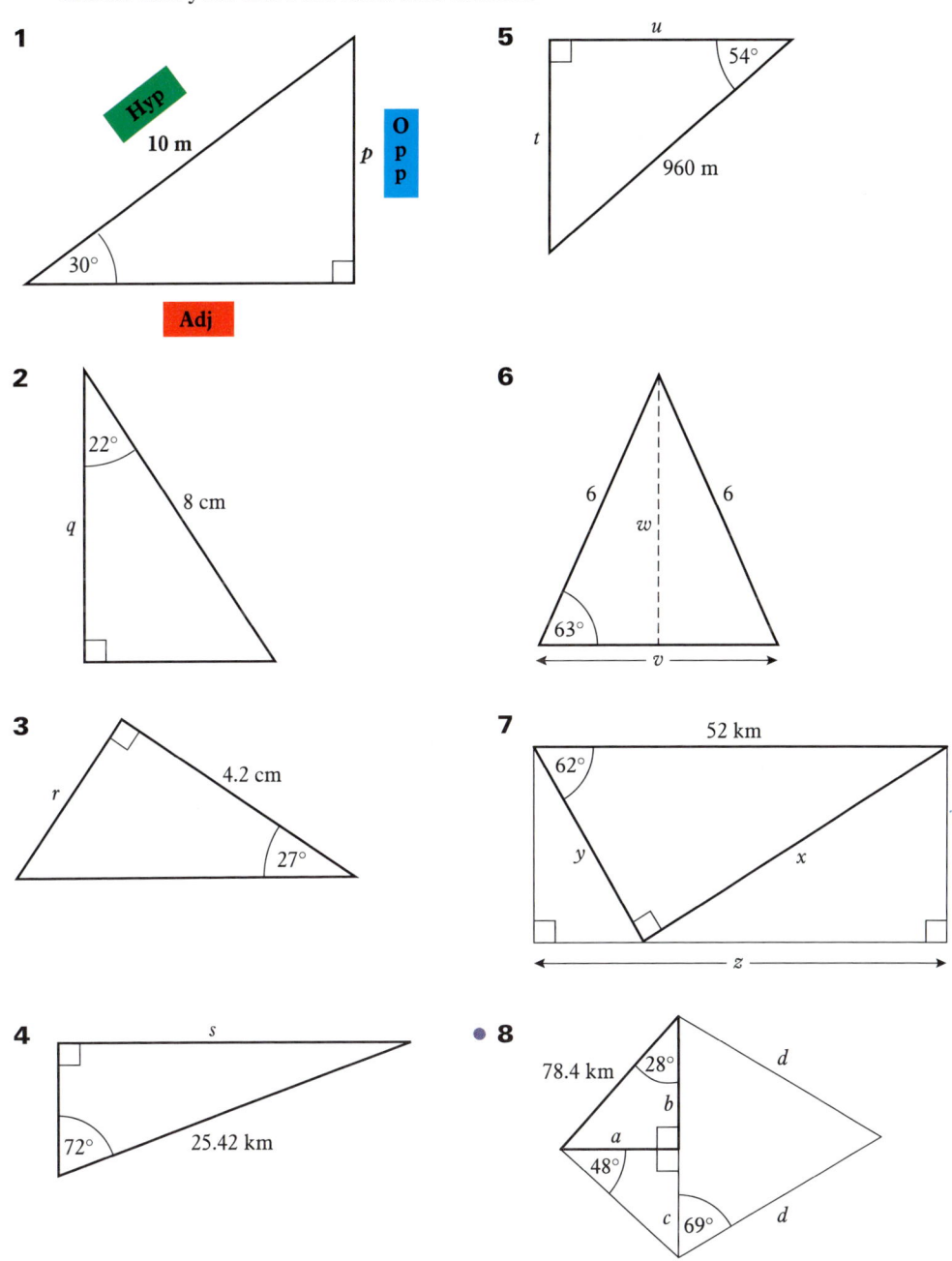

1

Hyp
10 m
p
O
p
p
30°
Adj

2

22°
8 cm
q

3

r
4.2 cm
27°

4

s
72°
25.42 km

5

u
54°
t
960 m

6

6
w
6
63°
v

7

52 km
62°
y
x
z

8

78.4 km
28°
b
a
48°
c
69°
d
d

Exercise 12:9

In this exercise, round all your answers to 3 sf.

1 Bamber is 27 metres from the base
of a tree. He measures the angle
shown to the top of the tree.
It is 42°.
Find the height of the tree.

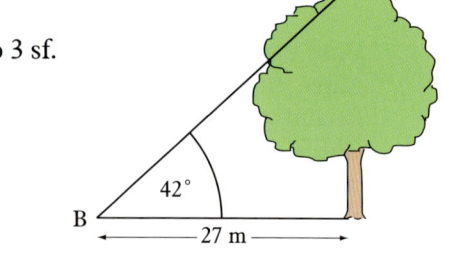

2 Sharon has climbed up the
Inaccessible Pinnacle in the
Cuillin Hills. She sees her
companion Jacqui further along
on the ridge. Another friend takes
this picture and measures the
angle shown. Jacqui is 120 m from
the base of the pinnacle.
Find the height of the pinnacle.

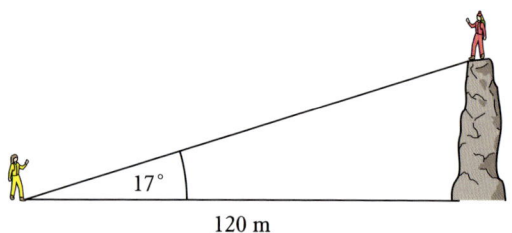

3 Rebecca is running down a cliff
path. If she runs along the path
marked in red, write down:
a how far she has descended
vertically
b how far to the left or right of
point A she is when she
reaches B.

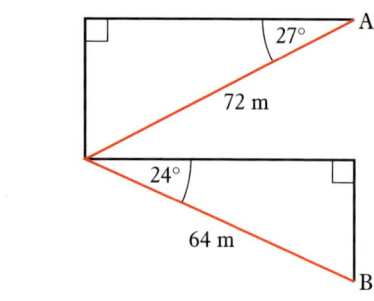

4 Steve has to drive his dumper up the track in a
quarry. The track is a collection of slopes shown
in red on the diagram. After a lot of excavation
Steve's boss asked him to work out the depth of
the quarry. This is Steve's diagram. He
measured the angles shown with a clinometer.
a What is the depth of the quarry?
b What is the width of the quarry used
for the tracks?

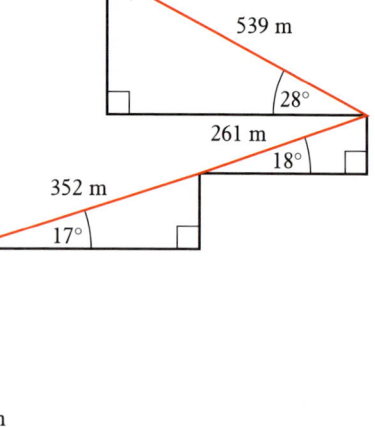

5 This is a section of the Grand Canyon.

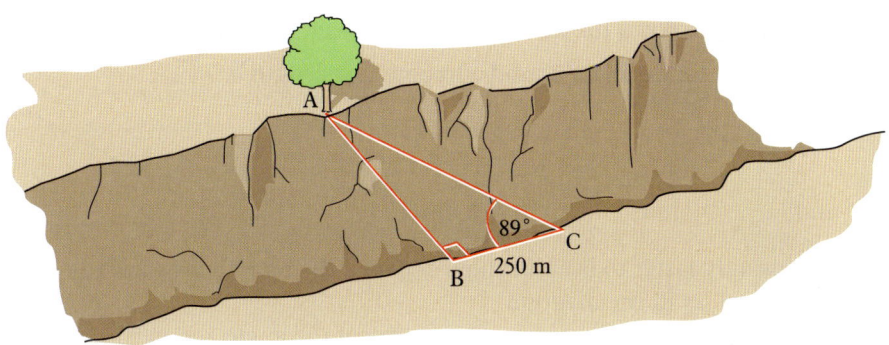

Lauren stands at B. This is the point directly opposite the tree at A.
She then walks 250 m to C. Lauren measures the angle BCA to be 89°.
Use Lauren's measurements to find the distance AB across the Grand
Canyon.

Using components to speed up calculations

Exercise 12:10

1 Fill in the table for the triangle on the right. What do you notice?

x	$\sin x$	$\cos x$	a	b
10				
30				
45				
60				

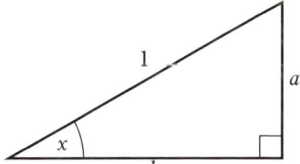

2 Fill in the table for the triangle on the right. What do you notice?

x	$\sin x$	$\cos x$	a	b
10				
30				
45				
60				

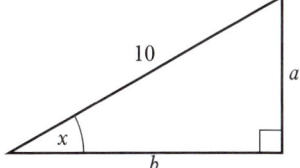

3 Write down what you think the results would be if the hypotenuse was:
   a 100   **b** 1000   **c** h

Here is a right-angled triangle where you know the hypotenuse and an angle.
You can write down the formula for the opposite and adjacent sides immediately.

In general, for an angle $x°$ and a hypotenuse length h:

$$\frac{a}{h} = \cos x \quad \text{so} \quad a = h \cos x$$

and $\quad \dfrac{b}{h} = \sin x \quad \text{so} \quad b = h \sin x$

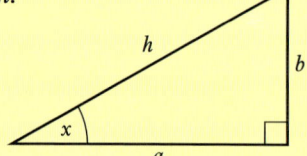

It is usually faster to use the angle between the hypotenuse and the horizontal, as in the diagram.
Then horizontal distances use the cosine of the angle and vertical distances use the sine of the angle.
These are the horizontal and the vertical components of the distance.

Distance 15 km, angle to the horizontal 20°.
The horizontal distance is 15 cos 20°.
The vertical distance is 15 sin 20°.

Distance 74 km, angle to the horizontal 27°.
The horizontal distance is 74 cos 27°.
The vertical distance is 74 sin 27°.

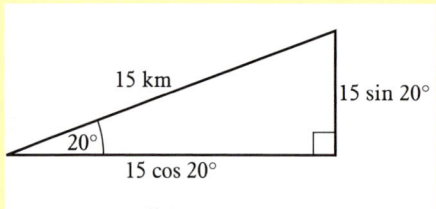

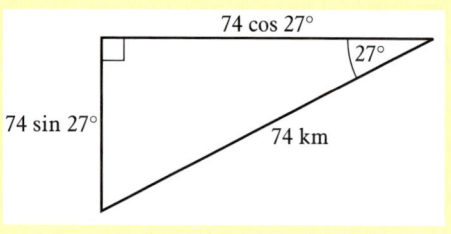

4 For each part find: (1) the horizontal component of the distance given
(2) the vertical component of the distance given

a

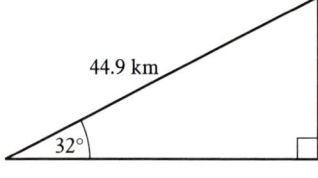

c

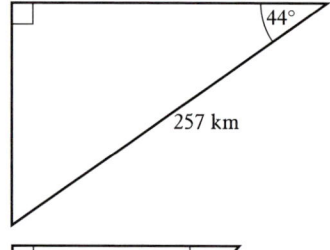

b

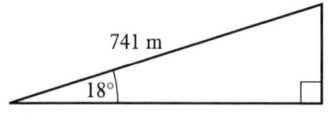

• **d**

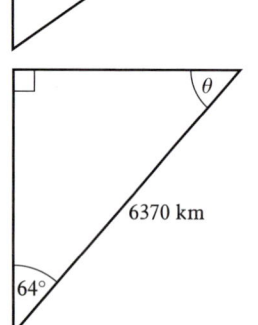

Game: Cop a load of this!

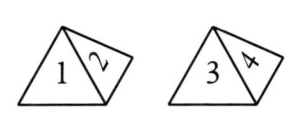

This is a game for two players. You need two tetrahedral dice.

One of you is a Bronx Cop and the other is a Criminal fleeing from justice. Both players roll the two dice. The numbers on the dice act like co-ordinates. The first player's score is the traffic island where the cop is. The second player's score is the traffic island where the criminal is.

The map overleaf shows a series of blocks. The distances given are diagonals for each block. You can only move along the dotted blue lines between the blue dots. All the distances from the traffic islands to the nearest block corners are 14 m. All roads are 20 m wide.

Each player then calculates (with **full working out**) the distance between the cop and the criminal. You will need to have a time limit of 4 minutes for each go.

Scoring
1 point for each completely correct line of working **before** the final answer.
2 points for a correct final answer.
A completely correct calculation by the cop scores a bonus point.
The player with the highest point score is the cop for the next turn.
The game is over when one player's total is 10 points more than the other.

Suppose you had to get from point A to point B in the game.

Record it like this, and give all distances to the nearest metre.

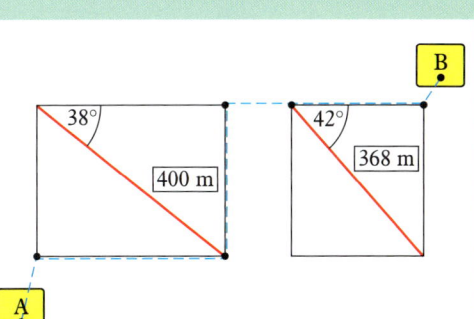

Cop's score sheet

Move	Full working	Distance	Pts
1	diagonal	14	1
2	horiz = 400 cos 38°	315	1
3	vert = 400 sin 38°	246	1
4	cross road	20	1
5	horiz = 368 cos 42°	273	1
6	diagonal	14	1
	Total	882	2
	Correct answer	bonus	1

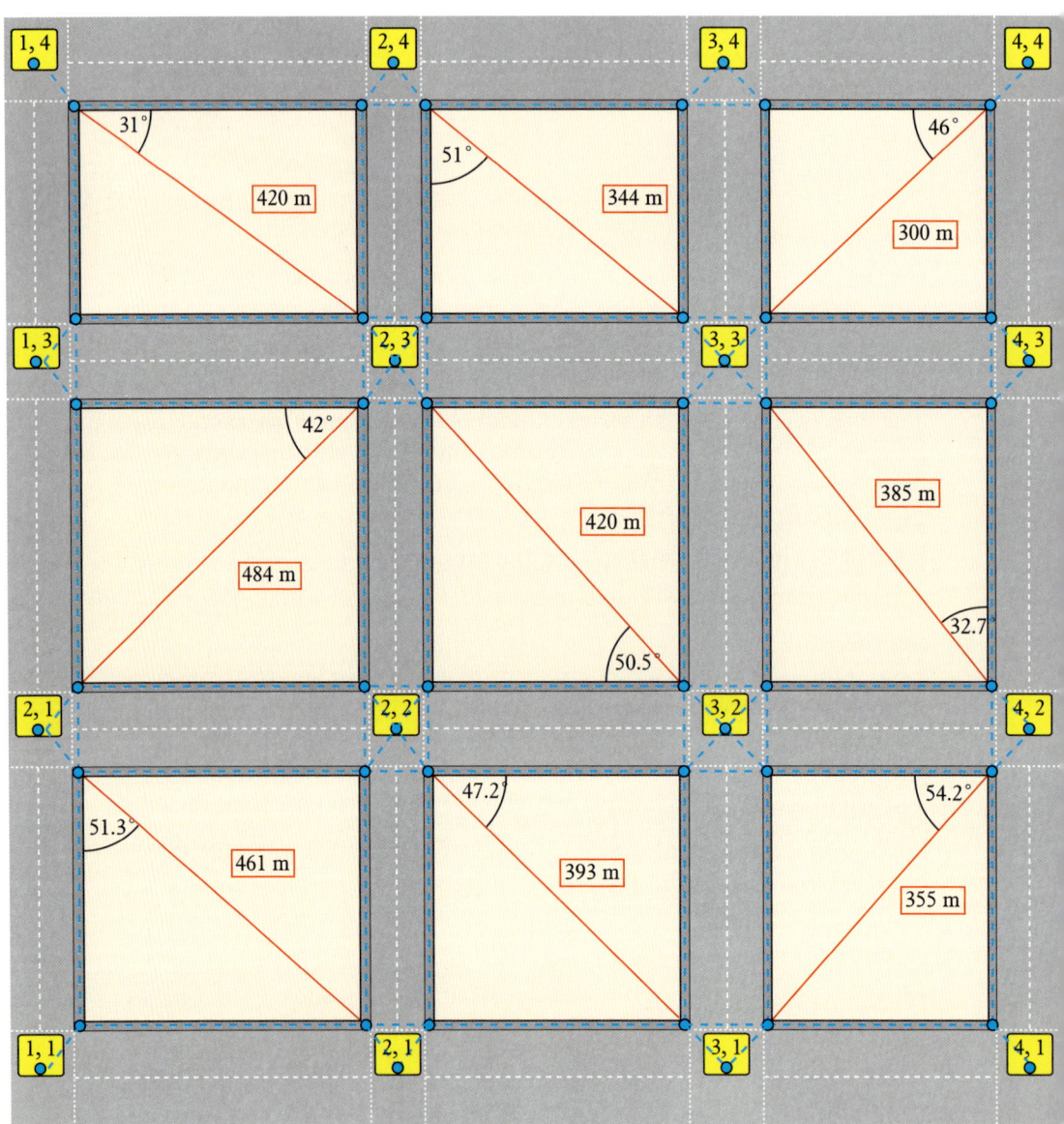

Finding the hypotenuse

Look at this triangle. Suppose you need to find the hypotenuse *a*.
You cannot use Pythagoras' theorem, because you only have one side.

To find the side marked *a* in this triangle, write out

SOHCAHTOA

Cross out the side that you know.
Cross out the hypotenuse because
you want to find it.

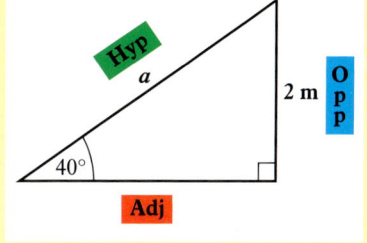

$$\boxed{\text{S}\cancel{\text{O}}\cancel{\text{H}}} \quad \boxed{\text{C A}\cancel{\text{H}}} \quad \boxed{\text{T}\cancel{\text{O}}\text{A}}$$

The formula you need is where two sides are crossed out together.

$$\sin 40° = \frac{\text{Opposite}}{\text{Hypotenuse}}$$

Substitute into the formula:

$$\sin 40° = \frac{2}{a}$$

You need to make *a* the subject of the formula.
Here it is a denominator, so multiply by *a* on both sides.

So $\qquad a \times \sin 40° = 2$

Now divide both sides by sin 40°

$$a = \frac{2}{\sin 40°}$$

Make sure that your calculator is working in degrees.

Key in:

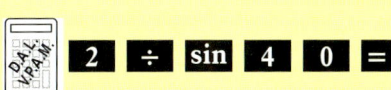

to get ***a*** = 3.11 m (3 sf)

You can use the other two formulas in the same way.

Exercise 12:11

Find the sides marked with letters in each of these triangles.
Round your answers to 3 sf.

1

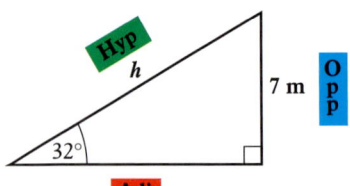

3

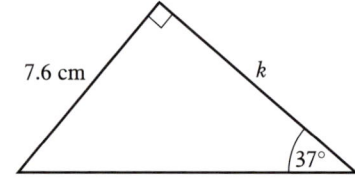

2

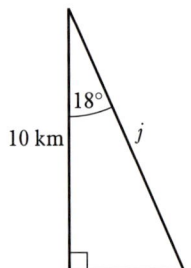

4

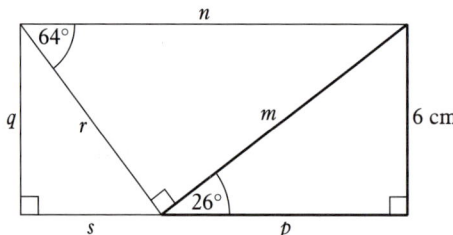

5 Forester Fred patrols three rectangular woods. Every day he walks along the diagonal of each wood, finishing at 'Old Harry Oak'. How far does he walk altogether?

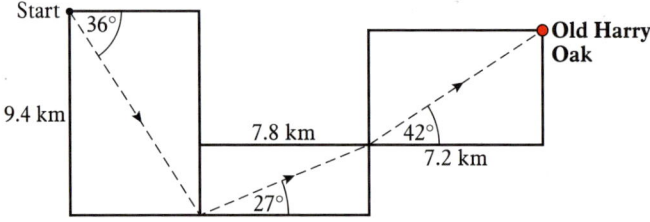

6 Pete is a pylon painter. One of the sections he has to paint looks like this.

Find the total length, $p + q + r + s$ of the girders that he paints.

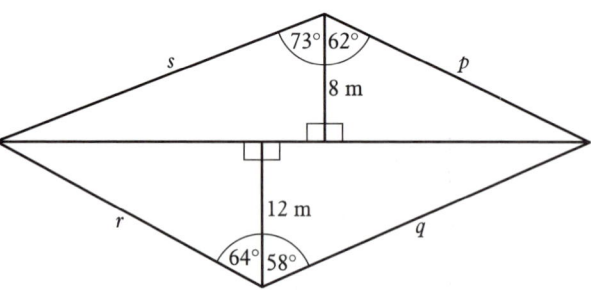

1 Find the length of the hypotenuse in each of these triangles.
Give your answers to part **a** to 1 dp.

a
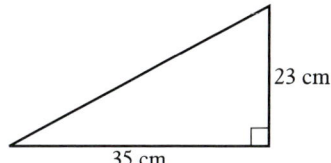
23 cm
35 cm

b
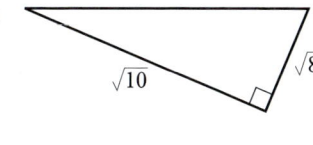
$\sqrt{10}$
$\sqrt{8}$

2 Find the length of the missing side in each of these triangles.
Give your answers to 1 dp.

a
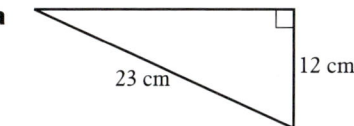
12 cm
23 cm

b
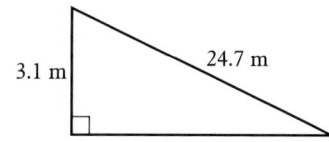
3.1 m
24.7 m

3 Find the height of an equilateral triangle of side 12 cm.

4 The diagram shows a chord of a circle.
The circle has radius 8 cm.
The chord is 13 cm long.
Find the distance from the
centre of the circle, O, to the chord.

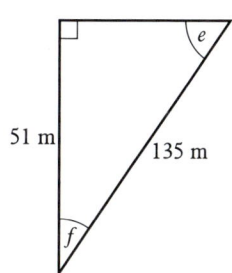

5 Find the labelled angles in these triangles.
Give your answers to the nearest degree.

a
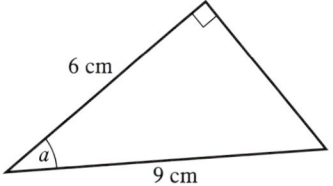
6 cm
a
9 cm

b
e
51 m
135 m
f

6 Find the missing sides in these triangles.
Give your answers to 3 sf.

a
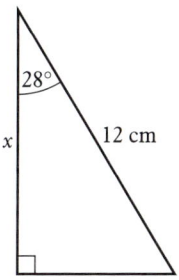
28°
x
12 cm

b
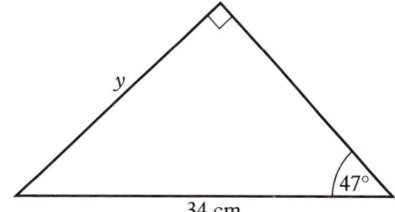
y
47°
34 cm

7 This diagram shows a chord in a sector of a circle.
The radius of the circle is 6 cm.
The length of the chord is 10 cm.
Find the angle in the sector.

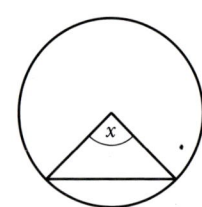

8 Find the hypotenuse in both of these triangles.
Give your answers to 3 sf.

a

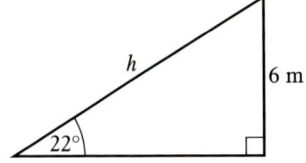

b

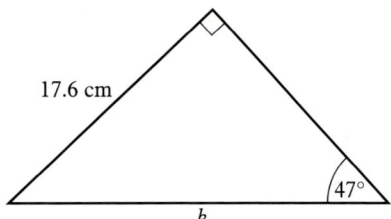

9 This diagram shows the position of three ports.
Two of the ports are on one side of the river
and the other port is on the opposite side.

The distance from A to C is 65 km.
The distance from B to C is 75 km.
Find the distance between ports A and B.

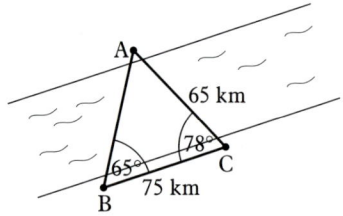

10 Gerald is taking a stroll around the grounds of Holkom Hall.
He walks along the red route.

The paths are shown in blue.

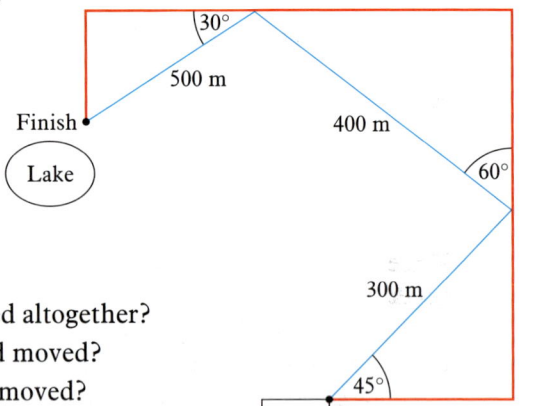

a How far has Gerald walked altogether?
b How far North has Gerald moved?
c How far West has Gerald moved?
d How far is Gerald from his starting point?
e Gerald returns home along the paths.
He walks at 1 m/s. How much quicker is his return journey?

1 Here is a table showing some Pythagorean Triples.

3	4	5
5	12	13
7	24	25

    a Copy the table. Add 5 extra rows.
    b There is a pattern in each column.
        Fill in the next 5 entries in each column.
    c Check that your 5 extra rows are all Pythagorean Triples.
    d Write down the entry in the nth row in each column.
        Show algebraically that these entries also give a Pythagorean Triple.

2 Use Pythagoras' theorem to find the value of x.

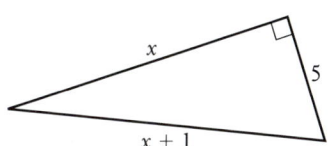

3 Show that the distance between the two points (x_1, y_1) and (x_2, y_2) is:

$$\sqrt{(x_2 - x_1)^2 + (y_2 - y_1)^2}$$

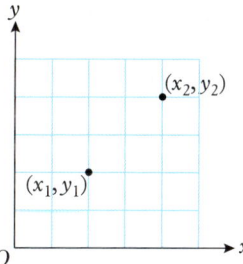

 4 Work out the angles marked in this diagram.
Show all your working.

2 cm

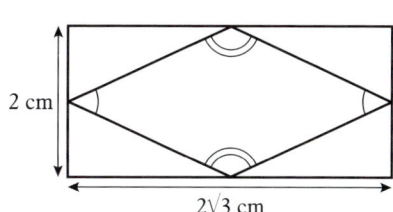

$2\sqrt{3}$ cm

5   **a** Write down the values of $\sin A$, $\cos A$ and $\tan A$ in this right-angled triangle.
      You only need the letters a and b.
  b Use your answers to part **a** to show that
      (1) $(\sin A)^2 + (\cos A)^2 = 1$
      (2) $\tan A = \dfrac{\sin A}{\cos A}$

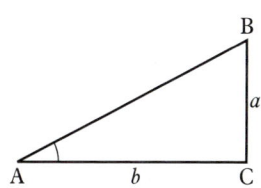

1 Find the length of the side marked with a letter in each of these triangles.
Give your answer to 1 dp where you need to round.

a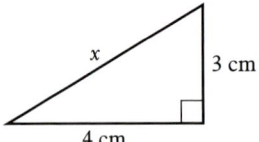

b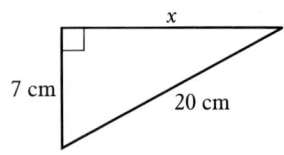

2 Find the length of the side marked with a letter in each of these triangles.
Leave your answers in surd form.

a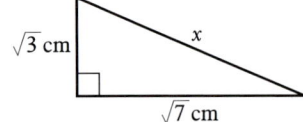

b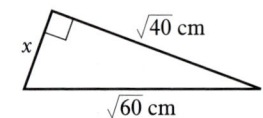

3 Find the angles marked with letters in these triangles.

a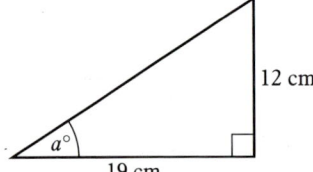

b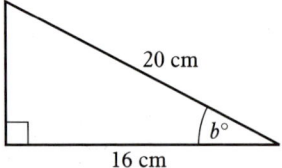

4 Find the length of the side marked with a letter in each of these triangles.
Give your answers to 1 dp.

a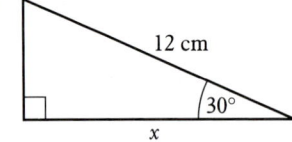

b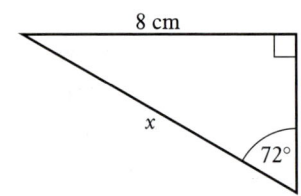

5 Find the height of an equilateral triangle of side 10 cm.

6 Howard leans a ladder against a wall.
The ladder is 3 m long and its base is 1 m from the wall.
a How far up the wall does the ladder reach?
b What angle does the base of the ladder make with the ground?

13 Mainly quadratics

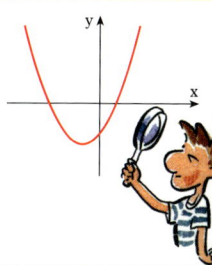

CORE

QUESTIONS

EXTENSION

TEST YOURSELF

1   Quadratic equations

Ken needs to find the x co-ordinates of the points where his curve cuts the x axis to 2 decimal places. He cannot find a sheet of graph paper that lets him draw the graph big enough to give this degree of accuracy.

He uses algebra to find out the answer.

You have already seen the face method for multiplying out brackets in algebra.
You can also multiply out $(x + 4)(x - 2)$ like this.

Multiply the second bracket by each term in the first bracket.

$$(x + 4)(x - 2) = x(x - 2) + 4(x - 2)$$
$$= x^2 - 2x + 4x - 8$$
$$= x^2 + 2x - 8$$

Coefficient   The number in front of a letter is called a **coefficient**. In $x^2 + 2x - 8$, 2 is called the coefficient of x.

Constant term   The number on the end of the equation is known as the **constant term**. In $x^2 + 2x - 8$, -8 is the constant term.

Exercise 13:1

1   Multiply out each of these pairs of brackets.
    a $(x + 3)(+ 7)$ **c** $(x + 3)(x - 9)$ **e** $(x + 5)(x - 3)$
    b $(x + 4)(x - 7)$ **d** $(x - 4)(x + 5)$ **f** $(3x - 4)(2x + 2)$

2   Copy this table. Use your answers to question **1** parts **a** to **e** to fill it in. The first one is done for you. Can you find a rule for your answers?

	number at end of 1st bracket	number at end of 2nd bracket	coefficient of x	constant term
a	3	7	10	21
b	4	−7		
c	3	−9		
d	−4	5		
e	5	−3		

In question **2** you should have noticed that when you multiply out two brackets that both start with x:

a the **coefficient of** x is found by adding the two numbers at the end of the brackets.

b the **constant term** is found by multiplying the two numbers at the end of the brackets.

When you multiply out $(x + 4)(x - 7)$ you get:

$$(x + 4)(x - 7) = x^2 - 3x - 28$$
$$+4 + -7 = -3 \text{ which is the coefficient of } x$$
$$\text{and } +4 \times -7 = -28 \text{ which is the constant term.}$$

Once you know these facts, you can use them to reverse the process.
This means taking a quadratic equation and splitting it back into two brackets.
This process is known as **factorising**.

Example

Factorise $x^2 + 5x + 6$.

The brackets will be $(x + ?)(x + ?)$.

The two numbers at the end of the brackets will
add together to give 5 and
multiply together to give 6.

The two numbers that do this are 2 and 3.
So $x^2 + 5x + 6 = (x + 2)(x + 3)$

3 Factorise these quadratic expressions.

a $x^2 + 7x + 10$ **f** $x^2 - 3x - 18$

b $x^2 + 10x + 16$ **g** $x^2 - 7x - 30$

c $x^2 + 12x + 27$ **h** $x^2 + 4x - 32$

d $x^2 + 14x + 40$ **i** $x^2 + 6x - 40$

e $x^2 + 15x + 36$ **• j** $x^2 - x$

You will also find it helpful to look at the signs in the equation you are factorising.

Examples

$x^2 + 5x + 6$ The number at the end is $+6$.
$= (x + ?)(x + ?)$ The numbers must be the same sign so that they multiply to give a $+$.
They must both be $+$ because they add to give $+5$.

$x^2 - 7x + 10$ The number at the end is $+10$.
$= (x - ?)(x - ?)$ The numbers must be the same sign so that they multiply to give a $+$.
They must both be $-$ because they add to give -7.

$x^2 + 3x - 10$ The number at the end is -10.
$= (x + ?)(x - ?)$ The numbers must have different signs so that they multiply to give a $-$.
The $+$ number must be bigger because they add to give a $+$ total.

4   Factorise these quadratic expressions.

   a $x^2 + 5x - 14$ **f** $x^2 - x - 12$

   b $x^2 - 4x - 5$ **g** $x^2 + x - 12$

   c $x^2 - 12x + 32$ **h** $x^2 - 7x - 44$

   d $x^2 + 17x + 60$ ● **i** $x^2 + x + 0.25$

   e $x^2 + 8x - 20$ ● **j** $x^2 - 9$

Difference of two squares

A quadratic expression which is in the form $x^2 - a^2$ is known as the **difference of two squares**. Difference means subtract. The same rules still work when you are factorising it.

Example

Factorise $x^2 - 16$.
The numbers in the two brackets add to give 0 and multiply to give -16.
They are $+4$ and -4.
$x^2 - 16 + (x - 4)(x + 4)$

The general rule is $x^2 - a^2 = (x - a)(x + a)$

Exercise 13:2

1 Factorise these quadratic expressions.

  a $x^2 - 25$ **e** $x^2 - 49$

  b $x^2 - 36$ ● **f** $x^2 - b^2$

  c $x^2 - 100$ ● **g** $x^2 - 0.25$

  d $x^2 - 1$ **h** $x^2 - 289$

2 Draw graphs of the following quadratics.
Put all the graphs on the same diagram.

  a $y = x^2 - 1$ **b** $y = x^2 - 4$ **c** $y = x^2 - 9$

3 Look at the graphs that you drew in question **2**.

  a Factorise the equations of the graphs.

  b What do you notice about the points where the graphs cross the x axis?

  c Why does this happen?

Not all quadratic expressions start with just x^2.
Many start with $2x^2$ or $3x^2$, etc.
These quadratics require a slightly different method to factorise them.

Example   Factorise $2x^2 + 7x + 3$.

1 Decide what goes at the beginning of each bracket.
One of the brackets must begin with a $2x$.
This is the only way to get $2x^2$ at the beginning.
So $2x^2 + 7x + 3 = (2x + ?)(x + ?)$

2 Draw a table and write down all the pairs of numbers that multiply to give the constant term.

$2x$	3	1
x	1	3

3 Multiply the numbers in diagonal pairs with the terms in the first column. Add the answers together.

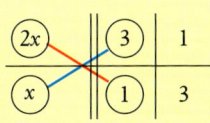

$2x \times 1 + x \times 3 = 2x + 3x = 5x$
This is not the required $7x$, so try the next pair.

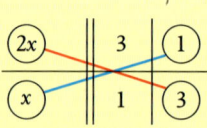

$2x \times 3 + x \times 1 = 6x + x = 7x$

This is correct.

4 Read across the table to write down the brackets.

So $2x^2 + 7x + 3 = (2x + 1)(x + 3)$

Exercise 13:3

1 Look at the quadratic $2x^2 + 13x + 15$.

a Copy this table.

b Fill in all the possible pairs of numbers that multiply to give 15. You should have 4 pairs.
c Multiply the pairs to find the correct one.
d Factorise $2x^2 + 13x + 15$.

2 Look at the quadratic $3x^2 + 20x + 12$.

a Copy this table.

b Fill in all the possible pairs of numbers that multiply to give 12. You should have 6 pairs.
c Multiply the pairs to find the correct one.
d Factorise $3x^2 + 20x + 12$.

3 Factorise these quadratics. Follow the steps that you used in question **2**.

a $2x^2 + 7x + 3$
b $3x^2 + 13x + 4$
c $2x^2 + 11x - 6$
d $2x^2 - 7x + 5$
e $5x^2 - 7x - 6$
f $5x^2 - 17x - 12$

g $7x^2 + 22x + 3$
h $5x^2 - 27x - 18$
i $3x^2 - 35x + 72$
j $11x^2 + 42x - 8$
k $17x^2 - 11x - 6$
● **l** $4x^2 + 10x + 6$

Once you can factorise a quadratic expression, you can solve quadratic equations.
Solving quadratic equations, tells you where the graph of a quadratic crosses the x axis.

Example   Solve $x^2 + 5x + 6 = 0$.

1   Factorise the quadratic.

$(x + 2)(x + 3) = 0$

You now have two brackets *multiplied* together to give 0.
The only way this can happen is if one of the brackets is 0.
It is very important that the equation is always **equal to 0**.

2   Put the two brackets equal to 0.

Either $x + 2 = 0$ or $x + 3 = 0$.

3   Solve these simple equations.

$x + 2 = 0$ $x + 3 = 0$
$x = -2$ $x = -3$

These are both solutions of
$x^2 + 5x + 6 = 0$
They are also the points where
the graph of $y = x^2 + 5x + 6$
crosses the x axis.

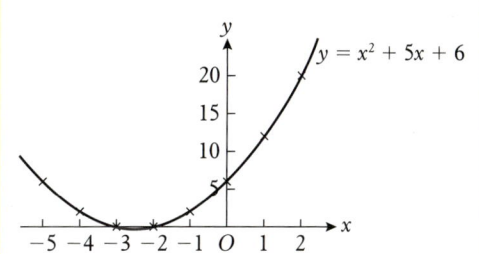

Exercise 13:4

1   Solve these quadratic equations.

   a $x^2 + 4x + 3 = 0$ **g** $2x^2 + 7x - 30 = 0$

   b $x^2 + 13x + 42 = 0$ **h** $6x^2 - 11x - 7 = 0$

   c $x^2 + x - 6 = 0$ **i** $3x^2 + 5x - 2 = 0$

   d $x^2 - 7x + 12 = 0$ **j** $11x^2 + 42x - 8 = 0$

   e $x^2 + 6x = 0$ ● **k** $x^2 + x = 6$

   f $x^2 - 11x - 26 = 0$ ● **l** $2x^2 + 11x = 6$

2   **a** Plot the graph of $y = x^2 - 2x - 8$.
       Use x values from -3 to 5.

   b Solve $x^2 - 2x - 8 = 0$.

   c Check that your solutions to part **b** match the graph.

2 Quadratic methods

Not all quadratic equations will factorise.

There is a formula that you can use to solve this type of equation.

Fortunately you do not have to be able to work out the formula for yourself!

Quadratic formula

The **quadratic formula** works for any quadratic that is written in the form $ax^2 + bx + c = 0$.
a, b and c are all numbers.

In the equation $2x^2 + 6x - 3 = 0$,
$a = 2$, $b = 6$, and $c = -3$

The **quadratic formula** is $x = \dfrac{-b \pm \sqrt{b^2 - 4ac}}{2a}$

±

The ± means that you have to work out the formula twice, once using the + and once using the −.

Example

Solve the equation $2x^2 + 6x - 3 = 0$ using the quadratic formula.

(1) Write down the values of a, b and c.
$a = 2 \quad b = 6 \quad c = -3$

(2) Fill these values into the formula and tidy up.

$$x = \frac{-6 \pm \sqrt{6^2 - 4 \times 2 \times (-3)}}{2 \times 2}$$

$$x = \frac{-6 \pm \sqrt{36 + 24}}{4}$$

$$x = \frac{-6 \pm \sqrt{60}}{4}$$

(3) Work out the two values of x.
Use the $+$ for the first and the $-$ for the second.

$$x = \frac{-6 + \sqrt{60}}{4} \qquad \text{or} \qquad x = \frac{-6 - \sqrt{60}}{4}$$

$$x = \frac{-6 + 7.746}{4} \qquad \text{or} \qquad x = \frac{-6 - 7.746}{4}$$

$$x = 0.44 \ (2 \ \text{dp}) \qquad \text{or} \qquad x = -3.44 \ (2 \ \text{dp})$$

Exercise 13:5

1 You are going to solve the equation $x^2 + 5x + 1 = 0$.
  a Write down the values of a, b and c.
     $a = 1 \qquad b = \dots \qquad c = \dots$
  b Write down the quadratic formula.
  c Put in the values of a, b and c.
  d Work out the two values of x.
     Round your answers to 2 dp.

2 You are going to solve the equation $x^2 + 7x - 2 = 0$.
  a Write down the values of a, b and c.
  b Write down the quadratic formula.
  c Put in the values of a, b and c.
  d Work out the two values of x.
     Round your answers to 2 dp.

3 Solve these quadratic equations.
  Round your answers to 2 dp.
  a $x^2 + 6x + 3 = 0$
  b $x^2 + 11x + 7 = 0$
  c $x^2 + x - 8 = 0$
  d $x^2 - 3x + 1 = 0$
  e $x^2 - 8x - 3 = 0$
  f $x^2 - 11x - 9 = 0$
  g $2x^2 + 10x - 3 = 0$
  h $3x^2 - 11x - 1 = 0$
  i $5x^2 - 9x - 2 = 0$
  j $5x^2 + 42x - 2 = 0$
  • **k** $3x^2 + x = 6$
  • **l** $4x^2 + 12x = 3$

Not all quadratics come in ready-to-solve form!

Sometimes you have to rearrange them before you can begin to solve them.
It is very important that quadratics are **equal to zero** before you solve them.

You can't tell which quadratics will factorise and which will not just by looking. It does not matter if you use the formula on an equation that will factorise. It will still work!

Some quadratics are in the form of a problem.

The following exercise is a mixture of questions.

Exercise 13:6

1 Rearrange these quadratic equations so that they are equal to 0.
Solve them using factorising or the quadratic formula.

   a $x^2 = 6x - 2$ **e** $10 = 6x^2 - 11x$

   b $x^2 - x = 6$ **f** $x^2 = 17x - 3$

   c $5x^2 = 3x^2 - 4x + 2$ **g** $5x^2 = 9x$

   d $(x - 3)^2 = 4$ **h** $(x + 4)^2 = (x - 3)^2$

2 Look at this right-angled triangle.
The lengths are marked in centimetres.

   a Write down a quadratic equation using Pythagoras' theorem.

   b Simplify and rearrange this equation.

   c Solve the equation.
      Round your answers to 2 dp.

   d Write down the lengths of the sides of the triangle.
      Why is only one of the answers a possible solution to the problem?

3 Solve the equation $2x + 2 = \dfrac{7}{x} - 1$.

(Hint: You will need to multiply by x first.)

4 Use the difference of two squares to work out the exact value of:

   a $1001^2 - 999^2$

   b $10\,000\,000\,001^2 - 9\,999\,999\,999^2$

Completing the square

There is another way of solving quadratics that don't factorise.
It is called completing the square.
It gets its name because there is always a bracket squared in the final expression.

The aim is to change an equation which is in the form $ax^2 + bx + c$ into the form $p(x + r)^2 + s$. Doing this makes it possible to get x as the subject of the formula.

Example   Express $x^2 + 8x + 11$ in the form $(x + r)^2 + s$.

Look at the first two terms of the quadratic $x^2 + 8x$.
If you halve the coefficient of x, in this case 8, you get 4.

Put this 4 in a bracket in the form $(x + 4)^2$.
If you multiply this bracket out you get $x^2 + 8x + 16$.
This is not exactly what you want but the first two terms are correct.

The original quadratic has $+11$ as its number term whereas this bracket produces $+16$. We need to subtract 5. $16 - 5 = 11$.

So $x^2 + 8x + 11 = (x + 4)^2 - 5$.

Once you have a quadratic in this form, it is possible to use it to solve equations.

Example   Solve the equation $x^2 + 8x + 11 = 0$ by completing the square.
Give your answers to 2 dp.

Start with the original equation.
$$x^2 + 8x + 11 = 0$$
Complete the square.
$$(x + 4)^2 - 5 = 0$$
Take the 5 to the RHS.
$$(x + 4)^2 = 5$$
Square root both sides. Remember to put in a positive and a negative square root.
$$x + 4 = \pm\sqrt{5}$$
Finally, take the 4 to the RHS.
$$x = \pm\sqrt{5} - 4$$
The two solutions are $\sqrt{5} - 4 = -1.76$
and $-\sqrt{5} - 4 = -6.24$

Exercise 13:7

1 Express each of these quadratic expressions in the form $(x + r)^2 + s$.

a $x^2 + 8x + 13$ **f** $x^2 - 16x + 27$
b $x^2 + 6x + 7$ **g** $x^2 + 3x + 1$
c $x^2 + 10x - 3$ **h** $x^2 + 5x + 6$
d $x^2 - 4x + 2$ **i** $x^2 - 3x - 4$
e $x^2 - 8x + 1$ **j** $x^2 - 5x - 8$

2 Use your answers to question **1** to solve these quadratic equations.
Give your answers to 2 dp.
Remember there are two solutions to each equation.

a $x^2 + 8x + 13 = 0$ **f** $x^2 - 16x + 27 = 0$
b $x^2 + 6x + 7 = 0$ **g** $x^2 + 3x + 1 = 0$
c $x^2 + 10x - 3 = 0$ **h** $x^2 + 5x + 6 = 0$
d $x^2 - 4x + 2 = 0$ **i** $x^2 - 3x - 4 = 0$
e $x^2 - 8x + 1 = 0$ **j** $x^2 - 5x - 8 = 0$

You can also complete the square when the coefficient of x^2 is not 1.
There are a couple of extra stages to the process.

Example   Express $2x^2 + 4x + 15$ in the form $p(x + r)^2 + s$.

Look at the first two terms of the quadratic $2x^2 + 4x$.
Take the coefficient of x^2 outside a bracket: $2(x^2 + 2x)$.
Now complete the square on the inside of the bracket as before.
Halving the coefficient of x gives 1.
Put this 1 in a bracket but don't forget the 2 outside: $2(x + 1)^2$.

If you multiply this bracket out you get

$$2(x^2 + 2x + 1) = 2x^2 + 4x + 2.$$

Now sort out the number term.
The original quadratic has $+15$ as its number term, whereas this
bracket produces $+2$. We need to add 13.

So, $2x^2 + 4x + 15 = 2(x + 1)^2 + 13$.

---

3 Use the method of completing the square to solve these quadratic equations.

a $2x^2 + 8x + 5 = 0$.   **f** $6x^2 - 12x - 10 = 0$
b $2x^2 + 6x + 3 = 0$ ● **g** $3x^2 + 3x - 1 = 0$
c $2x^2 + 10x - 3 = 0$ ● **h** $2x^2 + 5x - 6 = 0$
d $4x^2 - 4x - 7 = 0$ ● **i** $3x^2 - 8x - 2 = 0$
e $4x^2 - 8x + 1 = 0$ ● **j** $5x^2 - 16x + 4 = 0$

Now that you can solve quadratic equations, you can look at more complicated simultaneous equations. You first saw these in Chapter 11, where both equations were linear.

In this example, one equation is quadratic and the other one is linear.

You will need several of the skills you have learned in this chapter to solve them.

The method is:

1 rearrange the linear equation to make either x or y the subject.

2 substitute this equation into the quadratic equation so that it now has just one letter in it.

3 solve the quadratic equation. You will get two answers.

4 substitute these answers back into the linear equation.

Example   Solve the equations $x^2 + y^2 = 17$

$2x + y = 6$

1 Rearrange the linear equation to make y the subject.

$$y = 6 - 2x$$

2 Substitute $y = 6 - 2x$ into the quadratic equation to replace the y^2.

$$x^2 + y^2 = 17$$
$$x^2 + (6 - 2x)^2 = 17$$

3 To solve the quadratic, first multiply out the bracket.

$$x^2 + (36 - 24x + 4x^2) = 17$$
$$5x^2 - 24x + 36 = 17$$
$$5x^2 - 24x + 19 = 0$$

You can use any method to solve this.

$$(5x - 19)(x - 1) = 0$$

So $x = 3.8$ or $x = 1$

4 Substitute these answers back into the linear equation.

$$y = 6 - 2x$$
$$y = 6 - 2 \times 3.8 \quad \text{or} \quad y = 6 - 2 \times 1$$
$$y = -1.6 \quad \text{or} \qquad\qquad y = 4$$

The final answers are $x = 1, y = 4$ or $x = 3.8, y = -1.6$

Exercise 13:8

1   Solve these pairs of simultaneous equations.
   Remember that you need two solutions for each one.

   a $x^2 + y^2 = 13$ **b** $x^2 + y^2 = 10$ **c** $x^2 + y^2 = 20$
   $3x + y = 9$ $2x + y = 5$ $2x + y = 2$

2 Solve these pairs of simultaneous equations.

  a $x^2 + y^2 = 10$ **b** $x^2 + y^2 = 29$ **c** $2x^2 + y^2 = 34$
   $4x + 2y = -10$ $x - 2y = 12$ $2x - y = 2$

In fact, an equation in the form $x^2 + y^2 = r^2$ is the equation of a circle.
The circle has its centre at the origin and r is its radius.

The equation $x^2 + y^2 = 16$ represents a circle of radius **4**, centre $(0, 0)$.

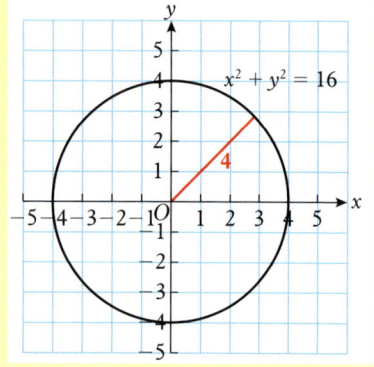

When you solve a pair of equations where one is in this form and one is a straight line, you are actually finding the co-ordinate of the points where the straight line crosses the circle.

The solutions to the equations $x^2 + y^2 = 25$
                                and $x + y = 7$
are $x = 3, y = 4$ and $x = 4, y = 3$.

You can see the line and the circle on the graph. Notice that the points of intersection match the answers to the simultaneous equations.

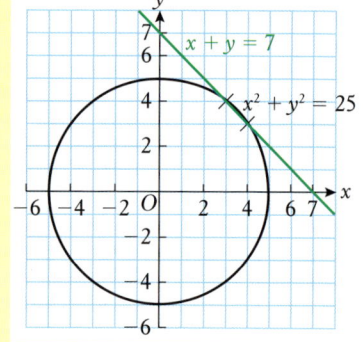

3 **a** Draw the circle $x^2 + y^2 = 25$ on a graph.
  b Draw the line $x + y = -1$ on the same graph.
  c Write down the points of intersection of the circle and the line.
  d Write down the solutions of the equations
     $x^2 + y^2 = 25$ and $x + y = -1$.

4 **a** Draw the circle $x^2 + y^2 = 36$ on a graph.
  b Draw the line $y = x$ on the same graph.
  c Write down the points of intersection of the circle and the line.
     Give your answers to 1 dp.
  d Write down the solutions of the equations $x^2 + y^2 = 36$ and $y = x$.
  e Solve these simultaneous equations using algebra to check your answers.

3 Trial and improvement

You have seen a formula in the last section that tells you how to solve any quadratic equation using the coefficients of the terms.

Evariste Galois (1811–1832) was a French mathematician who was killed in a duel at the age of only 20. The night before the duel he stayed up and wrote down all of his ideas. It took mathematicians more than 100 years to deal with what he wrote down in one night!

Galois proved that there is no formula for solving an equation using the coefficients (as there is for a quadratic) when the highest power of x is 5 or more.

You need a different way of solving these equations.
You can use trial and improvement.
You can also use trial and improvement for easier equations if you are told to do so.

Example

Solve $x^4 = 104\,976$ using trial and improvement.

Value of x	Value of x^4	
10	10 000	too small
20	160 000	too big
18	104 976	correct

Answer $x = 18$.
This is only part of the answer.
You may need to think about negative values.

Value of x	Value of x^4	
-10	10 000	too small
-20	160 000	too big
-18	104 976	correct

So $x = -18$ as well.

Exercise 13:9

Solve these equations using trial and improvement.
Draw a table to help you set out your working.

1   **a** $x^4 = 531\,441$
      b $x^4 = 74\,120.0625$

2   **a** $x^3 = 216$ There is only one answer for this equation.
      b $x^3 - 3x = 488$ There is only one answer for this equation.
 ●   **c** $x^3 - 4x^2 + x + 6 = 0$ There are three answers for this equation.

3   The length of this cuboid is x cm.

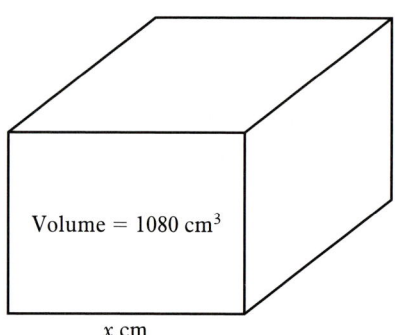

Volume $= 1080$ cm^3

      a   The width is 2 cm less than the length.
         Write down an expression for the width.
      b   The height is 3 cm less than the length.
         Write down an expression for the height.
      c   The volume of the cuboid is 1080 cm^3.
         Show that x satisfies the equation

$$x^3 - 5x^2 + 6x = 1080$$

      d   Solve the equation $x^3 - 5x^2 + 6x = 1080$
         using trial and improvement.
      e   Write down the length, width and height
         of the cuboid.

x cm

Sometimes answers do not work out exactly.
When this happens you may have to give your answer correct to 1 dp.

Example   Solve $x^3 = 135$

Value of x	Value of x^3		
5	125	too small	
6	216	too big	x is between 5 and 6
5.5	166.375	too big	x is between 5 and 5.5
5.1	132.651	too small	x is between 5.1 and 5.5
5.2	140.608	too big	x is between 5.1 and 5.2
5.15	136.590 875	too big	x is between 5 and 5.15

this value is halfway between 5.1 and 5.2

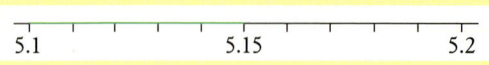

x must be somewhere in the green part of the number line.
Any number in the green part rounds down to 5.1 to 1 dp.
Answer: $x = 5.1$ to 1 dp.

Exercise 13:10

Solve these equations by trial and improvement.
Draw a table to help you find each solution.
Give all of your answers to 1 dp.

1 $x^3 = 250$

3 $x^3 + x = 45$

2 $x^5 = 21\,892$

4 $x^3 + 4x = 70$

5 Solve these equations using trial and improvement.
You need to rearrange the equations to get all the xs on the same side.
Part **a** has been rearranged for you.
All of these equations only have one answer.
Give your answers to 1 dp.

a $x^2 + 1 = \dfrac{1}{x}$ This is the same as $x^2 + 1 - \dfrac{1}{x} = 0$ **c** $\sqrt{x} = \dfrac{1}{x} + 5$

b $x^3 = \dfrac{1}{x}$ **d** $x^3 = \dfrac{1}{x} + 3$

You can give greater accuracy than 1 dp in your answers.
$x^2 = 135$ gives $x = 11.6$ to 1 dp but you can carry on to get the answer to 2 dp.

Value of x	Value of x^2		
11.6	134.56	too small	x is between 11.6 and 11.7
11.7	136.89	too big	x is between 11.6 and 11.65
11.65	135.7225	too big	x is between 11.61 and 11.65
11.61	134.7921	too small	x is between 11.61 and 11.62
11.62	135.0244	too big	x is between 11.615 and 11.62
11.615	134.908 225	too small	

this value is halfway between 11.61 and 11.62

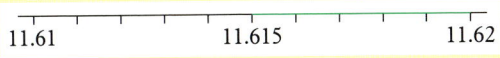

11.61   11.615   11.62

x must be somewhere in the green part of the number line.
Any number in the green part rounds up to 11.62 to 2 dp.
Answer: $x = 11.62$ to 2 dp.

---

6 **a** Solve the equation in question **3** giving your answer to 2 dp.
  • **b** Solve the equation in question **4** giving your answer to 3 dp.

1 Multiply out each of these pairs of brackets.
  a $(x + 4)(x + 6)$ **c** $(2x - 3)(2x + 3)$
  b $(2x - 6)(x + 3)$ **d** $(5x - 2)(6x - 4)$

2 Factorise these quadratic expressions.
  a $x^2 + 5x + 6$ **c** $2x^2 - 13x - 7$
  b $x^2 - 3x - 28$ **d** $6x^2 - 6$

3 Write down where these graphs cut the x axis.
  a $y = x^2 - 9$ **b** $y = x^2 - 16$ **c** $y = x^2 - 36$

4 Solve these quadratic equations.
  a $x^2 + 3x + 2 = 0$ **c** $2x^2 + 11x - 21 = 0$
  b $x^2 - 3x - 4 = 0$ **d** $6x^2 + x - 2 = 0$

5 Solve these quadratic equations.
  Give your answers to 2 dp.
  a $x^2 + 8x + 1 = 0$ **c** $2x^2 + 10x - 3 = 0$
  b $x^2 - 3x - 6 = 0$ **d** $5x^2 + 12x = 6$

6 Look at this rectangle.
  The width is 5 units less than the length.
  a Write down an expression for the
    area of the rectangle.
  b The area of the rectangle is 104 cm².
    Write down an equation in terms of x.
  c Solve your equation.
  d Write down the values of the length
    and width of the rectangle.

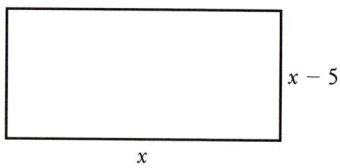

7 Look at this triangle.
  a Write down an expression for the
    area of the triangle.
  b The area of the triangle is 20 cm².
    Write down an equation in terms of x.
  c Solve your equation.
  d Write down the base and height of the
    triangle.

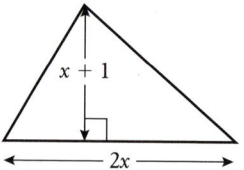

8 Use algebra to find where these graphs cut the x axis.
  Do not draw the graphs.
  a $y = x^2 + 3x - 10$ **c** $y = x^2 - 2x - 3$
  b $y = x^2 + 11x + 28$ **d** $y = x^2 - 5x + 4$

9 Look at this rectangle.

The length is 4 units longer than the width.

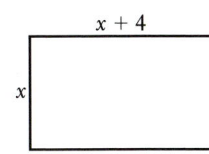

a Write down an expression for the area of the rectangle.

Another rectangle is drawn.
Its length is half the length of the rectangle above.

b Write down an expression for the length of the new rectangle.

The width of the new rectangle is 5 units less than the width of the rectangle above.

c Write down an expression for the width of the new rectangle.

d Write down an expression for the area of the new rectangle.

e The area of the new rectangle is 55 less than the rectangle above. Find the value of x.

10 The diagram shows a rectangle ABCD and a square EBGF.
AG = 3 cm and EC = 5 cm.
The length of the side of the square EBGF is x cm.

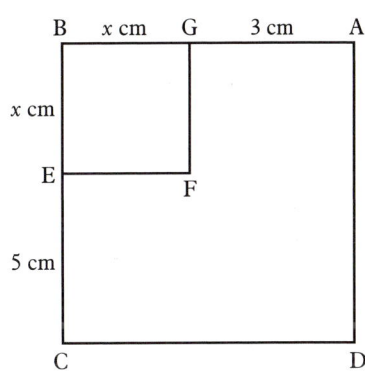

a The rectangle ABCD has an area of 120 cm^2.
Form an equation in terms of x.
Show that it can be written in the form $x^2 + 8x - 105 = 0$.

b Solve $x^2 + 8x - 105 = 0$ and hence calculate the area of the square EBGF.

11 a Write down an expression, in terms of x, for the area of a square of side $2x$

b Write down an expression, in terms of x, for the area of this rectangle.

c The square and the rectangle have the same area.
Form an equation in x and show that it can be written in the form $x^2 - 4x = 0$.

d Solve the equation.

e Write down the area of the square.

12 Express each quadratic expression in the form $p(x + r)^2 + q$.

a $x^2 + 6x + 16$

b $x^2 + 8x - 20$

c $x^2 - 8x + 16$

d $x^2 - 7x + 1$

e $2x^2 + 6x + 10$

f $3x^2 - 12x - 13$

13 Solve these quadratic equations by completing the square.

  a $x^2 + 8x - 10 = 0$

  b $2x^2 - 8x - 13 = 0$

14 Solve these simultaneous equations.
Remember that you need two pairs of answers.

$$x^2 + y^2 = 34$$
$$x - 2y = -7$$

15 These are equations of circles.
For each circle write down   (1) the centre
                                                   (2) the radius.

  a $x^2 + y^2 = 36$

  b $x^2 + y^2 = 81$

  c $x^2 + y^2 - 9 = 0$

16 **a** Draw the circle $x^2 + y^2 = 9$ on a graph.

  b Draw the line $y = x + 1$ on the same graph.

  c Write down the points of intersection of the circle and the line.
Give your answers to 1 dp.

  d Write down the solutions of the equations $x^2 + y^2 = 9$ and $y = x + 1$.

  e Solve these simultaneous equations using algebra to check your answers.

17 Solve these equations using trial and improvement.
Draw a table to help you set out your working.

  a $x^3 = 3375$ There is only one answer for this equation.

  b $x^3 - 4x = 2688$ There is only one answer for this equation.

18 Solve these equations using trial and improvement.
Give all of your answers to 1 dp.

  a $x^2 + 4 = \dfrac{1}{x}$ **b** $4x^2 = \dfrac{1}{x} + 2$

1   The perimeter of a rectangle is 42 cm.
The diagonal is 15 cm long.
What is the length and the width of the rectangle?

2 a and b are consecutive whole numbers.
Prove that the difference between their squares is equal to their sum.

3   Here is a proof which shows you why the quadratic formula is true.

   a   Multiply out $\left(x + \dfrac{b}{2a}\right)^2$

   b   Rearrange your answer to part **a** to get $x^2 + \dfrac{b}{a}x = \ldots$

    The general quadratic formula is $ax^2 + bx + c = 0$

    If you divide this equation by a you get $x^2 + \dfrac{b}{a}x + \dfrac{c}{a} = 0$

   c   Substitute your answer for part **b** into this expression. Show that

$$\left(x + \frac{b}{2a}\right)^2 - \frac{b^2}{4a^2} + \frac{c}{a} = 0$$

   d   Show that you can rearrange this equation to get

$$\left(x + \frac{b}{2a}\right)^2 = \frac{b^2 - 4ac}{4a^2}$$

   e   Now square root your equation in part **d**. You need to include the $\pm$ symbol to show that there are two possible answers when you square root. Show that

$$x + \frac{b}{2a} = \pm \frac{\sqrt{b^2 - 4ac}}{2a}$$

   f   Now rearrange the equation in part **e** to prove the quadratic formula!

4   **a**   Find all the solutions of this equation by trial and improvement.

$$x^4 + 3x^3 - 15x^2 - 19x + 30 = 0$$

   b   Sketch the graph of $y = x^4 + 3x^3 - 15x^2 - 19x + 30$.

5   Simplify these expressions.

   a $\dfrac{x}{(x + 2)} + \dfrac{2}{(x^2 + 5x + 6)}$ **b** $\dfrac{x^2 + 3x - 4}{x} \times \dfrac{x^2}{x^2 + 2x - 3} \div \dfrac{x}{2x + 6}$

1   Multiply out each of these pairs of brackets.

   a $(x + 3)(x + 4)$ **c** $(2x - 5)(3x - 3)$

   b $(x + 2)(x - 7)$ **d** $(7x - 4)(6x + 2)$

2   Factorise these quadratic expressions.

   a $x^2 + 5x + 6$ **c** $x^2 - 3x - 28$

   b $x^2 + 10x + 21$ **d** $x^2 + 7x - 30$

3   Factorise these quadratic expressions.

   a $2x^2 + 13x + 6$ **c** $3x^2 + 17x - 6$

   b $3x^2 + 22x + 7$ **d** $4x^2 - 16x + 15$

4   Solve these quadratic equations using the quadratic formula.
Give your answers to 2 dp.

   a $x^2 + 9x + 2 = 0$ **c** $5x^2 + 19x - 6 = 0$

   b $3x^2 + 12x + 1 = 0$ **d** $7x^2 - 3x - 15 = 0$

5   Solve these quadratic equations by completing the square.
Give your answers to 2 dp.

   a $x^2 + 4x + 2 = 0$ **c** $2x^2 + 12x - 9 = 0$

   b $x^2 + 12x + 1 = 0$ **d** $3x^2 - 12x - 15 = 0$

6   Solve the equation $x^3 - 9x = 850$ using trial and improvement.
Use this table to help you.
Give your answer to 2 dp.

Value of x	Value of $x^3 - 9x$	
5	80	too small
12	1701	too big

7   Solve these simultaneous equations.

      $x^2 + y^2 = 34$

      $2x - y = 13$

14 Vectors

1 Vectors and scalars
Defining vectors and scalars
Using vector notation
Adding and subtracting vectors
Multiplying a vector by a scalar
Combining vectors
Defining magnitude

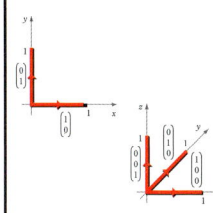

2 Vector geometry
Defining position vector
Using vectors for geometrical proof

3 This is for real
Doing real vector problems with velocities
and with forces

CORE

QUESTIONS

EXTENSION

TEST YOURSELF

1 Vectors and scalars

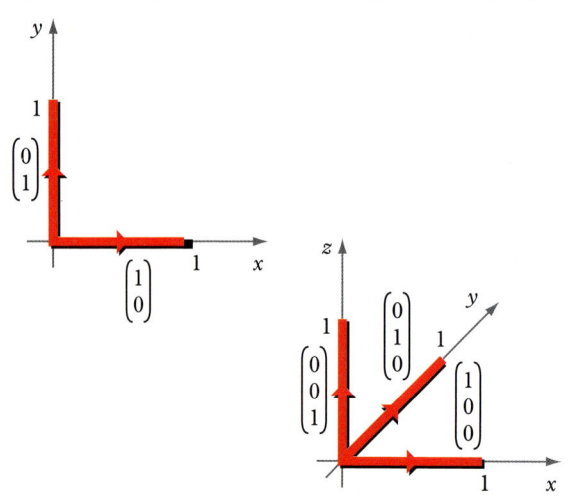

In two dimensions the vectors $\begin{pmatrix}1\\0\end{pmatrix}$ and $\begin{pmatrix}0\\1\end{pmatrix}$ are perpendicular.

In three dimensions the vectors

$\begin{pmatrix}1\\0\\0\end{pmatrix}$ $\begin{pmatrix}0\\1\\0\end{pmatrix}$ and $\begin{pmatrix}0\\0\\1\end{pmatrix}$ are perpendicular.

What about $\begin{pmatrix}1\\0\\0\\0\end{pmatrix}$ …?

Scalar	A **scalar** quantity has size but no direction. Distance is a scalar. All numbers are scalars.
Vector	A **vector** quantity has both size and direction. Displacement is a vector.

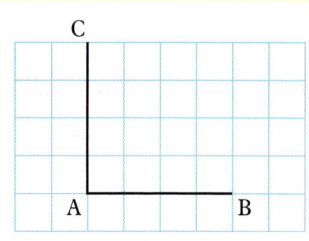

The distance from A to B is written as AB.
The distances AB and AC are the same.

The vector from A to B is written as $\overrightarrow{AB}$.

The vectors $\overrightarrow{AB}$ and $\overrightarrow{AC}$ are not the same.
They have different directions.

$\overrightarrow{AB} = \begin{pmatrix}4\\0\end{pmatrix}$ and $\overrightarrow{AC} = \begin{pmatrix}0\\4\end{pmatrix}$

$\begin{pmatrix}4\\0\end{pmatrix}$ means 4 units to the right.

$\begin{pmatrix}0\\4\end{pmatrix}$ means 4 units up.

Exercise 14:1

1 State whether each of these is a vector or a scalar.

a 5 km due north	**d** 7	**g** 10 ms^{-1} on a bearing of 060°
b 40 ms^{-1}	**e** $\sqrt{3}$	**h** 20° C
c −50° C	**f** 46 cm^2	**i** 3 m vertically upwards

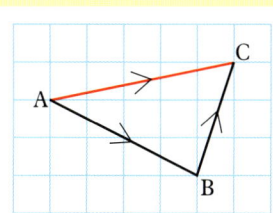

$$\overrightarrow{AB} = \begin{pmatrix} 4 \\ -2 \end{pmatrix} \quad \overrightarrow{BC} = \begin{pmatrix} 1 \\ 3 \end{pmatrix} \quad \overrightarrow{AC} = \begin{pmatrix} 5 \\ 1 \end{pmatrix}$$

You add column vectors by adding the numbers in corresponding positions.

$$\begin{pmatrix} 4 \\ -2 \end{pmatrix} + \begin{pmatrix} 1 \\ 3 \end{pmatrix} = \begin{pmatrix} 4+1 \\ -2+3 \end{pmatrix} = \begin{pmatrix} 5 \\ 1 \end{pmatrix}$$

In the diagram $\overrightarrow{AB} + \overrightarrow{BC} = \overrightarrow{AC}$.

2 a Write these as column vectors.

(1) $\overrightarrow{PQ}$ (2) $\overrightarrow{QR}$ (3) $\overrightarrow{RS}$ (4) $\overrightarrow{PS}$

b Show that $\overrightarrow{PQ} + \overrightarrow{QR} + \overrightarrow{RS} = \overrightarrow{PS}$.

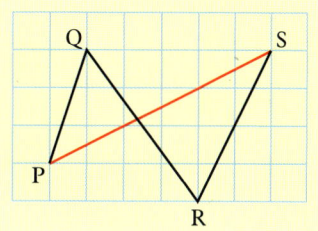

3 Copy these. Fill in the gaps.

a $\begin{pmatrix} 5 \\ 2 \end{pmatrix} + \begin{pmatrix} -1 \\ \ldots \end{pmatrix} = \begin{pmatrix} \ldots \\ 6 \end{pmatrix}$ **c** $\overrightarrow{AF} + \overrightarrow{FQ} = \ldots$ **e** $\ldots + \overrightarrow{QY} = \overrightarrow{AY}$

b $\begin{pmatrix} \ldots \\ -3 \end{pmatrix} + \begin{pmatrix} 4 \\ \ldots \end{pmatrix} = \begin{pmatrix} -3 \\ 0 \end{pmatrix}$ **d** $\overrightarrow{PV} + \ldots = \overrightarrow{PH}$ **f** $\overrightarrow{LN} + \ldots + \overrightarrow{WA} = \overrightarrow{LA}$

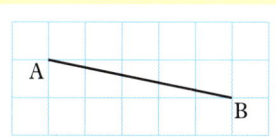

$$\overrightarrow{AB} = \begin{pmatrix} 5 \\ -1 \end{pmatrix} \quad \text{and} \quad \overrightarrow{BA} = \begin{pmatrix} -5 \\ 1 \end{pmatrix} = -\begin{pmatrix} 5 \\ -1 \end{pmatrix}$$

$\overrightarrow{AB}$ and $\overrightarrow{BA}$ are the same length but go in opposite directions.

This means that $\overrightarrow{AB} = -\overrightarrow{BA}$.

4 $\overrightarrow{AG} = \begin{pmatrix} 2 \\ -3 \end{pmatrix} \quad \overrightarrow{GL} = \begin{pmatrix} -1 \\ 7 \end{pmatrix}$

Write these as column vectors:

a $\overrightarrow{GA}$ **b** $\overrightarrow{LG}$ **c** $\overrightarrow{AL}$ **d** $\overrightarrow{LA}$

You can also label a vector with a small letter.

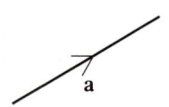

These small letters are shown in **bold** print in the book.
You should <u>underline</u> them when you write them.

Two vectors are equal if they have the same size *and* the same direction.
You can label equal vectors with the same letter.

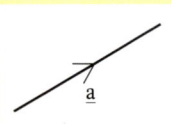

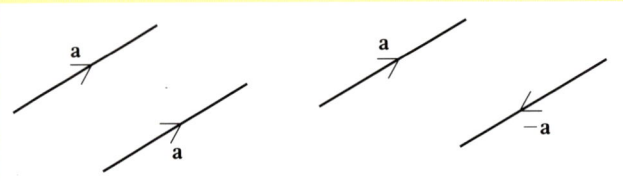

−**a** is the same size as **a** but points in the opposite direction.

a + **b** is the same as **a** followed by **b**.
The vectors **a**, **b** and **a** + **b** look like this.
This is called a vector triangle.

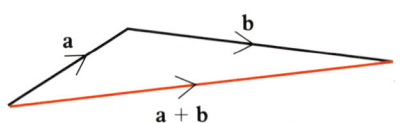

5 $a = \begin{pmatrix} 1 \\ 3 \end{pmatrix}$ $b = \begin{pmatrix} -2 \\ 1 \end{pmatrix}$

Copy the diagram. Label each of the vectors in terms of **a** and **b**.

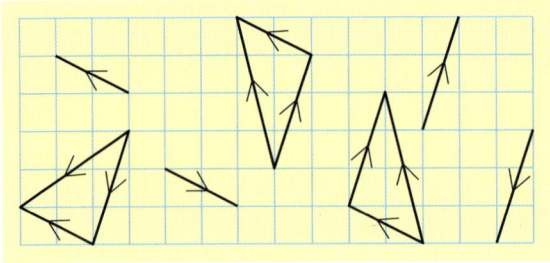

6   **a**   Draw a diagram of **p** + **q**.
     b   Draw a diagram of **q** + **p**.
     c   Explain why **p** + **q** = **q** + **p**.

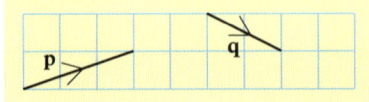

7 $\mathbf{p} = \begin{pmatrix} 5 \\ 2 \end{pmatrix}$ $\mathbf{q} = \begin{pmatrix} 6 \\ -1 \end{pmatrix}$ $\mathbf{r} = \begin{pmatrix} -8 \\ 4 \end{pmatrix}$

    a Show that $\mathbf{p} + (\mathbf{q} + \mathbf{r}) = (\mathbf{p} + \mathbf{q}) + \mathbf{r}$.
    b Copy the diagram. Complete it to show the result in part **a**.

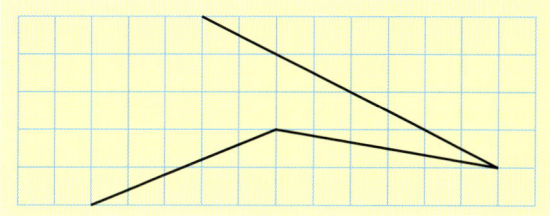

$\mathbf{a} = \begin{pmatrix} 3 \\ 2 \end{pmatrix}$ $\mathbf{b} = \begin{pmatrix} 1 \\ -2 \end{pmatrix}$

To subtract column vectors you subtract the numbers in corresponding positions.

$$\mathbf{a} - \mathbf{b} = \begin{pmatrix} 3 \\ 2 \end{pmatrix} - \begin{pmatrix} 1 \\ -2 \end{pmatrix}$$

$$= \begin{pmatrix} 3 - 1 \\ 2 - -2 \end{pmatrix} = \begin{pmatrix} 2 \\ 4 \end{pmatrix}$$

On the diagram, you subtract the vector **b** by adding $-\mathbf{b}$.
So, $\mathbf{a} - \mathbf{b}$ means **a** followed by $-\mathbf{b}$.
$\mathbf{a} - \mathbf{b} = \mathbf{a} + -\mathbf{b}$

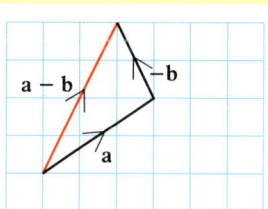

The vectors $\mathbf{a}$, $-\mathbf{b}$ and $\mathbf{a} - \mathbf{b}$ make a vector triangle.

Exercise 14:2

1 $\mathbf{p} = \begin{pmatrix} 4 \\ 1 \end{pmatrix}$ $\mathbf{q} = \begin{pmatrix} 3 \\ 2 \end{pmatrix}$

    a Write $\mathbf{p} - \mathbf{q}$ as a column vector.
    b Draw a diagram to show $\mathbf{p}$, $-\mathbf{q}$ and $\mathbf{p} - \mathbf{q}$ in a vector triangle.

2 **a** Copy the diagram. Label each of the vectors in terms of **p** and **q**.

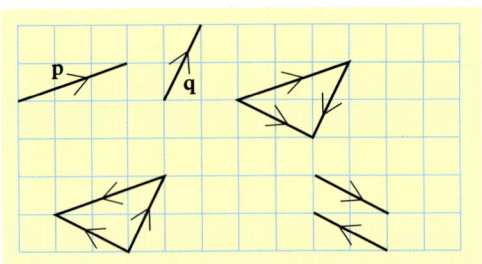

b What is the connection between **p** − **q** and **q** − **p**?

3 Copy these. Fill in the gaps.

    a $a - b = -(b \dots)$

    b $\overrightarrow{AB} - \overrightarrow{CB} = \overrightarrow{AB} + \dots = \dots$

    c $\overrightarrow{AJ} + \overrightarrow{KN} - \overrightarrow{KJ} = \overrightarrow{AJ} + \dots + \overrightarrow{KN} = \dots$

4 Simplify these vector expressions.
You need to use the same methods as in question **3**.

    a $\overrightarrow{PQ} - \overrightarrow{RQ}$ **c** $\overrightarrow{FG} + \overrightarrow{RS} - \overrightarrow{RG}$ **e** $\overrightarrow{MN} - \overrightarrow{GW} - \overrightarrow{WN}$

    b $\overrightarrow{ML} - \overrightarrow{TL} + \overrightarrow{TR}$ **d** $\overrightarrow{VW} - \overrightarrow{CW} - \overrightarrow{KC}$ **f** $\overrightarrow{JW} - \overrightarrow{KS} + \overrightarrow{WJ} + \overrightarrow{KT}$

5 **a** Write $\overrightarrow{AB}$ in terms of **p**, **q**, **r** and **s**.

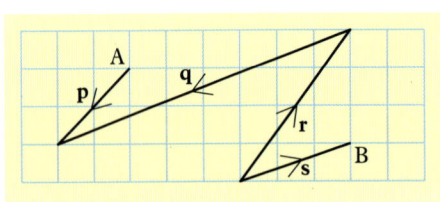

    b Write $\overrightarrow{BA}$ in terms of **p**, **q**, **r** and **s**.

6 **a** Find $\overrightarrow{PQ}$ in terms of **a**, **b** and **c**.

You need to start at P and get to Q using the vectors **a**, **b** and **c**.
Remember that you can subtract vectors as well as add them.

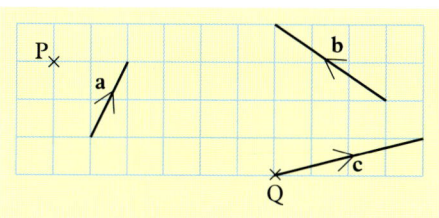

b Find $\overrightarrow{QP}$ in terms of **a**, **b** and **c**.

7 $\mathbf{p} = \begin{pmatrix} 8 \\ 7 \end{pmatrix}$ $\qquad \mathbf{q} = \begin{pmatrix} 3 \\ 5 \end{pmatrix}$ $\qquad \mathbf{r} = \begin{pmatrix} 2 \\ 4 \end{pmatrix}$

Show that $(\mathbf{p} - \mathbf{q}) - \mathbf{r} \neq \mathbf{p} - (\mathbf{q} - \mathbf{r})$.

You can multiply a vector by a scalar.

Using $\mathbf{p} = \begin{pmatrix} 4 \\ -2 \end{pmatrix}$

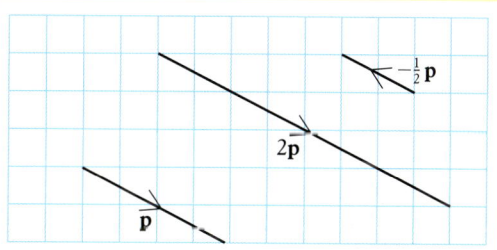

$$2\mathbf{p} = 2\begin{pmatrix} 4 \\ -2 \end{pmatrix} = \begin{pmatrix} 2 \times 4 \\ 2 \times -2 \end{pmatrix} = \begin{pmatrix} 8 \\ -4 \end{pmatrix}$$

$$-\tfrac{1}{2}\mathbf{p} = -\tfrac{1}{2}\begin{pmatrix} 4 \\ -2 \end{pmatrix} = \begin{pmatrix} -\tfrac{1}{2} \times 4 \\ -\tfrac{1}{2} \times -2 \end{pmatrix} = \begin{pmatrix} -2 \\ 1 \end{pmatrix}$$

In the diagram: **2p** is **twice** as long as **p** and in the same direction.
$-\tfrac{1}{2}\mathbf{p}$ is **half** as long as **p** and in the **opposite** direction.

Exercise 14:3

1 $\mathbf{p} = \begin{pmatrix} 3 \\ -2 \end{pmatrix}$ $\qquad \mathbf{q} = \begin{pmatrix} -1 \\ 4 \end{pmatrix}$

Write these as column vectors.

a $2\mathbf{p}$ **d** $\tfrac{1}{2}\mathbf{q}$ **g** $\mathbf{p} - 2\mathbf{q}$

b $-\mathbf{q}$ **e** $-\tfrac{1}{3}\mathbf{p}$ **h** $\tfrac{1}{2}(\mathbf{p} + \mathbf{q})$

c $-3\mathbf{p}$ **f** $2\mathbf{p} + \mathbf{q}$ **i** $-2(3\mathbf{p} + \mathbf{q})$

2 Copy the diagram. Label each vector in terms of the vectors **a** and **b**.

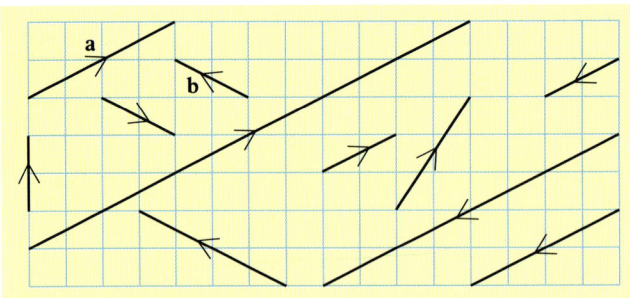

3 **a** Copy the diagram. Complete it to show that $3\mathbf{a} + 3\mathbf{b} = 3(\mathbf{a} + \mathbf{b})$.

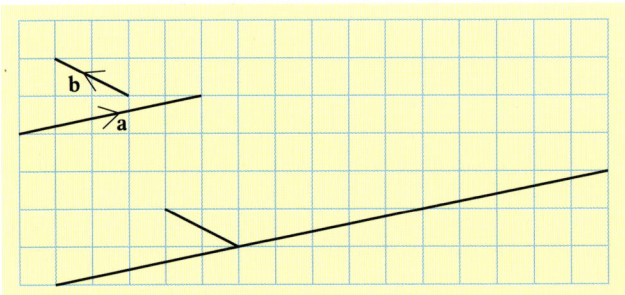

b Show that $2\mathbf{a} + 2\mathbf{b} = 2(\mathbf{a} + \mathbf{b})$.

Linear combination

If p and q are scalars then $p\mathbf{a} + q\mathbf{b}$ is a **linear combination** of **a** and **b**.

$2\mathbf{a} + 3\mathbf{b}$ is a linear combination of **a** and **b** with $p = 2$ and $q = 3$.
$5\mathbf{a} - 2\mathbf{b}$ is a linear combination of **a** and **b** with $p = 5$ and $q = -2$.

Example

$$\mathbf{a} = \begin{pmatrix} 3 \\ 4 \end{pmatrix} \quad \mathbf{b} = \begin{pmatrix} -1 \\ 6 \end{pmatrix}$$

Find a linear combination of **a** and **b** that is parallel to the x axis.

A column vector that is parallel to the x axis must have a zero in the bottom row.

You only need to look at the numbers in the bottom rows of **a** and **b** to find a possible linear combination.

$3 \times 4 - 2 \times 6 = 0$ so one possible linear combination is $3\mathbf{a} - 2\mathbf{b}$.

Exercise 14:4

1 $\mathbf{m} = \begin{pmatrix} -3 \\ 10 \end{pmatrix}$ $\mathbf{n} = \begin{pmatrix} 2 \\ 5 \end{pmatrix}$

     a Find a linear combination of **m** and **n** that is parallel to the x axis.
     b Find a linear combination of **m** and **n** that is parallel to the y axis.

2 $\mathbf{a} = \begin{pmatrix} -3 \\ 4 \end{pmatrix}$ $\mathbf{b} = \begin{pmatrix} 4 \\ 2 \end{pmatrix}$

     a Find a linear combination of **a** and **b** that is parallel to the x axis.
     b Find a linear combination of **a** and **b** that is parallel to the y axis.

3

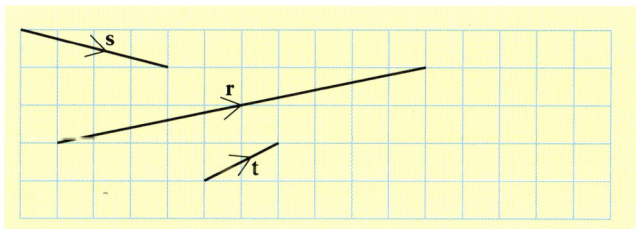

     a Write down **r**, **s** and **t** as column vectors.
     b Find values of p and q so that $\mathbf{r} = p\mathbf{s} + q\mathbf{t}$.
     c Find **s** as a linear combination of **r** and **t**.
  • **d** Find **t** as a linear combination of **r** and **s**.

4 $\mathbf{m} = \begin{pmatrix} 4 \\ 0 \end{pmatrix}$ $\mathbf{n} = \begin{pmatrix} 3 \\ -1 \end{pmatrix}$

Write each of these column vectors as a linear combination of **m** and **n**.

     a $\begin{pmatrix} 10 \\ -2 \end{pmatrix}$ **b** $\begin{pmatrix} -2 \\ 2 \end{pmatrix}$ **c** $\begin{pmatrix} 17 \\ -3 \end{pmatrix}$ **d** $\begin{pmatrix} 1 \\ 5 \end{pmatrix}$

| Magnitude of a vector | The **magnitude of a vector** is its size. This is the length of the vector on a vector diagram. |

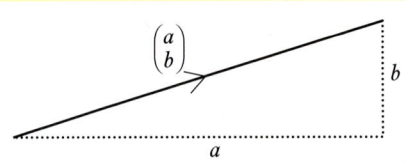

Using Pythagoras' theorem the column vector $\begin{pmatrix} a \\ b \end{pmatrix}$ has length $\sqrt{a^2 + b^2}$.

So the magnitude of $\begin{pmatrix} a \\ b \end{pmatrix}$ is $\sqrt{a^2 + b^2}$.

The magnitude of $\begin{pmatrix} 6 \\ 8 \end{pmatrix}$ is $\sqrt{6^2 + 8^2} = \sqrt{100} = 10.$

When you square $(-n)$ you get $(-n) \times (-n) = n^2$.

So the magnitude of $\begin{pmatrix} 5 \\ -3 \end{pmatrix}$ is $\sqrt{5^2 + (-3)^2} = \sqrt{5^2 + 3^2}$

$$= \sqrt{34} = 5.83 \text{ (to 3 sf)}$$

Exercise 14:5

1 Find the magnitude of each of these vectors.

a $\begin{pmatrix} 5 \\ 12 \end{pmatrix}$ **b** $\begin{pmatrix} -5 \\ 12 \end{pmatrix}$ **c** $\begin{pmatrix} 8 \\ 7 \end{pmatrix}$ **d** $\begin{pmatrix} -9 \\ -3 \end{pmatrix}$ **e** $\begin{pmatrix} -8.63 \\ 9.47 \end{pmatrix}$

2 Find three column vectors that have the same magnitude as $\begin{pmatrix} 1 \\ 3 \end{pmatrix}$.

3 Write the magnitude of each of these vectors in surd form.

a $\begin{pmatrix} 1 \\ 1 \end{pmatrix}$ **b** $2\begin{pmatrix} 1 \\ 1 \end{pmatrix}$ **c** $\begin{pmatrix} 3 \\ 3 \end{pmatrix}$ **d** $\begin{pmatrix} 5 \\ -5 \end{pmatrix}$

4 a Show that the magnitude of $\begin{pmatrix} 2 \\ 2 \end{pmatrix}$ is $2 \times$ the magnitude of $\begin{pmatrix} 1 \\ 1 \end{pmatrix}$.

b Show that the magnitude of $\begin{pmatrix} ka \\ kb \end{pmatrix}$ is $k \times$ the magnitude of $\begin{pmatrix} a \\ b \end{pmatrix}$.

5 Find the vector with magnitude 50 that is in the same direction as $\begin{pmatrix} 3 \\ -4 \end{pmatrix}$.

2 Vector geometry

Sir William Rowan Hamilton (1805–1865) was a brilliant mathematician and physicist.

He spent many years developing a theory of quaternions that could be used to solve problems in applied mathematics.

Unfortunately his theory was never used because vectors could be used to solve the same problems and vectors are much easier!

Origin

The **origin** is a point chosen as a starting point to measure from. The origin is usually labelled O.

Position vector

The vector $\overrightarrow{OP}$ starts at the origin and finishes at P.

$\overrightarrow{OP}$ is called the **position vector** of P.

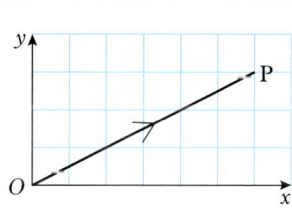

The co-ordinates of P are (6, 3).

The position vector of P is $\begin{pmatrix} 6 \\ 3 \end{pmatrix}$.

The position vector of Q is $\mathbf{a} + \mathbf{b}$.

Exercise 14:6

1 Write down the position vector of P and Q in each diagram.

a

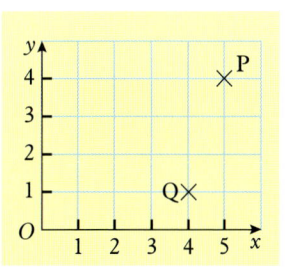

b

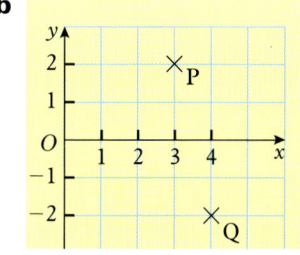

c

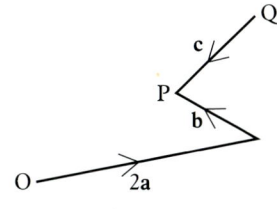

2   The diagram shows a tessellation made from a parallelogram.
Find the position vector of each of the labelled points.

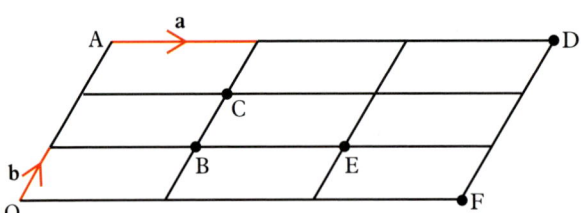

In the diagram, the points A and B have
position vectors **a** and **b**. Using this notation
you can write down two important results.

1   The vector from A to B is $-\mathbf{a} + \mathbf{b}$
so $\overrightarrow{AB} = \mathbf{b} - \mathbf{a}$.

2   M is the midpoint of AB.
$$\overrightarrow{OM} = \mathbf{a} + \tfrac{1}{2}\overrightarrow{AB}$$
$$= \mathbf{a} + \tfrac{1}{2}(\mathbf{b} - \mathbf{a})$$
$$= \mathbf{a} + \tfrac{1}{2}\mathbf{b} - \tfrac{1}{2}\mathbf{a}$$
$$= \tfrac{1}{2}\mathbf{a} + \tfrac{1}{2}\mathbf{b}$$
$$= \tfrac{1}{2}(\mathbf{a} + \mathbf{b})$$

So the midpoint of AB has position vector $\tfrac{1}{2}(\mathbf{a} + \mathbf{b})$.

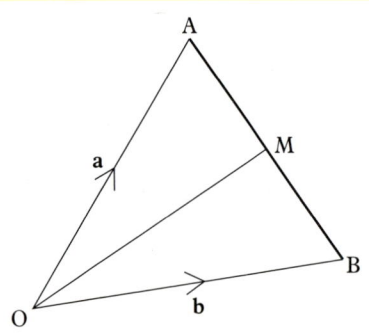

Example   A has position vector $2\mathbf{p} + 3\mathbf{q}$ and B has position vector $4\mathbf{p} - \mathbf{q}$.

Find   **a** $\overrightarrow{AB}$ **b**   the position vector of the
midpoint of A and B.

a   You can think of $\overrightarrow{AB}$ as $\mathbf{b} - \mathbf{a}$ where $\mathbf{b} = 4\mathbf{p} - \mathbf{q}$ and $\mathbf{a} = 2\mathbf{p} + 3\mathbf{q}$.

So $\overrightarrow{AB} = (4\mathbf{p} - \mathbf{q}) - (2\mathbf{p} + 3\mathbf{q})$
$$= 4\mathbf{p} - \mathbf{q} - 2\mathbf{p} - 3\mathbf{q}$$
$$= 2\mathbf{p} - 4\mathbf{q}$$

b   The midpoint of A and B has position vector $\tfrac{1}{2}(\mathbf{a} + \mathbf{b})$.

$\tfrac{1}{2}(\mathbf{a} + \mathbf{b}) = \tfrac{1}{2}((4\mathbf{p} - \mathbf{q}) + (2\mathbf{p} + 3\mathbf{q})) = \tfrac{1}{2}(6\mathbf{p} + 2\mathbf{q}) = 3\mathbf{p} + \mathbf{q}$

So the position vector of the midpoint of A and B is $3\mathbf{p} + \mathbf{q}$.

Exercise 14:7

1 A has co-ordinates $(7, -1)$ and B has co-ordinates $(3, 5)$.
    a Write down the position vectors of A and B.
    b Find $\overrightarrow{AB}$.
    c Find the position vector of the midpoint of A and B.

2 $\overrightarrow{OP} = 3\mathbf{m} + 5\mathbf{n}$. $\overrightarrow{OQ} = \mathbf{m} - \mathbf{n}$.
    a Find $\overrightarrow{PQ}$ in terms of $\mathbf{m}$ and $\mathbf{n}$.
    b Find the position vector of the midpoint of PQ.

3 OABC is a parallelogram.
    a Find the position vector of the midpoint of AC.
    b Find the position vector of the midpoint of OB.
    c Explain what your answers to **a** and **b** show
       about the diagonals of a parallelogram.

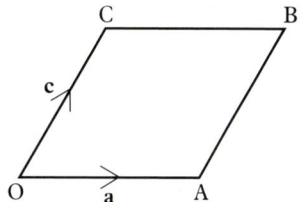

4 In the diagram P divides
    AB in the ratio $2 : 1$.
    a Write $\overrightarrow{AP}$ in terms of $\overrightarrow{AB}$.
    b Write $\overrightarrow{AP}$ in terms of $\mathbf{a}$ and $\mathbf{b}$.
    c Show that $\overrightarrow{OP} = \dfrac{\mathbf{a} + 2\mathbf{b}}{3}$

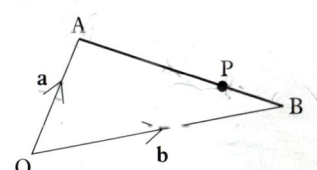

5 In triangle ABC, the position vectors
    of A, B and C are $\mathbf{a}$, $\mathbf{b}$ and $\mathbf{c}$, respectively.
    M, N and P are the midpoints of
    AC, BC and AB, respectively.
    a Write down the position vectors
       of M, N and P.
    b Find the position vector of the point
       that divides BM in the ratio $2 : 1$.
    c Find the position vector of the point
       that divides AN in the ratio $2 : 1$.
    d Show that AN, BM and CP pass
       through the same point.

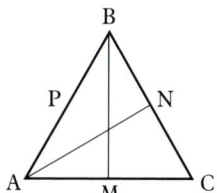

Example

In the diagram, M is the midpoint of AB and N is the midpoint of BC. Show that MN is parallel to AC and is half its length.

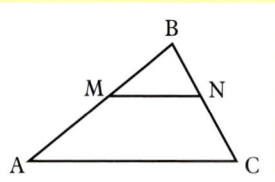

You can write $\overrightarrow{AC}$ in terms of $\overrightarrow{AB}$ and $\overrightarrow{AC}$.

$\overrightarrow{AC} = \overrightarrow{AB} + \overrightarrow{BC}$

$\overrightarrow{MN}$ can also be written in terms of $\overrightarrow{AB}$ and $\overrightarrow{BC}$:

M is the midpoint of AB so $\overrightarrow{MB} = \frac{1}{2}\overrightarrow{AB}$

N is the midpoint of BC so $\overrightarrow{BN} = \frac{1}{2}\overrightarrow{BC}$

$\overrightarrow{MN} = \overrightarrow{MB} + \overrightarrow{BN}$

$\quad\quad = \frac{1}{2}\overrightarrow{AB} + \frac{1}{2}\overrightarrow{BC}$

$\quad\quad = \frac{1}{2}(\overrightarrow{AB} + \overrightarrow{BC})$

$\quad\quad = \frac{1}{2}\overrightarrow{AC}$

This shows that the vector $\overrightarrow{MN}$ is half the vector $\overrightarrow{AC}$, so MN is parallel to AC and half its length.

Exercise 14:8

1 In the diagram PQ and SR are parallel and equal in length.

   a Write $\overrightarrow{QP}$ and $\overrightarrow{SR}$ in terms of **a**.

   b Show that $\overrightarrow{QR} =$ **b**.

   c Explain why PQRS must be a parallelogram.

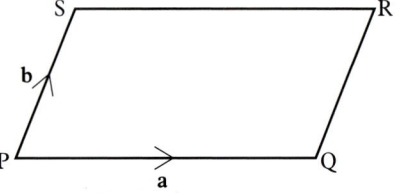

2 ABCD is a parallelogram.
The ratio of BE to EC is 2 : 1.
The ratio of CF to FD is 1 : 2.

   a Write $\overrightarrow{BD}$ in terms of **a** and **b**.

   b Write $\overrightarrow{EF}$ in terms of **a** and **b**.

   c What is the connection between EF and BD?

   d What shape is BDFE?

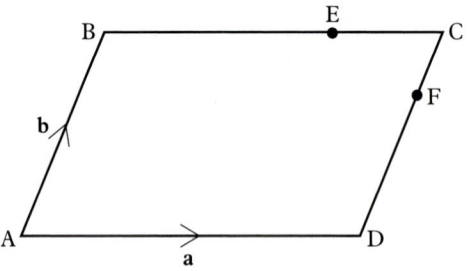

Collinear Points that lie on the same straight line are **collinear**.

X, Y and Z are not collinear.

$\overrightarrow{XY}$ and $\overrightarrow{YZ}$ have a common point but different directions.

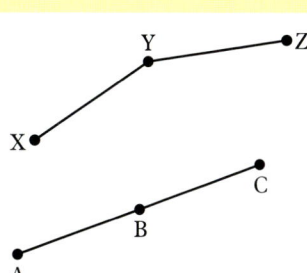

A, B and C are collinear.

$\overrightarrow{AB}$ and $\overrightarrow{BC}$ have a point in common and are in the same direction.

Whenever this happens you know that the points are collinear.

Example $\overrightarrow{OP} = 2\mathbf{a} + 3\mathbf{b}$, $\overrightarrow{OQ} = 5\mathbf{a} - \mathbf{b}$ and $\overrightarrow{OR} = 11\mathbf{a} - 9\mathbf{b}$.
Show that P, Q and R are collinear.

$$\begin{aligned}\overrightarrow{PQ} &= \overrightarrow{OQ} - \overrightarrow{OP} \\ &= (5\mathbf{a} - \mathbf{b}) - (2\mathbf{a} + 3\mathbf{b}) \\ &= 5\mathbf{a} - \mathbf{b} - 2\mathbf{a} - 3\mathbf{b} \\ &= 3\mathbf{a} - 4\mathbf{b} \qquad [1]\end{aligned}$$

$$\begin{aligned}\overrightarrow{QR} &= \overrightarrow{OR} - \overrightarrow{OQ} \\ &= (11\mathbf{a} - 9\mathbf{b}) - (5\mathbf{a} - \mathbf{b}) \\ &= 11\mathbf{a} - 9\mathbf{b} - 5\mathbf{a} + \mathbf{b} \\ &= 6\mathbf{a} - 8\mathbf{b} \qquad [2]\end{aligned}$$

From [1] and [2], $\overrightarrow{PQ} = \tfrac{1}{2}\overrightarrow{QR}$.

$\overrightarrow{PQ}$ and $\overrightarrow{QR}$ have a common point, Q, and the same direction so P, Q and R are collinear.

3 $\overrightarrow{OA} = 3\mathbf{a} - 5\mathbf{b}$, $\overrightarrow{OB} = \mathbf{a} + 3\mathbf{b}$, $\overrightarrow{OC} = -3\mathbf{a} + 19\mathbf{b}$.
Show that A, B and C are collinear.

4 $\overrightarrow{OP} = 7\mathbf{q} + 5\mathbf{r}$, $\overrightarrow{OQ} = 3\mathbf{q} - 2\mathbf{r}$, $\overrightarrow{OR} = 5\mathbf{q} + 6\mathbf{r}$, $\overrightarrow{OS} = \mathbf{q} + 8\mathbf{r}$
Which three of the points P, Q, R and S lie on the same straight line?

5 In the diagram P is a point $\tfrac{2}{3}$ of the
way from O to A.
Q is a point $\tfrac{2}{3}$ of the way from A to B.
A has position vector $\mathbf{a}$.
B has position vector $\mathbf{b}$.
R has position vector $k\mathbf{b}$.
P, Q and R are collinear.
Find the value of k.

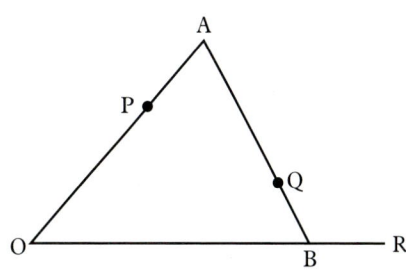

3 This is for real

Hamish has just rowed across this river.
He tried to row straight across.
He finished quite a long way downstream.

This is a real example of vector addition.

Speed is a scalar. Speed is the magnitude of velocity.
Velocity is a vector because it is a speed *in a particular direction.*

Hamish tried to row straight across the river.
He rowed at 2 m/s.
This is the vector showing his velocity on the water.

The river is flowing from left to right at 1 m/s.
This is the vector showing the velocity of the river.

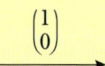

Hamish actually travels at an angle, instead of perpendicular to the river.
He also travels faster than 2 m/s because the river increases his speed.
To find Hamish's actual velocity, you need to add the two vectors together.

Resultant vector   When you add two or more vectors together, the vector that you
get is called the **resultant vector**.

This is the vector triangle for Hamish's
journey.
The resultant vector is the red vector
in this triangle.

The magnitude is:

$\sqrt{1^2 + 2^2} = \sqrt{5} = 2.2$ m/s to 1 dp.

and the direction is α to the right of the perpendicular where $\tan\alpha = \dfrac{1}{2} = 0.5$

so $\alpha = 26.6°$ to 1 dp.

The resultant vector is Hamish's actual velocity as he crosses the river.
Hamish's velocity is 2.2 m/s at 26.6° to the right of the perpendicular.

Exercise 14:9

1 Gerald is rowing across a river. The speed of the river is 3 m/s.
He tries to row straight across at 4 m/s.
  a How fast does he travel?
  b What direction does he travel across the river?

2 Terry is going to row across a river. The speed of the river is 4 m/s.
He tries to row straight across at 2 m/s.
  a How fast does he travel?
  b What direction does he travel across the river?

The width of the river is 80 metres.
  c How far down the river does Terry
       reach the opposite side?
  d How far is Terry's actual journey?
       Use Pythagoras' theorem in the triangle.
  e How long does the journey take him?
  f If Terry had gone straight across the 80 m
       width of the river at 2 m/s how long would
       the journey have taken him?
  g Write down what your answers to parts **e** and **f** tell you.

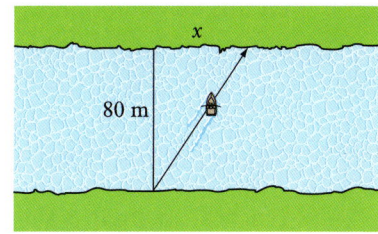

3 Hayley wants to swim straight
across this river.
She knows that she will be
carried downstream if she
aims straight across.
She decides to aim upstream at α to
the perpendicular.
She knows that she can swim at 2 m/s.
The river is flowing at 1 m/s.
  a Find the angle, α, that Hayley should use
       so that her resultant velocity will be straight across the river.
       You will need to use trigonometry to help you.
  b What speed will Hayley actually go across the river?

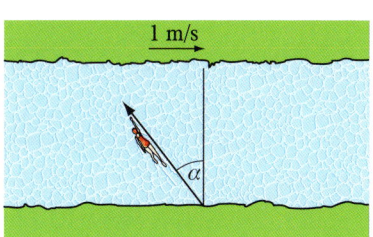

The river is 100 metres wide.
  c How long does Hayley take to cross the river?
       You should be able to work this out using your answer to part **b**.

As well as using vectors to solve problems about velocities, you can also solve problems that involve forces.

A force is a vector because it has size and direction.

Forces are measured in newtons. You write 15 newtons as 15 N.

If you want to find out what a combination of forces will do, you need to find the resultant force.

This vector represents a force of 15 N up. $\begin{pmatrix} 0 \\ 15 \end{pmatrix}$

This vector represents a force of 17 N across. $\begin{pmatrix} 17 \\ 0 \end{pmatrix}$

The resultant force is the force shown on this diagram in red.

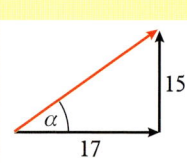

The magnitude of the resultant force is $\sqrt{17^2 + 15^2} = 22.7$ N to 1 dp.

It acts at an angle α above the horizontal where

$$\tan \alpha = \frac{15}{17} \text{ so } \alpha = 41.4° \text{ to 1 dp.}$$

So the resultant of forces of 15 N up and 17 N horizontally is a force of 22.7 N at 41.4° above the horizontal.

4 Find the resultant of each of these pairs of forces.

a

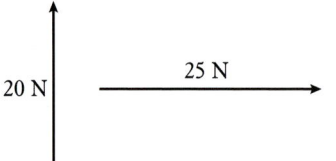

b

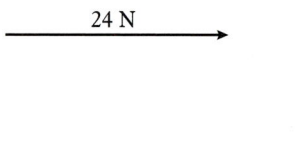

5 Two tug boats are pulling a ship that is stuck on the bank of a river.
The diagram shows the forces on the ship.
The ship needs to be pulled with a force with a magnitude of at least 100 000 N to get it free.
Will the ship be pulled off the bank?

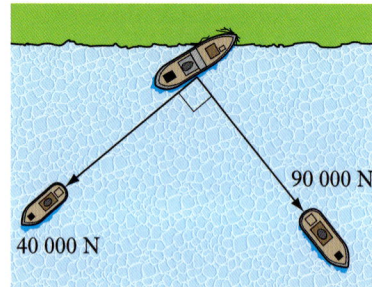

When you are dealing with vectors you can think about components.
Splitting a vector into components is doing the opposite of finding the resultant of two vectors.

Component

A **component** of a vector is the amount of the vector that acts in a given direction. Components are often very useful when you are looking at forces.

If you have a force **F** acting at an angle α above the horizontal you can split the force into components.
You can find the amount of the force that acts horizontally and the amount that acts vertically.

The horizontal component of the force is the force **h** on the diagram.

The vertical component of the force is the force **v** on the diagram.

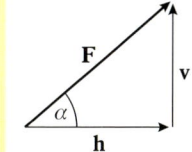

Using trigonometry you can find the magnitude of these components.
Using F for the magnitude of the force **F**:

$$\sin \alpha = \frac{v}{F} \qquad\qquad \cos \alpha = \frac{h}{F}$$

so $\qquad v = F \sin \alpha \qquad$ and $\qquad h = F \cos \alpha$

Exercise 14:10

1 Find the exact values for each of these forces of:
(1) the horizontal component
(2) the vertical component

a
15 N
30°

c
20 N
60°

e
30 N
30°

g
40 N

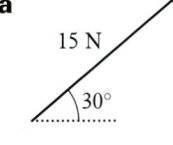
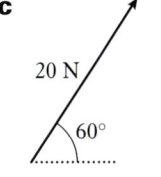
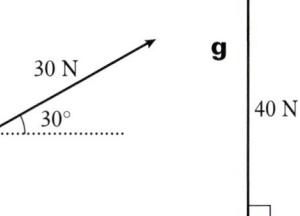

b
25 N
60°

d
50 N
30°

f
60 N

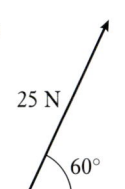
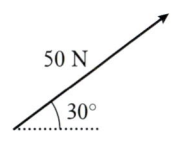
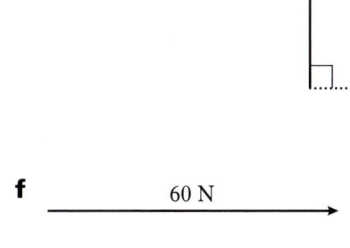

2 a Add the horizontal components of the forces in parts **a** to **g** of question **1**.
  b Add the vertical components of the forces in parts **a** to **g** of question **1**.
  c Find the resultant force of the forces in parts **a** and **b** of this question.
  d Draw a diagram to show the resultant force.

3 Find the exact values for each of these forces of:
  (1) the horizontal component
  (2) the vertical component

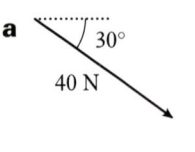

a 30°
40 N

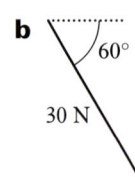

b 60°
30 N

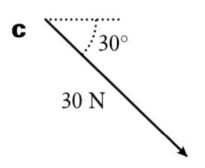

c 30°
30 N

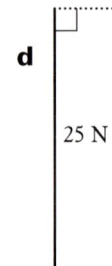

d
25 N

4 a Add the horizontal components of the forces in parts **a** to **d** of question **3**.
  b Add the vertical components of the forces in parts **a** to **d** of question **3**.
  c Find the resultant force of the forces in parts **a** and **b** of this question.
  d Draw a diagram to show the resultant force.

5 a Write each of these vectors as column vectors.
    You need to work out the horizontal and vertical components.

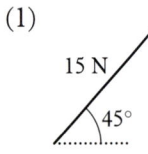

(1)
15 N
45°

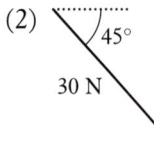

(2) 45°
30 N

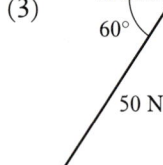

(3) 60°
50 N

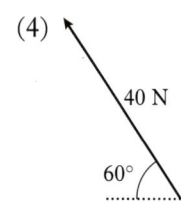

(4)
40 N
60°

  b Find the resultant of the four forces by adding the column vectors.
  c Find the magnitude and direction of the resultant force.
  d Draw a diagram to show the resultant force.

6 Jenny and Aisha are pulling a sledge.
Jenny is pulling with a force of 500 N
at 30° above the horizontal.
Aisha is pulling with a force of 800 N
at 60° above the horizontal.
Which way will the sledge go?

1 Copy these. Fill in the gaps.

a $\begin{pmatrix} 3 \\ 2 \end{pmatrix} + \begin{pmatrix} -4 \\ \cdots \end{pmatrix} = \begin{pmatrix} \cdots \\ 6 \end{pmatrix}$ **c** $\overrightarrow{SD} + \overrightarrow{DU} = \cdots$ **e** $\cdots + \overrightarrow{PB} = \overrightarrow{AB}$

b $\begin{pmatrix} \cdots \\ -2 \end{pmatrix} + \begin{pmatrix} 5 \\ \cdots \end{pmatrix} = \begin{pmatrix} 3 \\ 2 \end{pmatrix}$ **d** $\overrightarrow{CP} + \cdots = \overrightarrow{CH}$ **f** $\overrightarrow{DB} + \cdots + \overrightarrow{JG} = \overrightarrow{DG}$

2 a Write these as column vectors.

(1) $\overrightarrow{PQ}$ (2) $\overrightarrow{QR}$ (3) $\overrightarrow{RS}$ (4) $\overrightarrow{PS}$

b Show that $\overrightarrow{PQ} + \overrightarrow{QR} + \overrightarrow{RS} = \overrightarrow{PS}$.

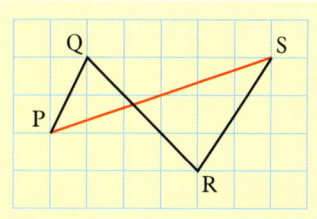

3 $p = \begin{pmatrix} 5 \\ 2 \end{pmatrix}$ $q = \begin{pmatrix} 5 \\ -2 \end{pmatrix}$ $r = \begin{pmatrix} 7 \\ -3 \end{pmatrix}$

Find:

a $p + q$ **c** $q + r$ **e** $p - q - r$

b $p - q$ **d** $p + q + r$ **f** $r - q - p$

4 $p = \begin{pmatrix} 3 \\ -2 \end{pmatrix}$ $q = \begin{pmatrix} -1 \\ 4 \end{pmatrix}$

Write these as column vectors:

a $3p$ **d** $\frac{1}{3}q$ **g** $2p - 3q$

b $-2q$ **e** $-\frac{1}{2}p$ **h** $\frac{1}{2}(p - q)$

c $-2p$ **f** $3p + q$ **i** $-3(4p + 2q)$

5 Copy the diagram. Label each vector in terms of the vectors **a** and **b**.

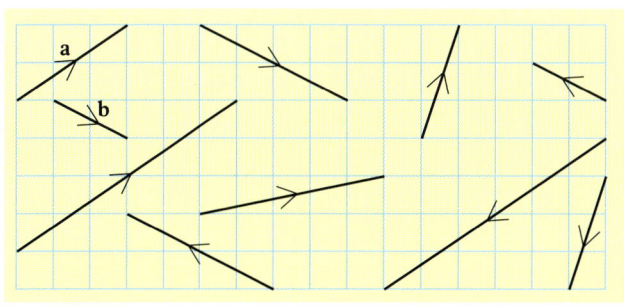

6 $\mathbf{p} = \begin{pmatrix} -2 \\ 8 \end{pmatrix}$ $\mathbf{q} = \begin{pmatrix} 3 \\ 6 \end{pmatrix}$

    a Find a linear combination of **p** and **q** that is parallel to the x axis.
    b Find a linear combination of **p** and **q** that is parallel to the y axis.

7 $\mathbf{m} = \begin{pmatrix} 3 \\ 0 \end{pmatrix}$ $\mathbf{n} = \begin{pmatrix} 4 \\ -2 \end{pmatrix}$

    Write each of these column vectors as a linear combination of **m** and **n**.

    a $\begin{pmatrix} 7 \\ -2 \end{pmatrix}$ **b** $\begin{pmatrix} -1 \\ 2 \end{pmatrix}$ **c** $\begin{pmatrix} 10 \\ -2 \end{pmatrix}$ **d** $\begin{pmatrix} 2 \\ 2 \end{pmatrix}$ **e** $\begin{pmatrix} -5 \\ 4 \end{pmatrix}$

8 Find the magnitude of each of these vectors.

    a $\begin{pmatrix} 3 \\ 4 \end{pmatrix}$ **b** $\begin{pmatrix} -3 \\ -4 \end{pmatrix}$ **c** $\begin{pmatrix} 7 \\ 24 \end{pmatrix}$ **d** $\begin{pmatrix} 4 \\ -7 \end{pmatrix}$ **e** $\begin{pmatrix} -2.15 \\ 4.5 \end{pmatrix}$

9 Find three column vectors that have the same magnitude as $\begin{pmatrix} 2 \\ -4 \end{pmatrix}$.

10 Write down the position vector of P in each diagram.

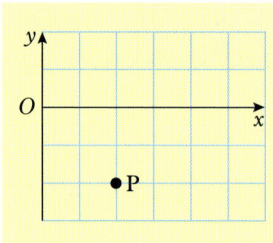
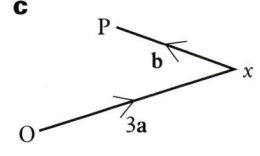

11 A has co-ordinates $(6, -1)$ and B has co-ordinates $(2, 7)$.
    a Write down the position vectors of A and B.
    b Find $\overrightarrow{AB}$.
    c Find the position vector of the midpoint of A and B.

12 In the diagram P divides
AB in the ratio $3 : 1$.
Find the position vector
of P in terms of **a** and **b**.

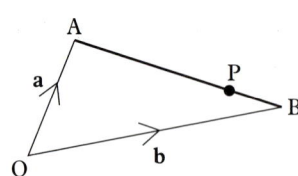

13 $\overrightarrow{OQ} = 2\mathbf{a} + \mathbf{b}$, $\overrightarrow{OR} = 4\mathbf{a} - 2\mathbf{b}$, and $\overrightarrow{OS} = 8\mathbf{a} - 8\mathbf{b}$.

    a Show that Q, R and S are collinear.

    b Show that R divides QS in the ratio 1 : 2.

14 When an aeroplane flies it can be
blown off course by the wind.
In the old days planes were quite slow
and flew at low heights.

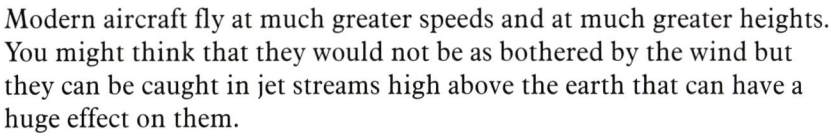

    a What velocity does a plane have if it is
flying due North at 100 knots in a wind
blowing at 40 knots due East?

    b How far off course is the plane if it flies
for what the pilot thinks is 200 miles due North?

Modern aircraft fly at much greater speeds and at much greater heights.
You might think that they would not be as bothered by the wind but
they can be caught in jet streams high above the earth that can have a
huge effect on them.

    c What velocity does a plane have if it is flying due North at
2000 knots in a wind blowing at 200 knots due East?

    d How far off course is the plane if it flies for what the pilot thinks is
500 miles due North?

15 Sam and Josie are fighting over a teddy bear.
Sam pulls with a force of 10 N at 30° above the
horizontal.
Josie pulls with a force of 15 N at 60° above the
horizontal.
Will the teddy start to move towards Sam
or Josie?

16 One of the events in the competition to
find the World's Strongest Man is to
pull a juggernaut.

Why do the competitors try to get themselves
and the rope as close to the horizontal as
possible?

1   Solve these vector equations.

a $3\begin{pmatrix} a \\ b \end{pmatrix} + \begin{pmatrix} 5 \\ -3 \end{pmatrix} = \begin{pmatrix} 11 \\ 9 \end{pmatrix}$

b $2\begin{pmatrix} s \\ t \end{pmatrix} + \begin{pmatrix} 5s \\ -3t \end{pmatrix} = \begin{pmatrix} 14 \\ -4 \end{pmatrix}$

2   Solve these vector equations.
You need to use simultaneous equations to do these.

a $2\begin{pmatrix} s \\ t \end{pmatrix} + \begin{pmatrix} 5t \\ -3s \end{pmatrix} = \begin{pmatrix} 19 \\ 0 \end{pmatrix}$

b $\begin{pmatrix} 13 \\ 1 \end{pmatrix} = a\begin{pmatrix} 4 \\ 1 \end{pmatrix} + b\begin{pmatrix} 5 \\ 2 \end{pmatrix}$

3 $\mathbf{p} = \begin{pmatrix} 1 \\ 4 \end{pmatrix}$ $\mathbf{q} = \begin{pmatrix} 3 \\ 6 \end{pmatrix}$

a   Find a linear combination of **p** and **q** that is equal to the vector $\begin{pmatrix} 7 \\ 16 \end{pmatrix}$.

b   Find a linear combination of **p** and **q** that is equal to the vector $\begin{pmatrix} -1 \\ 2 \end{pmatrix}$.

4   In the diagram P divides
AB in the ratio $m : n$.
Find the position vector
of P in terms of **a** and **b**.

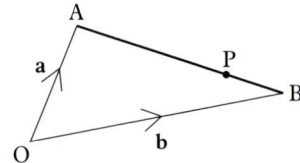

5   Fiona is going to row across a river. The speed of the river is s m/s.
She tries to row straight across at r m/s. The width of the river is m metres.
a   How fast does she travel?
b   What direction does she travel across the river?
c   How long does the journey take her?

6   This diagram shows a sign held by two
strings.
The forces on the sign are the weight of
the sign, W, and the tensions in the two strings.
a   For the sign to stay still, what must be true
about the upward and downward forces on
the sign?
b   Find the weight of the sign.

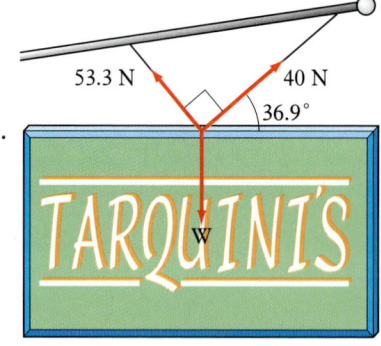

1 Copy these. Fill in the gaps.

  a $\begin{pmatrix} 4 \\ -1 \end{pmatrix} + \begin{pmatrix} -3 \\ \dots \end{pmatrix} = \begin{pmatrix} \dots \\ 7 \end{pmatrix}$

  b $\overrightarrow{LZ} + \overrightarrow{ZY} = \dots$

2 Write $\overrightarrow{AB}$ in terms of **p**, **q** and **r**.

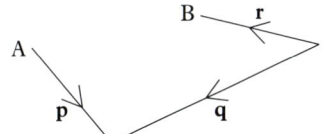

3 $\mathbf{m} = \begin{pmatrix} 2 \\ 3 \end{pmatrix}$ $\mathbf{n} = \begin{pmatrix} -2 \\ 4 \end{pmatrix}$

  Find:

  a $\mathbf{m} + \mathbf{n}$ **c** $3\mathbf{m}$

  b $\mathbf{m} - \mathbf{n}$ **d** $-\dfrac{1}{2}\mathbf{n}$

4 **a** Find the magnitude of the vector $\begin{pmatrix} -5 \\ 12 \end{pmatrix}$.

  b Write down three more column vectors with the same magnitude as the vector in part **a**.

5 The diagram shows a circle with centre O passing through the point P(4, 7.5)

  a Write down the position vector of P.
  b Find the radius of the circle.

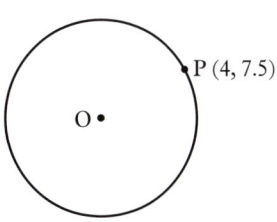

6 P has position vector $\begin{pmatrix} 6 \\ -3 \end{pmatrix}$.

  Q has position vector $\begin{pmatrix} 4 \\ 1 \end{pmatrix}$.

  Write down the position vector of the midpoint of PQ.

7 $\overrightarrow{OA} = 2\mathbf{a} - 3\mathbf{b}$ $\qquad$ $\overrightarrow{OB} = 5\mathbf{a} + \mathbf{b}$ $\qquad$ $\overrightarrow{OC} = 8\mathbf{a} + 5\mathbf{b}$
Show that A, B and C are collinear.

8 In the diagram, P divides
MN in the ratio 4 : 1.
Find the position vector
of P in terms of **m** and **n**.

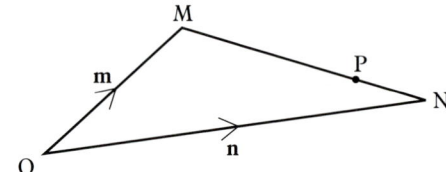

9 Solve these vector equations.

a $2\begin{pmatrix} x \\ y \end{pmatrix} + \begin{pmatrix} 4 \\ -1 \end{pmatrix} = \begin{pmatrix} 12 \\ 9 \end{pmatrix}$
$\qquad$
b $p\begin{pmatrix} 2 \\ 7 \end{pmatrix} + q\begin{pmatrix} -3 \\ 5 \end{pmatrix} = \begin{pmatrix} 12 \\ 11 \end{pmatrix}$

10 $\mathbf{t} = \begin{pmatrix} -4 \\ 5 \end{pmatrix}$ $\qquad$ $\mathbf{v} = \begin{pmatrix} 3 \\ 2 \end{pmatrix}$

a Find a linear combination of **t** and **v** that is parallel to the *x* axis.
b Find a linear combination of **t** and **v** that is parallel to the *y* axis.

11 Write $\begin{pmatrix} 16 \\ 3 \end{pmatrix}$ as a linear combination of $\begin{pmatrix} 4 \\ -1 \end{pmatrix}$ and $\begin{pmatrix} -2 \\ -3 \end{pmatrix}$.

12 Find the exact value for this force of:

a the horizontal component
b the vertical component

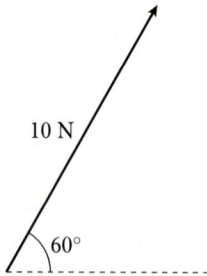

15 Back to the drawing board

1 Angles
Finding angles in triangles
Finding angles in quadrilaterals
Looking at parallel lines
Proving that the angles in a triangle add up to 180°
Working out interior and exterior angles of polygons

2 Similarity
Introducing similarity
Using the rules for similar triangles to find missing sides
Proving that triangles are similar

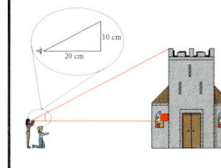

3 Congruence
Introducing congruence
Using the 4 rules of congruence for triangles

4 Loci
Defining a locus
Drawing loci

5 Circle theorems
Looking at tangents to circles
Looking at angles in circles
Discovering the circle theorems
Using the circle theorems
Proving the circle theorems

CORE

QUESTIONS

EXTENSION

TEST YOURSELF

1 Angles

The angles in this bike frame are very important to its strength.

Designing all sorts of structures involves calculating angles. Look at the entrance to the Louvre in Paris on the cover of this book!

Angles in a triangle	**Angles in a triangle** add up to 180°.

Exercise 15:1

Calculate the angles marked with letters.

1

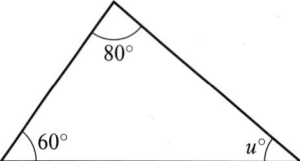

4

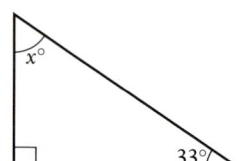

2

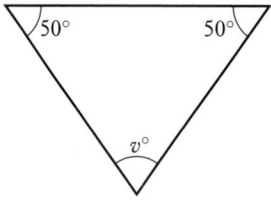

5

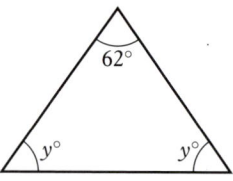

3

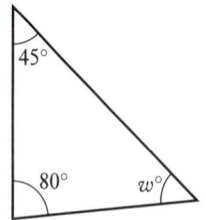

6

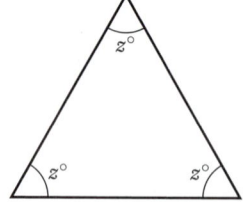

All quadrilaterals are made up of two triangles.

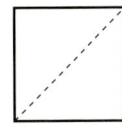 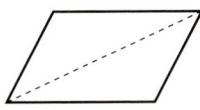 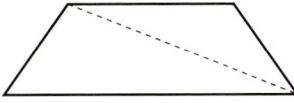

Because the angles in a triangle add up to 180°, the angles in a quadrilateral add up to 2 × 180° = 360°.

Example   Find the angle marked $x°$.

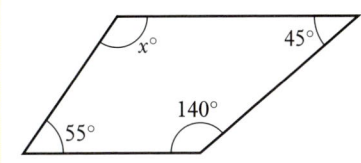

$x° = 360° - 140° - 45° - 55°$
$x° = 120°$

Exercise 15:2

Calculate the angles marked with letters.

1
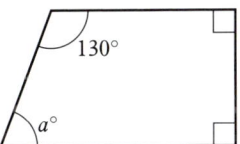

4
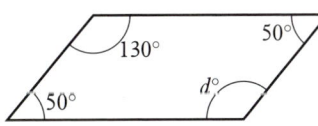

2
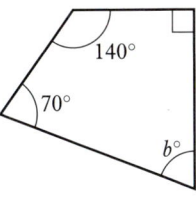

●5
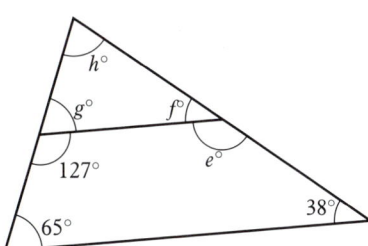

3
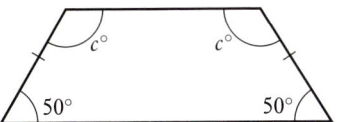

●6
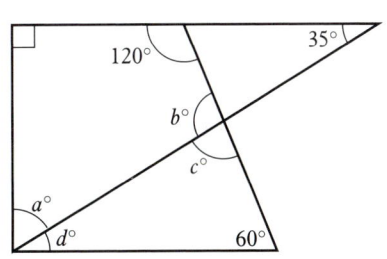

You have been told that the angles in a triangle add up to 180°.
How do you know that this is always true?
To prove this result you need to know some angle facts about parallel lines.

Parallel lines

Parallel lines are always the same distance apart.

You show parallel lines with arrows like this.

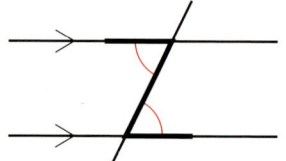

When you draw a line across a pair of parallel lines you get these angles.

Alternate angles
Z angles

The red angles are called **alternate angles.**

They are the angles in the Z shape.
They are sometimes called **Z angles.**

The blue angles are also alternate angles.
They don't look much like a Z, but they are still alternate angles.

Alternate angles are equal.

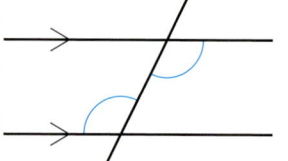

Corresponding angles
F angles

The red angles are **corresponding angles.**
They are the angles in the F shape so they are sometimes called **F angles.**

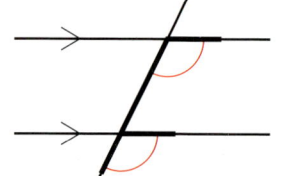

All of the angles in the same place in the top part of the diagram and the bottom part of the diagram are corresponding angles.

Corresponding angles are equal.

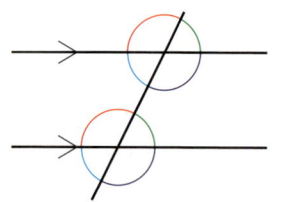

Opposite angles
X angles

Opposite angles are the angles that are opposite each other at a cross.
They are sometimes called **X angles.**
Opposite angles are equal.

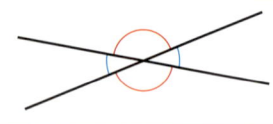

Exercise 15:3

For each question, write down the angle marked with a letter.
Give a reason for each answer.

1

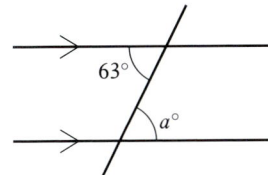

3

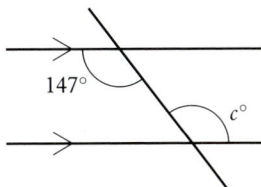

2

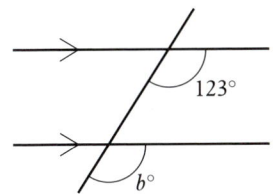

4

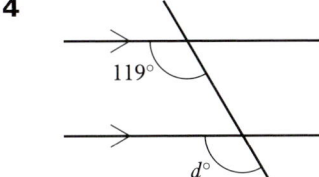

Now you're ready to prove that the angles in a triangle add up to 180°.
You already know that the angles on a straight line add up to 180°.
When you're writing out a proof you need to give a reason for every line
of your working.

This is triangle ABC.
The angles inside triangle ABC
are labelled a, b and c.
You need to show that $a + b + c = 180°$.

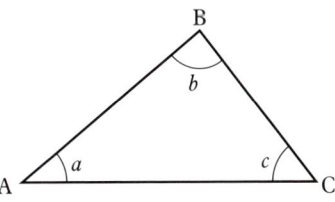

5 a Extend the line AC to the right and draw a line parallel to AB from C
to get the diagram below. Label the angles p and q as shown.

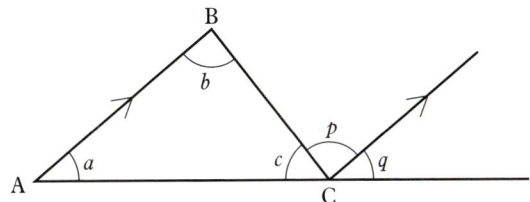

b Copy this. Fill it in.

$$c + p + q = \ldots \qquad \text{(Angles on } \ldots\ldots\ldots\ldots\ldots\ldots\text{)}$$
$$p = b \qquad (\ldots\ldots\ldots\ldots \text{ angles are equal)}$$
$$q = a \qquad (\ldots\ldots\ldots\ldots \text{ angles are equal)}$$

So $\ldots\ldots\ldots = 180°$

and you have proved the result!

6 Prove that the angle outside triangle ABC at C is equal to the angles inside the triangle at A and B added together.

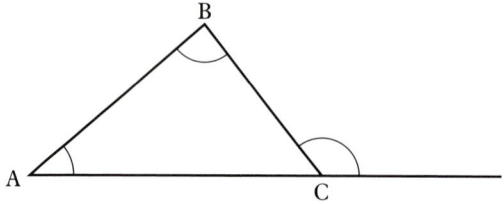

Exterior angles	To find an **exterior angle**:

To find an **exterior angle**:
(1) make one side longer.
(2) mark the angle between your line and the next side.
(3) this is the exterior angle. The blue angles are all exterior angles.

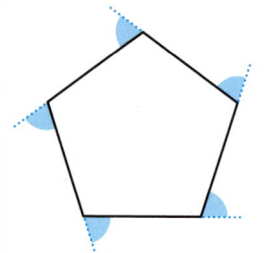

The diagram shows a regular pentagon.
It has rotational symmetry of order 5 about the point C.

The pentagon fits onto itself 5 times in one rotation.

The size of each turn is $360° \div 5 = 72°$.
This is the size of the exterior angle.

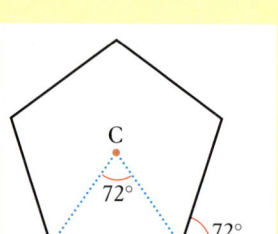

If a regular polygon has n sides then:

1 it has rotational symmetry of order n

2 the exterior angle $= \dfrac{360°}{n}$

3 $n = \dfrac{360°}{\text{the exterior angle}}$

Exercise 15:4

1 Work out the exterior angle of a regular hexagon.

2 Work out the exterior angle of a regular decagon.

3 The exterior angle of a regular polygon is 12°.
How many sides does it have?

4 The exterior angle of a regular polygon is 15°.
How many sides does it have?

5 **a** Write down which of these is not an exterior angle of a regular polygon.
   (1) 40°   (2) 22.5°   (3) 50°   (4) 8°
   b Explain how you were able to decide.

6 Each diagram shows two sides of a regular polygon.
Work out the number of sides for each one.

a
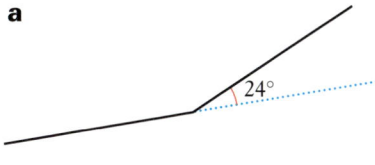

c
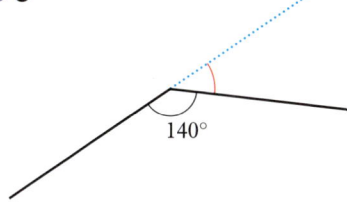

b

d
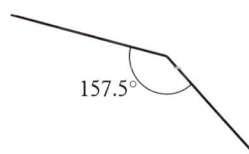

| Interior angles | An **interior angle** is the angle inside a shape where two sides meet. The red angles are all interior angles. |

The interior angle always makes a straight line with the exterior angle.

This means that interior angle + exterior angle = 180°.

7 Write down the interior angle when the exterior angle is:

    a 72°   **b** 9°   **c** 60°   **d** 3°

8 A regular polygon has 30 sides.

    a Find the size of the exterior angle.

    b Write down the interior angle.

9 The interior angle of a regular polygon is 172°.

    a Write down the exterior angle.

    b Work out how many sides the polygon has.

You can find the sum of the interior angles of any polygon.

(1) Draw the polygon.

(2) Join one vertex to all the others.
You divide the shape into triangles.
All the interior angles are now inside one of the triangles.

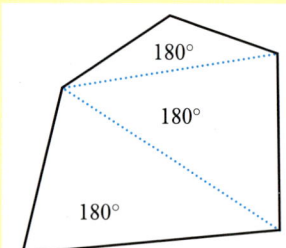

(3) Count the number of triangles.
Multiply by 180° to find the total.

Example   Find the sum of the interior angles of a pentagon.
The pentagon splits into **3** triangles.

Total = **3** × 180° = 540°

The sum of the interior angles of a pentagon is 540°.
This is true for all pentagons.

Exercise 15:5

1 Calculate the size of the missing angle in each of these pentagons.

a

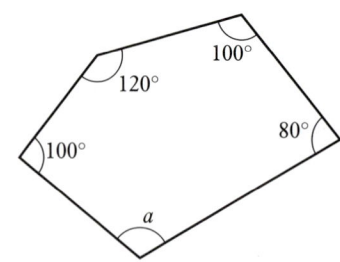

b

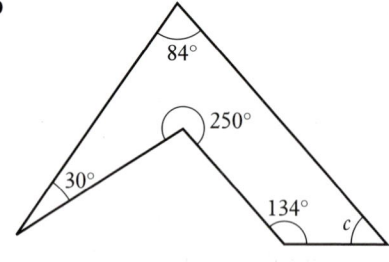

c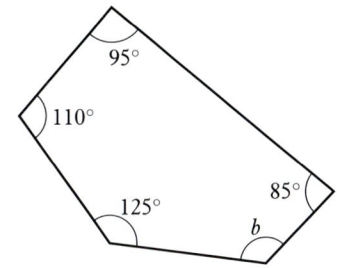

d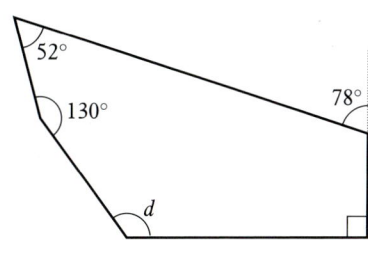

2 **a** A hexagon has 6 sides. Draw a hexagon.

    b Join one vertex to all of the others.

    c Count the number of triangles.

    d Find the sum of the interior angles of a hexagon.

3 **a** A heptagon has 7 sides. Draw a heptagon.

    b Join one vertex to all of the others.

    c Count the number of triangles.

    d Find the sum of the interior angles of a heptagon.

4 **a** An octagon has 8 sides. Draw an octagon.

    b Join one vertex to all of the others.

    c Count the number of triangles.

    d Find the sum of the interior angles of an octagon.

5 **a** A nonagon has 9 sides. Draw a nonagon.

    b Join one vertex to all of the others.

    c Count the number of triangles.

    d Find the sum of the interior angles of a nonagon.

6 **a** A decagon has 10 sides. Draw a decagon.

    b Join one vertex to all of the others.

    c Count the number of triangles.

    d Find the sum of the interior angles of a decagon.

7 **a** Copy the table. Fill it in.

Name of polygon	Number of sides	Number of triangles	Sum of interior angles
	5	3	$3 \times 180°$
	6		
	7		
	8		
	9		
	10		

b Use the results in your table to find a formula for the sum of the interior angles of a polygon with n sides.

> The sum of the interior angles of a polygon with n sides is $(n - 2) \times 180°$.
>
> The sum of the exterior angles of any polygon is 360°.

8 The exterior angles of a pentagon are 64°, 78°, 80°, 36° and $x°$. Find the value of x.

9 The exterior angles of a hexagon are $x°$, $x°$, $2x°$, $2x°$, $3x°$, $3x°$.
    a Find the value of x.
    b How many of these angles are right angles?
    c How many of the interior angles are obtuse? Explain your answer.

10 Find the sum of the interior angles of a polygon with 22 sides.

11 The sum of the interior angles of a polygon is 3240°.
    a Use n to stand for the number of sides. Write an equation for n.
    b Solve your equation. How many sides does the polygon have?

2 Similarity

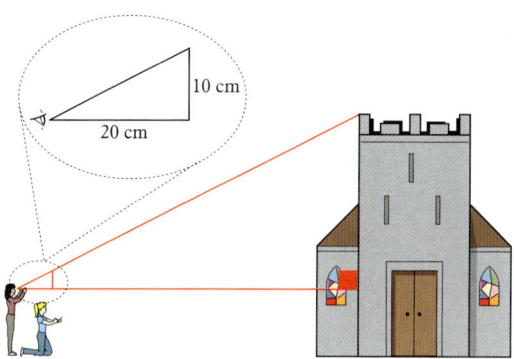

Lin and Karina are finding the height of the church tower. They haven't got a clinometer to measure the angle. They are using a triangle made from card.

This section will show you how to find a height like this.

Exercise 15:6

1 a You will need a piece of 1 cm squared paper.
You will need to draw these triangles accurately.
Start near the bottom left-hand corner of your paper.
Draw triangle AB_1C_1 with a right angle at B_1.
$AB_1 = 4$ cm, $B_1C_1 = 2$ cm.

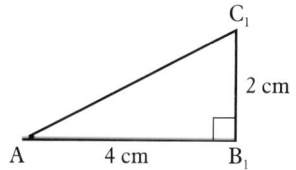

b Now draw AB_2 8 cm long.
Draw another right angle at B_2 and draw in B_2C_2.

c Carry on drawing triangles like this to get this diagram.

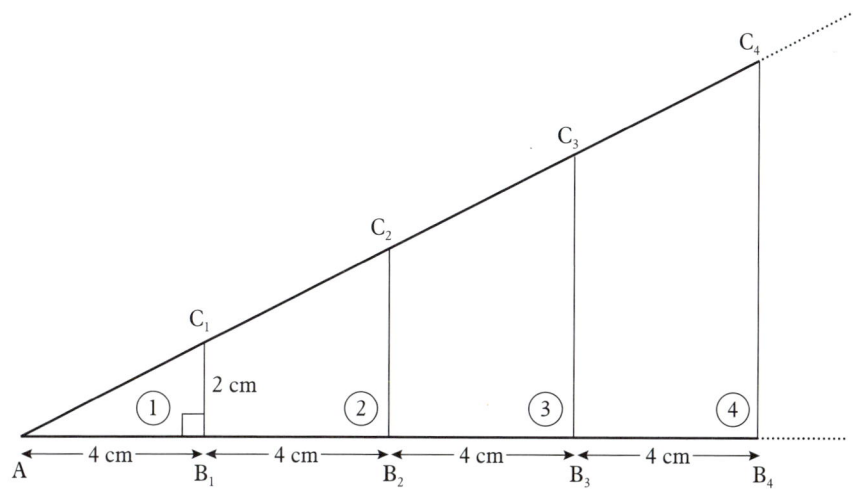

d Copy this table. Fill it in.
The first row has been filled in for you.

Triangle number	Length	Length	Length	Angle (2 sf)	Angle (2 sf)	Ratio	Ratio	Ratio
1	$AB_1 = 4$ cm	$B_1C_1 = 2$ cm	$AC_1 = \sqrt{20}$ cm $= 2\sqrt{5}$ cm	$\angle C_1AB_1 = 27°$	$\angle B_1C_1A = 63°$	$\dfrac{AB_1}{AB_1} = 1$	$\dfrac{B_1C_1}{B_1C_1} = 1$	$\dfrac{AC_1}{AC_1} = 1$
2	$AB_2 = ...$	$B_2C_2 = ...$	$AC_2 = ...$	$\angle C_2AB_2 = ...$	$\angle B_2C_2A = ...$	$\dfrac{AB_2}{AB_1} = ...$	$\dfrac{B_2C_2}{B_1C_1} = ...$	$\dfrac{AC_2}{AC_1} = ...$

e Continue your table for at least 5 triangles.

2 **a** What do you notice about the angles $\angle C_1AB_1$, $\angle C_2AB_2$, ...?
b What do you notice about the angles $\angle B_1C_1A$, $\angle B_2C_2A$, ...?
c What do you know about the angles at B_1, B_2, B_3, ...?
d What do your results to parts **a**, **b** and **c** tell you about the angles in these triangles?

3 **a** Write down the lengths AB_1, AB_2, AB_3, ... as a sequence.
b Find the general term for this sequence.
c Write down the lengths B_1C_1, B_2C_2, B_2C_3, ... as a sequence.
d Find the general term for this sequence.
e Use surds to write down the lengths AC_1, AC_2, AC_3, ... as a sequence.
• **f** Find the general term for this sequence.
• **g** What do your results to parts **b**, **d** and **f** tell you about the sides in these triangles?

4 **a** What do you notice about the ratios $\dfrac{AB_2}{AB_1}$, $\dfrac{B_2C_2}{B_1C_1}$, $\dfrac{AC_2}{AC_1}$ ...?

b What do you notice about the ratios $\dfrac{AB_3}{AB_1}$, $\dfrac{B_3C_3}{B_1C_1}$, $\dfrac{AC_3}{AC_1}$ ...?

c What do your results suggest about the ratios of corresponding sides in these triangles?

Similar	If two objects are **similar**, one is an enlargement of the other. They have the same shape but different sizes.

Exercise 15:7

For each pair of triangles: **a** construct the triangles.
b write down if they are similar or not.

1 (1) Triangle ABC: AB = 2 cm   BC = 3 cm   CA = 4 cm
    (2) Triangle DEF: DE = 5 cm   EF = 7.5 cm   FD = 10 cm

2 (1) Triangle GHI: GH = 8 cm   ∠HGI = 54°   ∠GHI = 42°
    (2) Triangle JKL: JK = 5 cm   ∠JKL = 42°   ∠KJL = 54°

3 (1) Triangle MNP: MN = 4 cm   NP = 5 cm   ∠MNP = 60°
    (2) Triangle QRS: QR = 8 cm   RS = 9 cm   ∠QRS = 60°

4 (1) Triangle TUV: TU = 5 cm   TV = 4 cm   ∠UTV = 60°
    (2) Triangle WXY: WX = 6 cm   XY = 7.5 cm   ∠WXY = 60°

5 (1) Triangle ABC: AB = 5 cm   BC = 7 cm   CA = 9 cm
    (2) Triangle DEF: DE = 2.5 cm   EF = 4.5 cm   FD = 3.5 cm

---

Similar triangles

In **similar triangles** all 3 pairs of angles are equal.
Their 3 pairs of sides are in the same ratio.

To show that two triangles are similar, you have to show that one of these rules is true.

Rule 1 All three pairs of angles are equal.

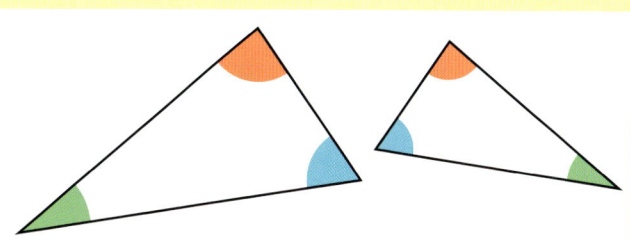

If you can show that 2 pairs of angles are equal then the third pair must be equal.

Rule 2 All pairs of corresponding sides are in the same ratio.

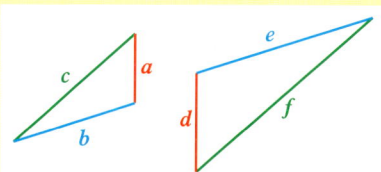

So $\dfrac{a}{d} = \dfrac{b}{e} = \dfrac{c}{f}$

Rule 3 Two pairs of corresponding sides are in the same ratio and the angles *between* the pairs of sides are also equal.

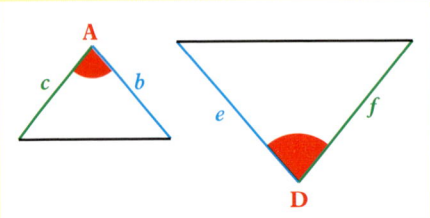

Here $\dfrac{b}{e} = \dfrac{c}{f}$

and $\angle A = \angle D$

Exercise 15:8

For each pair of triangles in questions **1–5**:
a sketch the diagram
b find the missing angles if you can
c decide if the triangles are similar. If they are, write down the similarity rule

1

2

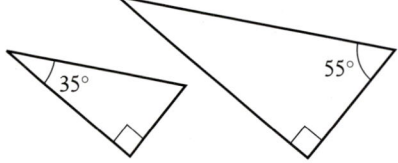

3

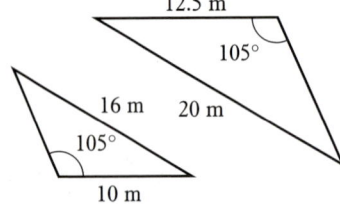

4

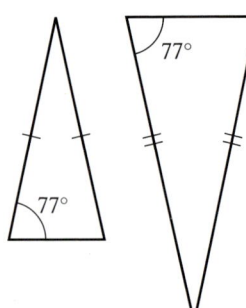

5

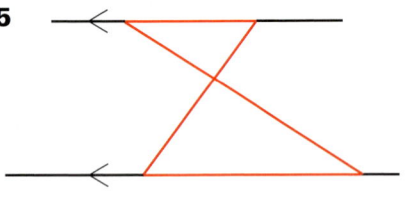

Triangles ABC and FGH are similar. ∠BCA = ∠GHF and ∠CAB = ∠HFG. Find the missing lengths.

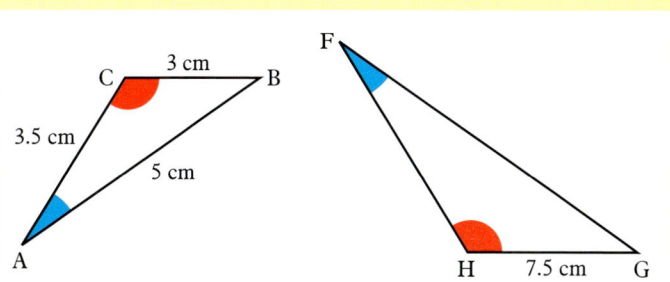

You need to look carefully to decide which sides correspond in each triangle. The colours show the pairs of corresponding angles.
If you write these like this:

∠B**CA** = ∠**GH**F

then   **CA** corresponds to **HF**
         BC corresponds to **GH**
and   **BA** corresponds to **GF**

Now use common sense. Triangle GHF is bigger than triangle BCA so the scale factor going from left to right is **more than 1**.

So, from triangle BCA to triangle GHF, scale factor $= \dfrac{GH}{BC} = \dfrac{7.5}{3} = 2.5$

So HF = 2.5 × 3.5 = 8.75 cm and GF = 2.5 × 5 = 12.5 cm

For each pair of triangles in questions **6–10**:
a sketch the diagrams
b write down which pairs of angles are equal
c use colours to show angles in corresponding positions
d find the lengths marked with letters

6

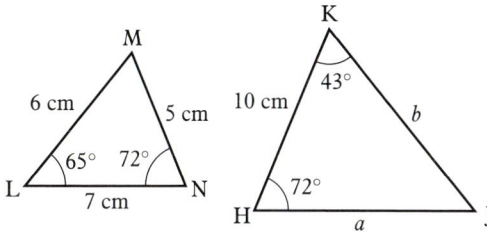

7

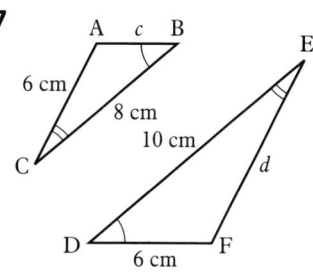

8

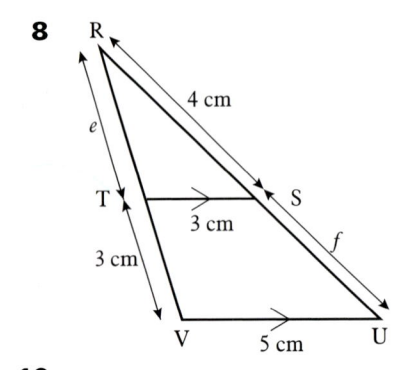

9

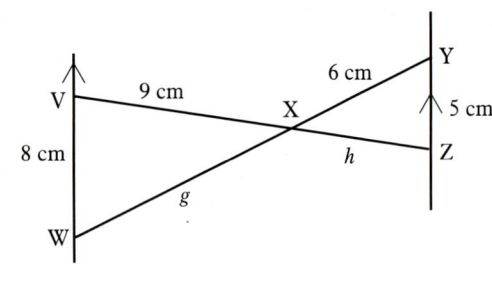

10

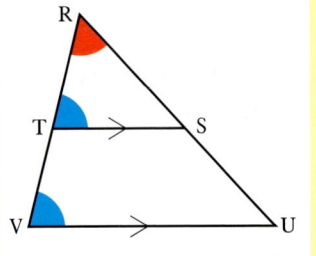

Proving that triangles are similar

You have seen that there are three different rules for similar triangles.
To prove that two triangles are similar, you must show that one of these three rules is true.

Here is a proof that triangles RST and RUV are similar.

∠SRT = ∠URV (**common angle**)

∠RTS = ∠RVU (**corresponding angles, // lines**)

So ∠RST = ∠RUV (angle sum of a triangle = 180°)

So triangles $\begin{cases} \text{RST} \\ \text{RUV} \end{cases}$ are similar (3 equal angles)

Put corresponding letters in the triangles above each other. Then you will be ready to work out any sides that you need.
You need to give a reason for every fact that you give in a proof.

11 Prove that each of these pairs of triangles are similar:
  a triangles RST and RUV in question **8**
  b triangles XVW and XZY in question **9**
  c triangles ACD and CBD in question **10**

Exercise 15:9

1
  a Copy these axes.
  b Draw the quadrilateral ABCD
     with co-ordinates:
     A (0, 1)   B (3, 4)   C (6, 1)   D (5, −1)
  c Measure all the angles in this
     quadrilateral.
  d Enlarge quadrilateral ABCD with:
     (1) scale factor 2 centre the origin
     (2) scale factor $-\frac{1}{2}$ centre (0, 1)
  e Measure all the angles in each
     enlargement. Write down what you
     notice about your answers.
  f What can you say about the three quadrilaterals?

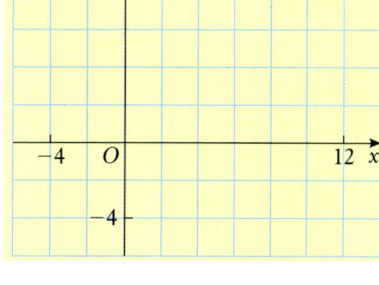

2
  a Copy these axes.
     Draw any convex pentagon
     within the rectangle made by
     (0, 0), (6, 0), (0, 4), (6, 4).
  b Measure the angles of the pentagon.
  c Draw any enlargement of the
     pentagon that will fit on these axes.
  d Measure all the angles of your
     enlargement.
  e Write down what you notice about
     your answers to parts **b** and **d**.
  f What can you say about the two pentagons?

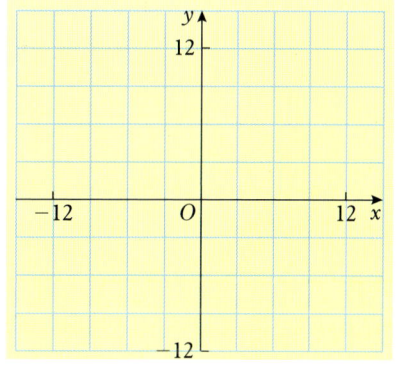

3 For any polygon and its enlargement:
  a write down a rule linking the angles of an object and its image
  b write down a rule linking the corresponding sides of an object and its image

4 An alien spaceship is able to shrink when under attack. When it shrinks, all its
   angles stay the same. These are plan views of the ship before and after attack.

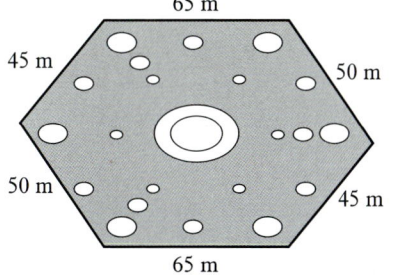
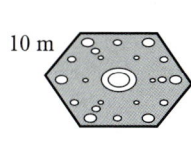

Work out the lengths of all the remaining sides after attack.
Give your answers to 1 dp if you need to round.

3   Congruence

Cranes have triangles in their structures.
This gives them extra strength.

Many of the triangles are exactly the same shape and size.

Congruent
Two objects are **congruent** if they are identical to each other.
They must be exactly the same shape *and* size.

To show that two triangles are congruent, you have to show that one of these rules is true.

Rule 1 All three pairs of sides are equal.

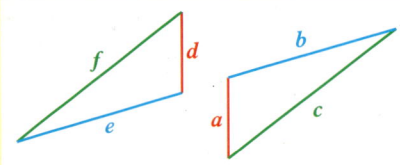

Here $a = d$
       $b = e$
       $c = f$

You can remember this as **SSS**.

Rule 2 Right angle, hypotenuse and side are equal.

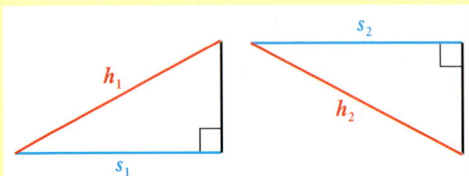

Here $h_1 = h_2$
       $s_1 = s_2$

and both triangles have a right angle.
You can remember this as **RHS**.

Rule 3 Two pairs of corresponding sides are equal and the angles *between* the pairs of sides are also equal.

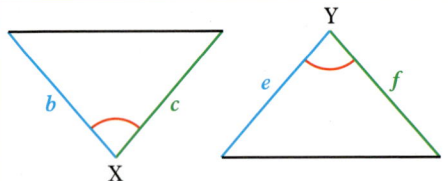

Here $b = e$
       $c = f$

and $\angle X = \angle Y$

You can remember this as **SAS**.

You write the A in the middle to remind you that the angle is *between* the two sides.

Rule 4 Two pairs of angles are equal and a pair of corresponding sides is also
.equal.

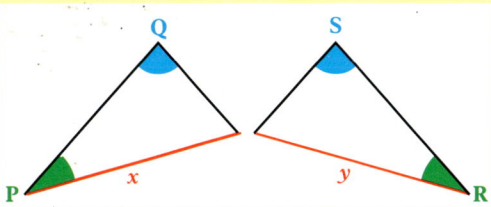

Here $x = y$

$\angle P = \angle R$

and $\angle Q = \angle S$

Remember this as **AA corr. S.**

Exercise 15:10

For each pair of triangles in questions **1–5**:
a sketch the diagrams
b find the missing angles or sides, if you need to
c decide if the triangles are congruent. If they are, write down the
congruence rule that you have used

1

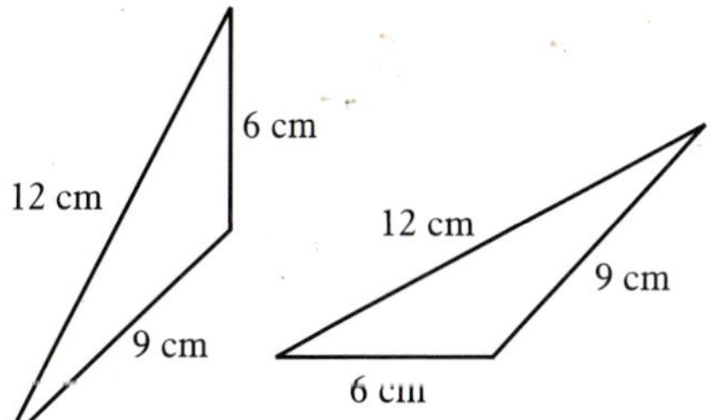

6 cm
12 cm
12 cm
9 cm
9 cm
6 cm

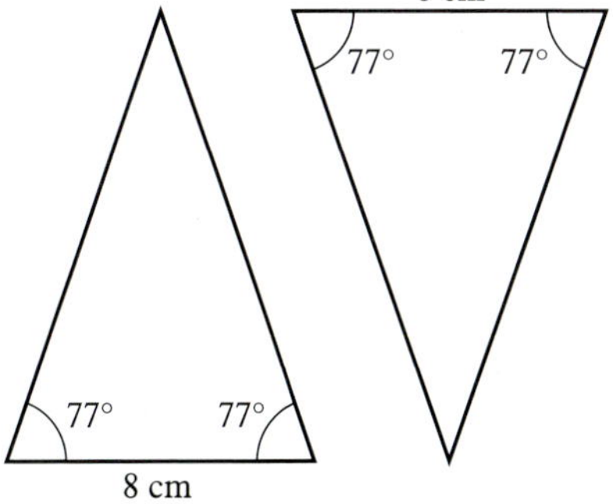

4

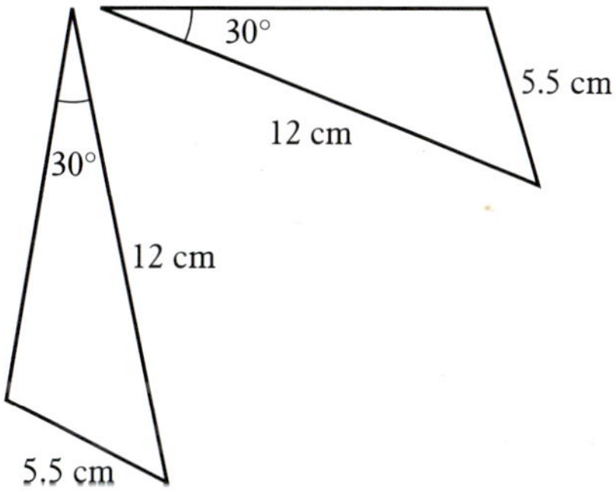

30°
5.5 cm
30°
12 cm
12 cm
5.5 cm

2

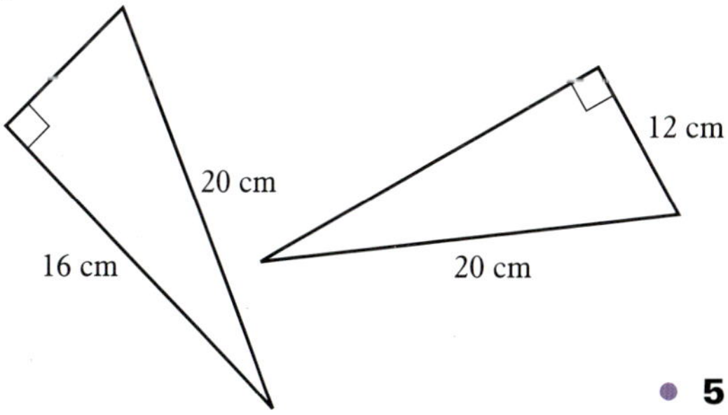

20 cm
16 cm
12 cm
20 cm

5

33°
39°
108°
33°

3

8 cm
77°   77°
77°   77°
8 cm

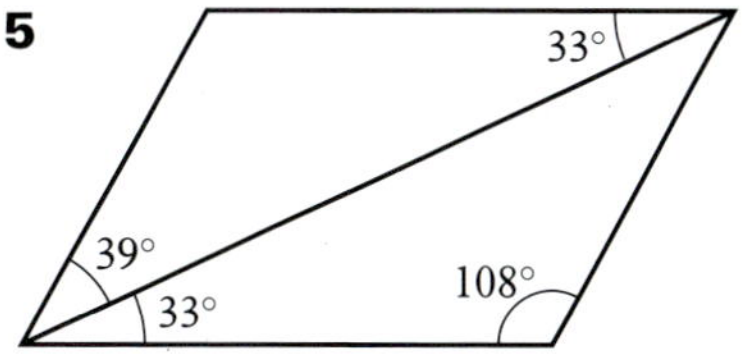

Proving that triangles are congruent

You have seen that there are four different rules for congruent triangles. To prove that two triangles are congruent, you must show that one of these four rules is true.

Here is a proof that triangles WXV and ZXY are congruent.

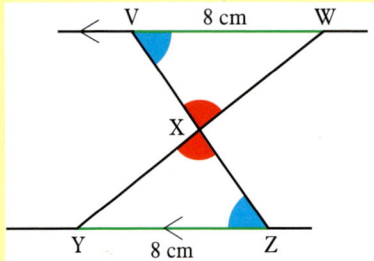

$\angle$WXV = $\angle$ZXY (**vertically opposite angles**)

$\angle$XZY = $\angle$XVW (**alternate angles, // lines**)

WV = ZY (**given in the question**)

So triangles $\begin{cases} \text{RST} \\ \text{RUV} \end{cases}$ are congruent (AA corr. S)

You need to give a reason for every fact that you give in a proof.

Exercise 15:11

1 ABCD is a rectangle.
Prove that triangles ABD and BCD are congruent.

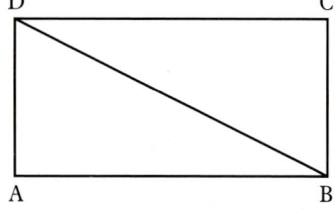

2 FH is perpendicular to IG.
H is the centre of a circle.
Prove that triangles IJH and GJH are congruent.

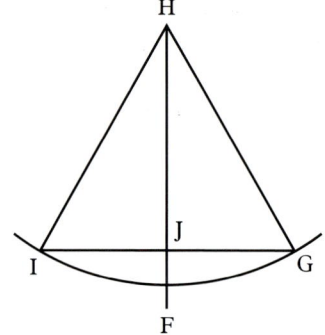

3 JKLMN is a regular pentagon.
Prove that triangles JKL and JKN are congruent.

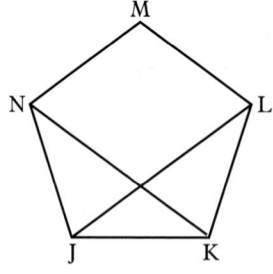

4 This is a plan view of some railway lines.
AB and CD are sleepers.
The sleepers are the same length,
but have *not* been fitted exactly
at right angles to the track.
Despite this, show there is
sufficient evidence to prove that
triangles ABC and BCD are congruent.

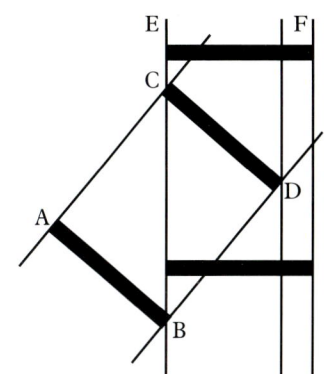

5 Marvo the clown is walking on electric stilts.
The stilts always remain parallel.
Braces AD and BC are jointed at E.
The braces are joined the same distance
apart on each leg, so AB is equal to CD.
Prove that triangles ABE and CDE are
always congruent.

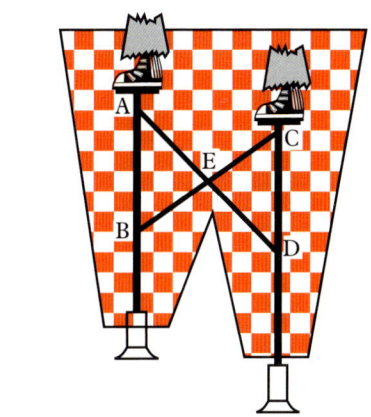

6 GHIJ is a circus trapeze.
Ladders GJ and IH are the same length.
Supporting cables run from G to I and H to J.
  a Prove that triangles GHJ and
  HIG are congruent.
  b Use part **a** to prove that triangles
  JIG and JIH are congruent.
  c Find another pair of triangles that
  look alike.
  d Prove that the triangles in part **c**
  are congruent.

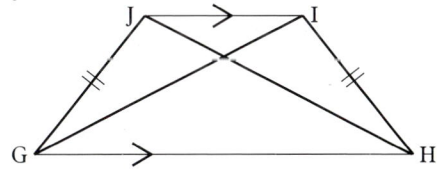

7 ABCD is a school playing field.
It has two pairs of equal sides,
AD = CD and AB = BC.
An area is to be fenced off for the school fete.
This is done by joining the midpoints of all
the sides.
Show, by using congruent triangles, that the
fete will be held in a rectangle.

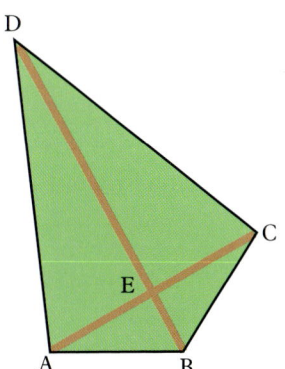

377

4   Loci

In Norway it is not unusual for people to keep animals on the roof!
It is important to keep Sven tied up so that he doesn't fall off.
Sven is attached to a post.
He can eat the grass in a circle.
The radius of the circle is the length of the rope.
The centre of the circle is the post.
Sven can be anywhere inside the circle.

When something can only be on a line or a curve then this line or curve is called a locus.

Locus

The **locus** of an object that is moving according to a rule is the path of the object.
You can describe a locus in words or with a diagram.

The tip of the hour hand on this clock moves in a circle.

The hour hand is 3 cm long.

The locus of the tip of the hour hand is a circle of radius 3 cm.
The centre of the circle is the centre of the clock.

You can also draw the locus.
The locus of the tip of the hour hand is the blue circle.

Exercise 15:12

In questions **1–6**:   **a** describe the locus in words
                         b draw a diagram to show the locus

1 The locus of the tip of the minute hand on a clock. The hand is 5 cm long.

2 The locus of the midpoint of the minute hand in question **1**.

3 The locus of a point that is always 4 cm from point O.

4 The locus of a point that is always 3 cm away from this line.

A ————————————— B

5 The locus of a point that moves so that it is always the same distance from the points A and B in question **4**.
What is the mathematical name of this locus?

6 The locus of a point that moves so that it is the same distance from the lines AB and AC in this diagram.
What is the mathematical name of this locus?

7 Draw a diagram to show the locus of the following.
 a The midpoint of this ladder as the ladder slides down the wall.

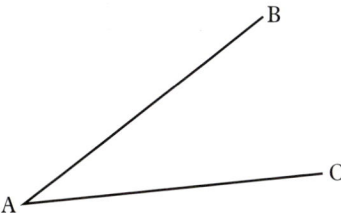

 b A point on the rim of a bicycle wheel as the bicycle rolls forwards.

 c The path of a ball that Richard throws to Thomas.
The ball leaves Richard's hand at 45° above the horizontal.

 d The centre of the coin as the coin moves along the edges of the box.

 e A point on the edge of the coin in part **d** if the coin rolls around the edges of the box and does not slip.

You can also use regions to describe where something can be.

Example   Sven the goat is tethered to a post in the centre of a roof.
The roof is 8 m long and 7 m wide.
The rope is 3 m long.
Make a scale drawing to show the area where Sven can graze.
Use a scale drawing of 1 cm to 2 m.

You need to draw a rectangle 4 cm by 3.5 cm.
The post, P, is at the centre of the rectangle.
Now draw a circle, centre P, with radius 1.5 cm.

Sven can eat grass anywhere inside the red circle.

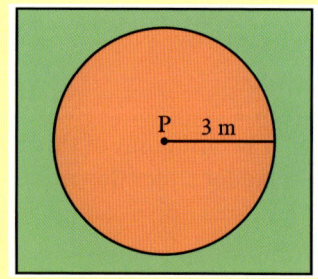

8   A horse is tied to a wall at W.
The length of the rope is 3 m.
Make a scale drawing to show where the horse can graze.
Use a scale of 1 cm to 1 m.

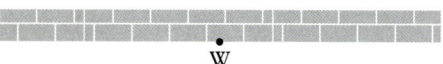

9   A bull is tethered to a ring at R.
The rope is 9 m long.
Make a scale drawing to show where the bull can move.
Use a scale of 1 cm to 2 m.

• R

   You need Worksheets 15:2 and 15:3 – Regions.

5 Circle theorems

This is a picture of Michaela Melinte of Romania throwing the hammer.

She set the world record for women in March 1997. Her throw was 69.58 m.

She throws the hammer after turning it round in circles. When she releases the hammer, it flies off at a tangent to the circle.

Tangent

A **tangent** to a circle is a straight line that touches the circle at one point.

Point of contact

The point where the tangent touches the circle is called the **point of contact**.

The red line is a tangent to the circle.

The blue line is not a tangent to the circle because it crosses the circle.

A tangent to a circle is perpendicular to the radius of the circle drawn to the point of contact.
The angle between the tangent and the radius is 90°.

If you draw any chord of a circle, the line from the centre of the circle to the midpoint of the chord is perpendicular to the chord.
This gives you two right-angled triangles.

You need to remember these results.

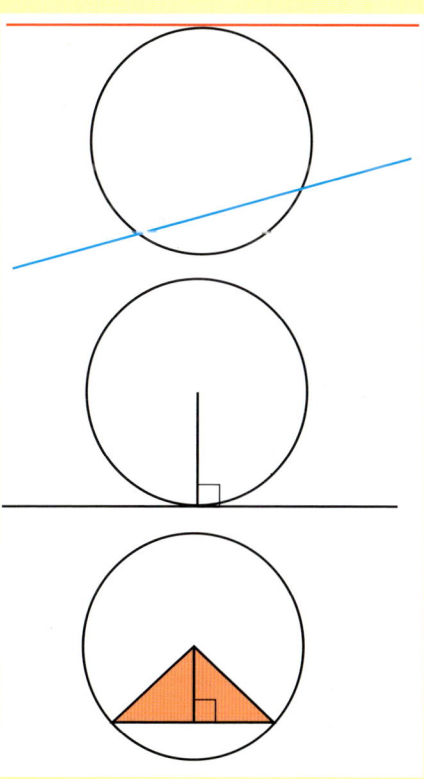

Exercise 15:13

1 Find the angles marked with letters in each part.

a

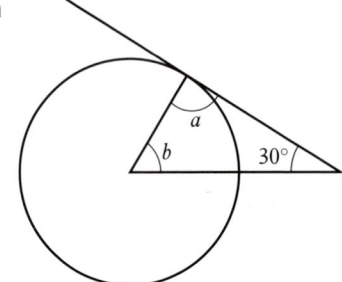

c

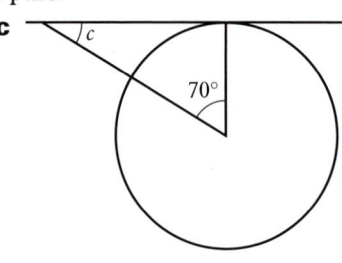

b

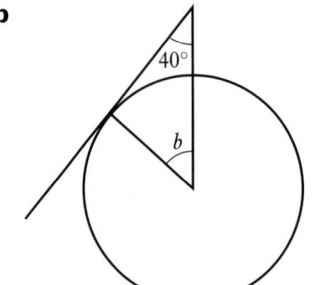

d

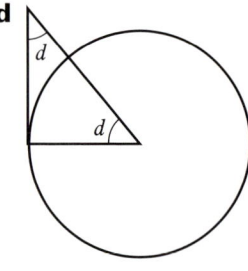

You can draw two tangents to a circle from any point outside the circle.

There are two tangents from the
point P to this circle.

They touch the circle at the
points A and B.
PA and PB are the two tangents
from P to the circle.
The two tangents are equal.
So   PA = PB.
This is an important result to
remember.
This means that triangle ABP is an
isosceles triangle.
So the angles ∠PAB and ∠PBA are equal.

The centre of the circle is O.
OA is a radius of the circle. OB is also a radius.
So   OA = OB.
This means that triangle AOB is also an isosceles triangle.
So the angles ∠OAB and ∠OBA are equal.

2 Find the angles marked with letters in each part.
You might need to draw extra lines to help you solve the problem.

a

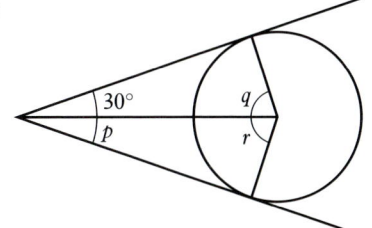

d

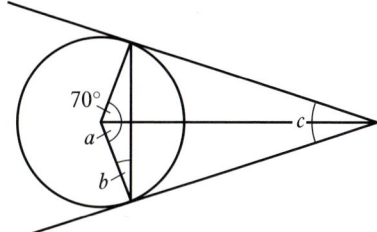

b

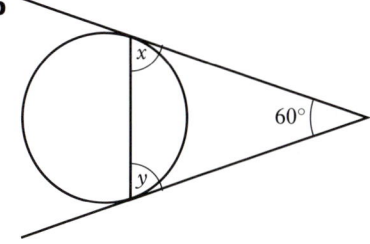

e

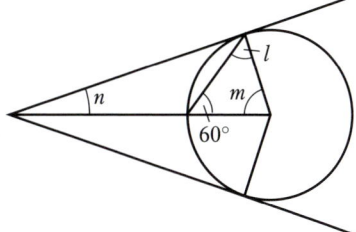

c

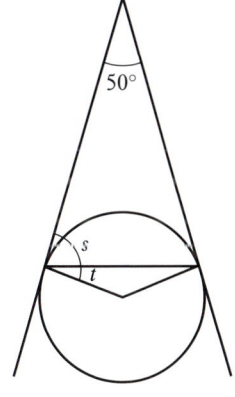

f

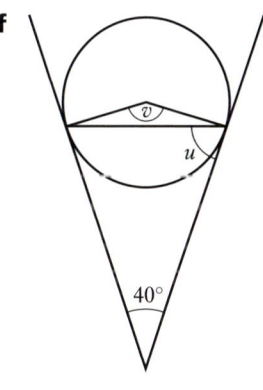

Cyclic quadrilateral

If you draw 4 points on a circle and join them together like this you get a **cyclic quadrilateral**.
ABCD is a cyclic quadrilateral.

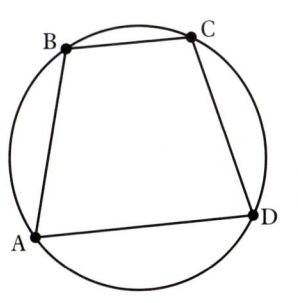

3 **a** Draw a circle with radius 5 cm.
  b Draw any cyclic quadrilateral ABCD using your circle.
    You need to label the vertices so that A is opposite C and B is opposite D.
  c Copy this table.

A	C	B	D

    Measure the angles inside the cyclic quadrilateral at A, B, C and D.
    Fill in your results in the first row of the table.
  d Draw two more cyclic quadrilaterals. Label them ABCD.
    Measure the angles. Fill in the other two rows of the table.
  e Look at your angles.
    Find a rule that connects the angles A and C, and the angles B and D.
    Write down the rule.
    You need to know the rule before you can do the next question.

4 Find the angles marked with letters in each part.

a 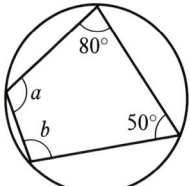   **b** 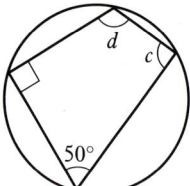   **c**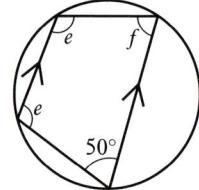

If you draw a chord in a circle you split the circle into two segments.

The red segment is bigger than the blue segment.

The red segment is called the **major segment**.

The blue segment is called the **minor segment**.

You can draw angles in a segment by joining both ends of the chord to a point on the circumference.

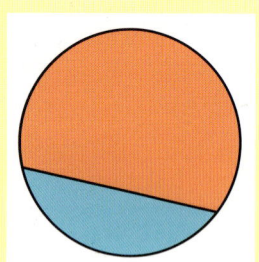

This is an angle drawn in the major segment.

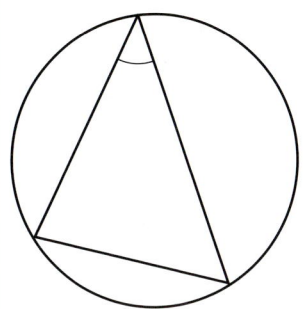

This is an angle drawn in the minor segment.

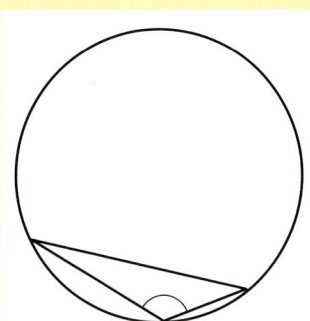

Exercise 15:14

1 **a** Draw a circle with radius 5 cm.
  b Draw a chord AB in your circle.
  c Draw three angles in the *major* segment in your diagram.
  d Measure each of the angles you have drawn.
  e Copy this. Fill it in.

  The angles in the major segment are ....

2 **a** Draw a circle with radius 5 cm.
  b Draw a chord AB in your circle.
  c Draw three angles in the *minor* segment in your diagram.
  d Measure each of the angles you have drawn.
  e Copy this. Fill it in.

  The angles in the minor segment are ....

  f Write one sentence that summarises the results in the last two questions. Check that you have the right answer before you do the next question.

3 Find the angles marked with letters in each part.

a

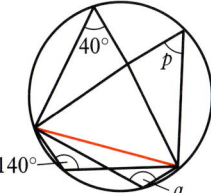

b

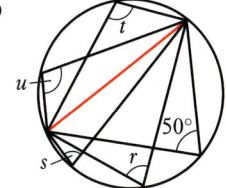

• c

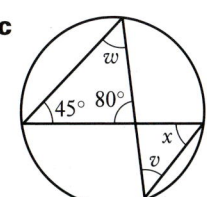

385

An angle in a segment is sometimes called an **angle at the circumference**.

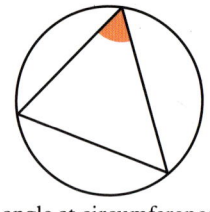 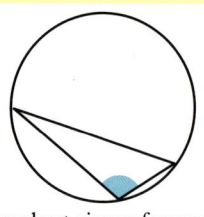

angle at circumference in major segment   angle at circumference in minor segment

You can join the ends of the chord to the centre of the circle.

This gives you two **angles at the centre**.

There is a connection between the angle at the circumference and one of the angles at the centre.

The one that you use depends on which segment you're looking at.

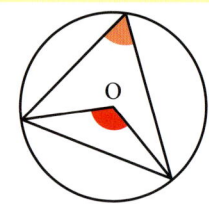 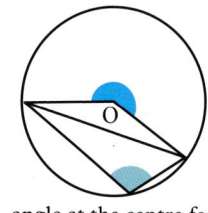

angle at the centre for angle at circumference in major segment   angle at the centre for angle at circumference in minor segment

4 **a** Draw a circle with radius 5 cm.
  b Draw a chord AB in your circle.
  c Draw an angle in the *major* segment in your diagram.
  d Draw the angle at the centre for the angle in the segment you have drawn.
  e Measure the angle at the centre and the angle at the circumference.
     Copy this. Fill it in.
     The angle at the centre is equal to .... the angle at the circumference.

5 **a** Draw a circle with radius 5 cm.
  b Draw a chord AB in your circle.
  c Draw an angle in the *minor* segment in your diagram.
  d Draw the angle at the centre for the angle in the segment you have drawn.
  e Measure the angle at the centre and the angle at the circumference.
     Copy this. Fill it in.
     The angle at the centre is equal to .... the angle at the circumference.

6 **a** Draw a circle with radius 5 cm.
  b Draw a diameter AB in your circle.
  c Draw and measure three angles in either segment in your diagram.
  d Copy this. Fill it in.
     The angle in a semi-circle is equal to ....°

7 In this diagram the line XY
is a tangent to the circle at A.
AB is a chord of the circle.
P is a point on the circumference
of the circle.
 a Copy the diagram.
 b Measure the angles
  ∠BAY and ∠APB.
 c Write down what you notice.

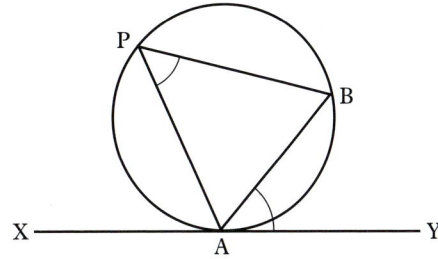

8 In this diagram the line XY
is a tangent to the circle at A.
AB is a chord of the circle.
P is a point on the circumference
of the circle.
 a Copy the diagram.
 b Measure the angles
  ∠BAY and ∠APB.
 c Write down what you notice.

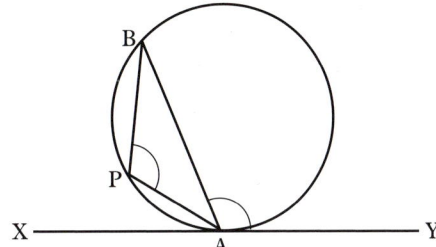

You can write the result in questions **7** and **8** in a short way.
You need to know a new name for the segment that P is in.
The angle between the chord and the
tangent crosses one segment of the
circle.
It does not cross the segment with
P in it.

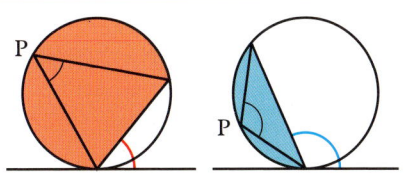

The segment that the angle does not
cross is called the **alternate segment**.

**The angle between a tangent and a chord drawn to the point of contact is
equal to the angle in the alternate segment.**

This is the last result that you need to learn from this section!
Now you need to be able to use all the results that you've discovered.

Opposite angles in a cyclic quadrilateral add up to 180°.
Angles in the same segment are equal.
The angle at the centre is twice the angle at the circumference.
The angle in a semi-circle is 90°.

Exercise 15:15

Find the angles marked with letters.

1

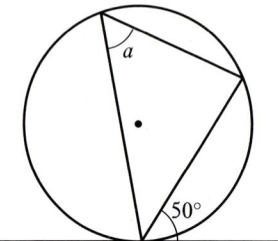

5

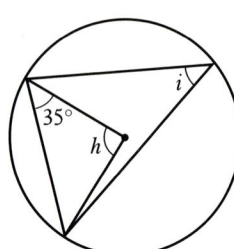

2

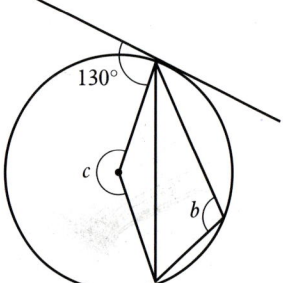

6

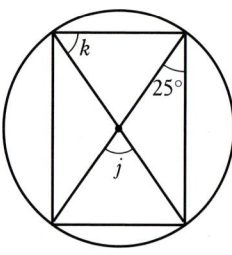

3

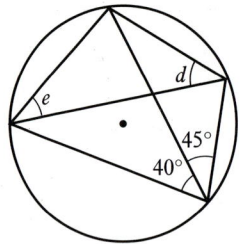

● **7**

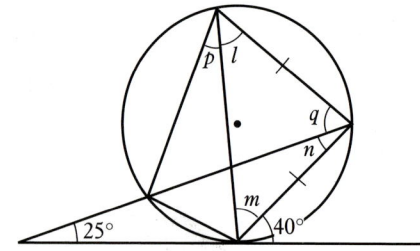

4

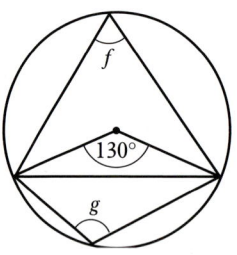

● **8**

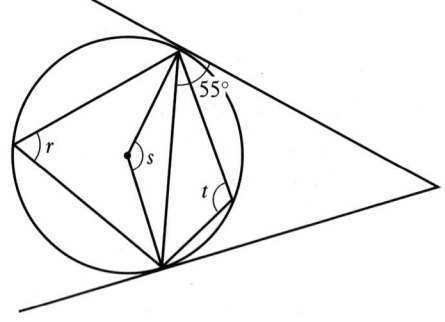

W   You need Worksheets 15:4 and 15:5 – Proofs of the circle theorems

1 Find the angles marked with letters.

a

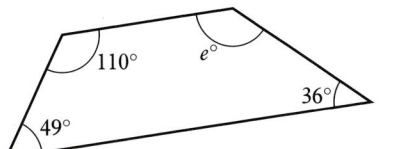

c

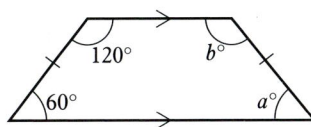

b

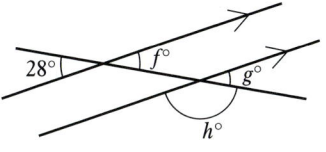

d

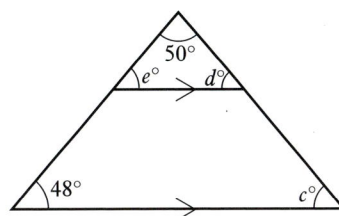

2 Find the angles marked with letters.

a

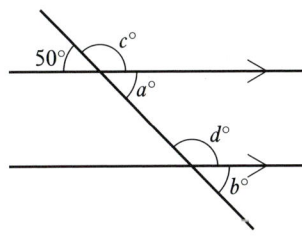

c

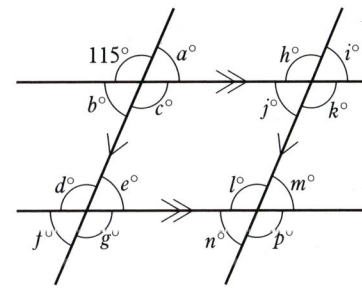

b

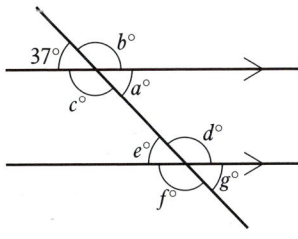

d

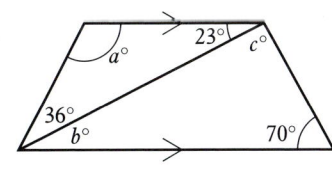

3 The diagram shows two of
the sides of a regular polygon.
How many sides does the polygon have?

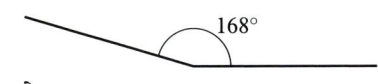

4 The interior angles of a pentagon are $2x°$, $3x°$, $3x°$, $4x°$ and $6x°$.
 a Find the value of x.
 b Write down the size of each of the interior angles.

5 The diagram shows a sculpture entitled:
'What's the point?'
LM is parallel to NP.

  a Prove that triangles KLM and KNP
     are similar.

  b Find the lengths marked with letters.

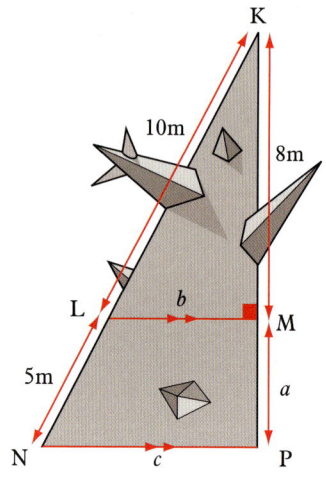

6 The picture shows a heavy metal
drum fixed by cables on a lorry.
O is the centre of the drum.

  a Prove that triangles
     ATC and ATB are
     similar.

  b Prove that triangles
     ATB and TBC are
     similar.

  c Write down what your
     results to parts **a** and **b**
     tell you about
     triangles ATC and TBC.

  d How many other pairs of similar triangles can you find?
     Write these pairs down.

  e Cables AD and DT are the same length.
     Prove that triangles ADT and DTE are congruent.

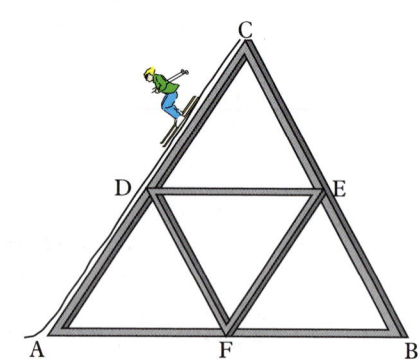

7 The diagram shows a ski slope.
The main structure is braced
by a triangle DEF.
DEF joins the midpoints of girders
AC, BC and AB together.
Let $\vec{AB} = \mathbf{a}$, $\vec{BC} = \mathbf{b}$
Use the vectors to prove that:

  a triangle ABC is similar to DEF

  b triangles DEF, ADF, BFE and CDE
     are all congruent

8 Captain Fortiz is patrolling a hazardous piece of coastline.

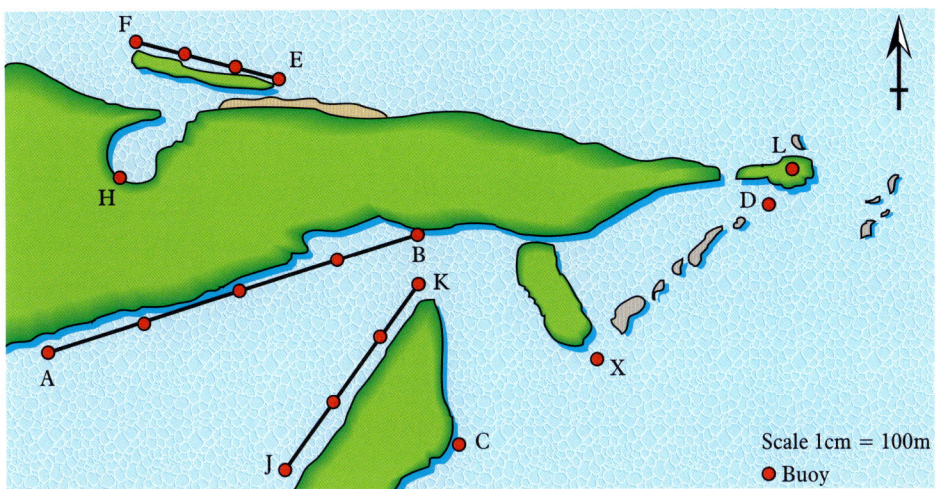

He starts from a point 150 m south of A.

From here he pilots his boat so it is equidistant from the lines of buoys AB and JK.

He continues on this course until he reaches the line BK.

He then steers his boat so that it is always equidistant from buoys C and X.

He continues on this course until he is due east of buoy C.

At this point Captain Fortiz pilots the boat so that it is parallel with the line XD, until he is due south of lighthouse L.

He then travels so that the boat is always 50 m from the lighthouse, until he is due north of it.

Then he sets a course so that he finishes 50 m due north of buoy E.

Now he stays the same distance from the line of buoys EF. He continues on this course until he comes around to the entrance to the harbour north east of H. He then sails directly to a mooring buoy at H.

    a Trace the diagram.   **b** Draw Captain Fortiz's course.

9 Billy the buffalo is tethered by a rope 28 m long to two posts F and G.

The distance FG is 20 m.

The rope can move freely through a ring on Billy's collar. Billy can then be in a region on either side of the rail.

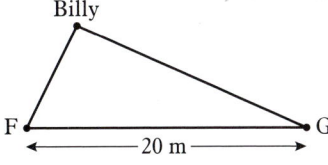

    a Draw the locus of the perimeter of the region that Billy can be in.

Billy is then moved.

He is tethered by a rope 28 m long to the point A.

    b A is on the outside of a barn that is 20 m long and 10 m wide.

       Show the region that Billy can be in.

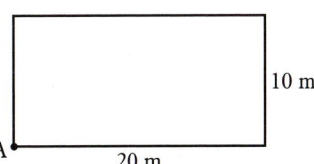

1 George and Will are moving a wardrobe. The wardrobe is 1.8 m tall, and 1 m wide. They rotate the wardrobe anticlockwise 90° about the point P.
  a Draw the locus of the point S.
  b Draw the locus of the point R.

    The light bulb is 2 m above the floor.
  c Will the wardrobe hit the light bulb? Show how you work out your answer.

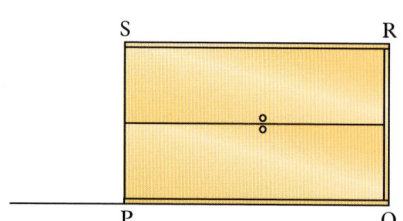

2 Two spotlights at A and B are used to light the stage DEC of a circular theatre. They both cast a beam of light that spreads from C to D.
  a Prove that triangles ABC and ABD are similar.
  b The lengths AD and BC are equal. Prove that triangles ABC and ABD are congruent.
  c At the end of the performance a spotlight at E is turned on the audience. It shines a beam that spreads from A to B. How many similar triangles are there in the diagram?

3 Draw the quadrilateral ABCD. Mark on the midpoints M, N, P, Q of AB, BC, CD, DA respectively. Prove that triangles MPQ and MNP are congruent. (Hint: use vectors.)

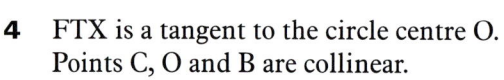

4 FTX is a tangent to the circle centre O. Points C, O and B are collinear.
Reflex ∠AOT = 316°.
Reflex ∠AOD = 314°. ∠BTO is 62°.
  a Write down every distinct angle that can be written with three of the letters on the diagram that appears on the diagram.
  b Find the value of all the angles in part **a**. Give a reason for each one.

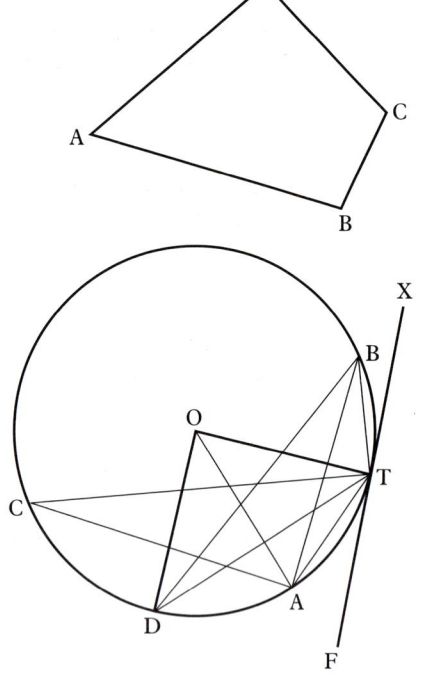

1 For each part, write down the angles marked with letters.
Give a reason for each answer.

a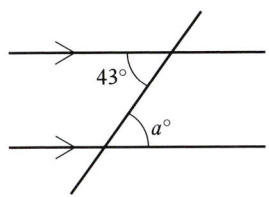

c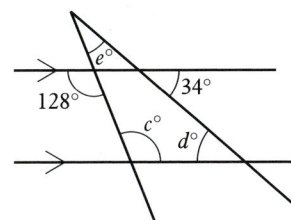

b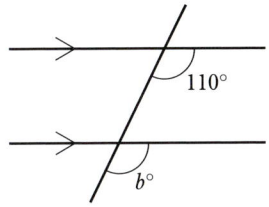

d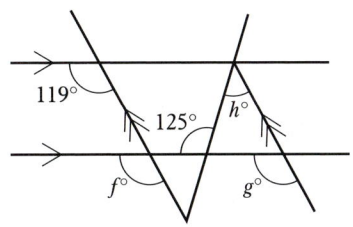

2 Prove that the angles in a triangle add up to 180°

3 Prove that angle *a* is equal to
angle *b* + angle *c*.

4 A dodecagon has 12 sides.
  a Find the size of an exterior angle of a regular dodecagon.
  b Work out the sum of the interior angles of a dodecagon.

5 A regular polygon has an interior angle of 165°
How many sides does the polygon have?

6 Triangles ABC and XYZ are similar.
  a Use colours to show equal angles.
  b Work out the lengths marked with letters.

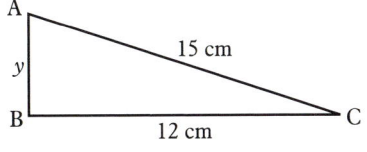

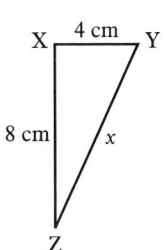

7 ABCD is a parallelogram.
Prove that triangles ABC
and CDA are congruent.

8 Billski is attached to a point X
at the corner of a shed in a
large field by a rope that is
3.5 m long.
Draw the boundary of the region
in which Billski can graze.

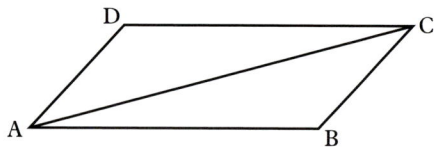

9 For each part, write down the angles marked with letters.
Give a reason for each answer.

a

c

b

d

10 a Prove that the angle at the centre of a circle is twice the angle at the
circumference.
   b Use your proof in **a** to prove that the angle in a semi-circle is 90°.

16 Using trigonometry

1 Get your bearings
Looking at bearings
Using trigonometry in bearing problems
Looking at angles of elevation and depression

CORE

2 The next dimension
Looking at perpendicular lines in 3-D
Doing two-stage problems
Finding the angle between a line and a plane

QUESTIONS

EXTENSION

TEST YOURSELF

1 Get your bearings

The rescue services need to be able to accurately pinpoint the location of someone in trouble.

They use bearings to help them.

A bearing is an angle.

It is always measured in the same way so that no-one is confused about what the angle means.

Bearing	A **bearing** is an angle.
	Bearings are *always* measured clockwise starting from north.
	A bearing must always have 3 figures.
	If the angle is less than 100° put a zero as the first digit.
	030° is the bearing for an angle of 30° clockwise from north.

Bearing of B from A

The **bearing of B from A** means that you are at A.

The **bearing of B from A** is the angle in red.
You start at A.
You face north.
You turn clockwise until you are facing B.

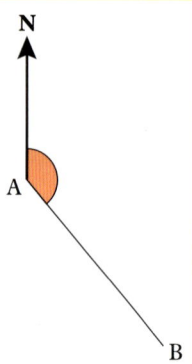

Bearing of A from B

The **bearing of A from B** means that you are at B.

The **bearing of A from B** is the angle in blue.
You start at B.
You face north.
You turn clockwise until you are facing A.

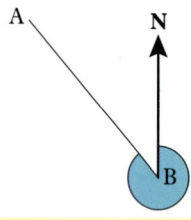

You have already found bearings without using trigonometry.
You use simple angle facts.

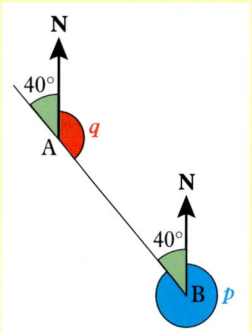

Example   Work out:
a the bearing of B from A
b the bearing of A from B

a You want angle q.
$q = 180° − 40°$
$q = 140°$

b You want angle p.
$p = 360° − 40°$
$p = 320°$

Exercise 16:1

1 In each of these find: (1) the bearing of A from B
(2) the bearing of B from A

a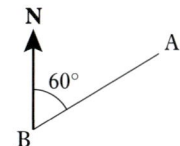

c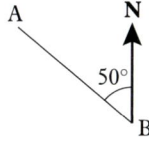

e

b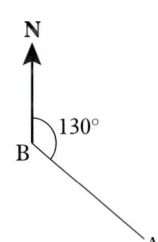

d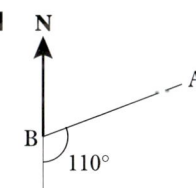

f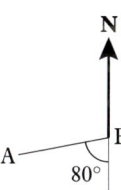

2 Asif is in charge of a lifeboat.
These are some of his journeys to rescues.
The lifeboat starts at A. The rescue is at B.
The diagrams show you the bearing that he uses to get to the rescue.
Find the bearing for his return journey.

a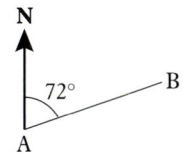

b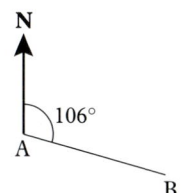

c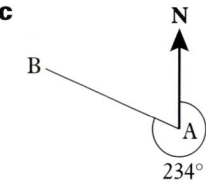

3 When Asif sets off to a rescue, the bearing that he uses is sometimes called an outward bearing.
When he returns home the bearing that he uses is then called a back bearing.
You have worked out three back bearings in question **2**.
In **a** and **b** the outward bearing was less than 180°.
In **c** the outward bearing was more than 180°.
Write down a rule to work out the back bearing for any outward bearing.

You often need to use trigonometry in questions involving bearings.
You need to make sure that you remember the work from Chapter 12.

Example   The map shows the positions of two lighthouses, A and B.

The bearing of B from A is 075°.
B is 35 km east of A.
How far north of A is B?

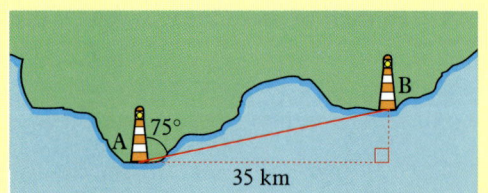

You need to find the length x.
Draw a right-angled triangle to help you.

C is the point that is directly east of A and directly south of B.
So $\angle ACB$ is 90°.

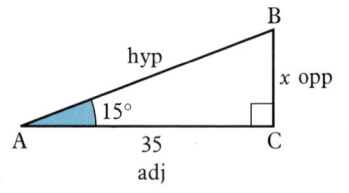

In triangle ABC
$\angle CAB = 90 - 75 = 15°$.

Using trigonometry gives:

$$\tan 15° = \frac{x}{35}$$

$$x = 35 \times \tan 15$$

$$\boxed{S \cancel{O} H} \; \boxed{C \cancel{A} H} \; \boxed{T \cancel{O} A}$$

Make sure that your calculator is working in degrees.

$x = 9.4$ km to 1 dp.
So B is 9.4 km north of A.

Exercise 16:2

1 The diagram shows the position of two ships A and B.
The bearing of B from A is 075°.
B is 25 km east of A.
  a Copy the diagram.
    Show the information on your diagram.
  b How far north of A is B?

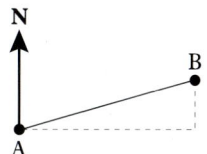

2 The diagram shows the position of two ships A and B.
The bearing of A from B is 244°.
A is 80 km west of B.
  a Copy the diagram.
    Show the information on your diagram.
  b How far south of B is A?

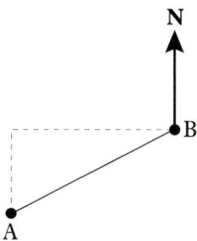

3 The diagram shows the position of two
lighthouses P and Q.
The bearing of P from Q is 305°.
P is 63 km west of Q.
  a Copy the diagram.
    Show the information on your diagram.
  b How far north of Q is P?

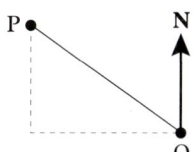

4 The diagram shows the position of two jets Y and Z.
The bearing of Z from Y is 115°.
Z is 377 km east of Y.
  a Copy the diagram and
    fill in the given information.
  b How far south of Y is Z?

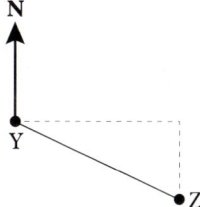

5 The diagram shows the position of two boats A and B.
The bearing of B from A is 122°.
The distance of B from A is 36 miles.
  a Copy the diagram and
    fill in the given information.
  b How far south of A is B?

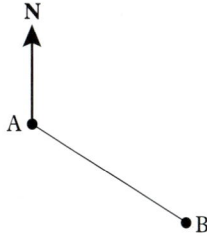

Angles of elevation and depression

Start by looking horizontally.
When you look *up* at something, the angle is called an angle of *elevation*.
When you look *down* at something, the angle is called an angle of *depression*.

Angle of elevation	If you are at A and you look up to a point B, the **angle of elevation of B**

from A is the angle between the horizontal
and the line AB. It is the angle *above* the
horizontal.

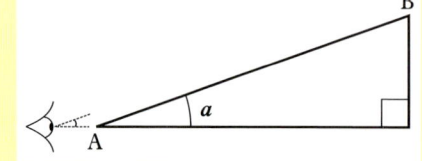

a is the angle of elevation of B from A.

Angle of depression	If you are at P and you look down to a point Q, the **angle of depression of Q from P** is

the angle between the horizontal and the line
PQ. It is the angle *below* the horizontal.

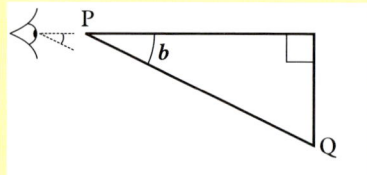

b is the angle of depression of Q from P.

Exercise 16:3

In this exercise, round your answers to 3 sf.

1 Sid is 26 m from the base of a tree.
The angle of elevation of the top
of the tree from Sid is 42°.
Find the height of the tree.

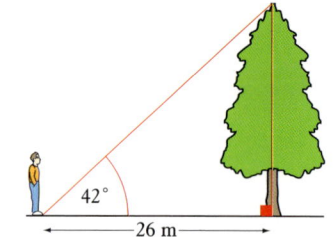

2 Graham is standing 52 m from a church tower.
The tower is 32 m high.
Work out the angle of elevation of the top
of the church tower from Graham.

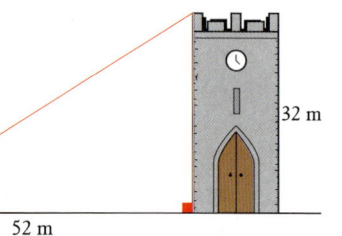

3 Fiona is at the edge at the top of a cliff.
She sees a boat on the water below.
The cliff is 105 m high. The angle of depression of the boat from Fiona is 7°.
a Draw a diagram to show this information.
b Work out the distance of the boat from the foot of the cliff.

2 The next dimension

The pointer of a sundial is called a gnomon.
The angle of the gnomon is the angle of
latitude where you are standing.
In England the angle is 52°.
This is so that the shadow from the sun will
fall at the right place on the dial.
The shadow makes a triangle in two
dimensions on the surface of the sundial.
When you want to find lengths and angles
in 3-D you need to break the problem down
so that you can work in 2-D.
You still need to use right-angled triangles.
The problem is finding the right triangles to
work in!

A vertical line is perpendicular to a horizontal plane.
A vertical line is perpendicular to any line
drawn in a horizontal plane.

This vertical line is perpendicular
to the red line and the blue line.
The vertical line is perpendicular
to any line in the horizontal plane.

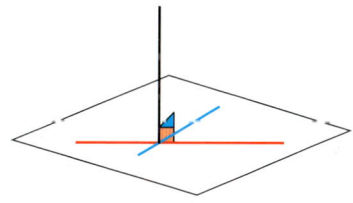

The red edge of this cuboid is perpendicular
to the top face and the bottom face.
So the red line is perpendicular to all of
the blue lines.

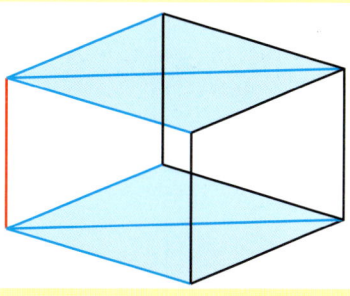

When you are doing trigonometry in 3-D:
(1) think about lines that are perpendicular
(2) find a right-angled triangle to work in
(3) draw the triangle that you are using
    in 2-D so that you can see it clearly
(4) label the right angle and the sides or angles that you know in the triangle
(5) use the triangle to work out the side or the angle that you need.

Exercise 16:4

1 Write down the lines that are perpendicular to the line AB in each part.

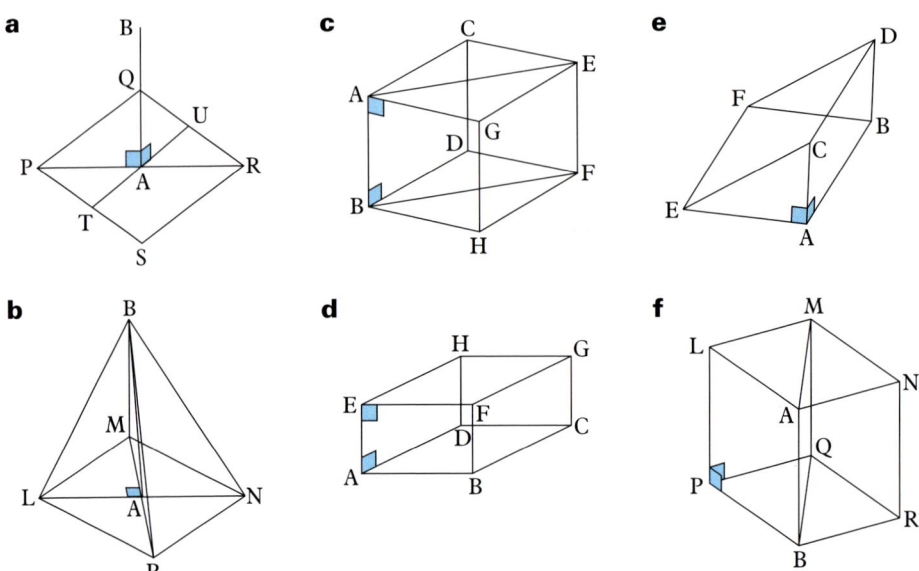

2 Work out the side or angle that is labelled in each part using trigonometry. Start by drawing and labelling the right-angled triangle in 2-D that you need to use.

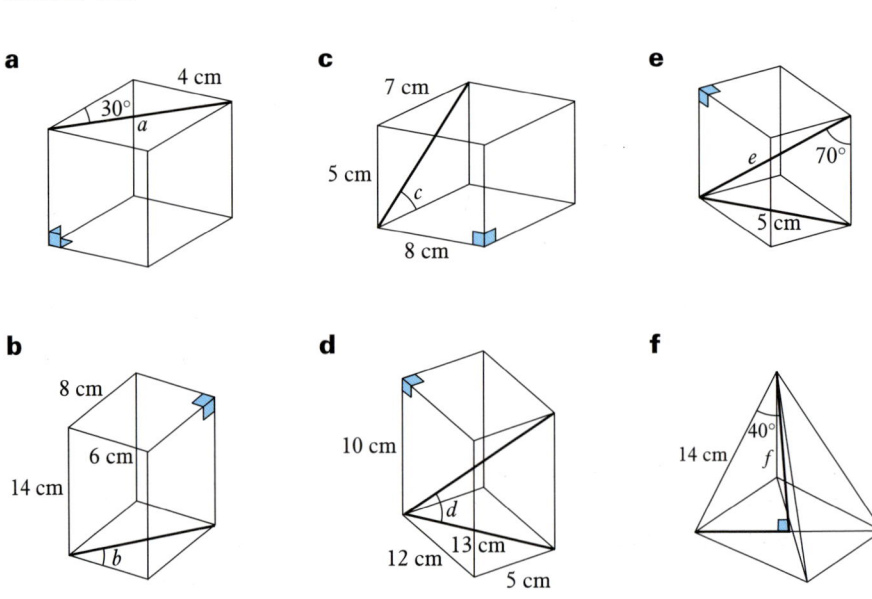

Sometimes you need to do an extra step before you can answer the question that you are asked.

Example   Find the angle between the red line and the blue line in this cuboid.

The red line is perpendicular to the green diagonal on the top face.

You have to work out the green length so that you can work out the angle *a*.

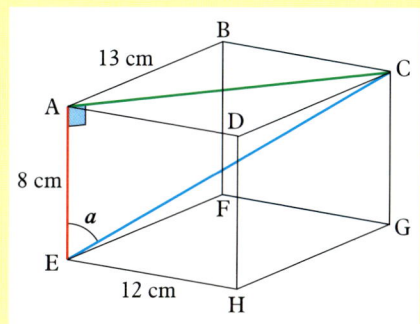

In triangle ABC
by Pythagoras' theorem:

$$AC^2 = AB^2 + BC^2$$
$$= 13^2 + 12^2$$
$$= 313$$
$$AC = \sqrt{313} \text{ cm}$$

In triangle ACE
using trigonometry: S Ø H   C A H   T Ø A

$$\tan a = \frac{\sqrt{313}}{8}$$
$$a = 65.7° \quad (1 \text{ dp})$$

The angle between the red and the blue lines is 65.7° (to 1 dp)

3   In this cuboid, find:
  a   the length of the green line
  b   the angle between the blue line and the green line

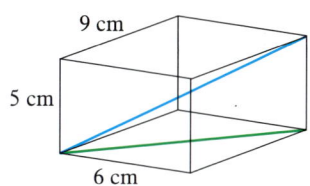

4   In this cuboid, find:
  a   the length of the green line
  b   the angle between the blue line and the green line

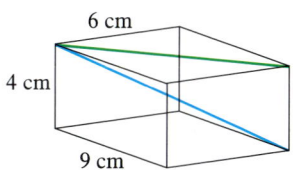

5 In this cuboid, find:
   a the length of EC
   b the angle between EC and AC

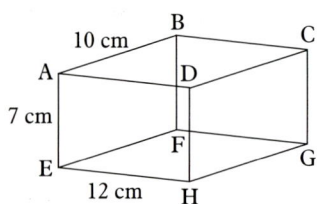

6 In this cuboid find the angle between EC and HC.

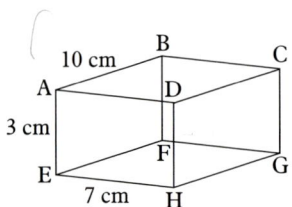

7 In this cuboid find the angle between BD and DF.

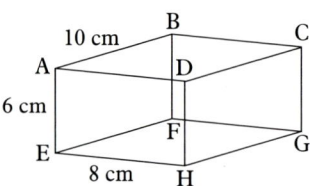

8 In this square-based pyramid find the angle between AE and AC.

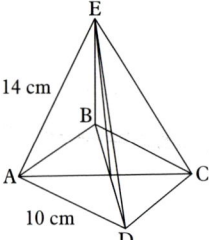

9 In this triangular prism find the angle between AQ and AC.

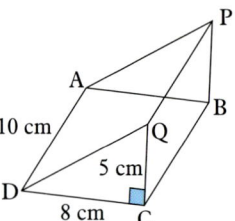

10 In this cube find:
   a the length of EC
   b the angle between EC and EG
   c the angle between EC and EB
   d the angle between EC and HC

Use your answers to parts **a** to **d** to write down:
   e the length of BH
   f the angle between BH and BD

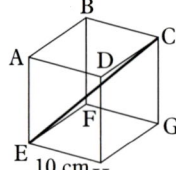

The angle between a line and a plane

The red line is not perpendicular to the horizontal plane.

The red line cuts the plane at an angle. The angle between the line and the plane is the angle shown in red.

It is the angle between the line and the dashed line in the plane.

You can think of this dashed line as the shadow that you would get if you shine a light perpendicular to the plane.

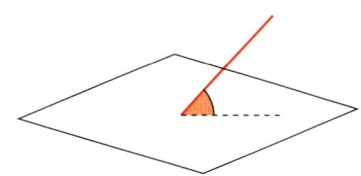
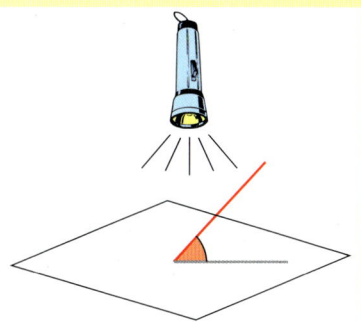
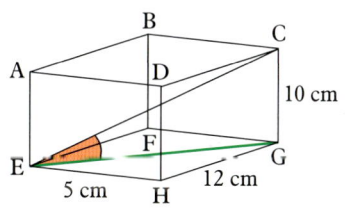

Example   Find the angle between the line EC and the plane EFGH.

The angle needed is the angle CEG. First find the length of EG.

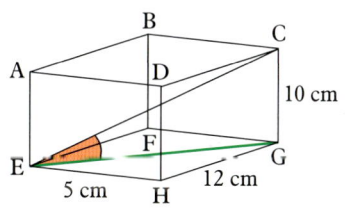

In triangle EGH by Pythagoras' theorem:

$EG^2 = EH^2 + GH^2$
$= 5^2 + 12^2$
$= 169$
$EG = 13\,cm$

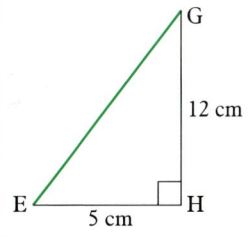

In triangle CEG using trigonometry: $\boxed{S\emptyset H}\ \boxed{C\!A\!H}\ \boxed{T\emptyset A}$

$\tan CEG = \dfrac{10}{13}$

$CEG = 37.6°$ (1 dp)

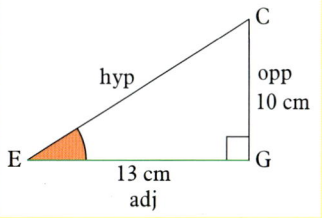

The angle between EC and EFGH is 37.6° to 1 dp.

Exercise 16:5

1 Find the angle between the red line and the blue plane in each of these.

a
18 cm
6 cm

c
8 m
9 m
5 m

e
13 cm
12 cm

b
14 cm
12 cm   9 cm

d
2 m
4 m   7 m

f
5 cm
13 cm
12 cm

2 A room is in the shape of a cube.
Find the angle between the
diagonal EC
and the wall BCGF.

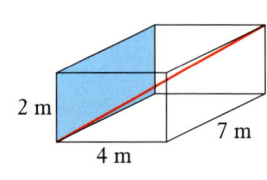

3 A shop sign is on a pole that
is perpendicular to a wall.
The pole is held in place by
two wires AP and AQ.
  a Find the angle between the wire AP and
  the wall.
  b Find the distance of A from the wall.

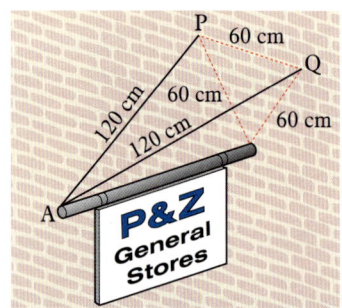

4 This is a picture of the Great Pyramid of
Khufu.
The base is a square of side 230 m.
The vertical height is 146.6 m.
Find the angle between a sloping edge
and the base.

1 In each of these find: (1) the bearing of A from B
                             (2) the bearing of B from A

a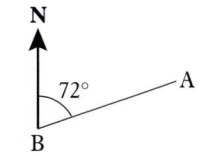
b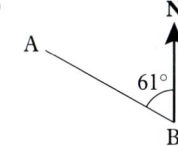
c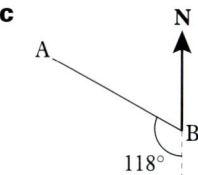

2 The diagram shows two aircraft A and B.
The bearing of B from A is 293°.
B is 615 km west of A.
a Copy the diagram.
b How far north of A is B?

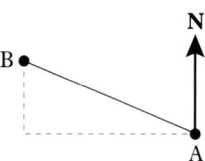

3 A helicopter flies 2500 km from Manchester on a bearing of 123°.
a Draw a diagram to show this information.
b How far east of Manchester is the helicopter?
c How far south of Manchester is the helicopter?
d What is the bearing of Manchester from the helicopter?

4 A jet flies 430 km from its base on a bearing of 305°.
a Draw a diagram to show this information.
b How far west of its base is the jet?
c How far north of its base is the jet?

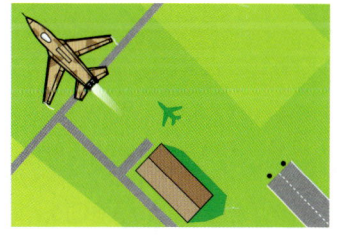

You often need to do bearing questions in stages.

5 The diagram shows two buildings.
The distance between the buildings is 80 m.
The smaller building is 34 m high.
The angle of elevation of the top
of the taller building from the top
of the smaller building is 27°.
Find the height of the taller
building.

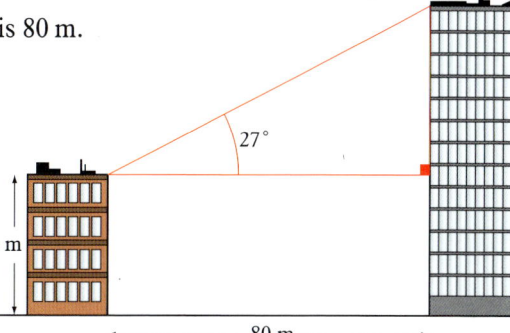

6 Canary Wharf tower in London's docklands
is the tallest building in Britain.
Nicki is at the top of the Canary Wharf tower.
She sees a boat on the river below.
The tower is 243.8 m high.
The angle of depression of the boat from Nicki is 37°.
a Draw a diagram to show this information.
b Work out the distance of the boat from the foot
of the tower.

7 Work out the side or angle that is labelled in each part using trigonometry.
Start by drawing and labelling the right-angled triangle in 2-D that you
need to use.

a

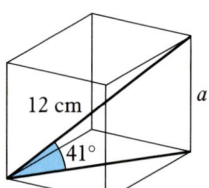

b

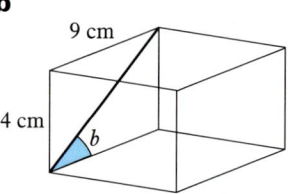

c

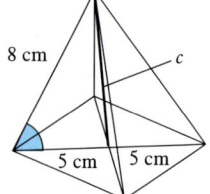

8 In this cuboid find:
a the length of WR
b the angle between WR and WS

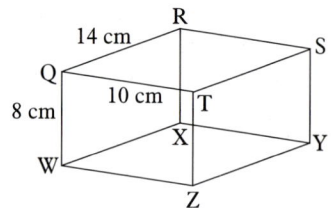

9 In this triangular prism
find the angle between AP and
the plane ABCD.

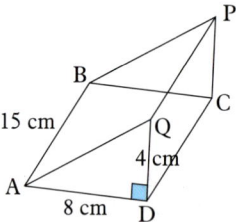

10 a In this gym find:
    (1) the angle between the rope EC
        and the floor EFGH
    (2) the angle between the rope EC
        and the wall ADHE
    (3) the angle between the rope EC
        and the wall ABFE

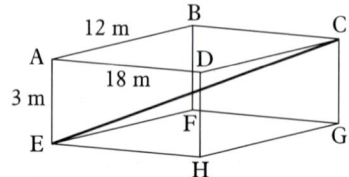

   b Use your answers to **a** to write down the angle between the rope EC and:
    (1) the ceiling ABCD   (2) the wall BCGF   (3) the wall DCGH

1   Gerry is trying to work out the width of
    a river.
    He stands at a point P which is directly
    opposite a tree, T.
    He measures the angle of elevation
    of the top of the tree from P as 45°.
    He then walks to a point Q that is 70 m
    along the bank from P.
    From here he measures the angle of
    elevation of the top of the tree as 35°.
    Let the width of the river be w.
    Let the height of the tree be h.
    Let the distance QT be x.
    a   Write down three equations that connect w, h and x.
    b   Find the height of the tree.
    c   Find the width of the river.

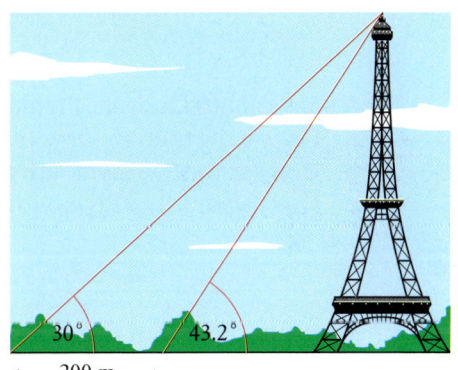

2   Tai is in Paris.
    She is looking at the Eiffel tower.
    The angle of elevation of the top
    of the tower from where she is
    standing is 30°.
    She walks 200 m towards the tower.
    The angle of elevation of the top
    of the tower is now 43.2°
    Work out:
    a   the height of the tower
    b   the horizontal distance of Tai
            from the tower when she started

3   The diagram shows a tetrahedron PQRS.
    The base of the tetrahedron, QRS, is an equilateral
    triangle of side 8.6 cm.
    The sides PQ, PR and PS are all 16.5 cm long.
    M is the midpoint of RS.
    a   Find the length of QM.
    b   Find the length of PM.

P is directly above the point S which is $\frac{2}{3}$ of the way along QM.
    c   Find the angle between PM and the plane QRS.
    d   Find the angle between PQ and the plane QRS.

1 In each of these find:
(1) the bearing of A from B
(2) the bearing of B from A

a

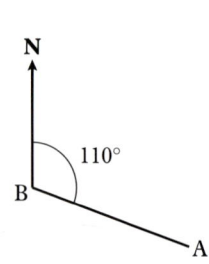

b

c

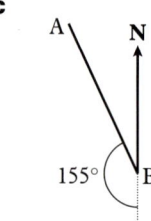

2 A helicopter flies 254 km from Aberdeen on a bearing of 072°.
   a Draw a diagram to show this information.
   b How far east of Aberdeen is the helicopter?
   c How far north of Aberdeen is the helicopter?

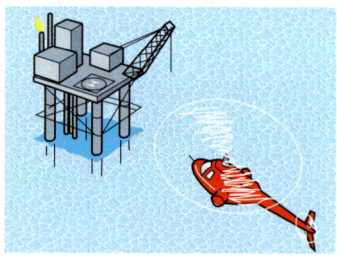

3 A ship sails 40 km from Plymouth on a bearing of 216°.
   a Draw a diagram to show this information.
   b How far west of Plymouth is the ship?
   c How far south of Plymouth is the ship?

4 Work out the length that is labelled in each part.

a

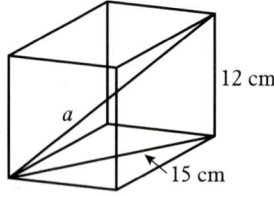

b

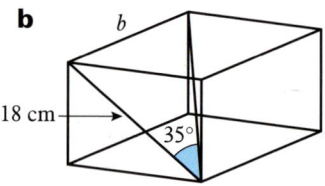

5 In this cuboid, find the angle between the diagonal EC and the plane ABCD.

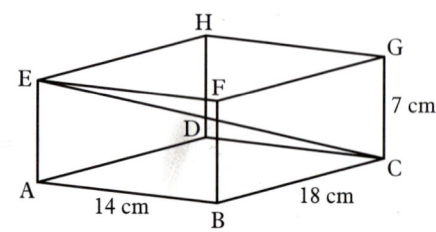

17 Graphs: moving on

1 Transforming graphs
Moving graphs vertically
Moving graphs horizontally
Reflecting and stretching
Combining transformations

CORE

2 Modelling with graphs
Searching for linear functions
Searching for quadratic functions
Looking at other functions
Breeding rabbits!

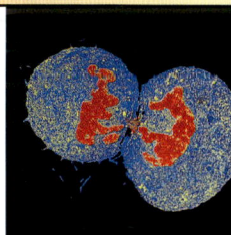

QUESTIONS

EXTENSION

TEST YOURSELF

1   Transforming graphs

You can use an oscilloscope to 'see' sound waves as a graph.

If you increase the volume, the peaks of the graph get higher. The graph stretches vertically.

If you increase the pitch, the peaks get closer together.

This chapter looks at how you transform graphs.

Exercise 17:1

Plot all the graphs for questions **1** to **3** on the *same* diagram.

1   **a**   Copy and complete this table of $y = x^2$

x	-5	-4	-3	-2	-1	0	1	2	3	4	5
y	25	16				0				16	25

    b   Draw an x axis from -5 to $+5$ and a y axis from -5 to 30.
    c   Draw the graph of $y = x^2$ from your table.

2   **a**   Copy and complete this table of $y = x^2 + 3$

x	-5	-4	-3	-2	-1	0	1	2	3	4	5
y	28	19				3				19	28

    b   Draw the graph of $y = x^2 + 3$ from your table.

3   **a**   Copy and complete this table of $y = x^2 - 4$

x	-5	-4	-3	-2	-1	0	1	2	3	4	5
y	21	12				-4				12	21

    b   Draw the graph of $y = x^2 - 4$ from your table.

4   Compare your three graphs.
    a   Describe how $y = x^2$ has moved to get the graph of $y = x^2 + 3$
    b   Describe how $y = x^2$ has moved to get the graph of $y = x^2 - 4$

Adding a constant to $y = x^2$ moves the graph **up**.

The graph of $y = x^2 + a$ is the graph of

$y = x^2$ translated by $\begin{pmatrix} 0 \\ a \end{pmatrix}$.

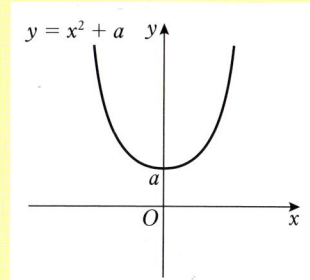

Subtracting a constant from $y = x^2$ moves the graph **down**.

The graph of $y = x^2 - a$ is the graph of

$y = x^2$ translated by $\begin{pmatrix} 0 \\ -a \end{pmatrix}$.

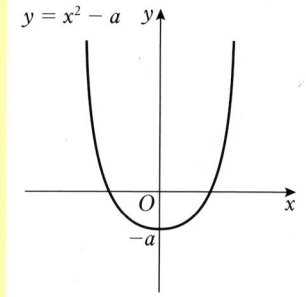

Example Sketch the graph of $y = x^2 + 6$

The graph of $y = x^2$ **+ 6** is the graph of

$y = x^2$ translated by $\begin{pmatrix} 0 \\ 6 \end{pmatrix}$.

The graph is moved **up 6**.

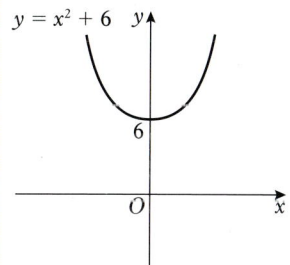

Exercise 17:2

Sketch each of these graphs.

1 $y = x^2 + 3$

2 $y = x^2 + 7$

3 $y = x^2 - 2$

4 $y = x^2 - 5$

5 $y = x^2 + 10$

6 $y = x^2 + 3\frac{1}{2}$

7 $y = x^2 - 5\frac{1}{2}$

8 $y = x^2 + 3.2$

You can use this method to transform any graph.

Example   Here is a sketch of $y = x^3 + x$

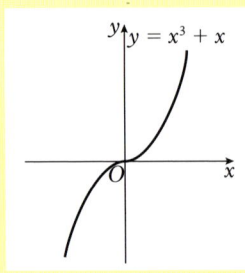

The graph of $y = x^3 + x + 5$ is the graph of $y = x^3 + x$ moved up 5.

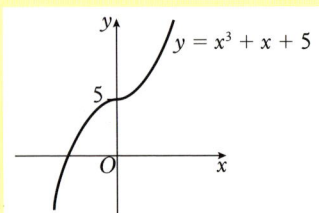

Sketch $y = x^3 + x + 5$

Exercise 17:3

1 Look at this graph of $y = x^3$
Use it to sketch:
a $y = x^3 + 3$
b $y = x^3 - 5$

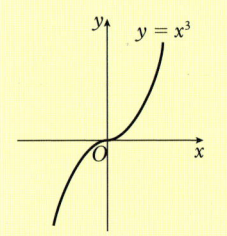

2 Look at this graph of $y = x^3 - x^2$
Use it to sketch:
a $y = x^3 - x^2 - 2$
b $y = x^3 - x^2 + 6$

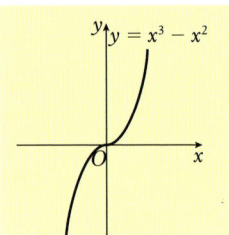

3 Look at this graph of $y = \dfrac{1}{x}$
Use it to sketch:

a $y = \dfrac{1}{x} - 3$

b $y = \dfrac{1}{x} + 4$

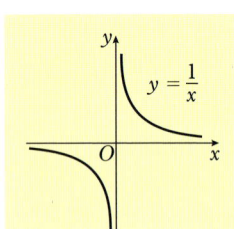

It is possible to translate graphs in other ways.

Exercise 17:4

Plot all the graphs for questions **1–3** on the *same* diagram.

1 **a** Draw an x axis from -5 to $+5$ and a y axis from 0 to 30.
b Draw the graph of $y = x^2$ on your axes.

2 a Copy and complete this table of $y = (x - 3)^2$

x	-2	-1	0	1	2	3	4	5
y	25	16	9					

b Draw the graph of $y = (x - 3)^2$ from your table.

3 a Copy and complete this table of $y = (x + 2)^2$

x	-4	-3	-2	-1	0	1	2	3
y	4	1					16	

b Draw the graph of $y = (x + 2)^2$ from your table.

4 Compare your three graphs.
  a Describe how $y = x^2$ has moved to get the graph of $y = (x - 3)^2$
  b Write the translation as a vector.
  c Describe how $y = x^2$ has moved to get the graph of $y = (x + 2)^2$
  d Write the translation as a vector.

5 Write down the translations you would have to make to the graph of $y = x^2$ to sketch these graphs:
  a $y = (x - 4)^2$ **b** $y = (x + 6)^2$ **c** $y = (x + 2.5)^2$

Adding or subtracting a constant from x *before* squaring it moves the graph left or right.

The graph of $y = (x + a)^2$ is the graph of $y = x^2$ translated by $\begin{pmatrix} -a \\ 0 \end{pmatrix}$

Notice that **adding** a constant moves the graph to the **left**.

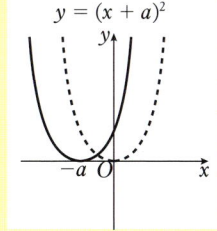

The graph of $y = (x - a)^2$ is the graph of $y = x^2$ translated by $\begin{pmatrix} a \\ 0 \end{pmatrix}$

Notice that **subtracting** a constant moves the graph to the **right**.

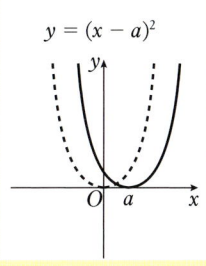

Example   Sketch the graph of $y = (x + 6)^2$

The graph of $y = (x + 6)^2$ is the graph of

$y = x^2$ translated by $\begin{pmatrix} -6 \\ 0 \end{pmatrix}$.

The graph is moved **6 to the left**.

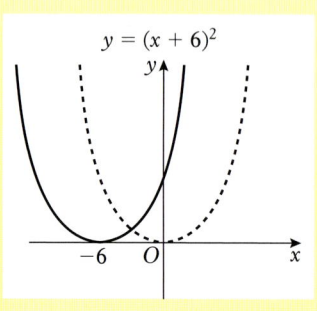

Exercise 17:5

Sketch each of these graphs.

1 $y = (x + 5)^2$

5 $y = (x + 5\frac{1}{2})^2$

2 $y = (x + 9)^2$

● **6** $y = (x - 3\frac{1}{4})^2$

3 $y = (x - 1)^2$

● **7** $y = (x + 2)^2 + 1$

4 $y = (x - 2)^2$

● **8** $y = (x - 1)^2 - -1$

You can write transformations of graphs in function notation.

These transformations will work for *any* function $f(x)$.

1 $y = f(x)$ is shown in black.

The red graph is $y = f(x) + a$

It is $y = f(x)$ translated by $\begin{pmatrix} 0 \\ a \end{pmatrix}$

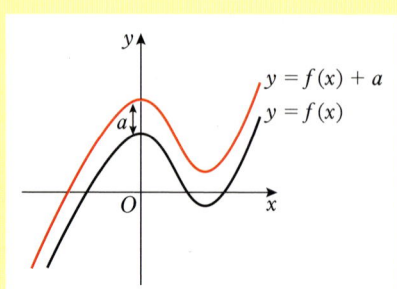

2 The red graph is $y = f(x - a)$

It is $y = f(x)$ translated by $\begin{pmatrix} a \\ 0 \end{pmatrix}$

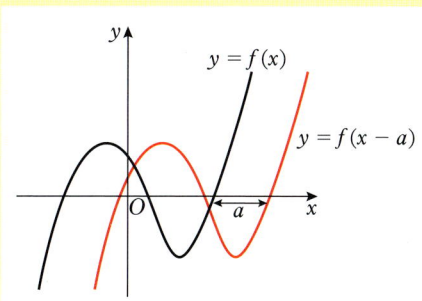

3 The red graph is $y = f(-x)$

It is $y = f(x)$ reflected in the y axis.

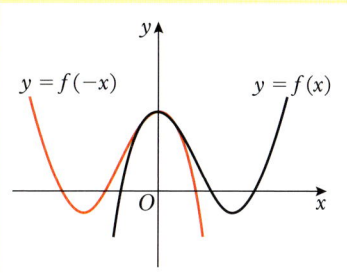

4 The red graph is $y = -f(x)$

It is $y = f(x)$ reflected in the x axis.

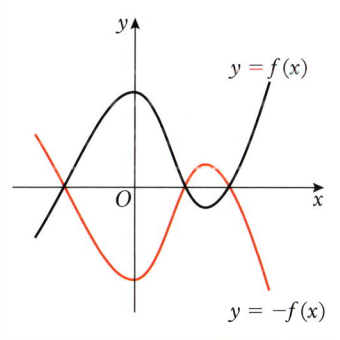

5 The red graph is $y = kf(x)$

It is $y = f(x)$ stretched by scale factor k in the y direction.

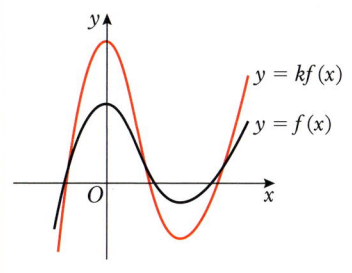

Exercise 17:6

1 Here is a sketch of $y = f(x)$ where
$f(x) = x^3$.
Sketch each of the following graphs.
a $y = f(x) + 3$ **c** $y = f(-x)$
b $y = f(x - 4)$ **d** $y = -f(x)$

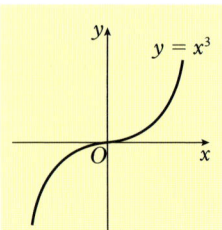

2 Here is a sketch of $y = f(x)$ where
$f(x) = \sqrt{x}$.
Sketch each of the following graphs.
a $y = f(x) + 1$ **c** $y = 4f(x)$
b $y = f(x) - 9$ **d** $y = -f(x)$

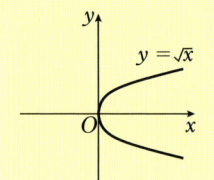

3 Here is a sketch of $y = f(x)$ where

$f(x) = \dfrac{1}{x^2}$

Sketch each of the following graphs.
a $y = f(x) + 3$ **c** $y = f(-x)$
b $y = f(x) - 2$ **d** $y = -f(x)$

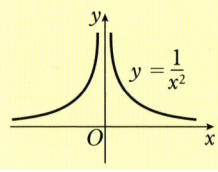

It is possible to combine several transformations in one graph.

Example   Sketch the graph of $y = 2(x + 3)^2 + 4$
There are three transformations to do:

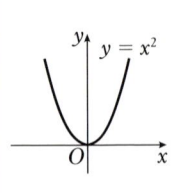
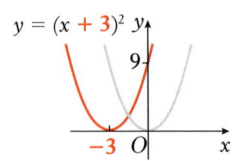
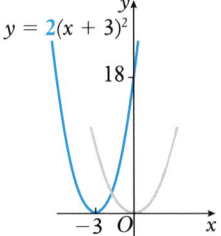
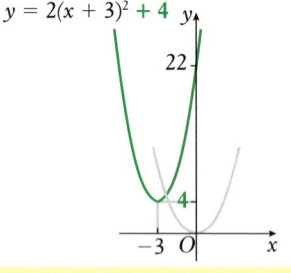

| Start with the graph of $y = x^2$ | (1) The **+3** moves the graph **3** to the left | (2) The **2** stretches the graph by factor **2** in the y direction | (3) The **+4** moves the graph up **4** |

Exercise 17:7

1 Sketch the graph of $y = (x + 4)^2 + 3$

2 Sketch the graph of $y = (x - 4)^2 + 3$

3
  a Sketch the graph of $y = 3(x - 2)^2$
  b Describe the transformations that you have done to $y = x^2$

4
  a Sketch the graph of $y = 2(x + 1)^2 - 2$
  b Describe the transformations that you have done to $y = x^2$

5 This is a sketch of $y = f(x)$
  Sketch the graph of $y = -f(x) + 3$

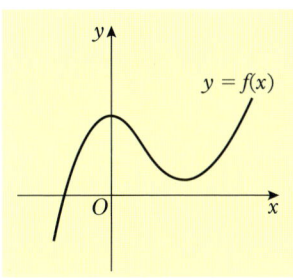

6 This is a sketch of $y = g(x)$
  Sketch the graph of $y = 2g(x) - 1$

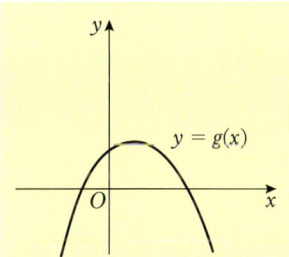

7 This is a sketch of $y = h(x)$
  Sketch the graph of $y = 2h(-x) + 3$

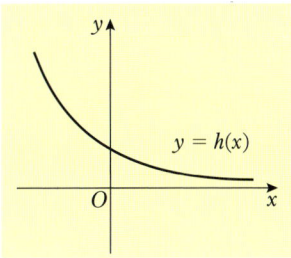

8 A function $f(x) = \dfrac{1}{x}$

  a Write $y = \dfrac{1}{(x + 4)}$ in terms of $f(x)$

  b Sketch the graph of the function in part **a**.
  c Sketch the function $y = f(x) + 4$

  d Sketch the graph of $y = \dfrac{1}{(x + 4)} + 4$

2   Modelling with graphs

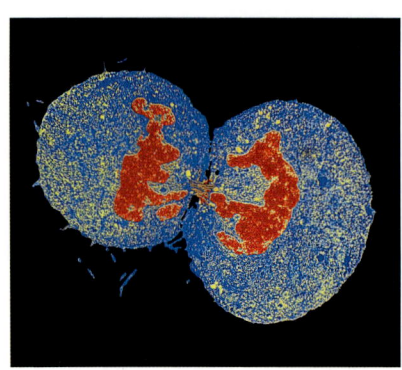

Under laboratory conditions, bacteria double their population every 30 minutes.

This is known as exponential growth.

Human cells divide in a similar way when an embryo is developing.

You will see this type of growth at the end of this section.

You can also use graphs to help you with proportionality problems. You saw these in Chapter 6.

Graphs are often used to plot experimental data. They can show how two variables are related and whether they are proportional to each other.

Example   Nick is doing an experiment in science to show Hooke's Law. He hangs masses on the end of a spring and measures the extension. He records his results in a table.

Mass (g)	100	200	300	400	500
Extension (cm)	5	9.5	15.2	20.4	25.7

Nick plots a graph of these results.
They form an approximate straight line.
Nick draws a line of best fit through the points.
He calculates the gradient of the line: $5 \div 100 = 0.05$
Nick can now write a formula connecting the mass and the extension

$E = 0.05m$

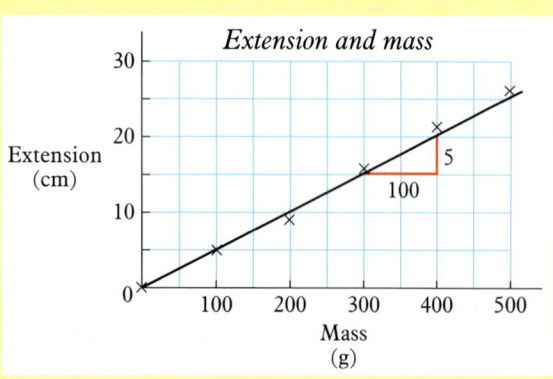

Exercise 17:8

1 Here are the results from another Hooke's Law experiment using a different spring.

Mass (g)	100	200	300	400	500
Extension (cm)	9	18.8	26.4	36	44.7

  a Plot these points on a graph.
  b Draw a line of best fit through the points. It must go through $(0, 0)$.
  c Work out the gradient of the line.

2 The value of an antique vase increases each year.
This table shows its approximate value for 5 years.

Year	1	2	3	4	5
Value (£)	400	445	510	555	615

  a Plot these values on a graph.
  b Draw a line of best fit through the points. It will *not* go through $(0, 0)$ – why not?
  c Work out the gradient of the line.
  d Write down the intercept of the line with the 'value' axis.
  e Write down an equation linking the value with the year number. It should be in the form $V = aY + b$ where a and b are numbers.

3 Dan is doing an experiment to see if alcohol affects human reaction times. He asks his father to take a reaction test on a computer.
Dan asks him to repeat the test another 5 times after drinking 200 ml of beer between each test.
Here are his results.

Test number	1	2	3	4	5	6
Time (milliseconds)	18.1	20.1	22.4	24.9	26.7	28.8

  a Plot these values on a graph.
  b Draw a line of best fit through the points. It will *not* go through $(0, 0)$.
  c Work out the gradient of the line.
  d Write down the intercept of the line with the 'time' axis.
  e Write down an equation linking the time with the test number. It should be in the form $T = aN + b$ where a and b are numbers.

Not all variables are linked by linear equations.
Some may be linked by quadratic equations or other types of function.
Amazingly, you can still use straight line graphs to find the equations.

Example   Tom is doing an experiment in science.
He thinks that the temperature of liquid is related to the square of the pressure it is under.
He has the following data.

Pressure (atm)	1	2	3	4	5
Temperature (°C)	20.2	23.1	26.4	35.8	45.2

Tom plots temperature against pressure.
He thinks the graph looks like a quadratic.

To check this, Tom plots temperature against (pressure)^2.
This gives an approximate straight line.
This shows that the temperature of the liquid *is* proportional to the square of the pressure it is under.

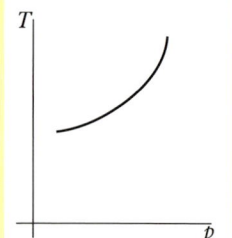

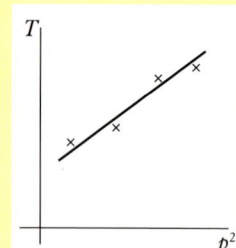

To find the equation, Tom finds the gradient and intercept from his straight line graph.
The gradient is **1.2** and the intercept is **18.5**
The equation is $T = $ **1.2**$p^2 + $ **18.5**

This can be done with any type of function.

For example, if you have two variables p and q and you suspect that p is related to $\dfrac{1}{q}$, plot a graph of p and $\dfrac{1}{q}$

If this graph is a straight line, your suspicion is correct.
You can work out the gradient and write down the intercept from the *straight line* graph. From this you can write down the full equation.
If the gradient is m and the intercept is c the formula will be:

$$p = m \times \frac{1}{q} + c = \frac{m}{q} + c$$

If $c = 0$ then p is proportional to $\dfrac{1}{q}$

Exercise 17:9

1 In each of the following sets of data y is related to x^2.

For each one: (1) plot a graph of y against x^2
(2) find the gradient of the line
(3) write down the intercept with the y axis
(4) write down an equation connecting y and x^2

a

x	1	2	3	4
y	13	16	21	28

c

x	0.2	0.4	0.6	0.8
y	1.04	1.16	1.36	1.64

b

x	1	2	3	4
y	3	6	11	18

2 Herman has some results from a science experiment.

He suspects that y is related to $\dfrac{1}{x}$

These are Herman's results:

x	1	2	3	4	5
y	3.1	2.55	2.4	2.2	2.15

a Plot a graph of y against $\dfrac{1}{x}$

b Find the gradient of the line.

c Write down the intercept with the y axis.

d Write an equation connecting y and $\dfrac{1}{x}$

e On separate axes, draw a graph of your equation from part **d**.
Use x values from 0 to 5.

f Plot the points from the table on your graph.
Use a different colour.

g Comment on the fit of the graph to the data.

3 The following data was collected during an experiment.

x	1	2	3	4	5
y	1.1	1.5	1.7	2.1	2.3

Investigate the connection between x and y.

Choose from y related to x^2, $\dfrac{1}{x}$ and $\sqrt{x}$

Growth curves

You saw exponential equations in Chapter 12. These are equations where the variable is a power.

Cell division is often modelled using exponential curves.

For example if a cell divides into two every hour, the formula for the number of cells N present after time t hours is $N = 2^t$

The graph of this formula looks like this:

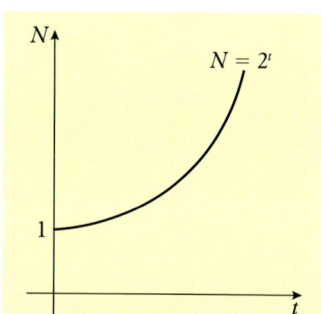

This also works for population growth.

If you have data that you think fits an exponential pattern you can use the method you have seen in this section to work out the equation connecting the variables.

Example Dr Taylor is doing an experiment on cell division. She has the following data and she suspects it fits an exponential pattern.

t (hours)	1	2	3	4	5
N	3	6	12	24	48

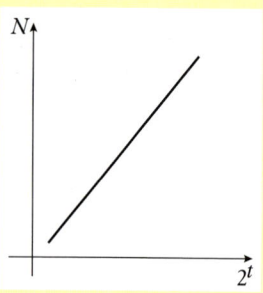

Dr Taylor draws a graph of N against 2^t. The graph forms a straight line.

She measures the gradient of the line. The gradient is 1.5

The formula she wants is $N = 1.5 \times 2^t$

Exercise 17:10

1 Here are the results of another experiment on cell division.

t (hours)	1	2	3	4	5
N	4	8	16	32	64

a Plot a graph of N against 2^t
b Find the gradient of the line.
c Write and equation connecting N and 2^t

2 Linda is researching into how washing powder dissolves in water.
She puts 100 g of powder into water.
She measures how much of the powder is left every minute.
Here are Linda's results.

t (mins)	0	1	2	3	4	5
Powder remaining (g)	100	50	25	12.5	6.25	3.13

Linda thinks that P is connected to $(0.5)^t$
Use a suitable graph to find a formula linking P and t.

3 George likes to monitor the price of his house.
He has it valued each year.
Here are his results for the last 5 years.

Year	1	2	3	4	5
Value (£)	50 000	53 500	57 250	61 250	65 550

George thinks that the price is rising by about 9% each year.
He wants to predict the value of the house in another 5 years.
He wants to find a formula to do this.
He tries to fit the data to a formula involving $(1.09)^Y$

a Use a suitable graph to find a formula involving $(1.09)^Y$
b Use your formula to predict the value of the house after another 5 years.

4 Howard started breeding rabbits 2 years ago.
He now has 24 rabbits.
In another 2 years, he will have 96 rabbits if none have died.
a Suggest a formula to fit this data.
b Use a graph to find the complete formula.
c Use your formula to find out how many rabbits Howard had to start with.

1 Sketch each of these graphs:

    a $y = x^2 + 6$ **d** $y = x^2 + 1$

    b $y = x^2 + 9$ **e** $y = x^2 + 1\frac{1}{2}$

    c $y = x^2 - 3$ **f** $y = x^2 - 7\frac{1}{2}$

2 Look at this graph of $y = x^4$.
Use it to sketch:

    a $y = x^4 + 5$

    b $y = x^4 - 7$

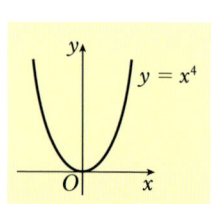

3 Look at this graph of $y = x^3 + x$.
Use it to sketch:

    a $y = x^3 + x - 4$

    b $y = x^3 + x + 5$

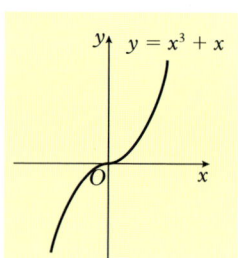

4 Sketch each of these graphs:

    a $y = (x + 3)^2$ **c** $y = (x - 2\frac{1}{2})^2$

    b $y = (x - 9)^2$ **d** $y = (x + 0.25)^2$

    e For each of your graphs write down how the graph of $y = x^2$ has been transformed to get your graph. Use vector notation.

5 Look at this graph of $y = -x^2$.
Use it to sketch:

    a $y = -(x + 3)^2$

    b $y = 4 - x^2$

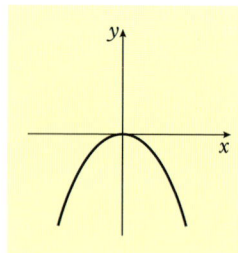

6 Here is a sketch of $y = f(x)$ where

$$f(x) = \frac{1}{x}$$

Sketch each of the following graphs:

    a $y = f(x) + 3$ **c** $y = f(-x)$

    b $y = f(x) - 4$ **d** $y = -f(x)$

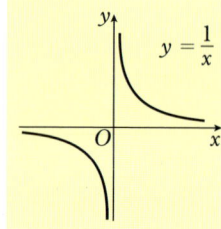

7 Sketch the graph of $y = (x + 3)^2 + 2$

8 Sketch the graph of $y = (x - 4)^2 - 1$

9 **a** Sketch the graph of $y = 2(x - 5)^2$
 b Describe the transformations to $y = x^2$ that you have done.

10 **a** Sketch the graph of $y = 3(x + 6)^2 - 4$
 b Describe the transformations to $y = x^2$ that you have done.

11 Here is a sketch of $y = f(x)$.
Sketch each of these following graphs.
 a $y = f(x) - 3$ **c** $y = f(x + 2)$
 b $y = f(-x)$ **d** $y = -f(x)$

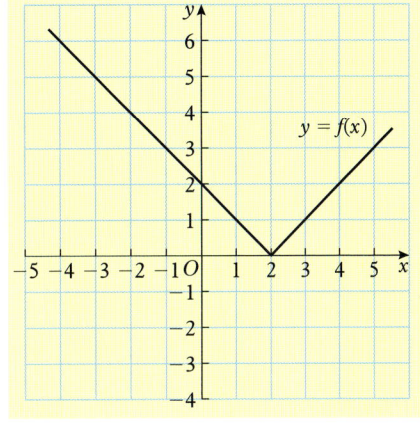

12 The value of a veteran car increases each year.
This table shows its approximate value for 5 years.

Year	1	2	3	4	5
Value (£)	15 000	18 500	21 300	24 700	28 000

 a Plot these values on a graph.
 b Draw a line of best fit through the points.
 c Work out the gradient of the line.
 d Write down the intercept of the line with the 'value' axis.
 e Write down an equation linking the value with the year number.

13 Here are the results of another experiment on cell division.

t (hours)	1	2	3	4	5
N	6	12	24	48	96

 a Plot a graph of N against 2^t
 b Find the gradient of the line.
 c Write an equation connecting N and 2^t

1 This is the graph of $y = x^2 - 7x + 10$.
Use it to sketch:

   a $y = x^2 - 7x$
   b $y = x^2 - 7x + 12$

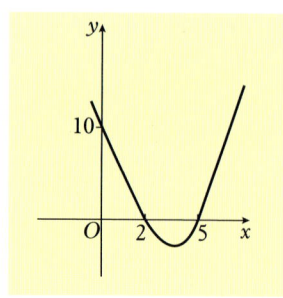

2 This is a sketch of the graph of $y = f(x)$, where
$f(x) = (x - 3)(x - 5)(x + 2)$.

   a Write down the value of $f(-1)$.
   b Sketch the graph of $y = -f(x)$.
   c Describe fully the transformation you have
      used to obtain the graph in part **b**.
   d Describe how you would obtain the graph
      of $y = f(-x)$ from the graph of $f(x)$.

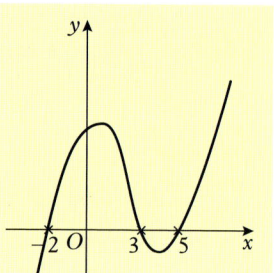

3 The table gives experimental values for x and y.

x	16	48	60	72	80
y	254	472	612	775	912

   a Plot a graph of y against x.
   b By examining your graph, suggest the relationship between y and x.
   c Draw a suitable straight line graph to confirm your suggestion.
   d Write down the gradient and intercept of your straight line.
   e Write down an equation connecting y and x.

4 Kepler's third law states that:

> 'When a moon orbits a planet the square of the time taken to
> complete one orbit is proportional to the cube of the radius of
> the orbit.'

Here is some data relating to this law:

Radius of orbit (millions of km)	1.1	1.9	11.1	11.5	11.7
Time (days)	7.2	16.9	239	251	259

Investigate how well this data fits the law.

1 This is the graph of $y = x^2$.
   Sketch the graph of:
   a $y = x^2 - 3$
   b $y = (x + 2)^2$
   c $y = 2(x - 3)^2 + 1$

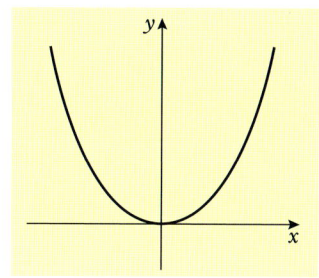

2 **a** Sketch the graph of $y = (x + 2)^2 - 4$
   b Describe the transformations to $y = x^2$ that you have done.

3 This is the graph of the
   function $y = f(x)$.

   a Sketch the graph of
      $y = 2f(x)$.
   b Sketch the graph of
      $y = f(x + 1)$.
   c Sketch the graph of
      $y = f(-x)$.

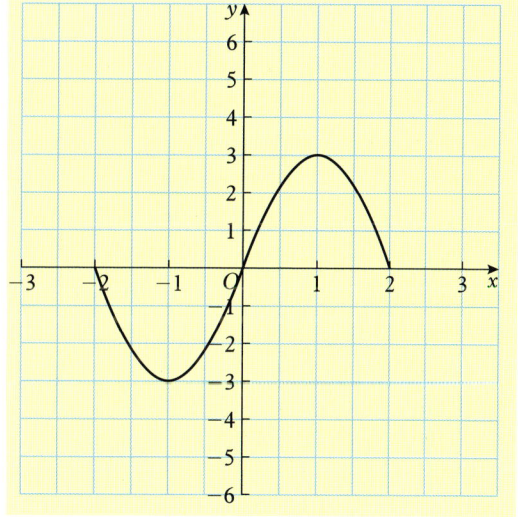

   d This is a sketch of the
      function $y = f(x) + a$.
      Write down the value of a.

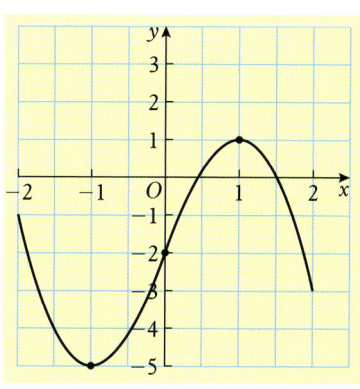

4 **a** Sketch the graph of $y = 3(x + 1)^2$
   b Describe the transformations to $y = x^2$ that you have done.

5 **a** Sketch the graph of $y = -x^2$
   b Sketch the graph of $y = 7 - (x - 2)^2$
   c Describe the transformations to $y = -x^2$ that you have done.

6 This is a sketch of $f(x) = \dfrac{1}{2x^2}$.

Sketch the graph of $y = -f(x)$.

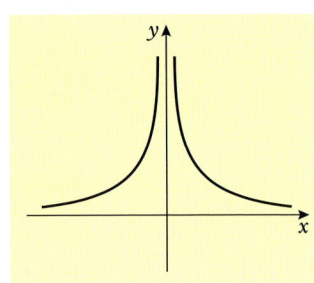

7 Gail has collected some data in a mechanics experiment.
   This is her data.

t	2	4	6	8	10	12	14	16
v	14	22	15	31	38	45	48	56

   a Plot this data on a graph.
      Use t for the horizontal axis and v for the vertical axis.
   b Gail made a mistake in one of her readings.
      For what time did she make the mistake?
   c Gail knows that the variables t and v are connected by the equation
         $v = u + at$
      Draw a line of best fit for your graph and use it to find the values of
      u and a.

18 Shape: the final frontier

1 Circles
Revising circumference and area
Finding arc lengths
Finding sector areas
Finding segment areas

2 Areas and volumes
Finding the volume and surface area of a prism
Finding the volume and surface area of a pyramid
Finding the volume and surface area of a cone
Finding the volume and surface area of a sphere
Converting area and volume units

CORE

3 Areas and volumes of similar figures
Investigating ratios of areas of similar shapes
Finding areas given the length factor
Finding lengths given areas
Investigating ratios of volumes of similar shapes
Finding volumes given the length factor
Finding lengths given volumes
Finding volumes given areas
Finding masses of similar solids

4 Dimensional analysis
Using dimensions to analyse formulas for length, area and volume

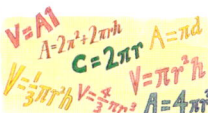

QUESTIONS

EXTENSION

TEST YOURSELF

1 Circles

The Earth moves in an orbit around the Sun. It takes the Earth 365 days, 5 hours, 48 minutes and 46 seconds to complete one orbit.

The Earth moves so that it is always between 91.4 and 94.6 million miles from the Sun.

If you assume that the orbit is a circle of radius 93 million miles that takes 365 days to complete, then we are hurtling through space at more than 66 700 miles per hour!

Circumference   Circumference $= \pi \times d$iameter
                   or in symbols $C = \pi d$

Example   Find the circumference of this circle.

   $C = \pi d$
       $= \pi \times 8$ Key in: $\boxed{\pi}$ $\boxed{\times}$ $\boxed{8}$ $\boxed{=}$
       $= 8\pi$ cm
       $= 25.1$ cm to 1 dp   *25.132741*

Exercise 18:1

1 Find the circumference of these circles. Give your answers in terms of π and to 1 dp.

  a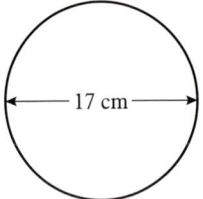
  17 cm

  b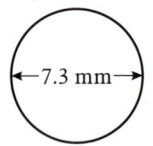
  7.3 mm

2 Henry lives in a circular windmill.
He is a bit eccentric.
Every day he walks around the outside wall of his house 100 times.
The windmill has a radius of 3.2 m.

  a How far does Henry walk each time he goes round his house?

  b How many kilometres does Henry walk each day? Give your answer to the nearest metre.

Example The circumference of a circle is 38 cm.

Find: **a** the diameter **b** the radius

a Start with the formula $C = \pi d$

You rearrange
this to get $d = \dfrac{C}{\pi}$

so $d = \dfrac{38}{\pi}$ Key in: **3** **8** **÷** **π** **=**

$d = 12.1$ cm to 1 dp. *12.095776*

b The radius is half the diameter.
Don't use the rounded value for the diameter.

Keep the exact value from part **a** in *12.095776*
your calculator display and halve that.

Key in: **÷** **2** **=**

Then round your answer. *6.0478878*

$r = 6.0$ cm to 1 dp.

3 Find: **a** the diameter **b** the radius
of a circle with a circumference of:
(1) 80 cm (2) 47 cm (3) 123 cm (4) 243 cm
Give all your answers to the nearest millimetre.

Area of a circle *A*rea of a circle $= \pi \times (\text{radius})^2$
or in symbols $A = \pi r^2$

Example Find the area of this circle.

$A = \pi r^2$
$= \pi \times 4^2$
$= 16\pi \text{ cm}^2$
$= 50.3 \text{ cm}^2$ to 1 dp

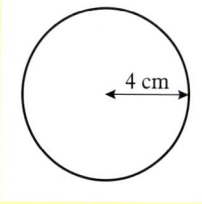

4 cm

4 Find the area of a circle with:
a radius 7.4 cm **b** diameter 25.2 cm
Give your answers in terms of π and to 1 dp.

5 Show that the radius of a circle can be found from the area by using the
formula:

$$r = \sqrt{\dfrac{A}{\pi}}$$

6 Find the radius of a circle that has an area of:
   a 100 cm²   **c** 1 m²   **e** 54 m²
   b 300 cm²   **d** 400 mm²   **f** 1640 mm²
   Give each answer to a sensible degree of accuracy.

Arc length

A length around part of the circumference of a circle is called an **arc length**. This circle has a diameter of d.

The red length around half of the circumference is $\dfrac{180}{360} \times \pi d$

The blue length around a quarter of the circumference is $\dfrac{90}{360} \times \pi d$

If the angle in a sector of a circle is θ then the arc length, s, is given by

$$s = \frac{\theta}{360} \times \pi d$$

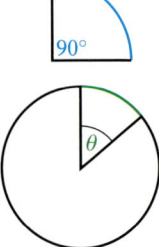

Exercise 18:2

Give your answers to a sensible degree of accuracy in each question in this exercise.

1 Find the length of the coloured arc in each of these circles.

a
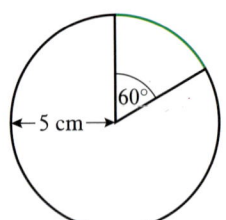

c
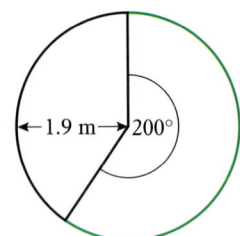

b
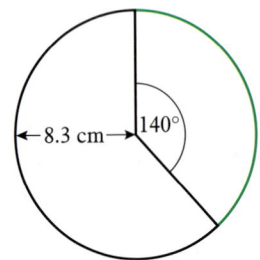

d
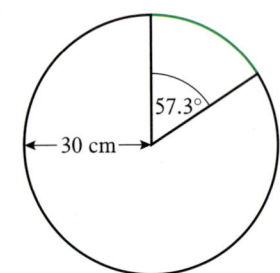

2 Assume that the Earth travels in a circle of radius 93 million miles around the Sun in 365 days. How far does it travel in 1 day?

3 The diagram shows you a roundabout of radius 21.5 m. Work out the shortest distance around the roundabout between:

a A and B
b A and D
c C and A
d D and B

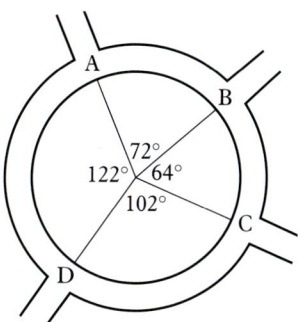

Sector	A **sector** of a circle is a region that is bounded by two radii and an arc of the circle.

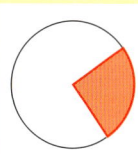

Area of a sector	If the angle in a sector of a circle is θ then the **area of the sector, A,** is given by $A = \dfrac{\theta}{360} \times \pi r^2$ where r is the radius of the circle.

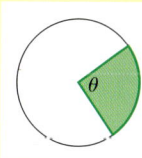

Exercise 18:3

1 Find the coloured sector area in each of these.

a

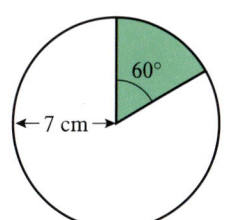

60°

←7 cm→

c

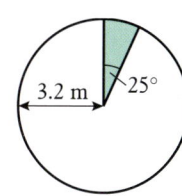

3.2 m 25°

b

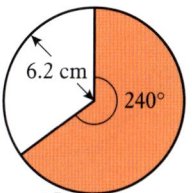

6.2 cm 240°

• d

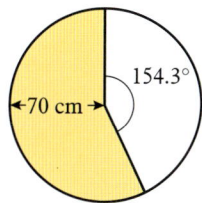

154.3°

←70 cm→

2 This is a picture of a spinner that is being used in a probability experiment.
The *diameter* of the spinner is 7.8 cm. The angle in each sector is shown in the table.

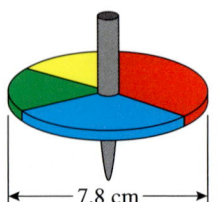

Colour	red	blue	green	yellow
Angle	130°	110°	65°	55°

Find the area of each coloured sector.

3 This is a picture of the *Countdown* clock. The radius of the clock is 0.8 m. Find the area of the sector of the clock that lights up for each passing second.

4 In the diagram OAB is a quarter of a circle. OA and OB are radii.
  a Find the area of sector OAB.
  b Find the area of triangle OAB.
  c Use your answers to **a** and **b** to write down the blue area. The blue region is called a **segment**.

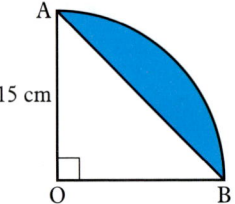

5 In the diagram OAB is a sector of a circle. OA and OB are radii. Angle AOB = 60°.
  a Find the area of sector OAB.
  b Find the area of triangle OAB.
  c Use your answers to parts **a** and **b** to write down the area of the blue segment.

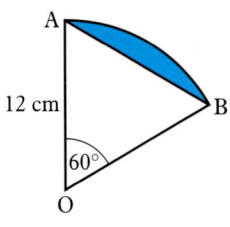

6 Work out the coloured area in each of these.

a

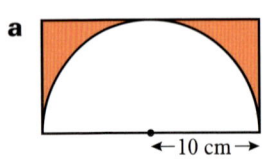

b

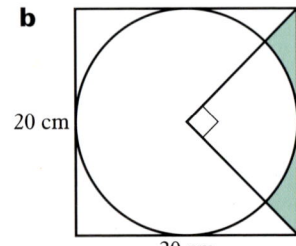

c

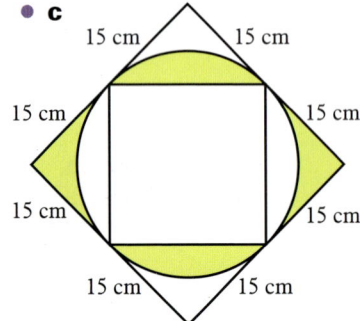

You have seen segments of a circle in Chapter 15.

To find the area of a minor segment you need to work out the area of the sector that contains the segment and subtract the area of the triangle.

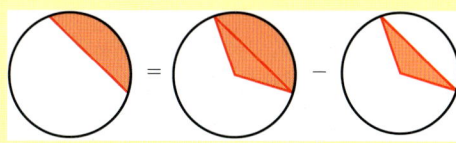

Area of a triangle There is a special formula that you can use to work out the area of a triangle if you know two sides and the angle in between them.

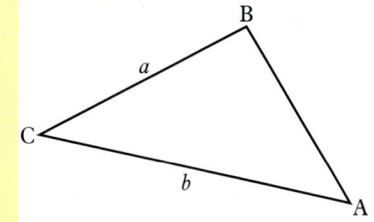

The area of this triangle is $\frac{1}{2}ab \sin C$.

Area of a segment The **area of a segment** contained in a sector of a circle of radius r with angle θ is therefore

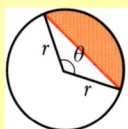

$$\frac{\theta}{360} \times \pi r^2 - \frac{1}{2}r^2 \sin\theta$$

7 Find the coloured segment area in each of these.

a
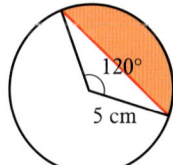
120°
5 cm

c
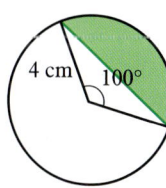
4 cm 100°

b
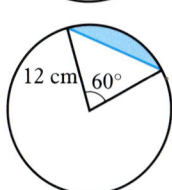
12 cm 60°

d
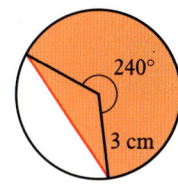
240°
3 cm

● **8** Show that the area of the red segment is $25(\pi - 2)$ cm².

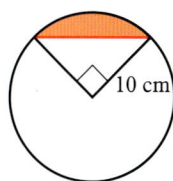
10 cm

2   Areas and volumes

The use of shapes in this building speaks volumes about the architect!

Cross section

A **cross section** through a solid is the shape that you get when you make a cut perpendicular to the length. This is a picture of a block of cheese. The cross section is a trapezium.

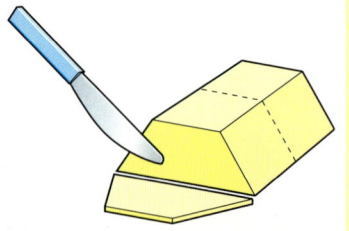

Prism

A **prism** is a solid that has the same cross section all the way through. The cross section must be a polygon.

The shape of a cross section is often used to name a prism. This is a *triangular* prism.

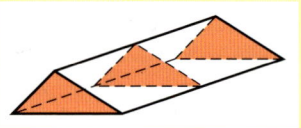

A cylinder is like a prism but has a circle as its cross section.

Volume of a prism = Area of cross section × length

Example

Find the volume of this cylinder.

The cross sectional area is a circle so $A = \pi r^2$ where r is the radius.

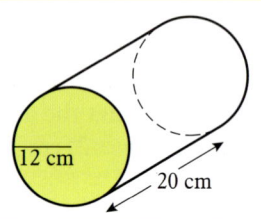

Here $r = 12$ Area $= \pi \times 12^2$

$$\begin{aligned} \text{Volume} &= \pi \times 12^2 \times 20 \\ &= 9047.78\ldots \\ &= 9050 \text{ cm}^3 \text{ to 3 sf} \end{aligned}$$

Exercise 18:4

Work out the volumes of these storage tanks. All the tanks are prisms.
You will need to use trigonometry in questions **4–6**. Round your answers to 3 sf.

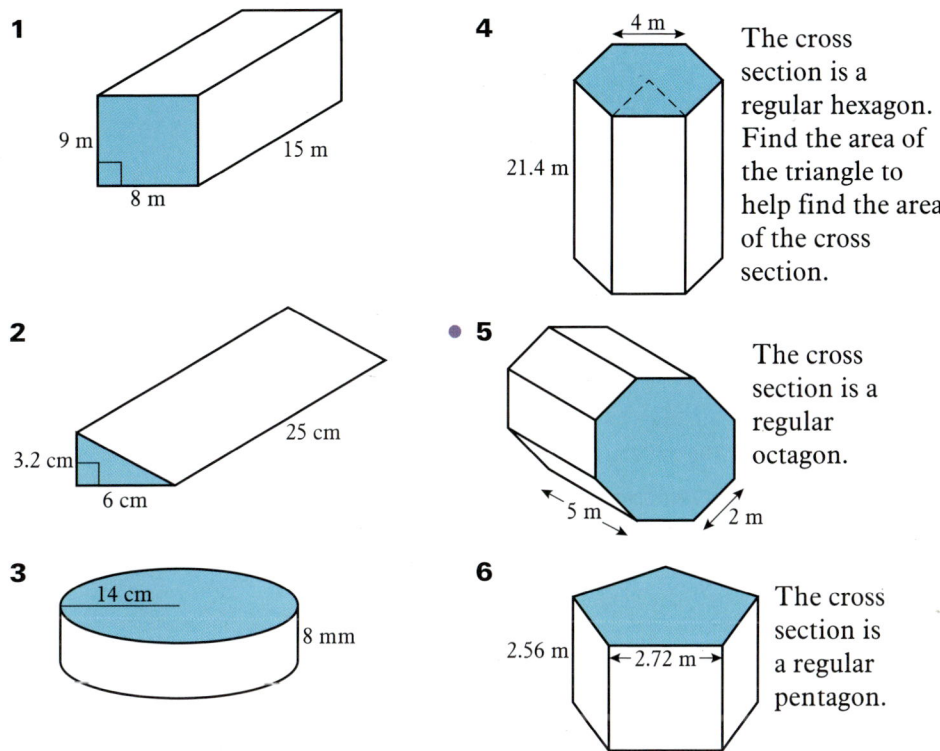

1 9 m 8 m 15 m

4 4 m 21.4 m The cross section is a regular hexagon. Find the area of the triangle to help find the area of the cross section.

2 3.2 cm 6 cm 25 cm

5 5 m 2 m The cross section is a regular octagon.

3 14 cm 8 mm

6 2.56 m 2.72 m The cross section is a regular pentagon.

7 The trailer of a wine lorry carries a cylinder. The cylinder is 10 m long and the radius of the cross section is 1.2 m. How many litres of wine does it carry? (1000 litres = 1 m³)

8 A very large concrete pipe has a hexagonal cross section.
Within the pipe 4 cylindrical tubes carry liquid gases.
Each tube has a radius of 82 cm.
Work out:
a the volume of gas in 100 m of one tube
b the volume of concrete in 1 km of pipe

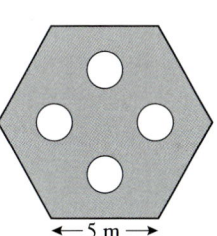
5 m

9 Find the cross sectional areas of these prisms.

a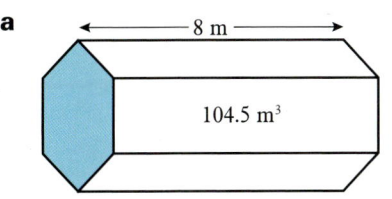
8 m 104.5 m³

b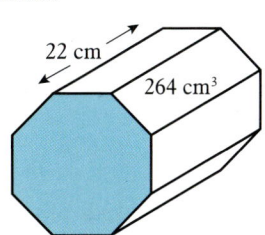
22 cm 264 cm³

10 a Find the length of this prism.   **b** Find the length of this cylinder.

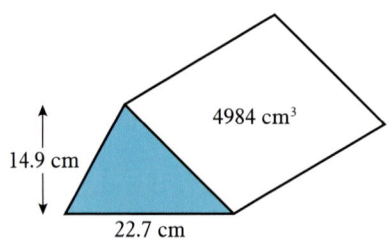

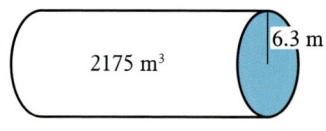

Finding the surface areas of prisms

A simple way to do this is to sketch the net so you will not miss any faces.

To find the surface area of a prism:
(1) Sketch the net.
(2) Work out the areas of the different faces.
(3) Find the total of all the areas

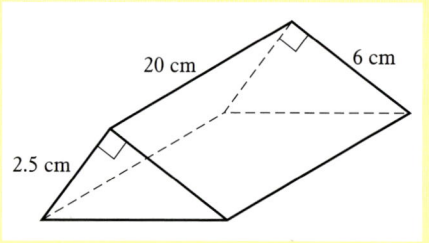

Example   For this prism, right-angled triangles A and B are congruent so they have the same area. The hypotenuse of triangle A is the width of rectangle C.
The hypotenuse is worked out by Pythagoras' theorem:
$h^2 = 6^2 + (2.5)^2$ so that $h = 6.5$ cm

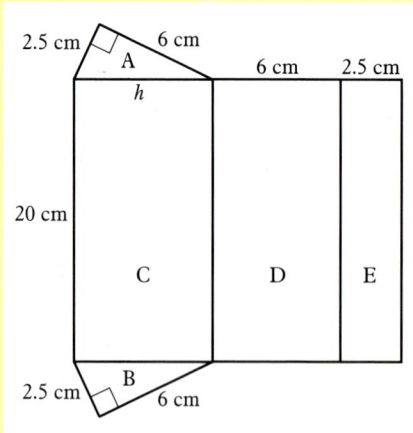

Area of triangle A $= \frac{1}{2} \times 6 \times 2.5 \quad = \quad 7\frac{1}{2}$ cm²
Area of triangle B $= \frac{1}{2} \times 6 \times 2.5 \quad = \quad 7\frac{1}{2}$ cm²
Area of rectangle C $= 20 \times 6.5 \quad\quad = 130$ cm²
Area of rectangle D $= 20 \times 6 \quad\quad\quad = 120$ cm²
Area of rectangle E $= 20 \times 2.5 \quad\quad = \quad 50$ cm²

Total surface area $\quad\quad\quad\quad\quad = 315$ cm²

11   Work out the surface area of the tanks in questions **1–2, 4–6**.

12 Work out the surface area of these prisms.

a

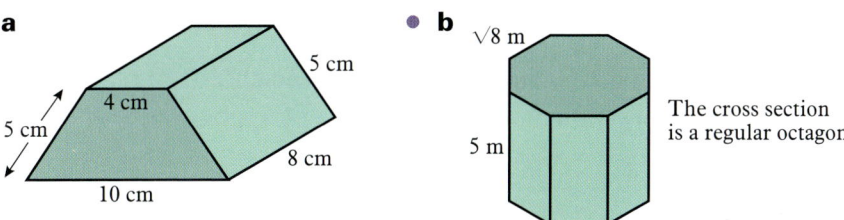

5 cm
4 cm
5 cm
8 cm
10 cm

• b √8 m

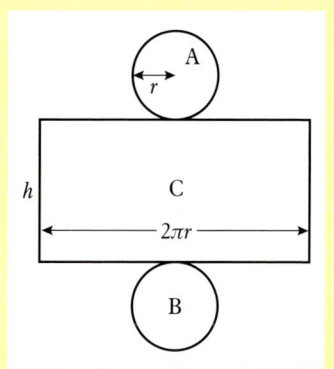

5 m

The cross section
is a regular octagon

The surface area of a cylinder is worked out in the
same way.

Think of an unrolled tin can.
The net is shown here. The circles have a radius of r.
The length of rectangle C is the same as the
circumference of the circles A and B. This is $2\pi r$.
So the area of rectangle C is $2\pi rh$.
The area of the 2 circles, A and B is $2\pi r^2$.

This gives a total surface area of
$2\pi r^2 + 2\pi rh = 2\pi r(r + h)$

A
r
h
C
$2\pi r$
B

---

13 Work out the surface areas of these cans. Ignore any lips.

a

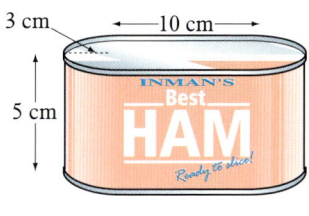

4 cm
15 cm
Sutton's
BEANS
in tomato sauce

b Each end of this cross
section is a semi-circle.

3 cm ◄—10 cm—►
5 cm
INMAN'S
Best
HAM
Ready to slice!

c Each corner of this
cross section is a quarter-circle.

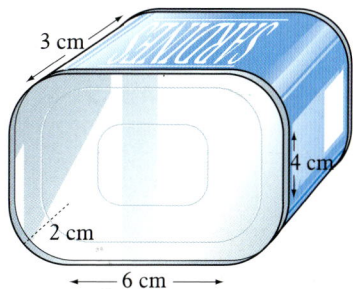

3 cm
4 cm
2 cm
◄— 6 cm —►

Volume of a pyramid

The *V*olume of a pyramid is $\frac{1}{3}\times$ base *A*rea $\times$ vertical *h*eight, or in symbols $V=\frac{1}{3}Ah$

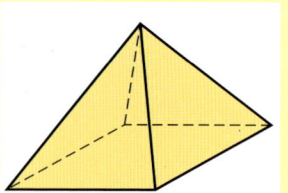

As you increase the number of sides on the base of a pyramid … eventually you end up with a cone!

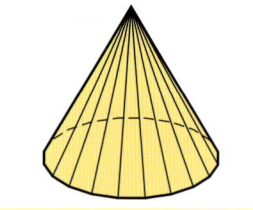

So the *V*olume of a cone is also $\frac{1}{3}\times$ base *A*rea $\times$ vertical *h*eight. A cone has a circle for a base,

so $A=\pi r^2$ and $V=\frac{1}{3}\pi r^2 h$

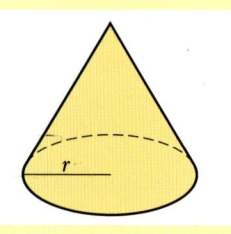

Exercise 18:5

Work out the volume of each of these shapes. Round all your answers to 3 sf.

1

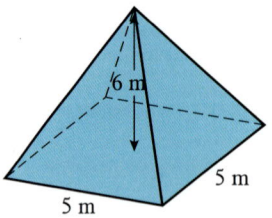

6 m

5 m

5 m

2

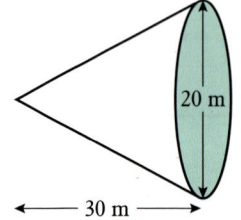

20 m

30 m

3 The picture shows a wheel from a child's trolley. It is made from two congruent cones and a cylinder.

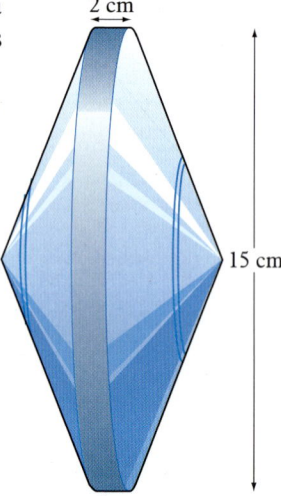

2 cm

15 cm

6 cm

4 The Great Pyramid at Giza was originally
147 m high.
It has a square base of side 230 m.
Work out:
a the volume in m^3
b the surface area in m^2 (including the base)

5 A Millenium Cone is made by building a cone and then removing a
smaller cone from the top. The radius of the large cone is 72 m. The
height of the large cone is 100 m.
The radius of the small cone is $\frac{1}{8}$ of the radius of the large cone.
Work out: **a** the volume of the original cone
             b the volume of the small cone
             c the volume of the remaining building
The shape of the building is called a frustum.

6 A grain hopper is a cylinder with a
frustum beneath. Work out the
volume of grain which can be stored
in the hopper.

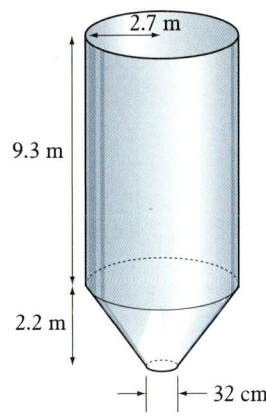

Finding the surface area of a cone

This is a picture of a cone that has a base radius of r and a slant height l.
If you slice down the edge of the cone and open it out you get a sector of a circle.

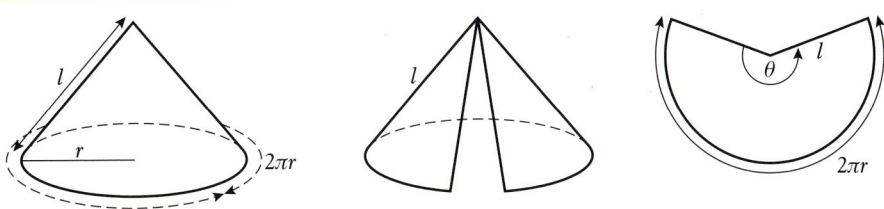

In the picture of the cone the circumference of the base is $2\pi r$.
So the arc length of the sector of the circle is also $2\pi r$.

The arc length of the sector is also $\dfrac{\theta}{360} \times 2\pi l$

so $\dfrac{\theta}{360} \times 2\pi l = 2\pi r$

dividing by $2\pi l$ gives $\dfrac{\theta}{360} = \dfrac{2\pi r}{2\pi l}$

so $\dfrac{\theta}{360} = \dfrac{r}{l}$

The area of the sector is $\dfrac{\theta}{360} \times \pi l^2$

But $\dfrac{\theta}{360} = \dfrac{r}{l}$ $= \dfrac{r}{l} \times \pi l^2$

This is the curved surface area of a cone $= \pi r l$

The total surface area of a cone is $\pi r^2 + \pi r l$

$= \pi r (r + l)$

Exercise 18:6

1 Find the surface area in each part.

a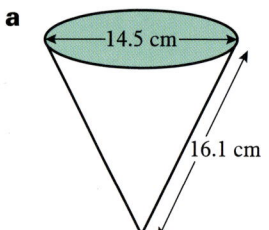

b

2 Find the surface areas of the solids in questions **2** and **3** of Exercise 18:5.

The volume and surface area of a sphere

The volume of a sphere of radius r is $\frac{4}{3}\pi r^3$.

The surface area of a sphere of radius r is $4\pi r^2$.

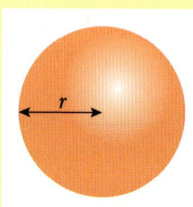

Exercise 18:7

1 For each sphere work out: (1) the volume (2) the surface area
Round all your answers to 3 sf.

a

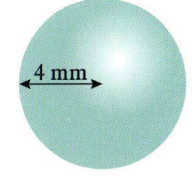

4 mm

c

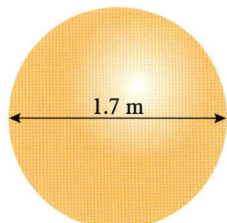

1.7 m

b

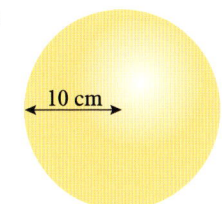

10 cm

d

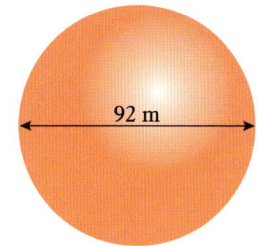

92 m

2 This is a picture of a hot air balloon.
Its radius is 25 m.
Work out:
a the volume of hot air required in this balloon
b the surface area of the material used
c If the material is 4 mm thick, work out the volume of material. Assume the balloon is a perfect sphere.

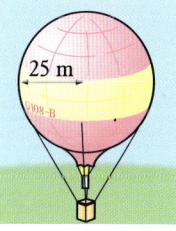

25 m

3 Mr Ophseid, the Head of PE, stores footballs in a chest.
The chest has been designed so that the balls fit exactly as shown in the diagram. The chest is exactly 3 layers deep.
Each ball is 28 cm in diameter. Work out the volume of:
a the chest **c** all the balls
b 1 football **d** the wasted space

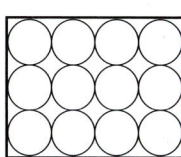

4 A vat is built in the shape of a hemisphere, 1.4 m deep.
It is filled with water at the rate of 50 litres per minute.
a What is the volume of water in the vat when full?
b How long does it take to fill?

Water has a density of 1 g/cm³. The vat has a mass of 120 kg.
c What is the total mass the floorboards under the vat must be able to support?

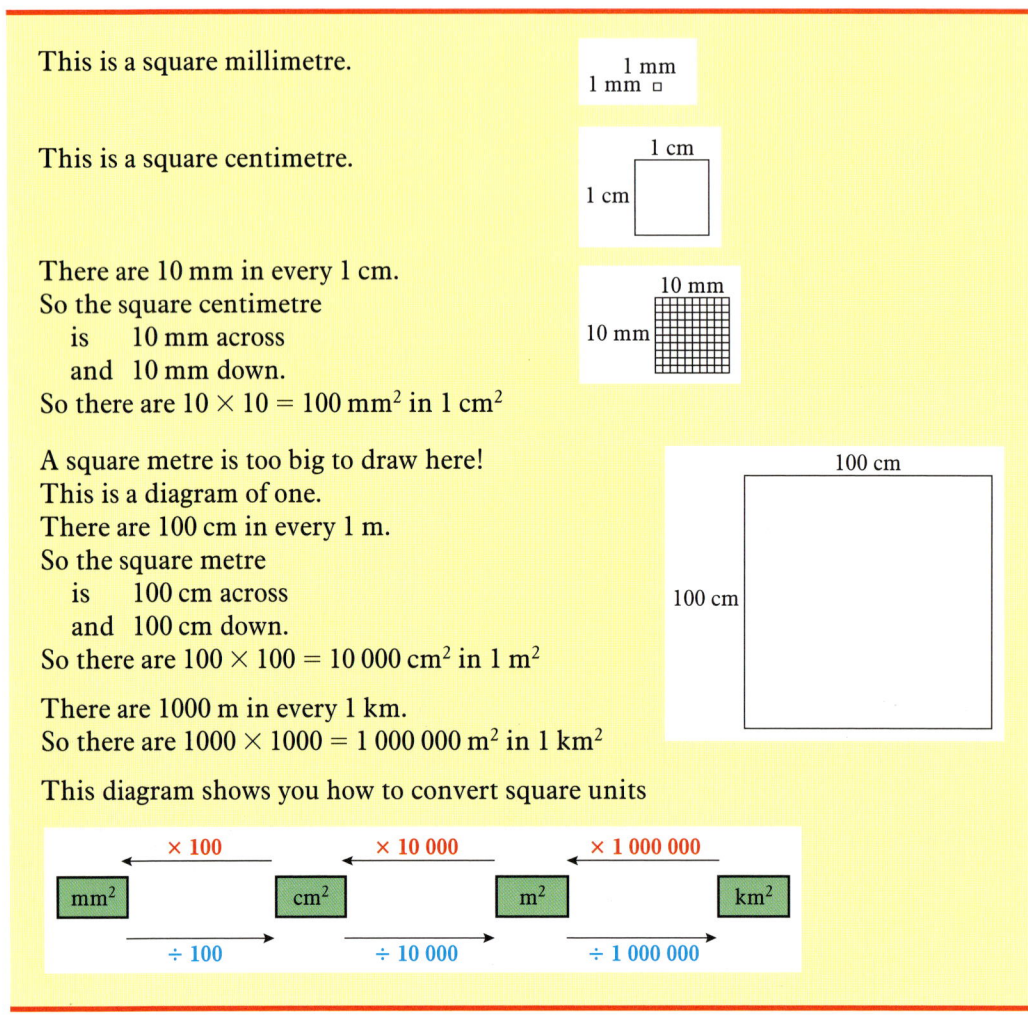

This is a square millimetre.

1 mm
1 mm □

This is a square centimetre.

1 cm
1 cm

There are 10 mm in every 1 cm.
So the square centimetre
   is   10 mm across
  and 10 mm down.
So there are $10 \times 10 = 100$ mm^2 in 1 cm^2

10 mm
10 mm

A square metre is too big to draw here!
This is a diagram of one.
There are 100 cm in every 1 m.
So the square metre
   is   100 cm across
  and 100 cm down.
So there are $100 \times 100 = 10\,000$ cm^2 in 1 m^2

100 cm
100 cm

There are 1000 m in every 1 km.
So there are $1000 \times 1000 = 1\,000\,000$ m^2 in 1 km^2

This diagram shows you how to convert square units

	$\times$ 100		$\times$ 10 000		$\times$ 1 000 000	
mm^2		cm^2		m^2		km^2
	$\div$ 100		$\div$ 10 000		$\div$ 1 000 000	

Exercise 18:8

1   Draw a square 2 cm by 2 cm. Find the area in square millimetres.

2   Change each of these areas into square centimetres.
      a 2 m^2 **c** 12 m^2 **e** 0.43 m^2 **g** 128 mm^2 **i** 2050 mm^2
      b 8 m^2 **d** 0.9 m^2 **f** 400 mm^2 **h** 672 mm^2 **j** 25 mm^2

3   Change each of these areas into square metres.
      a 40 000 cm^2 **b** 7900 cm^2 **c** 0.4 km^2 **d** 8.95 km^2

4 Change each of these areas into square kilometres.
    a $10\,000\,\text{m}^2$ ● **c** $10^9\,\text{m}^2$
    b $7\,500\,000\,\text{m}^2$ ● **d** $2.3 \times 10^7\,\text{m}^2$

This is a cubic millimetre.
All the sides are 1 mm.

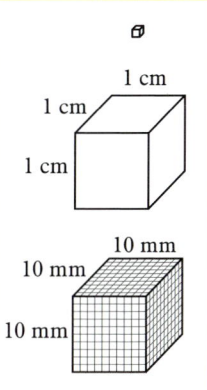

This is a cubic centimetre.

There are 10 mm in every 1 cm.
    So in the cubic centimetre
    the width is 10 mm
    the length is 10 mm
    the height is 10 mm
    So there are $10 \times 10 \times 10 = 1000\,\text{mm}^3$ in $1\,\text{cm}^3$

A cubic metre is too big to draw here.
This is a diagram of one.
There are 100 cm in every 1 m.
    So in the cubic metre
    the dimensions are $100\,\text{cm} \times 100\,\text{cm} \times 100\,\text{cm}$
So there are $100 \times 100 \times 100 = 1\,000\,000\,\text{cm}^3$ in $1\,\text{m}^3$

This diagram shows you
how to convert cubic units

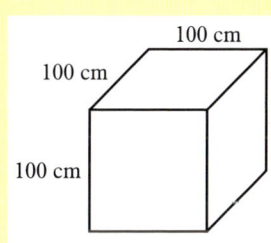

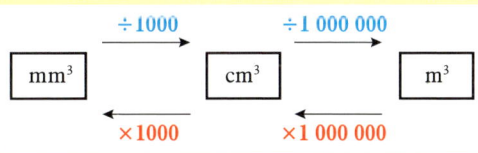

---

5 Draw a sketch of a cube 2 cm by 2 cm by 2 cm. Find the volume in mm^3.

6 Change each of these volumes into cm^3.
    a $6\,\text{m}^3$ **c** $12.36\,\text{m}^3$ **e** $672\,\text{mm}^3$
    b $0.4\,\text{m}^3$ **d** $2050\,\text{mm}^3$ **f** $86\,\text{mm}^3$

7 Change each of these volumes into m^3.
    a $40\,000\,000\,\text{cm}^3$ **b** $7\,900\,000\,\text{cm}^3$ **c** $459\,000\,\text{cm}^3$

3 Areas and volumes of similar figures

Alphonse has a set of similar stainless steel saucepans.

He knows that a pan that has double the radius of another one holds far more than twice as much soup. But how much soup does it hold?

| **Similar** | If two objects are **similar**, one is an enlargement of the other. They have the same shape but different sizes. This is true for 3D solids as well as 2D shapes. |

Exercise 18:9

1

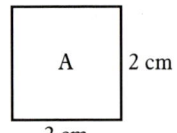

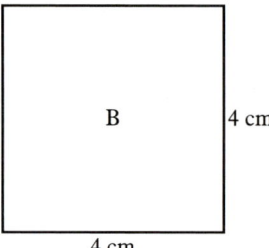

Square B is similar to square A.
a Write down the scale factor for the enlargement from A to B.
This is the *linear* scale factor (the scale factor for the lengths).
b Write down the area of square A.
c Write down the area of square B.

d Work out the scale factor given by $\dfrac{\text{area of square B}}{\text{area of square A}}$

This is the *area* scale factor for the enlargement from A to B.
e Write down what you notice about your answers to parts **a** and **d**.

2 Repeat each part of question **1** for these two squares.

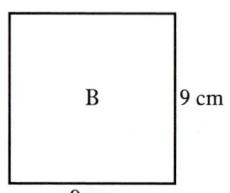

3

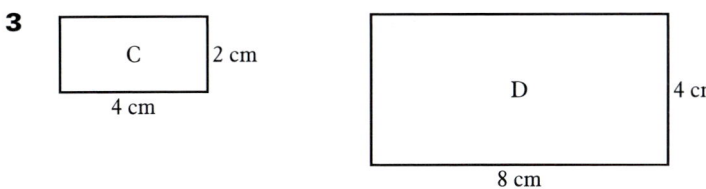

    a Are rectangles C and D similar? Explain your answer.
    b Write down the linear scale factor for the enlargement from C to D.
    c Work out the area scale factor for the enlargement from C to D.
    d Write down what you notice about your answers to parts **b** and **c**.

4

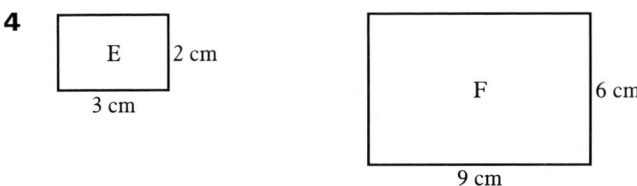

    a Write down the linear scale factor for the enlargement from E to F.
    b Work out the area scale factor for the enlargement from E to F.
    c Write down what you notice about your answers to parts **a** and **b**.

5 Copy this table. Fill it in for each pair of similar shapes.
    Write down what you notice about your answers.

	Type of shape	Shape A		Shape B		Linear scale factor from A to B	Area scale factor from A to B
a	Square	length 4 m		length 12 m		…	…
b	Rectangle	length 3 cm	width 2 cm	length 12 cm	width …	…	…
c	Triangle	base 5 cm	height 2 cm	base 25 cm	height …	…	…
d	Parallelogram	base 3 cm	height 1 cm	base …	height 6 cm	…	…
e	Circle	radius 8 cm		radius 4 cm		…	…
● **f**	Square	length 1 cm		length a cm		…	…
● **g**	Rectangle	length 2 cm	width 1 cm	length …	width a cm	…	…

For *any* pair of similar shapes A and B

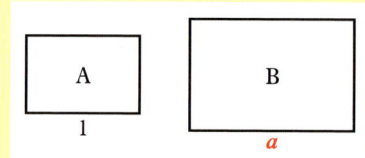

if the **linear** scale factor for the enlargement from A to B is *a*,
then the **area** scale factor for the enlargement from A to B is $a \times a = a^2$

This means the area of shape B is a^2 times the area of shape A.

Sign A and sign B are two
similar signs.
Sign A is 4 m long.
Sign B is 10 m long.
The area of sign A is 256 cm².
To work out the area of sign B
you need to find the area scale factor.

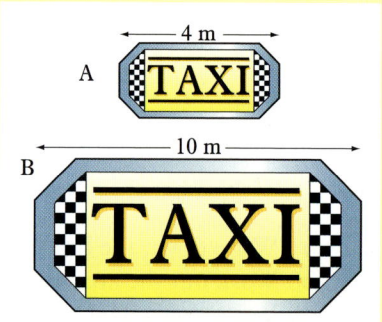

The linear scale factor from A to B is $\dfrac{10}{4} = 2.5$

so the area scale factor from A to B is $(2.5)^2 = 6.25$

and the area of sign B is $256 \times 6.25 = 1600 \text{ cm}^2$

Exercise 18:10

1 These are the linear scale factors for some enlargements.
Work out the area scale factors.
a 2   **c** 4   **e** 2.8   **g** $\frac{1}{4}$
b 3   **d** $1\frac{1}{2}$ **f** $\frac{1}{2}$ **h** $\frac{2}{5}$

2 A metre is an enlargement of a centimetre using a linear scale factor
of 100.
Work out how many square centimetres are in a square metre using an
area scale factor.

3 Use the method in question **2** to work out:
a how many m² are in a km²   **b** how many cm² are in a km²

4 Fred has drawn a plan of a flint path that he is going to lay.

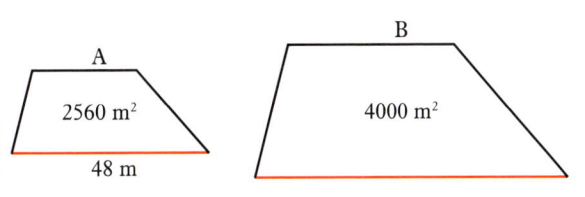

2 cm

30 cm

On the plan it is 30 cm long and 2 cm wide.
The plan is drawn to the scale 1:50.
a Work out the area of the path on the plan.
b Work out the area of the real path.

5 Lizzy is a talented artist. She paints large pictures from postcards.
She is copying from a postcard that is 17.5 cm long and 12 cm wide.
To cover this area on canvas she needs 25 ml of paint.
She enlarges the picture on the postcard to cover a canvas 70 cm long.
How many ml of paint does she need?

Sometimes you need to use areas to find lengths. These are two playing fields, A and B. Each one has a path along one edge. You need to find the length of the path at the edge of the large field.

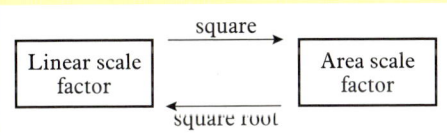

To go from a linear scale factor to an area scale factor, you need to square.
To *undo this*, you need to square root.

Linear scale factor	square → ← square root	Area scale factor

Here the area scale factor from A to B is

$4000 \div 2560 = 1.5625$

so the linear scale factor is

$\sqrt{1.5625} = 1.25$

and the length of the path on the edge of field B is

$48 \times 1.25 = 60$ m

---

6 This is a diagram of a model car racing circuit.
The area enclosed is 2.5 m^2.
It is similar to a real car racing circuit.
The area enclosed by the real life circuit is 2560 m^2.
Work out the length of its grandstand.

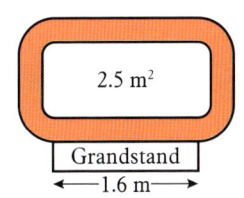

2.5 m^2

Grandstand

←—1.6 m—→

7 A2 paper is four times the area of A4 paper.
A5 paper is half the area of A4 paper. All A sizes of paper are similar.
If A4 paper measures 21.0 cm by 29.7 cm, work out the dimensions of:
a A2 paper
b A5 paper

Exercise 18:11

1

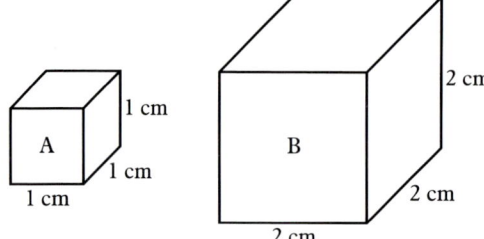

Cube B is similar to cube A.
a Write down the linear scale factor for the enlargement from A to B.
b Work out the surface area of cube A.
c Work out the surface area of cube B.
d Work out the area scale factor for the enlargement from A to B.
e Write down what you notice about your answers to parts **a** and **d**.
f Work out the volume of cube A.
g Work out the volume of cube B.
h Work out the volume scale factor given by $\dfrac{\text{volume of cube B}}{\text{volume of cube A}}$

This is the *volume* scale factor for the enlargement from A to B.
Write down what you notice about your answers to parts **a** and **h**.

2 Copy this table. Fill it in for each pair of similar shapes.

Type of shape	Shape A			Shape B			Linear scale factor from A to B	Volume scale factor from A to B
a Cube	length 4 m			length 12 m			...	...
b Cuboid	length 4 cm	width 3 cm	height 2 cm	length 12 cm	width ...	height ...	...	...
c Triangular prism	cross section 8 cm²		length 5 cm	cross section ...		length 10 cm	...	...
d Pyramid	base area 3 cm²		height 1 cm	base area ...		height 6 cm	...	...
e Sphere	radius 2 cm			radius 6 cm			...	...
• f Cube	length 1 cm			length a cm			...	...
• g Cuboid	length 4 cm	width 3 cm	height 2 cm	length ...	width ...	height 2a cm	...	...

For *any* pair of similar solids A and B

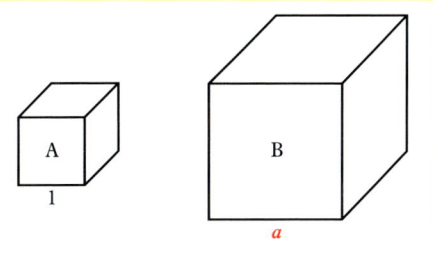

if the **linear** scale factor going from A to B is a
then the surface **area** scale factor going from A to B is $a \times a = a^2$
and the **volume** scale factor going from A to B is $a \times a \times a = a^3$

This means the surface **area** of shape B is a^2 times the surface area of shape A and the **volume** of shape B is a^3 times the volume of shape A.

Drum A and drum B are two similar oil drums.
Drum A has a height of 40 cm.
Drum B has a height of 1.6 m.
The volume of drum A is 120 litres.
To work out the volume of drum B you need to find the volume scale factor.

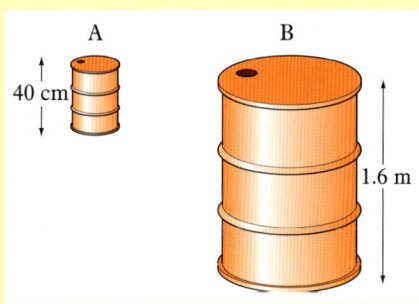

The linear scale factor from A to B is $\dfrac{1.6}{0.4} = 4$ (40 cm = 0.4 m)

so the volume scale factor from A to B is $4^3 = 64$

and the volume of drum B is $120 \times 64 = 7680$ litres

Exercise 18:12

1 These are the linear scale factors for some enlargements.
Work out the volume scale factors.
a 2 **c** 5 **e** 2.4 **g** $\frac{3}{4}$
b 3 **d** $3\frac{1}{2}$ **f** $\frac{1}{3}$ **h** $\frac{2}{9}$

2 Two cereal packs are similar.
The volume of the small packet is 240 cm³. What is the volume of the large packet?

10 cm

25 cm

3 A Valentine's day post-box is made so that it is similar to a real post-box.
It has an internal volume of 11.5 litres and a radius of 11 cm.
If a real post-box has a radius of 24.5 cm, what is the internal volume of a real post-box?

11 cm

11.5 *l*

4 Two skyscrapers are similar. Each floor of both buildings is divided into office units. The number of office units in each building is directly proportional to their overall volume. The tall skyscraper is 250 m high. How many office units does it have?

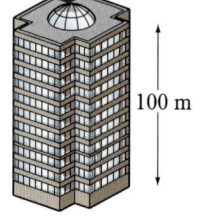

100 m

250 000 m³, 416 office units

Sometimes you need to use volumes to find lengths. These are two similar hot air balloons A and B. Jules will be flying balloon B under a bridge. He needs to know the height.

To go from a linear scale factor to a volume scale factor, you need to cube.
To *undo this*, you need to cube root.

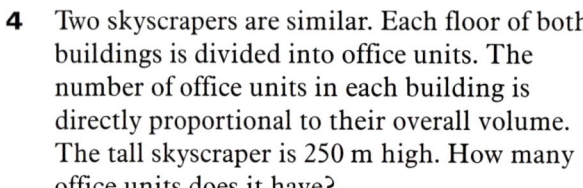

	cube →	
Linear scale factor		Volume scale factor
	← cube root	

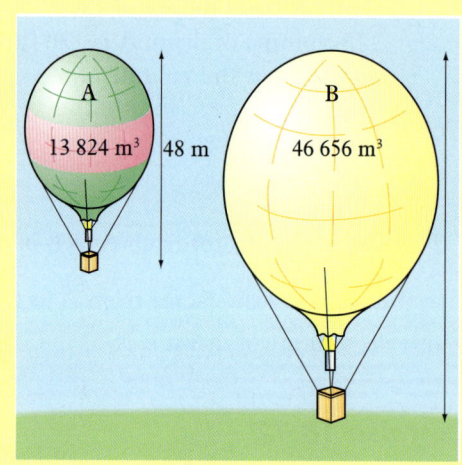

13 824 m³ 48 m   46 656 m³

Here the volume scale factor from A to B is $46\,656 \div 13\,824 = 3.375$

so the linear scale factor is $\sqrt[3]{3.375} = 1.5$

and so the height of balloon B is $48 \times 1.5 = 72$ m

5 The volume of a mini rugby ball is 2400 cm³.
It has a diameter of 12 cm.
A bigger rugby ball has a volume of 5500 cm³.
What is its diameter?

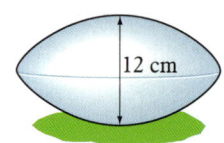

12 cm

6 A big top is built in the shape shown.
A small circus uses a similar big top.
The volume of the small circus big
top is 10 000 m³.
Work out the radius of the smaller big top.
Give your answer to 1 dp.

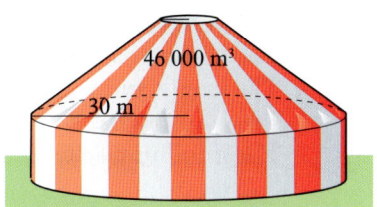

To go from a volume scale factor to an area scale factor you need to work out the linear scale factor.

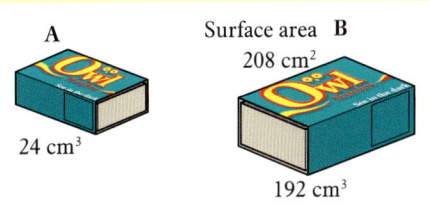

Example A and B are two similar matchboxes.
The surface area of B is 208 cm².
Find the surface area of A.

To work out the surface area of A, first find the linear scale factor.

Here the volume scale factor from B to A is $24 \div 192 = \frac{1}{8}$

Cube root this to find the linear scale factor. $\sqrt[3]{\frac{1}{8}} = \frac{1}{2}$

Square this to find the area scale factor. $(\frac{1}{2})^2 = \frac{1}{4}$

The surface area of A is $208 \times \frac{1}{4} = 52 \text{ cm}^2$

This diagram summarises how to get from one scale factor to another.

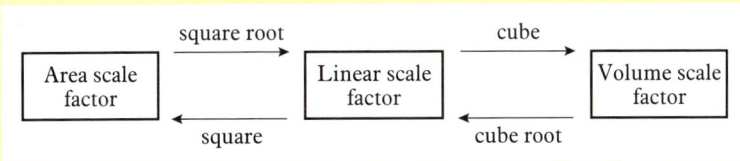

To get from an area scale factor to a volume scale factor:
(1) square root to get the linear scale factor
(2) cube to get the volume scale factor

Notice that you always find the *linear* scale factor first.

7 A venture scout expedition has a choice of two similar tents.
The Ultimo has a volume of 27 m³.
The length and width of the Ultimo are 4 m and 3 m.
The Minimo has a volume of 15.625 m³.
The minimum space for each person to sleep is a rectangle 2 m by 0.75 m.

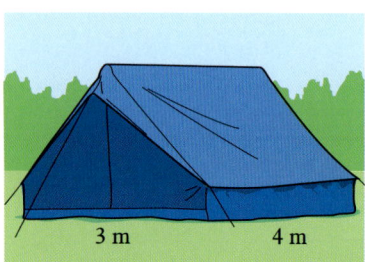

a Will 2 Minimos or 1 Ultimo sleep more people?
Explain your answer, showing your working.

The Ultimo has a surface area of 64.5 m² including the ground sheet.
1 m² of material has a mass of 50 g.
b Will 2 Minimos or 1 Ultimo be heavier to carry?
Explain your answer, showing your working.

The mass of a solid is proportional to its volume.

This is because: $\text{Density} = \dfrac{\text{Mass}}{\text{Volume}}$

and, by definition, the density of a particular substance must be constant.

If two solids are similar, their masses are related by the volume scale factor.

Example   A blue whale calf is 7 m long and has a mass of 2.8 tonnes.
The mother is 24.5 m long and she is similar to her calf.
Find the mass of the mother to the nearest tonne.

The linear scale factor from calf to mother is $\dfrac{24.5}{7} = 3.5$

so the volume scale factor is $(3.5)^3 = 42.875$

so the mother's mass is
$2.8 \times 42.875 = 120$ tonnes to the nearest tonne.

Exercise 18:13

1 John has built the Statue of Hope.
It is 4 m high, with a volume of
2 m^3 and a surface area of 12.4 m^2.
The local council have
commissioned a similar statue
5 times the height.
Work out:

  a the surface area of the new
    statue

  b the volume of the new statue

  c the mass of the statue if it is
    made from steel with a density
    of 7800 kg/m^3

2 A model of a bridge has a mass of
17.6 kg. It is made from material
with an average density of
2300 kg/m^3. The model is made
from the same material as the real
bridge to a scale of 1:50. Find the
mass of the real bridge.

3 A model locomotive built to a
scale of 1:72 has a mass of 0.24 kg.
Find the mass of the real
locomotive if it is built from the
same material as the model.

4 Dimensional analysis

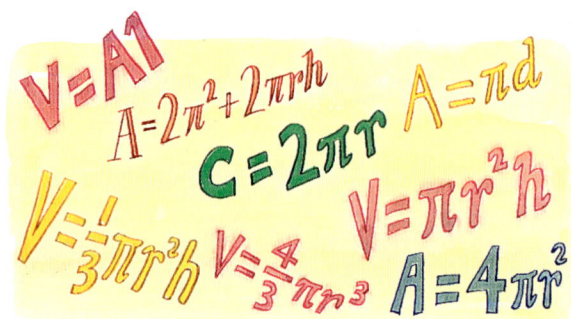

These are some of the formulas that you have seen in this chapter. Some of them are for lengths, some are for area and some are for volume. You can tell quickly what a formula is for by looking at the dimension of the formula.

Dimension The **dimension** of a formula is the number of lengths that are multiplied together.

Constant A **constant** has no dimension. It is just a number.

Length has one dimension.
Any formula for length can only involve constants and length.

$C = \pi d$ is a length formula.
π is a constant.
d is a length.

Area has two dimensions.
Any formula for area can only involve constants and length $\times$ length.

$A = \pi r^2$ is an area formula.
π is a constant.
$r^2 = r \times r$
which is length $\times$ length.

Volume has three dimensions.
Any formula for volume can only involve constants and length $\times$ length $\times$ length.

$V = \frac{4}{3}\pi r^3$ is a volume formula.
$\frac{4}{3}$ and π are constants.
$r^3 = r \times r \times r$
which is length $\times$ length $\times$ length.

Example Write down the dimension of the expression $\dfrac{3\pi r^2}{4t}$ where r and t are lengths.

This expression is $\dfrac{\text{constant} \times \text{constant} \times \text{length} \times \cancel{\text{length}}}{\text{constant} \times \cancel{\text{length}}}$

This cancels down to give only one **length**.
So the dimension is 1.

Exercise 18:14

1 In this question, p, q and r are lengths, c and k are constants.
Write down the dimension of each of these expressions.

a pqr **e** $3kp^2q$ **i** $\dfrac{3rp}{q}$ **m** $\dfrac{r^2p^2}{q^3}$

b $3pq$ **f** $5ckr$ **j** $\dfrac{3pr^2}{q}$ **n** $\dfrac{4c^2krp^3}{q^2}$

c $2rq^2$ **g** $3kpq$ **k** $\dfrac{7ckp^3}{q^2}$ **o** $\dfrac{5ck\,\pi pq^2r}{p^2q}$

d $4cpq$ **h** $5ckp$ **l** $\dfrac{ckpqr}{p^2}$ **p** $\dfrac{\pi r^3p^2}{ckp^2q}$

2 Jennie is trying to find a formula for the volume of a bottle.
She is testing different formulas to see which works best.
The radius of the base of the bottle is r and the height is h.
These are the formulas that she is using.

$$V = \tfrac{3}{5}\pi r^2h \qquad V = \tfrac{3}{5}\pi r^3h \qquad V = \tfrac{3}{5}\pi rh^2 \qquad V = \tfrac{3}{5}\pi rh^3$$

  a Explain why Jennie should only be testing two of these formulas.
● **b** Which of the two formulas that she should be testing is more likely
to be correct?

3 Phil thinks that the total surface area
of this cylinder is $A = 2\pi r(r + h)$.
  a Explain how Phil can show that
this formula has the right
dimension.
  b Does this mean that his formula
is correct?

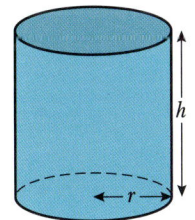

4 Cath thinks that the area of material
needed to cover this lampshade is

$$A = \pi h(b - a)^2$$

Explain why Cath has to be wrong.

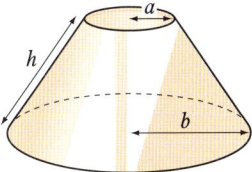

5 In this question l, b, h and r are lengths.
Write down what each of these formulas could represent.
  a lbh **b** $2\pi l^2r$ **c** $\pi r(r + h)$ **d** $2\pi h^2(r + b)$

6 In this question l, b, h and r are lengths.
Write down what each of these formulas could represent.

   a $\sqrt{r^2 + l^2}$ **b** $\dfrac{\pi h^2 \sqrt{r^4 + h^4}}{b}$ **c** $\dfrac{3r^2 \sqrt{h^2 + b^2}}{h}$ **d** $\sqrt[3]{4r^3 + 5\pi h^3}$

Some formulas have more than one part.
When this happens all of the parts must have the same dimension if the formula is
for length or area or volume.
This is a formula for the total surface area of a cylinder.

$$A = 2\pi r^2 + 2\pi rh$$

The first part is   constant $\times$ constant $\times$ length^2 which is an area.
The second part is   constant $\times$ constant $\times$ length $\times$ length   which is also an area.

This formula for a volume, V, cannot be right.

$$V = 2\pi r^3 + 2rh$$

The first part is   constant $\times$ constant $\times$ length^3 which is a volume.
The second part is   constant $\times$ length $\times$ length   which is an area.

So it is impossible for this formula to give you a volume.

---

7 In this question p, q, r, s and t are lengths, c and k are constants.
Write down what each formula could represent.
If a formula is impossible, explain why.

   a $pqr + s^2 t$ **e** $kp^2 q + crst$ **i** $\dfrac{2rp}{q} + \dfrac{r^2 p^2}{q^3}$

   b $3pq + 5rst$ **f** $5ckr + 3cr^2$ **j** $\dfrac{\pi pr^2}{qs} + \dfrac{4crp}{q}$

   c $2rq^2 + 4s^2 t$ **g** $kp^2 q + cr^3$ **k** $\dfrac{8ckp^3}{q^2} - \dfrac{5\pi pq^2 r}{s^2 t} + \dfrac{r^2 p^2}{q^3}$

   d $4cpq + 2ckr$ **h** $5ckp + cr$ **l** $\dfrac{ckpqr}{t^2} + \dfrac{\pi r^3 p^2}{cks^2 q} - \dfrac{t^2 p^2}{q^3}$

8 Harry is trying to find a formula for the volume of a jar.
r, h and b are lengths.

He thinks that the volume is $V = 3\pi r^2 h + \frac{3}{4}\pi rb^2$.

Harry's friend Fiona thinks that the volume is $V = 3\pi r^2 h + \frac{3}{4}\pi r^2 b^2$.

Explain why Fiona has to be wrong.

1 Copy this table. Fill it in.
Use the values given to work out the missing quantities.

	radius r	circumference C	area A
a	12 cm		
b	2.84 km		
c		56 m	
d			256 mm^2
e		48π cm	

2 For a circle with radius r:
  a write down the formula for the arc length, s, of a sector with angle θ
  b rearrange the formula to show that (1) $r = \dfrac{180s}{\pi\theta}$ (2) $\theta = \dfrac{180s}{\pi r}$

So if you have any two of radius, arc length and angle, you can work out the other one.
  c Write down the formula for the sector area, A, of a sector with angle θ.
  d Rearrange the formula to find: (1) r (2) θ
So if you have any two of radius, sector area and angle, you can work out the other one.

3 Copy this table. Fill it in.
Use the values given and your
answers to question **2** to work out the
missing quantities.

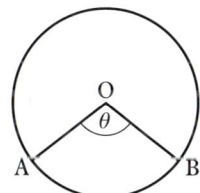

	radius r	angle θ	arc length AB	sector area AOB
a	12 cm	46°		
b	7.25 km	103°		
c		84°	207 mm	
d	17 m			148 m^2

4 O is the centre of the circle.
  a Find the area of the minor sector AOB.
  b Find the area of the triangle AOB.
  c Use your results to parts **a** and **b** to find the
     area of the minor segment shaded in red.
  d Find the area of the major sector AOB.
  e Use your results to parts **b** and **d** to find the
     area of the major segment.

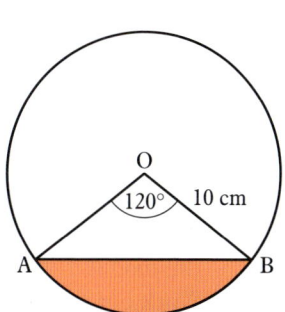

5 The largest volcano in the solar system is Olympus Mons on Mars. It has a radius of approximately 250 km and a height of about 26 km. Assuming it it roughly conical in shape,
a work out its volume in km³.
b If 1 km³ = 10^9 m³, how many times bigger than a great pyramid is it? You need to use your answer to Exercise 18:5, question **4**.

6 A concrete path runs around a park. The external radius of the path is R and the internal radius of the path is r.
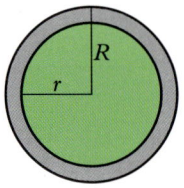
a Write down the area of the circle radius R.
b Write down the area of the circle radius r.
c Use your answers to parts **a** and **b** to write down an expression for the area of the path. Factorise your answer as fully as possible.
The area you have found is called an annulus.
d Calculate the area of the path if $R = 70$ m and $r = 65$ m.

7 Concrete piping 7 km long has an external radius of 50 cm and an internal radius of 40 cm.
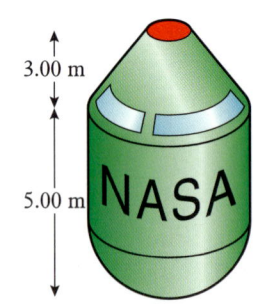
a Find the volume of concrete used to make the piping.
Water flows out of the pipe at the rate of 2500 litres per second.
b Find the speed of the water in: (1) m/s (2) km/h
The water flows into a reservoir in the shape of a cuboid.
The base of the reservoir is a rectangle 500 m by 450 m.
c Calculate the rise in the water level over 24 hours. Give your answer to the nearest centimetre.

8 In this question round all your answers to 3 sf.
A space capsule is made from a hemisphere, a cylinder and a frustum as shown.
The radius of the hemisphere, cylinder and frustum base is 2.40 m. The radius of the top of the frustum is 0.40 m.
a Work out the volume of the capsule.
b Work out the surface area of the capsule.
A model of this capsule has a volume of 0.840 m³.
c Work out the height of the cylindrical part of the model.
d Work out the surface area of the model.

1 The diagram shows the circular cross section of a submarine. ABCD is a rectangle. BOD and AOC are straight lines. The main operating space of the submarine is a cylinder of length 42 m.

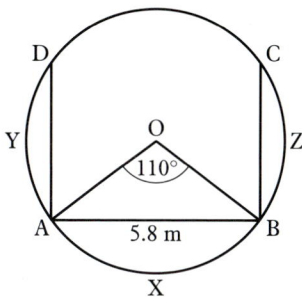

 a Work out the volume of this part of the submarine.

Segments AXB, AYD and BZC are for storage of cabling, pipes etc.

 b Work out the volume for storage.

2 A radian is a measure of turn. It is defined as the angle made at the centre of the circle by an arc with the same length as the radius of the circle.

 a How many radians are in a circle?
 b How many radians are equivalent to
  (1) 360° (2) 180° (3) 90°?
 c Work out a formula for arc length using radians instead of degrees.
 d Work out a formula for sector area using radians instead of degrees.

3 Mr Ferrwey likes to play golf in the garden. Unfortunately he regularly loses golf balls in the pond. The pond is a cylinder with a 1 m radius. To his astonishment, when draining the pond, Mr Ferrwey discovered he had lost 2645 golf balls. These were all of radius 2 cm. How much had they raised the water level? Round your answer in centimetres to 1 dp.

4 Complete this table for the planets.
Express your answers in standard form where appropriate.
You can assume that the planets are spherical and therefore similar.

Planet	Radius (km)	Surface area (km^2)	Volume (km^3)
Mercury	2440		
Venus	6052		
Earth	6378		
Mars			1.6420×10^{11}
Jupiter		6.5039×10^{10}	
Saturn		4.5644×10^{10}	
Uranus			6.8334×10^{13}
Neptune		8.0239×10^{9}	
Pluto			7.6625×10^{9}

5 Find the surface area.

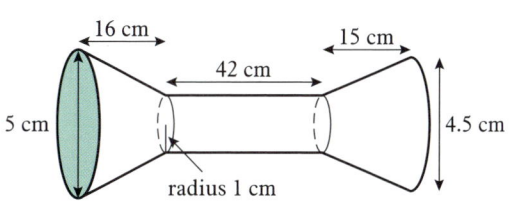

1 In each of these, find in terms of π

(1) the length of the bold arc
(2) the area of the shaded sector

a

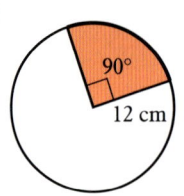

90°

12 cm

b

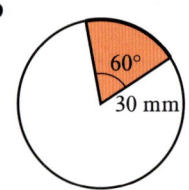

60°

30 mm

c

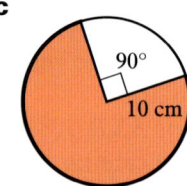

90°

10 cm

2 Find the area of the shaded segment.
Give your answer to 3 sf.

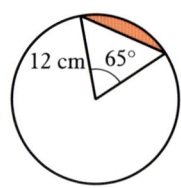

12 cm 65°

3 For each of these shapes, find in terms of π

(1) the surface area
(2) the volume

a

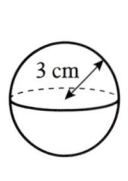

3 cm

sphere

b

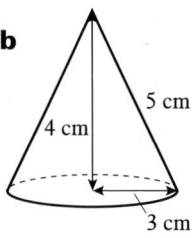

5 cm

4 cm

3 cm

cone

c

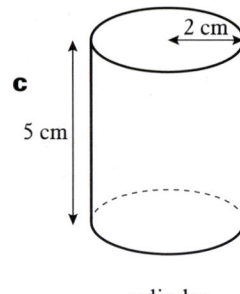

2 cm

5 cm

cylinder

4 **a** This flower pot is a frustum of a cone.
The base is a circle of radius 15 cm.
The top is a circle of radius 30 cm.
Find the exact volume of the pot.
You will need to use similar triangles.

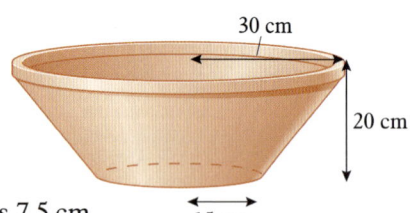

30 cm

20 cm

15 cm

b A similar pot is made with a base of radius 7.5 cm.
Write down the exact volume of the smaller pot.

5 In this question, x, y and z are lengths, and a and k are constants.
Write down what each of these formulas could represent.

a $xyz + ax^2y$

b $\dfrac{ax^2z}{ky}$

c $\dfrac{kxy}{a} + \dfrac{az^3}{x}$

19 <Inequalities>

1 Solving inequalities using algebra
Showing simple inequalities on the number line
Solving linear inequalities
Multiplying and dividing by a negative number
Solving inequalities with several parts
Solving quadratic inequalities

CORE

2 Solving inequalities using graphs
Showing inequalities with lines parallel to the axes
Showing two inequalities on the same graph
Graphing inequalities involving both x and y
Showing multiple inequalities on the same graph
Using inequalities to solve problems
Solving complicated inequalities using graphs

QUESTIONS

EXTENSION

TEST YOURSELF

1   Solving inequalities using algebra

The angle at which a rocket re-enters the earth's atmosphere is critical.

If the angle is too steep then the rocket will travel too quickly.

If it is too shallow, the friction will be too great and the rocket will burn up.

There is only a small range of angles that are suitable.

You use inequalities to describe a range of numbers.

$x > 3$

$x > 3$ means that x can take any value **greater than 3**. It cannot be 3. On a number line, this is shown like this:

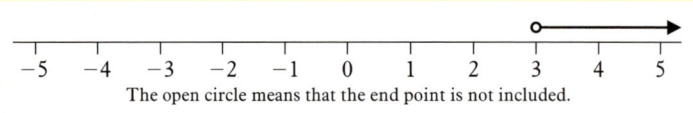

The open circle means that the end point is not included.

$x \leqslant 1$

$x \leqslant 1$ means that x can take any value **less than or equal to 1**. This includes 1. On a number line, this is shown like this:

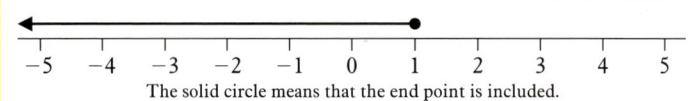

The solid circle means that the end point is included.

$-2 \leqslant x < 4$

$-2 \leqslant x < 4$ means that x is bigger than or equal to -2.
$-2 \leqslant x < 4$ means that x is less than 4.
So $-2 \leqslant x < 4$ means that x **is between -2 and 4.**
-2 is included, 4 is not.

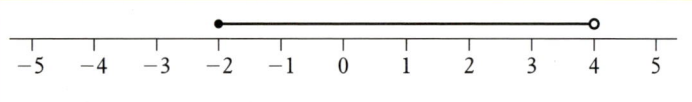

Exercise 19:1

1 Write down inequalities to describe each of these number lines.

a
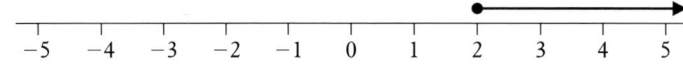

b
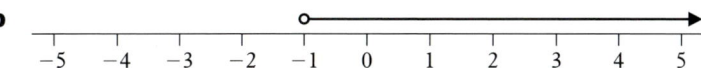

c
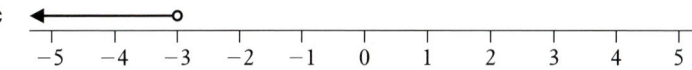

d
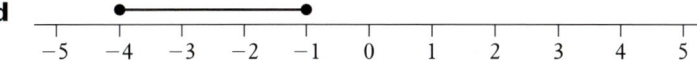

e
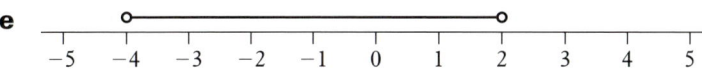

f
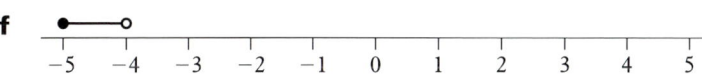

g
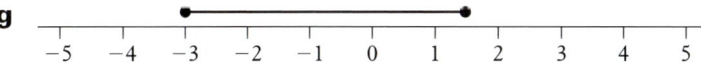

2 Draw each of these inequalities on a number line.
a $x > 2$ **c** $x \leqslant -3$ **e** $1 < x < 2$ **g** $-3 \leqslant x \leqslant -1$
b $x < 1$ **d** $x \geqslant -2$ **f** $-1 < x < 4$ **h** $-5 < x \leqslant 4.5$

Integer	An **integer** is a whole number.
	Integers are ... $-3, -2, -1, 0, 1, 2, 3, 4, 5$ ...

3 List the integers that are included in each of these inequalities.
a $1 < x < 4$ **c** $-3 < x < 2$ **e** $-2 \leqslant x \leqslant 6$ **g** $-3 \leqslant x \leqslant -2$
b $1 \leqslant x \leqslant 4$ **d** $-4 < x < 4$ **f** $0 < x < 7$ **h** $-3 < x < -2$

Most inequalities you will see are written in algebra. They are used to solve problems.

Inequalities are solved in a very similar way to equations. This means you can:
- add the same number to both sides of an inequality
- subtract the same number from both sides of an inequality
- multiply or divide both sides of an inequality by any **positive** number.

If you multiply or divide by a **negative** number there is a new rule which you will see later.

Examples **1** Solve $3x - 5 > 8$

$$3x - 5 > 8$$

Add 5 to both sides. $\qquad 3x > 13$

Divide both sides by 3. $\qquad x > \dfrac{13}{3}$

2 Solve $5 - x < 2x - 1$

$$5 - x < 2x - 1$$

Add x to both sides. $\qquad 5 < 3x - 1$

Add 1 to both sides. $\qquad 6 < 3x$

Divide both sides by 3. $\qquad 2 < x$

This should be written as $\qquad x > 2$

Exercise 19:2

Solve each of these inequalities.

1 $x + 4 < 7$

2 $3x - 3 > 9$

3 $5x - 6 \leqslant 9$

4 $y + 2.4 > 8$

5 $\dfrac{y}{5} - 6 > 20$

6 $\dfrac{3f}{2} + 7 \geqslant -10$

7 $4(3t + 10) < 20$

8 $\dfrac{3x - 7}{4} \leqslant 6$

9 $6x - 4 > 2x + 6$

10 $3.5g - 2 < 7 - g$

11 $\dfrac{2x}{3} - 6 \leqslant \dfrac{x}{3} + 7$

● **12** $\dfrac{5n + 2}{4} \geqslant \dfrac{3n - 5}{3}$

Look at this simple statement.   14 > 4   Clearly this is true.
Now add 2 to both sides.   16 > 6   It is still true.

Multiply both sides by 3.   48 > 18   Still true!

But, dividing both sides by -2 gives $-24 > -9$ This is **not** true.

-24 is *less* than -9, not greater than it.

This is because of the way negative numbers work.
If numbers go **up** in twos, you can write: $2 < 4 < 6 < 8 < 10$
But if they go **down** in twos,
the inequalities are the other way around: $-2 > -4 > -6 > -8 > -10$

You need a new rule to deal with this.
- If you multiply or divide an inequality by a **negative** number then you must **change the direction** of the inequality sign.

This means that taking an inequality like $14 > 4$
and multiplying both sides by -1 gives $-14 < -4$

Example   Solve the inequality $6 - 2x < 12$

$$6 - 2x < 12$$

Subtract 6 from both sides. $-2x < 6$

Divide both sides by -2 **and** change the direction of the inequality. $x > -3$

Exercise 19:3

Solve each of these inequalities.
Be careful if you multiply or divide by a negative number.

1 $4 - x < 7$

2 $3x - 3 > 9 + 6x$

3 $5x - 6 \leqslant 20 + 7x$

4 $-7 - 3y > -8 - 5y$

5 $-4(3t + 10) < 50$

6 $\dfrac{7 - 2x}{4} \leqslant 6$

7 $3 - 5x \geqslant -2x + 6$

8 $6 - 4g < 7 - g$

Some inequalities have three parts to them.

Example Solve $15 < 4x + 7 < 19$

This is the same as the two separate inequalities $15 < 4x + 7$ and $4x + 7 < 19$.
You can solve this by working on both at once.
The aim is to leave a single x in the middle of the inequality.

First remove the **+7**.
To do this, subtract **7** from all three parts.
Now divide through by **4**.

$$15 < 4x + 7 < 19$$
$$8 < \quad 4x \quad < 12$$
$$2 < \quad x \quad < 3$$

Exercise 19:4

Solve each of these inequalities.

1 $4 < 2x - 4 < 8$

2 $12 \leqslant 3t + 9 \leqslant 27$

3 $55 \leqslant 3x + 1 < 64$

4 $51 \leqslant 8y + 19 \leqslant 75$

5 $3 > \dfrac{t}{4} - 6 > 20$

6 $-6 < -x + 5 < 7$

7 $-9 < 3z + 2 < 20$

8 $-2 \leqslant \dfrac{3x - 7}{4} \leqslant 6$

9 $2x - 4 < 6x - 4 < 2x + 6$

10 $-3 < 3 - 10x < 15$

11 $26 - x < 32 < 42 - x$

● **12** $8 - 3x \geqslant 6 + x \geqslant 5 - 3x$

Some double inequalities can't be solved in this way.
They have to be split into two parts.
A number line is helpful to find the final answer.

Example Solve the inequality $x - 1 \leqslant 2x \leqslant 6$

First, solve the left-hand parts.

$$x - 1 \leqslant 2x \leqslant 6$$
$$-1 \leqslant x$$

So

$$x \geqslant -1$$

Now solve the right-hand parts.

$$x - 1 \leqslant 2x \leqslant 6$$
$$x \leqslant 3$$

Now look at both of these answers on the number line.

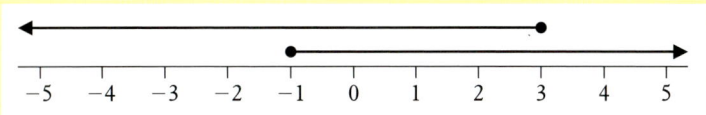

The inequalities are both true for values of x between -1 and 3.
So the solution is $\mathbf{-1 \leqslant x \leqslant 3}$.

Exercise 19:5

Solve each of these inequalities.

1 $0 < x + 12 < 2x + 7$

2 $-4 < 3x + 4 < x + 10$

3 $x - 1 \leqslant 2x \leqslant 10$

4 $x + 4 > 2x - 1 > 5$

5 $x - 1 < 2x - 3 < 9$

6 $3 < 3 - x < 2x + 5$

7 $2x + 6 \leqslant 3x + 15 \leqslant x + 26$

8 $6 - x \leqslant 12 + x \leqslant 70$

● **9** $6 - 2x > 1 + 3x > 2x + 12$

10 $2x + 5 \leqslant 3x \leqslant 16$

● **11** $18 < 3 - 5x < 2x - 11$

12 $x + 8 \leqslant 3x + 5 \leqslant 6x - 19$

Quadratic inequalities

If you come across an inequality with x^2 in it, you need to be very careful!
Solving the equation $x^2 = 16$
gives $x = \pm 4$
If you start with $x^2 \geqslant 16$
you might be tempted to say $x \geqslant \pm 4$
This means $x \geqslant 4$ and $x \geqslant -4$. Overall this gives $x \geqslant -4$.

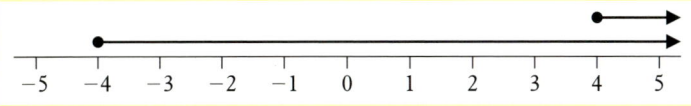

But think about $x = -2$ for example.
$(-2)^2$ is not greater than 16 so -2 does not fit the inequality.
But $(-5)^2 = 25$ which *is* bigger than 16.
So if $x^2 \geqslant 16$
then in fact $x \geqslant 4$ or $x \leqslant -4$

If you look at this on a number line, it looks like this.

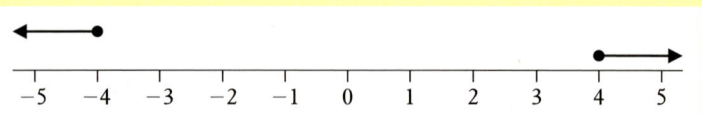

Example   Solve the inequality $x^2 + 5 > 30$

$$x^2 + 5 > 30$$

gives $$x^2 > 25$$

This means that $x > 5$ or $x < -5$.

Exercise 19:6

Solve each of these inequalities.

1 $x^2 + 5 > 21$ **4** $x^2 + 5 \geqslant 35$

2 $2x^2 + 5 > 37$ **5** $\dfrac{x^2}{2} < 8$

3 $3x^2 - 6 < 10$ **6** $\dfrac{x^2}{3} > 7$

Exercise 19:7

Write down an inequality to describe each problem.
Solve the inequality to answer the problem.

1 I think of a number, double it and add 5.
     The answer must be less than 70.
     What range of numbers can I choose?

2 Howard is given £10 to spend.
     He is told that he can buy as many CD singles as he likes but he must
     keep 75p for his bus fare. The CDs cost £2.05
     What is the maximum number of CDs he can buy?

3 The perimeter of this triangle must not
     be more than 50 cm.
     What is the maximum value x can be?

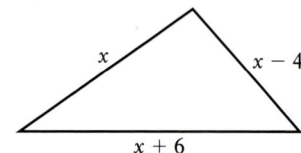

2 Solving inequalities using graphs

Ali and Graham are visiting a theme park.

They have a maximum of £25 to spend.

They can split their money between rides and food.

There are lots of ways they can do this.

You can use graphs to solve inequalities.
This gives you a 'picture' of the problem which often makes it easier to solve.

The easiest inequalities to show on a graph are those that have a boundary line that is parallel to one of the axes.

Example   Show the following inequalities on a graph.
   a $x \geqslant 3$ **b** $y < -2$

   a $x \geqslant 3$
   The line is $x = 3$.
   All the points in the shaded
   region have an x co-ordinate
   greater than 3.
   The solid line shows that the
   boundary **is** included.

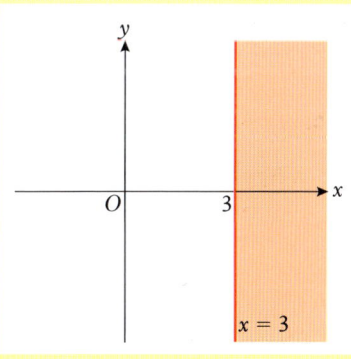

   b $y < -2$
   The line is $y = -2$.
   All the points in the shaded
   region have a y co-ordinate
   less than -2.
   The dashed line shows that the
   boundary is **not** included.

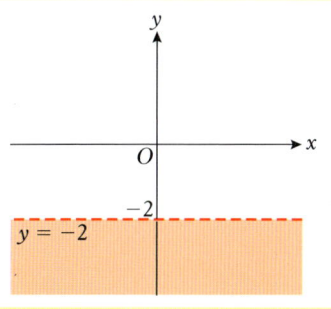

Exercise 19:8

Draw graphs to illustrate each of these inequalities.
Shade the region where each inequality is true.

1 $y \geqslant 3$

2 $x \geqslant 3$

3 $y < -1$

4 $y > -2$

5 $x > 5.5$

6 $x \leqslant -\frac{1}{2}$

7 $-2 \leqslant x \leqslant 3$

8 $-1 \leqslant y < 2$

9 $-3.5 < x \leqslant -0.25$

For each of the following graphs, write down the inequality that describes the shaded region.

10

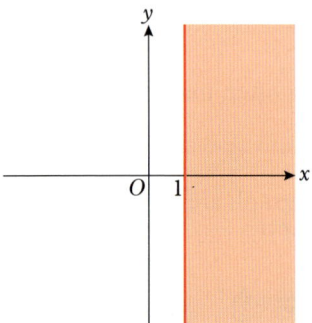

13

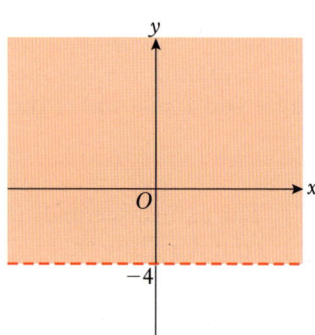

11

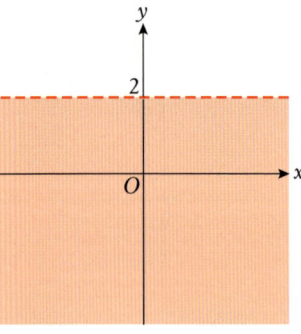

14

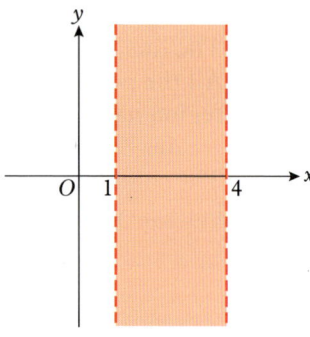

12

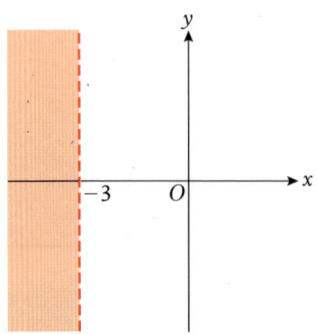

15

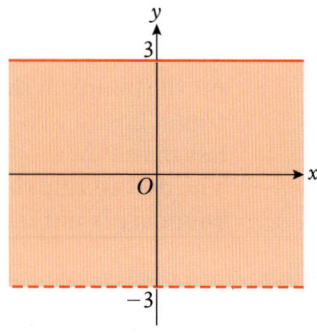

Sometimes you need to use more than one inequality to define a region.

Example　Draw a graph to show the region defined by the inequalities
$x \geqslant 1$ and $y < 5$.

This graph shows $x \geqslant 1$.　　　　　This graph shows $y < 5$.

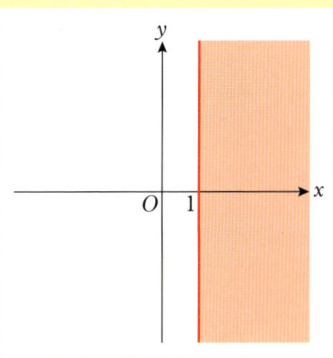
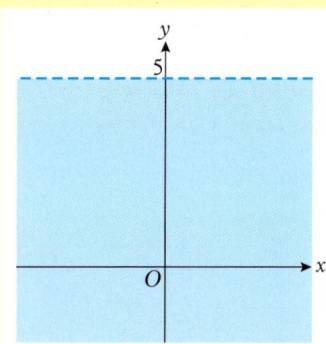

This graph shows both
inequalities together.
The purple area shows where
both inequalities are true.

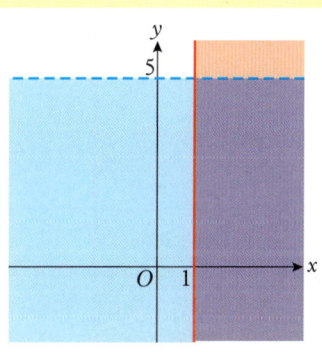

It is important that you label your graphs carefully.
You must say which area represents your answer.
You can use shading in different directions instead of colours.

Exercise 19:9

Draw graphs to show the regions defined by these inequalities.
Label each graph carefully.

1　$y \geqslant 3$ and $x > 3$　　　　　**5**　$x > -2$ and $0 \leqslant y \leqslant 3$

2　$x \geqslant 2$ and $y < 4$　　　　　**6**　$x \geqslant -2$ and $2 < y < 3$

3　$y < -2$ and $x > 0$　　　　　● **7**　$-2 \leqslant x \leqslant 4$ and $-3 \leqslant y \leqslant 4$

4　$-2 < x < 4$ and $y > 2$　　　　● **8**　$-2 < x \leqslant -1$ and $3 \leqslant y \leqslant 4$

Write down the inequality that describes the shaded region on each of these graphs.

9

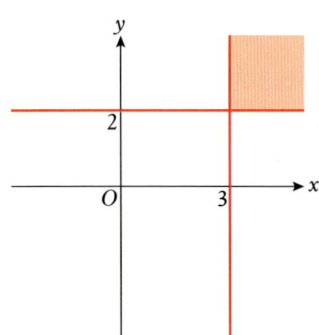

12

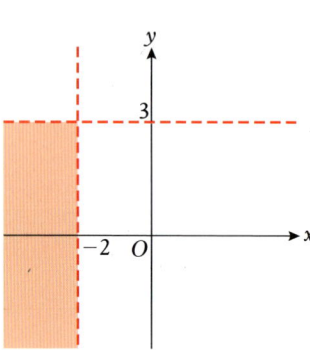

10

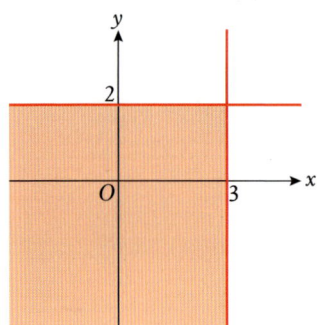

13

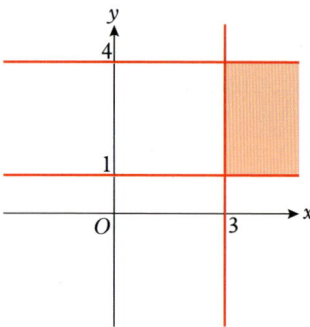

11

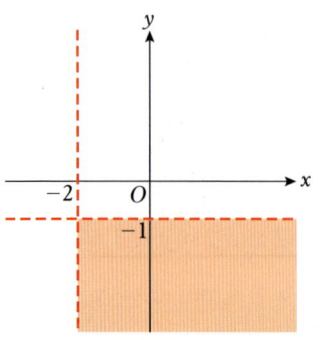

● **14**

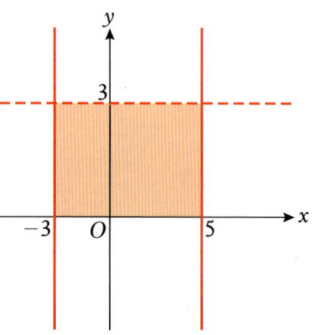

Inequalities with two variables

Sometimes, the lines that form the borders of the regions are not parallel to one of the axes. When this happens, the inequalities will have both x and y in them.

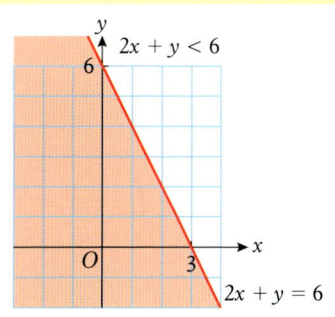

In this type of question, it can be more difficult to decide which side of the line you want. You often have to test a couple of points to help you to decide where to shade.

Example   Draw a graph to show the inequality $3x + 2y < 12$

First draw the boundary line on the graph. This is the line $3x + 2y = 12$.

To draw this line, find the points where it crosses the axes.

When $x = 0$: $2y = 12$ so $y = 6$ Crosses at $(0, 6)$
When $y = 0$: $3x = 12$ so $x = 4$ Crosses at $(4, 0)$

The graph of $3x + 2y = 12$ looks like this.

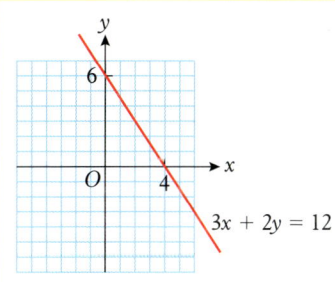

You now need to check which side of the line you want.
It may seem obvious in this case, but this will not always be true!
Pick one point below the line and one point above it. Substitute the co-ordinates into the inequality.

Below the line: $(0, 0)$ $3x + 2y = 0$
which is **less** than 12

Above the line: $(6, 6)$ $3x + 2y = 30$
which is **greater** than 12

So the required region is below the line. The boundary should be drawn with a dashed line as it is not included.

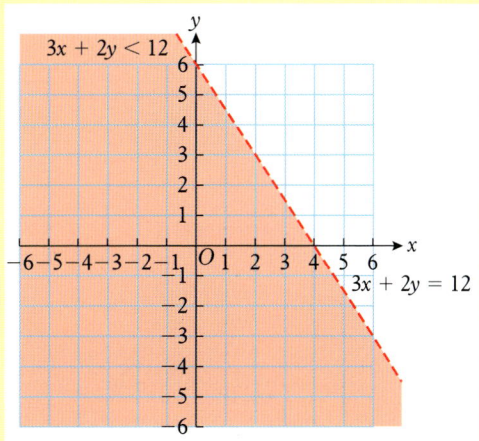

Exercise 19:10

Draw graphs to show the regions defined by these inequalities.
Label each graph carefully.

1 $2x + y > 8$

2 $3x + 2y \leqslant 6$

3 $x - 2y < 10$

4 $3x - 5y \geqslant 15$

5 $2x + 3y - 12 \leqslant 0$

6 $2x + 3y > 7$

● **7** $2y > 3x - 10$

● **8** $16x + 25y \leqslant 200$

Again, you need to be able to draw graphs that show more than one inequality. There can sometimes be three or even four separate inequalities to show on one diagram. It can become rather difficult to find the required region once the diagram is complete.
For this reason, it is sensible to shade the region you do **not** want. This is called **shading out**.
It means that the region you want is the region left with no shading at all.

Example   Show on a graph the region defined by the following set of inequalities: $x \geqslant 0$, $y \geqslant 0$, $x + y < 6$, $x + 3y > 6$

Separately, these inequalities are the unshaded regions shown.

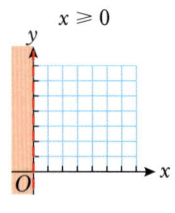

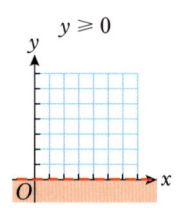

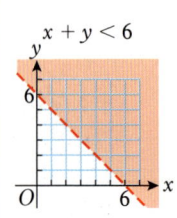

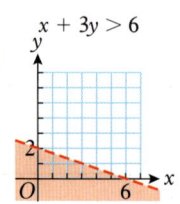

When you draw these on the same diagram, the area left white is the required region.

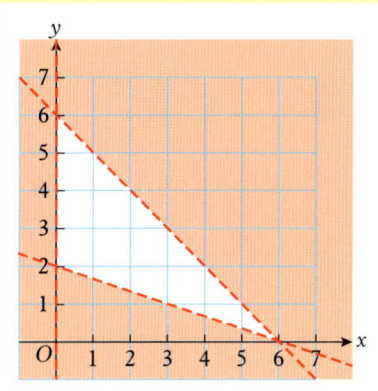

Exercise 19:11

Draw graphs to show the regions defined by these sets of inequalities.
Leave the required region unshaded.
Label each graph.

1 $x \geqslant 0$ $y \geqslant 0$ $x + 2y \leqslant 8$

2 $x \geqslant 0$ $y \geqslant 0$ $x + 2y \leqslant 10$ $x + 2y \geqslant 8$

3 $x \geqslant 0$ $y \leqslant 0$ $x - 2y \leqslant 8$

4 $y < x$ $y \geqslant 0$ $x < 6$

5 $3y - x > 0$ $x + y > 4$ $2y + x < 8$

6 $x + 2y < 6$ $y > x$ $x > -2$

7 $y > 2x$ $y < 3x$ $x + y > 4$ $x + y < 9$

● 8 $y > \dfrac{x}{3}$ $y < 6 - 2x$ $y < 2.5x$

Solving problems using inequalities

Many real life problems involve the use of limited quantities of materials or resources. These can range from allocating staff to jobs or buying stock from a limited budget. Inequalities can often be used to solve these problems. This can lead on to a more advanced technique known as **linear programming**.

In the final part of this chapter, you will see how inequalities can be used to solve problems. You will need the skills you have learnt in the first part of the chapter.

Example   A property developer has a plot of land with area 5400 m².
He builds two types of houses.
The 3 bedroomed Family requires an area of 450 m².
The 4 bedroomed Executive requires an area of 600 m².
The garden costs are £600 for a Family house and £1500 for an Executive house. The developer has £9000 available for gardens. He does not want more than 9 Family houses.

a Write down inequalities which describe the constraints on the builder.

b Draw a graph to show the possible combinations of the two types of house which can be built.

c If the profit on each house is £5500, calculate the maximum profit the builder can make.

a First give letters to each type of house.
Say that the developer builds f Family houses and e Executive houses.
Now write down the inequalities.

You can only build a positive number of houses so $e \geqslant 0$ and $f \geqslant 0$
You cannot exceed the total area of 5400 m² so $600e + 450f \leqslant 5400$
You can only spend £9000 on gardens so $1500e + 600f \leqslant 9000$
You want at most 9 Family houses so $f \leqslant 9$

b The graph of these inequalities looks like this:

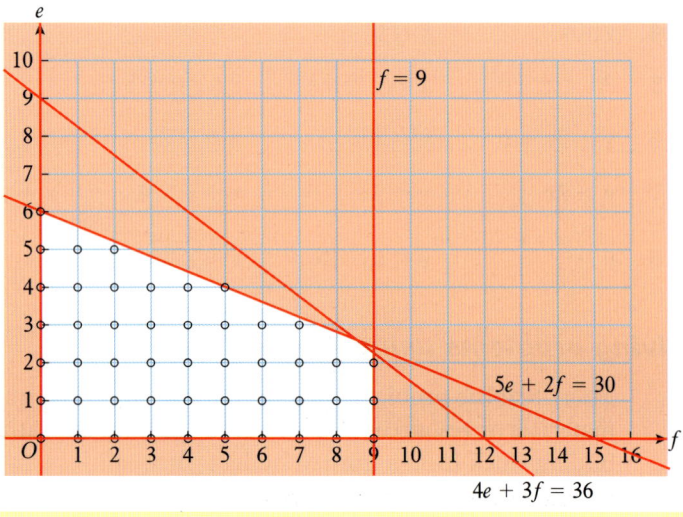

c The circled points on the grid show all the possible combinations of houses that the developer could build.

He will make the most profit if he builds 9 Family houses and 2 Executive houses, because this is the biggest number of houses.

His profit will be $11 \times £5500 = $ **£60 500**

You will notice that the point that gives the maximum profit is very close to one of the corners of the region.

This will always be the case. Because you are looking for an extreme value (a maximum or a minimum) this value will always be at or near one of the corners of the region.

These are the values you should test when you are looking for a maximum or minimum value.

You will need to consider whether the values you are looking for have to be whole numbers or not.

You also need to consider if the boundary lines are included or not.

Exercise 19:12

1 Alan wants to buy a combination of chart singles on CD and tape.
CDs cost £4 and tapes cost £3.
He has £24 to spend altogether.
He wants to buy at least one of each type of single.

a Copy each of these. Complete each one with an inequality.
Call the number of tapes t and the number of CDs c.
Alan buys at least one CD so ....
Alan buys at least one tape so ....
The total cost of the tapes and CDs must not exceed £24 so ....

b Draw a graph showing all of the inequalities you have written down in part a.

c Alan decides to buy 4 tapes.
Write down the possible numbers of CDs he can buy.

2 Fred the farmer needs to re-stock. He wants to buy at least 30 sheep and 12 cows.
Sheep cost £40 and cows cost £70. He has £5600 to spend altogether.

   a Write down three inequalities that describe the constraints on Fred.

   b Draw a graph showing all of the inequalities you have written down in part **a**.

   c Fred decides he wants to buy as near equal numbers of cows and sheep as possible. He also wants to spend as much of his money as possible. How many of each can Fred buy?

3 A radio DJ has to play a mixture of Chart Hits and Golden Oldies. He can only fit 35 records into his show. He wants to play at least 10 of each. Royalties on Chart Hits are £50 per record but on Golden Oldies are only £30 per record. The budget for the show is £1400.

   a Write down four inequalities to describe these constraints.

   b Draw a graph showing all of the inequalities you have written down in part **a**.

   c What is the largest number of Chart Hits that the DJ can play?

4 A lorry is loaded with two different sizes of box. Small boxes have a volume of 2 m^3 whilst large boxes have a volume of 3.5 m^3. The lorry has a maximum capacity of 70 m^3. The small boxes weigh 30 kg and the large boxes weigh 40 kg. The total weight of the load must not exceed 1225 kg.

   a Write down four inequalities to describe these constraints.

   b Draw a graph showing all of the inequalities you have written down in part **a**.

   c What is the maximum number of large boxes that the lorry can carry?

5 42 students are on a school ski trip in an Austrian hotel.
The hotel has two types of bedroom, one sleeps two people, the other three people. The 2-person rooms cost £150 per week and the 3-person rooms cost £200 per week. There is £3500 available for rooms. The hotel has only ten 3-person rooms.

   a Write down four inequalities and an equation to describe these constraints.
   b Draw a graph showing all of the constraints you have written down in part **a**.
   c What is the cheapest combination of rooms?

6 A taxi company uses 4-seater and 6-seater taxis.
James is organising a birthday party for 30 of his friends and wants them to travel by taxi. The cost of a 6-seater taxi is £10 and the cost of a 4-seater taxi is £7. The company owns 3 6-seater taxis and 6 4-seater taxis.

   a Write down inequalities which describe this situation.
   b Draw a graph of the inequalities you have written down. Show clearly the region which represents the possible combinations of taxis that James can use.
   c Which combination of taxis will be the cheapest?
   d Which combination uses the most taxis?

More complicated inequalities

It is possible to use graphs to solve inequalities that would be quite difficult to solve using algebra.

These can involve quite complicated functions. You will need to sketch or plot a graph of the function like you did in Chapter 7.

Example   **a** Sketch a graph of the function $f(x) = x^2 + 5x - 6$.
        b Use your graph to solve the inequality $x^2 + 5x - 6 > 0$.

a First solve $f(x) = 0$
$x^2 + 5x - 6 = 0$
$(x - 1)(x + 6) = 0$
$x = 1$ or $x = -6$
This means that the graph
cuts the x axis at $x = 1$
and $x = -6$.

b You want to know when
$x^2 + 5x - 6 > 0$
This is when $x^2 + 5x - 6$ is positive.
$x^2 + 5x - 6$ is positive when
the curve is above the x axis.
So $x^2 + 5x - 6 > 0$ when $x > 1$ or when $x < -6$.

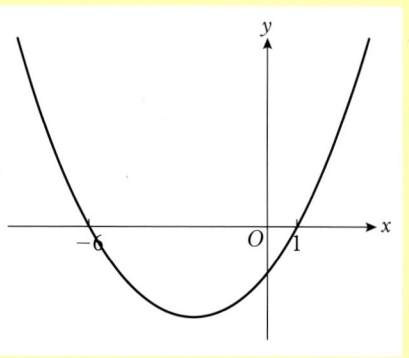

Exercise 19:13

1 **a** Sketch a graph of the function $f(x) = x^2 - x - 6$.
   b Use your graph to solve the inequality $x^2 - x - 6 > 0$.

2 **a** Sketch a graph of the function $f(x) = 9 - x^2$.
   b Use your graph to solve the inequality $9 - x^2 > 0$.

3 **a** Sketch a graph of the function $f(x) = x^2 - 3x$.
   b Use your graph to solve the inequality $x^2 - 3x < 0$.

4 **a** Sketch a graph of the function $f(x) = \dfrac{1}{x}$.

   b Use your graph to solve the inequality $\dfrac{1}{x} < 0$.

5 This is a sketch graph of the function $f(x) = (x + 3)(x - 1)(x - 4)$.

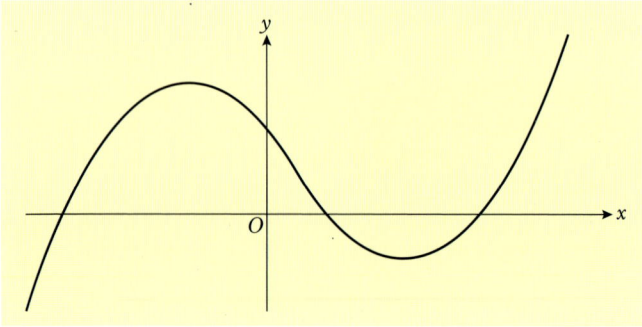

   a Write down the values of x where $f(x) = 0$.
   b Use your answer to part **a** to solve $f(x) \geqslant 0$.

6 **a** Draw axes with x from -5 to 5 and y from -10 to 35.
    b Copy and complete this table of $y = x^2 - 2x - 2$.

x	-5	-4	-3	-2	-1	0	1	2	3	4	5
y											

    c Plot the graph of $y = x^2 - 2x - 2$ from your table.
    d Copy and complete this table of $y = 2x + 2$.

x	-5	-4	-3	-2	-1	0	1	2	3	4	5
y											

    e Draw the graph of $y = 2x + 2$ over the top of your graph from part **c**.
    f Write down the x co-ordinates of the points of intersection of the curve and the line to 1 dp.
    g Use your answers to solve the inequality $x^2 - 2x - 2 > 2x + 2$.

7 **a** Draw a graph to solve the equation $x^2 - x + 3 = 0$.
       Draw your x axis from -3 to $+4$ and your y axis from 0 to 20.
    b Use your graph to solve $x^2 - x + 3 > 7$.
    c By drawing another line on your graph, solve the inequality $x^2 - x + 3 > x + 3$.

8 Look carefully at this graph.

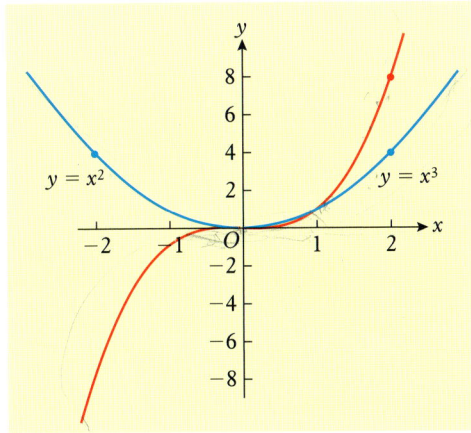

It shows parts of the graphs of $y = x^2$ and $y = x^3$.
Write down the values of x where:

a $x^3 = x^2$ **b** $x^3 > x^2$ **c** $x^3 < x^2$

1   Write down inequalities to describe each of these number lines.

a

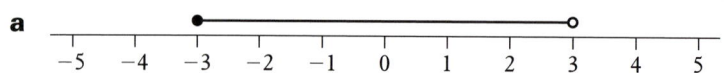

b

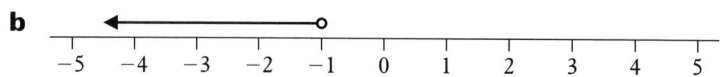

2   Solve each of these inequalities.

     a $2x + 4 < 18$ **e** $5(4t - 10) < 20$

     b $3z - 7 > 14$ **f** $\dfrac{8x - 2}{5} \leqslant 6$

     c $5x - 10 \leqslant 9$ **g** $4x - 7 > 2x + 19$

     d $3(r + 2.8) > 6$ **h** $3.5k - 8 < 7 - 2k$

3   Solve each of these inequalities.

     a $4 < x - 4 < 10$ **e** $-15 < 3z + 3 < -6$

     b $18 \leqslant 3p + 6 \leqslant 27$ **f** $-2 \leqslant 2(2x + 5) \leqslant 6$

     c $63 \geqslant 3x - 3 > 72$ **g** $17 < \dfrac{2x - 6}{3} < 20$

     d $96 \leqslant 8y + 12 \leqslant 100$

4   Solve each of these inequalities.

     a $0 < x + 5 < 3x + 17$ **c** $2x - 5 \leqslant 3x + 10 \leqslant 7x + 1$

     b $-10 < 2x + 4 < 5x + 10$ **d** $6 - 2x \leqslant 18 \leqslant 70 + x$

5   Draw graphs to illustrate each of these inequalities.
     Shade the region where each inequality is true.

     a $y \geqslant 4$ **b** $y > -3$ **c** $-6 \leqslant x \leqslant 1$

6 Write down the inequality that describes the shaded region for each of these graphs.

a

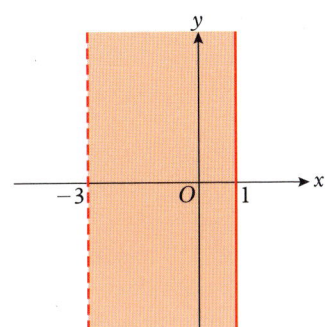

b

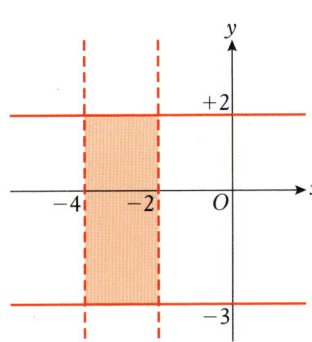

7 Draw graphs to show the regions defined by these inequalities.
- **a** $2x + y > 10$
- **b** $3x + 4y \leqslant 12$
- **c** $2x - 3y - 6 \leqslant 0$
- **d** $3x - 4y > 7$

8 Draw graphs to show the regions defined by these sets of inequalities. Leave the required region unshaded. Label each graph.
- **a** $x \geqslant 0$ $y \geqslant 0$ $x + 3y \leqslant 9$
- **b** $x \geqslant 1$ $y \geqslant 2$ $x + 2y \leqslant 10$
- **c** $x \geqslant 2$ $y \leqslant 10$ $x - 2y \leqslant 6$

9 A train company owns 50 diesel units. It can use them as single trains or couple two together to make a double train. The company employs 35 drivers.
- **a** Explain the inequality $s + 2d \leqslant 50$.
- **b** Write down three other inequalities that describe this situation.
- **c** Draw a graph to show all of the inequalities.
- **d** What is the maximum number of trains the company can run?

10 **a** Sketch a graph of the function $f(x) = x^2 + 2x - 15$.
- **b** Use your graph to solve the inequality $x^2 + 2x - 15 < 0$.

11 **a** Draw a graph to solve the equation $x^2 + 5x + 6 = 0$. Draw your x axis from -4 to $+2$ and your y axis from -5 to 15.
- **b** Use your graph to solve $x^2 + 5x + 6 > 2$.
- **c** By drawing the line $y = x$ on your graph, solve the inequality $x^2 + 5x + 6 > x$.

1 A computer company makes two types of laser printers. The details are given in this table.

	Model DB30	Model DB50
Cost to produce	£120	£90
Worker hours	2	2.5
Machine hours	3	4
Profit	£15	£20

In any one day, the factory has 80 worker hours and 150 machine hours available. They have £3600 to spend on production each day.
a Write down inequalities to describe the constraints described above.
b Draw a graph to show these inequalities.
c What combination of printers should the company make in order to make the most profit?

2 This is a graph of $f(x) = x^3 + 7x^2 + 7x - 15$.

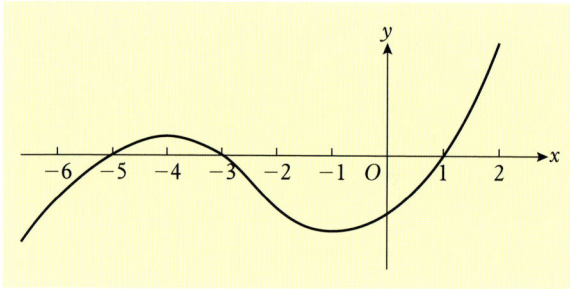

a Use the graph to write down the solutions to $x^3 + 7x^2 + 7x - 15 < 0$.
b Write $f(x)$ in the form $(x - a)(x + b)(x + c)$.

3 Look at this graph.
By looking carefully at the intercepts of each line, write down a series of inequalities which define the unshaded region.

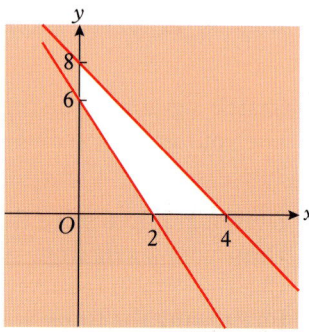

1 Write down inequalities to describe each of these number lines.

a

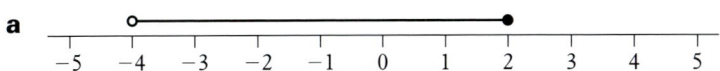

b

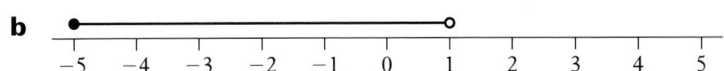

c

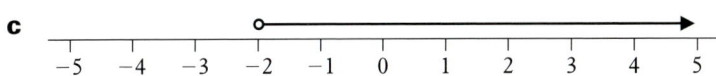

2 List the integers that are included in each of these inequalities.

a $2 < x \leqslant 5$ **c** $-5 \leqslant x \leqslant -1$

b $-3 \leqslant x < 1$ **d** $-3 < x < 3$

3 Solve each of these inequalities.

a $x - 3 < 8$ **e** $\dfrac{3x + 1}{5} < -4$

b $2x + 5 \geqslant 17$ **f** $5x + 11 \geqslant 3x + 7$

c $4x - 7 \leqslant 12$ **g** $\dfrac{3x}{5} - 1 < \dfrac{x}{5} + 3$

d $\dfrac{x}{4} - 9 > 2.3$ **h** $\dfrac{5x + 2}{6} \geqslant \dfrac{x}{3}$

4 Solve each of these inequalities.

a $11 - x > 3$ **c** $3x + 7 \leqslant 8x - 9$

b $\dfrac{5 - 2x}{7} < -3$ **d** $10 - 3x \geqslant -2x + 6$

5 Solve each of these inequalities.

a $5 \leqslant 2x - 1 \leqslant 11$ **c** $-8 \leqslant \dfrac{2x + 5}{3} < -1$

b $-3 < \dfrac{x}{2} + 5 \leqslant 0$ **d** $9 - x \leqslant x + 5 \leqslant 15 - x$

6 Write down the inequality that describes the shaded region on each of these graphs.

a

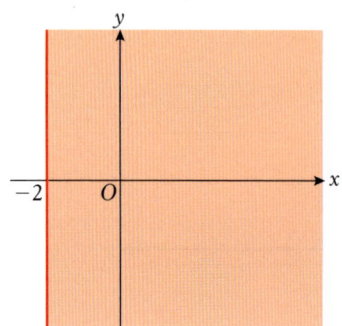

b

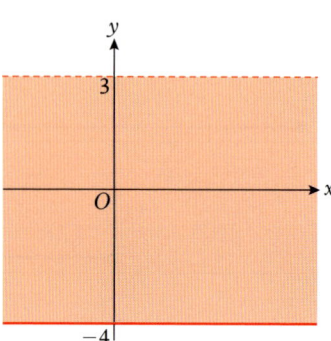

7 Write down inequalities to describe the shaded region on each of these graphs.

a

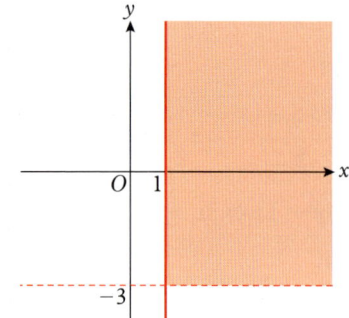

b

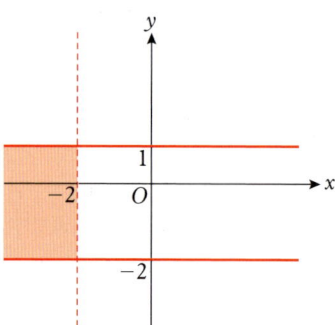

8 **a** Sketch the graph of the function $f(x) = x^2 - 3x + 2$.
   b Use your graph to solve the inequality $x^2 - 3x + 2 > 0$.

9 A bakery makes both sliced and unsliced loaves of bread. The maximum number of loaves it can make in a day is 800.
The number of sliced loaves made is always at least double the number of unsliced loaves. At least 200 unsliced loaves must be made.
   a Explain the inequality $s + u \leqslant 800$.
   b Write down four other inequalities to describe the situation.
   c Draw a graph to show all of the inequalities.
   d What is the maximum number of unsliced loaves that can be made?

20 Trigonometry: making waves

1 Beyond 90°
Doing trigonometry with angles of any size
Solving trig equations with angles of any size
Drawing the graphs of sin x, cos x and tan x
Transforming trig graphs

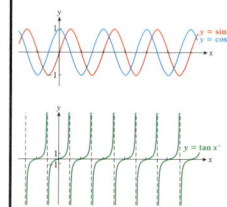

CORE

2 Solving triangles
Using the sine rule
Using the cosine rule
Finding the area of a triangle
Solving problems involving bearings
Solving problems in 3-D

QUESTIONS

EXTENSION

TEST YOURSELF

1   Beyond 90°

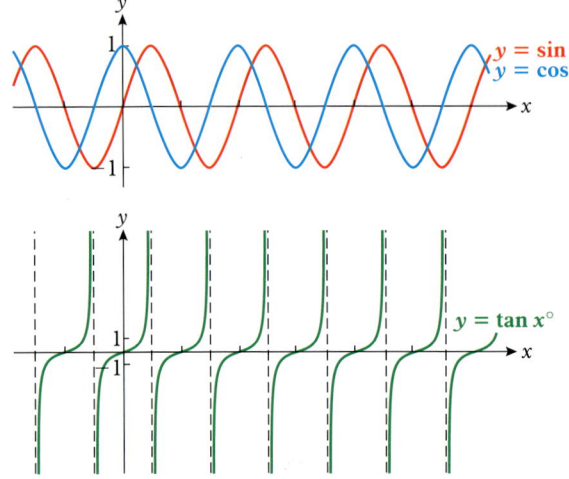

The trigonometric functions have a meaning for any angle and not just angles between 0° and 90°. In this section you are going to see how to use trigonometry with angles of any size.

In a right-angled triangle $\sin x = \dfrac{\text{opp}}{\text{hyp}}$

If you make the hypotenuse 1 unit long then

$\sin x = \dfrac{\text{opp}}{1} = \text{opp}$

So in the diagram $\sin x = PQ$

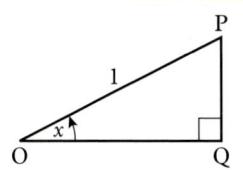

You can see from this diagram that $\sin 30° = PQ = 0.5$

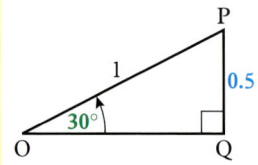

The same triangle OPQ has been drawn again, but inside a circle. The circle has radius OP = 1 unit. You can read the length of PQ on the vertical scale.

The blue arrow points to $\sin 30°$.

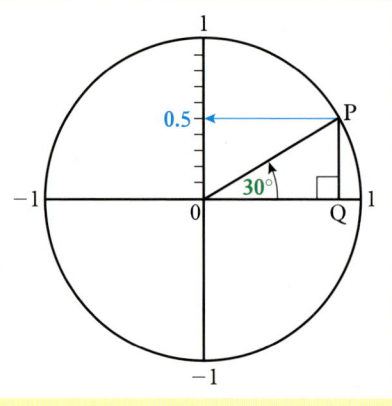

This diagram shows that
sin **24°** = **0.4** to 1 dp.

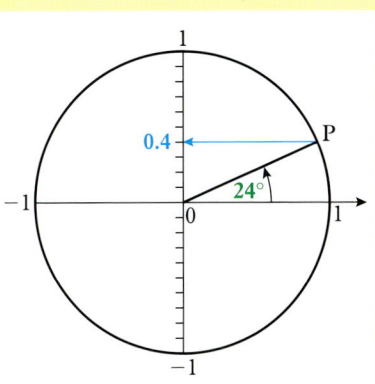

You can see how the sine of the angle changes
as the point P moves around the circle. The
angle of OP is measured positively in an anticlockwise direction from the positive horizontal.
The method works for angles of **any size**.

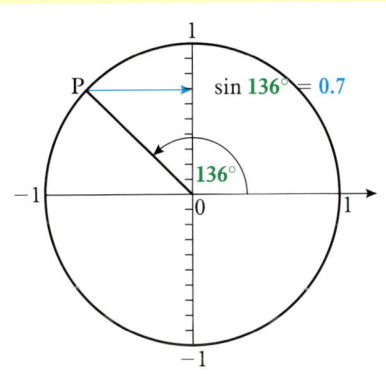

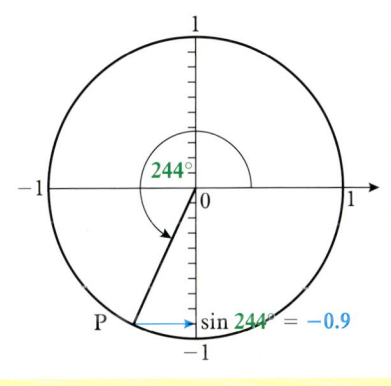

The sine of an obtuse angle is positive.

The sine of a reflex angle is negative.

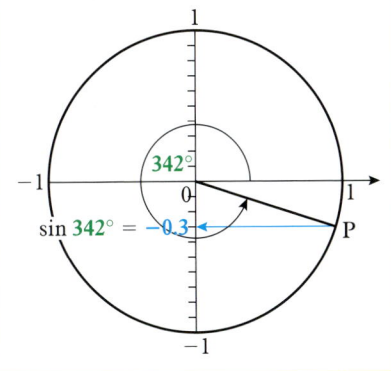

Negative angles are measured clockwise.

Exercise 20:1

1 Use the diagrams below to find the value of these to 1 dp.
You will need to use symmetry to answer some of the questions.

a	sin 12°	• **f**	sin (−156°)	**k**	sin 0°
b	sin 210°	**g**	sin 224°	**l**	sin 90°
c	sin 127°	• **h**	sin 136°	**m**	sin 180°
d	sin 316°	• **i**	sin 17°	**n**	sin 270°
e	sin 156°	• **j**	sin 163°	**o**	sin 360°

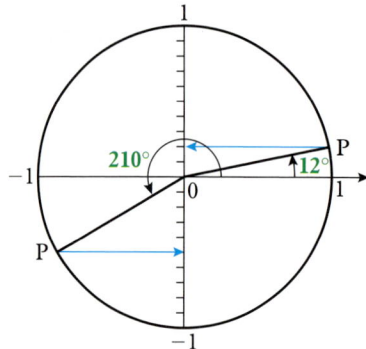
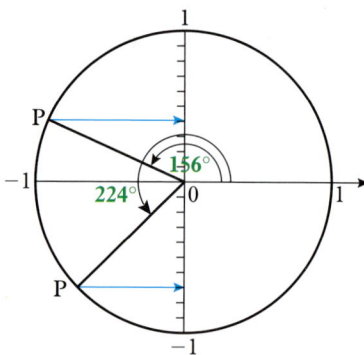

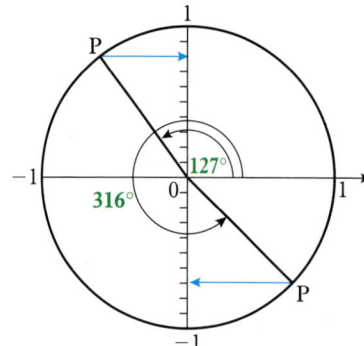
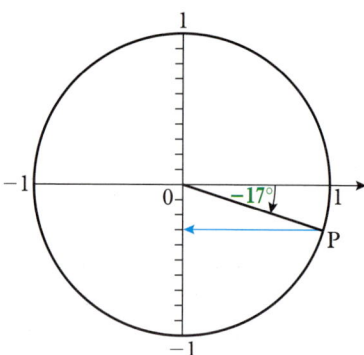

Use a circle diagram to answer these questions.

2 Describe how sin x changes as x increases from:
    a 0° to 90°   **b** 90° to 180°   **c** 180° to 270°   **d** 270° to 360°

3 What happens to the value of sin x as x increases beyond 360°?

4 **a** What is the largest possible value of sin x?
   b What is the smallest possible value of sin x?

5 The diagram shows a sketch of part of the graph of $y = \sin x$.
   a Copy the diagram.
   b The dotted line is a line of symmetry.
      Sketch the part of the curve from 90° to 180°.
   c The curve has rotational symmetry of order 2 about (180, 0).
      Sketch the part of the curve from 180° to 360° on the same diagram.
   d Check that your sketch matches the answers that you gave in
      question **1**.
   e Sketch the part of the curve from 360° to 720° on the same diagram.

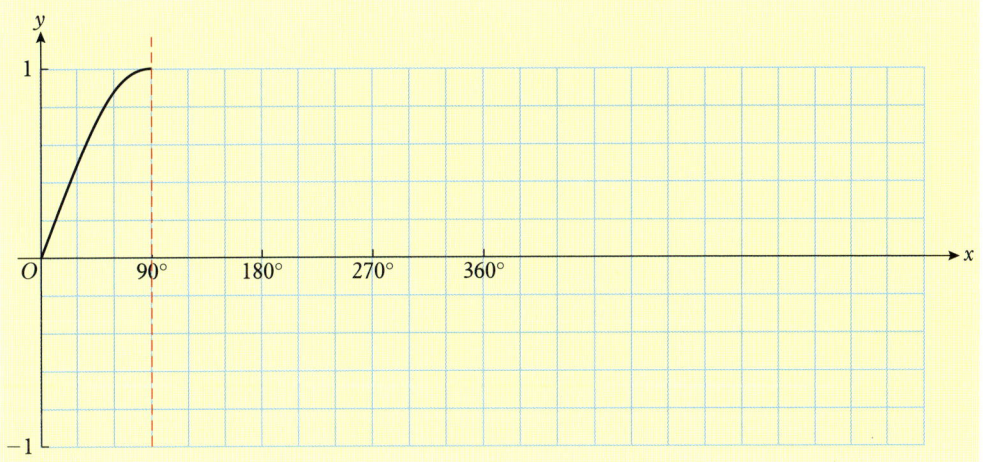

You can use the symmetry of your sketch to find more information
about sin x.

6 **a** Use your sketch of $y = \sin x$ to find the two values of x between
      0° and 360° that make sin $x = 0.5$
   b Find two values of x between 0° and 360° that make sin $x = -0.5$
   c Find two values of x between 360° and 720° that make sin $x = 0.5$
   d Use a calculator to check your answers.

7 sin 40° = 0.643 to 3 dp.
   Use your sketch of $y = \sin x$ to write down the value of these to 3 dp.
   a sin 140°   **b** sin 400°   **c** sin 220°
   Use a calculator to check your answers.

8 Write each of these in terms of sin x.
   a sin $(180° - x)$ **c** sin $(360° - x)$
   b sin $(180° + x)$ **d** sin $(360° + x)$

Example   Solve the equation sin $x = 0.45$ for values of x between $0°$ and $360°$.
Give your answers to 1 dp.

You can find one value of x from your calculator.

Key in:

to get $x = 26.7°$ to 1 dp.

Now use a circle diagram to
look for other values of x.

(1) Sketch the angle that you
have already found and
label P on the circumference.

(2) Use **symmetry** to find P′.

(3) Find the angle that
OP′ makes with the positive
horizontal.

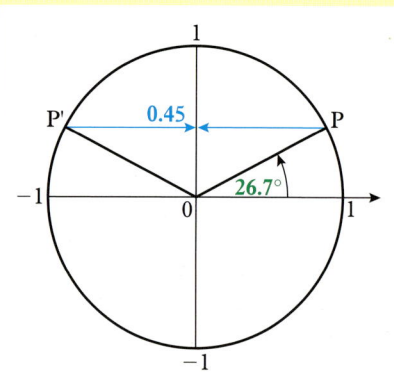

OP′ makes an angle of $180° − 26.7° = 153.3°$ with the positive horizontal.
The solutions are $x = 26.7°$ and $x = 153.3°$

Exercise 20:2

1   Solve these equations for values of x between $0°$ and $360°$.
Round your answers to 1 dp.

   a   sin $x = 0.76$ **c**   sin $x = 0.85$ **e**   sin $x = -0.45$
   b   sin $x = 0.23$ **d**   sin $x = -0.37$ **f**   sin $x = -0.62$

2   Find the values of x between $0°$ and $360°$ that solve these equations.

   a $\sin x = \dfrac{\sqrt{3}}{2}$ **b** $\sin x = \dfrac{1}{\sqrt{2}}$ **c** $\sin x = -\dfrac{\sqrt{3}}{2}$ **d** $\sin x = -\dfrac{1}{\sqrt{2}}$

3   Explain why the equation sin $x = 1$ only has one solution between $0°$ and $360°$.
Write down this solution.

In a right-angled triangle $\cos x = \dfrac{\text{adj}}{\text{hyp}}$

If you make the hypotenuse 1 unit long then

$\cos x = \dfrac{\text{adj}}{1} = \text{adj}$

So in the diagram $\cos x = OQ$

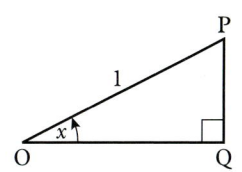

You can see from this diagram that
$\cos \mathbf{60°} = OQ = \mathbf{0.5}$

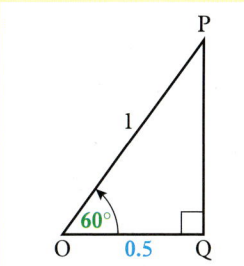

You can put triangle OPQ in a circle
as you did for the sine of an angle.

The circle has radius $OP = 1$ unit.
You can find the value of $\cos \mathbf{60°}$ on
the horizontal scale.

The blue arrow points to $\cos \mathbf{60°}$.

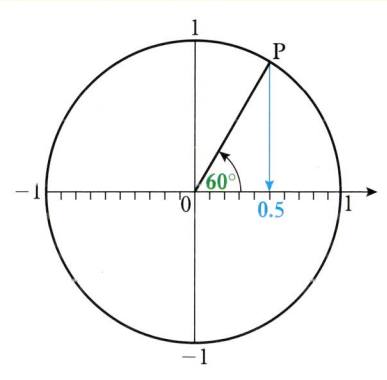

The method works for angles of any size.

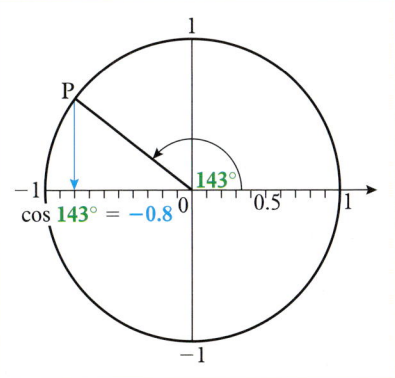

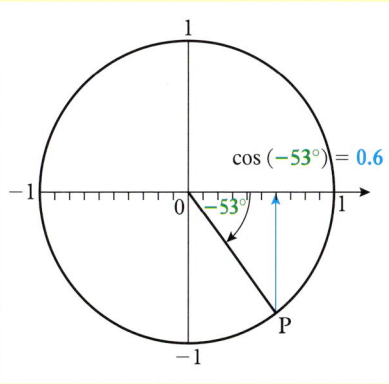

497

Exercise 20:3

1 Describe how cos x changes as x increases from:
    a 0° to 90°   **b** 90° to 180°   **c** 180° to 270°   **d** 270° to 360°

2 **a** What is the maximum value of cos x?
    b What is the minimum value of cos x?

3 **a** Copy the diagram.
    b Complete the sketch of $y = \cos x$ from 0° to 360°.

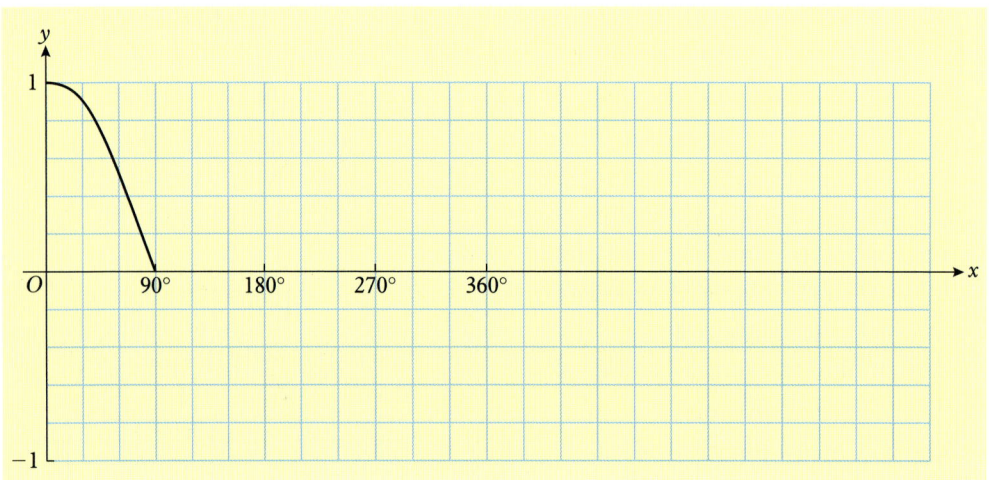

4 **a** What happens to the value of cos x as x increases beyond 360°?
    b Extend your sketch of $y = \cos x$ up to 720°.

5 The graph of $y = \cos x$ continues for ever in both directions.
    a Describe the positions of the lines of symmetry of the curve.
    b Describe the rotational symmetry of the curve.

6 **a** Use your sketch of $y = \cos x$ to find the two values of x between 0°
       and 360° that make cos $x = 0.5$
    b Find two values of x between 0° and 360° that make cos $x = -0.5$
    c Find two values of x between 360° and 720° that make cos $x = 0.5$
    d Use a calculator to check your answers.

7 Use your sketch to find 4 solutions of each of these equations.
    a cos $x = 0$ **b** cos $x = 1$ **c** cos $x = -1$

● **8** Write down the value of cos $(360n°)$ where n is an integer.

Example   Solve the equation $\cos x = -0.67$ for values of x between $0°$ and $360°$.
Give your answers to 1 dp.

You can find one value of x from your calculator.

Key in: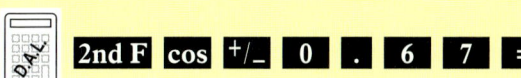

to get $x = 132.1°$ to 1 dp.

Now use a circle diagram to
look for other values of x.

(1) Sketch the angle that you
have already found and
label P on the circumference.

(2) Use **symmetry** to find P′.

(3) Find the angle that
OP′ makes with the positive
horizontal.

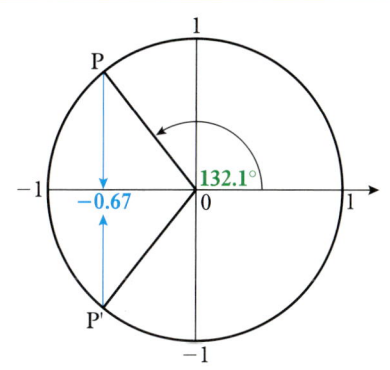

OP′ makes an angle of $360° - 132.1° = 227.9°$ with the positive horizontal.
The solutions are $x = 132.1°$ and $x = 227.9°$

Exercise 20:4

1   Solve these equations for values of x between $0°$ and $360°$.
Round your answers to 1 dp.

   a $\cos x = 0.76$ **c** $\cos x = 0.85$ **e** $\cos x = -0.45$

   b $\cos x = 0.23$ **d** $\cos x = -0.37$ **f** $\cos x = -0.62$

●   **2**   Find the values of x between $0°$ and $360°$ that solve these equations.

   a $\cos x = \dfrac{\sqrt{3}}{2}$ **b** $\cos x = \dfrac{1}{\sqrt{2}}$ **c** $\cos x = -\dfrac{\sqrt{3}}{2}$ **d** $\cos x = -\dfrac{1}{\sqrt{2}}$

In Chapter 13 you found that the graph of $y = kf(x)$ can be found by stretching the graph of $y = f(x)$ by scale factor k in the y direction. This works for any function.

You can use this result to sketch graphs based on the sine and cosine functions. To sketch $y = 2 \sin x$ you stretch the graph of $y = \sin x$ by a factor of 2 in the y direction.

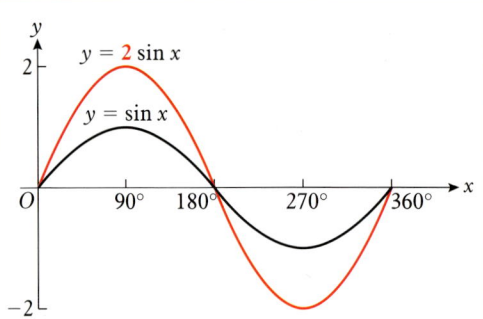

The maximum value of $2 \sin x$ is 2. The minimum value of $2 \sin x$ is -2.
If $k > 0$, the maximum value of $k \sin x$ is k. The minimum value of $k \sin x$ is $-k$.

The graphs of $y = \sin x$ and $y = \cos x$ repeat every $360°$.
A graph that has this kind of repeating pattern is said to be **periodic**.
The graphs of $y = \sin x$ and $y = \cos x$ both have a **period** of $360°$.

The graph of $y = f(kx)$ can be found by stretching the graph of $y = f(x)$ by scale factor $\dfrac{1}{k}$ in the x direction. This makes the graph appear compressed like a spring.

The graph of $y = f(kx)$ changes k times as fast as the graph of $y = f(x)$.
So, the graph of $y = \cos 2x$ changes **twice** as fast as the graph of $y = \cos x$.

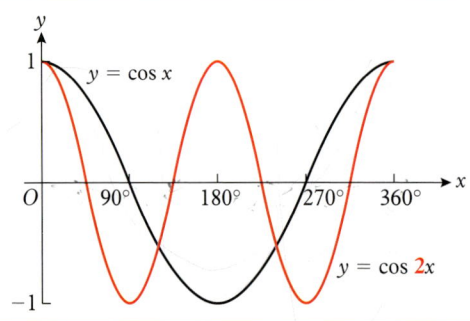

The graph of $y = \cos 2x$ has period $\dfrac{360°}{2} = 180°$. The graph repeats every $180°$.

Exercise 20:5

Write down the maximum and minimum value of y for each part of questions **1** to **3**. Sketch the graphs of the equations for $0° \leqslant x \leqslant 360°$.

1 **a** $y = 3 \sin x$
  b $y = 0.5 \sin x$
  c $y = 2 \cos x$
  d $y = 0.5 \cos x$

2 **a** $y = -\sin x$
  b $y = -2 \sin x$
  c $y = -3 \cos x$
  d $y = -0.5 \cos x$

3 **a** $y = \sin 2x$
  • **c** $y = \sin \dfrac{x}{2}$

  b $y = \cos 3x$
  • **d** $y = -0.5 \cos \dfrac{x}{3}$

You may need to transform a graph by stretching it in two directions. To sketch the graph of $y = a \sin bx$ you stretch the graph of $y = \sin x$ using a factor of a in the y direction and a factor of $\dfrac{1}{b}$ in the x direction.

You treat $y = a \cos bx$ in the same way starting from the graph of $y = \cos x$.

---

4 **a** What is the maximum possible value of $2 \sin 3x$?
  b What is the minimum possible value of $2 \sin 3x$?
  c What is the period of the graph of $y = 2 \sin 3x$?
  d Sketch the graph of $y = 2 \sin 3x$ for $0° \leqslant x \leqslant 360°$.

5 Write down the equation of the graph shown in this sketch.

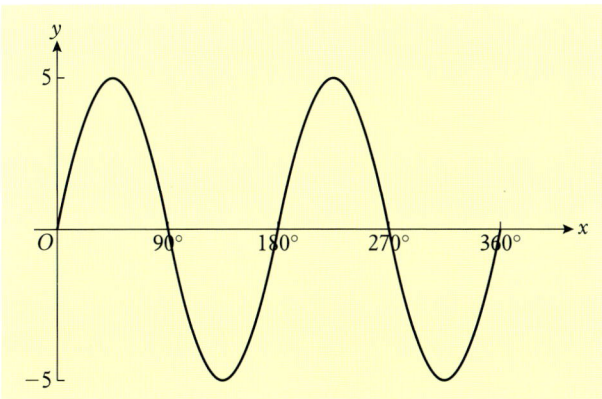

In a right-angled triangle $\tan x = \dfrac{\text{opp}}{\text{adj}}$

If you make the adjacent side 1 unit long then

$\tan x = \dfrac{\text{opp}}{1} = \text{opp}$

So in the diagram $\tan x = RQ$

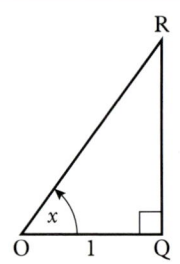

You can see from this diagram that

$\tan 60° = RQ = \sqrt{3}$

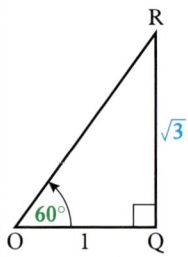

You can use a circle diagram again to show how the tangent of an angle changes with the size of the angle.

The circle has radius $OQ = 1$ unit.

You find the value of $\tan 60°$ by extending OP towards the vertical scale on the right.

The blue arrow points to $\tan 60°$.

In general, $\tan x$ is shown by the position where the line through O and P meets the vertical scale on the right.

The value of $\tan x$ is not defined whenever OP is parallel to the vertical scale. This happens when $x = 90°, 270°, 450°, \dots$

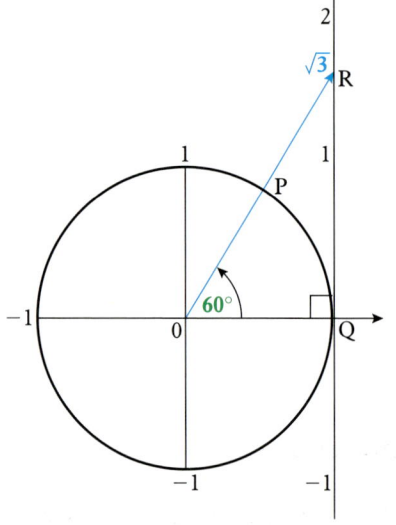

You can give a meaning to tan **150°** by extending PO towards the vertical scale on the right.

The blue arrow points to tan **150°**.

Using the **symmetry** of the diagram you can see that tan 150° = tan (−30°)

$$= -\tan 30°$$

You know that tan **30°** = $\dfrac{1}{\sqrt{3}}$ (from Chapter 12).

So tan **150°** = $-\dfrac{1}{\sqrt{3}}$

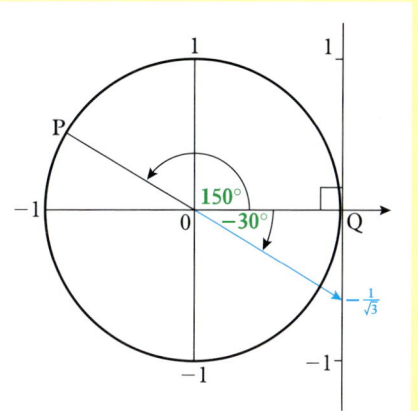

You can give a meaning to tan **240°** by extending PO towards the vertical scale on the right.

The green arrow points to tan **240°**.

You can see from the diagram that tan **240°** is the same as tan **60°**.

So tan **240°** = $\sqrt{3}$

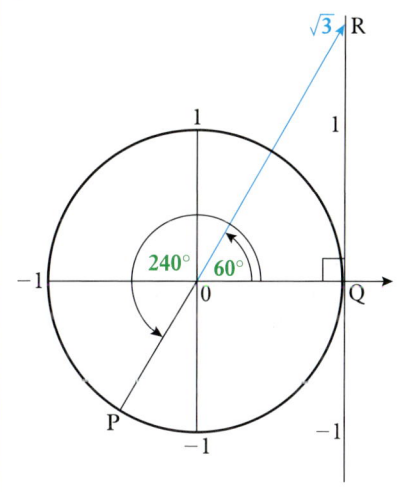

Exercise 20:6

1 Use a circle diagram to write down the value of each of these.
    a tan 0°   **b** tan 180°   ● **c** tan 45°

2 Use symmetry in a circle diagram to write each of these as:
    (1) the tangent of an acute angle   (2) an exact value
    a tan 225° **b** tan 135° **c** tan 330° **d** tan 210° **e** tan 120°

3 Use a circle diagram to find what happens to the value of tan x as x:
  a increases from 0° towards 90°   **c** increases from 180° towards 270°
  b reduces from 180° to 90°   **d** reduces from 360° towards 270°

4 The diagram shows a sketch of the curve $y = \tan x$ for $0° \leqslant x < 90°$.
  a Copy the diagram.
  b Sketch the part of the curve for $90° < x \leqslant 180°$.
  c Describe the symmetry of your diagram.
  d Complete the sketch for $180 \leqslant x \leqslant 360°$.

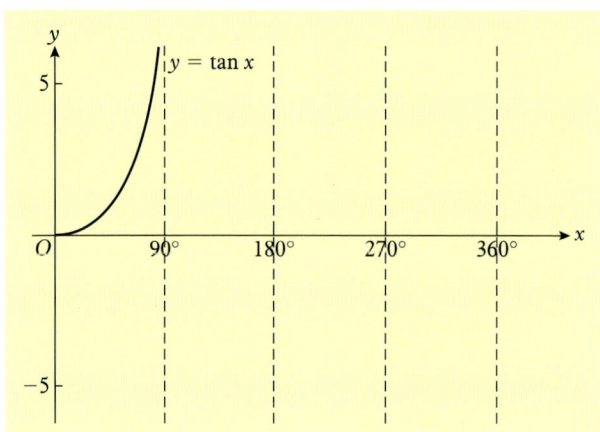

5 **a** What is the period of the graph of $y = \tan x$?
  b What is the period of the graph of $y = \tan 2x$?
  c What is the period of the graph of $y = \tan 3x$?

6 Write each of these in terms of tan x.
  a $\tan (x + 180°)$ **d** $\tan (180° - x)$
  b $\tan (x - 180°)$ **e** $\tan (360° + x)$
  c $\tan (-x)$ **f** $\tan (360° - x)$

7 Write down two differences between the graph of $y = \tan x$ and the graphs of $y = \sin x$ and $y = \cos x$.

8 One solution of the equation $\tan x = 2.5$ is $x = 68.2°$.
  a Use the sketch of $y = \tan x$ to find another solution between 0° and 360°.
  b Use the sketch to solve the equation $\tan x = -2.5$ for $0° \leqslant x \leqslant 360°$.

Example Solve tan x = 1.2 for $-180° \leqslant x \leqslant 180°$.

You can find one solution from your calculator.

Key in: 2nd F tan 1 . 2 =

 SHIFT tan 1 . 2 =

to get x = **50.2°** to 1 dp.

Using the diagram:

tan (**50.2°** − **180°**) = 1.2
so tan (−**129.8°**) = 1.2

The solutions are

x = 50.2° and x = −129.8°

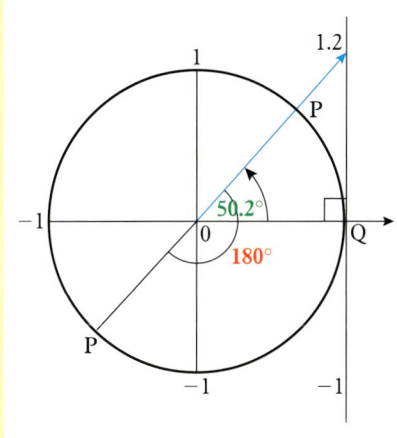

If you have one solution of an equation of the form tan x = k then you can find all of the others by adding or subtracting multiples of 180°.

Exercise 20:7

1 Solve these equations for $-180° \leqslant x \leqslant 180°$.
  a tan x = 0.9   **c** tan x = −0.8   **e** tan x = $\sqrt{5}$
  b tan x = 1.6   **d** tan x = −2.3   **f** tan x = $-3\sqrt{2}$

2 Solve these equations for $0° \leqslant x \leqslant 360°$.
  a tan x = 0.4   **c** tan x = −0.5   **e** tan x = $\sqrt{3} - 1$
  b tan x = 1.7   **d** tan x = −5.3   **f** tan x = $5 - 7\sqrt{2}$

3 Solve these equations for $-360° \leqslant x \leqslant 360°$.
  a tan x = 0.6   **c** tan x = −3.7   **e** 3 tan x = 7
  b tan x = 11.4   **d** tan x = −0.64   ● **f** $(\tan x)^2$ = 5

2 Solving triangles

There are some special rules that allow you to use trigonometry in any triangle. It does not have to be right-angled.
Astronomers use trigonometry to estimate the distance to stars.

After you have seen the work in this section, think about how they do it.

The sine rule

This triangle is labelled in a special way.

The angles are labelled with capital letters and the sides are labelled with lower case letters.
Each angle has the same letter as the opposite side.
This makes it easier to write some important rules in a way that you can remember.

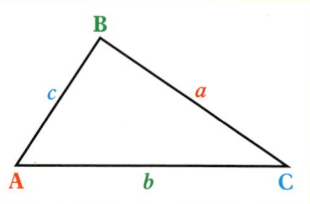

The sine rule is

$$\frac{a}{\sin A} = \frac{b}{\sin B} = \frac{c}{\sin C}$$

You can use the sine rule to find sides and angles in triangles that do not have a right angle.

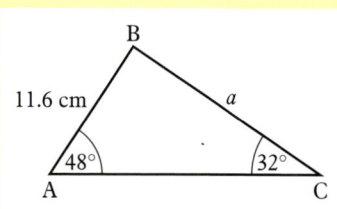

Example   Find the length of the side *a*.

Using the sine rule:

$$\frac{a}{\sin 48°} = \frac{11.6}{\sin 32°}$$

so $a = \dfrac{11.6}{\sin 32°}$

Key in: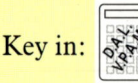

$a = 16.3$ cm to 1 dp.

Exercise 20:8

1 Find the length of side *a* in each diagram.

a

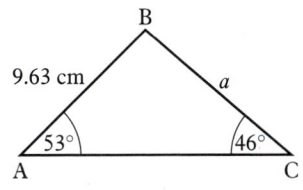

c

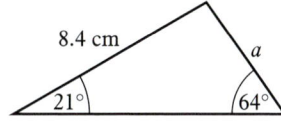

b

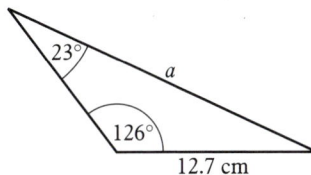

d

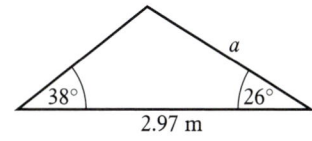

When you use the sine rule the unknown side can be in any position and might be labelled with any letter. You can think of the rule like this to help you.

$$\frac{\text{length of unknown side}}{\text{sine of opposite angle}} = \frac{\text{length of known side}}{\text{sine of its opposite angle}}$$

2 Find the lengths of the lettered sides in these diagrams.

a

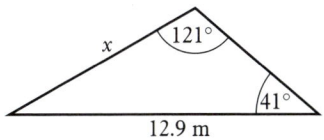

c

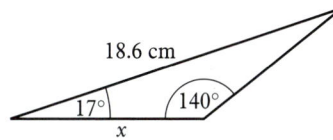

b

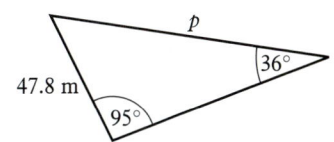

d

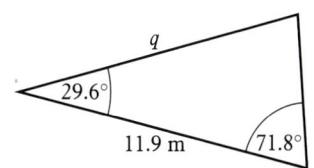

You can use the sine rule to find an unknown angle. In this case it is better to use the rule the other way up so that the unknown value is in the numerator.

$$\frac{\sin A}{a} = \frac{\sin B}{b} = \frac{\sin C}{c}$$

Again, the sides in your triangle might not be labelled this way so you can use:

$$\frac{\text{sine of unknown angle}}{\text{length of opposite side}} = \frac{\text{sine of known angle}}{\text{length of its opposite side}}$$

Example   Find the size of angle x.

$$\frac{\sin x}{10.4} = \frac{\sin 129°}{12.6}$$

$$\sin x = \frac{10.4 \sin 129°}{12.6}$$

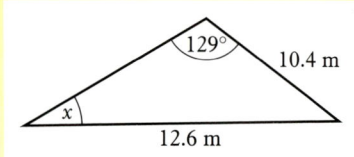

Key in: **2nd F** **sin** **(** **1** **0** **.** **4** **sin** **1** **2** **9** **÷** **1** **2** **.** **6** **)** **=**

 SHIFT **sin** **(** **1** **0** **.** **4** **sin** **1** **2** **9** **÷** **1** **2** **.** **6** **)** **=**

so $x = 39.9°$ to 1 dp.

Another angle with the same sine is $(180° - 39.9°) = 140.1°$
But this result is too big and so the only possible value of x is $39.9°$

Exercise 20:9

1   Find the size of angle x in each triangle.

a
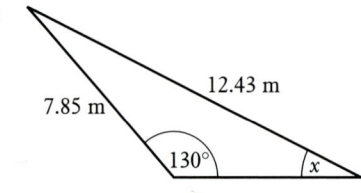

b
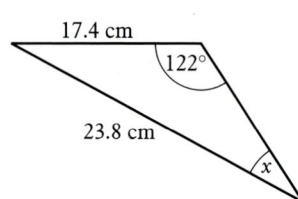

2 **a** Use compasses to construct the triangles shown below.

b Angle x is acute. Use the sine rule to find the size of angle x.

c Angle y is obtuse. Use the sine rule to find the size of angle y.

d Measure angles x and y on your diagrams.
Compare the results with your answers to parts **b** and **c**.

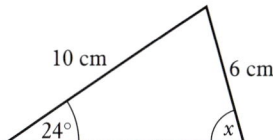 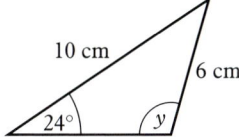

The cosine rule

The sine rule will not help you to find the length of side x in this diagram.

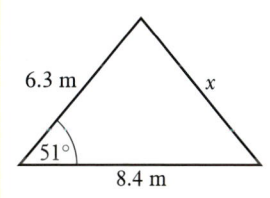

Whenever you know the lengths of two sides and the angle between them you can use the **cosine rule**.

Using the same notation as for the sine rule, the cosine rule is written as

$$a^2 = b^2 + c^2 - 2bc \cos A$$

From the diagram

$$x^2 = 6.3^2 + 8.4^2 - 2 \times 6.3 \times 8.4 \cos 51°$$

Key in: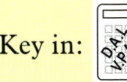

$x = 6.6$ cm to 1 dp.

Exercise 20:10

1 Use the cosine rule to find the lengths of the lettered sides in these triangles.

a

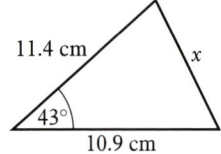

11.4 cm
43°
10.9 cm
x

c

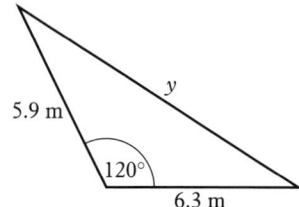

5.9 m
120°
6.3 m
y

b

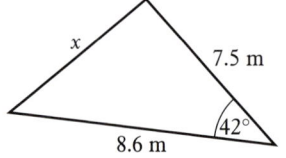

x
7.5 m
42°
8.6 m

d

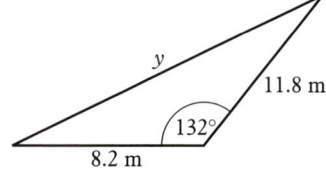

y
11.8 m
132°
8.2 m

The cosine rule can also be written as: $\cos A = \dfrac{b^2 + c^2 - a^2}{2bc}$

You use the rule in this form to find
an unknown angle.
You need to know all three sides of
the triangle.

8.5 m   6.9 m
9.2 m
x

Example   Find the size of angle x.

$$\cos x = \frac{9.2^2 + 6.9^2 - 8.5^2}{2 \times 6.9 \times 9.2}$$

Key in: **2nd** **cos** **((** **9** **.** **2** **x²** **+** **6** **.** **9** **x²** **−** **8** **.** **5**

x² **)** **÷** **(** **2** **×** **6** **.** **9** **×** **9** **.** **2** **)** **)** **=**

 SHIFT **cos** **((** **9** **.** **2** **x²** **+** **6** **.** **9** **x²** **−** **8** **.** **5**

x² **)** **÷** **(** **2** **×** **6** **.** **9** **×** **9** **.** **2** **)** **)** **=**

$x = 61.8°$ to 1 dp.

2 Use the cosine rule to find the angles marked with letters in these triangles.

a

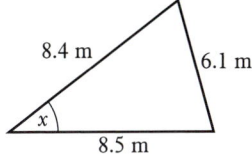

c

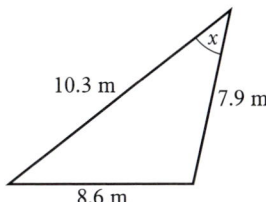

b

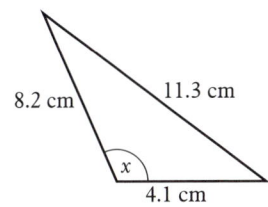

d

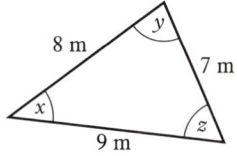

Area of triangle

You can use the same notation to write a formula for the area of any triangle as

$$\text{Area} = \tfrac{1}{2}\,ab\,\sin C$$

You can think of this as:

Area $= \tfrac{1}{2} \times$ the product of any two sides $\times$ the sine of the angle between them.

3 Find the area of these triangles.

a

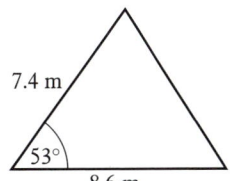

b

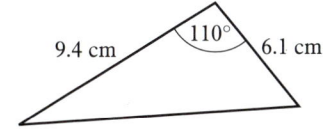

Bearings

You have seen simple bearing questions in Chapter 11.
Using the sine and cosine rules allows you to solve much more complicated
questions.

Example   A plane flies 20 km from Ampton to Boxford on a bearing of 044°.
It then flies 15 km on a bearing of 102° to Canborough.
a Find the distance from Ampton to Canborough.
b Find the bearing of Canborough from Ampton.

You need to start by drawing a diagram.
Show all of the information that you are given.
Use A, B and C for the towns.

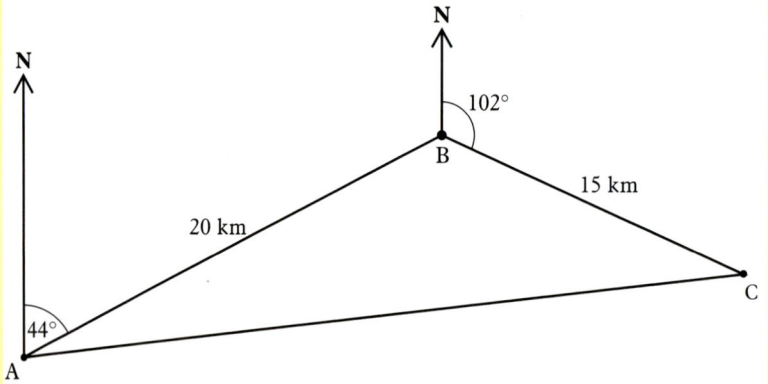

You want to find out about the length from A to C and the bearing of C from A.
For the bearing you need the angle at A in triangle ABC to add it to the 44°.
This means that you need to work in triangle ABC.
This triangle is not right-angled.

In triangle ABC you can find angle B.

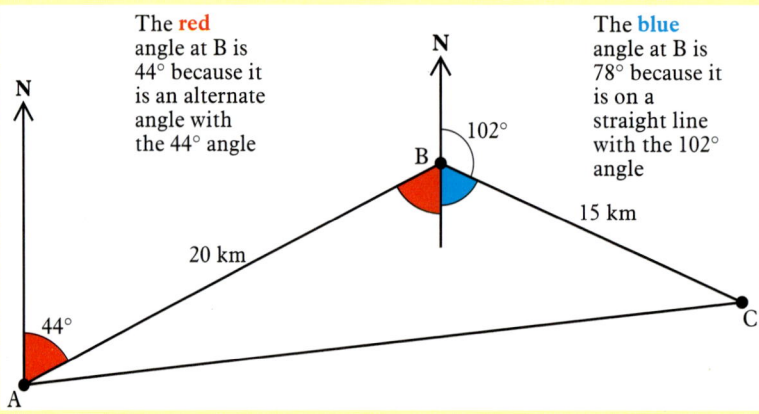

The **red**
angle at B is
44° because it
is an alternate
angle with
the 44° angle

The **blue**
angle at B is
78° because it
is on a
straight line
with the 102°
angle

So this is what you know in triangle ABC.

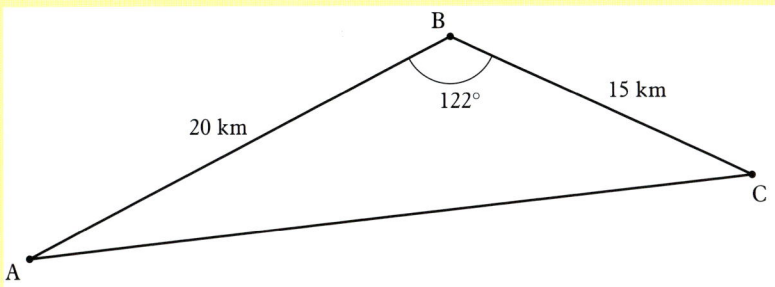

Now you can answer the question!

a In triangle ABC

$$AC^2 = 20^2 + 15^2 - 2 \times 20 \times 15 \times \cos 122° \qquad \text{(cosine rule)}$$
$$AC^2 = 942.952...$$
$$AC = 30.7 \text{ km (3 sf)}$$

So the distance from Ampton to Canborough is 30.7 km (to 3 sf).

Keep the exact value of AC in your calculator to use in the next part.
If you decide to write down and use a rounded value make sure that you work
to at least 4 sf if you want to give your final answer correct to 3 sf.

b In triangle ABC

$$\frac{\sin A}{15} = \frac{\sin 122}{AC} \qquad \text{(sine rule)}$$

$$\sin A = \frac{15 \times \sin 122}{30.7075...} = 0.41425...$$ ◄——— This is the exact value of AC kept in the calculator from part **a**.

$$A = 24.47° \text{ (to 4 sf)}$$

The angle needed for the bearing $= 44 + 24.47 = 68.47°$
So the bearing of Canborough from Ampton is 068° (to the nearest degree).

To do questions like these:
   (1) Draw a diagram that shows the information you are given.
   (2) Decide on which triangle you need to work in.
   (3) Work out any missing information about this triangle that you can.
   (4) Use the sine or cosine rules to work out the lengths and angles that you
       need.
   (5) Keep the exact value of any length or angle that you find in your
       calculator in case you need it in another part.
   (6) If you do use a rounded value make sure that you work to at least 4 sf if
       you want to give your final answer correct to 3 sf.
   (7) Remember to write down the answer to the actual question at the end of
       each part!

Exercise 20:11

In this exercise, give all distances to 3 sf and bearings to the nearest degree.

1 A plane flies 13 km from Abingdon to Bampton on a bearing of 285°.
It then flies 28 km on a bearing of 260° to Cirencester.
a Draw a diagram to show this information.
b Find the distance from Abingdon to Cirencester.
c Find the bearing of Cirencester from Abingdon.

2 A plane flies 15 km from Harlow to Chelmsford on a bearing of 100°.
It then flies 25 km on a bearing of 135° to Southend-on-Sea.
a Draw a diagram to show this information.
b Find the distance from Harlow to Southend-on-Sea.
c Find the bearing of Southend-on-Sea from Harlow.

3 A jet flies 300 km from Manchester on a bearing of 170°.
Then it flies 100 km on a bearing of 047° and arrives at Guildford.
a Draw a diagram to show this information.
b Find the shortest distance from Manchester to Guildford.
c Find the bearing of Guildford from Manchester.

4 A jet flies 8100 km from Dover in England on a bearing of 159°.
It then flies 5400 km on a bearing of 123° and arrives at Perth on the coast of Australia.
a Draw a diagram to show this information.
b Find the shortest distance from Dover to Perth.
c Find the bearing of Perth from Dover.

5 Frank is repairing lighthouses around the Irish Sea.
He flies by helicopter.
He sets off from Holyhead in Anglesey and flies for 50 km to Llandudno on a bearing of 089°.
Then he flies for 105 km to Douglas in the Isle of Man on a bearing of 330°.
His final call is to Fleetwood in Lancashire.
He flies 100 km from Douglas on a bearing of 105° to get there.

a Draw a diagram to show this information.
b Find the shortest distance from Holyhead to Fleetwood.
c Find the bearing of Fleetwood from Holyhead.

3-D problems

The sine and cosine rules can also be used in more complicated 3-D problems.
You still need to draw the triangle that you need to work in.
You did this in Chapter 11 but then the triangle was always right-angled.
You will still get some right-angled triangles here as well, and then you can use
Pythagoras' theorem and ordinary trigonometry.
If the triangle is not right-angled, then use the sine or cosine rules to work out
the lengths and angles that you need.
Remember to keep the exact value of any length or angle that you find in your
calculator in case you need it in another part.

Example   ABCD is a tetrahedron.
D is vertically above C.
AB = 12 cm, BC = 14 cm,
CD = 5 cm and ∠ABC = 60°.

Find:

   a   AC   **d**   ∠ADB

   b   AD   **e**   ∠ABD

   c   BD

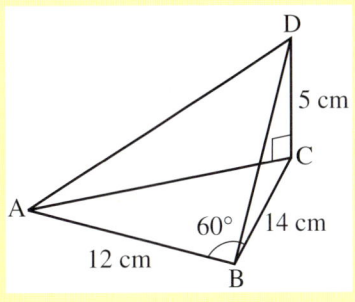

a   In triangle ABC
$AC^2 = 12^2 + 14^2 - 2 \times 12 \times 14 \cos 60°$ (cosine rule)
$AC^2 = 172$
$AC = \sqrt{172} = 13.1$ cm (3 sf)

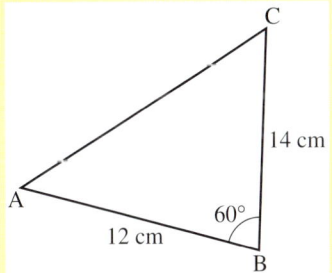

b   In triangle ACD, ∠ACD = 90°.
$AD^2 = (\sqrt{172})^2 + 5^2$ (Pythagoras)
$AD^2 = 197$
$AD = \sqrt{197} = 14.0$ cm (3 sf)

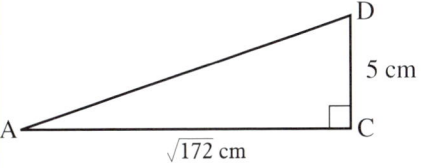

c   In triangle BCD, ∠BCD = 90°.
$BD^2 = 14^2 + 5^2$ (Pythagoras)
$BD^2 = 221$
$BD = \sqrt{221} = 14.9$ cm (3 sf)

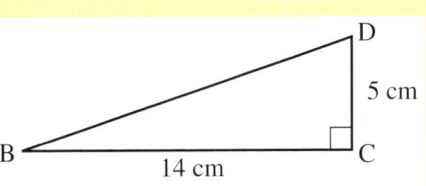

d In triangle ABD

$$\cos \angle ADB = \frac{(\sqrt{197})^2 + (\sqrt{221})^2 - 12^2}{2 \times \sqrt{197} \times \sqrt{221}} \quad \text{(cosine rule)}$$

$$= \frac{197 + 221 - 144}{2 \times \sqrt{197} \times \sqrt{221}} = 0.6565\ldots$$

$$\angle ADB = 48.96\ldots = 49.0° \text{ (3 sf)}$$

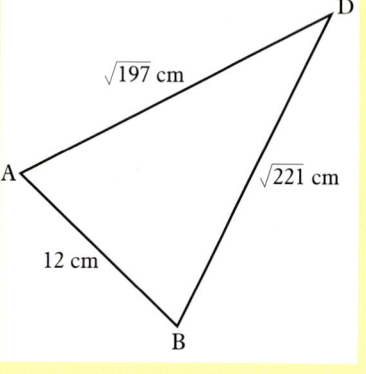

e In triangle ABD

$$\frac{\sin \angle ABD}{\sqrt{197}} = \frac{\sin \angle ADB}{12}$$

$$\sin \angle ABD = \frac{\sqrt{197} \times \sin 48.96\ldots}{12} = 0.882202\ldots$$

$$\angle ABD = 61.9° \text{ (3 sf)}$$

Exercise 20:12

1 WXYZ is a tetrahedron.
Z is vertically above Y.
WX = 11 cm, XY = 16 cm,
YZ = 4 cm and ∠WXY = 50°.
Find:

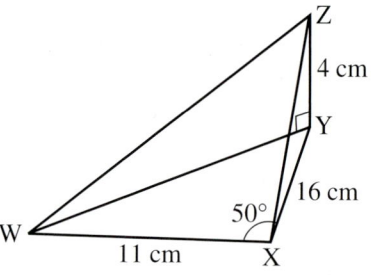

  a WY
  b WZ
  c XZ
  d ∠WZX
  e ∠WXZ

2 EFGH is a tetrahedron.
EF = 7 cm, FG = 10 cm,
GH = 3 cm and ∠EFG = 70°.
H is vertically above G.
Find:

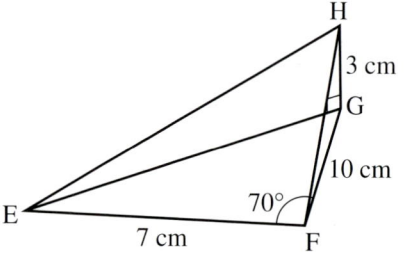

  a EG
  b ∠EGF
  c EH
  d HF
  e ∠EHF
  f ∠EFH

1 Solve these equations for values of x between $0°$ and $360°$.
   Round your answers to 1 dp.
   a $\sin x = 0.54$ **c** $\sin x = 0.76$ **e** $\sin x = -0.35$
   b $\sin x = 0.33$ **d** $\sin x = -0.24$ **f** $\sin x = -0.15$

2 Find the values of x between $0°$ and $360°$ that solve these equations.
   a $\sin x = \dfrac{1}{2}$ **b** $\sin x = \dfrac{\sqrt{3}}{2}$ **c** $\sin x = -\dfrac{1}{\sqrt{2}}$ **d** $\sin x = \dfrac{1}{\sqrt{2}}$

3 Explain why the equation $\sin x = -1$ only has one solution between $0°$ and $360°$.
   Write down this solution.

4 Solve these equations for values of x between $0°$ and $360°$.
   Round your answers to 1 dp.
   a $\cos x = 0.54$ **c** $\cos x = 0.76$ **e** $\cos x = -0.35$
   b $\cos x = 0.33$ **d** $\cos x = -0.24$ **f** $\cos x = -0.15$

5 Find the values of x between $0°$ and $360°$ that solve these equations.
   a $\cos x = \dfrac{1}{2}$ **b** $\cos x = \dfrac{\sqrt{3}}{2}$ **c** $\cos x = -\dfrac{1}{\sqrt{2}}$ **d** $\cos x = \dfrac{1}{\sqrt{2}}$

6 Sketch the graphs of these equations for $0° \leqslant x \leqslant 360°$.
   a $y = 2 \sin x$ **c** $y = 3 \cos x$ **e** $y = 1.5 \sin x$ **g** $y = 2.5 \cos x$
   b $y = 4 \sin x$ **d** $y = \frac{1}{2} \cos x$ **f** $y = 2.5 \sin x$ **h** $y = \frac{1}{4} \cos x$

7 Sketch the graphs of these equations for $0° \leqslant x \leqslant 360°$.
   a $y = \sin x$ **c** $y = \cos x$ **e** $y = 2 \sin x$ **g** $y = 3 \cos 2x$
   b $y = -\sin x$ **d** $y = -\cos x$ **f** $y = -2 \sin x$ **h** $y = -3 \cos 2x$

8 Sketch the graphs of these equations for $0° \leqslant x \leqslant 360°$.
   a $y = \sin 3x$ **b** $y = \cos 4x$ **c** $y = 2 \sin \dfrac{x}{3}$ **d** $y = -3 \cos \dfrac{x}{2}$

9 **a** What is the largest possible value of $4 \sin 2x$?
   b What is the smallest possible value of $4 \sin 2x$?
   c Sketch the graph of $y = 4 \sin 2x$ for $0° \leqslant x \leqslant 360°$.

10 One solution of the equation $\tan x = 1.5$ is $x = 56.3°$
   a Use the sketch of $y = \tan x$ to find another solution between $0°$ and $360°$.
   b Use the sketch to solve the equation $\tan x = -1.5$ for $0° \leqslant x \leqslant 360°$.

11 Solve these equations for $-180° \leqslant x \leqslant 180°$
   a $\tan x = 0.54$ **c** $\tan x = 0.76$ **e** $\tan x = -0.35$
   b $\tan x = 0.33$ **d** $\tan x = -0.24$ **f** $\tan x = -0.15$

12 Solve these equations for $-360° \leqslant x \leqslant 360°$
   a $\tan x = 0.3$ **c** $\tan x = -0.2$ **e** $\tan x = \sqrt{2} - 1$
   b $\tan x = 1.8$ **d** $\tan x = -4.7$ **f** $\tan x = 5 - 7\sqrt{3}$

13 Use the sine rule to find the marked side or angle in each of these.

a 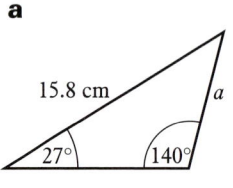 15.8 cm, 27°, 140°, *a*

b 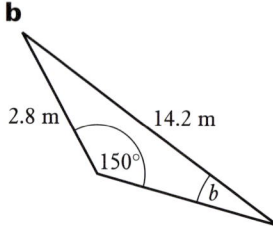 2.8 m, 14.2 m, 150°, *b*

c 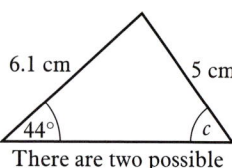 6.1 cm, 5 cm, 44°, *c*
There are two possible answers in this part.

14 Use the cosine rule to find the marked side or angle in each of these.

a 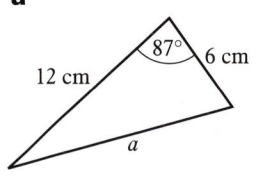 87°, 6 cm, 12 cm, *a*

b 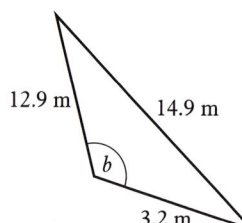 12.9 m, 14.9 m, *b*, 3.2 m

c 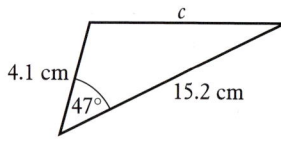 *c*, 4.1 cm, 47°, 15.2 cm

15 Find the area of each of these triangles.

a 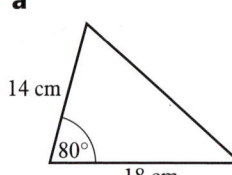 14 cm, 80°, 18 cm

b 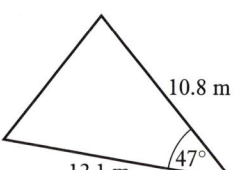 10.8 m, 12.1 m, 47°

c 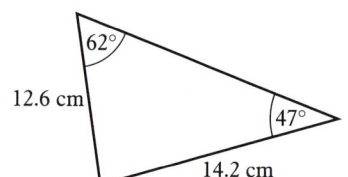 62°, 12.6 cm, 47°, 14.2 cm

16 A helicopter flies 22 km from Abingdon to Brize Norton on a bearing of 285°.
It then flies 25 km on a bearing of 250° to Cirencester.
  a Draw a diagram to show this information.
  Show all the information inside the triangle formed by the three towns.
  b Find the distance from Abingdon to Cirencester using the cosine rule.
  c Find the bearing of Cirencester from Abingdon.

17 WXYZ is a tetrahedron.
Z is vertically above W.
WX = 17 cm, XY = 18 cm,
WZ = 6 cm and $\angle$WXY = 30°.
Find:
  a WY
  b YZ
  c XZ
  d $\angle$XZY
  e $\angle$ZXY

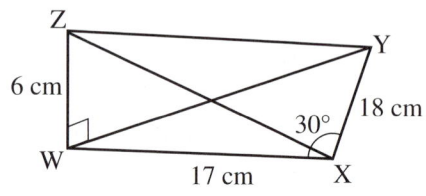
Z, Y, 6 cm, 18 cm, W, 17 cm, X, 30°

1 **a** Draw a pair of axes on 2 cm graph paper. Label the x axis from 0 to 180° using 2 cm per 20°. Label the y axis from 0 to 7 using 2 cm for each unit.

    b Draw the graph of $y = 2 \sin x + 4$.

    c Use the graph to solve the equation $2 \sin x + 4 = 5.1$
Show clearly on your graph how you found your answer.

2 You are going to prove that the sine rule is true.
Look at this triangle.
BX is perpendicular to AC.
h is the perpendicular height of the triangle.

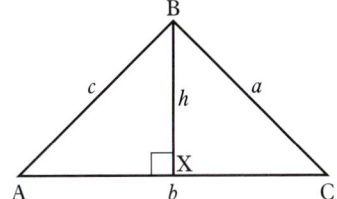

    a Use trigonometry in triangle ABX to find sin A.

    b Use trigonometry in triangle CBX to find sin C.

    c Use your answers to parts **a** and **b** to show that $c \sin A = a \sin C$.

    d Rearrange the equation in part **c** to prove that part of the sine rule is true.

    e Explain how this proves that the whole of the sine rule is true.

3 You are going to prove that the cosine rule is true.
Look at this triangle again.
Let AX $= x$.

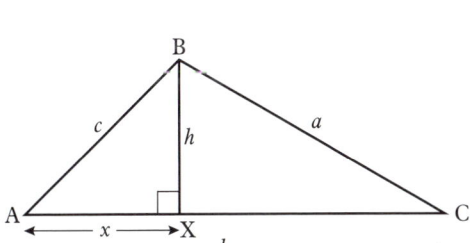

    a Use trigonometry in triangle ABX to show that $x = c \cos A$.

    b Use Pythagoras' theorem in triangle ABX to find h^2 in terms of x and c.

    c Use Pythagoras' theorem in triangle CBX to find a^2 in terms of h, b and x.

    d Use the equations in parts **a**, **b** and **c** to prove that the cosine rule is true.

4 Prove that the area of the triangle is
$\frac{1}{2} \times$ the product of two sides $\times$ the sine of the angle between them.

1 Solve the equation $\sin x = 0.43$ for values of x between $0°$ and $360°$. Round your answers to 1 dp.

2 Solve the equation $\cos x = 0.29$ for values of x between $0°$ and $360°$. Round your answers to 1 dp.

3 Find the exact values of x between $0°$ and $360°$ that solve each of these equations.

   a $\sin x = \dfrac{1}{\sqrt{2}}$ **b** $\cos x = -\dfrac{1}{\sqrt{2}}$

4 Sketch the graph of each of these equations for $0 \leqslant x < 360°$.

   a $y = \cos x$ **b** $y = \cos 2x$ **c** $y = \cos \dfrac{x}{2}$ **d** $y = \sin \dfrac{x}{3}$

5 **a** What is the maximum possible value of $6 \sin 2x$?
   b What is the minimum possible value of $6 \sin 2x$?
   c Sketch the graph of $y = 6 \sin 2x$ for $0° \leqslant x < 360°$.

6 Find the area of this triangle.

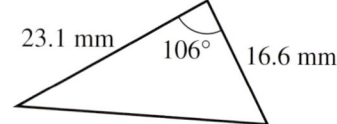

7 A ferry leaves a port P and travels 4.7 km on a bearing of $156°$ to a port Q. It then travels 8.2 km on a bearing of $054°$ to a port R.
   a Draw a diagram to show this information.
   b Show that $\angle PQR$ is $78°$.
   c Find the shortest distance from P to R.
   d Find the bearing of R from P.

8 ABCD is a tetrahedron.
   D is vertically above A.
   AB = 15 cm, BC = 7 cm,
   CD = 14 cm and $\angle ABC = 40°$.
   Find:

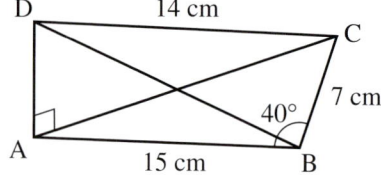

   a AC   **d** $\angle BDC$
   b AD   **e** $\angle DBC$
   c BD

21 Graphs: for real

1 Rates of change
Interpreting gradients of straight lines
Sketching graphs

2 Areas under graphs
Calculating areas under straight line graphs

CORE

3 Modelling
Modelling with exponential functions
Modelling with trigonometric functions

QUESTIONS

EXTENSION

TEST YOURSELF

1 Rates of change

How could you measure the speed at a particular point on the ride?

In Chapter 11 you used the fact that the gradient of a line tells you how steep it is. You can also use the gradient to measure how quickly the values on the vertical axis change compared with the values on the horizontal axis.

The gradient of this line is $\dfrac{20}{4} = 5$.

The units on the vertical axis are **metres**.
The units on the horizontal axis are **seconds**.

Distance is changing at the rate of **5 m/s**.

The **rate of change** of distance with respect to time is speed.
The gradient represents a speed of **5 m/s**.

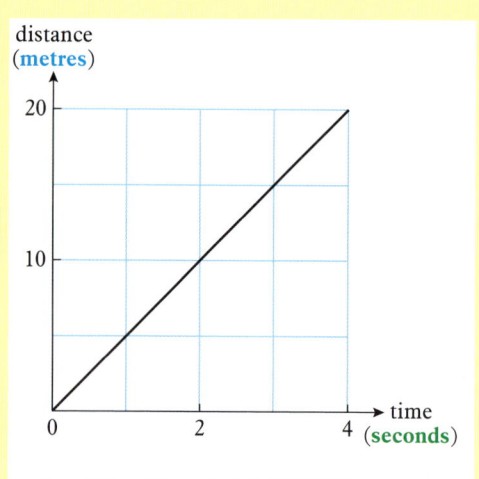

Exercise 21:1

1 What does the gradient of each graph represent?

a

b

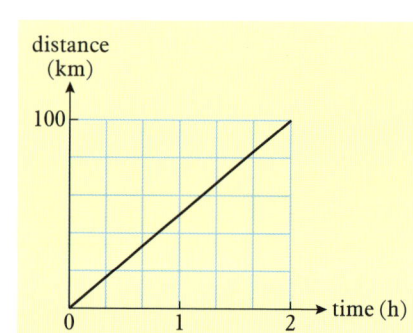

2 Steve and Jo are running a race over 5 miles.
The diagram shows the graphs of their progress.

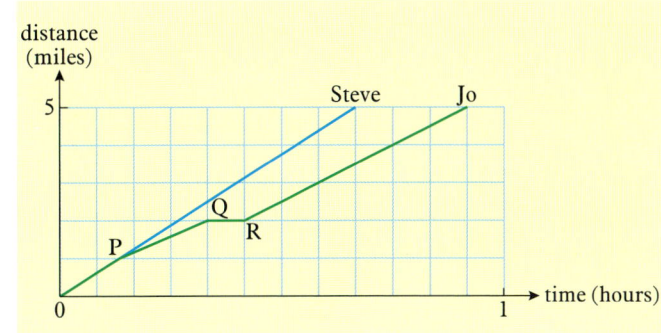

a Write down what you think happened at the points
(1) P   (2) Q   (3) R
b Describe Steve's speed during the race.
c Find Jo's average speed for the race. Give your answer to 1 dp.

Displacement is a vector. It stands for distance in a particular direction.

The gradient of this line is $-\dfrac{20}{5} = -4$

Displacement is changing at the rate of -4 **m/s**.

The rate of change of displacement with respect to time is velocity.
Velocity is a vector. It stands for speed in a particular direction.

The gradient represents a velocity of -4 **m/s**.
This is in the opposite direction to a velocity of **4 m/s**.

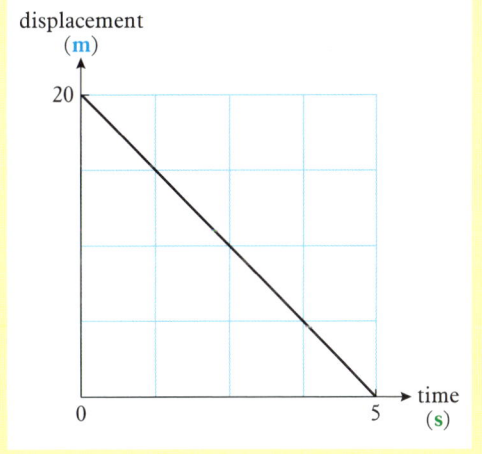

---

3 a Find the gradient of this line.
b What does the gradient represent?

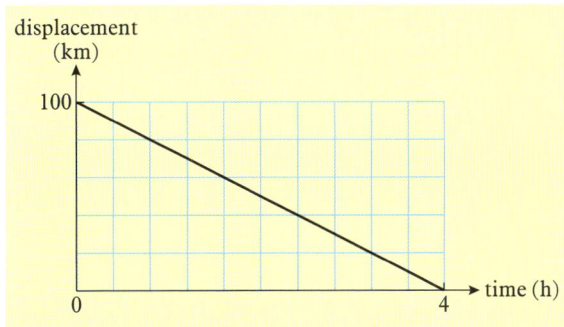

4 Kelly and Sam have a race over two lengths of a swimming pool.
This is the displacement–time graph for their race.

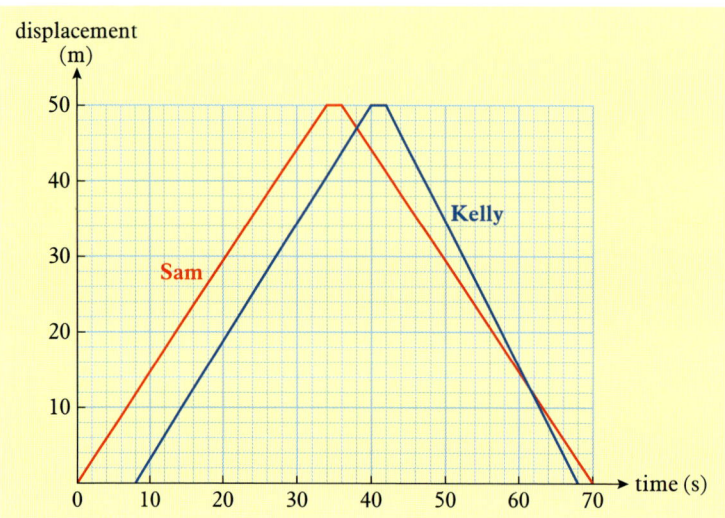

a How far did Sam swim before Kelly started the race?
b What was Kelly's velocity 40 seconds into the race?
c What was Sam's velocity 40 seconds into the race?
d Find the length of time that they were swimming in opposite directions.
e Who won the race?

Acceleration   Acceleration measures how quickly the velocity changes. It is the rate of change of velocity with respect to time.
The gradient of a velocity–time graph represents acceleration.

This graph shows how the vertical velocity of a parachutist changes during the first 4 seconds of fall.

The gradient of this line is $\dfrac{40}{4} = 10$

The units on the vertical axis are **m/s**.
The units on the horizontal axis are **s**.

Velocity is changing at the rate of **10** (m/s)/s. You write this as **10 m/s²**.

The gradient represents an acceleration of **10 m/s²**.

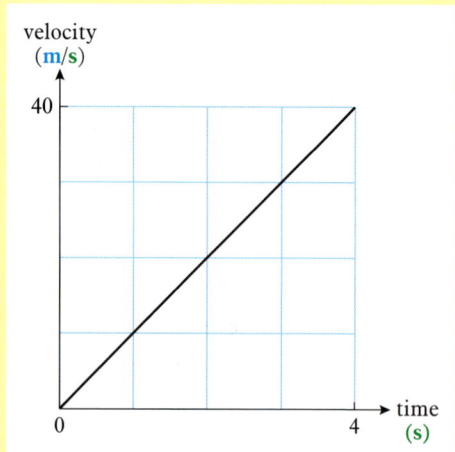

5 Find the acceleration shown by these graphs. Include the units in your answer.

a

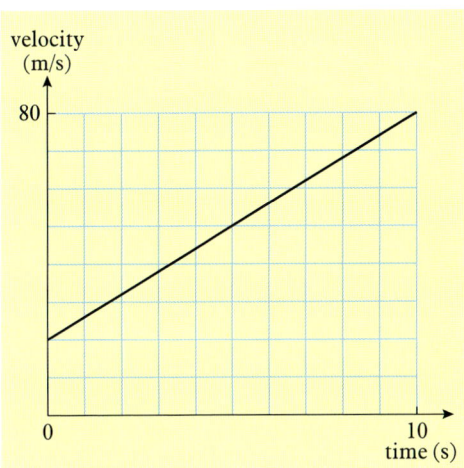

b

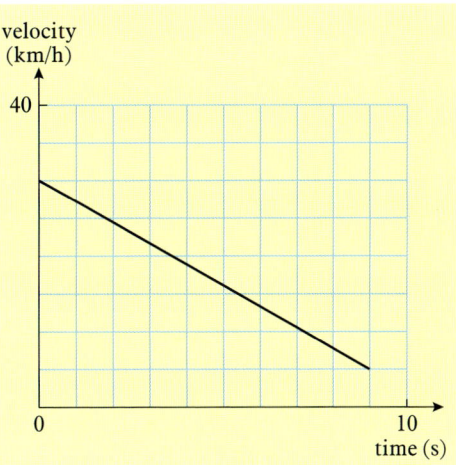

Constant acceleration	A straight line on a velocity–time graph always shows **constant acceleration**. This means that the acceleration does not change at any point along the straight line. It is also known as **uniform acceleration**.

---

6 A stationary car moves off and, with constant acceleration, reaches a speed of 15 m/s in 6 seconds.
   It travels at this speed for 60 seconds.
   The car then decelerates uniformly and stops in a further 4 seconds.
   a Draw a velocity–time graph to show this information.
   b Work out the acceleration of the car at each stage of its journey.

7 A sprinter accelerates uniformly from his starting blocks and reaches a speed of 12 m/s in the first 3 seconds. He maintains this speed for a further 7 seconds. He then decelerates uniformly to a stop in 5 seconds.
   a Draw a velocity–time graph to show this information.
   b Work out the acceleration of the sprinter at each stage of his journey.
   c How far would he run in 1 hour were he able to keep up the speed of 12 m/s?

Sketching graphs

Sometimes you will need to just sketch a graph rather than plot it accurately.
The important thing to consider is the gradient of the graph.
This will always be showing a rate of change.

Example　This milk bottle is filled with water from a tap flowing at a steady rate.
Sketch a graph to show how the height of water in the bottle changes as it
fills up. Describe and label each part of your graph.

a　At first the graph is a straight line as the height of the water is
changing at a steady rate. This is because the sides of the bottle are
vertical at this point.

b　As the bottle starts to narrow, the height changes more quickly.
This means that the gradient of the graph increases. As the bottle
narrows the height increases more quickly. So this part of the graph is
curved.

c　The final part of the graph shows what happens as the water reaches
the neck of the bottle. This is the steepest part of the graph. It is a
straight line again as the sides are vertical.

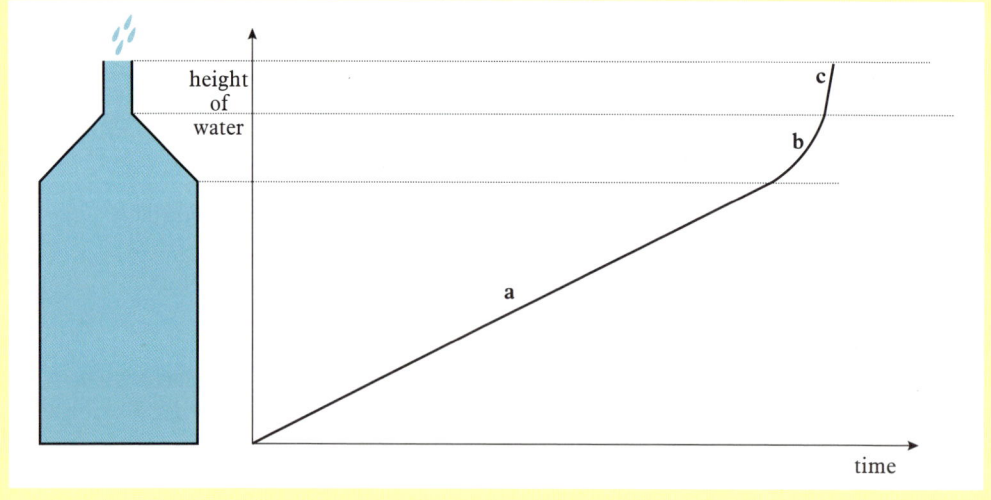

Exercise 21:2

1 Sketch graphs to show the height of water in each of these bottles as they are filled from a tap. Assume that the water is flowing at a steady rate. Describe and label each part of your graph.

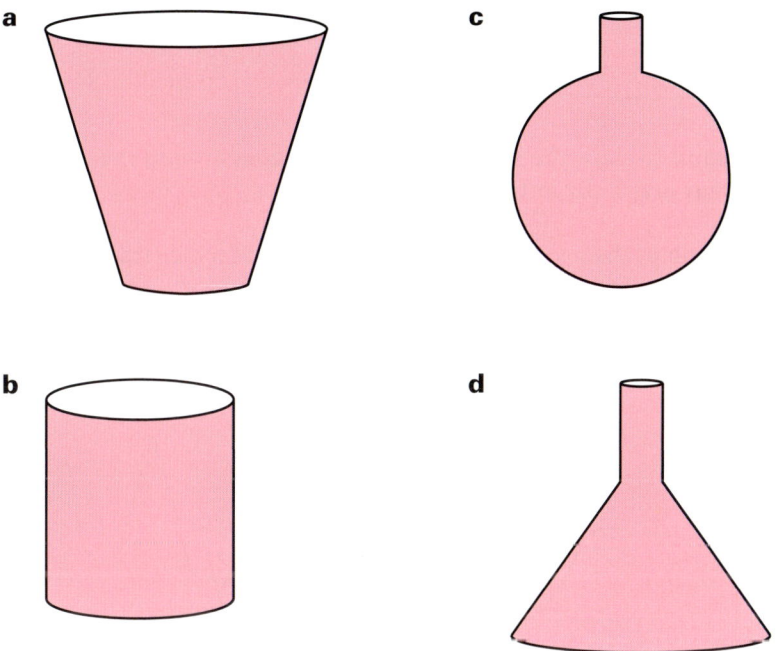

a

c

b

d

2 Sketch the bottles that go with each of these graphs.

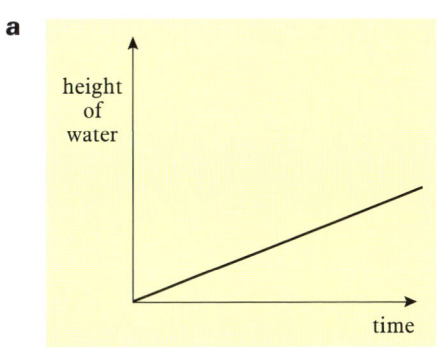

a

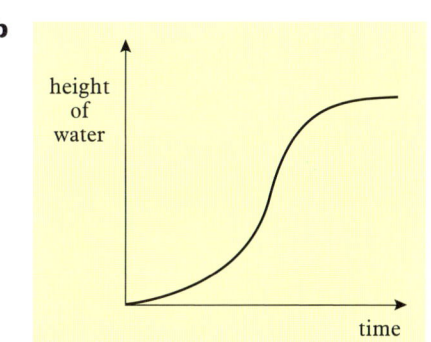

b

3   Look at this racing track.
    Think carefully about the speed of a car as it goes around the track.
    It will slow down as it approaches the corners and accelerate out of them.
    The car will maintain a steady speed on the straights.

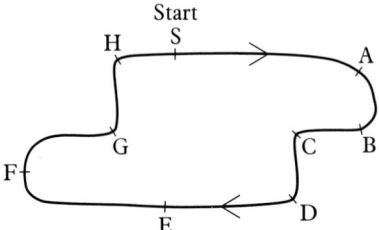

Sketch a graph to show the speed of the car as it goes around the track.
Mark on your graph the letters on the track.

4   Here is a graph of the speed of a car as it goes around a race track.
    Draw a sketch of the track.
    Mark the lettered points on the graph on the track.

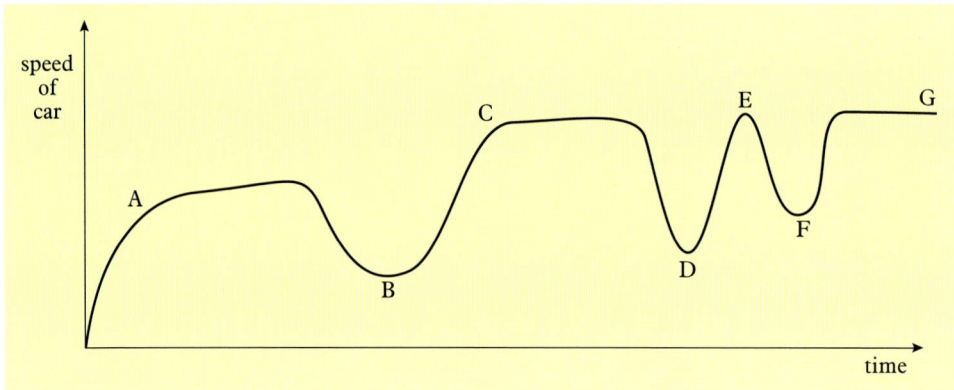

5   Raphy the cat suffers from fleas.
    The fleas are more common at certain times of the year.
    This graph shows the number of fleas on Raphy.

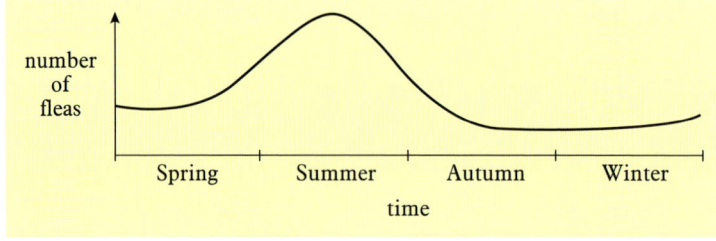

Describe the changes in the flea population.
Say when the population is decreasing most rapidly and when it is
increasing most rapidly.

2 Areas under graphs

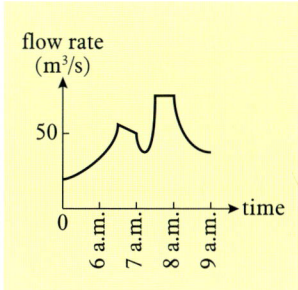

The flow rate of water from a reservoir varies throughout the day to meet the needs of consumers.

If you run for 10 seconds at 5 m/s you will cover a distance of $10 \times 5 = 50$ **m**.

You can show this on a graph.
The area under the graph represents the distance travelled in **metres**.

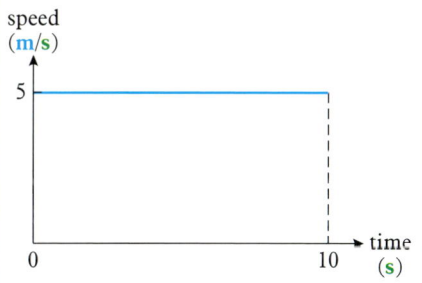

To see why this works, you need to look at how the units on the axes combine when you multiply them.

The graph has units of **m/s** on the vertical axis and **s** on the horizontal axis.

$$\boxed{\dfrac{\mathbf{m/s}}{\mathbf{s}}}$$

Each unit of area represents **m/s** $\times$ **s**.

You can think of **m/s** as $\dfrac{\mathbf{m}}{\mathbf{s}}$ so **m/s** $\times$ **s** is

the same as $\dfrac{\mathbf{m}}{\mathbf{s}} \times \mathbf{s} = \mathbf{m}$.

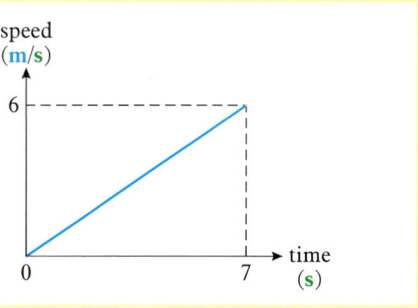

So, the area under any speed–time graph represents the distance travelled.

Using the formula for the area of a triangle, the area under this graph represents a distance of $\frac{1}{2} \times 7 \times 6 = 21$ m.

Exercise 21:3

1 Work out the area under each of these graphs.
Write down what the area represents.

a

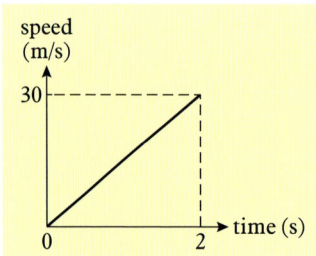

b

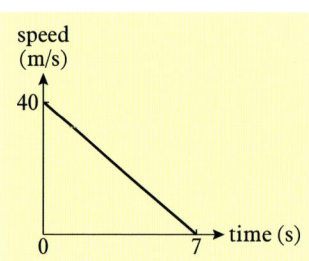

c

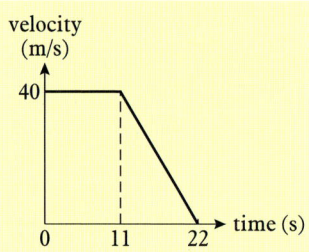

d

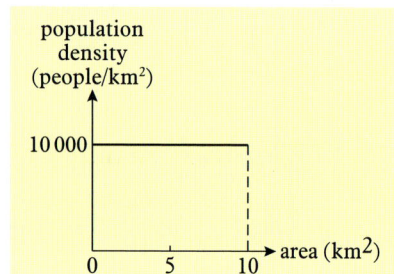

e

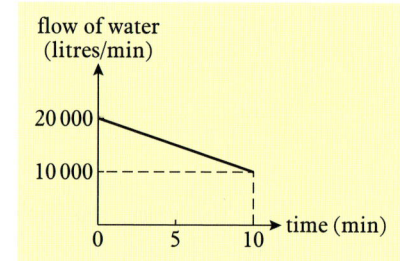

f

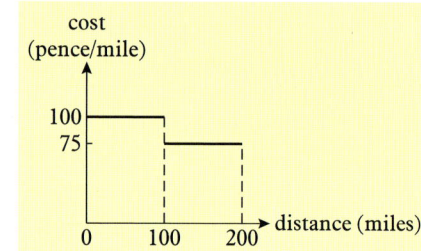

Example The graph shows the speed of
a train as it travels between
two stations.
a What is the maximum speed
of the train?
b What is the distance between
the stations?
c What is the average speed of
the train?

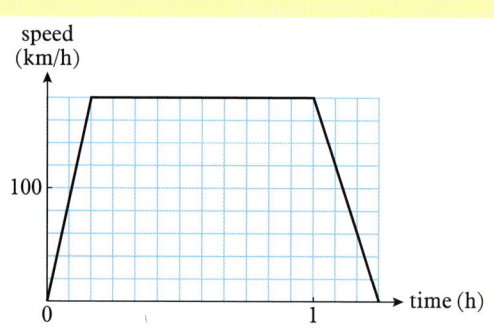

a The maximum speed of the train is shown at the highest point of the graph.
Each square on the vertical axis represents 20 km/h.
Maximum speed = 180 km/h.

b Each unit of area of the graph represents km/h × h = km.
You find the distance between the stations by working out the area under the graph. The answer will be in km.

The area of a trapezium is $\frac{1}{2}(a + b)h$.

Each square on the horizontal scale represents $\frac{1}{12}$ hour.

So the distance between the stations is

$$\frac{1}{2}(\tfrac{10}{12} + \tfrac{15}{12}) \times 180$$
$$= \frac{1}{2} \times \tfrac{25}{12} \times 180$$
$$= 187.5 \text{ km}$$

c The average speed of the train is $\dfrac{\text{total distance travelled}}{\text{total time taken}}$

$$= \dfrac{187.5}{\frac{15}{12}}$$

Key in: **1** **8** **7** **.** **5** **÷** **(** **1** **5** **÷** **1** **2** **)** **=**

$$= 150 \text{ km/h}$$

Exercise 21:4

1 The graph shows the speed of a car between two sets of traffic lights.
  a What is the maximum speed reached by the car?
  b What is the distance between the traffic lights?
  c What is the average speed of the car?

2 The graph shows the speed of a carriage on a fairground ride.
   a How far does the carriage travel during the ride?
   b What is its average speed?

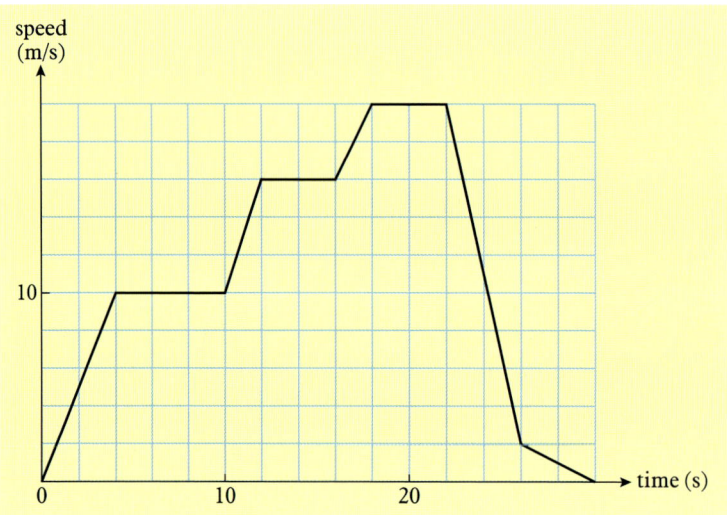

3 This graph shows the rate at which water is flowing into a bath in litres per second.
   a How much water is there in the bath when it is full?
   b What is the average rate of flow of water as the bath is filled up?

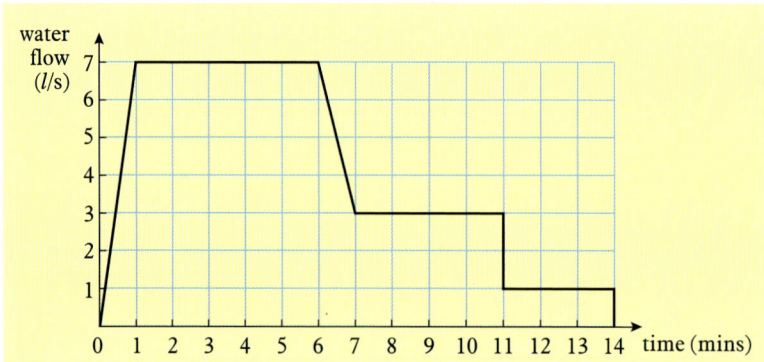

3 Modelling

You can use mathematics to predict the outcome of an experiment—usually.

Exponential function	Exponent is another word for power. An **exponential function** is a function where the variable is the power or exponent.

The exponential function $f(x) = pq^x$ is very important because its behaviour models the way that changes occur in many situations in everyday life.

Once you know the values of p and q you can use the function to predict how the situation will change in the future.

Example

The temperature $T\,°C$ of an object is modelled by $T = pq^t$.
t stands for the time in minutes since the object started to cool.
p and q are constants.

a Use the information in the sketch to find the values of p and q.

b Find the temperature of the object when $t = 5$.

a From the sketch $T = 100$ when $t = 0$.

$$\text{so } 100 = pq^0$$
$$q^0 = 1 \quad \text{so } 100 = p \times 1$$
$$p = 100.$$

You can also see from the sketch that

$T = 25$ when $t = 2$, so $25 = 100q^2$
$$q^2 = 0.25$$
$$\text{so } q = 0.5$$

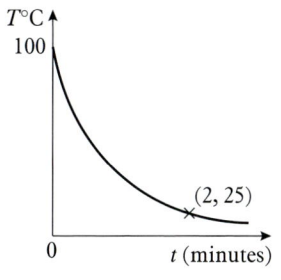

b You can now use the formula $T = 100(0.5)^t$ to find T at any time.

$$\text{When } t = 5, T = 100(0.5)^5$$
$$= 3.125$$

So the temperature of the object when $t = 5$ is 3.1°C to 1 dp.

Exercise 21:5

1 A large block of ice is allowed to melt. The sketch shows how the amount of ice that is left changes with time. The amount W kg that remains after t hours is modelled by $W = pq^t$. The values of p and q are constant.
  a Use the sketch to find p and q.
  b Find the amount of ice that is left after 8 hours.

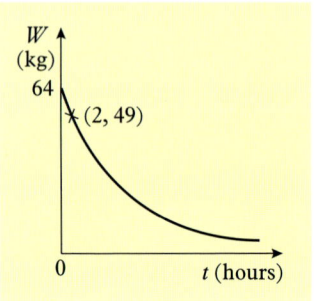

2 The amount of a drug d mg that remains in the body t hours after a dose is taken is modelled by $d = pq^t$. The values of p and q are constant.
  a Use the sketch to find p and q.
  b Find the amount of the drug that remains in the body after 5 hours.

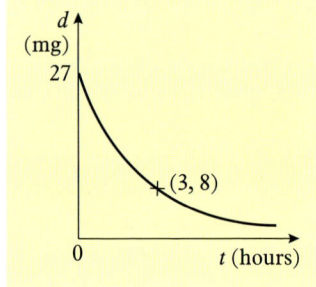

3 A colony of bacteria is placed in a culture dish. After t hours, the number of bacteria, N, is modelled by $N = pq^t$. The values of p and q are constant.
  a Use the sketch to find p and q.
  b Find the number of bacteria after 10 hours. Round your answer to 2 sf.
  ● c Do you think that the model will work for large values of t? Explain your answer.

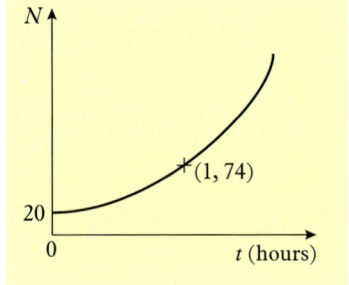

A different kind of function is needed to model behaviour that repeats itself in a cycle. You can use trigonometric functions to do this.

Example The depth of water in a harbour changes with the tide.

The depth d m is modelled by
$d = 2\cos(30t)° + 3.5$ where t is the number of hours after high tide.

  a How deep is the water at high tide?
  b How deep is the water at low tide?
  c High tide is at 12 noon. Find the depth of water at 5 pm.

a The largest possible value of $\cos(30t)°$ is 1.
  So at high tide $d = 2 \times 1 + 3.5 = 5.5$ m.
b The least possible value of $\cos(30t)°$ is -1.
  So at low tide $d = 2 \times -1 + 3.5 = 1.5$ m.
c At 5 pm $t = 5$. Using $d = 2\cos(30t)° + 3.5$
              gives $d = 2\cos(150)° + 3.5$
                  $= 1.767 ...$
  The depth of water at 5 pm is 1.8 m to 1 dp.

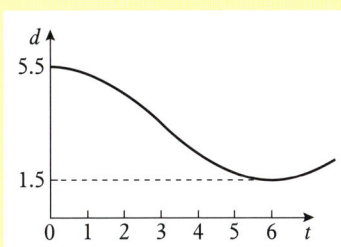

4 Use the formula $d = 2\sin(30t)° + 4$ to model the depth d m of water in a harbour. In the formula t is the number of hours after midnight.
  a What is the depth of the water at midnight?
  b What is the depth of the water at high tide?
  c What is the depth of the water at low tide?
  d What is the depth of water at 2 am?
  e What time is it when high tide first occurs?
  f What time is it when low tide first occurs?
  g Sketch the graph of d against t for $0 \leqslant t \leqslant 12$.

5 Paul tries to use the formula $d = 4\sin(30t)° + 3$ to model the depth d m of water in a harbour. He takes t to be the number of hours after midnight.
  a Use Paul's formula to predict the depth of the water at high tide.
  b Use Paul's formula to predict the depth of the water at low tide.
  c Explain how you know that the model must be wrong.

1 The graph shows the distance travelled by a car between noon and 2 pm.
The car is driven through town on to the motorway.

  a When does the car join the motorway?

  b What is the speed of the car through town?

  c What is the speed of the car on the motorway?

  d What is the average speed of the car between noon and 2 pm?

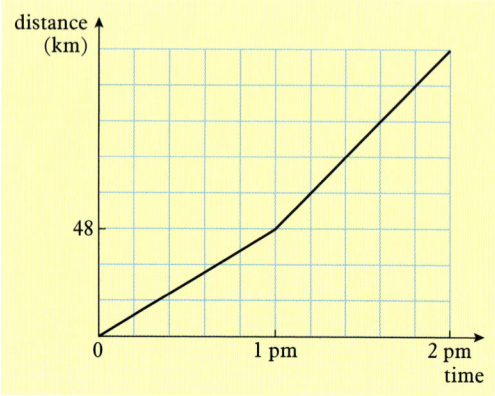

2 This graph shows how the volume of water changes in a storage tank.

  a Find the gradient of the line PQ.

  b What does this represent?

  c Write down the gradient of QR.

  d What does this show?

  e Write down the gradient of RS.

  f What information does the sign of the gradient give for this graph?

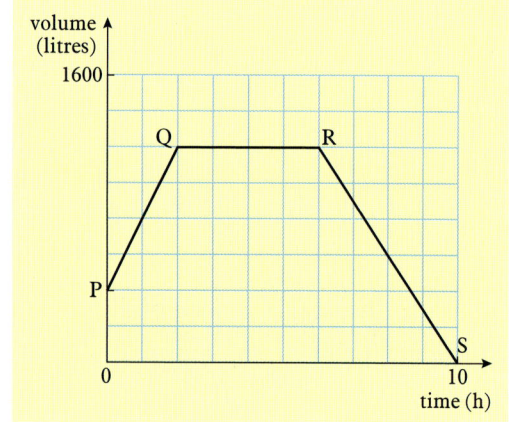

3 The graph shows how the flow rate of water from a pipe changes during a 3 minute interval.

  a Find the gradient of OP.

  b What does the gradient represent?
  Include the units in your answer.

  c Find the gradient of PQ.

  d What does the sign of the gradient show?

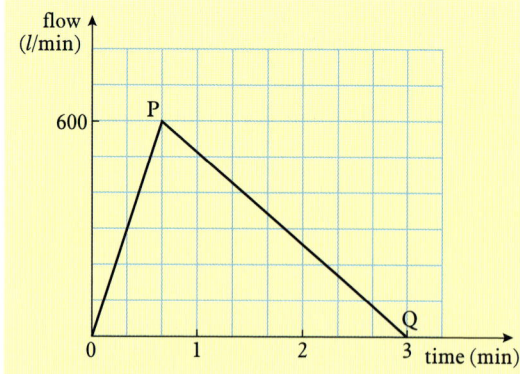

4 a What does the area of each square represent in the graph of question **3**?

  b Find the total area under the graph.

  c Write down what the area represents.

5 A stone is dropped from the top of a cliff and lands in the sea 4 seconds later.
The graph shows how the speed of the stone changes during its flight.

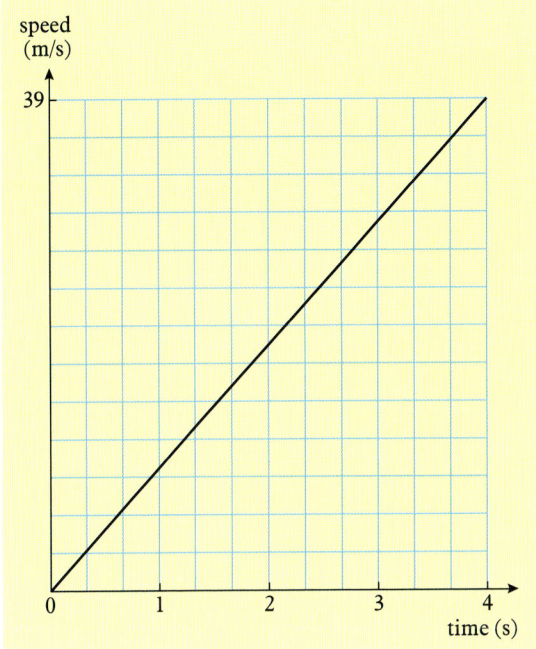

a What is the speed of the stone when it lands in the sea?
b What is the acceleration of the stone?
c What is the height of the cliff?

6 Sketch graphs to show the height of water in each of these bottles as they are filled from a tap. Assume the water is flowing at a steady rate. Describe and label each part of your graph.

a

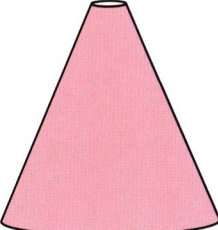

b

1   **a**   Write down the area of this trapezium.

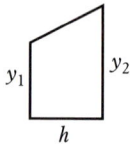

    b   Show that the area under this graph between P and Q is approximately

$$\frac{h}{2}(y_1 + 2y_2 + 2y_3 + y_4)$$

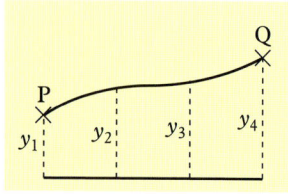

    c   The velocity v m/s of an object t seconds after it starts from rest is modelled by $v = t^2$.
       (1)   Sketch the graph of v against t for $0 \leqslant t \leqslant 4$.
       (2)   Use three trapeziums to estimate the distance that the object moves between $t = 1$ and $t = 4$. Use the formula in part **b** to help you.

2   The diagram shows Jane's velocity during a bungee jump.

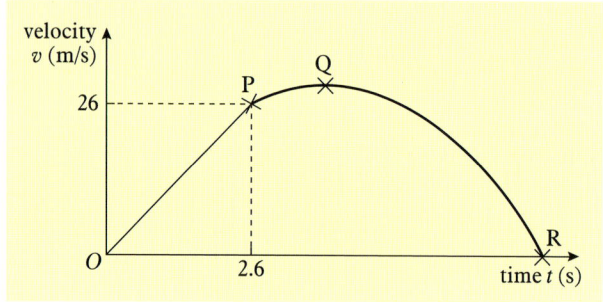

    a   Describe what is happening between these points on the sketch.
       (1) O and P   (2) P and Q   (3) Q and R
    b   Calculate the length of the rope.
    c   The velocity v m/s between points P and R on the graph is modelled by $v = 30 \cos(20t - 80)$. Use the model to find:
       (1)   Jane's maximum velocity
       (2)   the time taken for Jane to reach the lowest point
    d   Continue the sketch for Jane's upward movement. State any assumptions that you make.

1 This graph shows the distance Andrew covers during a race.

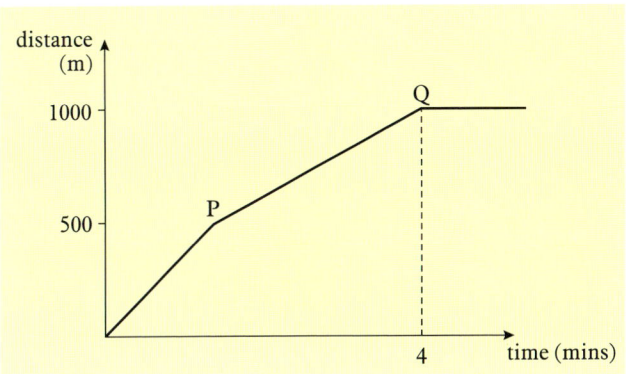

a Write down what happens at points P and Q.
b Find Andrew's average speed during the race.
Give your answer in metres per second.

2 This is a distance–time graph showing two trains.

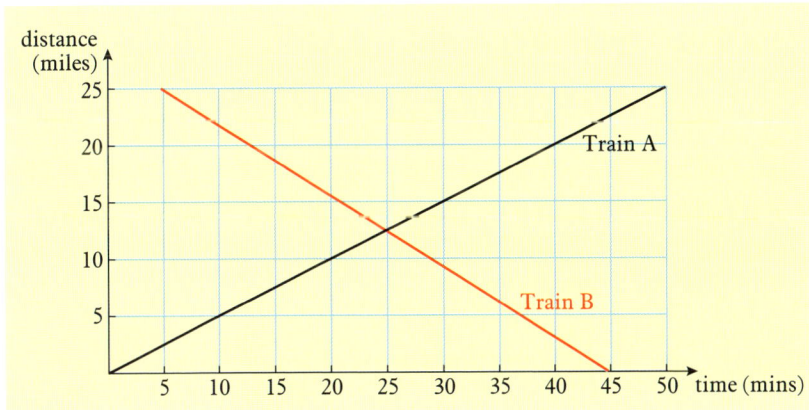

a Which train set off first?
b Explain how you can tell that the two trains are travelling in opposite directions.
c After how long did the trains pass each other?
d Work out the average speed of each train.

3 A stationary bus moves off with uniform acceleration.
It reaches a speed of 14 m/s in 10 s.
a Draw a velocity–time graph to show this information.
b Calculate the acceleration of the bus.

4 Sketch graphs to show the height of water in each of these bottles as they are filled with water. Assume that the water is flowing at a steady rate. Describe and label each part of your graph.

a

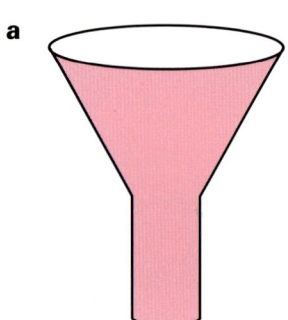

b

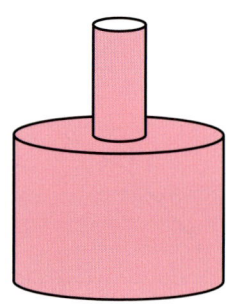

5 Sketch the bottles that go with each of these graphs showing the height of water in the bottle as they are filled at a uniform rate.

a

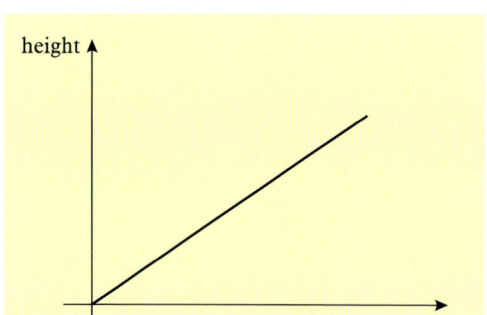

b

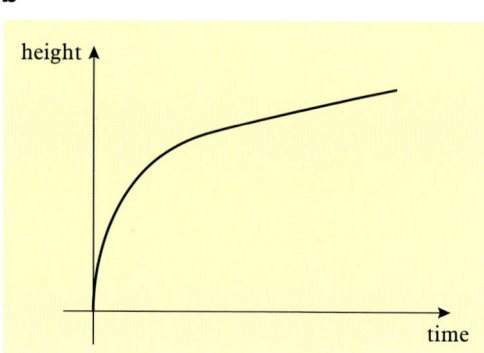

6 This graph shows the speed of a car between two sets of road works. Find the distance travelled by the car.

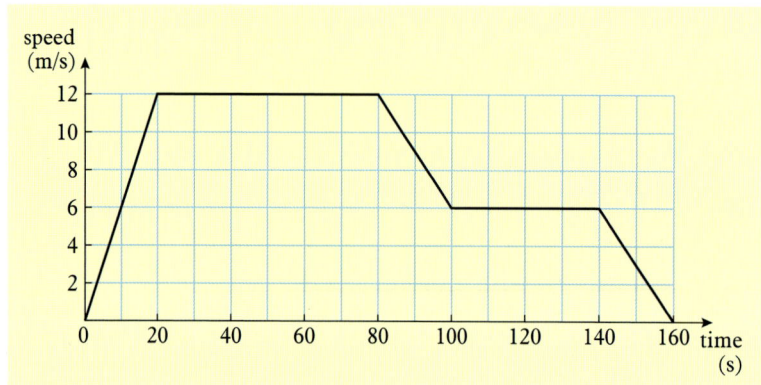

540

CHAPTER 1

1 a

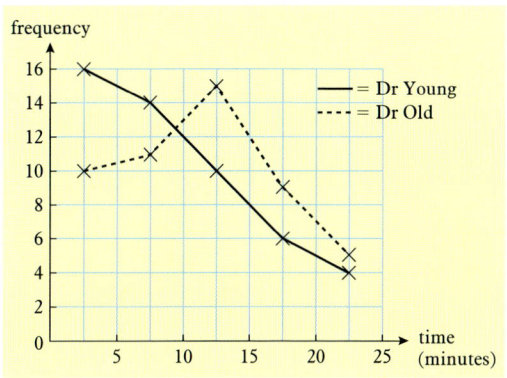

b Dr Young sees more patients in less time.
They both spend a long time with a few patients.

2

Area	$20 \leqslant A$ < 40	$40 \leqslant A$ < 60	$60 \leqslant A$ < 80	$80 \leqslant A$ < 100	$100 \leqslant A$ < 140	$140 \leqslant A$ < 180	$180 \leqslant A$ < 240	$240 \leqslant A$ < 300
Number of cards	8	18	17	15	12	11	6	3
Number of widths of 20 cm^2	1	1	1	1	2	2	3	3
Frequency per 20 cm^2	8	18	17	15	6	5.5	2	1

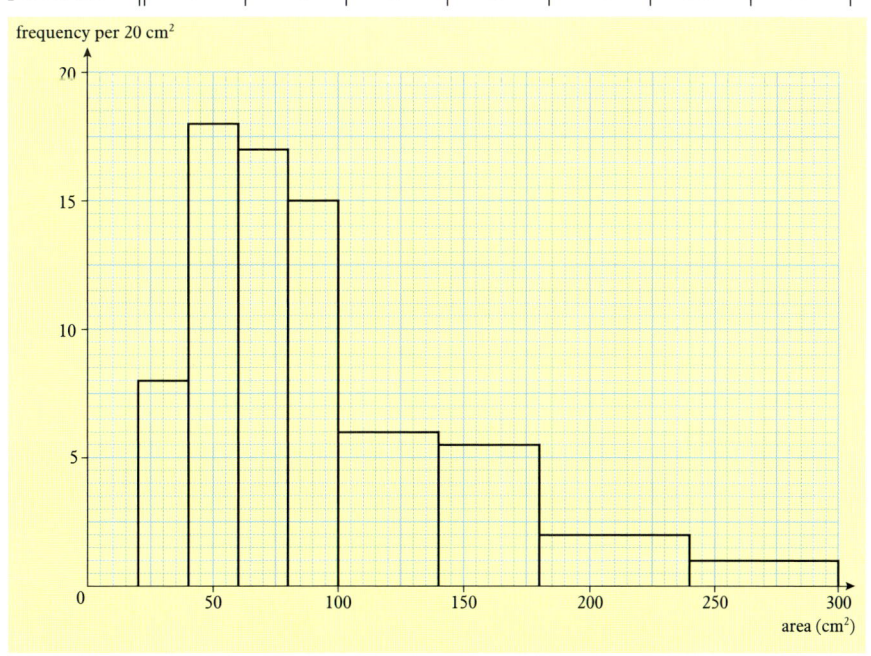

3

Rainfall	$0 \leqslant r < 2$	$2 \leqslant r < 5$	$5 \leqslant r < 10$	$10 \leqslant r < 15$	$15 \leqslant r < 30$
Town A, days	12	9	4	2	3
Width	2	3	5	5	15
Frequency density	6	3	0.8	0.4	0.2

Rainfall	$0 \leqslant r < 2$	$2 \leqslant r < 5$	$5 \leqslant r < 10$	$10 \leqslant r < 15$	$15 \leqslant r < 30$
Town B, days	4	3	8	12	3
Width	2	3	5	5	15
Frequency density	2	1	1.6	2.4	0.2

a

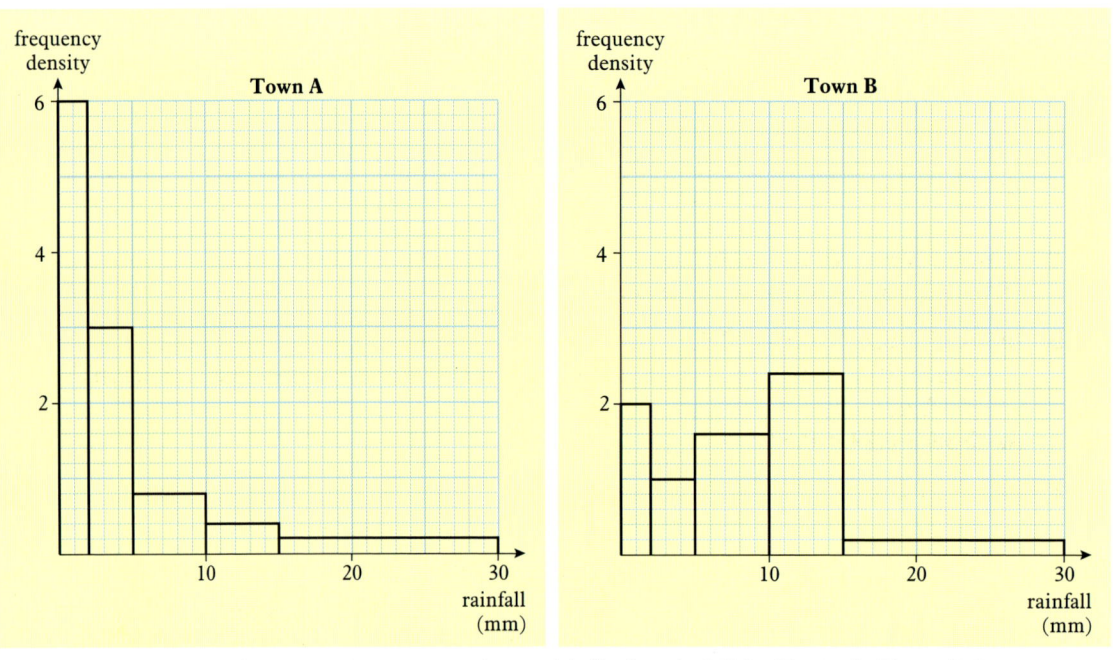

b There are many more days with little rainfall in Town A. Town B has more wetter days although both towns have the same number of very wet days.

CHAPTER 2

1 **a** $1 - 0.85 = 0.15$
   b $0.85 \times 0.6 = 0.51$
   c $0.15 \times 0.4 = 0.06$
   d $0.85 \times 0.4 = 0.34$
   e $0.85 \times 0.4 + 0.15 \times 0.6 = 0.34 + 0.09 = 0.43$

2 **a** $P(Q \text{ and } R) = P(Q) \times P(R) = \dfrac{1}{4} \times \dfrac{1}{3} = \dfrac{1}{12}$

b $P(S \text{ or } T) = P(S) + P(T) = \dfrac{2}{5} + \dfrac{1}{2} = \dfrac{4}{10} + \dfrac{5}{10} = \dfrac{9}{10}$

c If the events are independent,
$P(A \text{ and } B) = P(A) \times P(B) = 0.4 \times 0.2 = 0.08$
$0.08 \neq 0.075$ so the events are not independent

d $P(C) + P(D) = 0.85 + 0.3 = 1.15$
but probability can only lie between 0 and 1 so C and D are not
mutually exclusive

3 **a**

	3	4	5	6	7
1	1, 3	1, 4	1, 5	1, 6	1, 7
2	2, 3	2, 4	2, 5	2, 6	2, 7
3	3, 3	3, 4	3, 5	3, 6	3, 7
4	4, 3	4, 4	4, 5	4, 6	4, 7
5	5, 3	5, 4	5, 5	5, 6	5, 7

b $\dfrac{4}{25}$ **c** $\dfrac{3}{25}$ **d** $\dfrac{5}{25} = \dfrac{1}{5}$ **e** $\dfrac{3}{25}$ **f** $\dfrac{18}{25}$

4 $100\% - 35\% = 65\% = 0.65$
The probability it will not rain is 0.65

5 **a** $0.38 + 0.29 + 0.19 = 0.86$
Probabilities must add up to one so there must be at least one other colour in
the box.

b $0.38 + 0.29 = 0.67$

6 **a**

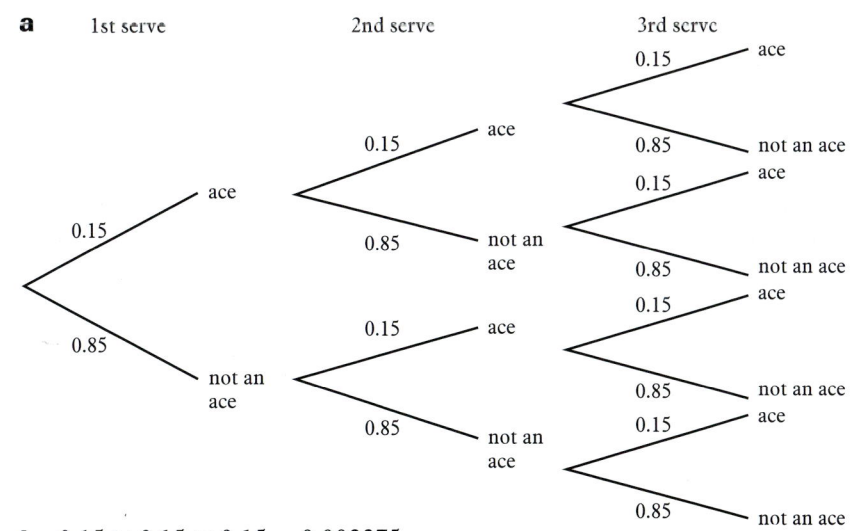

b $0.15 \times 0.15 \times 0.15 = 0.003375$
c $1 - \text{Probability (no aces)} = 1 - (0.85 \times 0.85 \times 0.85)$
$= 1 - 0.614125 = 0.385875$

d $0.15 \times 0.15 \times 0.85 + 0.15 \times 0.85 \times 0.15 + 0.85 \times 0.15 \times 0.15$
= 0.019125 + 0.019125 + 0.019125 = 0.057375

e 1 − Probability (3 aces) = 1 − 0.003375 = 0.996625

CHAPTER 3

1 a 256 + 328 + 156 + 208 + 297 = 1245   Mean = 1245 ÷ 5 = 249
  b 6 × 259 = 1554, 1554 − 1245 = 309

2 a

Amount, A (£)	Number of families, f	Mid-value, x	fx
$0 < A \leqslant 10$	6	5	30
$10 < A \leqslant 20$	14	15	210
$20 < A \leqslant 30$	22	25	550
$30 < A \leqslant 40$	17	35	595
$40 < A \leqslant 50$	8	45	360

$$\Sigma f = 67 \qquad \Sigma fx = 1745$$

$$\text{Estimate for the mean} = \frac{\Sigma fx}{\Sigma f} = \frac{1745}{67} = £26.04$$

b Because you use the mid-value to represent each group, not the actual data values.

3 a, c, d

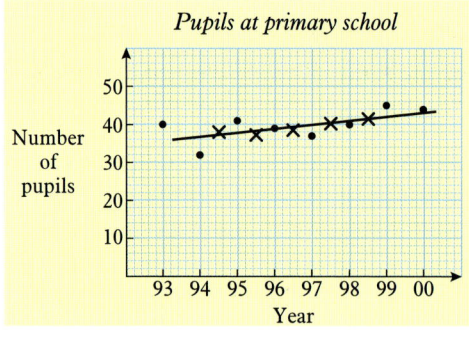

Pupils at primary school

b 40 + 32 + 41 + 39 = 152;   152 ÷ 4 = 38
  32 + 41 + 39 + 37 = 149;   149 ÷ 4 = 37.25
  41 + 39 + 37 + 40 = 157;   157 ÷ 4 = 39.25
  39 + 37 + 40 + 45 = 161;   161 ÷ 4 = 40.25
  37 + 40 + 45 + 44 = 166;   166 ÷ 4 = 41.5

e The numbers in the school could suddenly drop if a larger group of pupils than normal leave. The year 2001 is outside the range of the data.

4 **a** (1)

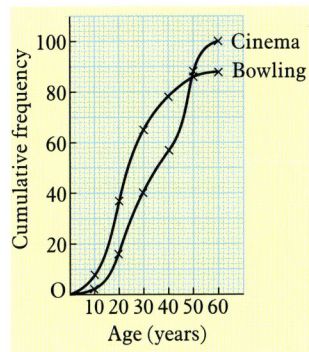

(2) Cinema median = 36 years
Bowling median = 22 years
Cinema interquartile range
= 46 − 25 = 21 years
Bowling interquartile range
= 30 − 15 = 15 years

b On average the people who go bowling are younger than those who go to the cinema and there is less variation in their ages

5 17, 17, 19, 19, 20, 20, 21, 23, 24, 26, 27, 27, 31, 33, 34, 36, 37, 38, 39, 41

a Median time $(26 + 27) \div 2 = 26.5$

b Lower quartile $(20 + 20) \div 2 = 20$
Upper quartile $(34 + 36) \div 2 = 35$

c

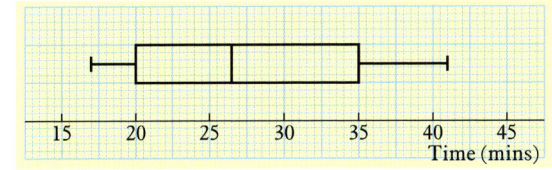

d (1) 27.5 minutes   (3) 20
(2) $31 - 23 = 8$ minutes   (4) 36

e They both take about the same time on average to drive to work. However Rudi's times are more consistent than those of Cara.

CHAPTER 4

1 **a** $\frac{2}{6} = \frac{1}{3}$

b $\frac{1}{3} \times \frac{1}{3} \times \frac{1}{3} = \frac{1}{27}$

c $P(\text{red}) = \frac{3}{6} = \frac{1}{2}$ $P(\text{black}) = \frac{1}{3}$
$P(\text{red followed by a black}) = \frac{1}{2} \times \frac{1}{3} = \frac{1}{6}$

d $\left(\frac{1}{3}\right)^n$ or $\left(\frac{2}{6}\right)^n$

e $P(\text{all black}) + P(\text{all red}) + P(\text{all white})$
$= \frac{1}{3} \times \frac{1}{3} \times \frac{1}{3} + \frac{1}{2} \times \frac{1}{2} \times \frac{1}{2} + \frac{1}{6} \times \frac{1}{6} \times \frac{1}{6}$
$= \frac{1}{27} + \frac{1}{8} + \frac{1}{216} = \frac{1}{6}$

f $P(\text{not a black on each throw}) = \frac{4}{6} = \frac{2}{3}$ so P (not a black on 3 throws) $= \frac{2}{3} \times \frac{2}{3} \times \frac{2}{3}$
$P(\text{at least 1 black}) = 1 - P(\text{no blacks}) = 1 - \frac{2}{3} \times \frac{2}{3} \times \frac{2}{3}$
$= 1 - \frac{8}{27}$
$= \frac{19}{27}$

g $200 \times \frac{1}{3} \approx 67$ blacks

2 **a** $0.06 \times 0.05 = 0.003$
   b $0.06 \times 0.05 \times 0.02 = 0.00006$
   c $(1 - 0.06) \times (1 - 0.05) \times (1 - 0.02) = 0.94 \times 0.95 \times 0.98 = 0.87514$
   d $P(\text{at least one}) = 1 - P(\text{none}) = 1 - 0.87514$
$$= 0.12486$$
   e $12\,000 \times 0.12486 = 1498.32$
$$\approx 1498 \text{ bottles}$$

3 **a** $\frac{3}{50}$ **b** $200 \times \frac{7}{50} = 28$ cars

4 **a**

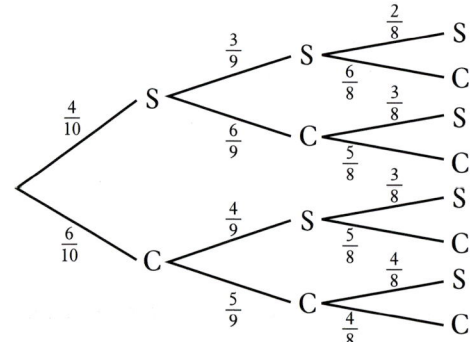

1st day   2nd day   3rd day

b $\dfrac{4}{10} \times \dfrac{3}{9} \times \dfrac{2}{8} = \dfrac{24}{720} = \dfrac{1}{30}$

c $\dfrac{4}{10} \times \dfrac{3}{9} \times \dfrac{6}{8} + \dfrac{4}{10} \times \dfrac{6}{9} \times \dfrac{3}{8} + \dfrac{6}{10} \times \dfrac{4}{9} \times \dfrac{3}{8}$

$$= \dfrac{72}{720} + \dfrac{72}{720} + \dfrac{72}{720} = \dfrac{1}{10} + \dfrac{1}{10} + \dfrac{1}{10} = \dfrac{3}{10}$$

d $1 - P(\text{no strawberry yoghurts}) = 1 - \dfrac{6}{10} \times \dfrac{5}{9} \times \dfrac{4}{8}$

$$= 1 - \dfrac{120}{720} = 1 - \dfrac{1}{6} = \dfrac{5}{6}$$

5 Total number of duvets $= 120$

   a $\dfrac{14}{120} = \dfrac{7}{60}$ **c** $8 + 5 + 2 = 15,\ \dfrac{15}{120} = \dfrac{1}{8}$

   b $17 + 12 + 2 = 31,\ \dfrac{31}{120}$ **d** $14 + 22 + 8 + 21 + 19 + 5 = 89,\ \dfrac{89}{120}$

6 Look back at recorded data.

CHAPTER 5

1 **a** $0.4 = \frac{4}{10} = \frac{2}{5}$

    b $0.\dot{7} = \frac{7}{9}$

    c $0.45 = \frac{45}{100} = \frac{9}{20}$

    d $0.\dot{4}\dot{5} = \frac{45}{99} = \frac{5}{11}$

    e $0.6\dot{7}\dot{2} = 0.6 + 0.0\dot{7}\dot{2}$

$$= 0.6 + (0.\dot{7}\dot{2} \div 10)$$
$$= 0.6 + (\tfrac{72}{99} \div 10)$$
$$= \tfrac{6}{10} + \tfrac{72}{990}$$
$$= \frac{6 \times 99 + 72}{990}$$
$$= \tfrac{666}{990} = \tfrac{37}{55}$$

2 **a** $20 = 2 \times 2 \times 5$
$26 = 2 \times 13$
HCF $= 2$

    b $30 = 2 \times 3 \times 5$
$45 = 3 \times 3 \times 5$
$60 = 2 \times 2 \times 3 \times 5$
HCF $= 3 \times 5 = 15$

3 **a** $6 = 2 \times 3$
$14 = 2 \times 7$
LCM $= 2 \times 7 \times 3 = 42$

    b $12 = 2 \times 2 \times 3$
$18 = 2 \times 3 \times 3$
LCM $= 2 \times 3 \times 3 \times 2 = 36$

4 $124 = 2 \times 2 \times 31$

5 $\frac{4}{60} = \frac{1}{15}$

    $15 = 3 \times 5$ The 3 means that this will produce recurring decimal

6 **a** $\sqrt{9 \times 2} = \sqrt{9} \times \sqrt{2} = 3\sqrt{2}$

    b $\sqrt{80} = \sqrt{4} \times \sqrt{20} = 2\sqrt{4 \times 5} = 2 \times 2\sqrt{5} = 4\sqrt{5}$

    c $\sqrt{99} = \sqrt{9} \times \sqrt{11} = 3\sqrt{11}$

    d $\sqrt{450} = \sqrt{9} \times \sqrt{50} = 3 \times \sqrt{25} \times \sqrt{2} = 3 \times 5\sqrt{2} = 15\sqrt{2}$

    e $\sqrt{7} \times \sqrt{7} = \sqrt{49} = 7$

    f $3\sqrt{11} \times 3\sqrt{11} = 9\sqrt{11} \times \sqrt{11} = 9 \times 11 = 99$

7 **a** $\sqrt{3 \times 5} = \sqrt{15}$

    b $\sqrt{84} = \sqrt{4 \times 21} = \sqrt{4} \times \sqrt{21} = 2\sqrt{21}$

    c $\dfrac{3\sqrt{5}}{5}$

    d $\sqrt{\dfrac{24}{2}} = \sqrt{12} = \sqrt{4 \times 3} = \sqrt{4} \times \sqrt{3} = 2\sqrt{3}$

8 **a** $1 + \sqrt{3} + \sqrt{5} + \sqrt{15}$ **b** $9 + 3\sqrt{2} - 3\sqrt{2} - 2 = 7$

9 **a** $\sqrt{6} + \sqrt{24}$
$= \sqrt{6} + 2\sqrt{6}$
$= 3\sqrt{6}$

    b $\sqrt{8} - \sqrt{2}$
$= 2\sqrt{2} - \sqrt{2}$
$= \sqrt{2}$

    c $\sqrt{12} + \sqrt{24}$
$= 2\sqrt{3} + 2\sqrt{6}$
$= 2(\sqrt{3} + \sqrt{6})$

    d $\sqrt{180} + \sqrt{45}$
$= \sqrt{9}\sqrt{4}\sqrt{5} + \sqrt{9}\sqrt{5}$
$= 3 \times 2 \times \sqrt{5} + 3\sqrt{5}$
$= 6\sqrt{5} + 3\sqrt{5}$
$= 9\sqrt{5}$

10 $\frac{5}{7} = 0.\dot{7}1428\dot{5}$

11 **a** 1 4 9 16 25 36   **c** 1 3 6 10 15 21

     b 1 8 27 64 125 216

CHAPTER 6

1 **a** 1.07 (100% + 7% = 107% = 1.07)   **c** 1.008
    b 1.12   **d** 2.5

2 £96 × 1.175 = £112.80

3 **a** 0.72 (100% − 28% = 72% = 0.72)   **c** 0.994
    b 0.835   **d** 0.007

4 100% − 4.2% = 95.8%
    £6520 × 0.958 = £6246.16

5 **a** 1.08 = 108%   **c** 0.789 = 78.9%
        This gives an increase of 8%   This gives a reduction
    b 2.36 = 236%   of 21.1%
        This gives an increase of 136%

6 **a** 405.3 ÷ 386 = 1.05   **b** 5%

7 **a** 40 : 38 : 10 : 6 = 20 : 19 : 5 : 3
    b Total number of parts = 20 + 19 + 5 + 3 = 47
        Value of one part − £6500 ÷ 47   − £138.2978 …
        Alan gets   20 × £138.2978 …   = £2765.96 (nearest p)
        Pat gets   19 × £138.2978 …   = £2627.66 (nearest p)
        Luke gets   5 × £138.2978 …   = £691.49 (nearest p)
        Katy gets   3 × £138.2978 …   = £414.89 (nearest p)

8 £904.75 ÷ 1.175 = £770

9 **a** 5 × 250 ml = 1250 ml (or 1.25 l)   **c** 0.5 × 450 = 225 ml
    b 1350 ÷ 450 = 3;
        3 × 300 ml = 900 ml

10 **a** £8400 × 1.06^3 = £10 004.53   **c** 1.06^3 = 1.191 016
    b £1604.53   19.1% increase to (1 dp)

11

Number of labels ordered	50	90	180	340
Cost	£1.25	£2.25	£4.50	£8.50

12 **a** $S = kp$: $12 = k \times 8$ **b** $126 = 1.5p$
        so $k = 12 \div 8 = 1.5$ $S = 1.5p$ so $p = 126 \div 1.5 = 84$

13 **a** $P = kr^2$ **b** When $r = 5$
        $28.8 = k \times 4^2$ $P = 1.8 \times 5^2 = 45$
        $k = 28.8 \div 4^2 = 1.8$
        $P = 1.8r^2$

14 **a** $H = \dfrac{k}{t}$; $16 = \dfrac{k}{3}$ **b** When $t = 4$
        so $k = 48$ $H = \dfrac{48}{4} = 12$
        $H = \dfrac{48}{t}$

15 1 bag will last one cat $5 \times 4 = 20$ days.
For 2 cats, 1 bag will last $20 \div 2 = 10$ days.

16 **a** $\dfrac{3}{x} + \dfrac{5}{2x} = \dfrac{6}{2x} + \dfrac{5}{2x} = \dfrac{11}{2x}$

c $\dfrac{\overset{2}{\cancel{10}}}{\cancel{x^2}} \times \dfrac{\overset{x}{\cancel{x^3}}}{\cancel{15}_{3}} = \dfrac{2x}{3}$

b $\dfrac{11}{3x} - \dfrac{1}{x} = \dfrac{11}{3x} - \dfrac{3}{3x} = \dfrac{8}{3x}$

d $\dfrac{21x}{8} \div \dfrac{35x}{12} = \dfrac{\overset{3}{\cancel{21x}}}{\cancel{8}_{2}} \times \dfrac{\overset{3}{\cancel{12}}}{{}_{5}\cancel{35x}} = \dfrac{9}{10}$

CHAPTER 7

1 a

x	-5	-4	-3	-2	-1	0	1	2	3
x^2	25	16	9	4	1	0	1	4	9
$3x$	-15	-12	-9	-6	-3	0	3	6	9
3	3	3	3	3	3	3	3	3	3
y	13	7	3	1	1	3	7	13	21

b–d

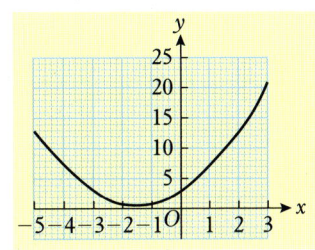

2 a $f(5) = (3 \times 25) - (7 \times 5) + 14 = 54$
b $f(0) = (3 \times 0) - (7 \times 0) + 14 = 14$
c $f(-2) = (3 \times 4) - (7 \times -2) + 14 = 40$

3 a $f(2) = \dfrac{1}{2}$

b $f\left(\dfrac{2}{3}\right) = \dfrac{1}{\frac{2}{3}} - \dfrac{1 \times 3}{\frac{2}{3} \times 3} = \dfrac{3}{2}$

c $f(-5) = \dfrac{1}{-5} = -\dfrac{1}{5}$

4 a

x	-3	-2	-1	0	1	2	3	4	0.5
x^2	9	4	1	0	1	4	9	16	0.25
$-x$	3	2	1	0	-1	-2	-3	-4	-0.5
-3	-3	-3	-3	-3	-3	-3	-3	-3	-3
y	9	3	-1	-3	-3	-1	3	9	-3.25

a, d

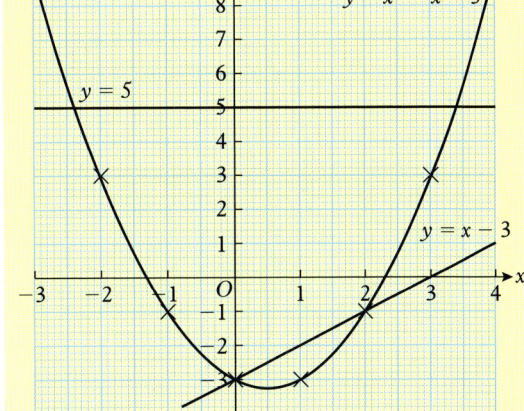

b $x = -1.3$ or 2.3
c $x = -2.4$ or 3.4
e $(0, -3), (2, -1)$
f
$$x^2 + x - 8 = 5$$
$$x^2 - x - 3$$
$$x^2 - x + 2x - 3 - 5 = 5$$
$$x^2 - x - 3 = 5 + 5 - 2x$$
$$= 10 - 2x$$
The line is $y = 10 - 2x$

5 a

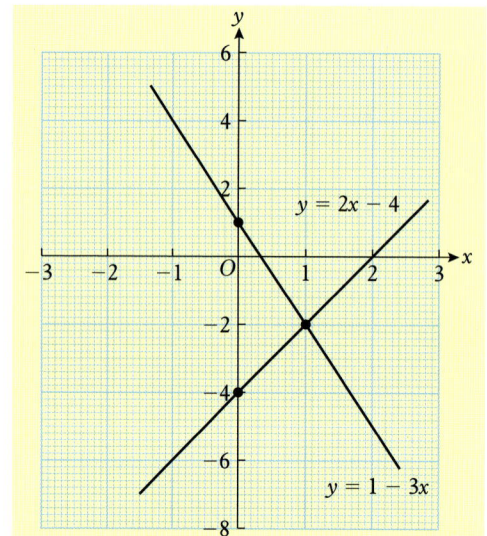

The solution is $x = 1$
$y = -2$

b

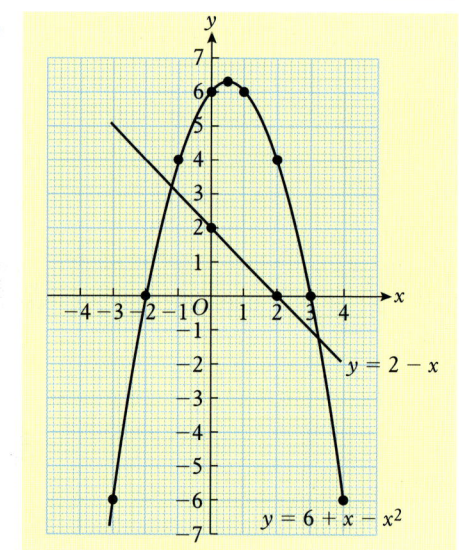

The solution is:
$x = 3.2$
$y = -1.2$
or
$x = -1.2$
$y = 3.2$

CHAPTER 8

1   **a** 7^5 **b** 4^3

2   **a**   1728   **b**   19   **c**   529   **d**   11   **e**   100 000   **f**   100

3   **a** $\frac{1}{8}$ **b**   5   **c** $\frac{3}{2} = 1\frac{1}{2} = 1.5$

4   **a**   1   **b** $\frac{1}{4}$ **c** $\frac{4}{3} = 1\frac{1}{3}$

5   **a** $\frac{1}{625}$ **b** $\frac{1}{7}$ **c** $\frac{1}{a}$

6   **a** y^7 **d** s **g** h^2 **j** a^{15}
    b $6c^3$ **e** $2x^6$ **h** w^9 **k** a^2
    c $35t^5$ **f** a^3b^{-3} **i** $3x^2y^{-3}$ **l**   1

7 **a** 4 **b** 5 **c** 9

8 **a** 11 **b** 44.89 **c** 4 **d** 7840

9 **a** 4.5×10^5 **c** 8.2×10^{-3} **e** 3×10^6

  b 3.683×10^8 **d** 3.751×10^{-1} **f** 6×10^{-8}

10 **a** 69 000 **b** 0.0024 **c** 0.000 000 04 **d** 361 800 000

11 **a** B, D, A, E, C, F **b** 8.25×10^{12}

12 $6.34 \times 10^9 \div 25 \text{ mins} = (6.34 \times 10^9 \div 25) \div 60 \text{ hours} = 4\,230\,000$
$$= 4.23 \times 10^6 \text{ hours}$$

13 **a** $35 \times 10^{5 + 8} = 3.5 \times 10 \times 10^{13} = 3.5 \times 10^{14}$

  b $\dfrac{1.5}{6} + 10^{4 - (-5)} = 0.25 \times 10^9 = 2.5 \times 10^{-1} \times 10^9 = 2.5 \times 10^8$

  c $40\,000 + 6000 = 46\,000 = 4.6 \times 10^4$

  d $300\,000 - 20\,000 = 280\,000 = 2.8 \times 10^5$

14 **a** 1.08×10^{17} **b** 9.69×10^{11} **c** 3.15×10^{-23}

CHAPTER 9

1 **a** 0.0507 **b** 350 000 **c** 600 100 **d** 0.0901 **e** 3×10^6 **f** 5×10^{-14}

2 **a** $(4 \times 10^{12}) \times (1 \times 10^{16}) = 4 \times 1 \times 10^{12} \times 10^{16}$
$$= 4 \times 10^{28}$$

  b $(9 \times 10^{-15}) \times (5 \times 10^8) = 9 \times 5 \times 10^{-15} \times 10^8$
$$= 45 \times 10^{-7}$$
$$= 4.5 \times 10^1 \times 10^{-7}$$
$$= 4.5 \times 10^{-6}$$

So, the estimate is about 4×10^{-6}. (The numbers 8.51 and 4.7 were both rounded up so 4.5 is rounded down.)

  c $\dfrac{8 \times 10^{23}}{2 \times 10^{-5}} = 4 \times 10^{23-(-5)} = 4 \times 10^{28}$

  d $\dfrac{3 \times 10^{-17}}{6 \times 10^8} = 0.5 \times 10^{-17-8} = 0.5 \times 10^{-25}$
$$= 5 \times 10^{-1} \times 10^{-25}$$
$$= 5 \times 10^{-26}$$

3 **a** answer = 4.86 to 3 sf estimate = $\dfrac{5 \times 3^2}{30 - 20} = \dfrac{45}{10} = 4.5$

  b answer = 37.8 to 3 sf estimate = $\dfrac{\overset{5}{\cancel{60}} \times 50}{7 \times \cancel{12}_1} = \dfrac{250}{7} \approx \dfrac{280}{7} = 40$

(or any similar method)

  c answer = 1.33 to 3 sf estimate = $\sqrt{\dfrac{70 \times 50}{200 \times 10}} = \sqrt{\dfrac{35}{20}}$
$$= \sqrt{\dfrac{7}{4}} \approx \sqrt{\dfrac{9}{4}} = \dfrac{3}{2} = 1.5$$

d answer $= 1.35$ to 3 sf   estimate $= \dfrac{-15 + \sqrt{225 + 20 \times 30}}{10}$

$$= \dfrac{-15 + \sqrt{825}}{10}$$

$$\approx \dfrac{-15 + 30}{10} = 1.5$$

4 a -30.4 to 3 sf   **b** $\dfrac{5}{\frac{1}{6} - \frac{1}{3}} = \dfrac{5}{\frac{1}{6} - \frac{2}{6}} = \dfrac{5}{-\frac{1}{6}} = -5 \times 6 = -30$

5 An error is always given as a positive number.

6 a $(20 \times 30) \div 2 = 300 \text{ cm}^2$
   b $(24.8 \times 27.2) \div 2 = 337.28 \text{ cm}^2$
   c Percentage error $= \dfrac{\text{error}}{\text{exact value}} \times 100\%$

$$= \dfrac{37.28}{337.28} \times 100\%$$

$$= 11\% \text{ (2 sf)}$$

7 a lower bound $= 7.6145 \times 10^6 \text{ km}^2$ upper bound $= 7.6155 \times 10^6 \text{ km}^2$
   b lower bound $= 18\,250\,000$ upper bound $= 18\,350\,000$
   c minimum $= \dfrac{18\,250\,000}{7.6155 \times 10^6} = 2.40$ to 3 sf   maximum $= \dfrac{18\,350\,000}{7.6145 \times 10^6} = 2.41$ to 3 sf

8 u: lower bound $= 22.5$ upper bound $= 23.5$
   t: lower bound $= 4.85$ upper bound $= 4.95$
   v: lower bound $= 22.5 - 4 \times 4.95 = 2.7$ upper bound $= 23.5 - 4 \times 4.85 = 4.1$

9 a lower bound $= 5 \times 33.5 = 167.5$ upper bound $= 5 \times 34.5 = 172.5$
   b lower bound $= 33.5 - 5.715 = 27.785$ upper bound $= 34.5 - 5.705 = 28.795$
   c lower bound $= 5.705 \div 0.55 = 10.37$ (4 sf)   upper bound $= 5.715 \div 0.45 = 12.7$
   d lower bound $= 3 \times 33.5 - 4 \times 5.715 = 77.64$
      upper bound $= 3 \times 34.5 - 4 \times 5.705 = 80.68$

10 a lower bound $= 5.85 \text{ cm}$ upper bound $= 5.95 \text{ cm}$
   b area of base   lower bound $= 5.85 \times 3.45 = 20.1825 \text{ cm}^2$
      upper bound $= 5.95 \times 3.55 = 21.1225 \text{ cm}^2$
   c length of diagonal   lower bound $= \sqrt{5.85^2 + 3.45^2} = 6.79 \text{ cm (3 sf)}$
      upper bound $= \sqrt{5.95^2 + 3.55^2} = 6.93 \text{ cm (3 sf)}$
   d volume   lower bound $= 5.85 \times 3.45 \times 3.95 = 79.7 \text{ cm}^3 \text{ (3 sf)}$
      upper bound $= 5.95 \times 3.55 \times 4.05 = 85.5 \text{ cm}^3 \text{ (3 sf)}$

CHAPTER 10

1 **a** $\begin{pmatrix} 5 \\ -3 \end{pmatrix}$

   b (1) 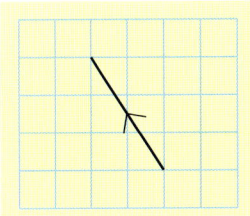 (2)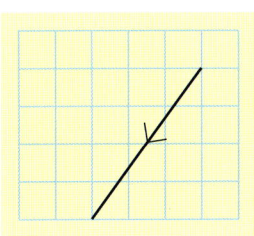

2

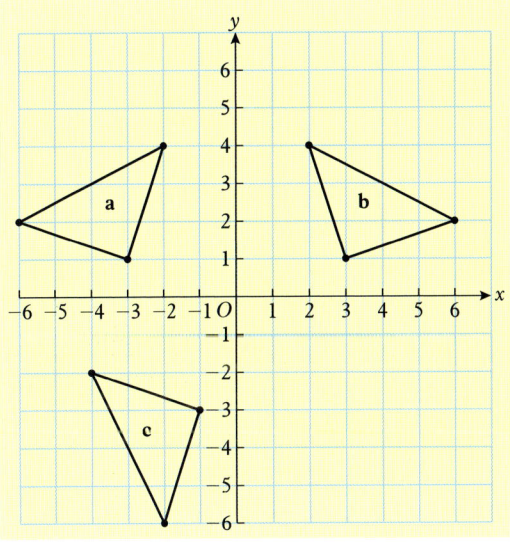

3 **a** a translation of 2 squares to the right and 3 squares down

   b a translation of $\begin{pmatrix} -5 \\ 4 \end{pmatrix}$

   c a rotation of 270° anti-clockwise about the point $(2, -3)$

   d a reflection in the line $y = 2x$

4 **a** $\frac{1}{4}$

   b -2

5 a, b

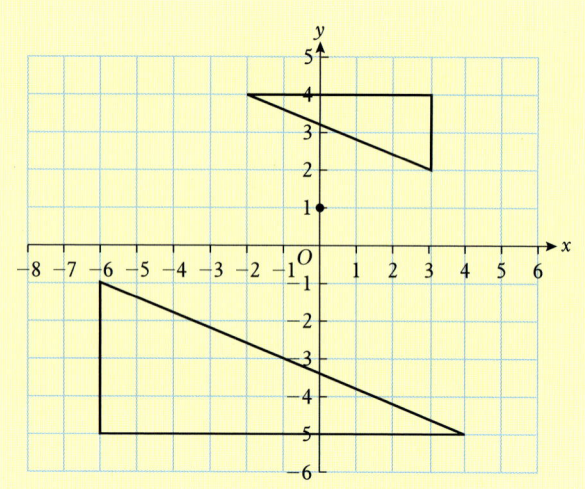

6 a–c

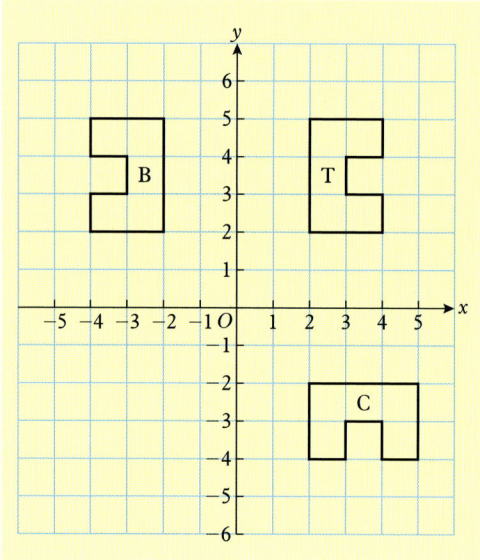

d Reflection in the line $y = x$

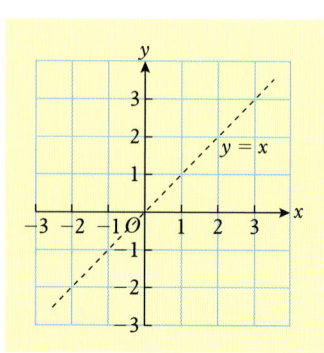

CHAPTER 11

1 a
$$t = \frac{3r + 4}{x}$$
$$tx = 3r + 4$$
$$tx - 4 = 3r$$
$$r = \frac{tx - 4}{3}$$

c
$$A = \pi r^2 h$$
$$\frac{A}{\pi h} = r^2$$
$$r = \sqrt{\frac{A}{\pi h}}$$

e
$$3x + y = \frac{x}{t}$$
$$(3x + y)t = x$$
$$3xt + yt = x$$
$$3xt - x = -yt$$
$$x(3t - 1) = -yt$$
$$x = \frac{-yt}{3t - 1}$$
$$\left(\text{or } \frac{yt}{1 - 3t}\right)$$

b
$$y = tx^2 + c$$
$$y - c = tx^2$$
$$\frac{y - c}{t} = x^2$$
$$x = \sqrt{\frac{y - c}{t}}$$

d
$$r = \frac{3t + 1}{t}$$
$$rt = 3t + 1$$
$$rt - 3t = 1$$
$$t(r - 3) = 1$$
$$t = \frac{1}{r - 3}$$

f
$$A = 2\pi rh + 2\pi r^2$$
$$A - 2\pi r^2 = 2\pi rh$$
$$h = \frac{A - 2\pi r^2}{2\pi rh}$$

2
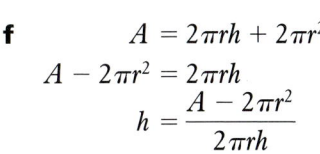
$$7 \xrightarrow{+5} 12 \xrightarrow{+5} 17 \xrightarrow{5} 22$$

$5n + 2$

3 a $6n + 3$
$= 6 \times 20 + 3$
$= 123$

b $\frac{1}{2}n - 7$
$= \frac{1}{2} \times 20 - 7$
$= 3$

4
$$4 \quad 10 \quad 18 \quad 28$$
$$+6 \quad +8 \quad 10$$
$$+2 \quad +2$$

Formula starts with n^2

Sequence	4	10	18	28
$-n^2$	1	4	9	16
$3n$	$+3$	$+6$	$+9$	$+12$

nth term $= n^2 + 3n$

5 a $n = 1$ $2 \times 1^2 + 3 \times 1 + 5 = 10$
$n = 2$ $2 \times 2^2 + 3 \times 2 + 5 = 19$
$n = 3$ $2 \times 3^2 + 3 \times 3 + 5 = 32$

b use trial and improvement
$n = 7$ $2 \times 7^2 + 3 \times 7 + 5 = 124$ too big
$n = 6$ $2 \times 6^2 + 3 \times 6 + 5 = 95$ ✓
so $n = 6$

6 a 3

b $\frac{1}{2}$

c -1

7 a $m = \frac{9 - 1}{3 - (-1)} = \frac{8}{4} = 2$

b $m = \frac{-7}{7} = -1$

555

8 a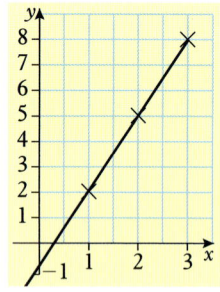

b $c = -1$ (where the line cuts the y axis)
$$m = \frac{8-2}{3-1} = \frac{6}{2} = 3$$

c $m = -\frac{1}{3}$

d $y = 3x +$ any number

9 a
$$2x - 7 = 15$$
$$2x = 22$$
$$x = 11$$

b
$$3x + 5 = 7x - 7$$
$$5 = 4x - 7$$
$$12 = 4x$$
$$x = 3$$

c
$$4(6 - x) = 10$$
$$24 - 4x = 10$$
$$24 = 10 + 4x$$
$$4x = 14$$
$$x = 3\frac{1}{2}$$

d
$$10(3x - 2) = 5(2 - x)$$
$$30x - 20 = 10 - 5x$$
$$35x - 20 = 10$$
$$35x = 30$$
$$x = \frac{30}{35} = \frac{6}{7}$$

10 a
$$4x + 2y = 6 \ (1)$$
$$x - 2y = 4 \ (2)$$
$$(1) + (2) \ 5x = 10$$
$$x = 2$$
Subst $x = 2$ in $4x + 2y = 6$
$$8 + 2y = 6$$
$$2y = -2$$
$$y = -1$$
Check $x - 2y = 2 + 2 = 4$ ✓

b
$$3x + 2y = 12 \ (1)$$
$$x - y = -1 \ (2)$$
$$(2) \times 2 \ 2x - 2y = -2 \ (3)$$
$$(1) + (3) \ 5x = 10$$
$$x = 2$$
Subst $x = 2$ in $3x + 2y = 12$
$$6 + 2y = 12$$
$$2y = 6$$
$$y = 3$$
Check $x - y = 2 - 3 = -1$ ✓

c
$$y = 6 - 3x (1)$$
$$x + 2y = -13 (2)$$
$$(1) \qquad 3x + y = 6 \quad (3)$$
$$(2) \times 3 \ 3x + 6y = -39 (4)$$
$$(4) - (3) \qquad 5y = -45$$
$$y = -9$$
Subst $y = -9$ in $x + 2y = -13$
$$x - 18 = -13$$
$$x = 5$$
Check $6 - 3x = 6 - 15 = -9$ ✓

11 a $c = 30$
(where the line cuts the vertical axis)
$$m = \frac{120 - 30}{5} = \frac{90}{5} = 18$$

b $m =$ cooking time per pound

c add 30 minutes for all weights

12 **a** perpendicular to $m = 2$

so $m = -\frac{1}{2}$

so $y = mx + c$

becomes $y = -\frac{1}{2}x + c$

$(0, 1)$ means $x = 0$ when $y = 1$

so $1 = 0 + c$

$c = 1$

Equation is $y = -\frac{1}{2}x + 1$

CHAPTER 12

1 **a** $x^2 = 3^2 + 4^2$
$= 9 + 16$
$= 25$
$x = 5$ cm

b $20^2 = 7^2 + x^2$
$400 = 49 + x^2$
$x^2 = 351$
$x = \sqrt{351}$
$= 18.7$ cm (1 dp)

2 **a** $x^2 = (\sqrt{3})^2 + (\sqrt{7})^2$
$= 3 + 7$
$= 10$
$x = \sqrt{10}$ cm

b $(\sqrt{60})^2 = (\sqrt{40})^2 + x^2$
$60 = 40 + x^2$
$20 = x^2$
$x = \sqrt{20}$ cm (or $x = 2\sqrt{5}$ since $\sqrt{20} = \sqrt{4 \times 5} = 2\sqrt{5}$)

3 **a** $\tan a° = \frac{12}{19}$
$= 0.6316$
$a° = 32.3°$ (1 dp)

b $\cos b° = \frac{16}{20}$
$= 0.8$
$b° = 36.9°$ (1 dp)

4 **a** $\cos 30° = \frac{x}{12}$
$0.8660 = \frac{x}{12}$
$x = 10.4$ cm (1 dp)

b $\sin 72° = \frac{8}{x}$
$0.9511 = \frac{8}{x}$
$0.9511x - 8$
$x = \frac{8}{0.9511} = 8.4$ cm (1 dp)

5

$\sin 60° = \frac{h}{10}$
$h = 10 \sin 60°$
$h = 8.7$ cm (1 dp)

OR

Using Pythagoras
$10^2 = h^2 + 5^2$
$h^2 = 100 - 25$
$= 75$
$h = 8.7$ cm (1 dp)

6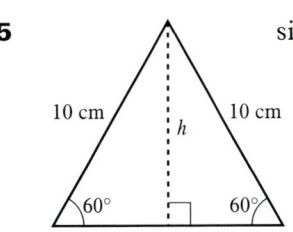

a $3^2 = 1^2 + h^2$
$9 = 1 + h^2$
$h^2 = 8$
$h = 2.8$ m (1 dp)

b $\cos b° = \frac{1}{3}$
$b° = 70.5°$

1 **a** $x^2 + 3x + 4x + 12 = x^2 + 7x + 12$ **c** $6x^2 - 6x - 15x + 15 = 6x^2 - 21x + 15$
 b $x^2 + 2x - 7x - 14 = x^2 - 5x - 14$ **d** $42x^2 + 14x - 24x - 8 = 42x^2 - 10x - 8$

2 **a** $(x + 2)(x + 3)$ **b** $(x + 7)(x + 3)$ **c** $(x - 7)(x + 4)$ **d** $(x + 10)(x - 3)$

3 **a** $(2x + 1)(x + 6)$ **b** $(3x + 1)(x + 7)$ **c** $(3x - 1)(x + 6)$ **d** $(2x - 3)(2x - 5)$

4 **a** $x = \dfrac{-9 \pm \sqrt{81 - 8}}{2}$

$x = -0.23, x = -8.77$

c $x = \dfrac{-19 \pm \sqrt{361 + 120}}{10}$

$x = 0.29, x = -4.09$

 b $x = \dfrac{-12 \pm \sqrt{144 - 12}}{6}$

$x = -0.09, x = -3.91$

d $x = \dfrac{3 \pm \sqrt{9 + 420}}{14}$

$x = 1.69, x = -1.27$

5 **a** $x^2 + 4x + 2 = 0$
$(x + 2)^2 - 2 = 0$
$(x + 2)^2 = 2$
$x + 2 = \pm\sqrt{2}$
$x = \pm\sqrt{2} - 2$
$x = -0.59, x = -3.41$

 c $2x^2 + 12x - 9 = 0$
$2(x^2 + 6x) - 9 = 0$
$2(x + 3)^2 - 27 = 0$
$2(x + 3)^2 = 27$
$(x + 3)^2 = 13.5$
$x = \pm\sqrt{13.5} - 3$
$x = 0.67, x = -6.67$

 b $x^2 + 12x + 1 = 0$
$(x + 6)^2 - 35 = 0$
$(x + 6)^2 = 35$
$x = \pm\sqrt{35} - 6$
$x = -0.08, x = -11.92$

 d $3x^2 - 12x - 15 = 0$
$3(x^2 - 4x) - 15 = 0$
$3(x - 2)^2 - 27 = 0$
$3(x - 2)^2 = 27$
$(x - 2)^2 = 9$
$x - 2 = \pm 3$
$x = 5, x = -1$

6 $x = 9.79$

7
$$x^2 + y^2 = 34 \quad (1)$$
$$2x - y = 13 \quad (2)$$
From (2) $\quad y = 2x - 13$
So in (1) $x^2 + (2x - 13)^2 = 34$
$x^2 + 4x^2 - 52x + 169 = 34$
$5x^2 - 52x + 135 = 0$
$(x - 5)(5x - 27) = 0$
$x = 5$ or $x = 5.4$
So $\quad y = -3, y = -2.2$

Answers are $x = 5, y = -3$ or $x = 5.4, y = -2.2$

CHAPTER 14

1 a $\begin{pmatrix} 4 \\ -1 \end{pmatrix} + \begin{pmatrix} -3 \\ 8 \end{pmatrix} = \begin{pmatrix} 1 \\ 7 \end{pmatrix}$

b $\overrightarrow{LZ} + \overrightarrow{ZY} = \overrightarrow{LY}$

2 $\overrightarrow{AB} = \mathbf{p} - \mathbf{q} + \mathbf{r}$

3 a $\begin{pmatrix} 2 \\ 3 \end{pmatrix} + \begin{pmatrix} -2 \\ 4 \end{pmatrix} = \begin{pmatrix} 0 \\ 7 \end{pmatrix}$

c $3 \times \begin{pmatrix} 2 \\ 3 \end{pmatrix} = \begin{pmatrix} 6 \\ 9 \end{pmatrix}$

b $\begin{pmatrix} 2 \\ 3 \end{pmatrix} - \begin{pmatrix} -2 \\ 4 \end{pmatrix} = \begin{pmatrix} 4 \\ -1 \end{pmatrix}$

d $-\dfrac{1}{2} \begin{pmatrix} -2 \\ 4 \end{pmatrix} = \begin{pmatrix} 1 \\ -2 \end{pmatrix}$

4 a $\sqrt{(-5)^2 + 12^2} = 13$

b $\begin{pmatrix} -5 \\ -12 \end{pmatrix}, \begin{pmatrix} 5 \\ 12 \end{pmatrix}, \begin{pmatrix} 5 \\ -12 \end{pmatrix}$

5 a $\begin{pmatrix} 4 \\ 7.5 \end{pmatrix}$

b $\sqrt{4^2 + 7.5^2} = \sqrt{72.25}$
radius $= \sqrt{72.25} = 8.5$

6 $\dfrac{1}{2}\left(\begin{pmatrix} 6 \\ -3 \end{pmatrix} + \begin{pmatrix} 4 \\ 1 \end{pmatrix} \right) = \begin{pmatrix} 5 \\ -1 \end{pmatrix}$

7 $\overrightarrow{AB} = 3\mathbf{a} + 4\mathbf{b}$ $\qquad \overrightarrow{AC} = 6\mathbf{a} + 8\mathbf{b}$
so, $\overrightarrow{AC} = 2\overrightarrow{AB}$, and A, B and C are collinear

8 position vector of P is $\dfrac{\mathbf{m} + 4\mathbf{n}}{5}$ or $\dfrac{1}{5}\mathbf{m} + \dfrac{4}{5}\mathbf{n}$

9 a $x = 4, y = 5$

b $p = 3, q = -2$

10 a $2\mathbf{t} - 5\mathbf{v}$

b $3\mathbf{t} + 4\mathbf{v}$

(any multiple of the answers given to parts **a** and **b** will also be correct)

11 $\begin{pmatrix} 16 \\ 3 \end{pmatrix} = 3\begin{pmatrix} 4 \\ -1 \end{pmatrix} - 2\begin{pmatrix} -2 \\ -3 \end{pmatrix}$

12 a $10 \cos 60° = 5 \text{ N}$

b $10 \sin 60° = 5\sqrt{3} \text{ N}$

CHAPTER 15

1 a $a = 43°$ (alternate angles)
 b $b = 110°$ (corresponding angles)
 c $c = 128°$ (alternate angles)
   $d = 34°$ (alternate angles)
   $e = 180° - 128° - 34°$ (angles in a triangle) $= 18°$
 d $f = 119°$ (corresponding angles)
   $g = 119°$ (corresponding angles with f)
   Angle above $g = 61°$ (angles on a straight line)
   Angle on right of $125° = 55°$ (angles on a straight line)
   $h = 180° - 61° - 55°$ (angles in a triangle) $= 64°$

2 In triangle ABC as shown, extend the line AC to the right and draw a line parallel to AB from C.
Let the angles formed be p and q as shown.

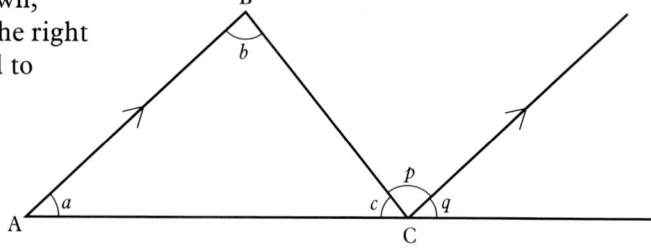

$c + p + q = 180°$ (angles on a straight line)
$\quad\quad p = b \quad$ (alternate angles)
$\quad\quad q = a \quad$ (corresponding angles)
so $a + b + c = 180°$

3 Split angle a as in question 2.

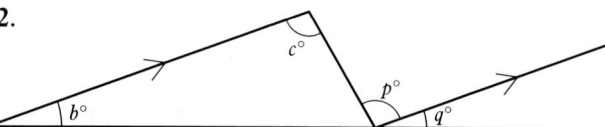

$\quad\quad a = p + q$
$\quad\quad p = c$ (alternate angles)
and $\quad q = b$ (corresponding angles)
so $\quad p + q = b + c$
i.e. $\quad\quad a = b + c$

4 a $\dfrac{360°}{12} = 30°$ **b** $(12 - 2) \times 180° = 1800°$

5 exterior angle $= 180° - 165° = 15°$

number of sides $\dfrac{360}{15} = 24$

6 a

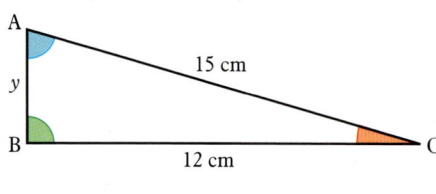

b ratio from ABC to XYZ $= \dfrac{8}{12} = \dfrac{2}{3}$

$x = 15 \times \dfrac{2}{3} = 10 \text{ cm} \quad\quad y = 4 \div \dfrac{2}{3} = 6 \text{ cm}$

7 AD = BC (opposite sides of a parallelogram)
DC = AB (opposite sides of a parallelogram)
AC = AC (common)
So triangles ABC and CDA are congruent (SSS).
This can also be proved using angles since the opposite angles in a parallelogram are equal.

8

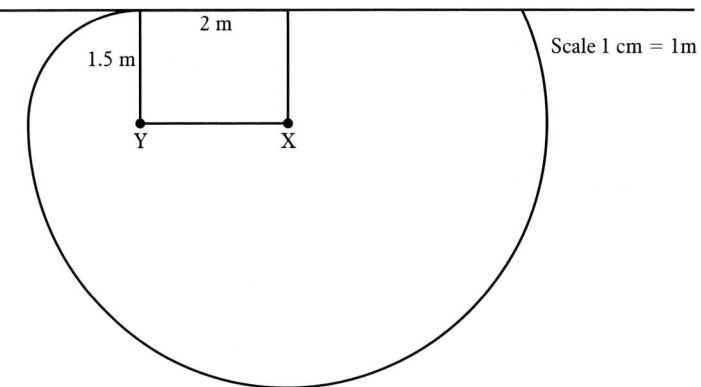

2 m

1.5 m

Scale 1 cm = 1m

Y   X

9   **a**   *a* = 38° (angle in the alternate segment)
         b = 76° (angle at the centre = 2 × angle at the circumference)
    b   *c* = 90° (angle in a semi-circle)
         d = 48° (angles in the same segment)
    c   *e* = 18° (angles in the same segment)
         f = 36° (angle at the centre = 2 × angle at the circumference)
         g = 18° (base angles isosceles triangle)
         h = 18° (angle in the same segment as *g*)
    d   angle on left of centre of circle
           = 2(180° − 90° − 34°)   (twice the angle in the triangle
                                  from tangent, radius and across
                                  the middle of the diagram)
           = 112°
         m = 56° (angle at the centre = 2 × angle at the circumference)
         n = 180° −56° = 124° (opposite angles in a cyclic quadrilateral)

10   **a**   Look at this diagram.
      O is the centre of the circle.
      A, B and C are points on the circumference.
      The line from B through O ends at P.

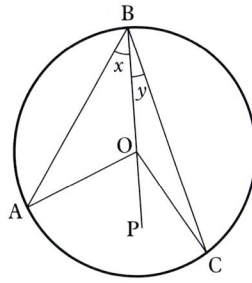

      Let the angle OBA be *x*
      and angle OBC be *y*.

            angle BAO = *x* (base angles isosceles triangle)
            angle AOB = 180° − 2*x*° (angles in a triangle)
            angle AOP = 2*x* (angles on a straight line)
            Similarly angle COP = 2*y*
      Now   angle ABC = *x* + *y*
      and   angle AOC = 2*x* + 2*y* = 2(*x* + *y*) = 2 × angle ABC
    b   In a semi-circle, AOC is a diameter and the angle at the centre = 180°.
      So, using **a**, the angle in a semi-circle is half of 180° = 90°.

CHAPTER 16

1 **a** (1) 065°
      (2) 180 + 65 = 245°
  b (1) 110°
      (2) 180 + 110 = 290°

c (1) 180 + 155 = 335°
    (2) 155°

2 **a**

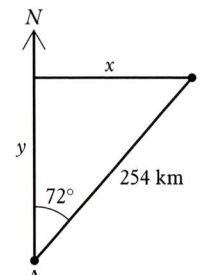

b $\sin 72 = \dfrac{x}{254}$
      $x = 241.6$ km (1 dp)

c $\cos 72 = \dfrac{y}{254}$
      $y = 78.5$ km (1 dp)

3 **a**

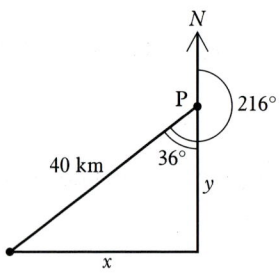

b $\sin 36 = \dfrac{x}{40}$
      $x = 23.5$ km (1 dp)

c $\cos 36 = \dfrac{y}{40}$
      $y = 32.4$ km (1 dp)

4 **a** $a^2 = 12^2 + 15^2$ (Pythagoras)
      $a^2 = 369$
      $a \ = 19.2$ cm (3 sf)

b $\tan 35 = \dfrac{b}{18}$
      $b = 12.6$ cm (3 sf)

5 In $\triangle$ABC

    $AC^2 = 14^2 + 18^2$ (Pythagoras)

    $AC^2 = 520$

    $AC = \sqrt{520}$

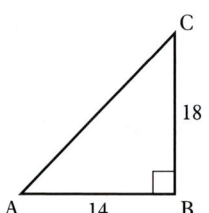

    In $\triangle$AEC, angle needed
    is $\angle$ECA = x
      $\tan x = \dfrac{7}{\sqrt{520}} = 0.30697\ldots$
        $x = 17.1°$ (3 sf)

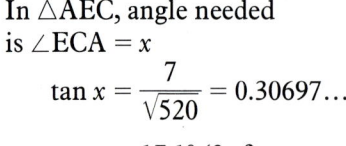

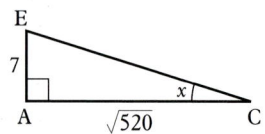

CHAPTER 17

1 a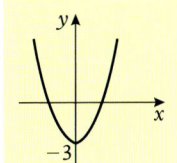

b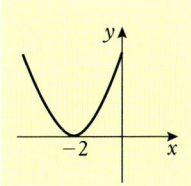

c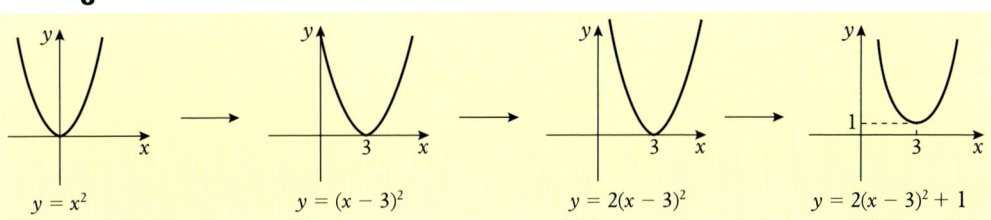

$y = x^2$ $y = (x - 3)^2$ $y = 2(x - 3)^2$ $y = 2(x - 3)^2 + 1$

2 a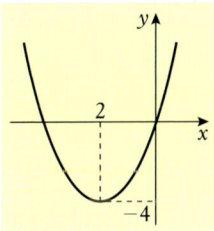

b The +2 moves the graph 2 units to the left, a translation of $\begin{pmatrix} -2 \\ 0 \end{pmatrix}$

The −4 moves the graph 4 units down, a translation of $\begin{pmatrix} 0 \\ -4 \end{pmatrix}$

3 a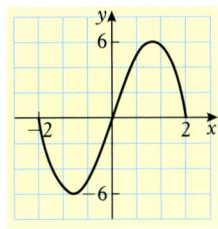

b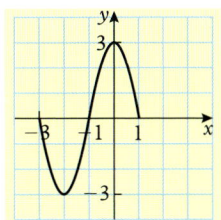

c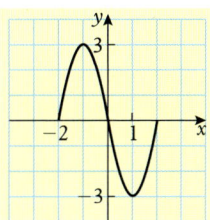

d $a = -2$ since the graph has moved down 2 units

4 a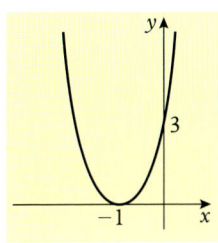

b The +1 moves the graph 1 unit to the left, a translation of $\begin{pmatrix} -1 \\ 0 \end{pmatrix}$

The 3 stretches the graph by a scale factor of 3 in the y direction

563

5 a 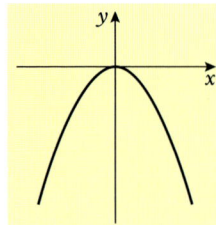 **b**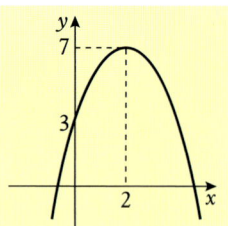

c The -2 moves the graph 2 units to the right, a translation of $\begin{pmatrix} 2 \\ 0 \end{pmatrix}$

The 7 moves the graph 7 units up, a translation of $\begin{pmatrix} 0 \\ 7 \end{pmatrix}$

6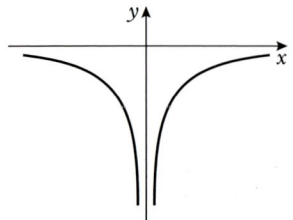

7 a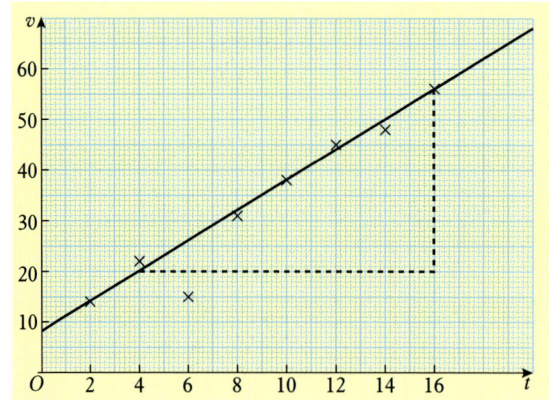

b $t = 6$

c $v = u + at$

a is the gradient: $\dfrac{56 - 20}{16 - 4} = \dfrac{36}{12} = 3$

u is where the line crosses the vertical axis:
so $u = 8$

CHAPTER 18

1 **a** (1) arc length
$$= \tfrac{90}{360} \times 2 \times \pi \times 12$$
$$= \tfrac{1}{4} \times 24\pi$$
$$= 6\pi \,\text{cm}$$

(2) sector area
$$= \tfrac{90}{360} \times \pi \times 12^2$$
$$= \tfrac{1}{4} \times 144\pi$$
$$= 36\pi \,\text{cm}^2$$

b (1) arc length
$$= \tfrac{60}{360} \times 2 \times \pi \times 30$$
$$= \tfrac{1}{6} \times 60\pi$$
$$= 10\pi \,\text{mm}$$

(2) sector area
$$= \tfrac{60}{360} \times \pi \times 30^2$$
$$= \tfrac{1}{6} \times 900\pi$$
$$= 150\pi \,\text{mm}^2$$

c (1) arc length
$$= \tfrac{270}{360} \times 2 \times \pi \times 10$$
$$= \tfrac{3}{4} \times 20\pi$$
$$= 15\pi \,\text{cm}$$

(2) sector area
$$= \tfrac{270}{360} \times \pi \times 10^2$$
$$= \tfrac{3}{4} \times 100\pi$$
$$= 75\pi \,\text{cm}^2$$

2 area of segment = area of sector − area of triangle
$$= \tfrac{65}{360} \times \pi \times 12^2 - \tfrac{1}{2} \times 12^2 \times \sin 65°$$
$$= 16.4 \,\text{cm}^2 \,(3 \,\text{sf})$$

3 **a** (1) surface area
$$= 4\pi r^2$$
$$= 4 \times \pi \times 3^2$$
$$= 36\pi \,\text{cm}^2$$

(2) volume
$$= \tfrac{4}{3}\pi r^3$$
$$= \tfrac{4}{3} \times \pi \times 3^3$$
$$= 36\pi \,\text{cm}^3$$

b (1) surface area
$$= \pi r^2 + \pi r l$$
$$= \pi \times 3^2 + \pi \times 3 \times 5$$
$$= 9\pi + 15\pi$$
$$= 24\pi \,\text{cm}^2$$

(2) volume
$$= \tfrac{1}{3}\pi r^2 h$$
$$= \tfrac{1}{3} \times \pi \times 3^2 \times 4$$
$$= 12\pi \,\text{cm}^3$$

c (1) surface area
$$= 2\pi r^2 \times 2\pi r h$$
$$= 2 \times \pi \times 2^2 + 2 \times \pi \times 2 \times 5$$
$$= 8\pi + 20\pi$$
$$= 28\pi \,\text{cm}^2$$

(2) volume
$$= \pi r^2 h$$
$$= \pi \times 2^2 \times 5$$
$$= 20\pi \,\text{cm}^3$$

4 **a** by similar triangles:
$$\frac{x}{15} = \frac{x + 20}{30}$$
$$30x = 15(x + 20)$$
$$30x = 15x + 300$$
$$15x = 300$$
$$x = 20$$
(or you can see that 15 is half of 30,
so x must be half of $x + 20$, i.e. $x = 20$)

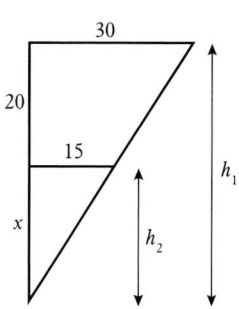

Volume of frustum $= \dfrac{1}{3}\pi r_1^2 h_1 - \dfrac{1}{3}\pi r_2^2 h_2$
$$= \frac{1}{3} \times \pi \times 30^2 \times 40 - \frac{1}{3} \times \pi \times 15^2 \times 20$$
$$= 12000\pi - 1500\pi$$
$$= 10500\pi \,\text{cm}^3$$

4 b The smaller pot has lengths half of the large pot. So:

$$\text{volume} = \left(\frac{1}{2}\right)^3 \times 10500\pi = \frac{1}{8} \times 10500\pi = 1312.5\pi \text{ cm}^3$$

5 a xyz = volume
ax^2y = volume
$\therefore$ volume + volume = volume

b $\dfrac{ax^2z}{ky} = \dfrac{\text{dimension 3}}{\text{dimension 1}}$ = dimension 2
$\therefore$ area

c $\dfrac{kxy}{a}$ = dimension 2

$\dfrac{az^3}{x} = \dfrac{\text{dimension 3}}{\text{dimension 1}}$ = dimension 2
$\therefore$ area + area = area

CHAPTER 19

1 a $-4 < x \leqslant 2$ **b** $-5 \leqslant x < 1$ **c** $x > -2$

2 a 3, 4, 5 **b** $-3, -2, -1, 0$ **c** $-5, -4, -3, -2, -1$ **d** $-2, -1, 0, 1, 2$

3 a $x < 11$ **c** $4x \leqslant 19$ **e** $3x + 1 < -20$ **g** $\dfrac{3x}{5} - \dfrac{x}{5} < 3 + 1$
$x \leqslant \dfrac{19}{4}$ $3x < -21$ $\dfrac{2x}{5} < 4$
$x < -7$ $2x < 20$
$x < 10$

b $2x \geqslant 12$ **d** $\dfrac{x}{4} > 11.3$ **f** $2x + 11 \geqslant 7$ **h** $5x + 2 \geqslant \dfrac{6x}{3}$
$x \geqslant 6$ $x > 45.2$ $2x \geqslant -4$ $5x + 2 \geqslant 2x$
$x \geqslant -2$ $3x \geqslant -2$
$x \geqslant -\dfrac{2}{3}$

4 a $11 > 3 + x$ **b** $5 - 2x < -21$ **c** $7 \leqslant 5x - 9$ **d** $10 \geqslant x + 6$
$x < 8$ $5 < -21 + 2x$ $16 \leqslant 5x$ $4 \geqslant x$
$26 < 2x$ $x \geqslant \dfrac{16}{5}$ $x \leqslant 4$
$x > 13$

5 a $6 \leqslant 2x \leqslant 12$ **d** $4 - x \leqslant x$ and $x \leqslant 10 - x$
$3 \leqslant x \leqslant 6$ $4 \leqslant 2x$ $2x \leqslant 10$
$x \geqslant 2$ $x \leqslant 5$

b $-8 < \dfrac{x}{2} \leqslant -5$ so $2 \leqslant x \leqslant 5$
$-16 < x \leqslant -10$

c $-24 \leqslant 2x + 5 < -3$ OR $9 - x \leqslant x + 5 \leqslant 15 - x$
$-29 \leqslant 2x < -8$ $4 - x \leqslant x$ $\leqslant 10 - x$
$-\dfrac{29}{2} \leqslant x < -4$ $4 \leqslant 2x$ $\leqslant 10$

$$2 \leqslant x \qquad \leqslant 5$$

6 **a** $x \geqslant -2$ **b** $-4 \leqslant y < 3$

7 **a** $x \geqslant 1, y > -3$ **b** $x < -2, -2 \leqslant y \leqslant 1$

8 **a** $x^2 - 3x - 2 =$ **9** **a** s represents the number of sliced loaves
$(x - 2)(x - 1)$ so u represents the number of unsliced loaves
graph crosses x at   The total number of loaves is less than or equal to 800
1 and 2.

            b $s \geqslant 0, u \geqslant 0, u \geqslant 200, s \geqslant 2u$

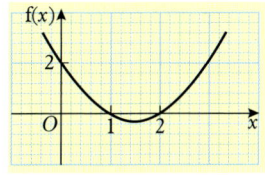

     c

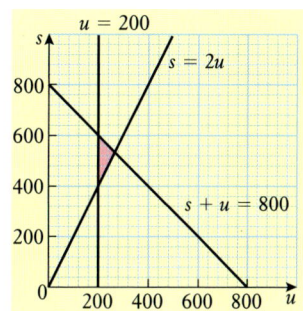

b $x < 1$ or $x > 2$

d maximum value of u is at point of intersection of
$s + u = 800$ and $s = 2u$
i.e. when $2u + u = 800$
$$3u = 800$$
$$u = 266 \text{ (Do not round up to 267.)}$$

CHAPTER 20

1 $x = 25.5°$ (3 sf) (from calculator)   **2** $x = 73.1°$ (3 sf) (from calculator)
$x = 154.5°$ (3 sf) $(180 - \text{first answer})$ $x = 286.9°$ (3 sf) $(360 - \text{first answer})$

3 **a** $x = 45°$ (from calculator)   **b** $x = 135°$ (from calculator)
$x = 135°$ $(180 - \text{first answer})$ $x = 225°$ $(360 - \text{first answer})$

4 **a** $y = \cos x$ **b** $y = \cos 2x$

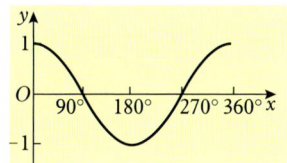   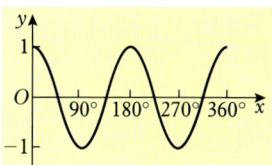

c $y = \cos \dfrac{x}{2}$ **d** $y = \sin \dfrac{x}{3}$

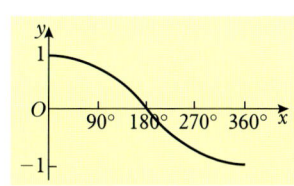   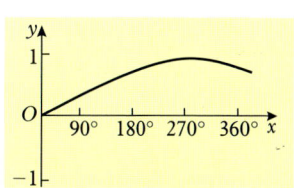

5 **a** 6
b −6

c
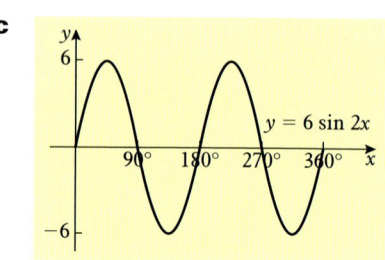

6 area $= \dfrac{1}{2}ab\sin c$

$= \dfrac{1}{2} \times 23.1 \times 16.6 \times \sin 106°$

$= 184\ \text{mm}^2$ (3 sf)

7 **a**
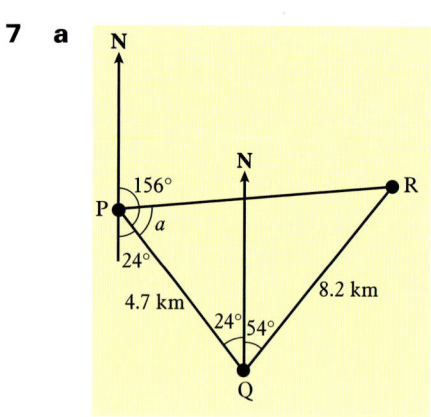

b angle at Q on left of
North line $= 24°$ (alternate angles)
$\therefore \angle PQR = 24 + 54 = 78°$

c $PR^2 = 4.7^2 + 8.2^2 - 2 \times 4.7 \times 8.2$
$\times \cos 78$ (cosine rule)
$= 73.304...$
$PR = 8.6\ \text{km}$ (1 dp)
so the shortest distance is 8.6 km

d $\dfrac{\sin a}{8.2} = \dfrac{\sin 78}{PR}$

$\sin a = \dfrac{8.2 \times \sin 78}{PR}$

$= 0.9368...$
$a = 69.52°$

so for bearing of R from P:
angle needed $= 180 - 24 - 69.52$
$= 86.48°$
$\therefore$ bearing $= 086°$ (nearest degree)

8 **a** in $\triangle ABC$
$AC^2 = 15^2 + 7^2 - 2 \times 15 \times 7$
$\times \cos 40$ (cos rule)
$= 113.13...$
$AC = 10.6\ \text{cm}$ (3 sf)
b in $\triangle ADC$
$AD^2 = 14^2 - AC^2$ (Pythagoras)
$= 82.8693...$
$AD = 9.10\ \text{cm}$ (3 sf)

c in $\triangle ADB$
$BD^2 = 15^2 + AD^2$ (Pythagoras)
$= 307.8693...$
$BD = 17.5\ \text{cm}$ (3 sf)
d in $\triangle BDC$
$\cos \angle BDC = \dfrac{14^2 + BD^2 - 7^2}{2 \times 14 \times BD}$
$= 0.9258...$
$\angle BDC = 22.2°$ (3 sf)

e   in △BDC

$$\frac{\sin \angle DBC}{14} = \frac{\sin \angle BDC}{7}$$

$$\sin \angle DBC = 14 \times \frac{\sin \angle BDC}{7}$$

$$= 0.75573\ldots$$

$$\angle DBC = 49.1° \text{ (3 sf)}$$

NB: You need to use the accurate answers to **a, b** and **c,** not the rounded answers, for the calculations in **d** and **e.**

CHAPTER 21

1 a Andrew slowed down at P
Andrew stopped at Q the end of the race.

  b $1000 ÷ (4 \times 60) = 4.17$ m/s

2 a train A

  b the gradients of the graphs are positive and negative

  c around 25 minutes

  d train A $25 ÷ 50 = 0.5$ miles/min $= 30$ mph
train B $25 ÷ 40 = 0.625$ miles/min $= 37.5$ mph

3 a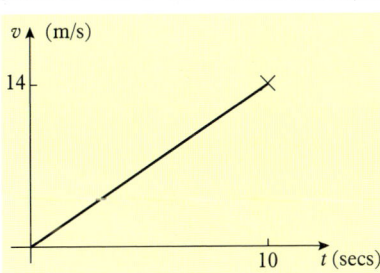

  b acceleration is given by the gradient $\dfrac{14}{10} = 1.4$ m/s²

4 a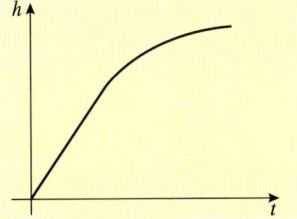

  b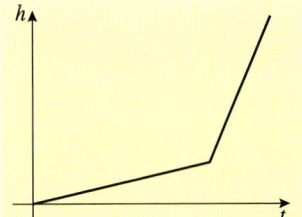

5 a

  b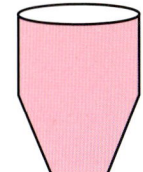

6 area

$$= (\tfrac{1}{2} \times 20 \times 12) + (60 \times 12) + (\tfrac{12 + 6}{2} \times 20) + (6 \times 40) + (\tfrac{1}{2} \times 20 \times 6)$$

$$= 120 + 720 + 180 + 240 + 60$$

$$= 1320 \text{ m}$$